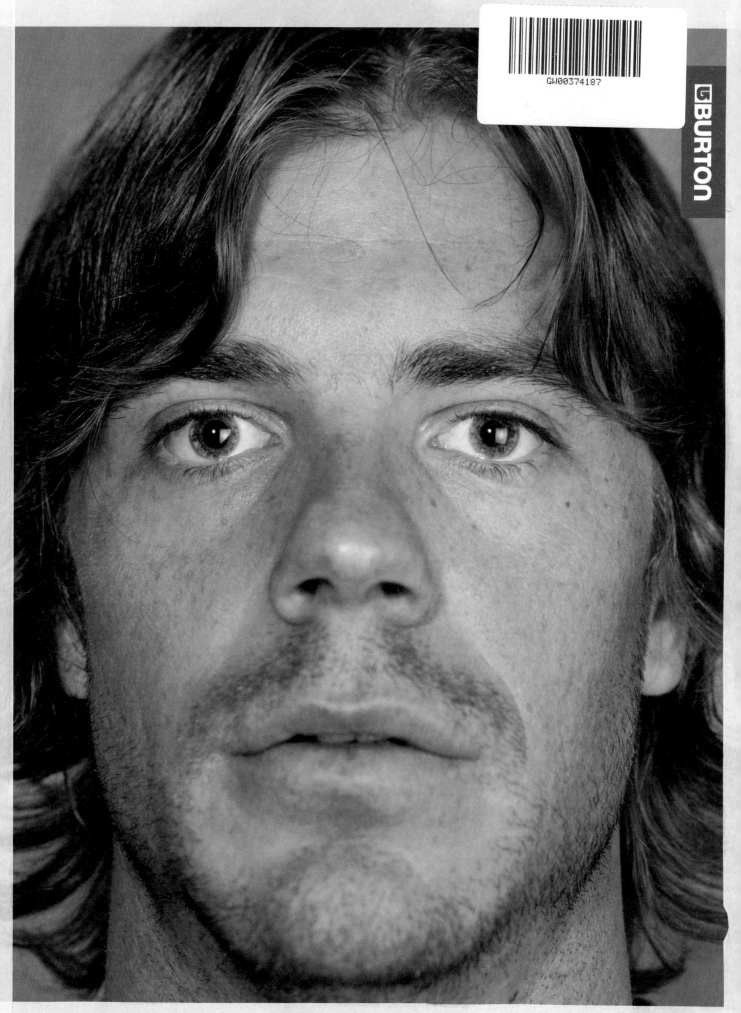

Who says you can't be all things to all people?

Snow Experience
- To some we are snow reports
- To some we are Club Reps
- To some we are a holiday

Information
- To some we are a website
- To some we are advisers
- To some we are a magazine

Benefits & Events
- To some we are insurance
- To some we are money savers
- To some we are party and event organisers

To some we are friends, to some we are memories

To all we are the
Ski Club of Great Britain

0845 45 807 80   www.skiclub.co.uk    FRESHTRACKS   Ski and board

European Snow Atlas 2005

ISBN
1 900916 14 2

Published by
Ice Publishing
45 Corrour Road
Dalfaber, Aviemore
Inverness-shire
PH22 1SS
Tel - 01479 810 362
www.snow-atlas.com
email - icep@btopenworld.com

Compiled by
Tony Brown
Design and Layout
Tony Brown

Mapping
Collins Bartholomew
0141 772 3200

Editing
Ian Samson
Eileen Brand

Advertising
Ashley Strain
Vivian Jenkins
DP Media

Distribution
Vine House
Tel - 01825 723 398
sales@vinehouseuk.co.uk

Special thanks to:
Bill Welch at Land Rover
Jenny Isaac at Land Rover.
Kathryn Kelly at Collins Bartholomew
Ewan Ross at Collins Bartholomew

Special mention for Lorraine,
baby Cara, the Muir household
and the Ossian clan.

Photography: as credited +
main cover - Land Rover.
1st small - Dean "blotto" Gray
Burton Snowboards.
2nd small - Rossingol.

PHOTO - Alvey & Towers

PHOTO - Ischgl Tourist Office

*European Snow Atlas is dedicated
to the fantastic memory of **Kaya,**
a very special friend.*

Headworx team rider Mark Ruparelia

Winter 2004
HEADWORX

Headworx
Stirling Group,
Atlantic Street, Broadheath,
Altrincham, WA14 5FY
T: +44 (0) 161 926 7000
F: +44 (0) 161 926 7011

Contents

5

Full Index:
www.snow-atlas.com

7

Introduction

Tony Brown
Publisher of ESA

The **European Snow Atlas** & **Guide** (ESA) is a unique publication and the only one of its kind in Europe aimed at ski-ers and snowboarders.

Sponsored by **Land Rover,** ESA is compiled with the very latest up to date maps by **Collins** (cartographers), making it the essential atlas which can not only be used to locate any one of 500 listed ski-resorts in the winter, but as an everyday UK/ European atlas to plan journeys at any time of the year. It includes a 60'000-location index via these pages and at www.snow-atlas.com

ESA has the support of the Ski Club of Great Britain and is endorsed by the UK's number one Olympic skier, Alain Baxter, who says, *"the Snow Atlas 'is a fantastic idea and the perfect travel companion. I believe that ESA will make getting to resorts so much easier, with ESA I will no longer have an excuses for turning up late for a race !"*

Whether you choose to fly/drive or set off from a ferry port, you will obviously need an atlas with you. No matter how good your onboard satellite navigation system is, or how detailed your route-planner may be, it makes sense to have a dedicated snow atlas for skiers and snowboarders in case you have to make a detour, or want to visit somewhere else.

ESA contains a snow-guide section with resort profiles and detailed route planners to use in conjunction with the Collins mapping section. When you view the route-planners, please note that they are a suggestion and not the only routes to take. The time, mileage, fuel and road-toll are based on averages, so again, use these as a guide when planning your trip. Your journey depends on how fast you drive, road and weather conditions, and the actual route you take. ESA information is given as a helpfull guide.

The European Snow Atlas is updated every year and new information is added i.e:- resort, bar and restaurant guide. Anyone with any new information on resorts-please contact us. We are currently working on a USA/Canada snow atlas so feel free to send in your resort reports.

*Please note that the A-Z places index in the **rear** mapping section on page **4** , is a listing for principal towns and cities across Europe. The full 60'000 - location index, with map reference and page number, can be found at - www.snow-atlas.com

NOTRE TOUTE NOUVELLE FIXATION CINCH

K2 CINCH BINDING

CINCHtechnologie

VITESSE. CONFORT. PERFORMANCE

ETAPE 1 Position fermé

EXCLUSIVE WORLD-WIDE PATENTS
BREVETS
US PAT. NO: 5,909,896
CA PAT. NO: 2,201,562
EP PAT. NO: 0,000,817 B1
JP PAT. NO: 1043730

FERME Position de glisse

POWER
PRO.BNDG.

VITESSE. CONFORT. PERFORMANCE

La nouvelle fixation Cinch est aussi facile à chausser et déchausser qu'un step-in, mais elle offre les sensations et la performance d'une coque traditionnelle. Le spoiler s'ouvre tandis que le strap de cheville s'élève en même temps, pour un chaussage et un déchaussage très rapides. Cela sans aucun compromis en matière de réglage, puisque les straps se règlent avec autant de précision qu'une coque traditionnelle et que le spoiler se règle également. Tu peux évidemment rider avec les boots de ton choix.

Testée par des experts, la nouvelle fixation Cinch rassemble le meilleur de deux mondes – le côté pratique du step-in et les performances des coques traditionnelles.

A. Spoiler Ergo avec TPU surmoulé – réglage en rotation

B. Molette de blocage du spoiler

C. Nouveau Strap de cheville Contour - entièrement adjustable et confortable

D. Nouveau Boucles en aluminium – rapidité de blocage et maintien parfait

E. Gas Pedal réglable avec pad amortissant en TPU surmoulé

F. Couvre-disque anti-vibrations et pad amortissants au talon en TPU surmoulé

G. Livrée avec disques en aluminium centrés ou décalés, compatibles 4X2 et 3D

ETAPE 2 système d'ouverture

DEBLOCAGE Prêt pour l'ouverture

ETAPE 3 Position ouverte

C. STRAP DE CHEVILLE CONTOUR

OUVERT Position d'entrée/ de sortie

A. SPOILER ERGO AVEC TPU SURMOULE

D. BOUCLES EN ALUMINUM

B. MOLETTE DE BLOCAGE DU SPOILER

G. LIVREE AVEC DISQUES EN ALUMINUM CENTRES OU DECALES, COMPATIBLES 4X2 et 3D

"SPOILER ENTIEREMENT ADJUSTABLE A LA BASE"

E. GAS PEDAL REGLABLE AVEC PAD AMORTISSANT EN TPU SURMOULE

K2snowboards
CINCH Binding

F. COUVRE-DISQUE ANTI-VIBRATIONS ET PAD AMORTISSANTS AU TALON EN TPU SURMOULE

info-k2snowboarding@k2sports.de   ph.49 8856 901 0   cell Toll free France 0800 907241
www.k2snow k2.com

POWER
PRO.BNDG.

Snow Bits- Land Rover Gear

LAND ROVER GEAR
For information on Land Rover Gear contact your local dealership, or telephone (0) 870 777 2779 - www.landrover.com

Land Rover Snow Jacket
Arctic jacket with snow skirt, removable hood and zippered underarm ventilation.
Red & Black XS S M L XL £199.00
JKT0369 www.landrover.com

Land Rover Garmin GPS
The Geko 301 is the world's smallest and lightest GPS system with electronic compass and barometric altimeter. £225.00
LRO 1078
www.landrover.com

Land Rover Zermatt Sunglasses
Metal framed, extreme wrap. UV protection
LRO 1121 £59.00
www.landrover.com

Land Rover Snow chains
Quick fitting high strength galvanised steel front wheels only 195 x 15"
STC7905 www.landrover.com

Land Rover Valais sunglasses
Wraparound sunglasses with impact resistant frames and scratch resistant 100% UV polycarbonate lenses. £59.00
LRO 0911 www.landrover.com

Land Rover TAC-Lite
One of the toughest flashlights in the world, five times brighter than other mini lights. £69.00
LRO0595 www.landrover.com

Land Rover Snow Traction System
Easy to fit for front wheels only 215 x 16" & 225 x 17"
STC50283 www.landrover.com

Land Rover Survival kit
Essential kit for all travellers including Gerber multi-tool, Maglite, Axe, Shovel, Sports Saw and First Aid Kit.
LRO 0487 £229.00 www.landrover.com

Land Rover Refrigerator/freezer
Tough polypropylene casing is impact resistant
STC8519AB www.landrover.com

Land Rover Multi tool 400
Versatile Gerber tool £59.00
LRO 0485 www.landrover.com

9

Snow Bits – Vehicle Gizmos

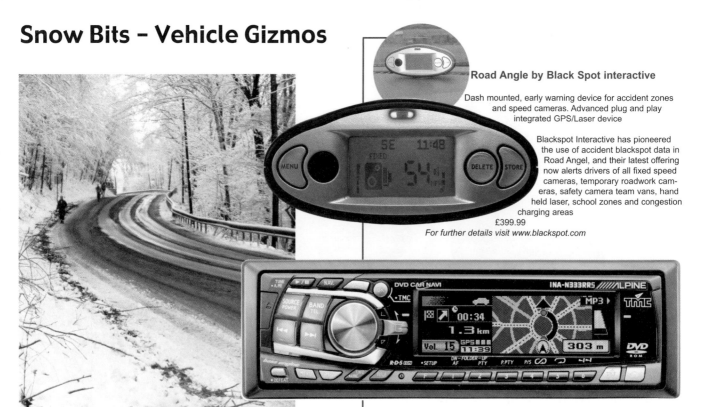

Road Angle by Black Spot interactive

Dash mounted, early warning device for accident zones and speed cameras. Advanced plug and play integrated GPS/Laser device

Blackspot Interactive has pioneered the use of accident blackspot data in Road Angel, and their latest offering now alerts drivers of all fixed speed cameras, temporary roadwork cameras, safety camera team vans, hand held laser, school zones and congestion charging areas
£399.99
For further details visit www.blackspot.com

Alpine Mobile media navigation system INA N333RS/RRS

The INA-N333RS is an advanced in-dash navigation system. This one-Din unit includes not only full navigation capabilities and a huge POI database but also a high quality Base Engine CD Receiver with a high-resolution display.

For details of the full range and prices visit www.alpine.com

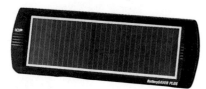

ICP Battery SAVER

The Battery Saver prevents dead car batteries and reduces the need for expensive battery replacements. The Battery Saver is efficient under all lighting conditions, including cloudy and rainy skies. It even works under 3 inches of snow! Excellent for cars in storage or parked for extended periods of time. Ensures quick starts on cold winter days.
Features - 1.8 watts rated power at 15 volts operating voltage
Connects in seconds via the cigarette lighter adapter.

For details of the full range of Batter Savers and prices visit www.icpsolar.com

Alpine Pulse Touch display monitor IVA d300R/RB

The IVA-D300R/RB 7" monitor is ideal choice for connecting an entire mobile entertainment system. Large, colourful menus make it easy to command the functions of a DVD player or change, a processor, amps, a TV turner, other monitors and all you need is your finger.

For details of the full range of displays and prices visit www.alpine.com

7" WIDE SCREEN OVERHEAD MONITOR TMX-R700

7" TFT Active Matrix LCD colour monitor with open, close, swivel and tilt mechanism. Supplied with a wireless remote control. IR transmitter for wireless headphones. 2-wired headphone outputs.

For details of the full range of monitors and prices visit www.alpine.com

Snow Bits - Stuff

The featured products are a small sample of whats new for this season. Further dtails about each produch can be obtained from manfactures or at your local stockist

First Ever Snowboard Specific Watch

The Nixon DELTA RRP £

It has arrived… Nixon proudly releases The Delta. Nixon fine tuned an old idea in altimeter watches and designed the first snowboard specific watch. No other watch in the world can do what The Delta does.

The Delta includes custom digital with barometer, altimeter, temperature, elevation tracking, pre-programmed snowboard base elevations, dual time, alarm, countdown timer, chrono, night light, Swiss barometric sensor, 50 meter, hardened mineral crystal, raised bezel and is available in either a stainless steel or polyurethane band.

Infor at www.freeride-dist.com

Photo - Jeff Curtes - Burton Snowboards

Apples I-Pod and I-Pod mini for tunes on the slopes

iPod

A musical dream come true, the fourth-generation iPod offers huge capacity, letting you easily slip up to 10,000 songs into your pocket. And enjoy it wherever you go. In the car, on the slopes or in you're chalets. Incorporating the fabulous Apple Click Wheel that was first introduced on iPod mini. Offering up to 12 hours of battery life. iPod continues to define the perfect digital music player for Mac and Windows. You can now purchase a 20GB iPod for £219. Or a 40GB iPod for £299.

www.apple.com/ipod

Monster iCase Travel pack

The iCase travel pack is the best way to protect your IPod on the move. Comes with a Monster iCar charger and Ispliter £48.99
www.apple.com/ipod/accessories

iPod mini

Everything you love about iPod just got tinier. iPod mini lets you bring along enough music for a three-day weekend get-away in a package so small you'll forget you're carrying it.
iPod mini lasts up to 8 hours on a single battery charge and like its (slightly) bigger brother, iPod mini gives you over 25 minutes of skip protection.
Storage 4Gb capable of 1000 songs.
iPod mini is available in five trend-setting colours: silver, gold, green, pink or blue, all shiny. £180
www.apple.com/ipod

Personal Attack Alarm
(also acts as a door & room alarm)

For that extra assurance why not carry a personal alarm which can also be used to protect your skis or snowboards. **£9.99**
www. maplin.co.uk

Metro Beam Benders

Universal headlamp converters for continental driving.
£12.99

The Snuggler

Innovative travel sleeping pillow. The new alternative to conventional travel pillows. Prevents head falling forward. Soft fleecy comfort jacket, fits snugly under the chin. **£5.99**
www. design-go.com

Splash Box

Splash box waterproof storage. Protects valuables from water, sand and snow. Comfortably worn around shoulder or neck.
£6.99
www. design-go.com

2 in 1 Gauge

Digital tire pressure gauge and tire track measure. PSI and Bar readings.
£
www. maplin.co.uk

PWP Go Bag

Revolutionary disposable urinal bag . The PWP Go Bag gives motorists, women, older people and familes the freedom to go whenever they want even on the move. **£**8.95
www. pwpdirect.com

Thermometer-Clock

Inside/Outside digital thermometer and clock.
Accurate digital C°/F° readout. Illuminating back light.
£
www. maplin.co.uk

Voice Travel Mate

Cross translate between 11 languages with 700 travel sentences per language. Individual topic keys for emergency, General, pharmacy, shopping, entertainment, shopping and restaurants.
£14.99   www. maplin.co.uk

11

Snow Bits – Snowboards +

Fleetwood £230
All Terrain

Sizes
146, 151,
156, 160
164.
158wide
165wide

Decade £230
All Terrain

Sizes
149, 152,
156, 159,
161, 164,
168.

Yuckon £270
Freeride

Sizes
159
164
169

Ride Snowboards 2005 The items shown are small selection of Rides 2005 range which contains 21 snowboards, 8 choices of bindings and 11 styles of boots

Ride Snowboards 2005
visit www. ridesnowboards.com

Amp
Boot
£150

Orion
Boot
£120

LX Viper *Bindngs*
£110

Timless £370
Freeride
Sizes
149, 152,
156, 159,
161, 164,
168.

K2 Snowboards 2005   www.k2skis.com
22 snowboards, 13 bindings and 19 boots

Mini Zeplin £200
All Terrain Juniors
Sizes
137
142
147

**Smiths Epic
Regulator goggles**

V12 *Binding*
£180

Recon Riser £400
All Terrain
Sizes
154
157
161
165

**Mens K2 Diem
Jacket £210**

**Womens K2 Versa
Hybrid Jacket
£250**

Smiths Gog Triad goggles

12

Burton Air

The all-new Air blends strength and a directional shape with smooth edge-to-edge transitioning for a technically superior ride. Designed to throw down, the Air possesses energetic snap, response and stompability unlike any other. All-terrain freestyle perfection is back among the living, at a price that will give you flashbacks of the mid-'90s. MSRP: £319.95

Sizes - 148 - 153 - 157 - 161 - 165.

Burton Feelgood ES

Female riders who demand high-end board construction should not have to settle for men's boards, so Burton created the all new Feelgood ES, a fully loaded, high-performance series. The super responsive Feelgood ES is fine-tuned to handle anything. Dragonfly core and Burton's Pressure Distribution Edge construction provides extra edge hold when you hit a gnarly patch of ice. Combine all this tech with a lightweight, lively ride, and the Feelgood's unrivalled women's-specific board. MSRP: £459.95

PHOTO - Jeff Curtes - Burton Snowboards

Red's Audio HiFi

in-mold polycarbonate shell super lightweight meshed flow through passive venting removable quick clip earflaps with speaker earpads earpads with volume and easy mute function included zip clip ratcheting chin buckle astm 2040 and ce1077 certified
£119.95

Burton Cartel Bindings

Armed with a lightweight, medium-flexing, short-fibre glass reinforced nylon baseplate for stability and response, the Cartel knows no mercy when attacking vicious rails and hell-bent booters. We re-engineered the Team Skyback® by coring out all the unnecessary material to reduce its overall weight by 13%, while providing the same great durability and response. MSRP: **£159.95.**

Salmon Era
£399

Da-Kine Cool tool £9.95

Da-Kine Binding tool £4.95

Da-Kine Wrist guard £14.95

Da-Kine Cool lock £14.95

Da-Kine Delux tune up kit £44.95

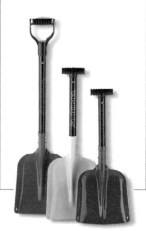

Da-Kine Mini tune up kit £24.95

13

Snow Bits – Ski's +

K2 Skis 2005 www.k2skis.com

K2 Fugative Skis £250

K2 Apache Chief Skis £380

K2 Burin Luv Skis £420 with bindings

Da Kine Poacher back pack
small **£94.95**
large **£97.95**

Rossingol Elite Bandit Boots: offering un-compromised quality and performance to explore the whole mountain. **£230**

Rossingol 2005 www.amg-outdoors.co.uk

Rossingol 9S Oversize Skis £440. Best for short-radius turns.

Rossingol B2 Skis £360. The B2 provides the lover of freedom skiing all - round performance true versatility on and off piste.

Rossingol Scratch 140 Binding. £160
Optimum informatiom flow from boot to ski

Rossingol Zenith 5 Skis £400. For aggressive skiers, offering multi-performance and unquestionable quality.

Rossingol Scratch FS Skis £300. Shaped for snowparks and tricks with excellent on trail performance too.

Salmon COURSE SPACEFRAME BOOTS £339.95

The ultimate performance boot for expert skiers featuring Spaceframe technology.

Salmon PERFORMA 8 Boots (W) £199.95
Second generation Performa boot is our best yet and set to maintain it's number one position this season with more features than ever.

Salmon PRO MODEL SPACE-FRAME £269.95
The reference freeski boot - Ride your dreams. Features Spaceframe technology.

Salmon
SALOMON STREETRACER 8 Skis (Womens) £369.955 Leader of the new women's ski generation with great on piste performance for multiradius turns.

Salmon
SCRAMBLER 77 Skis £299.95 The all mountain female ski, offering the perfect blend of flotation and autocarve.

Thank GOD, summer's over.

Drive Guide

First things first.

Pre-planning is essential if you are going to have a safe and trouble-free journey. Leaving every thing to the day of travel is stupid-you need to plan ahead and leave nothing to chance.

There are numerous web-sites that provide route planning services and advice. You can also contact one of the car associations, they will be able to supply you with a personal travel plan. It is important to note that whatever plan you come up with prior to leaving, even if you have an onboard satellite navigation system, you should always travel with an up-to-date map in-case you have to make detours etc.

Plan your route carefully from your departure point to your destination. Note down relevant information like mountain passes, toll-roads and border crossings. If you are heading to Austria and want to avoid toll-roads, travel via Holland, Luxembourg and Germany. Same for Switzerland. Do not be put off by toll roads, however, as these roads are often quiet and traffic free. what's more the charges are not that scary.

Before you set off its advisable to check the web for sites that give information on European road regulations for individual countries. You should also familiarise yourself with road signs and warnings. Although many signs are standardised across Europe each country has its own variation

A triangle sign depicts a warning.

A reversed triangle is for 'Give Way'.

A circle sign prohibits or restricts.

A rectangle sign carries information.

Stop signs are octagonal

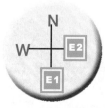

European route sign

Europe has a cross-border, main route numbering system displayed alongside national route numbers. European routes are displayed with the letter E placed before number. Markings are white on a green background. These signs are shown on motorways and other major roads. Minor roads do not generally display E signs.

The European road numbering system is divided into routes from east to west and north to south. Even numbers go from east to west, odd numbers north to south.

17

Even if you have an onboard satellite navigation system, you should always travel with an up-to-date map in-case you have to make detours etc.

Drive Guide

It is a legal requirement across Europe to wear a seat belt in the front seats and rear if fitted. Children under the age of 3 must be in a child restraint seat.

Rules, Regulations and Tips

Each European country has it's own traffic regulations, so do some home work and find out the basic rules for the country you are going to, and for those that you will pass through. Being ignorant of a countries laws is no defence when you run into trouble.

Speed limits in Europe vary, so be aware of the limits imposed in the country in which you are travelling, especially when crossing borders. German autobahns do not have an actual top-end speed limit unless signposted. Belgium has an upper limit of 120kph (75mph). In Norway it is as low as 90kph (50mph). France is extremely strict on motorway speed limits, which is 130kph (80mph), break the limits and the french police will stop you and administer an on-the-spot fine of up to 390 Euros (£250).
It is a fact that all European traffic cops will fine drivers on-the-spot. Having UK plates will not grant you immunity and if you don't pay cash at the time of the fine you may well find yourself arrested and whisked off to jail. Credit cards will not always be accepted, for payment of fines, so make sure you carry enough local currency at all times.

In Switzerland and Austria you are required, by law, to purchase a temporary road tax, or *Vignette*. This enables you to use the motorways. The Swiss tax disc can be bought at border checkpoints and lasts for a year, costing approximately £28. The Austrian version is much more flexible and can be bought for periods of ten days, two months or one year. There are also some areas where you can travel short distances without it. All the necessary information is available at border points and tourist offices.

Most European police forces take a very dim view of motorists who break down because they have run out of fuel. Should you find yourself in this situation you could face a hefty fine. Germany is particularly is strict on this so,- never let the tank go below a quarter full. It is always better to keep your tank topped up rather than carry a spare fuel can which is illegal in Italy and Portugal. Further more, fuel cans are not allowed to be carred in vehicles on cross channel ferries or on Euro Tunnel trains as they are deemed as a fire hazard.

Drivers of diesel vehicles, be aware that in extreme sub-zero temperatures diesel will freeze, although some oil companies now supply diesel that can with stand certain low temperatures. Drivers of cars that use Liquid Petroleum Gas (LPG) will find many garages in Europe where they can fill up – this excludes Spain. In remote mountain resort areas, LPG is not often widely available. Note also that LPG vehicles are baned on cross channel ferries and on Euro Tunnel trains.

FUEL RECOGNITION

Andorra	Essence Sans Plomb or Gasolina sin Plomb
Austria	Blyfrei
Bulgaria	Bezoloven Benzin
Czech Republic	Natural
	Diesel is *TT Diesel*
Finland	Lyyton Polttaine
France	Sans Plomb
	Diesel is as or Gaz -oil
Germany	Bleifrei
Italy	Benzina Sensa Piombo
	Diesel is Gaasolio
Liechtenstein	Bleifrei
Norway	Blyfritt Kraftstoff
Poland	Benzyna Bezolowlowa
Portugal	Gasolina Sin Plomo
	Diesel is Gasoleo
Romania	Benzina Fara Plumb
	Diesel is Motorina
Slovak Republic	Benzin Natura; 96 & 98
	Diesel is Nafta
Slovenia	Neosvincene Benzin
Spain	Gasolina Sin Piomo
	Diesel is Gas-oil
Sweden	Blyfrei
Switzerland	Bleifrei

Driving on the Right

The UK is the only European country to drive on the Left. When you arrive at ferry ports, on the continent, exit roads will usualy have signs warning you to drive on the right. This is not always the case at airports for those who fly/drive. Remember, when overtaking while driving on the oppsite side of the road - your view is going to be restricted, give your self extra space between you and the vehicle in front, especially on single carrage roads where you have to cross the other side in order to overtake.

The UK is also the only European country to use miles and kilometre's to measure distance, every where use only Kilometre's, so remember this when working out distances and reading road signs.

1 mile = 1.61 Kilometres. This can be calculated by mulitplying or dividing as follows-
Example: 300 miles x 1.61 = 483 kilometres
483 kilometres ÷ 1.61 = 300 miles

Head light convertors, or patches, are a legal requirement in most European countries. Patches are used to block out the blind spot that can affect drivers of on-coming vehicles as head-lights on a left hand drive vehicle are set to a different angle to a right hand drive.

Apart form a couple of countries, headlights are not required be be on at all times, but only a foul would drive in mountainous ares without dipped lights. Dipped lights should always be used in tunnels

Documents

It is important, when travelling to have all valid personal and vehicle documentation with you. Make sure you have the proper car insurance and breakdown cover the countries you will be visiting or passing through. If you don't, should the worst happen and you have an accident or breakdown, it will cost you a lot of money. You could also find yourself coming home minus your vehicle with the prospect of a court apperance at a later date. Contact your insurers, give them your itinerary and they will advise you of the best cover required. The same applies to travel insurance. Make sure you have adequate cover for all eventualities including flight/ferry cancellations etc.

Remembering your passport goes without saying, but make sure it is valid and up to date? Do not forget your driving licence. In many countries it is a legal requirement to carry it at all. To complicate matters, the UK has three different types of driving licence, but the only one that is easily recognised by European police forces, is the one that carries photographic identifaction. It is also advisable to take your valid vehicle registration document and MOT certificate as proof of ownership should the police ask to see it.

19

The UK is the only European country to drive on the Left.

Drive Guide

Snow Chains

Some countries make it a legal requirement for you to carry snowchains in your vehicle when you drive in mountain regions. There will often be road signs advising you to fit your chains. These fit around the outside of the drive wheel tyre. They are not always quick and easy to fit, especially during a snowstorm. A couple of tips - practice fitting snowchains before you leave home. To help chains stay in place, increase the tyre air pressure by about 10psi as chains sit better round a firm tyre rather than a soft one. It is a good idea to check with your vehicle manufacturer as to the appropriate snowchains for your vehicle.

You should never drive above 50kph (30mph) with the chains fitted and always remove them once you are back on clear roads.

If you don't want the expense of buying snowchains, there are a number of places where you can hire them. Check with motoring organisations, ski tour operators or your local ski shop.

Vehicle Check

Set off in clapped-out, unserviced vehicle and the only thing you are heading for is trouble! However, if you have the car serviced, take some precautions and do some pre-checks, you will at least minimise the chance of a breakdown.

Anti-freeze

Have the correct mixture in your system. This is normally 1 part antifreeze to 1 part water. Ideally, your antifreeze should be able to work in temperatures as low as –35⁰C. If you don't have the correct mixture you risk freezing your engine's cooling system, with disastrous results.

Battery

In cold conditions, your battery usage is much greater due to the constant use of electrical components such as heaters, wipers and lights. Your battery performance also decreases as the temperature drops. Ensure that all terminals are firmly connected and free from dirt. The battery indicator on your dash board should read 13-15 volts with the engine running and 12-13 volts, when the engine is switched off. If your vehicle is fitted with a catalytic convertor, take care not to start the car by turning the engine over for more than a few seconds at a time, as you can damage the convertor with a build-up of unburned fuel. You should also carry a set of jump leads in the event of a flat battery.

Brakes

Have brakes checked before starting your journey. It is advisable to change brake fluid once a year, especially when you are going to drive on mountain roads as you will be using your brakes a lot. You will also be driving a more slowly than on flat roads so, the brakes don't cool so efficiently. Brake discs and pads get covered in a of dirt and grit when driving in slush and snow. If the roads have been gritted, grit can cause a delay in the braking action.

Lights

Light bulbs don't like freezing conditions and will blow more often than usual. Always check your lights are fully operational. Always carry spare bulbs and during stops, clean all the lights and replace any blown bulbs.

Oil and Water

Don't put all your faith in warning lights on the dash board. Do a manual check, and even if the levels are fine when you leave, they won't stay like that-especially over long distances so, check all levels regularly. The normal pressure for engine oil is 55psi when driving and between 20 to 30psi when the engine is idling. In cold conditions it is very important to use the correct oil with the right viscosity. Low viscosity oil (thin oil) is best for starting the car when cold. Tt also helps to save fuel when the engine is warming up.
The recommended winter oil weight for most vehicles is 5w/30 oil. Check with a garage for further information.

Screen Wash

Keep topping up your reservoir at every opportunity. To prevent the wash from freezing, add a screen wash antifreeze solution to the mixture.

Tyres

Anyone not paying attention to the condition of their tyres is asking for trouble. Tyres should have an equal amount of depth to the tread. The law regarding the exact amount varies across Europe. In most countries, you will be within the law as long as you don't let the tread wear down below 1.6mm. If you're planning a lot of mountain driving where snow is likey on the roads, it would make sense to buy a set of snow-tyres. Keeping your tyres inflated at the manfactures recommended pressures will mean a safer trip and save fuel as under-inflated tyres require the engine to work harder. Finally, don't forget to check the spare tyre before you leave.

you will be within the law as long as you don't let the tread wear down below 1.6 mm.

Items for your vehicle

Check List

- ❏ **De-Icer & Scraper**
- ❏ **Fire Extinguisher**
- ❏ **First Aid Kit**
- ❏ **G.B. Sticker**
- ❏ **Headlight Patches**
- ❏ **Jump Leads**
- ❏ **Maps (ESA)**
- ❏ **Moblie Phone & Charger**
- ❏ **Snow Chains**
- ❏ **Snow Shovel**
- ❏ **Spare Bulbs**
- ❏ **Roof Racks/Boxes**
- ❏ **Tools**
- ❏ **Tourch & Batteries**
- ❏ **Tow Rope**
- ❏ **Warning Triangle**

Some countries insist that you carry certain safety equipment in your vehicle. First-aid kit, spare light-bulbs, fire extinguisher and breakdown warning triangle (placed 25 mtrs to the rear of vehicle to alert other drivers) are often compulsory.

First aid kit should consist of basic items i.e;- assorted waterproof plasters, crepe bandages, roll of micropore tape, cotton wool, 5 or 10cm gauze bandages, bottle of distilled water to clean wounds, anti-septic wipes, prepared wound dressings, small pair of scissors, triangular bandage, safety pins and some antiseptic cream.

Essential tools to carry in the boot are a foldaway camping shovel (to clear the snow if you get stuck), tow rope, torch with batteries, drinking water, food, blanket or sleeping bag, waterproof clothing and gloves (your ski/snowboard gear will suffice).

If your vehicle does not have a set of standard European number plates, you will require a country-of-orgin sticker on the rear of your car - this is the law in most European countries.

Roof Racks

Should you need to use a roof-rack or luggage box, ensure all items are securely attached and locked in. With racks, always pack bulky items towards the rear in order to reduce drag. If you intend to carry a snowboard in a rack, over a long distance, it would be advisable to put it in a board sack. Failing this, remove the bindings so that parts can't be dislodged in wind rush.

On average a roof rack or box will increase the fuel consumption by 10% at 20 mph and 15% at 70 mph. Your vehicles maximum speed will also be reduced by around 10 mph.

Remember to check the spare tyre

21

Drive Guide

Driving Safely

Snow and Ice

Driving on soft snow is the easiest and provided you take care, should pose few problems. Hard packed snow is a completely different matter and requires great care by the driver. Stay alert and drive slower than normal and keep your distance from other vehicles.

The most dangerous type of snow to drive on is impacted snow. This is snow that has been packed down and covered with a fresh layer. It is essential that extreme care is taken when driving in such conditions. Remember, snow will build up and block the tyre treads, reducing grip and making stopping and steering much trickier. Apply your brakes in a gentler way than normal.

Black Ice is one of the most dangerous problems you can encounter on roads and you can be driving on it before you even realise. Black ice is a sheet of ice, not normally visible to the eye. It is formed as rain hits the road in freezing temperatures. If you notice the steering seems lighter it is possible you have hit a stretch of black ice - so take the utmost care.

To avoid skidding, or locking the wheels, you must not brake and change direction at the same time. The way to deal with skidding is to gently apply the brakes with a pumping action without over steering. Both these actions should be carried out at very slow speed. How you deal with a skid varies according to whether you have a front or rear wheel drive vehicle. Rear wheel drives will skid from the rear. To get out of it you should ease off the brake and accelerator while turning the steering wheel in the same direction as the skid. Only apply the brakes or accelerator once you have full control of the skid and all wheels are straight. To control a front wheel skid, ease very gently off the accelerator and, as the speed drops, steer in to the corner. Once you have gained full control, carefully accelerate and steer in the correct direction. Remember, a sudden reduction in speed could act as braking and severely effect the control of your vehicle.

Breakdown

Even the best plans and precautions sometimes go out of the window and you may end up braking down. In the event of this happening, or at the first signs of trouble, you must take immediate action.

Your first priority is for the safety of your passengers, yourself, and other road users so get your vehicle off the road and into a safe parking place. If you break down on a motorway, stop on the hard shoulder and get your passengers to leave the vehicle from the side close to the verge. Make all possible effort to warn other road users by using your hazard lights and by placing a warning triangle about 25metres to the rear of your vehicle. If the light is poor, or it is night time, leave your side lights on.

Inform the local breakdown service of your problem. Use your mobile phone or locate a road-side emergency phone. At the earliest opptunity, contact your insurance company for advice, they will inform you of how any bills should be settled.

If you breakdown during a severe snow storm, contact the emergency services on your mobile phone and stay in your vehicle until the storm breaks or until the emergency services stumble across you on their routine patrols. <u>DO</u> <u>NOT</u> attempt to seek help by walking away from your vehicle.

Accidents

PHOTO - Auto Express

If you have an accident while travelling through Europe, there are a number key things that you will need to do in order to keep things safe, legal, and correct:

1- Asses the scene and prioritise casualties,
2- Secure the scene,
3- Call the emergency services,
4- Prevent fire and deal with any hazards.

PHOTO - Alvey & Towers

Immediately after any accident, attend to any casualties and if you need to, carry out emergency first aid. Establish who needs attention first but do not move a casualty unless they are in a danger area. Check the injured person's breathing and circulation and try to stop any bleeding.

The next thing to do is, make the accident area safe. Put out a warning triangle to the rear of the accident and in a place that is visable to other drivers. Switch on your hazard lights and direct traffic accordingly. Phone the police, which in some countries is a legal requirment even if no one has been injured. Asses if you need an ambulance or the fire brigade, and if so, call them or tell the police whats required. If you don't have a phone or can't find a road side one, get someone to go to a nearby house making sure they know your location.

To prevent fire switch of all engines at the scene. Don't smoke. If there is any petrol spillage, try to cover it with sand or earth. If you smell smouldering, check battery terminals and disconnet (buses and goods vehicles often have fuel cut-off switches located on the outside of the engine). If a casualty's clothes are on fire smother the flames with a blanket or coat. You should also roll and position them so the flames do not reach their face. If a persons clothers smell of petrol - try to remove them immediately and throw well away for the scene, but make sure you keep the casualty warm and not left bare.

Once you have made the accident area safe for drivers to pass and have done emergency first-aid, note down details about the accident for the police and insurance companies. Write the time of the accident, people involved, road and weather conditions at the time of the accident. If you have a camera, take some pictures of the scene. If there are any witness to the accident try to keep them them there till police arrive. A point to note when the police turn up, is not to admit liability for the accident. Leave the blame game to the police and the insurance companies.

Emergency First aid

- Treat injured people in a safe area.
- Prioritise and treat casualties in the following order-

A) Unconscious and non breathing,
B) Those with heavy bleeding.
C) Unconscious but are still breathing
D) Anyone who appears to be in shock.

Unconsciousness

An unconscious person who has stopped breathing may need mouth to mouth resuscitation. Carefully, shake and call out to them. Look, listen and feel for signs of breathing. Lay the casualty on their back, tilt back the head and open the airway. Clear away any obstructions i.e. false teeth or braces. Close the casualtys nose with one hand while supporting the jaw with the other. Place your lips over the mouth and in a controlled manner breath out watching as the chest rises then watch to see the chest go down. Repeat the whole procedure then check the patients pulse on the neck. If there is a pulse continue mouth to mouth every five seconds until breathing resumes.

Check the casualty's circulation and feel for the carotid pulse in the neck. If there is no sign of a circulation start chest compressions. Do this by placing the casualty on their back find the notch at the bottom of the breastbone. Measure two fingers widths above this. Place heel of hand on this spot and your other hand on top, press down firmly and smoothly 15 times at a rate of approx 100 times a minute. Repeat 2 breaths and 15 compressions until casualty shows signs of improvement or professional help arrives.

Bleeding

You must stop it. Lift the bleeding limb if there are no broken bones and apply direct pressure using a clean bandage or tissue. Once you control the bleeding, apply a sterile dressing. If there is a foreign body in the wound, do not attempt to remove it. Dress around it.

Burns

Always try and cool down burns swiftly to stop the
'cooking' action. Do this by pouring clean water directly over the burn - or with a damp cloth. Only cover a burn with a dry, none sticking material.

Fractures

Never move a fractured limb unless you have no other choice, leave it to the emergency crews. However, if you do have to move a casualty, support the limb by slinging an arm or tying an injured leg to the other at the knee and ankle.
If the wound is compounded (visible bones) carefully cover with a clean dressing.

23

PHOTO - Auto Express

Crossing the Channel

PHOTO - Super Fast

Ferries have, for years, been the only way to cross the Northsea/English Channel by car. The Channel Tunnel has changed all that, with it's fast freight and car transporters/train services. However, ferries still offer a more relaxed alternative to Eurotunel services. Ferries are slower at crossing the channel, with an average crossing time from Dover to Calais of approximately 1 hour 15 minutes compared to 35 minutes through the tunnel. Ferries have the advantage of allowing you to have a decent break before hitting the road's when you get off. You are able to relax, take a nap, have a meal or do some duty-free shopping on board.

Dover is the main UK departure and arrival port for travellers taking ferries to and from mainland Europe, but there are alternatives around the country, which includes Rosyth in Scotland which will suit travellers from the north. Dover has one main advantage over other ports, that is the number of daily sailings available. On average there are thirty sailing's a day where most other UK ports only offer one or two crossings per day.

Whichever port you chose, it's easy to book by phone or on the web. You don't always have to pre-book, and can often just turn up at a ferry terminal, buy a ticket and sail there and then. Prices are generally based on the length of your vehicle and the number of passenger's. Rates for cabins and lounge seats on long crossing vary between operators. Ticket prices also reflect the time of travel with late night and early morning sailing's having the lowest fares.

Ferry companies have set policies for passengers during crossings. For instance, once a ship has set sail, the vehicle decks are locked and passengers are not allowed back to their cars, so when you board, take whatever you need for the crossing.
To prevent fires, vehicles containing spare fuel cans are not allowed on board unless the can is empty. LPG (gas powdered cars) are not allowed on ferries.

On board ferries, you will find numerous bars and restaurants as well as duty-free shops and lounge areas. Some ships even provide Childrens' plays areas and mini-cinemas. On ferries making long crossings, there are various types of cabins and large reclining lounge-seats available so that you can have a sleep or merely chill out.

Superfast Ferries - *Rosyth Scotland*

Still in its infancy, a new service began between the UK and main land Europe back in 2002 and, for many, this could become the best way to cross the channel.

Superfast Ferries is the only operator sailing from Edinburgh, Scotland to Zeebrugge in Belgium. Ferries sail all year round with one daily return crossing taking 17 1/2 hours. However, the ship is so well equipped that it feels more like a cruise liner than a short-haul ferry.- What's more, if you're travelling from Carlisle, it would make far more sense and be cheaper to sail from Rosyth than drive all the way down to Dover simply to save on the crossing time. Sailing from Rosyth also means less time driving and more fuel saving.

Example.- *Carlisle to Courchevel*
via Roysth, - Driving 13 hours & 693 miles.
Via Dover , - Driving 17 hours & 963 miles.

Fares from Rosyth range from £54 return per person plus £59 for a car up to 6m long. Cabins start from £54 for a basic up to £124 for a luxury 2 bed.

On board, there is an excellent choice of restaurants, a bar, a casino and the Havana Club where you can relax. There is also a video games and internet corner, a jacuzzi-sauna and a children's playroom.

To book tel - 0870 055 1234
www.superfast.com

Eurotunnel offers you speed and convenience, for instance, you can travel down from London, go through customs, drive on and off the shuttle and arrive at Chamonix without ever leaving your car. This is not recommended as you should have sensible breaks in a long trip. Passport checks are done on departure, which means you simply drive off and away.

Eurotunnel fares are booked and priced in much the same way as on ferries i.e. based on length of vehicle, number of passengers and travel times.

Photo - Euro Tunnel

Although you don't have to pre-book, it is advisable, especially if you have a high vehicle. You will be allocated special space if your vehicle is over 1.85 metres high. Vehicles under 1.85m and carrying a roof rack/box will be charged the standard car price. Vehicles over 1.85m with a roof rack/box will be charged a higher rate.

As on ferries, LPG (gas powdered cars) vehicles and spare fuel cans (unless empty) are forbidden on all trains.

There are no services on board shuttles except for a few toilets. Drivers stay with their vehicles for the duration of the trip (35 minutes). You can get out of your car and stretch your legs, however.

Photo - Euro Tunnel

At the departure terminals there are numerous shops, banks and restaurants as well as cash dispensers - Travelex and an AA shop along with 24-hour information desks.

In the terminals' food villages you will find a variety of fast food bars ranging from Pret a Manger, Burger King and Little Chef. There are also delis, bakeries and self-service food stores.

Directions:
UK - To access the Eurotunnel Folkestone terminal from London, take the M20 southbound and exit at junction 11a.

Photo - Euro Tunnel

France - To access the Eurotunnel Calais/Coquelles Terminal from Paris, take the A16 north and exit junction 13.

Information
Eurotunnel fares, timetable and booking details:
Shuttles from Folkestone or Calais/Coquelles tel: 08705 35 35 35 www.eurotunnel.com

Cross Channel Operators

Brittany Ferries
(Portsmouth to Caen)
tel -08705 360 360 -
www.brittanyferries.co.uk

DFDS Seaways
(Newcastle sailings)
tel - 0870 333 000
www.dfdsseaways.co.uk.

Norfolkline
(Dover to Dunkerque)
tel -0870 870 1020 -
www.norfolkline.com

P&O North Sea Ferries
(Hull to Zeebrugge)
tel -0870 129 6002 -
www.ponsf.com

P&O Portsmouth
(Portsmouth to Cherbourg & Le Have)
tel -0870 242 4999
www.poportsmouth.com

P&O Stena Line
(Dover to Calais)
tel -0870 600 0600
www.posl.com

P&O Sea France
(Dover to Calais)
tel -08705 711 711
www.seafrance.com

Superfast Ferries
(Rosyth to Zeebruge)
tel - 0870 055 1234
www.superfast.com

25

THE **TICKET**
TODD RICHARDS
TEAM DESIGNED | CUSTOM BUILT
WWW.NIXONNOW.COM
PHOTO BY T.CAMPBELL

*See from page 28 for the full country index and mapping references for all 500 listed resorts.

PHOTO - Dean "blotto" Gray - Luke Mitrani *Burton Snowboards youth team rider*

27

Resort Guides

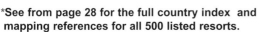

ANDORRA *(Review pages 30)*

Ordino 49 F7
▲ 2620m. 6 Lifts. 15 miles of pistes
Drive - Calais 728 miles - 12 hrs 20
Fly - Barcelona 128miles = 2 hrs 40

Pal 49 F7
▲ 2365m. 14 Lifts. 12 miles of pistes
Drive - Calais 730 miles - 12 hrs 10
Fly - Barcelona 127 miles = 2 hrs 40

AUSTRIA *(Review pages33)*

Abtenau 89 A6
▲ 1260m. 6 Lifts. 10 miles of pistes
Drive - Calais 724 miles - 11 hrs 30
Fly - Salzburg 29 miles = 42 mins

Altenmarkt - Zauchense 89 B6
▲ 2200m. 20 Lifts. 6 miles of pistes
Drive - Calais 724 miles - 11 hrs 30
Fly - Salzburg 50 miles = 42 mins

Annaberg 89 A6
▲ 1400m. 9 Lifts.
Drive - Calais 725 miles - 11 hrs 30
Fly - Salzburg 45 miles = 50 mins

Auffach 88 B4
▲ 1900m. 11 Lifts. 12 miles of pistes
Drive - Calais 674 miles - 11 hrs
Fly - Innsbruck 50 miles = 1 hr

Au & Schoppernau 88 B1
▲ 2090m. 7 Lifts.
Drive - Calais 566 miles - 9 hrs 50
Fly - Innsbruck 88 miles = 2 hrs

Bad Kleinkirchheim 89 C6
▲ 1965m. 20 Lifts. 16 miles of pistes
Drive - Calais 789 miles - 13 hrs
Fly - Klagenfurt 42 miles = 50 mins

Bad Mitterndorf 89 A7
▲ 1965m. 20 Lifts. 16 miles of pistes
Drive - Calais 751 miles - 12 hrs
Fly - Salzburg 50 miles = 1 hr 10 mins

Brixen in Thale 88 B4
▲ 1803m. 89 Lifts. 155 miles of pistes
Drive - Calais 676 miles - 11 hrs 20
Fly - Innsbruck 54 miles = 1 hr

Damüls 87 C7
▲ 2007m. 11 Lifts. 30 miles of pistes
Drive - Calais 570 miles - 10 hrs 10
Fly - Innsbruck 98 miles = 2 hrs

Ehrwald 88 B2
▲ 2964m. 22 Lifts. 30 miles of pistes
Drive - Calais 609 miles - 10 hrs 12
Fly - Innsbruck 54 miles = 1 hr 5

Filzmoos 89 B6
▲ 2500m. 14 Lifts. 22 miles of pistes
Drive - Calais 727 miles - 11 hrs 44
Fly - Salzburg 48 miles = 50 mins

Finkenberg 88 B3
▲ 3250m. 67 Lifts. 62 miles of pistes
Drive - Calais 699 miles - 10 hrs 30
Fly - Innsbruck 48 miles = 1 hr 5

Flachau 89 B6
▲ 1980m. 50 Lifts. 38 miles of pistes
Drive - Calais 727 miles - 11 hrs
Fly - Salzburg 46 miles = 50 mins

Fließ - Tirol West 88 B2
▲ 2212m. 7 Lifts.
Drive - Calais 614 miles - 10 hrs 25
Fly - Innsbruck 48 miles = 52 mins

Fügenberg 88 B3
▲ 2050m. 18 Lifts. 14 miles of pistes
Drive - Calais 685 miles - 10 hrs 50
Fly - Innsbruck 35 miles = 45 mins

Flumpes 88 B3
▲ 2260m. 10 Lifts. 12 miles of pistes
Drive - Calais 714 miles - 10 hrs 15
Fly - Innsbruck 14 miles = 18 mins

Gargellen 87 C7
▲ 2130m. 9 Lifts. 21 miles of pistes
Drive - Calais 586 miles - 10 hrs 20
Fly - Innsbruck 95 miles = 1 hr 50

Gerlos 88 B4
▲ 2300m. 23 Lifts. 44 miles of pistes
Drive - Calais 700 miles - 10 hrs 28
Fly - Innsbruck 52 miles = 1 hr 5

Going 88 A4
▲ 1829m. 6 Lifts. 32 miles of pistes
Drive - Calais 670 miles - 10 hrs 15
Fly - Innsbruck 52 miles = 1hr 5

Gosau 89 A6
▲ 1800m. 32 Lifts. 40 miles of pistes
Drive - Calais 720 miles - 11 hrs 10
Fly - Salzburg 38 miles = 55 mins

Großarl 89 B5
▲ 2027m. 20 Lifts. 50 miles of pistes
Drive - Calais 726 miles - 11 hrs
Fly - Salzburg 45 miles = 1 hr 20

Heiligenblut 89 C5
▲ 1300m. 14 Lifts.
Drive - Calais 744 miles - 11 hrs 5
Fly - Klagenfurt 105 miles = 2 hrs

Hopfgarten in Brixental 88 B4
▲ 1825m. 20 Lifts. 58 miles of pistes
Drive - Calais 670 miles - 10 hrs 15
Fly - Innsbruck 48 miles = 1 hr

Hittisau 88 B1
▲ 1600m. 5 Lifts.
Drive - Calais 556 miles - 9 hrs 50
Fly - Innsbruck 124 miles = 2 hrs 15

Igls 88 B3
▲ 2247m. 6 Lifts. 8 miles of pistes
Drive - Calais 648 miles - 10 hrs 5
Fly - Innsbruck 5 miles = 8 mins

Jerzens 88 B2
▲ 2450m. 19 Lifts.
Drive - Calais 634 miles - 9 hrs 50
Fly - Innsbruck 40 miles = 54 mins

Kirchberg in Tyrol 88 B4
▲ 2000m. 66 Lifts. 25 miles of pistes
Drive - Calais 677 miles - 10 hrs
Fly - Innsbruck 47 miles = 1 hr

Kirchdorf 88 A4
▲ 1000m. 8 Lifts. 6 miles of pistes
Drive - Calais 675 miles - 10 hrs
Fly - Innsbruck 62 miles = 1 hr 15

Kleinwaisertal 88 B1
▲ 2500m. 38 Lifts. 96 miles of pistes
Drive - Calais 600 miles - 9 hrs 45
Fly - Innsbruck 96 miles = 2 hrs 30

Koppl 89 A5
▲ 800m. 3 Lifts. 1 mile of pistes
Drive - Calais 696 miles - 10 hrs 12
Fly - Salzburg 14 miles = 24 mins

Kühtai 88 B2
▲ 2520m. 10 Lifts. 25 miles of pistes
Drive - Calais 645 miles - 10 hrs 15
Fly - Innsbruck 20 miles = 55 mins

Landeck 88 B1
▲ 2212m. 7 Lifts. 16 miles of pistes
Drive - Calais 609 miles - 10 hrs
Fly - Innsbruck 45 miles = 42 mins

Lermoos 88 B2
▲ 2200m. 9 Lifts. 16 miles of pistes
Drive - Calais 607 miles - 9 hrs 50
Fly - Innsbruck 42 miles = 58 mins

Leutasch 88 B2
▲ 1600m. 8 Lifts. 6 miles of pistes
Drive - Calais 641 miles - 10 hrs 12
Fly - Innsbruck 16 miles = 26 mins

Lofer 88 A5
▲ 1747m. 14 Lifts. 20 miles of pistes
Drive - Calais 689 miles - 10 hrs 8
Fly - Salzburg 23 miles = 38 mins

Mallnitz 89 C5
▲ 2650m. 12 Lifts. 20 miles of pistes
Drive - Calais 743 miles - 11 hrs 40
Fly - Salzburg 38 miles = 45 mins

Maria Alm 89 B5
▲ 1900m. 35 Lifts. 56 miles of pistes
Drive - Calais 700 miles - 10 hrs 30
Fly - Salzburg 54 miles = 1 hr 20

Mauterndorf 89 B6
▲ 2360m. 30 Lifts. 112 miles of pistes
Drive - Calais 754 miles - 10 hrs 55
Fly - Salzburg 74 miles = 1 hr 45

Mieders 88 B3
▲ 1780m. 4 Lifts.
Drive - Calais 656 miles - 10 hrs 10
Fly - Innsbruck 46 miles = 1 hr

Mühlbach am Hochkönig 88 B5
▲ 2954m. 48 Lifts. 99 miles of pistes
Drive - Calais 718 miles - 10 hrs 30
Fly - Salzburg 38 miles = 45 mins

Mutters 88 B3
▲ 1800m. 8 Lifts. 6 miles of pistes
Drive - Calais 652 miles - 10 hrs 10
Fly - Innsbruck 6 miles = 12 mins

Neustift 88 B3
▲ 3250m. 12 Lifts. 40 miles of pistes
Drive - Calais 662 miles - 10 hrs 15
Fly - Innsbruck 16 miles = 22 mins

Niederau 88 B4
▲ 1600m. 11 Lifts. 10 miles of pistes
Drive - Calais 668 miles - 10 hrs 10
Fly - miles = mins

Oberau 88 B4
▲ 1200m. 7 Lifts. 6 miles of pistes
Drive - Calais 670 miles - 10 hrs 20
Fly - Innsbruck 48 miles = 54 mins

Partenen 88 C1
▲ 2300m. 32 Lifts. 62 miles of pistes
Drive - Calais 589 miles - 10 hrs 12
Fly - Innsbruck 80 miles = 1 hr 50

Pettneu am Arlberg 88 B1
▲ 2040m. 4 Lifts. 10 miles of pistes
Drive - Calais 597 miles - 10 hrs 10
Fly - Innsbruck 58 miles = 1 hr 5

Pertisau 88 B3
▲ 1491m.
Drive - Calais 690 miles - 10 hrs 16
Fly - 690 miles = 10 mins 16

Radstadt 89 B6
▲ 1700m. 10 Lifts. 12 miles of pistes
Drive - Calais 729 miles - 10 hrs 40
Fly - Salzburg 44 miles = 52 mins

Ramsau am Dachstein 89 B6
▲ 2700m. 20 Lifts. 25 miles of pistes
Drive - Calais 700 miles - 10 hrs 30
Fly - Innsbruck 44 miles = 58 mins

Scheffau 88 A4
▲ 1829m. 15 Lifts. 155 miles of pistes
Drive - Calais 671 miles - 10 hrs 5
Fly - Innsbruck 52 miles = 1 hr 42

Schruns 87 C7
▲ 2400m. 13 Lifts. 25 miles of pistes
Drive - Calais 601 miles - 10 hrs 5
Fly - Innsbruck 88 miles = 1 hr 55

Serfaus 87 C8
▲ 2684m. 22 Lifts. 50 miles of pistes
Drive - Calais 659 miles - 10 hrs 30
Fly - Innsbruck 92 miles = 1 hr 10

Sillian 88 C4
▲ 2407m. 6 Lifts.
Drive - Calais 794 miles - 12 hrs 15
Fly - Innsbruck 92 miles = 1 hr 55

Spital am Pyhrn 89 A7
▲ 1870m. 10 Lifts. 11 miles of pistes
Drive - Calais 791 miles - 12 hrs 33
Fly - Salzburg 93 miles = 1 hr 40

St Christoph am Arlberg 88 B1
▲ 2811m. 35 Lifts. 106 miles of pistes
Drive - Calais 669 miles - 10 hrs 10
Fly - Innsbruck 65 miles = 1 hr 20

St Gallenkirch 87 C7
▲ 2370m. 13 Lifts. 62 miles of pistes
Drive - Calais 605 miles - 11 hrs
Fly - Innsbruck 90 miles = 2 rs

St Michael in Lungau 89 B6
▲ 2360m. 30 Lifts. 40 miles of pistes
Drive - Calais 756 miles - 10 hrs 25
Fly - Salzburg 68 miles = 1 hr 5

St Wolfgang 89 A6
▲ 1350m. 9 Lifts. 11 miles of pistes
Drive - Calais 726 miles - 10 hrs 35
Fly - Salzburg 38 miles = 58 mins

Stans 88 B3
▲ 791m. 2 Lifts. 1 mile of pistes
Drive - Calais 726 miles - 11 hrs
Fly - Innsbruck 24 miles = 30 mins

Sulzberg 87 B7
▲10 Lifts.
Drive - Calais 596 miles - 5 hrs
Fly - Zurich 90 miles = 1 hr 40

Tschagguns 87 C7
▲ 2085m. 9 Lifts. 20 miles of pistes
Drive - Calais 600 miles - 10 hrs
Fly - Innsbruck 88 miles = 1 hr 50

Unken 88 A5
▲ 18 Lifts.
Drive - Calais 689 miles - 10 hrs 16
Fly - Salzburg 20 miles = 34 mins

Uttendorf 88 B4
▲ 800m. 6 Lifts.
Drive - Calais 705 miles - 10 hrs 50
Fly - Salzburg 71 miles = 1hr 40

Vent 88 C1
▲ 2680m. 4 Lifts. 9 miles of pistes
Drive - Calais 674 miles - 11 hrs 7
Fly - Innsbruck 62 miles = 1 hr 40

Villach 89 C6
▲ 2167m. 8 Lifts. 7 miles of pistes
Drive - Calais 799 miles - 12 hrs 30
Fly - Klagenfurt 19 miles = 24 mins

Wagrain 89 B6
▲ 2190m. 51 Lifts. 37 miles of pistes
Drive - Calais 730 miles - 12 hrs
Fly - Salzburg 45 miles = 1 hr 18

Waidring 88 B4
▲ 1900m. 12 Lifts. 16 miles of pistes
Drive - Calais 689 miles - 11 hrs
Fly - Salzburg 30 miles = 50 mins

Westendorf 88 B4
▲ 1865m. 21 Lifts. 40 miles of pistes
Drive - Calais 708 miles - 10 hrs 50
Fly - Innsbruck 51 miles = 58 mins

Wörgl 88 B4
▲ 815m. 3 Lifts. 2 miles of pistes
Drive - Calais 671 miles - 10 hrs
Fly - Innsbruck 42 miles = 45 mins

Zams 88 B2
▲ 2121m. 7 Lifts. 16 miles of pistes
Drive - Calais 645 miles - 10 hrs 5
Fly - Innsbruck 44 miles = 48 mins

Zell am Ziller 88 B3
▲ 2480m. 31 Lifts. 30 miles of pistes
Drive - Calais 697 miles - 11 hrs
Fly - Innsbruck 37 miles = 43 mins

Zurs 88 B1
▲ 2450m. 32 Lifts. 68 miles of pistes
Drive - Calais 614 miles - 10 hrs 5
Fly - Innsbruck 69 miles = 1 hr 23

BULGARIA *(Review pages 46)*

CZECH REPUBLIC

Harrachov 97 E6
▲ 1020m. 15 Lifts. 5 miles of pistes
Drive - Calais 727 miles - 12 hrs 50
Fly - Prague 80 miles = 1 hr 40

Janske Lazne 97 E6
▲ 1275m. 11 Lifts. 4 miles of pistes
Drive - Calais 760 miles - 13 hrs 45
Fly - Prague 100 miles = 2 hrs

Pec Pod Snezkou 97 E6
▲ 1602m. 45 Lifts. 7 miles of pistes
Drive - Calais 740 miles - 13 hrs 30
Fly - Prague 110 miles = 2 hrs 10

Spindleruv Mlyn 97 E6
▲ 1310m. 31 Lifts. 16 miles of pistes
Drive - Calais 752 miles - 13 hrs 30
Fly - Prague 105 miles = 2 hrs 10

Zelezna Ruda 92 D3
▲ 1200m. 26 Lifts. 10 miles of pistes
Drive - Calais 646 miles - 11 hrs 5
Fly - Prague 106 miles = 2 hrs 15

FINLAND *(Review pages 48)*

Isö-Syöte - Pudasjärvi 136 D4
▲ 430m. 12 Lifts. 9 miles of pistes
Drive - Helsinki 428 miles - 8 hrs 5
Fly - Oulo 99 miles = 1 hr 30

Jyväskylä 140 F2
5 Lifts.
Drive - Helsinki 164 miles - 3 hrs 5
Fly - Helsinki 164 miles = 3 hrs 5

Kasurila 140 C4
Drive - Helsinki 228 miles - 4 hrs 20
Fly - Helsinki 228 miles = 4 hrs 20

Levi - Sirkka 133 C6
▲ 531m. 16 Lifts. 20 miles of pistes
Drive - Helsinki 628 miles - 12 hrs 20
Fly - Kittila 10 miles = 2 mins

Olos - Muonio 133 C5
▲ 340m. 4 Lifts. 4 miles of pistes
Drive - Helsinki 631 miles - 12 hrs 35
Fly - Kittila 43 miles = 50 mins

Ounasvaara - Rovaniemi 135 A7
4 Lifts. 60 miles of pistes
Drive - Helsinki 514 miles - 9 hrs 50
Fly - Rovaniemi 6 miles = 12 mins

Pallas
▲ 807m. 4 Lifts. 3 miles of pistes
Drive - Helsinki 634 miles - 12 hrs 35
Fly - Kittila 48 miles = 1 hr

Pyhä
8 Lifts.
Drive - Helsinki 595 miles - 11 hrs 45
Fly - Rovaniemi 7 miles = 12 mins

Saariselkä - Ivalo 133 B8
6 Lifts. 6 miles of pistes
Drive - Helsinki 694 miles - 13 hrs 25
Fly - Ivalo 16 miles = 20 mins

Sappee 143 C6
Drive - Helsinki 229 miles - 4 hrs 20
Fly - Helsinki 229 miles = 4 hrs 20

Ylläs 133 D5
▲ 718m. 18 Lifts. 4 miles of pistes
Drive - Helsinki 571 miles - 11 hrs 5
Fly - Kittila 44 miles = 58 hrs

FRANCE *(Review pages 50)*

Alpe du Grand Serre 47 F6
▲2200m. 20 Lifts. 34 miles of pistes
Drive - Calais 556 miles - 8 hrs 50
Fly - Grenoble 50 miles = 1 hr 5

Argentière 47 D8
▲3275m. 11 Lifts. 20 miles of pistes
Drive - Calais 560 miles - 9 hrs
Fly - Geneva 56 miles = 1 hr 10

Auris en Oisans 47 F6
▲2175m. 15 Lifts.
Drive - Calais 571 miles - 8 hrs 55
Fly - Nice 58 miles = 1 hr 12

Auron 52 B4
▲2450m. 26 Lifts. 81 miles of pistes
Drive - Calais 633 miles - 11 hrs 32
Fly - Nice 58 miles = 1 hr 15

Aussois 47 E7
▲2750m. 11 Lifts.
Drive - Calais 595 miles - 9 hrs 20
Fly - Lyon 129 miles = 2 hr 7

Autrans 46 F5
▲1710m. 16 Lifts.
Drive - Calais 547 miles - 8 hrs 45
Fly - Grenoble 32 miles = 57 hr

Ax Les Thermes 49 E7
▲2400m. Lifts. 26 runs
Drive - Calais 688 miles - 10 hrs 54
Fly - Toulouse 85 miles = 1 hr 50

Barèges 49 E5
▲2450m. 21 Lifts. 38 miles of pistes
Drive - Calais 697 miles - 10 hrs 17
Fly - Nice 114 miles = 2 hrs 8

Bellevaux 47 C7
▲1650m. 23 Lifts. 30 miles of pistes
Drive - Calais 535 miles - 9 hrs
Fly - Geneva 30 miles = 52 mins

Bonneval sur Arc 47 E8
▲3000m. 10 Lifts. 19 runs
Drive - Calais 620 miles - 9 hrs 30
Fly - Lyon 150 miles = 2 hr 40

Briancon 47 F7
▲3200m. 200 Lifts. 155 miles of pistes
Drive - Calais 627 miles - 10 hrs 12
Fly - Grenoble 79 miles = 2 hrs

Brides-les-Bains 47 E7
▲2952m. 58 Lifts. 370 miles of pistes
Drive - Calais 697 miles - 10 hrs 17
Fly - Grenoble 64 miles = 1 hr 18

Cauterets 48 E4
▲3843m. 49 Lifts. 20 miles of pistes
Drive - Calais 733 miles - 12 hrs
Fly - Toulouse 127 miles = 2 hrs 15

Champagny-en-Vanoise 47 E7
▲3250m. 8 Lifts. 130 miles of pistes
Drive - Calais 589 miles - 10 hrs
Fly - Grenoble 91 miles = 2 hrs 15

Combloux 47 D7
▲2350m. 25 Lifts. 87 miles of pistes
Drive - Calais 556 miles - 9 hrs
Fly - Geneva 51 miles = 57 mins

Cordon 47 D7
▲1600m. 6 Lifts. 6 miles of pistes
Drive - Calais 546 miles - 9 hrs 5
Fly - Geneva 30 miles = 52 miles

Corrençon-en-Vercors 47 F5
▲2170m. 11 Lifts. 80 miles of pistes
Drive - Calais 548 miles - 8 hrs 55
Fly - Grenoble 32 miles = 54 mins

Flumet 47 D7
▲2070m. 10 Lifts. 24 runs
Drive - Calais 553 miles - 9 hrs
Fly - Geneva 50 miles = 1 hr

Font Romeu 49 F8
▲2200m. 33 Lifts. 32 miles of pistes
Drive - Calais 722 miles - 11 hrs 50
Fly - Toulouse 114 miles = 2 hrs 40

Gourette 48 E4
▲2400m. 21 Lifts. 39 miles of pistes
Drive - Calais 692 miles - 11 hrs 35
Fly - miles = hr

Gresse en Vercors 47 F5
▲1700m. 18 Lifts. 20 miles of pistes
Drive - Calais 561 miles - 9 hrs 12
Fly - Grenoble 30 miles = 42 mins

Guzet-Neige 49 E7
▲2100m. 20 Lifts. 34 runs
Drive - Calais 688 miles - 10 hrs 40
Fly - Toulouse 82 miles = 1 hr 40

La Chapelle-d'Abondance 47 C7
▲1800m. 12 Lifts. 28 miles of pistes
Drive - Calais 515 miles - 8 hrs 35
Fly - Geneva 40 miles = 1 hr 7

La Grave 47 F7
▲3500m. 4 Lifts. 7 miles of pistes
Drive - Calais 586 miles - 9 hrs 15
Fly - Grenoble 54 miles = 1 hr 30

La Joue du loup 52 A3
▲2430m. 4 Lifts. 62 miles of pistes
Drive - Calais 589 miles - 9 hrs 10
Fly - Grenoble 60 miles = 1 hr 28

La Norma 47 E7
▲2750m. 18 Lifts. 40 miles of pistes
Drive - Calais 603 miles - 9 hrs 8
Fly - Lyon 137 miles = 2 hrs 24

La Tania 47 E7
▲3000m. 67 Lifts. 124 miles of pistes
Drive - Calais 590 miles - 9 hrs 22
Fly - Geneva 94 miles = 2 hrs 25

La Toussuire 47 E7
▲2620m. 19 Lifts. 25 miles of pistes
Drive - Calais 582 miles - 8 hrs 55
Fly - Geneva 115 miles = 1 hr 55

Lans en Vercors 47 F5
▲1870m. 16 Lifts. 15 miles of pistes
Drive - Calais 544 miles - 8 hrs 35
Fly - Grenoble 30 miles = 50 mins

Le Bonhomme 43 D5
▲1235m. 9 Lifts. 14 runs
Drive - Calais 394 miles - 6 hrs 22
Fly - Mulhouse 55 miles = 1 hr 10

Le Corbier 47 E7
▲2260m. 24 Lifts. 26 hrs 22
Drive - Calais 582 miles - 8 hrs 50
Fly - Geneva 115 miles = 1 hr 52

Le Collet d'Allevard 47 E6
▲2100m. 13 Lifts. 18 miles of pistes
Drive - Calais 697 miles - 9 hrs 50
Fly - Grenoble 25 miles = 33 mins

Le Grand Bornand 47 D7
▲2100m. 39 Lifts. 50 runs
Drive - Calais 540 miles - 8 hrs 30
Fly - Geneva 35 miles = 56 mins

Le Lioran 46 E1
▲1850m. 24 Lifts. 27 miles
Drive - Calais 508 miles - 8 hrs
Fly - Clemont 23 miles = 35 mins

Le Mont Doré 46 E1
▲1850m. 20 Lifts. 30 runs
Drive - Calais 471 miles - 7 hrs 20
Fly - Clemont 34 miles = 46 mins

Le Pleyney 47 E6
▲2400m. 24 Lifts. 38 runs
Drive - Calais 552 miles - 8 hrs 20
Fly - Grenoble 15 miles = 26 mins

Le Sauze Super Sauze 52 B4
▲2400m. 23 Lifts. 37 runs
Drive - Calais 645 miles - 10 hrs 50
Fly - Grenoble 111 miles = 3 hrs

Les Aillons 47 D6
▲1900m. 24 Lifts. 42 runs
Drive - Calais 530 miles - 8 hrs 20
Fly - Grenoble 48 miles = 1 hr 5

Les Angles 49 F8
▲2400m. 24 Lifts. 25 miles of pistes
Drive - Calais 711 miles - 10 hrs 54
Fly - Toulouse 99 miles = 1 hr 48

Les Carroz 47 D7
▲2480m. 15 Lifts. 80 miles of pistes
Drive - Calais 537 miles - 8 hrs 12
Fly - Geneva 31 miles = 48 mins

Les Contamines 47 D7
▲2500m. 26 Lifts. 75 miles of pistes
Drive - Calais 553 miles - 8 hrs 50
Fly - Geneva 50 miles = 1 hr

Les Gets 47 C7
▲544m. 53 Lifts. 80 miles of pistes
Drive - Calais 544 miles - 8 hrs 38
Fly - Geneva 30 miles = 50 mins

Les Houches 47 D7
▲1900m. 18 Lifts. 31 miles of pistes
Drive - Calais 550 miles - 9 hrs
Fly - Geneva 47 miles = 55 mins

Les Karellis 47 E7
▲2850m. 46 Lifts. 35 miles of pistes
Drive - Calais 580 miles - 8 hrs 55
Fly - Lyon 110 miles = 1 hr 48

Les Ménuires 47 E7
▲2850m. 46 Lifts. 75 miles of pistes
Drive - Calais 592 miles - 9 hrs 6
Fly - Geneva 94 miles = 2 hrs 10

Les Orres 52 B4
▲2700m. 24 Lifts. 40 miles of pistes
Drive - Calais 624 miles - 10 hrs 12
Fly - Grenoble 88 miles = 2 hrs 22

Les Rousses 47 C6
▲1680m. 40 Lifts. 43 runs
Drive - Calais 442 miles - 6 hrs 58
Fly - Annec y 62 miles = 1 hr 20

Les Saisies 47 D7
▲2000m. 24 Lifts. 30 runs
Drive - Calais 569 miles - 8 hrs 45
Fly - Geneva 64 miles = 1 hr 27

Les Sept Laux 47 E6
▲2400m. 31 Lifts. 62 miles of pistes
Drive - Calais 552 miles - 8 hrs 30
Fly - Grenoble 83 miles = 1 hr 30

Luz Ardiden 48 E4
▲2450m. 15 Lifts. 27 runs
Drive - Calais 739 miles - 11 hrs 30
Fly - Toulouse 132 miles = 2 hrs 25

Méaudre 47 F5
▲1600m. 46 Lifts. 13 runs
Drive - Calais 550 miles - 9 hrs 10
Fly - Grenoble 24 miles = 40 mins

Megève 47 D7
▲2350m. 79 Lifts. 135 runs
Drive - Calais 550 miles - 9 hrs 10
Fly - Geneva 84 miles = 2 hrs 25

Métabief 47 B7
▲1460m. 19 Lifts. 26 miles of pistes
Drive - Calais 435 miles - 7 hrs 20
Fly - Geneva 65 miles = 1 hr 10

Mijoux 47 C6
▲1680m. 29 Lifts.
Drive - Calais 451 miles - 7 hrs 15
Fly - Annecy 47 miles = 1 hr

Mont Jura 47 C6
▲1685m. 13 Lifts. 36 runs
Drive - Calais 475 miles - 7 hrs 35
Fly - Annecy 42 miles = 2 hrs 7

Montchavin les Coches 47 E7
▲3250m. 111 Lifts. 130 miles of pistes
Drive - Calais 594 miles - 9 hrs 20
Fly - 98 miles = 2 hrs 25

Morillon 47 C7
▲2500m. 47 Lifts. 79 miles of pistes
Drive - Calais 542 miles - 8 hrs 10
Fly - Geneva 38 miles = 56 hr

Notre Dame de Bellecombe 47 D7
▲2070m. 17 Lifts. 5 miles of pistes
Drive - Calais 557 miles - 8 hrs 45
Fly - Geneva 53 miles = 1 hr 6

Orcières - Merlette 52 A3
▲2725m. 29 Lifts. 44 runs
Drive - Calais 603 miles - 9 hrs 42
Fly - Grenoble 72 miles = 1 hr 56

Oz en Oisans 47 F6
▲2850m. 22 Lifts. 35 runs
Drive - Calais 567 miles - 8 hrs 50
Fly - Grenoble 35 miles = 1 hr 5

Peisey - Vallandry 47 E7
▲3226m. 76 Lifts. 124 miles of pistes
Drive - Calais 594 miles - 9 hrs 20
Fly - Geneva 98 miles = 2 hrs 25

Piau Engaly 49 E5
▲2500m. 21 Lifts. 22 miles of pistes
Drive - Calais 707 miles - 10 hrs 55
Fly - Toulouse 101 miles = 1 hr 50

Pra Loup 52 B4
▲2600m. 32 Lifts. 50 miles of pistes
Drive - Calais 643 miles - 10 hrs 48
Fly - Grenoble 106 miles = 2 hrs 55

Pralognan la Vanoise 47 E7
▲2400m. 14 Lifts. 22 miles of pistes
Drive - Calais 596 miles - 10 hrs
Fly - Geneva 100 miles = 2 hrs 40

Praz de Lys - Sommand 47 C7
▲2000m. 23 Lifts. 32 miles of pistes
Drive - Calais 539 miles - 8 hrs
Fly - Geneva 34 miles = 42 mins

Praz sur Arly 47 D7
▲2070m. 12 Lifts. 38 miles of pistes
Drive - Calais 550 miles - 8 hrs 10
Fly - Geneva 47 miles = 1 hr

Prémanon 47 C6
▲1680m. 40 Lifts. 43 runs
Drive - Calais 442 miles - 7 hrs
Fly - Geneva 30 miles = 40 mins

Puy Saint Vincent 47 F7
▲2750m. 16 Lifts. 30 miles of pistes
Drive - Calais 548 miles - 8 hrs 20
Fly - Turin 86 miles = 2 hrs

Réallon 52 B3
▲2115m. 7 Lifts. 17 runs
Drive - Calais 612 miles - 10 hrs 5
Fly - Grenoble 81 miles = 2 hrs 18

Saint Gervais 47 D7
▲2350m. 79 Lifts. 135 runs
Drive - Calais 553 miles - 8 hrs 15
Fly - Geneva 50 miles = 1 hr 10

Saint Jean Montclar 52 B3
▲639m. 16 Lifts. 20 runs
Drive - Calais 639 miles - 10 hrs 35
Fly - Grenoble 96 miles = 2 hrs 34

Saint Jeande Sixt 47 D7
2 Lifts. 4 runs
Drive - Calais 535 miles - 8 hrs
Fly - Geneva 30 miles = 45 mins

Saint Maurice sur Moselle 43 E5
▲1250m. 8 Lifts. 11 runs
Drive - Calais 399 miles - 6 hrs 35
Fly - Mulhouse 40 miles = 1 hr 5

Saint Nicolas de Véroce 47 D7
▲2350m. 10 Lifts. 26 runs
Drive - Calais 515 miles - 8 hrs 20
Fly - Geneva 50 miles = 1 hr 5

Sainte Foy en Tarentaise 47 D8
▲2620m. 5 Lifts. 14 runs
Drive - Calais 605 miles - 9 hrs 8
Fly - Geneva 101 miles = 2 hrs 30

Samoëns 47 C7
▲2480m. 16 Lifts. 20 miles of pistes
Drive - Calais 543 miles - 8 hrs 10
Fly - Geneva 40 miles = 55 mins

St François Longchamp 47 E7
▲2550m. 17 Lifts. 40 miles of pistes
Drive - Calais 582 miles - 8 hrs 50
Fly - Geneva 47 miles = 1 hr

Super Besse 46 E1
▲1850m. 22 Lifts. 25 runs
Drive - Calais 581 miles - 9 hrs 30
Fly - Grenoble 50 miles = 1 hr 26

Superbagnères 49 E5
▲2260m. 16 Lifts. 14 miles of pistes
Drive - Calais 700 miles - 11 hrs
Fly - Toulouse 94 miles = 1 hr 55

Superdévoluy 52 A3
▲2510m. 32 Lifts. 62 miles of pistes
Drive - Calais 589 miles - 9 hrs 15
Fly - Grenoble 60 miles = 1 hr 28

Termignon 47 E7
▲2480m. 9 Lifts. 15 runs
Drive - Calais 613 miles - 9 hrs 30
Fly - Turin 75 miles = 2 hrs

Thollon les Memises 47 C7
▲2000m. 18 Lifts. 30 miles of pistes
Drive - Calais 613 miles - 9 hrs 35
Fly - Geneva 40 miles = 1 hr 15

Val Cenis 47 E7
▲2800m. 22 Lifts. 43 miles of pistes
Drive - Calais 620 miles - 9 hrs 30
Fly - Turin 70 miles = 1 hr 38

Val d'Allos la Foux 52 B4
▲2600m. 33 Lifts. 32 runs
Drive - Calais 653 miles - 11 hrs
Fly - Grenoble 124 miles = 3 hrs 25

Val d'Allos le Seignus 52 B4
▲2426m. 14 Lifts. 15 runs
Drive - Calais 471 miles - 8 hrs 10
Fly - Grenoble 126 miles = 3 hrs 30

Valberg Peone 52 C4
▲21000m. 24 Lifts. 58 runs
Drive - Calais 684 miles - 12 hrs
Fly - Grenoble 146 miles = 4 hrs

Valfréjus 47 F7
▲2737m. 12 Lifts. 32 miles of pistes
Drive - Calais 603 miles - 9 hrs 10
Fly - Turin 80 miles = 1 hr 40

Valmeinier 47 F7
▲2600m. 35 Lifts. 95 miles of pistes
Drive - Calais 595 miles - 9 hrs 10
Fly - Geneva 125 miles = 2 hrs 10

Vars 52 A4
▲2750m. 56 Lifts. 60 miles of pistes
Drive - Calais 660 miles - 10 hrs 30
Fly - Turin 102 miles = 2 hrs 20

Vaujany 47 F6
▲2800m. 18 Lifts. 30 miles of pistes
Drive - Calais 568 miles - 9 hrs
Fly - Grenoble 40 miles = 1 hr 15

Ventron 43 E5
▲1110m. 8 Lifts. 10 runs
Drive - Calais 400 miles - 5 hrs 20
Fly - Mulhouse 50 miles = 1 hr

Vic Sur Cère 46 F1
▲1850m. 24 Lifts. 40 runs
Drive - Calais 522 miles - 8 hrs
Fly - Clemont 88 miles = 1 hr 45

Villard de Lans 47 F5
▲2170m. 29 Lifts. 80 miles of pistes
Drive - Calais 588 miles - 8 hrs 20
Fly - Grenoble 22 miles = 38 mins

Villard Reculas 47 F6
▲3330m. 9 Lifts. 16 miles of pistes
Drive - Calais 568 miles - 8 hrs 45
Fly - Grenoble 38 miles = 58 mins

Xonrupt 43 D5
▲1300m. 2 Lifts.
Drive - Calais 393 miles - 6 hrs 20
Fly - Mulhouse 44 miles = 1 hr 10

GERMANY (Review pages 64)

Balderschwang 88 B1
▲1500m. 10 Lifts. 16 miles of pistes
Drive - Calais 607 miles - 9 hrs 20
Fly - Munich 125 miles = 2 hrs 24

Bayerisch Eisenstein 92 D3
▲1450m. 7 Lifts. 5 miles of pistes
Drive - Calais 642 miles - 9 hrs 40
Fly - Munich 121 miles = 2 hr 14

Bayrischzell 88 A4
▲1580m. 22 Lifts. 25 miles of pistes
Drive - Calais 652 miles - 9 hrs 47
Fly - Munich 50 miles = 1 hr 10

Berchtesgadener Land 89 A5
▲1800m. 21 Lifts. 34 miles of pistes
Drive - Calais 690 miles - 10 hrs 12
Fly - Munich 86 miles = 1 hr 28

Bischofsmais 92 D3
▲1121m. 7 Lifts. 2 miles of pistes
Drive - Calais 620 miles - 9 hrs 10
Fly - Munich 103 miles = 1 hr 44

Bolsterlang 88 B1
▲1665m. 9 Lifts. 11 miles of pistes
Drive - Calais 601 miles - 9 hrs 5
Fly - Munich 118 miles = 2 hrs 12

Grainau 88 B2
▲2830m. 12 Lifts. 75 miles of pistes
Drive - Calais 656 miles - 9 hrs 55
Fly - Munich 60 miles = 1 hr 18

Jenner 89 A5
▲1800m. 5 Lifts. 6 miles of pistes
Drive - Calais 703 miles - 10 hrs 30
Fly - Salzburg 42 miles = 60 hr

Mittenwald 47 C7
▲2244m. 8 Lifts. 14 miles of pistes
Drive - Calais 658 miles - 10 hrs
Fly - Munich 65 miles = 1 hr 15

Oberammergau 88 A2
▲1683m. 9 Lifts. 20 miles of pistes
Drive - Calais 648 miles - 9 hrs 40
Fly - Munich 56 miles = 1 hr

Oberaudorf 88 A4
▲900m. 4 Lifts. 5 miles of pistes
Drive - Calais 660 miles - 9 hrs 40
Fly - Munich 58 miles = 1 hr 10

Oberjoch 88 A1
▲1630m. 17 Lifts. 19 miles of pistes
Drive - Calais 603 miles - 9 hrs 10
Fly - Munich 90 miles = 1 hr 50

Oberstaufen 88 A1
▲1340m. 13 Lifts. 12 miles of pistes
Drive - Calais 600 miles - 9 hrs 20
Fly - Munich 110 miles = 2 hrs 5

Oberstdorf 88 B1
▲2200m. 31 Lifts. 27 miles of pistes
Drive - Calais 601 miles - 9 hrs 10
Fly - Innsbruck 95 miles = 2 hrs 26

Pfronten 88 A1
▲1678m. 16 Lifts. 12 miles of pistes
Drive - Calais 592 miles - 8 hrs 45
Fly - Munich 80 miles = 1 hr 40

Reit im Winkl 88 A4
▲1850m. 21 Lifts. 30 miles of pistes
Drive - Calais 676 miles - 8 hrs 45
Fly - Munich 70 miles = 1 hr 20

Rettenberg 88 A1
▲1670m. 14 Lifts. 25 miles of pistes
Drive - Calais 593 miles - 8 hrs 45
Fly - Munich 88 miles = 1 hr 50

Ruhpolding 88 A5
▲1645m. 8 Lifts. 9 miles of pistes
Drive - Calais 674 miles - 10 hrs
Fly - Munich 70 miles = 1 hr 10

Sankt Englmar 92 D2
▲1035m. 14 Lifts. 7 miles of pistes
Drive - Calais 620 miles - 9 hrs 10
Fly - Munich 116 miles = 1 hr 50

Schönau am Königssee 89 A4
▲1800m. 4 Lifts. 6 miles of pistes
Drive - Calais 706 miles - 10 hrs 45
Fly - Munich 45 miles = 1 hr 12

Winterberg 37 B7
▲809m. 8 Lifts. 25 miles of pistes
Drive - Calais 341 miles - 5 hrs 18
Fly - Dortmund 93 miles = 1 hr 10

Zwiesel 92 D3
▲750m. 8 Lifts. 4 miles of pistes
Drive - Calais 633 miles - 9 hrs 25
Fly - Munich 111 miles = 2 hrs

GREAT BRITAIN (Review pages 66)

Castleford Xscape 27 D6
1 Lift. 1 mile of pistes
Drive - London 187 miles - 3 hrs 26
Fly - Manchester 66 miles = 1 hr 20

Glenshee 21 A6
▲1060m. 26 Lifts. 25 miles of pistes
Drive - London 490 miles - 8 hrs
Fly - Aberdeen 71 miles = 1 hr 45

Glencoe 20 B4
▲1097m. 6 Lifts. 7 miles of pistes
Drive - London 491 miles - 8 hrs 20
Fly - Inverness 99 miles = 2 hrs 25

Milton Keynes Xscape 31 C5
1 Lift. 1 mile of pistes
Drive - London 54 miles - 1 hrs 20
Fly - Birmingham 67 miles = 1 hr 35

Tamworth Snow Zone 30 B4
2 Lifts. 1 mile of pistes
Drive - London 120 miles - 2 hrs 20
Fly - Birmingham 19 miles = 40 mins

ITALY (Review pages 68)

Abetone 82 D1
▲1900m. 25 Lifts. 30 miles of pistes
Drive - Calais 831 miles - 13 hrs 5
Fly - Milan 168 miles = 3 hr 25

Alagna Valsesia 84 B3
▲3550m. 5 Lifts. 14 miles of pistes
Drive - Calais 720 miles - 11 hrs 30
Fly - Milan 94 miles = 2 hrs 20

Alba 53 A6
▲2441m. 5 Lifts. 6 miles of pistes
Drive - Calais 807 miles - 12 hrs 45
Fly - Innsbruck 95 miles = 1 hr 45

Alleghe 88 D4
▲2100m. 8 Lifts. 20 miles of pistes
Drive - Calais 810 miles - 12 hrs 36
Fly - Innsbruck 108 miles = 2 hr 10

Alpe di Siusi / Seiser Alm 88 D3
▲2454m. 19 Lifts. 44 miles of pistes
Drive - Calais 772 miles - 11 hrs 40
Fly - Innsbruck 70 miles = 1 hr 30

Artesina 53 B6
▲2064m. 12 Lifts. 38 miles of pistes
Drive - Calais 723 miles - 11 hrs 15
Fly - Turin 68 miles = 1 hr 38

Asiago 88 E3
▲2010m. 22 Lifts. 62 miles of pistes
Drive - Calais 826 miles - 12 hrs 30
Fly - Milan 170 miles = 2 hrs 55

Bardonecchia 47 F7
▲2750m. 22 Lifts. 88 miles of pistes
Drive - Calais 604 miles - 9 hrs 5
Fly - Turin 60 miles = 1 hr 10

Barzio 85 A5
▲2359m. 19 Lifts. 32 miles of pistes
Drive - Calais 645 miles - 10 hrs
Fly - Milan 23 miles = 30 mins

Bellamonte 88 D3
▲2500m. 9 Lifts. 46 miles of pistes
Drive - Calais 820 miles - 12 hrs 35
Fly - Innsbruck 103 miles = 2 hrs

Brixen / Plose 88 C3
▲2574m. 10 Lifts. 25 miles of pistes
Drive - Calais 755 miles - 11 hrs 5
Fly - Innsbruck 52 miles = 1 hr 5

Campitello di Fassa 88 D3
▲2428m. 7 Lifts. 9 miles of pistes
Drive - Calais 794 miles - 12 hrs
Fly - Innsbruck 92 miles = 2 hrs

Campo Felice 78 C3
▲2064m. 30 Lifts. 25 miles of pistes
Drive - Calais 1055 miles - 16 hrs
Fly - Rome 90 miles = 1 hr 42

Cavalese 88 D3
▲2230m. 9 Lifts. 12 miles of pistes
Drive - Calais 763 miles - 12 hrs
Fly - Innsbruck 93 miles = 1 hr 50

Cesana 47 F7
▲2700m. 25 Lifts. 25 miles of pistes
Drive - Calais 621 miles - 9 hrs 40
Fly - Turin 63 miles = 1 hr 12

Champoluc 84 B3
▲2727m. 15 Lifts. 38 miles of pistes
Drive - Calais 684 miles - 9 hrs 40
Fly - Turin 66 miles = 1 hr 16

Chiesa 88 D4
▲2336m. 10 Lifts. 16 miles of pistes
Drive - Calais 800 miles - 12 hrs 50
Fly - Milan 144 miles 2 hrs 40

Cimone - Montecreto 82 C1
▲1976m. 27 Lifts. 50 miles of pistes
Drive - Calais 809 miles - 12 hrs 26
Fly - Milan 147 miles = 2 hrs 45

Corvara 78 B4
▲2550m. 57 Lifts. 80 miles of pistes
Drive - Calais 1052 miles - 15 hrs 40
Fly - Rome 114 miles = 1 hr 55

Dobbiaco / Toblach 88 C4
▲2200m. 26 Lifts. 30 miles of pistes
Drive - Calais 788 miles - 12 hrs
Fly - Innsbruck 85 miles = 1 hr 45

Falcade 88 D3
▲2428m. 11 Lifts. 25 miles of pistes
Drive - Calais 812 miles - 12 hrs 25
Fly - Innsbruck 109 miles = 2 hrs

Folgaria 85 A8
▲2007m. 40 Lifts. 30 miles of pistes
Drive - Calais 798 miles - 12 hrs 10
Fly - Milan 143 miles = 2 hrs 35

Gressoney-La-Trinité 84 B3
▲2861m. 12 Lifts. 30 miles of pistes
Drive - Calais 644 miles - 10 hrs
Fly - Turin 67 miles = 1 hr 20

Gressoney-St-Jean 84 B3
▲2020m. 4 Lifts. 7 miles of pistes
Drive - Calais 636 miles - 9 hrs 45
Fly - Turin 60 miles = 1 hr 15

Kastelruth/Castelrotto 88 D3
▲1500m. 3 Lifts. 2 miles of pistes
Drive - Calais 770 miles - 11 hrs 20
Fly - Innsbruck 68 miles = 1 hr 12

Macugnaga 84 A3
▲2970m. 12 Lifts. 24 miles of pistes
Drive - Calais 623 miles - 11 hrs 5
Fly - Milan 91 miles = 2 hrs 20

Malga San Giorgio 85 B8
▲1806m. 7 Lifts. 10 miles of pistes
Drive - Calais 778 miles - 12 hrs
Fly - Milan 123 miles = 2 hrs 20

Marilléva 88 D2
▲2050m. 30 Lifts. 66 miles of pistes
Drive - Calais 829 miles - 12 hrs 28
Fly - Innsbruck 126 miles = 2 hrs 20

Merano 2000 88 C2
▲2350m. 7 Lifts. 20 miles of pistes
Drive - Calais 796 miles - 11 hrs 40
Fly - Innsbruck 94 miles = 1 hr 30

Moena di Fassa 88 D3
▲2513m. 18 Lifts. 26 miles of pistes
Drive - Calais 803 miles - 12 hrs 15
Fly - Innsbruck 102 miles = 1 hr 55

Nova Levante 88 D3
▲2337m. 16 Lifts. 24 miles of pistes
Drive - Calais 807 miles - 12 hrs 20
Fly - Innsbruck 86 miles = 1 hr 30

Obereggen 88 D3
▲2220m. 20 Lifts. 21 miles of pistes
Drive - Calais 780 miles - 11 hrs 30
Fly - Innsbruck 78 miles = 1 hr 22

Pejo 88 D2
▲2400m. 7 Lifts. 9 miles of pistes
Drive - Calais 781 miles - 13 hrs
Fly - Milan 126 miles = 3 hrs 20

Piancavallo 88 E4
▲1830m. 18 Lifts. 12 miles of pistes
Drive - Calais 873 miles - 13 hrs 10
Fly - Venice 61 miles = 1 hr 10

Pinzolo 88 E2
▲2100m. 9 Lifts. 19 miles of pistes
Drive - Calais 844 miles - 12 hrs 46
Fly - Milan 131 miles = 3 hrs 8

Pozza di Fassa 88 D3
▲2153m. 6 Lifts. 6 miles of pistes
Drive - Calais 799 miles - 12 hrs 10
Fly - Innsbruck 99 miles = 1 hr 55

Roccaraso 78 C4
▲2140m. 31 Lifts. 68 miles of pistes
Drive - Calais 1083 miles - 16 hrs 15
Fly - Naples 86 miles = 1 hr 50

San Cassiano 88 D4
▲751m. 57 Lifts. 80 miles of pistes
Drive - Calais 751 miles - 11 hrs 30
Fly - Innsbruck 68 miles = 1 hr 22

San Martino Di Castrozza 88 D3
▲2609m. 19 Lifts. 25 miles of pistes
Drive - Calais 832 miles - 12 hrs 33
Fly - Venice 90 miles = 2 hrs 10

San Sicario 47 F7
▲2566m. 11 Lifts. 25 miles of pistes
Drive - Calais 617 miles - 9 hrs 14
Fly - Turin 60 miles = 1 hr 5

San Vigilio di Marebbe 88 C4
▲2275m. 33 Lifts. 58 miles of pistes
Drive - Calais 757 miles - 11 hrs 48
Fly - Turin 60 miles = 1 hr 5

Santa Caterina 88 D1
▲2726m. 8 Lifts. 25 miles of pistes
Drive - Calais 698 miles - 12 hrs 5
Fly - 698 miles = 12 hrs 10

Santa Cristina 88 D3
▲2454m. 0 miles of pistes
Drive - Calais miles - hrs
Fly - Milan 114 miles = 3 hrs 10

Sappada 89 D5
▲2050m. 17 Lifts. 30 miles of pistes
Drive - Calais 817 miles - 12 hrs 40
Fly - Innsbruck 102 miles = 2 hrs 10

Sella Nevea 89 D6
▲1850m. 8 Lifts. 7 miles of pistes
Drive - Calais 822 miles - 12 hrs
Fly - Klagenfurt 46 miles = 50 mins

Solda 88 D2
▲3150m. 11 Lifts. 19 miles of pistes
Drive - Calais 671 miles - 11 hrs 32
Fly - Milan 150 miles = 3 hrs

Trafoi 88 D1
▲2550m. 4 Lifts. 6 miles of pistes
Drive - Calais 669 miles - 11 hrs 18
Fly - Verona 147 miles = 2 hrs 45

Valtournenche 84 A3
▲3085m. 9 Lifts. 38 miles of pistes
Drive - Calais 620 miles - 9 hrs 35
Fly - Milan 73 miles = 1 hr 25

Vigo di Fassa 88 D3
▲2062m. 8 Lifts. 8 miles of pistes
Drive - Calais 800 miles - 12 hrs 8
Fly - Innsbruck 92 miles = 1 hr 40

Watles 88 C1
▲2557m. 4 Lifts. 16 miles of pistes
Drive - Calais 676 miles - 11 hrs 40
Fly - Innsbruck 117 miles = 2 hrs 15

LIECHTENSTEIN

Malbun 87 C6
▲2000m. 7 Lifts. 14 miles of pistes
Drive - Calais 578 miles - 9 hrs 30
Fly - Zurich 85 miles = 1 hr 45

NORWAY (Review pages 80)

ÅL 117 F5
▲980m. 6 Lifts. 7 miles of pistes
Drive - Oslo 94 miles - 3 hrs
Fly - Oslo 94 miles = 3 hrs

Filefjell Skiheiser (Vang) 117 E5
▲1250m. 3 Lifts. 5 miles of pistes
Drive - Oslo 141 miles - 3 hrs 35
Fly - Oslo 141 miles = 3 hrs 35

Gausdal 117 D6
▲1125m. 9 Lifts. 4 miles of pistes
Drive - Oslo 129 miles - 3 hrs 15
Fly - Oslo 129 miles = 3 hrs 15

Gaustablikk 110 B5
▲1100m. 5 Lifts. 6 miles of pistes
Drive - Oslo 104 miles - 2 hrs 5
Fly - Oslo 104 miles = 2 hrs 5

Gol 117 F5
▲1099m. 7 Lifts. 6 miles of pistes
Drive - Oslo 119 miles - 3 hrs 45
Fly - Oslo 119 miles = 3 hrs 45

Grong 121 B7
▲872m. 6 Lifts. 2 miles of pistes
Drive - Oslo 437 miles - 9 hrs 45
Fly - Oslo 437 miles = 9 hrs 45

Hafjell (Oyer) 117 D7
▲900m. 9 Lifts. 15 miles of pistes
Drive - Oslo 116 miles - 3 hrs
Fly - Oslo 116 miles = 3 hrs

Kvitfjell 117 D7
▲1044m. 7 Lifts. 12 miles of pistes
Drive - Oslo 136 miles - 3 hrs 10
Fly - Oslo 136 miles = 3 hrs 10

Narvik 127 D6
▲1272m. 5 Lifts. 9 miles of pistes
Drive - Oslo 843 miles - 19 hrs
Fly - Oslo 843 miles - 19 hrs

Nordseter 117 D7
▲1000m. 3 Lifts. 1 mile of pistes
Drive - Oslo 117 miles - 2 hrs 50
Fly - Oslo 117miles = 2 hrs 50

Norefjell 111 A6
▲1188m. 10 Lifts. 15 miles of pistes
Drive - Oslo 64 miles - 1 hr 42
Fly - Oslo 64 miles = 1 hr 42

Oppdal 117 A6
▲1260m. 16 Lifts. 48 miles of pistes
Drive - Oslo 247 miles - 5 hrs 30
Fly - Oslo 247 miles - 5 hrs 30

Rustadhøgda 127 C7
▲420m. 3 Lifts. 2 miles of pistes
Drive - Oslo 920 miles - 20 hrs
Fly - Oslo 920 miles = 20 hrs

Sjusjøen 117 D7
▲850m. 1 Lift. 1 mile of pistes
Drive - Oslo 110 miles - 2 hrs 30
Fly - Oslo 110 miles = 2 hrs 30

Tromsø 127 A7
▲420m. 6 Lifts. 2 miles of pistes
Drive - Oslo 999 miles -22 hrs
Fly - Oslo 999 miles = 22 hrs

Trysill 118 D2
▲1132m. 12Lifts. 40 miles of pistes
Drive - Oslo 133 miles - 3 hrs
Fly - Oslo 247 miles - 5 hrs 30

Uvdal Alpinsenter 110 A5
▲1209m. 4 Lifts. 12 miles of pistes
Drive - Oslo 129 miles - 3 hrs 15
Fly - Oslo 129 miles = 3 hrs 15

Valdres 117 E6
▲1040m. 4 Lifts. 0 miles of pistes
Drive - Oslo 61miles - 1 hr 38
Fly - Oslo 61 miles = 1 hrs 38

Vradal 110 C5
▲700m. 10 Lifts. 6 miles of pistes
Drive - Oslo 127 miles - 3 hrs 15
Fly - Oslo 127 miles = 3 hrs 15

POLAND

Szkarska Poreba 97 E6
▲1362m. 8 Lifts. 8 miles of pistes
Drive - Calais 723 miles - 12 hrs 40
Fly - Wroclaw 85 miles = 2 hrs 10

Zakopane 163 C7
▲1960m. 20 Lifts. 17 miles of pistes
Drive - Calais 992 miles - 18 hrs 47
Fly - Kracow 62 miles = 1 hr 15

PORTUGAL

Serra da Estrela 60 D4
▲1988m. 3 Lifts. 7 runs
Drive - Calais 1074 miles - 23 hrs
Fly - Lisbon 187 miles = 4 hrs 28

ROMANIA

Poiana Brasov 176 B4
▲1770m. 11 Lifts. 9 miles of pistes
Drive - Calais 1393 miles - 27 hrs 30
Fly - Bucharest 118 miles = 2 hrs 25

Sinaia 176 C5
▲2000m. 9 Lifts. 10 miles of pistes
Drive - Calais 1392 miles - 28 hrs
Fly - Bucharest 152 miles = 3 hrs 15

SLOVAK REPUBLIC

Donovaly 163 D6
▲1360m. 13 Lifts. 9 miles of pistes
Drive - Calais 982 miles - 18 hrs 40
Fly - Bratislava 185 miles = 3 hrs 45

Jasna 163 D6
▲2005m. 24 Lifts. 30 miles of pistes
Drive - Calais 968 miles - 18 hrs 20
Fly - Krakow 121miles = 2 hr 30

Martinske Hole 163 D5
▲1364m. 8 Lifts. 8 miles of pistes
Drive - Calais 935 miles - 17 hrs
Fly - Bratislava 138 miles = 2 hrs 33

Stary Smokovec 161 F1
▲1480m. 6 Lifts. 10 miles of pistes
Drive - Calais 1007 miles - 18 hrs 40
Fly - Bratislava 188 miles = 4 hrs 15

Tatranska Lomnica 161 F1
▲2627m. 9 Lifts. 7 miles of pistes
Drive - Calais 1033 miles - 19 hrs 20
Fly - Bratislava 207 miles = 4 hrs 50

SLOVENIA

Kobla 164 D1
▲1480m. 6 Lifts. 22 miles of pistes
Drive - Calais 863 miles - 15 hrs 15
Fly - Ljubljana 35 miles 1 hr

Kranjska Gora 164 D1
▲1623m. 20 Lifts. 19 miles of pistes
Drive - Calais 798 miles - 14 hrs
Fly - Ljubljana 53 miles 1 hr 10

Rogla 164 D3
▲1517m. 11 Lifts. 12 miles of pistes
Drive - Calais 881 miles - 15 hrs 38
Fly - Ljubljana 64 miles 1 hr 24

Vogel 164 D1
▲1800m. 9 Lifts. 22 miles of pistes
Drive - Calais 816 miles - 14 hrs 15
Fly - Ljubljana 52 miles 1 hr 15

Zantrnik 164 D1
▲1264m. 5 Lifts. 10 miles of pistes
Drive - Calais 797 miles - 13 hrs 50
Fly - Ljubljana 40 miles 1 hr

SPAIN

Astún 48 E4
▲2324m. 13 Lifts. 19 miles of pistes
Drive - Calais 745 miles - 12 hrs
Fly - Pamplona 92 miles = 2 hrs 20

Boi-Taull 49 F6
▲2457m. 8 Lifts. 17 runs
Drive - Calais 742 miles - 11 hrs 55
Fly - Barc elona 160 miles = 3 hrs 55

Candanchú 48 E4
▲2400m. 25 Lifts. 25 miles of pistes
Drive - Calais 725 miles - 12 hrs 12
Fly - Pamplona 84 miles = 2 hrs 18

Cerler 49 F5
▲2630m. 14 Lifts. 20 miles of pistes
Drive - Calais 767 miles - 13 hrs 10
Fly - Toulouse 160 miles = 4 hrs

El Formigal 48 E4
▲2200m. 24 Lifts. 35 miles of pistes
Drive - Calais 813 miles - 13 hrs 40
Fly - Pamplona 98 miles = 2 hrs 40

La Pinilla 56 F4
▲2273m. 12 Lifts. 16 runs
Drive - Calais 760 miles - 12 hrs
Fly - Barcelona 85 miles = 2 hrs 10

Lunada 56 B3
▲1710m. 7 Lifts. 7 miles of pistes
Drive - Calais 837 miles - 13 hrs
Fly - Pamplona 131 miles = 2 hrs 10

Manzaneda 54 D4
▲1780m. 6 Lifts. 13 runs
Drive - Calais 1121 miles - 17 hrs 15
Fly - Madrid 300 miles = 4 hrs 30

Masella 59 B5
▲2535m. 10 Lifts. 42 miles of pistes
Drive - Calais 768 miles - 12 hrs 35
Fly - Barcelona 77 miles = 1 hr 30

Navacerrada 62 C3
▲2222m. 11 Lifts. 12 miles of pistes
Drive - Calais 1027 miles - 15 hrs 45
Fly - Madrid 31 miles = 40 mins

Port Aine 49 F6
▲2440m. 6 Lifts. 18 runs
Drive - Calais 802 miles - 13 hrs 55
Fly - Barcelona 161 miles = 2 hrs 20

Port Del Comte 49 C5
▲2400m. 15 Lifts. 31 miles of pistes
Drive - Calais 804 miles - 14 hrs
Fly - Barcelona 100 miles = 2 hrs 25

San Isidro 55 B7
▲2155m. 13 Lifts. 13 miles of pistes
Drive - Calais 1022 miles - 16 hrs 45
Fly - Madrid 267 miles = 5 hrs 5

Super Espot 49 F6
▲2555m. 7 Lifts. 20 miles of pistes
Drive - Calais 803 miles - 14 hrs
Fly - Barcelona 100 miles = 2 hrs 18

Valcotos 62 C3
▲2275m. 8 Lifts. 7 runs
Drive - Calais 984 miles - 16 hrs
Fly - Madrid 80 miles = 1 hr 46

Valdelinares 64 C3
▲2024m. 5 Lifts. 67 runs
Drive - Calais 942 miles - 25 hrs
Fly - Madrid 205 miles = 4 hrs 35

Valdesqui 62 B4
▲2280m. 10 Lifts. 11 runs
Drive - Calais 967 miles - 15 hrs
Fly - Madrid 68 miles = 1 hr 10

Valdezcary 56 D4
▲2262m. 5 Lifts. 17 runs
Drive - Calais 1626 miles - 15 hrs 42
Fly - Madrid 116 miles = 2 hrs 20

Vallter 2000 49 F8
▲768m. 7 Lifts. 12 runs
Drive - Calais 768 miles - 11 hrs 45
Fly - Barcelona 77 miles = 1 hr 25

Val De Nuria 49 F8
▲2268m. 4 Lifts. 9 runs
Drive - Calais 770 miles - 12 hrs
Fly - Barcelona 954 miles = 2 hrs

SWEDEN (Review pages 88)

Björkliden 127 D7
▲958m. 5 Lifts. 14 miles of pistes
Drive - Stockholm 833 miles - 20 hrs
Fly - Kiruna 65 miles = 1 hr 40

Björnrike 118 B4
▲1010m. 11 Lifts. 9 miles of pistes
Drive - Stockholm 311 miles - 7 hrs
Fly - Stockholm 311 miles = 7 hrs

Funäsdalen 118 A2
▲1200m. 33 Lifts. 53 miles of pistes
Drive - Stockholm 368 miles - 9 hrs
Fly - Stockholm 368 miles = 9 hrs

Hovfjället 112 A5
▲592m. 6 Lifts. 5 miles of pistes
Drive - Stockholm 271 miles - 6 hrs
Fly - Stockholm 271 miles = 6 hrs

Idre Fjäll 118 C2
▲892m. 30 Lifts. 38 miles of pistes
Drive - Stockholm 289 miles - 7 hrs
Fly - Stockholm 289 miles = 7 hr

Kiruna 88 B4
▲598m. 3 Lifts. 2 miles of pistes
Drive - Stockholm 768 miles - 19 hrs
Fly - Kiruna 5 miles = 10 mins

Lofsdalen 118 B3
▲1125m. 8 Lifts. 14 miles of pistes
Drive - Stockholm miles - hrs
Fly - Stockholm miles = hr

Nya Dundret 132 E2
▲320m. 4 Lifts. 9 miles of pistes
Drive - Stockholm 656 miles - 17 hrs
Fly - Nya Dundret

Storlien 121 E6
▲831m. 8 Lifts. 3 miles of pistes
Drive - Stockholm 420 miles - 10 hrs
Fly - Stockholm 420 miles = 10 hrs

Sundsvall 119 B7
▲179m. 2 Lifts. 2 miles of pistes
Drive - Stockholm 237 miles - 5 hrs
Fly - Stockholm 237 miles = 5 hr

Sunne 119 A7
▲365m. 8 Lifts. 8 miles of pistes
Drive - Stockholm 234 miles - 5 hrs
Fly - Stockholm 234 miles = 5 hrs

Tärnaby 124 E4
▲830m. 5 Lifts. 10 miles of pistes
Drive - Stockholm 311 miles - 7 hrs
Fly - Stockholm 311 miles = 7 hrs

SWITZERLAND (Review pages 86)

Beatenberg 86 D4
▲1950m. 5 Lifts. 9 miles of pistes
Drive - Calais 551 miles - 8 hrs 28
Fly - Zurich 89 miles = 1 hr 38

Bettmerlap 86 E4
▲2709m. 12 Lifts. 19 miles of pistes
Drive - Calais 552 miles - 8 hrs 48
Fly - Zurich 90 miles = 1 hr 42

Champoussin 47 C7
▲2277m. 35 Lifts. 13 miles of pistes
Drive - Calais 520 miles - 8 hrs 55
Fly - Geneva 83 miles = 1 hr 44

Château d'Oux 47 C8
▲1800m. 29 Lifts. 31 miles of pistes
Drive - Calais 528 miles - 8 hrs 50
Fly - Geneva 90 miles = 1 hr 40

Einsiedeln 43 F8
▲1113 m. 3 Lifts. 4 miles of pistes
Drive - Calais 527 miles - 8 hrs 45
Fly - Zurich 32 miles = 45 mins

Fiesch 87 E4
▲2869m. 10 Lifts. 28 miles of pistes
Drive - Calais 579 miles - 9 hrs 26
Fly - Geneva 142 miles = 2 hrs 28

Flumserberg 87 C6
▲2222m. 18 Lifts. 31miles of pistes
Drive - Calais 560 miles - 9 hrs
Fly - Zurich 65 miles = 1 hr 18

Giswil 86 D4
▲1850m. 5 Lifts. 9 miles of pistes
Drive - Calais 529 miles - 8 hrs 16
Fly - Zurich 58 miles = 1 hr 10

Grächen 84 A3
▲2890m. 13 Lifts. 25 miles of pistes
Drive - Calais 577 miles - 9 hrs 45
Fly - Zurich 142 miles = 1 hr 50

Grimentz 84 A3
▲3000m. 12 Lifts. 31 miles of pistes
Drive - Calais 559 miles - 9 hrs 50
Fly - Geneva 122 miles = 2 hrs 15

Kandersteg 86 E3
▲2000m. 7 Lifts. 0 miles of pistes
Drive - Calais miles - hrs
Fly - miles = hr

La Tzoumaz 47 C8
▲3300m. 9 Lifts. 124 miles of pistes
Drive - Calais 538 miles - 9 hrs
Fly - Geneva 100 miles = 2 hrs

Lauterbrunnen 86 D4
▲2591m. 49 Lifts. 116 miles of pistes
Drive - Calais 550 miles - 8 hrs 35
Fly - Zurich 89 miles = 1 hr 35

Le Chable 47 C8
▲2445m. 6 Lifts. 19 miles of pistes
Drive - Calais 532 miles - 8 hrs 30
Fly - Geneva 96 miles = 1 hr 30

Lenk 47 C8
▲2099m. 18 Lifts. 40 miles of pistes
Drive - Calais 560 miles - 9 hrs
Fly - Zurich 128 miles = 3 hrs

Lenzerheide - Valbella 87 D6
▲1470m. 36 Lifts. 96 miles of pistes
Drive - Calais 586 miles - 9 hrs 50
Fly - Zurich 92 miles = 1 hr 38

Les Bivio 87 E6
▲2560m. 4 Lifts. 20 miles of pistes
Drive - Calais 617 miles - 9 hrs 40
Fly - Zurich 122 miles = 2 hr 15

Les Diablerets 86 E3
▲3000m. 28 Lifts. 37 miles of pistes
Drive - Calais 517 miles - 8 hrs 50
Fly - Geneva 80 miles = 1 hr 22

Maloja 87 E7
▲2159m. 3 Lifts. 3 runs
Drive - Calais 632 miles - 10 hrs 5
Fly - Zurich 137 miles = 2 hrs 33

Meiringen Hasliberg 86 D4
▲2433m. 16 Lifts. 37 miles of pistes
Drive - Calais 495 miles - 8 hrs 40
Fly - Zurich 72 miles = 1 hr 16

Montreaux 47 C8
▲2000m. 6 Lifts. 8 miles of pistes
Drive - Calais 495 miles - 8 hrs 30
Fly - Geneva 58 miles = 1 hr 5

Morgins 47 C7
▲2000m. 16 Lifts. 43 miles of pistes
Drive - Calais 517 miles - 8 hrs 40
Fly - Geneva 48 miles = 1 hr 20

Pontresina 88 D1
▲3005m. 13 Lifts. 55 miles of pistes
Drive - Calais 632 miles - 10 hrs 10
Fly - Zurich 136 miles = 2 hrs 34

Rougemont 47 C8
▲2156m. 3 Lifts. 12 miles of pistes
Drive - Calais 531 miles - 8 hrs 50
Fly - Geneva 94 miles = 1 hr 50

S - Chanf 88 C1
▲1950m. 1 Lift. 1 mile of pistes
Drive - Calais 621 miles - 10 hrs
Fly - Zurich 135 miles = 2 hrs 35

Saas Grund 84 A3
▲3100m. 7 Lifts. 16 miles of pistes
Drive - Calais 576 miles - 9 hrs 45
Fly - Geneva 139 miles = 2 hrs 45

Samnaun 88 C1
▲2872m. 42 Lifts. 124 miles of pistes
Drive - Calais 644 miles - 10 hrs
Fly - Zurich 130 miles = 2 hrs 45

Scuol 88 C1
▲2783m. 15 Lifts. 50 miles of pistes
Drive - Calais 622 miles - 10 hrs 6
Fly - Zurich 106 miles = 2 hrs 6

Sedrun 87 D5
▲2200m. 13 Lifts. 31 miles of pistes
Drive - Calais 570 miles - 9 hrs
Fly - Zurich 90 miles = 1 hr 44

Sils - Maria 87 E7
▲2800m. 6 Lifts. 24 miles of pistes
Drive - Calais 628 miles - 10 hrs
Fly - Zurich 134 miles = 2 hrs 30

Silvaplana 87 E7
▲3030m. 7 Lifts. 25 miles of pistes
Drive - Calais 625 miles - 9 hrs 48
Fly - Zurich 130 miles = 2 hrs 22

Täsch 84 A3
▲3899m. 1 Lift. 1 mile of pistes
Drive - Calais 501 miles - 9 hrs
Fly - Geneva 76 miles = 1 hr 32

Torgon 47 C7
▲2001m. 12 Lifts. 22 miles of pistes
Drive - Calais 514 miles - 8 hrs 50
Fly - Geneva 76 miles = 1 hr 32

Veysonnaz 47 C8
▲2700m. 17 Lifts. 30 miles of pistes
Drive - Calais 542 miles - 9 hrs 10
Fly - Geneva 105 miles = 1 hr 45

Wilderswil 86 D4
▲2591m. 2 Lifts. 1 mile of pistes
Drive - Calais 545 miles - 9 hrs
Fly - Geneva 134 miles = 2 hrs

Wildhaus 87 C6
▲3885m. 9 Lifts. 33 miles of pistes
Drive - Calais 583 miles - 9 hrs
Fly - Zurich 64 miles = 1 hr 25

Zinal 84 A3
▲2895m. 9 Lifts. 43 miles of pistes
Drive - Calais 561 miles - 9 hrs 15
Fly - Geneva 124 miles = 2 hrs 15

Andorra

France
Valira
Vella
Spain
Espagne

Resorts Featured
30 Arinsal
31 Pas de la Casa
31 Soldeu
See page 28 for the index of all resorts.

See page 28 for the index of all resorts.

30

DRIVE ON THE RIGHT

Priority road

Restriction continues **RAPPEL**

Snow Chains

Snow on road

Tunnel

Country identification **AND**

Motorway speed	**90kph**
Rural speed	**50kph**
Urban speed	**30kph**
Alcohol limit	**80mgs**
Front seatbelts	✔
Rear seatbelts	✔
Kids in front seat	**12 years**
Legal age to drive	**18**
Warming triangle	Required
First aid kit	Required
Fire extinguisher	Required
Snowchains	Advisable

FACT FILE

Country - Andorra
Location - Western Europe
Geography
Andorra is located in the Pyrenees between France to the north and Spain to the south. It thefore shares two boarders.
Highest Mountain
Coma Pedrosa - 2959m
Coast line & Seas
No seas, land Locked
Land Area
467.8 sq km (180.6 sq miles)
Capital - Andorra la Vella
Populartion - 20,845
Language - Catalan
Religion - Roman Catholic
Currecny - Euros
Time
GMT + 1 hour, (GMT + 2 hours between March & October)
Electricity Supply - 240volts
Communications
International Country code 00376
Fire 17
Police 18
Ambulance 18
National Tourism www.andorra.ad
Rail Information www.andorra.ad
Bus Information
email - novatel@andornet.ad
Air Information www.andorra.ad
Gateway International Airports
Toulouse in France
Barcelona in Spain
Madrid in Spain
Weather Information www.andorra.ad
Avalanche Information
France 0033 (0) 836 68 10 20 99
Spain 0034 (0) 906 365 380
Passports
French and Spannish nationals don't need a passport, everyone else needs a vaild one. **Visas** Not needed
Duty Free - Duty Free Zone

Motoring Organisations
Automobil Club d'Andorra
(ACA)
Carrer Babot Camp 13, Andorra la VELLA
tel +(376) 80 34 00
fax +(376) 82 25 60
http:// www.aca.ad
e-mail: automobilclub@aca.ad
AIT   FIA

Andorra
Arinsal

Top Lift	2560m.
Resort Height	1470m.
Vertical Drop	1092m.
Total Runs	22
Longest Run	6km
Slopes	64km of piste

● **Beginner**
50% of the runs
● *Intermediate*
40% of the runs
● **Advanced**
10% of the runs

Cross-Country
4km of tracks
Snowboarding
Half-pipe & Park
Snow Season
Dec to April
Snowmaking
300 cannons
Number of lifts
29
Up Lift Capicity
11,600 per hour
Mountain Cafes
9

On the Slopes - Arinsal is a favourite of Tour Operators throughout Europe, yet it is Andorra's least appealing resort. Every winter it is invaded by hordes of package deal holiday makers, leading to a somewhat downmarket feel. Arinsal is a cheap resort, and a good snowfall means that beginners will love it – but such conditions are infrequent and the novice runs into the resort never seem to have enough snow to be usable. The mountain has some 22 marked runs that snake through tight trees and stretch down to the base area. A recently installed cable car link to the nearby resort of Pal means that should Arinsal prove too boring, at least you can try somewhere else (Pal is not particularly hot, however). Advanced skiers will, in all likelihood, find Arinsal has little to offer them after a couple of days – intermediates will also quickly exceed the resort's limits as the red runs are quite short and not up to much. Being an inexpensive, and thus popular, winter holiday destination, one would expect long lift queues, but they are surprisingly short and apart from the odd bottleneck in the morning and at weekends, crowding is not a problem. Cross-country skiers and snowboarders will struggle in Arinsal, no matter how short the lift queues are – there are no facilities for slow slip-sliders and naff all for airheads.

Off the Slopes - While the resort is a dull, miserable and unattractive haunt, it caters extremely well for groups of lads and girls on a booze, ski/snowboard, trip. There is an abundance of self-catering accommodation to choose from and plenty of decent hotels. Rates are low wherever you stay, but if you're looking for the five star treatment, you've come to the wrong place. The restaurants are reasonable; you can get a decent grill at the Rocky Mountain for example, which is also a popular nightspot. Evenings can be summed up as loud, sleazy, cheap and very drunken.

Verdict - Tedious, ugly and not the sort of place you would to re-visit   **3**/10

COST INDICATOR

Budget   Moderate   Very Expensive   Criminal

i - Information - 00376 737 020
www.palarinsal.com

ROUTE PLANNER

CALAIS 0 miles
along the A16 E402
Toll Road
➡ **ARRAS** 69 miles
1hr 13   A11 E15
➡ **PARIS** 162 miles
2hrs 44   Ring road south via
Antony to the A10 E05
➡ **ORLEANS** 245 miles
4hrs 14   A71 E09
➡ **VIERZON** 297miles
5hrs 6   A20 E09
➡ **MONTAUBAN** 572 miles
9hrs 40   A62 E09 E72
➡ **TOULOUSE** 585 miles
10hrs   south around Toulouse,
pick up the A61 E80
then the A66 E09
Tolls End
➡ **PAMIERS** 630 miles
10hrs 45   N20 E09
➡ **FOIX** 638 miles
11hrs   N20 E09 south into
Andorra via the N22
to the
➡ **ARINSAL**

KM	**Distance**	**720** miles *(1160 km)*
⏱	**Drive time**	**12** hours **56** mins
⛽	**Fuel**	**£65**
€	**Tolls**	**£35**

Airports & Fly Drive Guide

1st- Toulouse (F) - **3** hrs
➡ A61 E80 and all routes south via Foix = **130** miles
2nd- Barcelona (S) - **4** hrs **12**
➡ C16, 16, 260, 145, 1 = **134** miles
3rd- Madrid (S) - **9** hr **20**
➡ A7 E15 north and all routes via Lleida = **386** miles

⏱ **DRIVE TIME** - **nixon** ® www.nixonnow.com

Andorra

Pas de la Casa

Mapping Page 49 F7

Top Lift
2600m.
Resort Height
2100m.
Vertical Drop
590m.
Total Runs
55
Longest Run
2.5km
Slopes
100km of piste
● *Beginner*
34% of the runs
● *Intermediate*
42% of the runs
● *Advanced*
24% of the runs

Cross-Country
15km of tracks
Snowboarding
Half-pipe & Park
Snow Season
Dec to April
Snowmaking
427 cannons
Number of lifts
30
Up Lift Capicity
47,000 per hour
Mountain Cafes
8

On the Slopes - If you are looking for an inexpensive, no-frills resort which still offers a lively winter sports experience, then look no further. Pas de la Casa is extremely popular with tour operators who offer cheap package deals and is linked by ski lift to nearby Grau Roig – pronounced 'Grau Rosh' – and is accessible on the same lift ticket. Together these resorts offer easy-to-master beginner and intermediate terrain, and a few advanced black runs. A week in Pas de la Casa would be ideal for novice and intermediates, offering easy access to the lower nursery slopes, but the same length stay may well bore the more adventurous skier or snowboarder. While the area is comparatively small compared to European mega-resorts, Pas de la Casa/Grau Roig is well serviced by some 30 lifts and, with the exception of main holiday periods, lift lines are seldom problematic. The popularity of Andorra for entry-level winter sports enthusiasts can lead to somewhat 'lively' slopes, whose users are more enthusiastic than they are competent, but the extensive array of snow-cannons, coupled with the resort's altitude, lends itself to good snow cover from mid-December to early April.

Off the Slopes - Services and local facilities are based at the foot of the slopes, where you will also find a large number of concrete apartment blocks that make up the bulk of the resort's accommodation facilities. Pas de la Casa is unlikely to ever win any beauty contests, but that is not where it's attraction lies – a host of duty-free shops, supermarkets and restaurants offer good value services while a number of lively (and late opening) bars and clubs see a good deal of hardcore partying. Most amenities are a short stroll from the accommodation areas, doing away with the need for a car or public transport in the evenings. Despite numerous eateries, Pas de la Casa is not noted for its culinary delights – put simply, the eating options are basic, with little of note. The hottest night-spots are Bar Marseilles and Milwaukee.

ROUTE PLANNER

🏠 **CALAIS** 0 miles
along the A16 E402
Toll Road

➡ **ARRAS** 69 miles
1hr 13 **A11** E15

➡ **PARIS** 162 miles
2hrs 44 Ring road south via Antony to the **A10** E05

➡ **ORLEANS** 245 miles
4hrs 14 **A71** E09

➡ **VIERZON** 297miles
5hrs 6 **A20** E09

➡ **MONTAUBAN** 572 miles
9hrs 40 **A62** E09 E72

➡ **TOULOUSE** 585 miles
10hrs south around Toulouse, pick up the **A61** E80 then the **A66** E09
Tolls End
➡ **PAMIERS** 630 miles
10hrs 45 **N20** E09

➡ **FOIX** 638 miles
11hrs **N20** E09 south into Andorra via the N22 to the

➡ **PAS de la CASA**

🔢 **Distance** 698 miles *(1123 km)*
🕐 **Drive time** 12 hours 15 mins
⛽ **Fuel** £63
€ **Tolls** £35

5/10

COST INDICATOR
Budget   Moderate   Very Expensive   Criminal

ℹ - **Information -** 00376 80 10 60
www.pasgrau.com

✈ **Airports & Fly Drive Guide**
1st- Toulouse (F) - **2** hrs 20
➡ **A61** E80 and all routes south via **Foix** = 105 miles

2nd- Barcelona (S) - **3** hrs 50
➡ **C16, 16, 260, 145, 1** = 121 miles

3rd- Madrid (S) - **9** hr 30
➡ **A7** E15 north and all routes via **Lleida** = 394 miles

Andorra

Soldeu

Mapping Page 49 F7

Top Lift
2560m.
Resort Height
1710m.
Vertical Drop
850m.
Total Runs
52
Longest Run
8.2km
Slopes
92km of piste
● *Beginner*
56% of the runs
● *Intermediate*
36% of the runs
● *Advanced*
8% of the runs

Cross-Country
3km of tracks
Snowboarding
Half-pipe & Park
Snow Season
Dec to April
Snowmaking
32km of piste
Number of lifts
32
Up Lift Capicity
38,700 per hour
Mountain Cafes
8

On the Slopes - While it's not Andorra's largest, Soldeau/El Tarter's 90km of marked runs and low prices means that it has long been on the hit list for budget-conscious skiers – and it's fast becoming a popular snowboard destination, too. The double-edged honour of being the country's most popular resort often leads to busy lift lines and crowded slopes, however. Despite having one of the largest mountain areas in Andorra, there is still not a great deal of adventurous terrain and those looking for black runs will have limited success. Soldeu, like the rest of Andorra, is nonetheless a good choice for those intending to build their confidence or progress from the ranks of novice to intermediate. Perhaps inevitably, large tour operators have seized on this fact and made Soldeu/El Tarter one of their most popular resorts and ship in large numbers of holidaymakers, so be prepared for some long lift lines, busy nursery slopes and raucous evenings. There is however a good snowboard scene, with plenty of natural hits to catch air from although the halfpipe and man made hits are not up to much. Best thing to do is seek out a local and get them to show you where the best hits are. As for cross-country skiing, Soldeu is not up to much with only a few kilometers of cross-country tracks in resort, more suitable terrain, including a 20km cross country track, can be found at La Rabassa near the Spanish border.

Off the Slopes - A rather unappealing cluster of apartment blocks, hotels and chalets are situated near the slopes offering inexpensive lodging. In tune with most Andorran resorts, facilities are basic although perfectly adequate for a week's stay, especially if you are on a tight budget. Nightlife can be raunchy, with partying into the early hours the norm. Holiday reps rule proceedings in many bars, so expect lively fun and games and while booze is cheap if brought in a supermarket, bar prices can be expensive. Check out the Pussycat, Fat Albert's or the Esquirol for the best action. All open early and close late attracting a mixed crowd.

ROUTE PLANNER

🏠 **CALAIS** 0 miles
along the A16 E402
Toll Road

➡ **ARRAS** 69 miles
1hr 13 **A11** E15

➡ **PARIS** 162 miles
2hrs 44 Ring road south via Antony to the **A10** E05

➡ **ORLEANS** 245 miles
4hrs 14 **A71** E09

➡ **VIERZON** 297miles
5hrs 6 **A20** E09

➡ **MONTAUBAN** 572 miles
9hrs 40 **A62** E09 E72

➡ **TOULOUSE** 585 miles
10hrs south around Toulouse, pick up the **A61** E80 then the **A66** E09
Tolls End
➡ **PAMIERS** 630 miles
10hrs 45 **N20** E09

➡ **FOIX** 638 miles
11hrs **N20** E09 south into Andorra via the N22 to the

➡ **SOLDEU**

🔢 **Distance** 700 miles *(1127km)*
🕐 **Drive time** 12 hours 25 mins
⛽ **Fuel** £63
€ **Tolls** £35

5/10

COST INDICATOR
Budget   Moderate   Very Expensive   Criminal

ℹ - **Information -** 00376 89 05 00
www.soldeu.com

✈ **Airports & Fly Drive Guide**
1st- Toulouse (F) - **2** hrs 30
➡ **A61** E80 and all routes south via **Foix** = 110 miles

2nd- Barcelona (S) - **4** hrs
➡ **C16, 16, 260, 145, 1** = 126 miles

3rd- Madrid (S) - **9** hr 18
➡ **A7** E15 north and all routes via **Lleida** = 387 miles

DRIVE TIME - nixon® www.nixonnow.com

TRAVEL INSURANCE

Annual cover

from

£60.75*

with winter sports included.

With Direct Line travel insurance you don't just get great value. From sunglasses to ski passes, our annual policy provides the cover you need. And, because we cover you for up to 120 days a year, including an optional 22 days of winter sports, you'll be covered for your summer holidays and weekends away too.

0845 246 1899
call or buy online
directline.com

DIRECT LINE®

Lines open 8am-9pm weekdays, 9am-5pm Saturdays, 10am-5pm Sundays.

Austria

FACT FILE

Country - Republik Osterich
Location - Western Europe
Geography
Austria borders 9 countries:
Czech Republis, Gernmany
Hungary, Italy, Liechtenstein,
Slovak Republic, Slovenia and
Switzerland.
Highest Mountain
Grossglockner - 3797m
Coast line & Seas
No seas, land Locked
Land Area
83,858 sq km (32,378 sq miles)
Capital - Vienna
Populartion - 8 million
Language - German
Religion - 78% Roman Catholic
Currecny - Euros
Time
GMT + 1 hour, (GMT + 2 hours
between March & October)
Electricity Supply - 240volts
Communications
International Country code 0043
Fire 122
Police 133
Ambulance 144
National Tourism
0043 (0)1 58 72 000
www.austria-tourism.at
Rail Information
05 1717 -
www.oebb.at
Bus Information
www.austria-tourism.at
Air Information
www.austria-tourism.at
Weather Information
www.wetter.at
www.winterline.at
Avalanche Information
Karnten 0043 (0)463 1588
Oberosterreich 0043 (0) 732 1588
Salzburg 0043 (0) 662 1588
Steiermark 0043 (0) 316 1588
Tirol 0043 (0) 512 1588
Vorarlberg 0043 (0) 5522 1588
www.lawine.at
www.wetter.at

Passprts & Visa Requirments

	Passports	Visa
Australian	Yes	No
British	Yes	No
Canadian	Yes	No
USA	Yes	No
EU		No

Duty Free - None EU travellers
200 cigarettes or 100 cigarillos or
50 cigars or 25g of tobacco. 1ltr of
spirits over 22% or 21% of fortified
wine or spirits up to 22% or 21% of
sparkling wine or liqueur and 21 %
of still wine. 50g of perfume and
€175 worth of goods.
EU travellers - No tarrifs

Motoring Organisations

Osterreichischer Automobil-
Motorrad -und Touring Club
OAMTC
Schubertring 1-3, 1010 Wein
tel +43 (0) 1 711 990
fax +43 (0) 1 713 18 07
http:// www.oeamtc.at
e-mail: oeamtc@apaned.at

Photo - Tourismusverband Ischgl- Austria

ROAD SIGNS AND WARNINGS

Abblendlicht *Dipped headlights*
Alle Richtungen *All directions*
Ausfahrt *Exit*
Autobahnkreuz *Autobahn junction*
Bauarbeiten *Roadworks*
Durchfahrt verboten *No through traffic*
Einbahnstraße *One-way street*
Einfahrt *Entrance*
Fahrbahnwechsel *Change lanes*
Gefahr/gefährlich *Danger, risk*
Glatteisgefahr *Icy road*
Grenze *Border*
Grenze Kontrolle *Customs inspection*
Halt *Stop*
Haltestelle *Bus/tram stop*
Keine, Kein *No*
Keine einfahrt *No entry*
Krankenfahrzeuge frei *Ambulances only*

Links einbiegen *Turn left*
Parkschein *Parking permit ticket*
Parkuhr *Parking meter*
Polizei *Police*
Rechts einbiegen *Turn right*
Rechts fahren *Keep right*
Rollsplitt *Loose material*
Sperrgebiet *Restricted area*
Sperrung *Closure*
Spur *Traffic lane*
Stadtzcentrum *Town center*
Tankstelle *Fuel Station*
Umleitung *Detour*
Verboten *Prohibited*
Verengte Fahrbahn *Road narrows*
Verkehr *Traffic*
Vorfahrtstraße *Priority road*
Vorsicht *Be careful*
Zufahrt frei *Access permitted*

DRIVE ON THE RIGHT

Street lights not on all night

Diversion — Umleitung

Snow Chains

Police — POLIZEI POLICE

Trams turns at yellow or red.

Federal road with priority — **16**

Federal road with out priority — 17

Country identification — Ⓐ

Stop - *Halt* — STOP

33

Motorway speed	130kph
Rural speed	100kph
Urban speed	50kph
Alcohol limit	50mgs
Front seatbelts	✔
Rear seatbelts	✔
Kids in front seat	12 years
Legal age to drive	18
Warning triangle	Required
First aid kit	Required
Fire extinguisher	No rules
Snowchains	Advisable

Alpbach

ROUTE PLANNER

| | CALAIS | 0 miles |
along the **A16 - A26**
E15 / E17
Toll Road

➡ **REIMS** 168 miles
2hrs 53 A4 **E17 / 50**

➡ **METZ** 270 miles
4hrs 47 A4 **E25** *Dir Strasbourg*
Tolls End

✕ A35 north to the D4
⚠ **Enter Germany** 401 miles
B500 to the **E35 - 5**

➡ **KARLSRUHE** 424 miles
7hrs 16 A8 **E52**
via Pforzheim

➡ **STUTTGART** 459 miles
7hrs 50 A8 **E52**

➡ **MUNICH** 589 miles
9hrs 55 Travel around Munich
and follow all directions
south for Salzburg along
the A8 **E45/E52**. Then
pick up the **E45/ E60**
for **Innsbruck**.

⚠ **Enter Austria** 660 miles
Head south along the
A12 in the direction of
Innsbruck.

➡ Rattenberg 660 miles
11hrs 15 B171, L5

⬇ **ALPBACH**

Top Lift
2025m.
Resort Height
1000m.
Vertical Drop
1212m.
Total Runs
12
Longest Run
3km
Slopes
45km of piste
● Beginner
15% of the runs
● Intermediate
70% of the runs
● Advanced
15% of the runs

Cross-Country
22km of tracks
Snowboarding
Half-pipe
Snow Season
Dec to April
Snowmaking
25km of pistes
Number of lifts
19
Up Lift Capicity
19,000 per hour
Mountain Cafes
9

34

On the Slopes - Alpbach is a fine example of a traditional Austrian resort and a great alternative to some of its more famous and nearby cousins. This picture-perfect postcard destination comes complete with traditional charming chalets dotted on and around the gently rising mountain slopes that surround the village. Alpbach has something of a reputation where skiers seem to spend more time sunning themselves on the restaurant decking rather than enjoying the mostly gentle intermediate slopes. The majority of the 45km of pistes are spread out across north-facing slopes, initially accessed via a six person gondola to the Hornboden lift station where you will not only find some gentle slopes that descend back to the village (snow permitting), but also gives access to a number of highly-rated runs on the slopes of the Wiedersbergerhorn. Alpbach also has a reputation for extremely well prepared and laid out slopes, making it an easy place to negotiate, even for first time visitors. It is not a mountain that will take too long to conquer, however – a week is sufficient to come to terms with what the resort has to offer, certainly not a whole season. Snowboarders have a halfpipe and snowboard park of sorts plus some cool trees to shred, while cross-country skiers have a reasonable choice of tracks to explore.

Off the Slopes - Most of Alpbach's accommodation options are located a short bus ride from the base station, although there are some slope side beds to be found. The village is everything you'd expect of a Tyrolean hamlet: a relaxed, beautiful and generally quiet place – except for when the après-ski drinking sessions are under way. Local facilities, while of a good standard, are limited to an indoor swimming pool, outdoor ice-skating rink and little else. There is a good choice of restaurants, most of which offer traditional Austrian dishes, with the exception of a Mexican restaurant. Nightlife is largely pub-based, with no late night club action. The Waschkuchl Pub and the Weinstadl are the most popular places to check out.

Verdict - A stunning picture-postcard area, with good intermediate slopes. **6/10**

COST INDICATOR

Budget   Moderate   Very Expensive   Criminal

i - **Information** - 0043 (0) 5336 6000
www.alpbach.at

⬇ **Distance** 685 miles *(1102 km)*
🕐 **Drive time** 11 hours 50 mins
⛽ **Fuel** £62
€ **Tolls** £26

✈ **Airports & Fly Drive Guide**
1st- **Innsbruck** - 56 minutes
➡ A12, E60, E45 L5 via
Brixegg = 38 miles

2nd- **Salzburg** - 1 hr 40
➡ Routes A8, A93, A12 via
Rattenberg = 89 miles

3rd- **Munich** (D) - 2 hrs
➡ A94, A99, E45, A8, A12 via
Rattenberg = 105 miles

Axamer Lizum

ROUTE PLANNER

| | CALAIS | 0 miles |
along the **A16 - A26**
E15 / E17
Toll Road

➡ **REIMS** 168 miles
2hrs 53 A4 **E17 / 50**

➡ **METZ** 270 miles
4hrs 47 A4 **E25** *Dir Strasbourg*
Tolls End

✕ A35 north to the D4
⚠ **Enter Germany** 401 miles
B500 to the **E35 - 5**

➡ **KARLSRUHE** 424 miles
7hrs 16 A8 **E52**
via Pforzheim

➡ **STUTTGART** 459 miles
7hrs 50 A8 **E52**

➡ **ULM** 523 miles
8hrs 55 A7 **E532**

➡ **KEMPTEN** 573 miles
9hrs 50 A7 **E532** south via
Nesselwang along the
B309 & **B179**.
⚠ **Enter Austria** 600 miles
Head south along the
B179 via the **Fernpaß**
to the **B189**.

➡ **TELFS** 646 miles
11hrs 35 A12 **E60**

➡ **INNSBRUCK** 658 miles
11hrs 50

⬇ **AXAMER LIZUM**

Top Lift
2388m.
Resort Height
868m.
Vertical Drop
1420m.
Total Runs
14
Longest Run
6km
Slopes
40km of piste
● Beginner
30% of the runs
● Intermediate
80% of the runs
● Advanced
10% of the runs

Cross-Country
40km of tracks
Snowboarding
Half-pipe & Park
Snow Season
Dec to April
Snowmaking
20 cannons
Number of lifts
10
Up Lift Capicity
12,400 per hour
Mountain Cafes
7

On the Slopes - Built in 1964 for the Innsbruck Winter Olympics, Axamer Lizum may not be the biggest of resorts, nor particularly popular with package tour operators, but it remains a fantastic, unpretentious resort that is becoming one of Austria's most popular snowboarder's hangouts, especially with locals from nearby Innsbruck. Axamer Lizum is a natural freeride and freestyle boarder's paradise and a great intermediate skier's retreat. The slopes, most of which are reached after a short funicular ride, are usually quiet and crowd-free, with lift lines almost non-existent during the week – weekends can be extremely busy, however. This is not a high resort and as such can hardly be considered snow-sure – if Austria suffers from poor snowfall, Axamer Lizum is one of the places that can miss out. Snowboarders and freestyle skiers will get the best out of these slopes, with loads of great hits, big banks, and gullies that form natural half-pipes to ride in and out. Provided there is good snow cover, cross-country skiers are in for a great treat, with some very long trails through trees that stretch way down the mountain into Axmams and beyond. Whatever you have on your feet, Axamer Lizum will have something for you.

Off the Slopes - There is some accommodation at the base of the slopes, but it is very basic with no facilities – having a car to visit Axamer Lizum is a good idea. The village of Axams is only a few miles away and has a good selection of local services, which includes a few shops and a sports centre. The best, and most economic option is to stay in Innsbruck as there is a regular bus service to and from the city and once there, you are bombarded with all sorts of facilities: large shops, an Olympic ice rink, swimming pools and concert halls: the list is endless. Innsbruck is an inexpensive and friendly place, nightlife and eating out are superb with an extensive choice of great restaurants and bars – there's even an Irish pub on the high street.

Verdict - One of the best snowboard resorts in Austria and great value. **9/10**

COST INDICATOR

Budget   Moderate   Very Expensive   Criminal

i - **Information** - 0043 (0) 5234 681 78
www.axamer-lizum.at

⬇ **Distance** 668 miles *(1075km)*
🕐 **Drive time** 12 hours 30 mins
⛽ **Fuel** £62
€ **Tolls** £25

✈ **Airports & Fly Drive Guide**
1st- **Innsbruck** - 50 minutes
➡ B171, A12, L13 via **Axams**
= 15 miles

2nd- **Salzburg** - 2 hrs 40
➡ Routes A8, A93, A12 via
Innsbruck = 126 miles

3rd- **Munich** (D) - 3 hrs
➡ A95, E533 via **Garmisch**
and **Innsbruck** = 120 miles

Austria
Bad Gastein

Mapping Page 89 B5

Top Lift
2230m.
Resort Height
1080m.
Vertical Drop
1150m.
Total Runs
64
Longest Run
8km
Slopes
200km of piste
● ● *Beginner*
30% of the runs
● *Intermediate*
12% of the runs
● *Advanced*
15% of the runs

Cross-Country
90km of tracks
Snowboarding
Half-pipe & Park
Snow Season
Dec to April
Snowmaking
30% of pistes
Number of lifts
48
Up Lift Capacity
23,400 per hour
Mountain Cafes
35

On the Slopes - Bad Gastein is an old spa town along the Gastein Valley in the Tyrol region and located at an altitude of 1080 metres. It's a large, but relatively unknown area, split into four separate resorts each of which offers something different. Altogether there are over 200km of marked pistes to explore, although they're not all connected by lifts and some road travel may be necessary. The Stubnerkogel is the most challenging of the areas, with a good selection of red runs, while over on the Graukogel there is some decent treelined runs. The Schlossalm, which links directly with Bad Hofgastein, offers a choice of easy novice slopes with a smattering of red runs at the top section for the more adventurous to try – and also where you'll find the area's main halfpipe and terrain park. The Sportgastein area, which is some six miles from Bad Gastein, is known for having the best snow conditions in the area and favours those at an intermediate level, whether skiing or snowboarding. Cross-country skiers have an extensive selection of trails mostly located in the lower areas, which can be a drawback if snow conditions are poor. It's worth noting that in general the slopes tend to be crowd-free and lift queues never seem to be a problem.

Off the Slopes - Bad Gastein and its surrounding villages provide a varied selection of hotels, chalets and B&B's. In Bad Gastein itself, which is a strange mixture of the old and new, the shops and main centre are well appointed and easy to get to. Wherever you choose to stay, accommodation is not expensive for the area and cheap lodgings are available. There's not a huge choice of restaurants, but you can dine Austrian style in one of the many hotel restaurants or opt for Chinese fare. As for a lively night out, forget it – Bad Gastein mainly caters for those who like to hit the slopes early. There are nice places to while away the evenings in, but nothing major. Bars are traditional and quaint where locals like to mingle with visitors while downing a few beers.

Verdict - Good resort in which to spend a week enjoying crowd-free slopes. **5/10**

COST INDICATOR
Budget   Moderate   Very Expensive   Criminal

i - **Information** - 0043 (0) 6434 25310
www.gastein.com

ROUTE PLANNER

🚢 **CALAIS** *0 miles*
along the **A16 - A26**
E15 / E17
Toll Road

➡ **REIMS** *168 miles*
2hrs 53 **A4 E17 / 50**

➡ **METZ** *270 miles*
4hrs 47 **A4 E25** *Dir Strasbourg*
Tolls End

🚗 **A35** north to the D4
⚠ **Enter Germany** *401 miles*
B500 to the **E35 - 5**

➡ **KARLSRUHE** *424 miles*
7hrs 16 **A8 E52**
via Pforzheim

➡ **STUTTGART** *459 miles*
7hrs 50 **A8 E52**

➡ **MUNICH** *586 miles*
9hrs 58 Travel around Munich and follow all directions south for Salzburg along the **A8 E45/E52**. Then pick up the **E45/ E60**

⚠ **Enter Austria** *689 miles*

➡ **SALZBURG** *690 miles*
11hrs 50 Head towards the airport and pick up the **A10 E55** south. Exit junction 46 for **Bischofschofen** along the **311** to **Lend**, then finally south down the **167** via **Bad Hofgastein**

➡ **BAD GASTEIN**

KM **Distance** 756 miles *(1217km)*
🕐 **Drive time** 13 hours 40 mins
⛽ **Fuel** £70
€ **Tolls** £25

✈ **Airports & Fly Drive Guide**

1st- Salzburg - 2 hrs
➡ **A10 E55** - **Bischofschofen**
311 to **Lend**, **167** = 65 miles

2nd- Innsbruck - 3 hrs 30
➡ **A12, 312, 311** and the **167**
via **Lend** = 124 miles

3rd- Munich (D) - 3 hrs 40
➡ **A8 E45/E52 & E45/E60**
A10, 311, 167 = 170 miles

Austria
Ellmau

Mapping Page 88 B4

Top Lift
1829m.
Resort Height
820m.
Vertical Drop
1009m.
Total Runs
28
Longest Run
7km
Slopes
53km of piste
● ● *Beginner*
43% of the runs
● *Intermediate*
48% of the runs
● *Advanced*
9% of the runs

Cross-Country
80km of tracks
Snowboarding
Half-pipe & Park
Snow Season
Dec to April
Snowmaking
135km of pistes
Number of lifts
20
Up Lift Capacity
113,750 per hour
Mountain Cafes
65

On the Slopes - Ellmau is part of the massive Ski Welt region, which, with over 250km of pistes served by 92 lifts, is claimed to be Austria's largest linked ski and snowboard area. Located is a part of the extensive Tyrol region and lies a mere 90 minutes from the city of Salzburg. Unfortunately, the resort's relatively low altitude means that annual snowfall is lower than elsewhere in Europe but to be fair, there is a good snowmaking system to help out when the real stuff is lacking. The Ski Welt, which combines Brixen Ellmau, Going, Hopfgarten, Itter, Scheffau and Söll, generally lacks good advanced pistes with only 9% of the slopes graded black. Novices and intermediates are better served, with some low prices and excellent, wide-open nursery slopes that are easy to access, although this can lead to busy slopes. As an extremely popular resort, Ellmau occasionally has long queues, but new lifts have helped to improve the situation. What's more, as well as this being a responsibly inexpensive resort, Ellmau can boast having some excellent wide open nursery slopes that are easy to reach, although in some instances it does mean bussing to and from the slopes. The snowboard scene in the Ski Welt is good, even though the terrain is best suited to intermediate freeriders or lazy carvers who stick with red and blue pistes. Freestylers have a half-pipe but it's not always maintained, unlike the excellent terrain park at Söll.

Off the Slopes - Ellmau is a quaint Austrian village full of charm and generations-old chalets – it is also one of the best-equipped villages in the area, with a good selection of facilities, yet remains far quieter than its neighbours. Local public transport services are poor which can make getting around difficult, but accommodation is affordable with a great variety of hotels and pensions to choose from. Restaurants and cafes are in abundance with good spots to eat such as the Bettina Cafe and La Cantina, but nightlife is rather dull, unless you're into aprés ski games.

Verdict - Despite an average snow record, the Ski Welt has lots to offer. **5/10**

COST INDICATOR
Budget   Moderate   Very Expensive   Criminal

i - **Information** - 0043 (0) 5358 2301
www.ellmau.com

ROUTE PLANNER

🚢 **CALAIS** *0 miles*
along the **A16 - A26**
E15 / E17
Toll Road

➡ **REIMS** *168 miles*
2hrs 53 **A4 E17 / 50**

➡ **METZ** *270 miles*
4hrs 47 **A4 E25** *Dir Strasbourg*
Tolls End

🚗 **A35** north to the D4
⚠ **Enter Germany** *401 miles*
B500 to the **E35 - 5**

➡ **KARLSRUHE** *424 miles*
7hrs 16 **A8 E52**
via Pforzheim

➡ **STUTTGART** *459 miles*
7hrs 50 **A8 E52**

➡ **MUNICH** *586 miles*
9hrs 58 Travel around Munich and follow all directions south for Salzburg along the **A8 E45/E52**. Then pick up the **E45/ E60** for **Innsbruck**.

⚠ **Enter Austria** *660 miles*
Head south along the **A12** in the direction of Innsbruck.

➡ **KUFSTEIN** *660 miles*
11hrs 15 **B173**

➡ **ELLMAU**

KM **Distance** 676 miles *(1088 km)*
🕐 **Drive time** 11 hours 40 mins
⛽ **Fuel** £62
€ **Tolls** £25

✈ **Airports & Fly Drive Guide**

1st- Salzburg - 1 hr 20
➡ Routes **B1, B21, E60, B178**
= 45 miles

2nd- Innsbruck - 1 hr 20
➡ **A12, E45, E60, B178** via
Worgl = 55 miles

3rd- Munich (D) - 1 hr 55
➡ Routes **A99, E45, A8, A93**
via **Kufstein** = 95 miles

35

🕐 DRIVE TIME - nixon. www.nixonnow.com

Fieberbrunn

Top Lift
2020m.
Resort Height
878m.
Vertical Drop
1220m.
Number of Runs
25
Longest Run
8km
Slopes
45km of piste
● ● *Beginner*
34% of the runs
● *Intermediate*
50% of the runs
● **Advanced**
16% of the runs

Cross-Country
-
Snowboarding
Half-pipe & Park
Snow Season
Dec to April
Snowmaking
30 cannons
Number of lifts
10
Up Lift Capicity
-
Mountain Cafes
-

On the Slopes - Despite being largely ignored by the ski world, Fieberbrunn is well-known and respected in snowboarding circles. While not a high-altitude, nor particularly testing resort, Fieberbrunn nonetheless appeals to riders of all levels and skiers who like a mountain off the beaten track. Most people will be able to cover the place within three or four days however, especially if they are at an advanced level. The resort's popularity with snowboarders must have something to do with it's fantastic halfpipe that is flood-lit and stays open until 10pm most evenings – or perhaps it's because the area lies in a natural snow pocket and regularly receives 50% more snow than nearby Kitzbuhel. Either way, Fieberbrunn has not attracted large UK tour operators, even though it's popular with locals and their cousins from Germany. The well-prepared pistes do have busy periods (mainly at weekends and over holiday times, like everywhere else), but don't be put off: Fieberbrunn is a friendly place and the lift queues are usually minimal. A few years ago the resort added a high-speed quad chair and the Sky-Liner gondola from the car park to the top of the Doischberg, which has greatly improved the uplift capacity and reduce lift queues, which at times were horrendous. The options for cross-county skiing is rather limited with only a few miles of accessable tracks.

Off the Slopes - Fieberbrunn is a small and pleasant village with a good selection of hotels and pensions. Much of the accommodation is situated around the car-free village centre, which is some distance from the base slopes. Room rates are reasonable and start from around 16 Euros a night. Local facilities are a bit sparse, but you could try out the Go-Karts in Saalfelden (20 minutes away), or just pig out in one of the standard local Austrian restaurants. For a drink or somewhere to chill out in the evenings, then Cheers and the Riverhouse are both popular bars, as is the Tenne club, which is the local's favorite late night hangout for drinking and dancing.

Verdict - A good resort that is particularly popular with snowboarders. 6/10

COST INDICATOR

Budget   Moderate   Very Expensive   Criminal

i - **Information** - 0043 (0) 5356 304
www.fieberbrunn.com

ROUTE PLANNER

CALAIS	0 miles
along the **A16 - A26**	
E15 / E17	
Toll Road	

→ **REIMS** 168 miles 2hrs 53
A4 E17 / 50

→ **METZ** 270 miles 4hrs 47
A4 E25 *Dir Strasbourg*
Tolls End

✈ A35 north to the D4
⚠ **Enter Germany** 401 miles
B500 to the **E35 - 5**

→ **KARLSRUHE** 424 miles 7hrs 16
A8 E52
via Pforzheim

→ **STUTTGART** 459 miles 7hrs 50
A8 E52

→ **MUNICH** 589 miles 9hrs 58
Travel around Munich and follow all directions south for Salzburg along the **A8 E45/E52.** Then pick up the **E45/ E60** for **Innsbruck.**

⚠ **Enter Austria** 660 miles
Head south along the **A12** in the direction of Innsbruck.

→ **KUFSTEIN** 660 miles 1hr 35
B173, B164

→ **FIEBERBRUNN**
9hr 22

KM Distance **689** miles *(1109 km)*
⏱ **Drive time** **12 hours**
⛽ **Fuel** **£62**
€ **Tolls** **£25**

✈ **Airports & Fly Drive Guide**
1st- Salzburg - 1 hr 25
→ Routes B1, B21, **E60**, B178, B164 = **50 miles**

2nd- Innsbruck - 1 hr 40
→ A12, **E45, E60**, B178 via Worgl B164 = **68 miles**

3rd- Munich (D) - 2 hrs 10
→ Routes A99, **E45**, A8, A93 via Kufstein = **110 miles**

Galtur

Top Lift
2292m.
Resort Height
1584m.
Vertical Drop
700m.
Number of Runs
-
Longest Run
2km
Slopes
48km of piste
● ● *Beginner*
10% of the runs
● *Intermediate*
60% of the runs
● **Advanced**
30% of the runs

Cross-Country
40km of tracks
Snowboarding
Half-pipe & Park
Snow Season
Dec to April
Snowmaking
10% of the pistes
Number of lifts
12
Up Lift Capicity
-
Mountain Cafes
-

On the Slopes - Galtur, the lesser-known neighbour of Ischgl, hit the headlines for all the wrong reasons during the winter of '98/'99 when the resort suffered a huge avalanche that covered much of the village. While Galtur is a relatively small resort, it's a perfect example of a traditional Austrian ski village and manages to prove that size doesn't always matter, and is a particularly suitable destination for families. Whilst it's larger neighbour, Ischgl, gets the media attention, Galtur is left alone, making for a generally quieter feel to enjoy – although it should be pointed out that the slopes can become very busy during main holiday times, as mountain users spill over from Ischgl. Galtur has a good annual snow record and well is well worth a week's stay – what's more, you can buy a lift ticket for the Silvretta region, of which Galtur and Ischgl are a part, opening up a total a area of 330km of skiable pistes. With this much terrain, there is no reason for any one to get bored. The joint lift pass also includes free travel on the region's shuttle bus, so getting around is made easier. A notable feature of Galtur is the flood-lit slopes that offer evening skiing and snowboarding – very uncommon for Austria. Overall Galtur will suit beginners and intermediates who like well-groomed flat pistes, while those who class themselves as experts, will find Ischgl offers far more challenging terrain.

Off the Slopes - As a typical Austrian village Galtur, offers a whole range of accommodation options, from well priced and simple Pensions, to expensive five star hotels. Everything is within easy access of the slopes and for such a small resort, there are plenty of things to do when you're not on the mountain including a modern and well-equipped sports centre. Action in the evenings is somewhat muted and far quieter than Ischgl's, however there are some good restaurants in and around the village square, most notable of which is the Alpenrose which has a good menu and is worth a visit. Amongst the popular night spots, La Tschuetta is a good choice.

Verdict - Galtur is a great resort for intermediate skiers. 9/10

COST INDICATOR

Budget   Moderate   Very Expensive   Criminal

i - **Information** - 0043 (0) 5443 521
www.galtuer.com

ROUTE PLANNER

CALAIS	0 miles
along the **A16 - A26**	
E15 / E17	
Toll Road	

→ **REIMS** 168 miles 2hrs 53
A4 E17 / 50

→ **METZ** 270 miles 4hrs 47
A4 E25 *Dir Strasbourg*
Tolls End

✈ A35 north to the D4
⚠ **Enter Germany** 401 miles
B500 to the **E35 - 5**

→ **KARLSRUHE** 424 miles 7hrs 16
A8 E52
via Pforzheim

→ **STUTTGART** 459 miles 7hrs 50
A8 E52

→ **ULM** 523 miles 8hrs 55
A7 E532

→ **MEMMINGEN** 553 miles 9hrs 30
A96 E43/54, south in the direction of **Lindau**

⚠ **Enter Austria** 595 miles
Head further south along the **A14 E60** via **Feldkirch** and exit at junction 61 to the **B188**

→ **GALTUR**

KM Distance **642** miles *(1034km)*
⏱ **Drive time** **11 hours 40 mins**
⛽ **Fuel** **£59**
€ **Tolls** **£25**

✈ **Airports & Fly Drive Guide**
1st- Innsbruck - 1 hr 35
→ A12 via **Landeck** along the B188 = **69 miles**

2nd- Zurich (CH) - 2 hrs 33
→ A1 **E60**, A14 - Feldkirch, A14, B188 = **130 miles**

3rd- Salzburg - 3 hrs 20
→ All roads to **Innsbruck** A12 & via **Landeck** = **180 miles**

⏱ **DRIVE TIME -** **nixon** www.nixonnow.com

Austria
Hintertux

Mapping Page 88 B3

Top Lift
3250m.
Resort Height
1500m.
Vertical Drop
1750m.
Number of Runs
133 (Tux valley)
Longest Run
8km
Slopes
90km of piste
⬤⬤ Beginner
28% of the runs
⬤ Intermediate
57% of the runs
⬤ Advanced
15% of the runs

Cross-Country
15km of tracks
Snowboarding
Half-pipe & Park
Snow Season
All year round
Snowmaking
86% of pistes
Number of lifts
24
Up Lift Capicity
30,100 per hour
Mountain Cafes
4

On the Slopes - Located at the very end of the Ziller valley, Hintertux is a peculiar mix of good and bad. On the plus side, the lowest point of the resort sits at 1500m and climbs to the glacier at well over 3000m, ensuring that there is always snow, even during the summer months when the resort can boast having more snow that many other resorts get in the winter. The terrain has something to offer skiers and snowboarders of all levels. On the down side if there is poor snowfall, Hintertux can be the only resort in the area with snow on the slopes and becomes hellishly busy as mountain users flock from as far away as Munich, which is only a couple of hours down the motorway – weekends in particular see a large influx of city dwellers. Another disadvantage is that due to it's treeless nature, the resort is somewhat exposed, which means that when its cold here even the polar bears wear gloves – always have the correct clothing or you could suffer dearly. Initial access to the slopes is via a twenty-minute, three-stage gondola and once up you'll find the open expanse of treeless terrain is excellent, with good advanced slopes and nice powder fields that are seldom tracked out. All the pistes are well marked and connect nicely with each other by a series of chair and draglifts. In terms of snowboarding, they don't come much better – Hintertux often hosts major competitions.

Off the Slopes - The village area, if it could be called that, is little more than an enormous car park for day and weekend trippers and a few, overpriced hotels. The village totally lacks local services and with a captive audience (the next closest accommodation is around 25 minutes away) prices in general are steep. The few hotels and restaurants are good, however, and there are some lively watering holes, particularly during the après ski hours. If you want variety, the best choice is to stay in the bustling Mayrhofen, about 25 minutes down the valley which has a lot going for it with more hotels, restaurants, shops and pubs.

ROUTE PLANNER

🛫 **CALAIS** 0 miles
along the **A16 - A26**
E15 / E17
Toll Road

➡ **REIMS** 168 miles
2hrs 53 **A4 E17 / 50**

➡ **METZ** 270 miles
4hrs 47 **A4 E25** *Dir Strasbourg*
Tolls End

✈ **A35** north to the **D4**
⚠ **Enter Germany** 401 miles
B500 to the **E35 - 5**

➡ **KARLSRUHE** 424 miles
7hrs 16 **A8 E52**
via Pforzheim

➡ **STUTTGART** 459 miles
7hrs 50 **A8 E52**

➡ **MUNICH** 589 miles
9hrs 58 Travel around Munich and follow all directions south for Salzburg along the **A8 E45/E52**. Then pick up the **E45/ E60** for **Innsbruck**.

⚠ **Enter Austria** 660 miles
Head south along the **A12** towards Innsbruck. Leave the **A12** at the Munster junction for the Zillertal valley.

➡ **MAYRHOFEN** 707 miles
12hrs 15 **B169, L6**

➡ **HINTERTUX**

KM Distance 720 miles *(1160 km)*
🕐 **Drive time** 12 hours 45 mins
⛽ **Fuel** £66
€ **Tolls** £25

✈ **Airports & Fly Drive Guide**
1st- Innsbruck - **1 hr 40**
➡ **A12 E60. B169, L6** via
Mayrhofen = 60 miles

2nd- Salzburg - **2 hrs 30**
➡ Routes **A8, E52. E45, A93** and the **B169, L6 = 120 miles**

3rd- Munich (D) - **2 hrs 50**
➡ **A8 E45/E52 & E45/E60**
A12 & B169, L6 = 135 miles

Verdict - A decent place to ride or ski throughout the year. **5/10**

COST INDICATOR

Budget　　Moderate　　Very Expensive　　Criminal

💯

ℹ **- Information -** 0043 (0) 5287 8506
www.hintertuxergletscher.com

Austria
Innsbruck

Mapping Page 88 B3

Top Lift
3200m.
Resort Height
850m.
Vertical Drop
1460m.
Longest Run
9.6km
Slopes
323km of piste
⬤⬤ Beginner
54% of the runs
⬤ Intermediate
40% of the runs
⬤ Advanced
6% of the runs

Cross-Country
200km of tracks
Snowboarding
Half-pipe & Park
Winter Season
Dec to April
Summer Season
May to Sept
Snowmaking
45% of pistes
Number of lifts
210
Up Lift Capicity
-
Mountain Cafes
20

On the Slopes - As Austria's second city, Innsbruck is not actually a ski area, but the gateway to dozens of nearby of resorts – five of which (Axamer Lizum, Igls, Seegrübe, Mütters and Stubai) are either in the city, on the outskirts or within a very short drive. All the Innsbruck resorts (except the Stubai Glacier) are low altitude and not always snow sure – none of them are particularly large or challenging, with the exception of the ultra-extreme black run that descends from Seegrübe (the nearest resort to the city centre). Innsbruck's main resorts are covered by a joint pass that includes a regular shuttle bus between them: you can simply hop on or off at each resort. Although local bus services are excellent in this region, it may be an advantage to have your own car so you can travel around the resorts or further afield at your leisure. Road links are superb, so you won't have problems getting around, but remember to take snow-chains, especially if you intend to visit the glacier resort of Stubai. Snowboard fans may be interested to know that Burton Snowboards set up their first non-American headquarters in Innsbruck in 1982 and the Snowboard Klinik are also based here, making Innsbruck the snowboard capital city of Europe which becomes apparent when you see the number of snowboarders on the slopes at any one of the resorts.

Off the Slopes - Innsbruck may not be New York, London or Paris, but it's still a damn fine and beautiful city set along both banks of the river Inns and is steeped in history, with cobbled streets and overhanging buildings. You have huge choice of accommodation options, from international five star hotels, guesthouses, pensions, bunkhouses and youth hostels to choose from with price tags to suit everyone. There are dozens of restaurants, loads of shops, Olympic ice rink, concert halls and cinemas. Nightlife, although superb, is quite muted and centered on the bars and clubs along the main high street or traditional bierkellers that are tucked away in the old town.

ROUTE PLANNER

🛫 **CALAIS** 0 miles
along the **A16 - A26**
E15 / E17
Toll Road

➡ **REIMS** 168 miles
2hrs 53 **A4 E17 / 50**

➡ **METZ** 270 miles
4hrs 47 **A4 E25** *Dir Strasbourg*
Tolls End

✈ **A35** north to the **D4**
⚠ **Enter Germany** 401 miles
B500 to the **E35 - 5**

➡ **KARLSRUHE** 424 miles
7hrs 16 **A8 E52**
via Pforzheim

➡ **STUTTGART** 459 miles
7hrs 50 **A8 E52**

➡ **ULM** 523 miles
8hrs 55 **A7 E532**

➡ **KEMPTEN** 573 miles
1hr 35 **A7 E532** south via **Nesselwang** along the **B309 & B179.**
⚠ **Enter Austria** 600 miles
Head south along the **B179** via the **Fernpaß** to the **B189.**

TELFS 646 miles
A12 E60

➡ **INNSBRUCK**

KM Distance 658 miles *(1059km)*
🕐 **Drive time** 11 hours 55 mins
⛽ **Fuel** £61
€ **Tolls** £25

✈ **Airports & Fly Drive Guide**
1st- Innsbruck - **10 minutes**
➡ **B174, B171 = 3 miles**

2nd- Salzburg - **2 hrs**
➡ Routes **A1, A8, A12 = 114 miles**

3rd- Munich (D) - **2 hrs 25**
➡ **A8, A93, A12 = 130 miles**

Verdict - Superb place to base yourself with world class resorts nearby.. **5/10**

COST INDICATOR

Budget　　Moderate　　Very Expensive　　Criminal

💯

ℹ **- Information -** 0043 (0) 512 598 50
www.innsbruck-tourism.at

🕐 DRIVE TIME - nixon® www.nixonnow.com

Ischgl

Mapping Page 88 C1

Top Lift
2864m.
Resort Height
1400m.
Vertical Drop
1472m.
Number of Runs
98 (in Silvretta)
Longest Run
7km
Slopes
53km of piste
● Beginner
25% of the runs
● Intermediate
60% of the runs
● Advanced
15% of the runs

Cross-Country
48km of tracks
Snowboarding
Half-pipe & Park
Snow Season
Dec to April
Snowmaking
52km of pistes
Number of lifts
41
Up Lift Capacity
58,200 per hour
Mountain Cafes
11

On the Slopes - Ischgl has gained a reputation as one of Austria's best resorts with the likes of St Anton – and it's a worthy accolade at that. While it's not the most testing of ski areas, Ischgl still has plenty to offer everyone, with well-groomed slopes and fine off-piste runs serviced by fast, modern lifts with a total uplift capacity of over 60,000 people an hour – making long queues a thing of the past. All the slopes are high up, which usually means a good covering of snow throughout each season – indeed, the average annual snowfall record is in excess of 160cm. If you feel the need to explore, you can ski or ride into the neighbouring Swiss duty-free resort of Samnaun which can be reached by a series of connecting lifts, including one of the biggest cable cars in Europe. Uplift is covered on the Silvretta lift pass, which includes access to the nearby resorts of Galtur, Kappl and See. Freestyle snowboarders are in for a real treat as the terrain-park is one of the best in Europe with all sorts of obstacles and marked areas for certain styles – there is also a good competition standard halfpipe. The one drawback in Ischgl is a lack of good total beginners slopes, but if you're a fast learner, there are great opportunities to improve with lots of well laid out runs that cover the area. Cross-country skiers are provided with almost 50 km of marked out tracks, and while this may not be the most adventurous place for flat skiing, it is certainly a spectacular one with nice wooded trails.

Off the Slopes - While a modern and pleasant village, Ischgl is busy and a little expensive – accommodation is of a high standard and convenient however. The village has an adventure swimming pool, indoor squash courts and tennis, a cinema and lots of good restaurants. However, fast food only exists when a shoplifter runs out of the supermarket without paying for a packet of biscuits. Nightlife is something of a love or hate affair; many places go in for an overdose of sickly aprés-ski, but there are plenty of good bars and late-night hangouts free of the silliness, but you'll need to be selective.

ROUTE PLANNER

✈ **CALAIS** 0 miles
along the **A16 - A26**
E15 / E17
Toll Road

➡ **REIMS** 168 miles
2hrs 53 **A4 E17 / 50**

➡ **METZ** 270 miles
4hrs 47 **A4 E25** *Dir Strasbourg*
Tolls End

✈ **A35** north to the **D4**

⚠ **Enter Germany** 401 miles
B500 to the **E35 - 5**

➡ **KARLSRUHE** 424 miles
7hrs 16 **A8 E52**
via Pforzheim

➡ **STUTTGART** 459 miles
7hrs 50 **A8 E52**

➡ **ULM** 523 miles
8hrs 55 **A7 E532**

➡ **MEMMINGEN** 553 miles
9hrs 30 **A96 E43/54**, south in the direction of **Lindau**

⚠ **Enter Austria** 595 miles
Head further south along the **A14 E60** via **Feldkirch** and exit at junction 61 to the **B188**

➡ **ISCHGL**
9hr 22

KM Distance 672 miles *(1082km)*
🕐 **Drive time** 11 hours 55 mins
⛽ **Fuel** £62
€ **Tolls** £25

Verdict - Excellent all-round mountain, but lacking for beginners. **6/10**

COST INDICATOR

Budget   Moderate   Very Expensive   Criminal

ℹ **· Information -** 0043 (0) 5445 2660
www.ischgl.com

✈ **Airports & Fly Drive Guide**

1st- Innsbruck - 1 hr 25
➡ **A12** via **Landeck** along the **B188** = 62 miles

2nd- Zurich (CH) - 3 hrs
➡ **A1 E60, A14 -** Feldkirch, **A14, B188** = 138 miles

3rd- Salzburg - 3 hrs 15
➡ All roads to **Innsbruck A12** & via **Landeck** = 172 miles

---

Kaprun

Mapping Page 89 B5

Top Lift
3029m.
Resort Height
786m.
Vertical Drop
800m.
Number of Runs
21
Longest Run
8km
Slopes
55km of piste
● Beginner
38% of the runs
● Intermediate
50% of the runs
● Advanced
12% of the runs

Cross-Country
50km of tracks
Snowboarding
Terrain Park
Snow Season
All year round
Snowmaking
15 cannons
Number of lifts
13
Up Lift Capacity
30,500 per hour
Mountain Cafes
8

On the Slopes - Kaprun is a small mountain that is open to snow sports in winter and summer, thanks to the Kitzsteinhorn Glacier - which reaches an altitude of 3,203 metres. This resort grabbed the world headlines in 2000 when the main funicular train caught fire, in a tunnel, resulting in a number of fatalities. The train has now been replaced by a modern, two stage, 24 person gondola which runs along side the old gondola and on up to the Alpencenter. It is a place which has always had a bit of a problem with lift-queues as visitors flock here when lower level resorts don't have sufficient snow cover. The new gondola has helped to reduce the base queues, but be prepared for some more queuing once up on the mountain. The high-level slopes are spread over a wide tree less bowl which in the winter is often knee deep in powder and a great place for intermediate skiers and snowboarders to enjoy. Experts won't find too much here to take up their time, with only a small number of advanced level runs, a good part of which is off-piste. The slopes of nearby Zell am See, far bigger and more popular, has a lot more varied and advanced terrain for those looking for hart-pumping rush. Cross country skiing in this area is excellent providing, of course, there is enough snow lower down, which is where the main tracks are located, such as those around Kaprun's golf course. Thanks to the summer snow available on the glacier, this place has become a very popular summer snowboard destination. Lots of training camps are held during May, June and July.

Off the Slopes - Kaprun is a large, sprawling-place. Having a car will save a lot of walking, although, there is a good and reliable local bus service. Around town, you get a mixture of the old-and the new with a typical Austrian flavour, offering good accommodation options to satisfy both the rich the and skint. Evenings in Kaprun are laid-back - check out the Austrian Pub, Bauber's, or the Fountain bar. Nothing great about any of them - but there are still good for a beer or a boogy.

ROUTE PLANNER

✈ **CALAIS** 0 miles
along the **A16 - A26**
E15 / E17
Toll Road

➡ **REIMS** 168 miles
2hrs 53 **A4 E17 / 50**

➡ **METZ** 270 miles
4hrs 47 **A4 E25** *Dir Strasbourg*
Tolls End

✈ **A35** north to the **D4**

⚠ **Enter Germany** 401 miles
B500 to the **E35 - 5**

➡ **KARLSRUHE** 424 miles
7hrs 16 **A8 E52**
via Pforzheim

➡ **STUTTGART** 459 miles
7hrs 50 **A8 E52**

➡ **MUNICH** 589 miles
10hrs Travel around Munich and follow all directions south for Salzburg via the **A8 E45/E52.** Then take the **A93 E45/ E60.**

⚠ **Enter Austria** 664 miles

➡ **ENDACH** 664 miles
11hrs 20 Pick up the **B173** and the **B178** via **Sperten** to the **B161** via **Kitzbuhel** to the **B168** via **Jesdorf** to the **L215**

➡ **KAPRUN**

KM Distance 720 miles *(1160km)*
🕐 **Drive time** 12 hours 50 mins
⛽ **Fuel** £66
€ **Tolls** £25

Verdict - Good for intermediates and summer snow, but big queues. **7/10**

COST INDICATOR

Budget   Moderate   Very Expensive   Criminal

ℹ **· Information -** 0043 (0) 6547 808 021
www.europa-sport-region.com

✈ **Airports & Fly Drive Guide**

1st- Salzburg - 1 hr 30
➡ **A10 E55. B311** = 62 miles

2nd- Innsbruck - 2 hrs 20
➡ **A12, B171, B178, L45, B170, B161, B168** = 92 miles

3rd- Munich (D) - 3 hrs 10
➡ **A8, A93, A12, B171, B178** to the **B161 & B168** = 140 miles

---

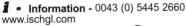

🕐 DRIVE TIME - **nixon** www.nixonnow.com

Austria
Kitzbühel

Mapping Page 88 B4

ROUTE PLANNER

Top Lift
2000m.
Resort Height
760m.
Vertical Drop
1200m.
Number of Runs
58
Longest Run
11km
Slopes
165km of piste
●● *Beginner*
45% of the runs
● *Intermediate*
40% of the runs
● *Advanced*
15% of the runs
Cross-Country
35km of tracks
Snowboarding
Half-pipe & Park
Snow Season
Dec to April
Snowmaking
43% of pistes
Number of lifts
56
Up Lift Capicity
76,000 per hour
Mountain Cafes
31

On the Slopes - Kitzbühel is world famous for the Hahnenkamm World Cup ski run and event, but despite all the press it generates, on the contrary, it is not the best resort in Austria. Far from it, in fact – the annual snow record is poor and being a low-level resort, relies heavily on snow cannons, particularly from mid-March until the end of the season as the lower runs often have only a thin covering. Despite this, UK tour operators love it and have subsequently made the resort one of their most-favoured Austrian destinations. Kitzbuhel can be good for week or so, particularly If you're a novice or intermediate standard or a family with kids. In fairness, the slopes aren't bad at all, it's just the mountain lacks a choice of advanced runs and the slopes can be annoyingly busy – lift queues can be a problem, but things have improved over recent years since the old Hahnenkamm cable car was replaced with a faster gondola. The runs are somewhat spread out, but easy to reach and once you do get going you will find lots of variety in terms of terrain features. Off-piste lovers won't be disappointed nor will skiers who like to hit moguls, however the number of nursery slopes is quite poor. For those who like to slide along wooded tracks, will find the cross-crountry terrain rather good so long as there is good snow cover on the lower areas.

Off the Slopes - Kitzbühel is a reasonably large resort with plenty going for it. It is both attractive and full of Tyrolean charm while at the same time being well equipped with a host of good visitor facilities. The choice of hotels and pensions is excellent as are the number and type of restaurants – there's even a well-known burger giant. In terms of evening action, there are loads of bars and lots of partying going on, which more than makes up for the sometimes disappointing slopes. The number of drinking holes is large and varied, with something for everyone, even those who actually like the whole aprés-ski thing. A good hang out is Seppi's Pub.

ROUTE PLANNER

🚗 **CALAIS**	0 miles	
	along the **A16 - A26**	
	E15 / E17	
	Toll Road	
→ **REIMS**	168 miles	2hrs 53
	A4 E17 / 50	
→ **METZ**	270 miles	4hrs 47
	A4 E25 *Dir Strasbourg*	
🛂 *Tolls End*		
→ **A35** north to the D4		1hr 35
⚠ **Enter Germany**	401 miles	
	B500 to the **E35 - 5**	
→ **KARLSRUHE**	424 miles	7hrs 16
	A8 E52	
	via Pforzheim	
→ **STUTTGART**	459 miles	7hrs 50
	A8 E52	
→ **MUNICH**	589 miles	10hrs
	Travel around Munich and follow all directions south for Salzburg via the **A8** E45/E52. Then take the **A93** E45/ E60.	
⚠ **Enter Austria**	664 miles	
→ **ENDACH**	664 miles	11hrs 20
	Pick up the **B173** and the **B178** via **Sperten** to the **B161**	
⬇		9hr 22
→ **KITZBUHEL**		

🇰🇲 **Distance**	682 miles *(1098km)*
🕐 **Drive time**	11 hours 50 mins
⛽ **Fuel**	£62
€ **Tolls**	£25

🛩 Airports & Fly Drive Guide

1st- Salzburg - 1 hr 15
→ **A1** E60. **B1, B21,** via Zell am See **B178, L40** = **42** miles

2nd- Innsbruck - 1 hr
→ **A12,** via Kufstein **B178, B161** = **62** miles

3rd- Munich (D) - 2 hrs
→ **A99, A8, A93** via Kufstein **B178, B161** = **100** miles

Verdict - Okay intermediate slopes but poor snow record. Good nightlife. **6/10**

COST INDICATOR

Budget Moderate Very Expensive Criminal

i - **Information** - 0043 (0) 5356 62155
www.kitzbuehel.com

Austria
Lech- Arlberg

Mapping Page 88 B1

ROUTE PLANNER

Top Lift
2444m.
Resort Height
1450m.
Vertical Drop
994m.
Number of Runs
32
Longest Run
5km
Slopes
97km of piste
●● *Beginner*
25% of the runs
● *Intermediate*
50% of the runs
● *Advanced*
25% of the runs
Cross-Country
18km of tracks
Snowboarding
Half-pipe & Park
Snow Season
Dec to April
Snowmaking
52km of pistes
Number of lifts
33
Up Lift Capicity
44,600 per hour
Mountain Cafes
18

On the Slopes - The Arlberg region, in the western part of Austria, is home to most of the classy resorts that the country has to offer. Lech is one of them, along with its close neighbours, Zurs, Stuben, St. Christoph and St. Anton. More closely linked with Zurs, Lech sits at the back of St Anton and is without doubt Austria's number one retreat for the wealthy: year in, year out, this high altitude resort attracts numerous royals and the finest from the film and pop worlds – many of whom come to be seen rather than ski, which is a crying shame – Lech has outstanding terrain for both skiing and snowboarding. Not only are the easy-to-access slopes ideal for all levels, but with the resort's neighbours within easy reach, the options for limitless adventure is superb. You may have to push past a fur coat or two, but you can explore a mountain where almost anything is possible: there are wonderful, wide-open powder bowls to glide down, tight trees to zip through and perfectly groomed pistes that favour intermediates who like to take it easy. Expert skiers and snowboarders can set the heart pumping down the steep blacks that descend back to the village, but be warned: treat the mountains with respect as a lot of snow falls in the region and avalanches are not uncommon. Despite the resort's upper class clientele, Lech has nevertheless long embraced snowboarding by providing a park and halfpipe, it is also a great freerider's resort and an excellent place for novices. Cross-country skiers will also like what's available here, just don't expect miles of marked out tracks.

Off the Slopes - At the base of the slopes is a picturesque – albeit expensive – resort dripping with people in fur coats, so expect to pay top prices for all services. Acccomodation is expensive throughout, however there are places to check out that are affordable. Local facilities are good, but there's not a great deal on offer. Nightlife is laid back, but there are good bars and restaurants to choose from such as Bistro Casarole which does a fine steak.

ROUTE PLANNER

🚗 **CALAIS**	0 miles	
	along the **A16 - A26**	
	E15 / E17	
	Toll Road	
→ **REIMS**	168 miles	1hr 35
	A4 E17 / 50	
→ **METZ**	270 miles	1hr 35
	A4 E25 *Dir Strasbourg*	
🛂 *Tolls End*		
→ **A35** north to the D4		1hr 35
⚠ **Enter Germany**	401 miles	
	B500 to the **E35 - 5**	
→ **KARLSRUHE**	424 miles	1hr 35
	A8 E52	
	via Pforzheim	
→ **STUTTGART**	459 miles	1hr 35
	A8 E52	
→ **ULM**	523 miles	1hr 35
	A7 E532	
→ **MEMMINGEN**	553 miles	9hrs 30
	A96 E43/54, south in the direction of Lindau	
⚠ **Enter Austria**	595 miles	
	Head further south along the **A14** E60 via **Feldkirch** to the **S16** via **Bings, Stuben** and **Zurs.**	
⬇		9hr 22
→ **LECH - ARLBERG**		

🇰🇲 **Distance**	657 miles *(1058km)*
🕐 **Drive time**	11 hours
⛽ **Fuel**	£56
€ **Tolls**	£25

🛩 Airports & Fly Drive Guide

1st- Innsbruck - 1 hr 40
→ **A12** via Landeck along the **B198** = **72** miles

2nd- Zurich (CH) - 2 hrs 30
→ **A1** E60, **A14** - Feldkirch, **S16** via Zurs = **125** miles

3rd- Salzburg - 2 hrs 30
→ All roads to Innsbruck **A12** & via Landeck = **124** miles

Verdict - First class mountain with great options, but nothing is cheap. **8/10**

COST INDICATOR

Budget Moderate Very Expensive Criminal

i - **Information** - 0043 (0) 5583 21610
www.lech.at

🕐 DRIVE TIME - 𝗻𝗶𝘅𝗼𝗻 www.nixonnow.com

Mayrhofen

Mapping Page 88 B3

Top Lift
2500m.
Resort Height
630m.
Vertical Drop
1870m.
Number of Runs
-
Longest Run
5.5km
Slopes
143km of piste
● Beginner
28% of the runs
● Intermediate
55% of the runs
● Advanced
17% of the runs

Cross-Country
20km of tracks
Snowboarding
Half-pipe & Park
Snow Season
Dec to April
Snowmaking
86km of pistes
Number of lifts
43
Up Lift Capacity
37,400 per hour
Mountain Cafes
20

On the Slopes - Mayrhofen has many factors. An ideal destination for both skiers and snowboarders. Only an hour's drive from Innsbruck along the Ziller Valley, Mayrhofen – which is linked with Finkenberg and Hippach on the slopes to give a pisted area of over 140km – has long been a popular family resort that has wonderful open snow fields that are truly excellent for beginners and intermediates alike. Even though the area boasts a fairly good snow record, should there be a lack of snow, you can head to the Hintertux glacier which is always snow sure, open all year round and reached by taking the free shuttle bus. Mayrhofen does have a few down points: for instance, the slopes can be so crowded that a walk down Oxford Street on a Saturday afternoon would be a breeze by comparison, furthermore there's not enough challenging terrain for advanced skiers and boarders and experts would be better off heading to Hintertux. In the past, uplift capacity had been a large problem queues used to be among the worst in the country, but extensive investment in state-of-the-art lifts means that has all changed and getting up to the main slopes has become a lot less problematic (not to say queues and bottlenecks don't exist in some areas). Mayrhofen is one of the best snowboard destinations in Austria, which can be highlighted by the number of riders who make the resort their winter home.

Off the Slopes - Mayrhofen can best be described as a 'quaint' resort, with a traditional Tyrolean style. The town isn't particularly large, but it still has lots to offer visitors with a good choice of accommodation, from large hotels to traditional pensions where a room and breakfast will set you back about 15 Euros a night. Cheap eating options are plentiful and evenings are pretty cool – you can party hard into the early hours in a couple of good bars and late discos, but be warned, this place is the Austrian capital for aprés-ski, giving the place a bit of cheap (which it's not) and cheesy feel about it. The Scotland Yard Pub is very popular.

ROUTE PLANNER

🏛	**CALAIS** 0 miles	
	along the **A16 - A26**	
	E15 / E17	
	Toll Road	
→	**REIMS** 168 miles	
2hrs 53	**A4 E17 / 50**	
→	**METZ** 270 miles	
4hrs 47	**A4 E25** Dir Strasbourg	
	Tolls End	
🚗	**A35** north to the D4	
⚠	**Enter Germany** 401 miles	
	B500 to the **E35 - 5**	
🏛	**KARLSRUHE** 424 miles	
7hrs 16	**A8 E52**	
	via Pforzheim	
→	**STUTTGART** 459 miles	
7hrs 50	**A8 E52**	
→	**MUNICH** 589 miles	
9hrs 58	Travel around Munich and follow all directions south for Salzburg along the **A8 E45/E52**. Then pick up the **E45/ E60** for **Innsbruck**.	
⚠	**Enter Austria** 660 miles	
	Head south along the **A12** towards Innsbruck. Leave the **A12** at the Munster junction for the Zillertal valley. **B181** and the **B169**.	

→ **MAYRHOFEN**

KM **Distance** 710 miles *(1143 km)*
🕐 **Drive time** 12 hours 20 mins
⛽ **Fuel** £64
€ **Tolls** £25

✈ **Airports & Fly Drive Guide**

1st- Innsbruck - **1 hr 12**
→ A12 **E60**. B169 = **47 miles**

2nd- Salzburg - **2 hrs 10**
→ Routes A1, A8, A93, B181 & B169 = **106 miles**

3rd- Munich (D) - **2 hrs 30**
→ A8 E45/E52 & E45/E60
A12 & B169 = **125 miles**

40

Verdict -An excellent, family-orientated resort with great facilities. **7**/10

COST INDICATOR

Budget   Moderate   Very Expensive   Criminal

ℹ️ • **Information** - 0043 (0) 5285 67600
www.mayrhofen.com

Obergurgl - *Hochgurgl*

Mapping Page 88 C2

Top Lift
3080m.
Resort Height
1800m.
Vertical Drop
1105m.
Number of Runs
35
Longest Run
8km
Slopes
110km of piste
● Beginner
32% of the runs
● Intermediate
50% of the runs
● Advanced
18% of the runs

Cross-Country
12km of tracks
Snowboarding
Half-pipe & Park
Snow Season
All year round
Snowmaking
90% of pistes
Number of lifts
13
Up Lift Capacity
33,000 per hour
Mountain Cafes
9

On the Slopes - Obergurgl sits at the head of the Otzal Valley, a mere 90 minutes from Innsbruck and twenty minutes from the more popular and larger resort of Solden. Both are located in the same valley and are base locations for summer riding on the Tiefenbach glacier, but the similarity ends there. Obergurgl (linked to the neighboring Hochgurgl) is far smaller and less diverse than Solden especially when it comes to type or terrain features. Obergurgl gets top marks when it comes to immaculately prepared pistes that will have beginners and intermediate snowboarders and skiers in heaven. The resort's high altitude also scores in its favour, offering a very good annual snow record with heaps of the stuff falling every year. Access to the slopes is almost direct from the village center and skiing back to your accommodation is not only possible, but also well worth the effort. Lift queues are virtually non-existent and with a recently installed gondola, direct access to Hochgurgl slopes are now possible which, in turn, gives greater opptunities and will make a two week trip that much more interesting. The runs are set out neatly and serviced by a series of lifts that go to a summit elevation of some 3035 metres. Most of the runs are of an intermediate level with a series of reds, a few easy blues and only a couple of advanced black trails to check out. Experts will need to head back down to Solden, which has a far greater choice of advanced slopes. Beginners should have no problems in Obergurgl with easy runs from the mid-point all the way back down to the village. It is fair to say that Obergurgl is not well known for is cross-country skiing, and while the choice of tracks is limited, its not actually bad.

Off the Slopes - The excitement on the slopes is not matched by what is available off them. Obergurgl is a small, almost car-free hamlet and facilities come in the form of a number of large hotels, a few guesthouses, half a dozen shops or so and a handful of restaurants and bars. Nearby Solden has more to offer.

ROUTE PLANNER

🏛	**CALAIS** 0 miles	
	along the **A16 - A26**	
	E15 / E17	
	Toll Road	
→	**REIMS** 168 miles	
2hrs 53	**A4 E17 / 50**	
→	**METZ** 270 miles	
4hrs 47	**A4 E25** Dir Strasbourg	
	Tolls End	
🚗	**A35** north to the D4	
⚠	**Enter Germany** 401 miles	
	B500 to the **E35 - 5**	
🏛	**KARLSRUHE** 424 miles	
7hrs 16	**A8 E52**	
	via Pforzheim	
→	**STUTTGART** 459 miles	
7hrs 50	**A8 E52**	
→	**ULM** 523 miles	
8hrs 55	**A7 E532**	
→	**KEMPTEN** 573 miles	
9hrs 50	**A7 E532** south via **Nesselwang** along the **B309 & B179**.	
⚠	**Enter Austria** 600 miles	
	Head south along the **B179** via the **Fernpaß** to the **B189**.	
→	**IMST** 636 miles	
11hrs 20	**B171, B186**	
→	**SOLDEN** 668 miles	
12hrs 10		

→ **OBERGURGL**

KM **Distance** 676 miles *(1075km)*
🕐 **Drive time** 12 hours 20 mins
⛽ **Fuel** £62
€ **Tolls** £25

✈ **Airports & Fly Drive Guide**

1st- Innsbruck - **1 hr 30**
→ A12 to junction *123* for the Otzal - B186 = **60 miles**

2nd - Munich (D) - **3 hrs 30**
→ A8 E45/E52 & E45/E60
A12 & B186 = **150 miles**

3rd - Salzburg - **3 hrs 15**
→ All roads to Innsbruck A12 & the B186 = **170 miles**

Verdict - A good, high mountain resort with easy slopes. **7**/10

COST INDICATOR

Budget   Moderate   Very Expensive   Criminal

ℹ️ • **Information** - 0043 (0) 6547 808 021
www.obergurgl.com

Austria
Oberturen

Mapping Page 89 B6

ROUTE PLANNER

CALAIS 0 miles
along the **A16 - A26**
E15 / E17
Toll Road

REIMS 168 miles
2hrs 53 **A4 E17 / 50**

METZ 270 miles
4hrs 47 **A4 E25** *Dir Strasbourg*
Tolls End

A35 north to the **D4**
⚠ **Enter Germany**
B500 to the **E35 - 5**

KARLSRUHE 424 miles
7hrs 16 **A8 E52**
via Pforzheim

STUTTGART 459 miles
7hrs 50 **A8 E52**

MUNICH 589 miles
9hrs 58 Travel around Munich
and follow all directions
south for Salzburg along
the **A8 E45/E52**. Then
pick up the **E45/ E60**.

⚠ **Enter Austria** 686 miles

SALZBURG 587 miles
11hrs 40 Head towards the
airport and pick up the
A10 E55 south.
Exit junction 63 for
Radstadt and pick up
the route **B99** south.

OBERTUREN

| **Top Lift** |
| 2335m. |
| **Resort Height** |
| 1740m. |
| **Vertical Drop** |
| 595m. |
| **Number of Runs** |
| 65 |
| **Longest Run** |
| 2.5km |
| **Slopes** |
| 120km of piste |
| ●● *Beginner* |
| *50% of the runs* |
| ● *Intermediate* |
| *35% of the runs* |
| ● *Advanced* |
| *15% of the runs* |
| **Cross-Country** |
| 18km of tracks |
| **Snowboarding** |
| Half-pipe & Park |
| **Snow Season** |
| Dec to April |
| **Snowmaking** |
| 30km of pistes |
| **Number of lifts** |
| 28 |
| **Up Lift Capicity** |
| 34,500 per hour |
| **Mountain Cafes** |
| 13 |

On the Slopes - Oberturen is one of those resorts that is often overlooked in favour of some Austrians more famous neighbours in the central region. Yet this wonderful place should not be given some serious consideration, especially if you are looking for a resort that offers both crowd free slopes with a good annual snow record. Located an hour south of Salzburg in the Niedere Tauren mountains, this semi purpose built resort has one of the best reputation in Austria for excellent annual snow cover. The slopes rise up the mountain and fan out to form a large open expanse of inter connecting slopes with runs from the summit back down into the village. Much of the mountain is graded blue for beginners with a selection of short, but good red runs for intermediates to try out. However, this mountains does suffer from a lack of testing runs for experts, although there are a few spots that will get the heart pumping, the best of which can be found on the Gamsleitenspitze area. However, there is good off piste skiing and snowboarding to be had. Because of enviable snow record here, when nearby resorts have poor snow cover, visitors flock to Obertauren, but it doesn't cause a major problem and the slopes don't tend to clog up, nor do the lifts. Cross-country skiers can practice their art around the 20km of tracks located close to the resort while snowboarders, who like backcountry areas, will find this a great freeriders hangout and when there has been a fresh dump of snow, the options for shredding deep powder is excellent. There is also a half-pipe at Hochalm but its not always maintained.

Off the Slopes - Despite being a purpose built resort, Obertauren remains an attractive place to visit, with a collection of high wooden chalets that straddle the roadside without giving the sense clutter. The resort has a good feel and is lively with good hotel accommodation at affordable prices, but apart form the sports complex – which lacks a swimming pool – there's little to do except go out. Nightlife is lively and entertaining for a small resort, however.

Verdict - An excellent snow record, simple slopes and a basic village. 6/10

COST INDICATOR

Budget   Moderate   Very Expensive   Criminal

i - **Information** - 0043 (0) 6456 7252
www.obertauren.com

KM Distance 743 miles *(1196 km)*
🕐 **Drive time** 12 hours 45 mins
⛽ **Fuel** £66
€ **Tolls** £25

✈ **Airports & Fly Drive Guide**
1st- Salzburg - 1 hr 10
→ **A10 E55** - to junction 63 to
Radstadt, **B99 = 56 miles**

2nd- Innsbruck - 3 hrs
→ **A12, 312, 311 A10 E55** to
Radstadt, **B99 = 166 miles**

3rd- Munich (D) - 3 hrs
→ **A8 E45/E52 & E45/E60**
A10 & B99 = 162 miles

Austria
Saalbach-Hinterglem

Mapping Page 88 B5

ROUTE PLANNER

CALAIS 0 miles
along the **A16 - A26**
E15 / E17
Toll Road

REIMS 168 miles
2hrs 53 **A4 E17 / 50**

METZ 270 miles
4hrs 47 **A4 E25** *Dir Strasbourg*
Tolls End

A35 north to the **D4**
⚠ **Enter Germany** 401 miles
B500 to the **E35 - 5**

KARLSRUHE 424 miles
7hrs 16 **A8 E52**
via Pforzheim

STUTTGART 459 miles
7hrs 50 **A8 E52**

MUNICH 589 miles
9hrs 58 Travel around Munich
and follow all directions
south for Salzburg via
the **A8 E45/E52**. Then
take the **A93 E45/ E60**.

⚠ **Enter Austria** 664 miles

KITZBUHEL 682 miles
11hrs 40 Pick up the **B164** and
the **B311** via **Kirchham**
to the **L111**

| **Top Lift** |
| 2864m. |
| **Resort Height** |
| 1003m. |
| **Vertical Drop** |
| 1095m. |
| **Number of Runs** |
| 61 |
| **Longest Run** |
| 7km |
| **Slopes** |
| 200km of piste |
| ●● *Beginner* |
| *50% of the runs* |
| ● *Intermediate* |
| *42% of the runs* |
| ● *Advanced* |
| *8% of the runs* |
| **Cross-Country** |
| 10km of tracks |
| **Snowboarding** |
| Half-pipe & Park |
| **Snow Season** |
| Dec to April |
| **Snowmaking** |
| 20% of pistes |
| **Number of lifts** |
| 63 |
| **Up Lift Capicity** |
| 62,000 per hour |
| **Mountain Cafes** |
| 40 |

On the Slopes - Saalbach-Hinterglem are two closely linked villages that lie along a valley floor where the mountain slopes rise up on either side. The first village you arrive at is Saalbach with its cousin Hinterglem a few minutes up the road and together they are one large ski area that covers 200 km of piste and forms a massive and first class ski and snowboard destination. For many years, Saalbach-Hinterglem has been a popular place for skiers and over recent years has become just as popular with snowboarders who are attracted by the high level of mountain facilities, such as the snowboard circuit.

The mountain area is split up with the main slope accessed via the lifts out of Hintertux at the north end. It is possible to reach the slope areas from either village, but it will mean some careful planning and detailed study of your piste map. As a resort that hosts world ski events, you would expect some good terrain and that is exactly what you get here, with piste preparation that is second to none – although it has to be said that not enough of it is challenging. There are trees, steeps, powder and natural hits, not to mention eight miles of snowboard-only runs for freeriders and carvers, as well as two halfpipes and a fun-park to suit all levels. If you get bored here, take up brass rubbing – it will suit you better. As for cross-country skiing, the best on offer are the trails between Saalbach and the village of Vorderglemm, but this area is not really one for 'slow sliding leisure louts'.

Off the Slopes - The resort is popular and can sometimes feel tacky and overpopulated – but don't let that put you off, as you'll find a high level of local services with plenty of things to do from shopping for tourist toys to body fitness adventures. Ice skaters also have a rink to play on, but a word of warning – nothing comes cheap here. Nightlife is very lively: Bobby's is a popular hangout and stays open late but it is also an après ski style haunt, so be warned. Castello's is a good place with live music.

Verdict - A large ski circuit, with good intermediate terrain and a nice village 8/10

COST INDICATOR

Budget   Moderate   Very Expensive   Criminal

i - **Information** - 0043 (0) 6541 680 068
www.saalbach.com

KM Distance 723 miles *(1164km)*
🕐 **Drive time** 13 hours 10 mins
⛽ **Fuel** £67
€ **Tolls** £25

✈ **Airports & Fly Drive Guide**
1st- Salzburg - 1 hr 50
→ **A1 E60. B1, B21,** via Zell
am See **B178, B311 = 54 miles**

2nd- Innsbruck - 2 hrs 40
→ **A12,** via Kitzbuhel **B178,**
B311 = 98 miles

3rd- Munich (D) - 3 hrs 20
→ **A92, A9, A99, A8** via
Kitzbuhel **B178, B311 = 140 miles**

🕐 DRIVE TIME - nixon. www.nixonnow.com

Schaldming

Mapping Page 89 B6

Top Lift
1850m.
Resort Height
745m.
Vertical Drop
1105m.
Number of Runs
74
Longest Run
7km
Slopes
53km of piste
● ● *Beginner*
25% of the runs
● *Intermediate*
71% of the runs.
● **Advanced**
4% of the runs

Cross-Country
300km of tracks
Snowboarding
Half-pipe & Park
Snow Season
All year round
Snowmaking
100% of pistes
Number of lifts
88
Up Lift Capacity
29,500 per hour
Mountain Cafes
47

42

On the Slopes - Schladming is a year-round resort, with summer skiing and snowboarding possible on the Dachstein Glacier. The terrain is spread out over a number of tree-lined areas, that offers basic intermediate level and perfect beginner slopes and while Schladming is not known as an advanced level destination, there are some testing runs to be found. Throughout the region the slopes are kept in top condition with excellent piste preparation, backed up by almost 100% coverage of snowmaking ability. The terrain is split into a number of mountains – Hauser Kaibling has some good intermediate runs, with a series of long reds which are ideal for carvers. There are also some excellent novice trails here, with the option to travel a long blue all the way back down to the base at the village of Haus. The Hochwurzen area rises to a height of 1,850m and has a number of red runs that descend back down through the trees to the base via Rohrmoos (snow permitting). The Planai mountain holds the main trails and is reached from the edge of Schladming by gondola. Planai's runs offer something for everyone, with interesting, intermediate, freeriding terrain for snowboarders and nice, cruising pistes for skiers. The Reiteralm is much the same as Hochwurzen and although a bigger area, it's less convenient for Schladming. If you can't make it here during the winter months, don't fret, the Dachstein Glacier is open all summer and a great place to visit in June. Cross country skiers will find themselves in their element, with some 300km of circuits throughout the region.

Off the Slopes - Accommodation is spread out around a large area, but the old town of Schladming has the biggest selection and offers the best facilities. Prices vary throughout the area, but there is a youth hostel with cheap bunks for those on a budget. The area offers a vast amount of sporting facilities as well as some good restaurants like Giovanni's. Nightlife is fun but with nothing outstanding.

Verdict - Nice mountain with plenty of cross-country ski trails. **7/10**

COST INDICATOR
Budget   Moderate   Very Expensive   Criminal

i - **Information** - 0043 (0) 3686 22340
www.haus.at

ROUTE PLANNER

🛣 **CALAIS** *0 miles*
  along the **A16 - A26**
  E15 / E17
  Toll Road

➡ **REIMS** *168 miles* 2hrs 53
  A4 **E17 / 50**

➡ **METZ** *270 miles* 4hrs 47
  A4 **E25** *Dir Strasbourg*
  Tolls End

✈ **A35** north to the **D4**
⚠ **Enter Germany** *401 miles*
  B500 to the **E35 - 5**

🛣 ➡ **KARLSRUHE** *424 miles* 7hrs 16
  A8 **E52**
  via Pforzheim

➡ **STUTTGART** *459 miles* 7hrs 50
  A8 **E52**

➡ **MUNICH** *589 miles* 9hrs 58
  Travel around Munich and follow all directions south for Salzburg along the **A8** **E45/E52**. Then pick up the **E45/ E60.**

⚠ **Enter Austria** *686 miles*

➡ **SALZBURG** *687 miles* 11hr 40
  Head south down the **A10** **E55** and exit at junction 63 for **Radstadt** and head along the **E651** **B99, B320** via **Mandling**

⬇

➡ **SCHLADMING**

KM **Distance** **742 miles** *(1195 km)*
🕐 **Drive time** **12 hours 40 mins**
⛽ **Fuel** **£67**
€ **Tolls** **£25**

✈ Airports & Fly Drive Guide

1st- Salzburg - **1 hr 10**
➡ **A10 E55** - to junction *63* the **B99, B320 = 55 miles**

2nd- Innsbruck - **3 hrs 4**
➡ **A12, 312, 311 A10 E55** to the **B99, B320 = 164 miles**

3rd- Munich (D) - **3 hrs**
➡ **A8 E45/E52 & E45/E60 A10, E651 B320 = 160 miles**

Seefeld

Mapping Page 88 B2

Top Lift
2170m.
Resort Height
1200m.
Vertical Drop
900m.
Number of Runs
36
Longest Run
6km
Slopes
35km of piste
● ● *Beginner*
38% of the runs
● *Intermediate*
42% of the runs
● **Advanced**
23% of the runs

Cross-Country
104km of tracks
Snowboarding
Halfpipe & Park
Snow Season
Dec to april
Snowmaking
90% of pistes
Number of lifts
26
Up Lift Capacity
20,000 per hour
Mountain Cafes
6

On the Slopes - Seefeld is a tiny, picturesque resort looking like everything you'd imagine an Austrian village to be. This low-key retreat is 20 kilometres from Innsbruck and can be reached with ease along the A12 Autobahn via Zirl. Seefeld is noted more for being a good cross country ski area rather than a downhill hotspot with over 100km of tracks in the resort and a further 180km in the region. There are even 50km of ice-skating tracks to try. Seefeld is a member of the 'Happy Card' group of resorts, a joint lift pass and discount scheme which offers the holder benefits at a number resorts throughout Europe. For instance you can ski here in the morning then make the short journey across the German border to Garmish, and snowboard in the afternoon with the same lift pass. Seefeld is not noted for its hardcore terrain or adventurous downhill skiing or snowboarding, but nevertheless this is still a fun mountain with access up to an altitude of 2100 metres and nice runs back down to the village outskirts. The mountain is split across two separate areas, that of the Gschwandtkopf and the Rosshutte – Gschwandtkopf is a bit limited with a few easy slopes while Rosshutte is a little more extensive with longer trails and wider slopes. Snowboarders will find riding here takes place at a sedate pace – nothing will take too long to conquer and good riders will have this place licked within a day or two at the most. If know your stuff a week might be a bit too long. However, novices should manage to stay interested as there are some really nice easy slopes.

Off the Slopes - Seefeld is quaint village with superb local facilities. The choice of accommodation, from five star hotels to simple pensions is excellent, with very good room rates available. The resort also boasts superb sporting facilities including a heated indoor and outdoor pool, a skating and curling rink, bowling and even an indoor golf range. In the evening, there are some fine restaurants to check out as well as a couple of lively bars and discos that stay open very late.

Verdict - Great cross country resort with excellent local services. **7/10**

COST INDICATOR
Budget   Moderate   Very Expensive   Criminal

i - **Information** - 0043 (0) 5212 2313
www.seefeld-tirol.com

ROUTE PLANNER

🛣 **CALAIS** *0 miles*
  along the **A16 - A26**
  E15 / E17
  Toll Road

➡ **REIMS** *168 miles* 2hrs 53
  A4 **E17 / 50**

➡ **METZ** *270 miles* 4hrs 47
  A4 **E25** *Dir Strasbourg*
  Tolls End

✈ **A35** north to the **D4**
⚠ **Enter Germany** *401 miles*
  B500 to the **E35 - 5**

➡ **KARLSRUHE** *424 miles* 7hrs 16
  A8 **E52**
  via Pforzheim

➡ **STUTTGART** *459 miles* 7hrs 50
  A8 **E52**

➡ **ULM** *523 miles* 1hr 35
  A7 **E532**

➡ **KEMPTEN** *573 miles* 1hr 35
  A7 **E532** south via **Nesselwang** along the **B309 & B179.**

⚠ **Enter Austria** *600 miles*
  Head south along the **B179** via the **Fernpaß** to the **B189.**

TELFS *646 miles*
  B171, L36

⬇

➡ **SEEFELD** 9hr 22

KM **Distance** **655 miles** *(1054km)*
🕐 **Drive time** **12 hours**
⛽ **Fuel** **£60**
€ **Tolls** **£25**

✈ Airports & Fly Drive Guide

1st- Innsbruck - **30 minutes**
➡ **A12, B177 & L36** via Leithen **= 14 miles**

2nd- Munich (D) - **2 hrs 10**
➡ **A9 A95, E533 B177 & L36** via Schamitz **= 120 miles**

3rd- Salzburg - **2 hrs 20**
➡ Routes **A8, A93, A12** via Innsbruck **= 125 miles**

Soll

ROUTE PLANNER

CALAIS 0 miles	along the **A16 - A26** **E15 / E17** *Toll Road*
REIMS 168 miles 2hrs 53	**A4** **E17 / 50**
METZ 270 miles 4hrs 47	**A4** **E25** *Dir Strasbourg* *Tolls End*
A35 north to the D4	**Enter Germany** 401 miles **B500** to the **E35 - 5**
KARLSRUHE 424 miles 7hrs 16	**A8** **E52** *via Pforzheim*
STUTTGART 459 miles 7hrs 50	**A8** **E52**
MUNICH 589 miles 9hrs 58	Travel around Munich and follow all directions south for Salzburg along the **A8** **E45/E52**. Then pick up the **E45/ E60** for **Innsbruck**.
Enter Austria	Head south along the **A12** in the direction of Innsbruck.
KUFSTEIN 660 miles 11hrs 15	**B173, B178**
SOLL	

Distance	**672 miles** *(1082 km)*
Drive time	**11 hours 30 mins**
Fuel	**£60**
Tolls	**£25**

Top Lift
1829m.
Resort Height
620m.
Vertical Drop
1129m.
Number of Runs
15
Longest Run
7.5km
Slopes
43km of piste
● ● *Beginner*
48% of the runs
● *Intermediate*
9% of the runs
● *Advanced*
15% of the runs

Cross-Country
30km of tracks
Snowboarding
Half-pipe & Park
Snow Season
Dec to April
Snowmaking
70 cannons
Number of lifts
12
Up Lift Capicity
111,800 per hour
Mountain Cafes
80

On the Slopes - Soll is a very traditional and appealing village with excellent slopes for beginners and as one of Austria's most popular resorts, is a favourite of package tour operators who send ski group's here en-masse. Located a short distance from the resorts of Ellmau, Scheffau, Going and the nearby hamlets of Brixen, Hopfgarten and Westendorf, they all combine to form Austria's largest linked ski and snowboard area, known as the Ski Welt. All the resorts are similar in style and character, yet are still unique in one way or another – Soll having two main areas of distinction. The first is that it's something of a paradise for beginner/intermediate skiers and snowboarders, with a wealth of easy to master slopes and secondly, the picturesque village offers a high level of good services. Getting to Soll is simplicity itself, with Salzburg only 90 minutes away or Innsbruck closer still. The downside is trying to appreciate the opportunities on the slopes when you arrive. Advanced mountain users will struggle to find challenging terrain and experts will soon tire of the resort even though slow carvers and beginners will love it. Soll is a cool destination if you're on a tight budget and want to take advantage of an inexpensive package holiday. Freeriding snowboarders will find this place a bit limiting but the black graded slope that runs down from the Hohe Salve is reasonable and not to be treated lightly – the same goes for the slope under the Brixen Gondola, but in truth Soll is not a particularly hot snowboarder's resort. As well as being a decent beginners mountain, this is a nice cross-country destination with vary levels of tracks to try out.

Off the Slopes - Soll is a small village that offers high quality services but the layout is not the most convenient for the slopes – you may find yourself staying a fair distance from the base lifts. Still, there are plenty of restaurants and surprisingly good nightlife. There is a good choice of bars and a few nightspots, most of which are well-priced.

Verdict - Good for a family with young children, but a disjointed village. **6/10**

COST INDICATOR

Budget   Moderate   Very Expensive   Criminal

Airports & Fly Drive Guide

1st- Innsbruck - 1 hr
A12 E60, E45 via **Worgl** to the **L213** B178 = **48 miles**

2nd- Salzburg - 1 hr 25
Routes B21 and the B178 south = **52 miles**

3rd- Munich (D) **- 2 hrs 40**
A99, A8, A93 via **Kufstein** = **92 miles**

i **· Information -** 0043 (0) 5333 5216
www.soll.com

Solden

ROUTE PLANNER

CALAIS 0 miles	along the **A16 - A26** **E15 / E17** *Toll Road*
REIMS 168 miles 2hrs 53	**A4** **E17 / 50**
METZ 270 miles 4hrs 47	**A4** **E25** *Dir Strasbourg* *Tolls End*
	A35 north to the D4
	Enter Germany 401 miles **B500** to the **E35 - 5**
KARLSRUHE 424 miles 7hrs 16	**A8** **E52** *via Pforzheim*
STUTTGART 459 miles 7hrs 50	**A8** **E52**
ULM 523 miles 8hrs 55	**A7** **E532**
KEMPTEN 573 miles 9hrs 50	**A7** **E532** south via **Nesselwang** along the **B309 & B179**.
	Enter Austria 600 miles Head south along the **B179** via the **Fernpaß** to the **B189**.
IMST 636 miles	**B171, B186**
SAUTENS 668 miles	**B186**
SOLDEN	

Distance	**668 miles** *(1075km)*
Drive time	**12 hours 5 mins**
Fuel	**£61**
Tolls	**£25**

Top Lift
3235m.
Resort Height
1377m.
Vertical Drop
1771m.
Number of Runs
-
Longest Run
12km
Slopes
180km of piste
● ● *Beginner*
32% of the runs
● *Intermediate*
52% of the runs
● *Advanced*
16% of the runs

Cross-Country
20km of tracks
Snowboarding
Half-pipe & Park
Snow Season
All year round
Snowmaking
28km of pistes
Number of lifts
33
Up Lift Capicity
60,700 per hour
Mountain Cafes
25

On the Slopes - Thirty minutes drive along the Otzal Valley and just an hour from Innsbruck, is the high altitude resort of Solden and its smaller cousin Hochsolden. Both are well-established haunts for snowboarders, skiers and many other adventure sports enthusiasts – summer even sees major canoeing events take place on the river that runs through the village. Solden offers year-round skiing and snowboarding thanks to its high altitude and snow sure slopes in the winter and the snow covered runs on the Tiefenbach Glacier in the summer which has access up to a height of 3312m although much of the glacier remains closed during the winter to preserve the runs for the summer months. Both Solden and Hochsolden will predominantly please piste-loving skiers who like long, wide carving runs and is a place where freeriding snowboarders can excel and fine-tune the talents down some great terrain. There are lots of options for riding off-piste and through trees, both thick and thin. Solden is a high resort, and reliable snow cover is almost guaranteed, but this can make the resort very busy, especially during the Christmas and New Year periods and during school holidays. The effect is that the base lifts can have long early queues up in the morning, but once up the mountain, lift lines are not a problem at all. At the end of the day skiing back down into the resort is possible on a number of very long trails with the option to go hard and fast down a black home run or slow and easy down some blue slopes.

Off the Slopes - Solden is a damn good resort but also an expensive place. You can walk from one end of the village to the other fairly easily or you can catch the free bus that goes past most of the hotels, nearly all of which are well located for the base lifts and slopes. The resort has an excellent centrally located sports complex as well as lots of good restaurants and cafes. Nightlife is rather lively with lots of drinking and dancing possible the Das Stampel Bar is a favorite hangout with locals and visitors alike.

Verdict - Snow sure mountain to suit all with excellent local facilities. **10/10**

COST INDICATOR

Budget   Moderate   Very Expensive   Criminal

Airports & Fly Drive Guide

1st- Innsbruck - 1 hr 15
A12 to junction **123** for the Otzal - B186 = **52 miles**

2nd - Munich (D) **- 3 hrs 15**
A8 **E45/E52 & E45/E60**
A12 & B186 = **140 miles**

3rd - Salzburg - 3 hrs
All roads to **Innsbruck** A12 & the B186 = **162 miles**

i **· Information -** 0043 (0) 5254 5100
www.solden.com

Stubai Glacier

Mapping Page 88 B3

ROUTE PLANNER

CALAIS 0 miles
along the **A16 - A26**
E15 / E17
Toll Road

REIMS 168 miles
2hrs 53 **A4** E17 / 50

METZ 270 miles
4hrs 47 **A4** E25 Dir Strasbourg
Tolls end

A35 north to the D4
⚠ **Enter Germany** 401 miles
B500 to the E35 - 5

KARLSRUHE 424 miles
7hrs 16 **A8** E52
via Pforzheim

STUTGART 459 miles
7hr 50 **A8** E52

ULM 523 miles
8hrs 56 **A7** E532

KEMPTEN 573 miles
9hrs 50 **A7** E532 south via
Nesselwang along the
B309 & B179.
⚠ **Enter Austria** 600 miles
Head south along the
B179 via the **Fernpaß**
to the B189.

TELFS 646 miles
A12, E60

INNSBRUCK xxx miles
A13 dir Brenner. Pick
up the **B183**, L232 via
Neustift

STUBAI GLACIER

KM **Distance 687 miles** (1106 km)
🕐 **Drive time 12 hours 40 mins**
⛽ **Fuel £64**
€ **Tolls £25**

Top Lift
3200m.
Resort Height
1721m.
Vertical Drop
1500m.
Number of Runs
38
Longest Run
9.6km
Slopes
152km of piste
●● Beginner
64% of the runs
◐ Intermediate
29% of the runs
● Advanced
7% of the runs

Cross-Country
5km of tracks
Snowboarding
Half-pipe & Park
Snow Season
All year round
Snowmaking
10% of pistes
Number of lifts
19
Up Lift Capicity
22,000 per hour
Mountain Cafes
3

On the Slopes - The Stubai Glacier sits at the head of the Stubai valley and not only is it the largest mountain in the Innsbruck area, it's also one of the most popular glaciers in Europe where you can ski or snowboard year round. It's not uncommon to see snowboarders and skiers hurtling down the slopes clad in short sleeves during the months of June and July. Summer is when a lot of Japanese and US students visiting Innsbruck take a day out from the museum trail and head up to Stubai for a day's snow fun, and it's also when a number of snowboard companies run summer camps. Winter is when things really happen on Stubai as there is much more terrain to ride where you'll find a mountain with wide-open slopes laid out well above the tree line. The marked runs offer inexcess of 150km of novice to intermediate rated slopes, but with only a few advanced runs. Unlike most Austrian resorts, the only action is on the slopes, as there is no resort at the base area at all, so skiing back down to your hotel is not an option. Access to the base area involves a twenty-minute cable car ride from the closest accommodation, and the same to get back down at the end of the day. As a high altitude mountain, it can be seriously cold here in the winter, so much so that it can be painful. If that wasn't enough, Stubai nearly always guarantees snow, and as a result the masses that head there can make the place very busy, especially at weekends.

Off the Slopes - Local services at Stubai are effectively zero, however there are a number of villages along the valley offering plenty of options for accommodation and places to get a meal. The village of Neustift, 20 minutes away, is the best bet in terms of choice of things to do in the evening and easy access to the mountain during the day. There are a number of hotels, pensions, restaurants, bars and a few shops, but Neustift doesn't have a great deal going on. Innsbruck (an hour away) offers a far greater choice – wherever you stay, having a vehicle is almost a must around here.

Verdict - A year-round destination but local services are spread out. 7/10

COST INDICATOR

Budget   Moderate   Very Expensive   Criminal

ℹ • **Information** - 0043 (0) 5226 2228
www.stubaiergletscherbahn.com

✈ **Airports & Fly Drive Guide**
1st- Innsbruck - **1 hr**
A13 dir Brenner & B183
via Neustift = 27 miles

2nd- Salzburg - **2 hrs 42**
A13, A12 via **Innsbruck**
A13 & B183 = 135 miles

3rd- Munich (D) - **3 hrs**
A8 E45/E52 & E45/E60
A12 & A13 = 150 miles

St Anton

Mapping Page 88 B1

ROUTE PLANNER

CALAIS 0 miles
along the **A16 - A26**
E15 / E17
Toll Road

REIMS 168 miles
2hrs 53 **A4** E17 / 50

METZ 270 miles
4hrs 47 **A4** E25 Dir Strasbourg
Tolls End

A35 north to the D4
⚠ **Enter Germany** 401 miles
B500 to the E35 - 5

KARLSRUHE 424 miles
7hrs 16 **A8** E52
via Pforzheim

STUTGART 459 miles
7hrs 50 **A8** E52

ULM 523 miles
8hrs 56 **A7** E532

MEMMINGEN 553 miles
9hrs 30 **A96** E43/54, south in the
direction of Lindau

⚠ **Enter Austria** 595 miles
Head further south along
the **A14** E60 via
Feldkirch to the **S16**
via **Bings, Stuben** and
St Christoph

ST ANTON
9hr 22

KM **Distance 619 miles** (997km)
🕐 **Drive time 11 hours**
⛽ **Fuel £56**
€ **Tolls £25**

Top Lift
2811m.
Resort Height
1304m.
Vertical Drop
1507m.
Number of Runs
10
Longest Run
8km
Slopes
260km of piste
●● Beginner
22% of the runs
◐ Intermediate
42% of the runs
● Advanced
36% of the runs

Cross-Country
40km of tracks
Snowboarding
Half-pipe & Park
Snow Season
Dec to April
Snowmaking
65% of psites
Number of lifts
83
Up Lift Capicity
115,300 per hour
Mountain Cafes
10

On the Slopes - St Anton is not only one of Austria's finest resorts both on and of the slopes, but it's also one of the country's largest ski areas. Located in the Arlberg region, St Anton has a worldwide reputation for being fantastic, with slopes offering thrill seekers of every ability level a challenge and makes even a two week stay seem too short. The vast expanse of marked and unmarked piste has it all, exhilarating steeps, 180km of amazing off-piste with deep powder fields, tight trees and great cruising trails. This is a snow sure mountain and can get very busy during certain times of the season, leading to some long waits in the lift queues but don't fret: it's not always bad and once you're off the base runs the main slopes never get overly busy. The pistes are kept in tip top condition by an army of overnight workers so every morning you are presented with wonderfully groomed trails. St Anton is known for its advanced level of terrain, but it still has plenty for intermediates and novices to sample, with good nursery slopes located close to the village centre. Snowboarders have an amazing freeriding mountain, with heaps of untracked terrain to explore, although it's best to ride with the assistance of a local guide, who will be able to show you where the best stuff is and keep you safe.

Off the Slopes - If there can be any criticism leveled against St Anton, then it would be the price as most things are expensive – although it's worth remembering that the best never comes cheap. However, the smart Tyrolean village is well-appointed with a host of attractions such as a modern sports complex, an array of shops and loads of restaurants. Lodging options are numerous with self-catering chalets a popular choice. There are plenty of hotels and guest houses close to the slopes and village centre, but nothing in the lower price bracket – standards are universally high, wherever you stay. Night life is very good and caters for most tastes especially party animals that like to watch the sun come up.

Verdict - Excellent mountain that is amongst the best in the world. 10/10

COST INDICATOR

Budget   Moderate   Very Expensive   Criminal

ℹ • **Information** - 0043 (0) 5446 22690
www.stantonamarlberg.com

✈ **Airports & Fly Drive Guide**
1st- Innsbruck - **1 hr 20**
A12 via Landeck along the
B198 = 60 miles

2nd- Zurich (CH) - **2 hrs 30**
A1 E60, A14 - Feldkirch,
S16 via Stuben = 122 miles

3rd- Salzburg - **3 hrs 10**
All roads to Innsbruck A12
& via Landeck = 170 miles

Austria
St Johann in Tirol

Mapping Page 88 A4

Top Lift	1700m.
Resort Height	670m.
Vertical Drop	1030m.
Number of Runs	20
Longest Run	7km
Slopes	60km of piste
●● *Beginner*	
41% of the runs	
● *Intermediate*	
47% of the runs	
● *Advanced*	
12% of the runs	
Cross-Country	75km of tracks
Snowboarding	Half-pipe & Park
Snow Season	Dec to April
Snowmaking	30km of pistes
Number of lifts	17
Up Lift Capacity	20,100 per hour
Mountain Cafes	12

On the Slopes - St Johann in Tyrol is Austrian through and through: read any one of the numerous ski guides and see how this place is often described as 'quaint, charming, traditional, lovely and picturesque'. All those descriptions of the town are true, but what counts is what it has to offer the skier or snowboarder, and frankly St Johann doesn't have a great deal going for it. There are 60km of pistes that, although immaculately looked after, is pretty poor for the region. St Johann is fine for first timers and slow learners but there is very little adventurous terrain, except for one fairly ordinary black run which is not hard to master. St Johann is located close to a lot of low-level resorts, none of which have a great annual snow record, which often leads to very busy slopes and long lift queues – this is largely down to the fact that many tour operators promote St Johann to family groups. This is not all gloom as a family can indeed have a great week here on a mountain that offers a collection of easy red runs with lots of nice easy blues and nursery slopes. Mountain facilities are very good, with an efficient modern lift system and unusually for a place of this size, some fifteen mountain cafes and bars. One area in which St Johann does shine is cross country skiing, which provided there is enough snow, is hard to beat with over 75km of marked tracks and lots more unmarked areas to slide along. Despite the halfpipe and terrain park, St Johann is not by any stretch of the imagination a snowboarder's mountain. It lacks any good natural terrain for freestylers while the pistes are not the greatest for carvers. Still the pipe is well maintained.

Off the Slopes - St Johann is a very pleasant, warm and welcoming resort. The village is traffic-free and you will find just about all you need to have an enjoyable, hassle-free stay. Hotels are plentiful with good rates and restaurants offer traditional Austrian food and although most are good, nothing stands out. The Ambiente bar is highly rated and a nice place for evening entertainment.

ROUTE PLANNER

	CALAIS 0 miles	
	along the **A16 - A26**	
	E15 / E17	
	Toll Road	
2hrs 53	**REIMS** 168 miles	
	A4 E17 / 50	
4hrs 47	**METZ** 270 miles	
	A4 E25 *Dir Strasbourg*	
	Tolls End	
	A35 north to the D4	
	Enter Germany 401 miles	
	B500 to the **E35 - 5**	
7hrs 16	**KARLSRUHE** 424 miles	
	A8 E52	
	via Pforzheim	
7hrs 50	**STUTTGART** 459 miles	
	A8 E52	
9hrs 58	**MUNICH** 589 miles	
	Travel around Munich and follow all directions south for Salzburg along the A8 **E45/E52**. Then pick up the **E45/ E60** for **Innsbruck.**	
	Enter Austria 660 miles	
	Head south along the **A12** in the direction of Innsbruck.	
11hrs 15	**KUFSTEIN** 664 miles	
	B173, B178	
	ST JOHANN IN TIROL	

KM **Distance**	682 miles *(1098km)*
Drive time	11 hours 45 mins
Fuel	£62
Tolls	£25

Airports & Fly Drive Guide

1st - Salzburg - 1 hr 10
Routes B1, B21, E60, B178 = **40 miles**

2nd - Innsbruck - 1 hr 20
A12, E45, E60, B178 via Worgl = **60 miles**

3rd - Munich (D) - 2 hrs
Routes A99, E45, A8, A93 via Kufstein = **100 miles**

Verdict - Traditional resort with excellent facilities, but poor terrain. **6/10**

COST INDICATOR

Budget   Moderate   Very Expensive   Criminal

i - **Information** - 0043 (0) 5352 63335
www.st.johann.tirol.at

Austria
Zell am See

Mapping Page 89 B5

Top Lift	1949m.
Resort Height	758m.
Vertical Drop	1191m.
Number of Runs	60
Longest Run	4km
Slopes	43km of piste
●● *Beginner*	
43% of the runs	
● *Intermediate*	
38% of the runs	
● *Advanced*	
19% of the runs	
Cross-Country	38km of tracks
Snowboarding	Half-pipe & Park
Snow Season	Dec to April
Snowmaking	25% of pistes
Number of lifts	31
Up Lift Capacity	74,000 per hour
Mountain Cafes	25

On the Slopes - Zell am See is an interesting lakeside resort which is a very popular destination for skiers during the winter months and equally so for summer holidaymakers. While not a 'typical' Austrian resort, what you have is a mountain that fans out from the centre of the village and one that will serve intermediate skiers and novice snowboarders very well but might leave experts feeling a little short-changed. Zell's slopes are finally tuned and the piste preparation is always first class but the mountain gets a lot of sun, so its not long before some of the lower areas start to thin out. A third of the runs are covered by snowmaking facilities – a good thing, as this resort doesn't have the greatest annual snow record. With over 130km of marked pistes on offer and only an hour from Salzburg airport, Zell has become a popular resort but a modern lift system helps ensure that queues are not a major problem. The nearby resort of Kaprun is a year-round glacial resort with guaranteed snow, but if you want to ride or ski, expect to wait a while in base area lift queues as it's a very busy place. Zell has long been popular with skiers and recently with snowboarders, but despite the abundance of trees, the management does not allow users to ride or ski off piste through the thick wooded sections dotted around the mountain as it causes damage to the trees and other terrain features. Beginners have lots of nursery areas as well as spots that allow for easy progression making this a good first timers resort, and country skiers certainly won't feel hard done by, with superb tracks both at Zell or at the nearby glacier resort of Kaprun.

Off the Slopes - Zell am See is an old town with lots of character and a car-free centre, but it is also a busy village with plenty of good local amenities and lots of accommodation at all price ranges. There is a large and good choice or restaurants spread around the resort ,mostly with an Austrian theme. Nightlife is rated as good and varied with something for all tastes and all ages.

ROUTE PLANNER

	CALAIS 0 miles	
	along the **A16 - A26**	
	E15 / E17	
	Toll Road	
2hrs 53	**REIMS** 168 miles	
	A4 E17 / 50	
4hrs 47	**METZ** 270 miles	
	A4 E25 *Dir Strasbourg*	
	Tolls End	
	A35 north to the D4	
	Enter Germany 401 miles	
	B500 to the **E35 - 5**	
7hrs 16	**KARLSRUHE** 424 miles	
	A8 E52	
	via Pforzheim	
7hrs 50	**STUTTGART** 459 miles	
	A8 E52	
9hrs 58	**MUNICH** 589 miles	
	Travel around Munich and follow all directions south for Salzburg via the A8 **E45/E52**. Then take the A93 **E45/ E60.**	
1hr 35		
	Enter Austria 664 miles	
	ENDACH 664 miles	
	Pick up the **B173** and the **B178** via **Sperten** to the **B161** via **Kitzbuhel** to the **B168** via **Jesdorf** to the **L215**	
9hr 22	**ZELL AM SEE**	

KM **Distance**	720 miles *(1160km)*
Drive time	12 hours 50 mins
Fuel	£66
Tolls	£25

Airports & Fly Drive Guide

1st - Salzburg - 1 hr 30
A10 E55. B311 = **62 miles**

2nd - Innsbruck - 2 hrs 20
A12, B171, B178, L45, B170, B161, B168 = **92 miles**

3rd - Munich (D) - 3 hrs 10
A8, A93, A12, B171, B178 to the B161 & B168 = **140 miles**

Verdict - Simple sunny slopes ideal for intermediates, but busy village. **8/10**

COST INDICATOR

Budget   Moderate   Very Expensive   Criminal

i - **Information** - 0043 (0) 6542 770
www.zellamsee.com

Bulgaria

Resorts Featured
46 Borovets
47 Pamporovo
47 Vitosha
*See page 28 for the
index of all resorts.*

See page 28 for the index of all resorts.

46

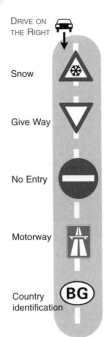

Drive on
the Right

Snow

Give Way

No Entry

Motorway

Country
identification   **BG**

Motorway speed	**120kph**
Rural speed	**90kph**
Urban speed	**50kph**
Alcohol limit	**50mgs**
Front seatbelts	✔
Rear seatbelts	✔
Kids in front seat	**10 years**
Legal age to drive	**18**
Warming triangle	Required
First aid kit	Required
Fire extinguisher	Required
Snowchains	Advisable

FACT FILE

Country - Narodna Republika Balgarija
Location - Eastern Europe
Geography
Bulgaria is located in the Balkans, and shares its boarders with, Greece, Macedonia, Romania, Serbia.
Highest Mountain - Mussala 2925m
Coast line & Seas - Black Sea
Land Area - 110,994 sq km (42,855 sq miles)
Capital - Sofia
Populartion - 7,949,000
Language - Bulgarian
Religion - 90% Christian
Currecny - Leva
Time - GMT + 2 hours, (GMT + 3 hours between March & October)
Electricity Supply - 220volts
Communications - International Country code 00359
Fire 160
Police 166
Ambulance 150
National Tourism - 359 (2) 987 9778
www.bulgariatravel.org
Rail Information - www.bulgariatravel.org
Bus Information - www.bulgariatravel.org
Air Information - www.bulgariatravel.org
Gateway International Airports
Sofia
Bourgas
Plovdiv
Varna
Weather Information - www.bulgariatravel.org
Avalanche Information - www.bulgariatravel.org
Motoring Organisations
Passports
All visitors require a valid passort.
Visas
All visitors require a visa apart from EU Nationals, and people from Cyprus, Iceland and Norway.
Duty Free
200 cigarettes or 50 cigars or 250g of tobacco. 1 Ltr of sprits and 21 lts of wine.
50g of perfume.

Motoring Organisations
Union des Automobilistes Bulgares (UAB)
3 Place Pozitano, BP 257
1090 Sofia
tel 00387 (2) 98 242

AIT   FIA

Borovets

Top Lift	2543m.
Resort Height	1317m.
Vertical Drop	193m.
Number of Runs	20
Longest Run	5km
Slopes	40km of piste
● Beginner	30% of the runs
● Intermediate	60% of the runs
● Advanced	10% of the runs
Cross-Country	16km of tracks
Snowboarding	None
Snow Season	Dec to April
Snowmaking	None
Number of lifts	15
Up Lift Capicity	2,000 per hour
Mountain Cafes	8

On the Slopes - Borovets is located in the Rila Mountains and is one of the highest ski-able areas in Eastern Europe. Snow cover in general is not assured – the resort has no snowmaking facilities and piste grooming is not a priority, so the runs can often be bare in mid season. Locals say that the season comes later than other areas and those in the know say April has the best snow. Still, when you can ski as cheaply as you can in Borovets then its well worth the risk and although this resort may not be up to the standards of some of the big western European resorts, it is still a place worth at least a week's visit. The 40km of piste is split across three areas, all of which offer open-pistes and lines through tight trees. The slopes are a little strange in their layout, with two of the areas only just connected on the slopes while the third is totally separate. All of the areas offer much the same terrain – a series of slopes that are, at best, suited to intermediates. There are a number of nursery slopes, but Borovets isn't the best beginner's resort, nor is it a hot place for advanced skiers. However, for freeriding snowboarders there are some good backcountry spots to ride, but be very careful as you won't want to get lost – ski patrol is not this resort's best feature. The quality of the lifts is another area that leaves a lot to be desired and queues can be a nightmare, especially for the six person gondola, that takes 25 minutes from the base to the top.

Off the Slopes - Borovets is a small place and the main hotels are the Rila, Samokov and the Olympic. Everything is cheap and caters well for budget-minded individuals and is especially suited for groups who enjoy partying as much as skiing. Evenings can be very lively, with cheap beer available everywhere – although few places accept credit cards or travellers cheques, so having cash is a must. Katy's is recommended for food, while the Black Tiger and Buzz bars are good places to damage your liver in.

Verdict - Rather dull slopes, but a fun holiday and very well priced.   **4/10**

COST INDICATOR

Budget   Moderate   Very Expensive   Criminal

i - Information - 00359 3021 336
www.bulgariatravel.org

ROUTE PLANNER

✈	**SOFIA**	0 miles
	south down the E80 I-12 **B82**	
1hr 35	**PANCHAREVO** **B82**	
1hr 35	**ZLOKUCHENE** **B82**	
1hr 35	**SAMOKOV** **B82**	
9hr 22	**BOROVETS** 50 miles	

KM Distance **50** miles *(80 km)*
⏱ Drive time **1 hour 5 mins**
⛽ Fuel **£6**
€ Tolls

✈	**Airports & Fly Drive Guide**
1st- Sofia - **1 hr 5**
E80 I-12 and the **B82 = 50** miles

Bulgaria
Pamporovo

Mapping Page 187 A5

ROUTE PLANNER

SOFIA 0 miles
south down the E80 A1

PLOVDIV 50 miles
55 mins B86

ASENOVGRAD 62 miles
75 mins B86

VASIL KOLAROV 99 miles
1hr 35 B86

PAMPOROVO

Distance 108 miles *(174km)*
Drive time 1 hour 55 mins
Fuel £10
Tolls

Top Lift	
1926m.	
Resort Height	
1600m.	
Vertical Drop	
480m.	
Number of Runs	
20	
Longest Run	
2.5km	
Slopes	
25km of piste	
● Beginner	
60% of the runs	
● Intermediate	
25% of the runs	
● Advanced	
15% of the runs	
Cross-Country	
40km of tracks	
Snowboarding	
Half-pipe	
Snow Season	
Dec to April	
Snowmaking	
None	
Number of lifts	
12	
Up Lift Capicity	
15,000 per hour	
Mountain Cafes	
10	

On the Slopes - Situated in the Snezhanka mountain range and around an hour away from Bulgaria's second city Plovdiv, Pamporovo is a popular destination for weekend city dwellers and foreign visitors alike. A common feature of many Eastern European resorts is their simplicity and that certainly rings true of Pamporovo which is by no means a big resort – what you have is a limited ski area offering short, low-gradient runs which are perfect for beginners on skis or a snowboard. Skiers who like to ski fast and steep should probably head elsewhere and even intermediates will soon tire of this place as there is nothing to keep the attention of thrill seekers for too long. The runs start from the summit and descend back down through trees to a base area that lies below the main village area, making things a little inconvenient. As well as being a good beginner's mountain this is also good place for cross-country skiers, with 40kms of tracks to glide around (snow permitting, of course). Good snowfall is not regular, but Pamporovo is at it's best when it does dump – unfortunately you won't find an abundance of off-piste terrain to enjoy. There are some decent spots but not a great deal, unless you are a freeride skier or snowboarder with an eye for such things and one who likes to hit off small stashes of snow along the piste lines and the suchlike. Riders who crave natural wind lips and big cliff jumps will be disappointed, however the guys from the Smolyan snowboard club regularly build and maintain a decent halfpipe.

Off the Slopes - Pamporovo is a purpose-built but resort with a good level of facilities located close to the slopes. Around the resort there are a number of well-appointed hotels offering cheap nightly room rates and good weekly packages. Hotels Perelik and Mourgavets are both popular places to stay with have pools, bars, restaurants and even a bowling alley. Bulgaria is not noted for it's cuisine, and eating out is a meat and potatoes affair. The nightlife in Bulgaria is stupidly cheap, very basic and loud but good fun.

Verdict - Okay for beginners and good value for money. **4**/10

COST INDICATOR

Budget   Moderate   Very Expensive   Criminal

i - **Information** - 00359 3021 336
www.bulgariatravel.org

Airports & Fly Drive Guide

1st- Plovdiv - **55 minutes**
B86 = 50 miles

2nd - Sofia - **1 hr 55**
E80 A1 and B86 = 108 miles

Bulgaria
Vitosha

Mapping Page 181 D6

ROUTE PLANNER

SOFIA 0 miles
south

VITOSHA

Distance 20 miles *(32 km)*
Drive time 15 mins
Fuel £2
Tolls

Top Lift	
2115m.	
Resort Height	
1515m.	
Vertical Drop	
600m.	
Number of Runs	
20	
Longest Run	
5km	
Slopes	
22km of piste	
● Beginner	
75% of the runs	
● Intermediate	
20% of the runs	
● Advanced	
5% of the runs	
Cross-Country	
16km of tracks	
Snowboarding	
None	
Snow Season	
Dec to April	
Snowmaking	
None	
Number of lifts	
12	
Up Lift Capicity	
8,600 per hour	
Mountain Cafes	
3	

On the Slopes - Vitosha gets it's name from the Vitosha National Park, where it is located and lies just half an hour from Sofia, the capital of Bulgaria – indeed, you can take a gondola from the outskirts of Sofia to Aleko, which sits at 1800m. Vitosha is a resort that punches above its weight and once considered itself good enough to host the winter Olympics – unfortunately, it wasn't. It's proximity to Sofia means that it's a popular hangout, with locals flocking here en-masse, particularly at weekends. As a result, the lift queues can be horrendous, as the twelve ancient lifts can only manage a measly 800 people an hour. Although a small resort with a worse than average snow record, Vitosha is still an interesting place to visit with noteworthy features, especially the views into the city. There are 22km of marked trails, all of which have 'easy' written all over them which makes the resort a first timer's paradise – intermediate and advanced users will soon run out of challenges, however. That said, there is a long 5km off-piste run and some nice tree runs to be found. As there are no UK tour operators promoting the resort, you can really get a feel for what its like to share a mountain with it's home grown natives. In fact the way they tackle lifts offers plenty of amusement. There are some cross-country tracks, but not many and you have to search for them (a sign would have helped here). Perhaps not surprisingly, Vitosha is not a hotspot for snowboarders, but freeriders with a sense of adventure will be pleasantly surprised especially if they head to the highest point of the Cherni Vrah peak, where they will find a mixture of uneven red and black runs. Snowboarders with freestyle boards will also find some natural hits and the locals are always building kickers, but there is no permanent terrain parks or halfpipes.

Off the Slopes - The resort has a number of convenient hotels with cheap rates and there are a few nightspots, but in truth this sleepy place is a little dull. For greater selection of local services visit Sofia, 23 km away.

Verdict - A good laugh, with easy slopes, but not much else. **3**/10

COST INDICATOR

Budget   Moderate   Very Expensive   Criminal

i - **Information** -00359 (2) 43331
www.bulgariatravel.org

Airports & Fly Drive Guide

1st- Sofia - **15 minutes**
A1 = 20 miles

Finland

Resorts Featured
48 Himos
49 Ruka
49 Tahko
*See page 28 for the
index of all resorts.*

48

DRIVE ON
THE RIGHT

Detour

Slippery
when wet

Falling
Rocks

No Parking
8am - 5pm **8-17**
Mon to Fri

Country
identification **FIN**

Hospital **H**

Motorway speed	**120kph**	
Rural speed	**100kph**	
Urban speed	**50kph**	
Alcohol limit	**50mgs**	
Front seatbelts	✔	
Rear seatbelts	✔	
Kids in front seat	-	
Legal age to drive	**18**	
Warming triangle	Required	
First aid kit	Advisable	
Fire extinguisher	Advisable	
Snowchains	Advisable	

FACT FILE

Country - Suomen Tasavalta
Location - Northern Europe
Geography
Finland is located in the far north of Europe in a region that is often called Scandinavia and shares its boarders with Estonia, Norway, Russia and Sweden.
Highest Mountain Haltiatunturi 1328m
Coast line & Seas Baltic Sea
Land Area - 338,145 sq km (130,559 sq miles)
Capital - Helsinki
Populartion - 5,181,115
Language - Finnish & Swedish
Religion - 85% Lutheran
Currecny - Euro
Time - GMT + 2 hours, (GMT + 3 hours between March & October)
Electricity Supply - 220volts
Communications - International Country code 00358
Fire 112
Police 112
Ambulance 112
National Tourism - 00358 (0) 417 6901
www.finland-tourism.com
Rail Information - www.vr.fi
Bus Information - www.finland-tourism.com
Air Information - www.finland-tourism.com
Gateway International Airports
Helsinki
Oulu
Weather Information - www.fmi.fi
Avalanche Information - www.fmi.fi
Passprts & Visa Requirments

	Passports	Visa
Australian	Yes	No
British	Yes	No
Canadian	Yes	No
USA	Yes	No
EU		No

Duty Free - None EU travellers
200 cigarettes or 100 cigarillos or 50 cigars or 25g of tobacco. 1ltr of spirits over 22% or 21% of fortified wine or spirits up to 22% or 21% of sparkling wine or liqueur and 21 % of still wine. 50g of perfume and €185 worth of goods.
EU travellers - No tarrifs.

Motoring Organisations
Autoliitto / Automobile and
Touring Club of Finland
Hameentie 105 - PO Box 35, 00551 HELSINKI.
tel +358 (0) 9 725 84 400
fax +358 (0) 9 725 84 460
http:// www.autoliitto.fi
e-mail: autoliitto@autoliitto.fi

Finland

Himos

Top Lift	220m.
Resort Height	80m.
Vertical Drop	140m.
Number of Runs	15
Longest Run	1km
Slopes	110km of piste
● *Beginner*	20% of the runs
● *Intermediate*	55% of the runs
● **Advanced**	25% of the runs
Cross-Country	15km of tracks
Snowboarding	Half-pipe & Park
Snow Season	Nov to May
Snowmaking	100% of pistes
Number of lifts	10
Up Lift Capicity	11,250 per hour
Mountain Cafes	2

On the Slopes - Three hours drive from the capital Helsinki, in the southern region of the country lies the unassuming and diverse outdoor adventure resort of Himos. . The resort opened in 1984 and is popular both in the winter for skiing and snowboarding and during the summer for mountain biking and outdoor pursuits. 'Quiet' is a fair way to describe Himos as the mountain is neither large nor is the village busy. Himos is a small hill rising from the shores of the frozen lake at its feet and is a world away from the mega resorts of France or Austria. The mountain is split into two slope areas with both offering much the same in terms of terrain and the degree of adventure. In general this is a mountain with a mixture of gentle, undulating slopes best suited to intermediate skiers with short skis and beginners on anything. The lack of natural terrain has led to Himos investing heavily in it's terrain parks and as a result it has become a popular playground for younger snowboaders and skiers with large numbers of freestylers enjoying the excellent halfpipe and park, which is regularly maintained and improved every season. Lots of major competitions are held here attracting top names in snowboarding, so it must have something to offer. Off-piste skiers and snowboarders are not going to find this place up to much as there's nothing really to excite them, nor are piste lovers who like long testing trails. The longest runs are to be found on the north slopes, where there is a black and a couple of red runs to try out. The slopes on the western side offer a few more challenges for advanced skiers, but your stamina is unlikely to be tested as nothing is more than a few turns long.

Off the Slopes - Accommodation is mainly offered in chalet form and is rather spread-out but within easy reach of the lifts. There are a number of hotels and while nothing is cheap, local services are very good. Restaurants are basic and nightlife is somewhat tame with only a few bars to visit, all of which have criminal prizes for booze.

Verdict - Those looking for a relaxed, easy holiday will find Himos perfect. **4/10**

COST INDICATOR

Budget	Moderate	Very Expensive	Criminal

i - **Information -** 00358 (42) 786 105
www.himos.fi

Mapping Page 143 B7

ROUTE PLANNER

HELSINKI 0 miles
north up the **E12, A3**

HAMEENLINNA 50 miles
52 mins **E12, A3**

TAMPERE 105 miles
2hrs 15 **E63, A9**

ORLIVESI 130 miles
2hrs 55 **A58 & B56**

HIMOS

KM	**Distance**	**168 miles** *(270 km)*
⏱	**Drive time**	**4 hours 25 mins**
⛽	**Fuel**	**£20**
€	**Tolls**	

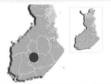

Airports & Fly Drive Guide

1st- Helsinki - **4 hr 20**
E12 and the **E63** via
Tampere = **168 miles**

Finland
Ruka

Mapping Page 137 B6

Top Lift 1300m.	
Resort Height 150m.	
Vertical Drop 200m.	
Number of Runs 28	
Longest Run 1.6km	
Slopes 20km of piste	
● *Beginner* 61% of the runs	
● *Intermediate* 32% of the runs	
● *Advanced* 7% of the runs	
Cross-Country 180km of tracks	
Snowboarding Half-pipe & Park	
Snow Season Oct to May	
Snowmaking 50 cannons	
Number of lifts 8	
Up Lift Capacity 21,000 per hour	
Mountain Cafes 5	

On the Slopes - The journey to Ruka involves no great uphill climbs or winding mountain passes, you simply arrive to see the hill popping out of the landscape like a volcano. Ruka is Finland's largest resort and back in 1996 it hosted the International Snowboard Federation's Junior World Championships, indicating that the place has something to offer and indeed it does – just don't get too excited as this is a small place and a week's skiing or snowboarding will be enough to see everything twice over. The main slopes offer a choice of evenly-matched intermediate and beginner's runs and it soon becomes clear why this is a perfect family resort. The slopes are well laid out, the lifts are easy to use and the local ski and snowboard school is simply excellent.

Like a lot of small resorts, it won't take an average skier more than a couple of days to conquer, and the runs can all be accessed via any one of the eight lifts that connect with one of four base car parks. Once up, the runs span out across three faces, one of which will see you heading down in the direction of Lake Talvijarvi. Trees cover much of the mountain, so most of the trails are cut through the forest giving you the feeling you are on a different run every time. Cross country skiers will love Ruka – as it has over 180km of tracks to explore which will take you through some stunning countryside with lots of tree-lined routes.

Off the Slopes - Ruka is a year-round tourist destination, so what you get is an expensive resort but one with excellent facilities. Most people stay in the well-equipped self catering cottages and while they are not all centrally located, there is a local shuttle bus operating through out the area. Eating out is not one of this place's strong points with little or nothing to choose from. What's more, this place is very costly, even the local supermarket will sting. The Ampan bakes a good pizza, while Ali-Baba does great grills to order. The only real night action takes place in the Restaurant Piste, which is a club/bar that is filled with youngsters.

ROUTE PLANNER

✈ **HELSINKI** 0 miles
north up the E75, 4

→ **LAHIT** 1hr 10
E75, 4

→ **HEINOLA** 2hrs 25
E75, 5

→ **MIKKELI** 3hrs 35
E63, 5

→ **KUOPIO** 5hrs 55
E63, 5, 5

→ **SIILINJARVI** 8hrs 35
E63, 5

KUUSAMO
E63, 5

→ **RUKA**

KM **Distance** 620 miles *(998 km)*
🕐 **Drive time** 11 hours 22 mins
⛽ **Fuel** £58
€ **Tolls**

Verdict - Interesting small mountain that will appeal to novices mostly. **4/10**

COST INDICATOR

Budget   Moderate   Very Expensive   Criminal

i - **Information** - 00358 (0) 888 600 200
www.ruka.fi

Finland
Tahko

Mapping Page 141 D5

Top Lift 220m.	
Resort Height 80.	
Vertical Drop 140m.	
Number of Runs 17	
Longest Run 1km	
Slopes 40 acres of piste	
● *Beginner* 50% of the runs	
● *Intermediate* 50% of the runs	
● *Advanced* 0% of the runs	
Cross-Country 10km of tracks	
Snowboarding Half-pipe & Park	
Snow Season Nov to May	
Snowmaking 100% of pistes	
Number of lifts 8	
Up Lift Capacity -	
Mountain Cafes 2	

On the Slopes - For some reason, many Finns regard Tahko as Finland's premier resort, and while it may be a cool hangout which attracts lots of snowboarders, it can hardly be regarded as a great skier's mountain. Located ten hours north of Helsinki by car, Tahko is not widely known outside the country and it's easy to see why as there is not much there to talk about. The so-called mountain is nothing more than a hill in drag, with a high point of just over 220 metres and only around 40 acres of pistes. Little on the hill will excite you and nothing will take long to check out. The season in Tahko usually starts in November and carries on until the following May when locals are still having fun on the slush often wearing nothing more than a T-shirt and jeans. The pistes are well looked after, with 100% snowmaking available when the real stuff is in short supply. All the runs are cut through trees along wide and narrow pistes that connect up nicely by the eight draglifts, which some beginners may find a bit tricky to use. If you prefer steeps, piste and deep powder gullies then this is not the place for you, as off-piste is not really an option. That said, there are areas with pockets of snow where you can experience some interesting skiing outside the marked trails. The slopes are evenly rated 50% beginner and 50% intermediate with simply nothing for those who consider themselves at an advanced level. Freestyle skiers and snowboarders have a well-shaped halfpipe located at the lower section alongside the tree line but many locals like to build their own hits away from the pistes. For cross-country skiers, there's not that much to this place.

Off the Slopes - Tahko may be a small place, but it does have a good selection of accommodation options close to the slopes. You can opt for a hotel, chalets or a bungalow, all of which are basic but cater nicely for a few nights stay. Prices are also not as bad as in many other Finnish tourists spots. As for facilities, bring all you need, there's not much at all here, including nightlife, which is very expensive.

ROUTE PLANNER

✈ **HELSINKI** 0 miles
north up the E75, 4

→ **LAHIT**
E75, 4

→ **HEINOLA**
E75, 5

→ **MIKKELI**
E63, 5

→ **KUOPIO**
E63, 5, 5

→ **SIILINJARVI**
E63, 5

NILSIA
75, 577

→ **TAHKO**

KM **Distance** 230 miles *(370km)*
🕐 **Drive time** 4 hours 20 mins
⛽ **Fuel** £34
€ **Tolls**

Verdict - Very limited and only good for slow learning skiers. **3/10**

COST INDICATOR

Budget   Moderate   Very Expensive   Criminal

i - **Information** -00358 (0) 71 464 8200

Airports & Fly Drive Guide
1st- Helsinki - 11 hr 22
→ E75, 4, E75, 5, E63, 5 =
620 miles

🕐 DRIVE TIME - nixon. www.nixonnow.com

France

See page 28 for the index of all resorts.

DRIVE ON THE RIGHT

Diversion

Give Way

50

Restriction Continues

Traffic on roundabout has priority

Keep over to the right

Country identification

End of priority

Truck no passing zone

Motorway speed	130kph
Rural speed	90kph
Urban speed	50kph
Alcohol limit	50mgs
Front seatbelts	✔
Rear seatbelts	✔
Kids in front seat	12
Legal age to drive	17
Warning triangle	Advisable
First aid kit	Advisable
Fire extinguisher	Advisable
Snowchains	Advisable

Photo - Christophe Guibbaud - Tourist Office Val d'IsereAlpe

Road Signs and Warnings

Allumez vos lanternes - *Turn on your lights*
Attention au feu - *Beware of traffic signal*
Attention travaux - *Beware roadworks*
Autre directions - *Other directions*
Barrière de dégel - *Trucks not allowed*
Chaussée déformée - *Bumpy road ahead*
Cédez le passage - *Give way (Give priority)*
Centre ville - *Town center*
Chambres d'Hôtes - *Bed and Breakfast*
Col - *Mountain pass*
Fermé - *Closed*
Gendarmerie - *Police station*
Gratuit - *Free of charge*
Gravillons - *Loose chippings*
Haute tension - *Electric line*

Interdit aux Piétons - *No pedestrians*
Nids de poules - *Potholes*
Ouvert - *Open*
Prochain échangeur - *No toll at next exit*
Rappel - *Remember*
Route barrée - *Road closed*
Sens unique - *One-way*
Serrez à droite - *Keep to the right*
Sortie - *Exit*
Suivre - *Follow*
Sur - *On*
Toutes directions - *All directions*
Vitesse adaptée sécurité - *Adapt your speed for safety*
Voie unique - *One-lane road*
Voitures - *Cars*

FACT FILE

Country - Republique Francaise
Location - Western Europe
Geography
France boarders 7 countries:
Andorra, Belgium, Germany, Italy,
Luxembourg, Switzerland, Spain.
Highest Mountain
Mont Blanc - 4807m
Coast line & Seas
North Sea, Atlantic Ocean and
the Mediterranean
Land Area
543,965 sq km (210,025 sq miles)
Capital - Paris
Popular tion - 58,890,000
Language - French
Religion - 79% Roman Catholic
Currecny - Euros
Time
GMT + 1 hour, (GMT + 2 hours
between March & October)
Electricity Supply - 220volts
Communications
International Country code 0033
Fire 18
Police 17
Ambulance 15
National Tourism
0043 (0)1 58 72 000
www.franceguide.com
Rail Information
www.sncf.com
Bus Information
www.franceguide.com
Air Information
www.franceguide.com
Gateway International Airports
Paris
Lyon
Toulouse
Geneva (CH)
Weather Information
www.metro.fr
Avalanche Information
Alpes Haute
0033 (0) 836 68 10 20 05
Alpes Maritimes
0033 (0) 836 68 10 20 06
Hautes -Alpes
0033 (0) 836 68 10 20 05
Haute Savoie
0033 (0) 836 68 10 20 74
Hautes Pyrenees
0033 (0) 836 68 10 20 65

Passprts & Visa Requirments

	Passports	Visa
Australian	Yes	No
British	Yes	No
Canadian	Yes	No
USA	Yes	No
EU		No

Duty Free - None EU travellers
200 cigarettes or 100 cigarillos or
50 cigars or 25g of tobacco. 1ltr of
spirits over 22% or 21% of fortified
wine or spirits up to 22% or 21% of
sparkling wine or liqueur and 21 %
of still wine. 50g of perfume and
€183 worth of goods.
EU travellers - No tarrifs

Motoring Organisations
Automobile Club de France
6-8 Place de la concorde,
75008 Paris.
tel +33 (0) 1 43 12 43 12.

France
Alpes-d'Huez

Mapping Page 47 F6

ROUTE PLANNER

CALAIS 0 miles	*along the* **A16 - A26** **E15 / E17** *Toll Road*
REIMS 168 miles 2hrs 55	**A26 A4 E17 / 50**
CHALONS en CHAMPAGNE 3hrs 15	**A26 E17**
TROYES 236 miles 4hrs	**A5 E17 / 54**
MARAC 295 miles 5hrs	**A31 E17 / 21**
DIJON 351 miles 6hrs 10	**A31 E17 & E15 A6**
MACON 395 miles 7hrs	**A6 E15**
LYON 471 miles 8hrs 50	**A43 E70 A48 E711**
GRENOBLE 537 miles 9hrs 26 Tolls End	Head south to **Le Pont de-claix** and pick up the **N91** in the direction of **Briancon**. Finally take the **D211** on the left up to the resort.

ALP d'HUEZ

KM **Distance**	**576 miles** *(927km)*
Drive time	**10 hours 25 mins**
Fuel	**£52**
€ **Tolls**	**£35**

Top Lift	
Top Lift 3330m.	

Top Lift
3330m.
Resort Height
1450m.
Vertical Drop
1880m.
Number of Runs
108
Longest Run
16km
Slopes
225km of piste
● ● *Beginner*
62% of the runs
● *Intermediate*
26% of the runs
● *Advanced*
13% of the runs

Cross-Country
50km of tracks
Snowboarding
Half-pipe & Park
Snow Season
Dec to April
Snowmaking
53km of pistes
Number of lifts
86
Up Lift Capicity
90,000 per hour
Mountain Cafes
16

On the Slopes - Alpe d'Huez is a high altitude resort with vast amounts of well-prepared sunny slopes and is quite possibly France's number one resort for beginners. A week's stay simply won't be enough, even for competent skiers and snowboarders as the terrain is both amazing and varied, with something for everyone. Alpe d-Huez receives good snow cover every year, usually from late November until mid April, and good powder days are a boast the resort lives up to, with excellent off-piste areas to explore. Although the terrain favours novices, intermediates and experts are not short-changed, which makes the resort ideal for mixed ability groups - inevitably, this leads to large numbers of package tour holidaymakers and results in many of the main runs resembling the M25 during rush hour. The lift system however is both excellent and modern, with an uplift of 90,000 people per hour, so long queues are rare. It's worth noting that much of this capacity is in the form of draglifts, so if you are a draglift virgin, expect a short, sharp, learning curve. Snowboarders who like to freeride will love this mountain and the backcountry terrain in areas such as Gorges de Sarenne and Glacier de Sarenne – seek advice from a local guide before going off-piste, no matter how good you are. There is a wealth of perfectly groomed pistes throughout the area and novices are bombarded with easy green runs in the lower area, the only bug being that these areas are usually very busy. Cross-country skiers should also warm to Alpe d'Huez with around 50km of high-level tracks, which are skied using a separate pass.

Off the Slopes - As a purpose built resort, Alpe d-Huez is hardly the prettiest of destinations yet in true French style it provides great all-round and affordable local services which are close to the slopes. Eating out is economical, with cheap pizza restaurants in abundance. Nightlife ranges from a cinema that shows English language films to loud partying in one of the multitude of bars and nightclubs.

Verdict - **Fantastic resort for all abilities. Well appointed, if tacky, town.** **8/10**

COST INDICATOR

Budget   Moderate   Very Expensive   Criminal

i **- Information** - 0033 (0) 476 114 444
www.alpedhuez.com

Airports & Fly Drive Guide

1st- Grenoble - 1 hr 40
Le Pont de-Claix - N91
D211 = 66 miles

2nd- Lyon - 2 hrs 5
Grenoble, N91 & D211 = 97 miles

3rd- Geneva (CH) - 2 hrs 50
A41 E712 to Grenoble, N91 & D211 = 132 miles

France
Avoriaz

Mapping Page 47 C7

ROUTE PLANNER

CALAIS 0 miles	*along the* **A16 - A26** **E15 / E17** *Toll Road*
REIMS 168 miles 2hrs 55	**A26 A4 E17 / 50**
CHALONS en CHAMPAGNE 3hrs 15	**A26 E17**
TROYES 236 miles 4hrs	**A5 E17 / 54**
MARAC 295 miles 5hrs	**A31 E17 / 21**
DIJON 351 miles 6hrs 10	**A31 E17 & E15 A6**
MACON 395 miles 7hrs	**A6 E15**
BOURG-en-BRESSE 426 miles 7hrs 15	**A40 E62**
GENEVA 491 miles 8hrs 20	**A40 E25**
CLUSES 530 miles 9hrs Tolls End	**D902** turning off to the right via **Montriond** to the resort.

AVORIAZ

KM **Distance**	**556 miles** *(895 km)*
Drive time	**10 hours 05 mins**
Fuel	**£52**
€ **Tolls**	**£28**

Top Lift
2277m.
Resort Height
1100m.
Vertical Drop
1470m.
Number of Runs
42
Longest Run
5km
Slopes
150km of piste
● ● *Beginner*
51% of the runs
● *Intermediate*
39% of the runs
● *Advanced*
10% of the runs

Cross-Country
45km of tracks
Snowboarding
Half-pipe & Park
Snow Season
Dec to April
Snowmaking
250 acres
Number of lifts
38
Up Lift Capicity
241,900 per hour
Mountain Cafes
60

On the Slopes - Avoriaz is a purpose built resort that sits on the edge of a cliff that towers some 2000ft above the ancient market town of Morzine. While it's easily accessible by road, the resort is car-free so many users prefer to park in Morzine and take the cable car to Avoriaz itself. The resort is the number one destination in the region known as the Portes du Soleil that straddles the French/Swiss border, and is the largest internationally linked ski area in the world. Avoriaz was one of the first European ski areas to offer a terrain park and as a result is very popular with snowboarders and freestyle skiers, with a freestyle only area that offers halfpipes and terrain parks - but long before snowboarders were shredding these slopes, skiers were doing their thing and this eclectic mix has helped make Avoriaz one of the major French resorts. The 150km of slopes greatly favour novices and while only 10% of the mountain is rated black, there is plenty of challenging terrain for those with an adventurous mind and who like steeps. White knuckle runs such as those down the Hauts Forts are particularly fun, where you get the chance to tackle different types of terrain from trees to cliffs and powder bowls. When the weather comes in, head for the tree runs that meander down to Les Lindarets for increased visibility – be careful about cutting off piste here, however, as there are a number of cliffs from small to absolutely huge – caution is the key word. The terrain park is no longer snowboarders only.

Off the Slopes - Purpose built resorts are often eyesore, but the architects of Avoriaz have at least attempted to make the concrete resort blend in with it's surroundings and used thousands of tons of wood in it's construction – somewhat succesfully. The resort provides excellent access from all accommodation to the slopes, with skiing to your door the norm. There are heaps of local attractions with a sporting complex and cinema. There are plenty of bars and inexpensive places to eat which makes the place pretty lively and often rowdy.

Verdict - **Great skiing and freeride boarding as well as intense partying.** **8/10**

COST INDICATOR

Budget   Moderate   Very Expensive   Criminal

i **- Information** - 0033 (0) 450 740 211
www.avoriaz.com

Airports & Fly Drive Guide

1st- Geneva (CH) - 1 hr 45
Cluses - A40 E25 & D907
56 = miles

2nd- Grenoble - 3 hr 10
A41 E712 upto the A40
E25, N91 & D211 = 140 miles

3rd- Lyon - 2 hrs 58
E611 A42 - Geneva A40
E25 & D907 = 140 miles

DRIVE TIME - **nixon.** www.nixonnow.com

France
Chamonix

Mapping Page 47 D7

ROUTE PLANNER

✈ **CALAIS**	0 miles	along the **A16 - A26** **E15 / E17** *Toll Road*
➡ **REIMS**	166 miles	2hrs 55 **A26 A4 E17 / 50**
➡ **CHALONS en CHAMPAGNE**		3hrs 15 **A26 E17**
➡ **TROYES**	236 miles	4hrs **A5 E17 / 54**
➡ **MARAC**	295 miles	5hrs **A31 E17 / 21**
➡ **DIJON**	351 miles	6hrs 10 **A31 E17 & E15 A6**
➡ **MACON**	395 miles	7hrs **A6 E15**
➡ **BOURG-en-BRESSE**	426 miles	7hrs 15 **A40 E62**
➡ **GENEVA**	491 miles	8hrs 20 **A40 E25**
➡ **CLUSES**	530 miles	9hrs **A40 E25** to the **N205 & N506** via Les Houches *Tolls End* the resort.
➡ **CHAMONIX**	681 miles	7hr 58

KM **Distance**	**556 miles** *(895km)*
⏱ **Drive time**	**9 hours 30 mins**
⛽ **Fuel**	**£50**
€ **Tolls**	**£35**

Top Lift
952m.
Resort Height
1400m.
Vertical Drop
1200m.
Number of Runs
76
Longest Run
3km
Slopes
150km of piste
⦿ *Beginner*
51% of the runs
⦿ *Intermediate*
37% of the runs
● *Advanced*
12% of the runs

Cross-Country
20km of tracks
Snowboarding
Half-pipe & Park
Snow Season
Dec to April
Snowmaking
90km of piste
Number of lifts
60
Up Lift Capicity
56,700 per hour
Mountain Cafes
14

On the Slopes - Chamonix is regarded by many as the European capital for extreme mountains, with stunning views across high peaks and down wide glaciers. The Chamonix valley is not the biggest region in France, nor come to that is it the most conveniently laid-out, but one thing is for certain – Chamonix is a jaw-dropping, heart-pumping place that will make even the most hardcore thrill seeker wet their pants with excitement. There are seven, largely un-connected, main slope areas spread along a twelve-mile valley floor and unless you have your own car, they can only be reached by using the various bus services. You should be aware that Chamonix is not a novice's place and although there are beginner's slopes, such as those at the Les Planards and Le Savoy. Chamonix is a destination noted for serious off-piste and extreme terrain. If there's a group of you visiting, be prepared to split up on a daily basis, as the novice's pistes are in one area while the intermediate and advanced slopes are in an entirely different one. However, the whole area does offer something for everyone and it's all covered by the one Mont Blanc lift pass. Despite being well spread-out, the slopes can still get very busy and lift queues can be long. For those in the know, Argentiere is the access point to some truly awesome off-piste runs, but be warned, this can be a very dangerous mountain and the only sensible way to explore any of the slopes is with a local guide.

Off the Slopes - Unlike many in France, Chamonix is not a purpose-built resort; instead, it's an old town oozing with alpine charm and atmosphere. Your choice of accommodation is very extensive, with everything from inexpensive bunkhouses in Argentiere, to centrally located five-star hotels, but nothing is cheap – not even the hostels. Restaurants are measured in the near hundreds. Casa Valerio does a mean pizza while the Jekyll serves good bar food. At night the whole place goes off, with dozens of bars and night spots. La Cantina and Wild Wallaby are cool young hangouts.

Verdict - Fantastic destination for those looking for a major thrill. **9/10**

COST INDICATOR

Budget   Moderate   Very Expensive   Criminal

✈ Airports & Fly Drive Guide
1st- Geneva (CH) - 1 hr 10
➡ Cluses - A40 E25 & D907 = 62 miles

2nd- Lyon - 2 hrs 26
➡ E611 A42 - Geneva A40 E25 & N506 = 135 miles

3rd- Grenoble - 2 hrs 40
➡ A41 E712 A43, A430, N212 & N506 = 135 miles

i - **Information** - 0033 (0) 450 530 024
www.chamonix.com

52

France
Chatel

Mapping Page 47 C7

ROUTE PLANNER

✈ **CALAIS**	0 miles	along the **A16 - A26** **E15 / E17** *Toll Road*
➡ **REIMS**	166 miles	2hrs 55 **A26 A4 E17 / 50**
➡ **CHALONS en CHAMPAGNE**		3hrs 15 **A26 E17**
➡ **TROYES**	236 miles	4hrs **A5 E17 / 54**
➡ **MARAC**	295 miles	5hrs **A31 E17 / 21**
➡ **DIJON**	351 miles	6hrs 10 **A31 E17 & E15 A6**
➡ **MACON**	395 miles	7hrs **A6 E15**
➡ **BOURG-en-BRESSE**	426 miles	7hrs 15 **A40 E62**
➡ **GENEVA**	466 miles	8hrs 20 **N5** *Tolls End*
➡ **THONON-les-BAINS**	488 miles	9hrs **D902** and the **D22** to the resort.
➡ **CHATEL**		

KM **Distance**	**513 miles** *(826 km)*
⏱ **Drive time**	**10 hours 5 mins**
⛽ **Fuel**	**£48**
€ **Tolls**	**£28**

Top Lift
2200m.
Resort Height
1200m.
Vertical Drop
1000m.
Number of Runs
47
Longest Run
6km
Slopes
130km of piste
⦿ *Beginner*
49% of the runs
⦿ *Intermediate*
39% of the runs
● *Advanced*
12% of the runs

Cross-Country
31km of tracks
Snowboarding
Half-pipe & Park
Snow Season
Dec to April
Snowmaking
10% of pistes
Number of lifts
41
Up Lift Capicity
41,600 per hour
Mountain Cafes
12

On the Slopes - Chatel is situated in the Portes du Soleil circuit and as a resort sits split between two relatively low altitude levels. The resort has long been a popular destination, especially for families as it is particulary suitable for them, offering a wide variety of runs. The local ski/snowboard schools (six at the last count) are well regarded and are able to handle all levels and all ages. The mountain is a mixture of wide-open areas knitted with trees and steep shaded runs although it's not likely to excite expert skiers and snowboarders. The steeps around the Pre-la-Joux area may get your heart pumping quicker. In the main, Chatel is a resort with a host of decent red trails that will give slow-learning skiers lots of time to progress on and improve their techniques. With the low altitude comes inconsistent snow cover, even though the resort makes extensive use of snow cannons to relieve the problem. There are however, a number of higher altititude resorts on the same lift ticket: Avoriaz is only a short bus ride away. The Portes du Soleil is a popular destination, which means that queues do exist and the nursery slopes can be a hassle to get on. For snowboarders who like to carve Chatel has decent groomed runs with wide pistes to blast about on. Freestylers are better off going to Avoriaz where they catered far better for with a halfpipe and a cool terrain park. Despite not being a hot-spot for cross-country skiers, there are some very nice and convenient tracks to enjoy, marked out over an area that covers some 30+ km.

Off the Slopes - Chatel is full of charm and is a nice alternative to some of the neighbouring purpose-built affairs. It's a rustic village that oozes Frenchness, but as a desirable place to holiday, it comes at a price. A high standard of accommodation is provided in the form of chalets and hotels. Eating out is also very good although the night-life is somewhat dull, and not for the hardcore. A nice restaurant to try out would be the Cornetts, while the Avalanche is a popular drinking hole.

Verdict - Good ski school reputation. Attractive village in a decent ski **5/10**

COST INDICATOR

Budget   Moderate   Very Expensive   Criminal

✈ Airports & Fly Drive Guide
1st- Geneva (CH) - 1 hr 40
➡ Cluses - N5, Thonon-les-Bains, D902, D22 = 83 miles

2nd- Lyon - 3 hrs 10
➡ A41 and all routes via Geneva = 135 miles

3rd- Grenoble - 3 hr 30
➡ A41 and all routes via Geneva = 150 miles

i - **Information** - 0033 (0) 450 732 244
www.chatel.com

France
Courchevel

Mapping Page 47 E7

Top Lift
3500m.
Resort Height
1250m.
Vertical Drop
1438m.
Number of Runs
102
Longest Run
5km
Slopes
600km of piste
●● *Beginner*
51% of the runs
● *Intermediate*
37% of the runs
● **Advanced**
12% of the runs

Cross-Country
66km of tracks
Snowboarding
Half-pipe & Park
Snow Season
Dec to April
Snowmaking
92km of piste
Number of lifts
65
Up Lift Capicity
243,260 per hour
Mountain Cafes
43

On the Slopes - Courchevel is the playground for the ridiculously rich and the just plain ridiculous and you'll find plenty of Z-list pop and TV stars posing on the slopes and around the resort. Despite it all, it's a fantastic resort in terms of the mountain and its hundreds of kilometres of linked terrain. A good annual snowfall adds to the attraction, as does the superb uplift system that can move a staggering 230,000 people up the slopes in a single hour. Courchevel, part of the vast Three Valleys ski region, consists of four purpose-built stations. At the bottom is 1300, otherwise known as Le Praz and is the only village of the group with pre ski history. Next up is 1550, followed closely by 1650 and finally (at the top) 1850, which also stands for 'ugly and expensive'. All four levels offer superb direct access on to the slopes with doorstep skiing and snowboarding an added attraction. No matter what level of skier or snowboarder you are, no one is going to feel left out here, because it's one of those rare places that has an abundance of every thing to suit everyone: Good expert slopes, wonderfully pisted intermediate runs, and lots of excellent nursery areas. It is, however, a busy place that caters for millions of visitors, so expect to queue up at some of the main lifts. In fairness, lifts lines throughout the region are surprisingly small for the amount of people using them

Off the Slopes - If you can put up with grim buildings and some of the twits that inhabit them, then your stay in Courchevel should be a pleasant one. Your Euro's will soon disappear, as this place is really expensive. There is a good choice of hotels on all levels as well as shops and local attractions. Each level has its popular restaurants offering just about any type of dish you hunger for, including veggie. Bars are full of tour reps playing après-ski games but for an early beer, try L'Equipe in 1850, or Le Signal in 1650 then the D'Arbeilo in Le Praz or Bang Bang. None are cheap, nor are they much to shout about, but you can have a good time partying with many like-minded souls.

Verdict - Fantastic skiing and boarding for all, but hellishly expensive. **9/10**

COST INDICATOR

Budget   Moderate   Very Expensive   Criminal

i **- Information -** 0033 (0) 479 080 029
www.courchevel.com

ROUTE PLANNER

CALAIS 0 miles
along the **A16 - A26**
E15 / E17
Toll Road

REIMS 168 miles
2hrs 55 **A26 A4 E17 / 50**

CHALONS en CHAMPAGNE
3hrs 15 **A26 E17**

TROYES 236 miles
4hrs **A5 E17 / 54**

MARAC 295 miles
5hrs **A31 E17 / 21**

DIJON 351 miles
6hrs 10 **A39 E21**

DOLE 363 miles
6hrs 10 **A39 E21**

BOURG-en-BRESSE 426 miles
7hrs 15 **E21 A40**

Tolls End

ALBERTVILE 537 miles
9hrs 30 **N90** to **Moutiers.**
Then take the **D915** & **D91** up to the resort.

COURCHEVEL

Distance 569 miles *(916km)*
Drive time 11 hours 44 mins
Fuel £52
Tolls £35

Airports & Fly Drive Guide

1st- Grenoble - **2 hr 30**
A41, E712 and all routes via **Albertville = 108 miles**

2nd- Geneva (CH) - **2 hr 25**
A41 E712 via Annecy & Albertville = **90 miles**

3rd - Lyon - **2 hrs 25**
A43 & **E70** all routes via Albertville = **115 miles**

France
Flaine

Mapping Page 47 D7

Top Lift
2500m.
Resort Height
1600m.
Vertical Drop
900m.
Number of Runs
107
Longest Run
km
Slopes
160km of piste
●● *Beginner*
50% of the runs
● *Intermediate*
38% of the runs
● **Advanced**
12% of the runs

Cross-Country
10km of tracks
Snowboarding
Half-pipe & Park
Snow Season
Dec to April
Snowmaking
0km of piste
Number of lifts
75
Up Lift Capicity
75,000 per hour
Mountain Cafes
7

On the Slopes - The person who designed this place must have either been high on every drug available or fresh out of a Russian Gulag – to say that Flaine is ugly is an understatement. Built in the 1960's, it is quite simply one of the world's most hideous resorts constructed out of what seems to be tons of recycled East German Concrete. The neighbouring villages and those en-route to Flaine are traditional and a pleasing alternative, however. The slopes of Flaine, however, are a refreshing change from the town itself with wonderful views across an area known as the Grand Massif, slopes to suit every one and a mountain that is extremely well laid out and serviced by a good lift system. Despite the resort's not so positive reputation, it is surprisingly popular, and queues do exist for base lifts and the home runs can get busy. Snow conditions are generally favourable with an average annual snow record of over 500cm a season. Intermediates are the ones who will fair best on these slopes with a good choice of red runs from the base up. Experts are not left out with some serious slopes to tackle such as the Diamant Noir run which will please mogul lovers. Flaine offers some good off-piste terrain, but it has its dangers off the beaten path, so hire a guide – don't go it alone. This is also a mountain suited to beginners with good nursery slopes; what's more the base lifts are free for learners.

Off the Slopes - Flaine is a car-free village and while it's not sprawling or particularly expensive, unlike other purpose built French resorts: it has however been presented something like a holiday camp on a mountain, and the Brits have done a good job of lowering the tone further. Lodging is basic, with apartments being the main choice, but there are a few hotels locally with further choices in one of the neighbouring villages. Local facilities are basic and eating out options poor. Nightlife is geared around hardcore boozing with lots of staged après-ski nights put on by tour reps. All the bars are similar, loud, tacky and not that appealing.

Verdict - Fine mountain with good skiing, but the resort is unappealing. **8/10**

COST INDICATOR

Budget   Moderate   Very Expensive   Criminal

i **- Information -** 0033 (0) 450 908 001
www.flaine.com

ROUTE PLANNER

CALAIS 0 miles
along the **A16 - A26**
E15 / E17
Toll Road

REIMS 168 miles
2hrs 55 **A26 A4 E17 / 50**

CHALONS en CHAMPAGNE
3hrs 15 **A26 E17**

TROYES 236 miles
4hrs **A5 E17 / 54**

MARAC 295 miles
1hr 35 **A31 E17 / 21**

DIJON 351 miles
6hrs 10 **A31 E17 & E15 A6**

MACON 395 miles
7hrs **A6 E15**

BOURG-en-BRESSE 426 miles
7hrs 15 **A40 E62**

GENEVA 491 miles
8hrs 20 **A40 E25**

CLUSES 521 miles
9hrs
Tolls End

FLAINE
7hr 58

Distance 549 miles *(884 km)*
Drive time 9 hours 35 mins
Fuel £50
Tolls £30

Airports & Fly Drive Guide

1st- Geneva (CH) - **1 hr 18**
Cluses - **A40 E25** & **D907** = **55 miles**

2nd- Lyon - **2 hrs 30**
E611 A42 - Geneva **A40 E25** via Cluses = **126 miles**

3rd- Grenoble - **2 hrs 45**
A41 E712 upto the **A40 E25, N91** & **D211 = 130 miles**

DRIVE TIME - nixon. www.nixonnow.com

Isola 2000

ROUTE PLANNER

Top Lift
2610m.
Resort Height
1800m.
Vertical Drop
810m.
Number of Runs
46
Longest Run
4km
Slopes
150km of piste
● ● *Beginner*
48% of the runs
● *Intermediate*
13% of the runs
● *Advanced*
13% of the runs

Cross-Country
10km of tracks
Snowboarding
Half-pipe & Park
Snow Season
Dec to April
Snowmaking
15% of pistes
Number of lifts
25
Up Lift Capicity
20,000 per hour
Mountain Cafes
4

On the Slopes - Isola 2000, is located in southern France just an hour north of Nice and it's attractions. Purpose-built in the sixties with the aim of attracting large numbers of package tour visitors, the resort planners over estimated how far clients would be willing to travel and the hordes of visitors they envisaged simply didn't materialise – mainly due to the somewhat difficult direct access from northern France. In the last few years however, an increasing number of visitors have started to make the journey and have been pleased with what they have found. The resort has easy access to the lifts, and the slopes offer enough terrain to keep most people busy for a good week or two. There are more than 150km of pistes, most of which favours novices, which is why the resort attracts large numbers of families. Weekends see a large influx of city dwellers from Nice as they take advantage of the good, regular snowfall throughout the season. Beginners have a massive designated area near the base lift station, which keeps them out of trouble in an area that aids progression, before they take on the higher-grade runs. Advanced skiers and snowboarders may not have a vast choice of runs but what is there, is good. Isola 2000 has ample tree coverage on the mid to lower areas with natural gullies near Melezes. Those looking for some off-piste should turn to the north-facing slope above Grand Tour, as it is well worth hiking the ridge to reach some decent powder fields.

Off the Slopes - The easiest option with accommodation would be to stay in one of the apartment blocks – comfortable, unfussy and just a stone's throw away from the lift station and amenities. If you're after a bit more style, take up space in one of the chalets on offer. Prices are not silly and you can stay either on, or close to the slopes. For food, why not try the Crocodile Bar, which serves up some decent Tex-Mex. It's also a good local snowboard hangout and stays open long into the early hours, with good measures and good sounds.

Verdict - Good resort for taking the kids to with excellent nursery slopes. **7**/10

COST INDICATOR
Budget   Moderate   Very Expensive   Criminal

i - **Information** - 0033 (0) 493 231 515
www.isola-2000.com

CALAIS 0 miles
along the A16 - A26
E15 / E17
Toll Road

→ **REIMS** 168 miles
2hrs 55   A26 A4 E17 / 50

→ **CHALONS en CHAMPAGNE**
3hrs 15   A26 E17

→ **TROYES** 236 miles
4hrs   A5 E17 / 54

→ **MARAC** 295 miles
5hrs   A31 E17 / 21

→ **DIJON** 351 miles
6hrs 10   A31 E17 & E15 A6

→ **MACON** 395 miles
7hrs   A6 E15

→ **LYON** 471 miles
8hrs 50   A43 E70 A48 E711

→ **GRENOBLE** 537 miles
9hrs 26   N85, N91, N94 D902
Tolls End south via **Guillestre** and St Paul to the D900 then along the SS21 towards **Vinadio** taking the SP255 & D97 right up to the resort.

→ **ISOLA 2000**

KM | **Distance** | 698 miles *(1124 km)*
Drive time | 13 hours 55 mins
Fuel | £66
Tolls | £38

Airports & Fly Drive Guide
1st- Nice - 1 hr 30
→ N202, D2205 and the D97 north via Clans = 52 miles

2nd- Grenoble - 5 hrs 5
→ N85, N91, and all routes via Guillestre, SP255 = 186 miles

3rd- Turin - 3 hr 10
→ SP2, A6, E74 and all roads south via Cuneo = 114 miles

La Clusaz

ROUTE PLANNER

Top Lift
2600m.
Resort Height
1100m.
Vertical Drop
1500m.
Number of Runs
84
Longest Run
3km
Slopes
132km of piste
● ● *Beginner*
60% of the runs
● *Intermediate*
30% of the runs
● *Advanced*
10% of the runs

Cross-Country
70km of tracks
Snowboarding
Half-pipe & Park
Snow Season
Dec to April
Snowmaking
25% of piste
Number of lifts
55
Up Lift Capicity
49,500 per hour
Mountain Cafes
20

On the Slopes - La Clusaz is a very French resort, full of rustic charm and beautifully set among trees and thankfully, the town planners of the sixties haven't had their wicked way as the resort has been allowed to develop naturally making this a pleasant alternative both on and off the slopes. Unlike some of the uglier, yet high altitude purpose-built affairs, La Clusaz can suffer from an indifferent snow record due in part to its low altitude and pine-clad slopes. What's more there isn't a great deal of snowmaking on offer. The resort is sandwiched among five mountains, which offer a combined piste area of 132km and good off-piste possibilities when snow permits. You can get around four of the five areas via a network of connecting lifts, while the fifth, the Massif de Balme, can be reached by road. 60% of the slopes are graded as beginner runs, but intermediates will enjoy it just as much by doing some exploring, it's just experts who may feel a little short changed – there are challenging slopes, but not a great deal. The Beauregard and L'Etale areas have good, easy slopes for beginners; the only potential problem is that they are mostly serviced by draglifts. On the other hand snowboarders should find this an okay hangout, noted for it's cool backcountry and freeride terrain such as the terrain at Combe de Balme. There is also a decent terrain park at Aguille. Cross-country enthusiasts should visit the tracks around Lac des Confins that will make for a few hours fun but, as with any low level resort, expect the best conditions after a good dump of snow.

Off the Slopes - The village has everything you would expect from a purpose built area, with plenty of hotels to choose from as well as cosy mountain chalets. You can also rent apartments from around 500euros a week for four people. Local facilities are good and the number and choice of restaurants is excellent. Restaurant Arbe is recommended for a hearty feed, while après fans should check out the Pub le Saalto or the Pressoir, but in truth neither are that hot.

Verdict - Good slopes to intermediate level, but not always snow sure. **5**/10

COST INDICATOR
Budget   Moderate   Very Expensive   Criminal

i - **Information** - 0033 (0) 4326 500
www.laclusaz.com

CALAIS 0 miles
along the A16 - A26
E15 / E17
Toll Road

→ **REIMS** 168 miles
2hrs 55   A26 A4 E17 / 50

→ **CHALONS en CHAMPAGNE**
3hrs 15   A26 E17

→ **TROYES** 236 miles
4hrs   A5 E17 / 54

→ **MARAC** 295 miles
5hrs   A31 E17 / 21

→ **DIJON** 351 miles
6hrs 10   A31 E17 & E15 A6

→ **MACON** 395 miles
7hrs   A6 E15

→ **BOURG-en-BRESSE** 426 miles
7hrs 15   A40 E62

→ **GENEVA** 491 miles
8hrs 20   A40 E25

→ **ANNEMASSE** 504 miles
Tolls End A40 E25 south towards **Toisinges**, turnig off for the D12 south to the D909 to the resort.

→ **LA CLUSAZ**

KM | **Distance** | 536 miles *(862 km)*
Drive time | 9 hours 25 mins
Fuel | £48
Tolls | £35

Airports & Fly Drive Guide
1st- Geneva (CH) - 1 hr 10
→ A40 and routes south via Annemasse, D909 = 44 miles

2nd- Lyon - 2 hrs 5 mins
→ A41 dir Geneva via Annecy to the D909 = 99 miles

3rd- Grenoble - 2 hrs 20
→ A48, E70, A41 to the D12 and D909 = 100 miles

DRIVE TIME - *nixon* www.nixonnow.com

France
La Plagne

Mapping Page 47 E7

ROUTE PLANNER

CALAIS	0 miles	
	along the **A16 - A26**	
	E15 / E17	
	Toll Road	
REIMS	168 miles	2hrs 55
	A26 A4 **E17 / 50**	
CHALONS en CHAMPAGNE		3hrs 15
	A26 **E17**	
TROYES	236 miles	4hrs
	A5 **E17 / 54**	
MARAC	295 miles	5hrs
	A31 **E17 / 21**	
DIJON	351 miles	6hrs 10
	A31 **E17** & **E15** A6	
MACON	395 miles	7hrs
	A6 **E15**	
BOURG-en-BRESSE	426 miles	7hrs 15
	A40 **E62**, N508	

Tolls End

ANNECY	510 miles	8hrs 50
	N508 south via	
	Albertville to the **N90**	
	and on to the **D220** up	
	to the resort.	

Top Lift
3250m.
Resort Height
1250m.
Vertical Drop
2000m.
Number of Runs
123
Longest Run
15km
Slopes
210km of piste
● Beginner
65% of the runs
◐ Intermediate
26% of the runs
● Advanced
9% of the runs

Cross-Country
90km of tracks
Snowboarding
Half-pipe & Park
Snow Season
Dec to April
Snowmaking
20 cannons
Number of lifts
108
Up Lift Capacity
116,800 per hour
Mountain Cafes
20

On the Slopes - La Plagne is a collection of villages spread out over a large area with almost 220km of pistes. It's also a part of the Paradiski area, which when combined brings the serviceable area up to a whacking 420km – you'd be hard pushed to not enjoy yourself, whatever your level and could spend a month here and still not get to see all that is on offer. Most of the main seven slopes sections are located above the tree lines, with easy access made possible via a network of fast lifts that seldom have major lift lines problems, even though some queuing is involved. With so many lifts and pistes, some planning is necessary to make the most of the, occasionally confusing, layout. The runs are well marked on the mountain itself, but with some 69 drag lifts to contend with, you could have a nightmare of a time if pomas are not your thing. La Plagne is a region that lends itself to beginners rapidly progressing into competent intermediates and where off-piste is possible on a grand scale. The resort's altitude and location means the snow record is good and cutting fresh powder in the morning is often possible. This is also a highly rated cross-country skiers resort and the 90km of trails that snake around the whole area are a joy. Likewise, snowboarders are provided with good natural hits and plenty of man-made ones in the form of a number of terrain parks and halfpipes.

Off the Slopes - The village has everything you would expect from a well-designed purpose-built resort: there's a good selection of accommodation ranging from expensive chalets to cheap self-catering options and you can lodge close to the slopes in a number of apartment blocks, while all the local amenities, such as shops and restaurants and so on, are located within easy reach of each other. Evenings are rather dull and uneventful, unless you're a into the whole après-ski scene, in which case you can party along with the tour reps in any one of many bars. Mat's and Cheyenne are two of the most popular bars to check out attracting louts and hard core boozers.

LA PLAGNE	

KM Distance 576 miles *(927km)*
Drive time 10 hours 37 mins
Fuel £52
€ **Tolls** £35

Verdict - Good resort if you like the whole purpose built scene. **7/10**

COST INDICATOR
Budget   Moderate   Very Expensive   Criminal

***i* - Information** - 0033 (0) 479 097 979
www.la-plagne.com

1st- Geneva (CH) **- 2 hrs 30**
➡ A41 **E712** south via **Annecy**
& **Albertville** = **96 miles**

2nd- Grenoble - 2 hrs 40
➡ A41, E712 and all routes
via **Albertville** = **115 miles**

3rd - Lyon - 2 hrs 45
➡ A43 & E70 and all routes
via **Albertville** = **122 miles**

France
La Tania

Mapping Page 47 E7

ROUTE PLANNER

CALAIS	0 miles	
	along the **A16 - A26**	
	E15 / E17	
	Toll Road	
REIMS	168 miles	2hrs 55
	A26 A4 **E17 / 50**	
CHALONS en CHAMPAGNE		3hrs 15
	A26 **E17**	
TROYES	236 miles	4hrs
	A5 **E17 / 54**	
MARAC	295 miles	5hrs
	A31 **E17 / 21**	
DIJON	351 miles	6hrs 10
	A39 **E21**	
DOLE	363 miles	6hrs 10
	A39 **E21**	
BOURG-en-BRESSE	426 miles	7hrs 15
	E21 A40	

Tolls End

ALBERTVILE	537 miles	7hrs 30
	N90 to **Moutiers**.	
	Then take the **D915** &	
	D91 up to the resort.	

Top Lift
2738m.
Resort Height
1350m.
Vertical Drop
1388m.
Number of Runs
102
Longest Run
km
Slopes
200km of piste
● Beginner
25% of the runs
◐ Intermediate
64% of the runs
● Advanced
11% of the runs

Cross-Country
66km of tracks
Snowboarding
Half-pipe & Park
Snow Season
Dec to April
Snowmaking
27km of piste
Number of lifts
67
Up Lift Capicity
243,260 per hour
Mountain Cafes
43

On the Slopes - La Tania is another of the resorts that forms part of the Three Valleys, claimed to be the largest linked ski region in the world. It's one of the smaller members, however, and consequently a pleasing alternative to its more famous neighbours such as Courchevel and Meribel, yet still linked to them on the mountain by the La Tania Gondola. Set back into a mountain face covered in trees, this is a modern, purpose-built station that has been attractively and conveniently designed. Lots of people are discovering that this place has the same opportunities to explore the whole Three Valleys, but from a quiet and hassle-free base – the only time you're likely to see a lift queue is in the mornings when the early punters get the main gondola. The actual slopes that lead in and out of the resort itself are limited, and consequently good for beginners, but higher up on the mountain there are countless options to ski off in many directions on slopes to suit all tastes. Beginners may get the lions shares of graded runs, but advanced and intermediates have plenty of challenging terrain to play on, as do cross-country skiers who are provided with over 65km of tracks that snake through trees and along open paths. Snowboarders are better off riding the slopes around Courchevel especially if they are freestylers, as thats where you will find the nearest halfpipe and terrain park. At the end of the day skiing or riding back down to your hotel is one of the joys of staying here, but the choice of final home runs are limited to only a few trails.

Off the Slopes - La Tania is a pleasant and low-key retreat and ideal for mum, dad and their 2.2 kids. The resort may have limited services but there is more than enough for a young family who are not looking for bright lights and fancy restaurants. Hotels and apartments are right on the slopes so you won't have to do a lot of walking or bussing around. There are some good restaurants and bars to choose from just don't expect too many of them. Le Ski Lodge is both good for its food and for evening drink.

LA TANIA	7hr 58

KM Distance 569 miles *(916km)*
Drive time 11 hours 44 mins
Fuel £52
€ **Tolls** £35

Verdict - A perfect base for a family holiday close to the Three Valleys. **7/10**

COST INDICATOR
Budget   Moderate   Very Expensive   Criminal

***i* - Information** - 0033 (0) 479 084 040
www.latania.com

1st- Grenoble - 2 hrs 30
➡ A41, E712 and all routes
via **Albertville** = **108 miles**

2nd- Geneva (CH) **- 2 hrs 25**
➡ A41 **E712** via **Annecy** &
Albertville = **90 miles**

3rd - Lyon - 2 hrs 25
➡ A43 & E70 and all routes
via **Albertville** = **115 miles**

La Rosiere

Mapping Page 47 D7

ROUTE PLANNER

Top Lift
2642m.
Resort Height
1150m.
Vertical Drop
1492m.
Number of Runs
61
Longest Run
4km
Slopes
150km of piste
● ● Beginner
48% of the runs
○ Intermediate
13% of the runs
● Advanced
13% of the runs

Cross-Country
25km of tracks
Snowboarding
Half-pipe & Park
Snow Season
Dec to April
Snowmaking
262 cannons
Number of lifts
36
Up Lift Capacity
26,000 per hour
Mountain Cafes
14

CALAIS 0 miles
along the A16 - A26
E15 / E17
Toll Road

➡ **REIMS** 168 miles
2hrs 55 A26 A4 E17 / 50

➡ **CHALONS en CHAMPAGNE**
3hrs 15 A26 E17

➡ **TROYES** 236 miles
4hrs A5 E17 / 54

➡ **MARAC** 295 miles
5hrs A31 E17 / 21

➡ **DIJON** 351 miles
6hrs 10 A39 E21

➡ **DOLE** 363 miles
7hrs A39 E21

➡ **BOURG-en-BRESSE** 426 miles
8hrs 50 E21, A40, N508, N90

Tolls End

➡ **MOUTIERS** 555 miles
10hrs D85, N90 to the resort.

➡ **LA ROSIERE**

Distance 586 miles (943km)
Drive time 10 hours 45 mins
Fuel £67
Tolls £30

On the Slopes - If you like the idea of being able to ski in two countries in the same day, then La Rosiere could be for you as this delightful medium-sized resort is linked with it's Italian, and much larger, neighbour La Thuile – set with views across the Mont Blanc, the Matterhorn and Monte Rosa. This is a resort with a good snow record, short lift queues and terrain for all levels with the bulk of the runs coloured red indicating that is an intermediate's place, which it largely is. Advanced skiers and snowboarders who like to pump down steep, uneven blacks don't have too many to choose from – if you can afford it and want the ultimate ski rush, then you can go heli-skiing/boarding from the Italian side, where you are flown out to some truly awesome off-piste terrain that will have you wetting your self with excitement. It's worth noting that it's not cheap nor are beginners allowed, but back on the main slopes, novices have plenty of easy blue runs to learn on which are close the village and allow for easy descents back home, doing away with the common practice of having to get a lift back down at the end of the day (unless the snow on the lower runs has thinned out that is). In terms of snowboarding, La Rosiere is not on the world snowboard events circuit, but La Thuile certainly is and it's easy to see why. Freeriders who can't afford to go heli-boarding need not fret, as there great option to ride close to home whether you access the runs from La Rosiere or La Thuile. Both have halfpipes. Nice cross-country ski area if you know what you're about.

Off the Slopes - La Rosiere is a purpose built resort with a simple and attractive appeal about it. This not a flash place and nor is over run with tour operators. The Hotels and chalets, which can house at any one time around 8,000 visitors, are of a traditional style, but local facilities are a bit sparse and apart from a few shops and a cinema (French speaking) there is little to do in the evenings. The choice of restaurants and bars are also limited, with little or no hardcore nightlife available in any of the pubs.

Verdict - Middle-of-the-road with good slopes but dull village. **6/10**

COST INDICATOR

Budget   Moderate   Very Expensive   Criminal

i - **Information** - 0033 (0) 479 068 051
www.larosiere.net

Les Arcs

Mapping Page 47 E7

ROUTE PLANNER

Top Lift
3226m.
Resort Height
1600m.
Vertical Drop
1626m.
Number of Runs
122
Longest Run
7km
Slopes
240km of piste
● ● Beginner
52% of the runs
○ Intermediate
30% of the runs
● Advanced
12% of the runs

Cross-Country
40km of tracks
Snowboarding
Half-pipe & Park
Snow Season
Dec to April
Snowmaking
25% of pistes
Number of lifts
56
Up Lift Capacity
85,600 per hour
Mountain Cafes
16

CALAIS 0 miles
along the A16 - A26
E15 / E17
Toll Road

➡ **REIMS** 168 miles
2hrs 55 A26 A4 E17 / 50

➡ **CHALONS en CHAMPAGNE**
3hrs 15 A26 E17

➡ **TROYES** 236 miles
4hrs A5 E17 / 54

➡ **MARAC** 295 miles
5hrs A31 E17 / 21

➡ **DIJON** 351 miles
6hrs 10 A39 E21

➡ **DOLE** 363 miles
7hrs A39 E21

➡ **BOURG-en-BRESSE** 426 miles
8hrs 50 E21, A40, N508, N90

Tolls End

➡ **MOUTIERS** 555 miles
10hrs D85, N90, D87, D226 to the resort.

➡ **LA ROSIERE**

Distance 577 miles (929km)
Drive time 10 hours 40 mins
Fuel £54
Tolls £30

On the Slopes - There are those who will delight in telling you that Les Arcs is a massive, concrete carbuncle – but those people probably haven't been here, let alone spent any sort of time in the place. Ignore such comments, come with an open mind, and enjoy one of the best mountain environments in the world. Les Arcs itself is split into four distinctive resorts - 1600, 1800, 2000 and Bourg-St-Maurice and each of the separate areas have a different feel, so choose wisely. 1600, where most of the chalets are situated, is quite chilled out with loads of trees. 1800 is the party place, while 2000 is a bit higher up and a little isolated, but it has good access to some amazing terrain. Bourg St Maurice is a low level traditional town that has a funicular train that links it speedily with the main ski area. Despite having a huge area, Les Arcs has managed to retain a cosy feel as it's dead easy to get from one area to another and you are only likely to run into heavy lift queues during the French holidays. On the mountain, Les Arcs has it all, from mellow beginner slopes to some of the most challenging runs anywhere in France and while there are plenty of visitors, there is a lot of terrain and a very efficient lift system. The slopes are left fairly quiet. Beginners are sorted here and it shouldn't be long before you're exploring the whole place aided by the quality of the piste and the fact that most areas are connected by fairly easy trails and lifts.

Off the Slopes - 1800 is the most popular place to stay, where there is a good selection of apartment blocks and hotels. The best thing about these areas is that prices for accommodation, eating out and partying are largely the same throughout, with something to appeal to everyone. The general feel is one of a gigantic, spread-out holiday camp that rocks 'til late, looks a little tacky, but has heaps going on with all manner of sporting facilities and shopping facilities. Night-life goes off where ever you stay. Cafe Sol being the number one hangout in 1600, while in 1800 its the Red Hot Saloon.

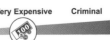
Verdict - An immense and near perfect popular resort in all aspects. **9/10**

COST INDICATOR

Budget   Moderate   Very Expensive   Criminal

i - **Information** - 0033 (0) 479 071 257
www.lesarcs.com

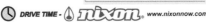

France

Les Deux Alpes

Mapping Page 47 F6

Top Lift	

Top Lift
3568m.
Resort Height
1270m.
Vertical Drop
2298m.
Number of Runs
70
Longest Run
16km
Slopes
200km of piste
● ● *Beginner*
30% of the runs
● *Intermediate*
60% of the runs
● *Advanced*
10% of the runs

Cross-Country
20km of tracks
Snowboarding
Half-pipe & Park
Snow Season
All year round
Snowmaking
25% of pistes
Number of lifts
58
Up Lift Capicity
66,100 per hour
Mountain Cafes
6

On the Slopes - Les 2 Alpes is one of the largest individual resorts and manages this without relying on linking with other nearby areas. It does link on the mountain to the small extreme resort of La Grave. Les 2 Alpes is notable for a number of reasons; it's a high altitude destination, with a good snow record. It is also a glacier resort with skiing and snowboarding during the summer as well as in winter and there a number of summer camps which are very popular with freestyle skiers and snowboarders. Indeed this place is a particularly freestyle-friendly hangout at the end of every October when the resort plays host to the legendary Des Mondial Du snowboard event which attracts over 5,000 people to a free demo session on the latest snowboards. However, don't fret skiers – Les 2 Alpes, is as much a skier's mountain as anyone else's. The 200km of piste can be accessed from a number of sections of the resort, a purpose built village that stretches down a long road with many access points to the slopes. The slopes favour all levels, with intermediates having the best facilities, but as you improve there are not many black trails to test your progress on. Mind, you one thing that there is on this mountain is some great off-piste areas and superb nursery slopes close to the base.

Off the Slopes - Les 2 Alpes is a modern, spread-out town, which can involve a fair bit of walking from one end to the other which can be a pain at night. Accommodation ranges from chalets and flash hotels, to lots of apartment blocks that wouldn't look out of place in a New York suburb. There are loads of off-slope services, including a cinema, bowling alley, sports complex and an outdoor climbing wall. There are the usual shopping outlets, and a mini-mall selling the usual tourist junk. There are some reasonably priced pizza and burger bars, a Thai takeaway and a disappointing Chinese. Being a busy tourist place, night-life is lively and very loud, it's common to see après-ski idiots throwing up early on the evenings after over-indulging at tea time sessions.

Verdict - Very good all year round resort, but rowdy in the evenings. 7/10

COST INDICATOR

Budget   Moderate   Very Expensive   Criminal

***i* - Information -** 0033 (0) 476 792 200
www.les2alpes.com

ROUTE PLANNER

CALAIS 0 miles
along the **A16 - A26**
E15 / E17
Toll Road

REIMS 168 miles 2hrs 55
A26 A4 E17 / 50

CHALONS en CHAMPAGNE 3hrs 15
A26 E17

TROYES 236 miles 4hrs
A5 E17 / 54

MARAC 295 miles 5hrs
A31 E17 / 21

DIJON 351 miles 6hrs 10
A31 E17 & E15 A6

MACON 395 miles 7hrs
A6 E15

LYON 471 miles 8hrs 50
A43 E70 A48 E711

GRENOBLE 537 miles 9hrs 26
Tolls End Head south to **Le Pont de-claix** and pick up the **N91** in the direction of Briancon. Finally taking the **D213** up to the resort.

LES DEUX ALPES 7hr 58

Distance 573miles *(922km)*
Drive time 10 hours 15 mins
Fuel £52
Tolls £35

Airports & Fly Drive Guide

1st- Grenoble - 1 hr 40
Le Pont de-Claix - N91 & D213 = 68 miles

2nd- Lyon - 2 hrs 5
Grenoble, N91 & D213 = 100 miles

3rd- Geneva (CH) - 2 hrs 50
A41 E712 to Grenoble, N91 & D213 = 135 miles

France

Meribel

Mapping Page 47 E7

Top Lift
2610m.
Resort Height
1800m.
Vertical Drop
810m.
Number of Runs
46
Longest Run
4km
Slopes
150km of piste
● ● *Beginner*
48% of the runs
● *Intermediate*
13% of the runs
● *Advanced*
13% of the runs

Cross-Country
10km of tracks
Snowboarding
Half-pipe & Park
Snow Season
Dec to April
Snowmaking
15% of pistes
Number of lifts
25
Up Lift Capicity
20,000 per hour
Mountain Cafes
4

On the Slopes - Meribel is certainly the place to avoid if you don't like large numbers of British holidaymakers as you could almost forget that you were in France at all. Don't be put off too easily, howver – Meribel is a great resort and one that is slap-bang in the middle of the world's largest linked ski and snowboard circuit, les Trois Vallees (Three Valleys). It's something of a cliché, but there really is something for every one here: even the mother in law (cliffs). Meribel has a serious amount of terrain of it's own before you even get into the Three Valleys ski region with over 600km of lift-linked piste. Access to the slopes from Meribel is not the most convenient, but once up, lift lines are not too much of a problem. On the down side, Meribel is very popular with most of the UK's tour operators, which means that the slopes can often fill up and become very crowded, especially around New Year, half term and Easter, which should be avoided at all costs. Cross-country skiers have a pleasant circuit around Lake Tueda to glide along, while the bulk of cross-country tracks can be found at Altiport. Meribel has not always been fashionable with snowboarders, due largely to a number of traverses between runs and because they were frowned upon in the early days. However, snowboarders are fully welcome and there is a lot for them to do including a number of pipes, parks and a boardercross run.

Off the Slopes - Meribel is a purpose-built affair, but not in the normal sense. What you have are lots of wooden buildings spread out along a winding street. Many of the chalets are owned and operated by Brits, so a traditional British breakfast isn't too hard to find. On the other hand, the cost of staying here is not as easy to accept and borders on being criminal. Mottaret, which is one of the neighbouring hamlets, has the cheapest lodging, but if you want any sort of local facilities then Meribel is the place, although nightlife is often ruined by too much themed aprés-ski going on. Still, Scott's Bar is a good lively hang out.

Verdict - Great slopes, good lifts, but too British and far too expensive. 8/10

COST INDICATOR

Budget   Moderate   Very Expensive   Criminal

***i* - Information -** 0033 (0) 479 086 001
www.meribel.net

ROUTE PLANNER

CALAIS 0 miles
along the **A16 - A26**
E15 / E17
Toll Road

REIMS 168 miles 2hrs 55
A26 A4 E17 / 50

CHALONS en CHAMPAGNE 3hrs 15
A26 E17

TROYES 236 miles 4hrs
A5 E17 / 54

MARAC 295 miles 5hrs
A31 E17 / 21

DIJON 351 miles 6hrs 10
A39 E21

DOLE 363 miles 6hrs 10
A39 E21

BOURG-en-BRESSE 426 miles 8hrs 50
E21 A40

Tolls End

ALBERTVILE 537 miles 9hrs 30
N90 to **Moutiers.** Then take the **D915 & D90** up to the resort.

MERIBEL 7hr 58

Distance 565 miles *(916km)*
Drive time 10 hours 20 mins
Fuel £52
Tolls £35

Airports & Fly Drive Guide

1st- Grenoble - 2 hrs 25
A41, E712 and all routes via Albertville = 104 miles

2nd- Geneva (CH) - 2 hrs 15
A41 E712 via Annecy & Albertville = 85 miles

3rd- Lyon - 2 hrs 25
A43 & E70 and all routes via Albertville = 114 miles

DRIVE TIME - nixon www.nixonnow.com

France
Montgenevre

Mapping Page 47 F7

Top Lift
2680m.
Resort Height
1850m.
Vertical Drop
1300m.
Number of Runs
45
Longest Run
7km
Slopes
100km of piste
● ● Beginner
40% of the runs
● Intermediate
39% of the runs
● Advanced
21% of the runs

Cross-Country
25km of tracks
Snowboarding
Half-pipe & Park
Snow Season
Dec to April
Snowmaking
15% of pistes
Number of lifts
25
Up Lift Capicity
6,500 per hour
Mountain Cafes
12

On the Slopes - Montgenevre is the only French part of the ski circuit known as the Milky Way, a collection of resorts that extends along a number of valley floors and criss-crosses into Italy. Montgenevre is essentially at one end of the Milky Way, while its more famous relation, the Italian resort of Sauze d 'Oulx, is at the other. Collectively, the circuit offers over 100km of ski and snowboarding terrain with slopes that have a good, reliable snow record. If one was to make a criticism of then it would be that the lifts are not the most modern in the Alps and there's a lack of steep runs for experts to explore but, as with many areas around the Milky Way, challenging terrain is not far away – even though getting to the best will involve some travelling by road.
Montgenevre offers an interesting mixture of mainly intermediate trails rising from the village, set at an altitude of 1850m. Although this is a popular tourist resort, it is not as tainted with package tours as some others in the region. Easy access to the slopes is made possible by a number of base lifts that take you to the main slopes of Les Anges and Le Querelay, or in the opposite direction to Le Chalvet which is rather limited in its scope and only has half a dozen runs. There are a surprisingly good number of beginner's slopes throughout the area and nursery slopes are well placed and can be reached with ease from the resort centre. While it is not a major snowboard resort, there are lots of opportunities for freeriders and some good carving pistes – there's also a number of parks.

Off the Slopes - Local facilities are based conveniently for the slopes with a mixture of apartment blocks, chalets, shops, sporting facilities and restaurants, refreshingly styled in a sober manner. The village is pleasant, and while there isn't a great deal to get excited about, the town planners seem to have resisted the French urge to build dozens of high rise buildings. Lodging is very affordable, and evenings can be very lively with a number of bars and the odd disco that have young crowds partying away.

Verdict - A decent resort, which will appeal to beginner and intermediate. 6/10

COST INDICATOR

Budget   Moderate   Very Expensive   Criminal

i - **Information** - 0033 (0) 492 215 252
www.montgenevre.com

ROUTE PLANNER

CALAIS 0 miles
along the **A16 - A26**
E15 / E17
Toll Road

➡ **REIMS** 168 miles
2hrs 55 **A26 A4 E17 / 50**

➡ **CHALONS en CHAMPAGNE**
3hrs 15 **A26 E17**

➡ **TROYES** 236 miles
4hrs **A5 E17 / 54**

➡ **MARAC** 295 miles
5hrs **A31 E17 / 21**

➡ **DIJON** 351 miles
6hrs 10 **A31 E17 & E15 A6**

➡ **MACON** 395 miles
7hr **A6 E15**

➡ **LYON** 471 miles
8hrs 50 **A43 E70 A48 E711**

➡ **GRENOBLE** 537 miles
9hrs 26 Head south to **Le Pont de-claix** and pick up
Tolls End the **N91** and **N94** via **Briancon**. Finally taking the **D2** and **N94** up to the resort.

➡ **MONTGENEVRE**

KM Distance **619 miles** (997km)
⏱ **Drive time** **10 hours 50 mins**
⛽ **Fuel** **£56**
€ **Tolls** **£35**

Airports & Fly Drive Guide

1st- Grenoble - 2 hrs 35
➡ Le Pont de-Claix - **N91** and all routes via **Briancon** = **105 miles**

2nd- Lyon - 2 hrs 40
➡ Grenoble, **N91** and all routes via **Briancon** = **145 miles**

3rd- Geneva (CH) - 2 hrs 55
➡ **A41 E712**, Grenoble, **N91** all roads via **Briancon** = **148 miles**

France
Morzine

Mapping Page 47 C7

Top Lift
2460m.
Resort Height
1000m.
Vertical Drop
1460m.
Number of Runs
66
Longest Run
11km
Slopes
138km of piste
● ● Beginner
50% of the runs
● Intermediate
40% of the runs
● Advanced
10% of the runs

Cross-Country
98km of tracks
Snowboarding
Half-pipe & Park
Snow Season
Dec to May
Snowmaking
15% of pistes
Number of lifts
67
Up Lift Capicity
55,200 per hour
Mountain Cafes
20

On the Slopes - Morzine is a major resort that is part of the Portes du Soleil region, which lift linked area with over 600km of terrain. This is also a resort that is greatly favoured by tour operators, especially British ones, but even though it gets a lot of visitors on a weekly basis, it seldom gets overpopulated, and while lift queues exist, there are resorts with far worse ones. Weekends see a few bottlenecks, however, especially the lift the links with Avoriaz, but persevere, the terrain is well worth the wait. Perhaps the only place where Morzine is let down, is it's relatively low altitude and the consequently, the low amount of natural snow cover it can get. Snowmaking facilities are generally poor, and you should consider the time of season that you want to visit. That aside, the resort is investing in new snow cannons all the time as well as new lifts. So if the snow is a bit thin in one area, then you can easily visit another spot higher up where better snow conditions exist. If you are a cross-country skier, then there are lots of opportunities and some really nice tracks to explore and as many of them are found up high, your are not always blighted by poor low level snow cover. The Vale de la is a superb area for cross-country skiing. Most of the lower nursery slopes can suffer once again for lack off snow, but don't be put of because there is stacks of easy terrain with great opportunities to progress to higher rated trails. If you go home from Morzine still a beginner after a week on snow, take up train spotting.

Off the Slopes - Morzine is a nice family resort with lots of good accommodation close to the slopes. Indeed is possible to book into a chalet with skiing to your door. Prices for most things here are reasonable, with room rates available from around A40 a night or a six person apartment from A430 per week. Around town restaurants are plentiful and you can eat cheaply in or dine out high on the hog. In the evenings, this is a lively resort where groups tend to party hard aided by tour reps. Dixie's is a cool sports bar, while Cavern is popular with locals. .

Verdict - The poor snow record here does let the place down a bit. 5/10

COST INDICATOR

Budget   Moderate   Very Expensive   Criminal

i - **Information** - 0033 (0) 450 747 272
www.morzine.com

ROUTE PLANNER

CALAIS 0 miles
along the **A16 - A26**
E15 / E17
Toll Road

➡ **REIMS** 168 miles
2hrs 55 **A26 A4 E17 / 50**

➡ **CHALONS en CHAMPAGNE**
3hrs 15 **A26 E17**

➡ **TROYES** 236 miles
4hrs **A5 E17 / 54**

➡ **MARAC** 295 miles
5hrs **A31 E17 / 21**

➡ **DIJON** 351 miles
6hrs 10 **A31 E17 & E15 A6**

➡ **MACON** 395 miles
7hr **A6 E15**

➡ **BOURG-en-BRESSE** 426 miles
7hrs 50 **A40 E62**

➡ **GENEVA** 491 miles
8hrs 20 **A40 E25**

➡ **CLUSES** 530 miles
9hrs **D902, D194 and D28**
Tolls End to the resort.

➡ **MORZINE**
7hr 58

KM Distance **548 miles** (882 km)
⏱ **Drive time** **9 hours 40 mins**
⛽ **Fuel** **£50**
€ **Tolls** **£28**

Airports & Fly Drive Guide

1st- Geneva (CH) - 1 hrs 25
➡ Cluses - **D902, D194** and **D28** = **52 miles**

2nd- Grenoble - 2 hrs 50
➡ **A41 E712** and all routes north via **Cluses** = **126 miles**

3rd- Lyon - 2 hrs 45
➡ **A43, A41** and all routes north via **Cluses** = **132 miles**

⏱ **DRIVE TIME -** nixon www.nixonnow.com

France
Risoul

Mapping Page 52 A4

ROUTE PLANNER

CALAIS	0 miles

along the **A16 - A26**
E15 / E17
Toll Road

REIMS	168 miles
2hrs 55	A26 **A4** **E17 / 50**
CHALONS en CHAMPAGNE	
3hrs 15	A26 **E17**
TROYES	236 miles
4hrs	A5 **E17 / 54**
MARAC	295 miles
5hrs	A31 **E17 / 21**
DIJON	351 miles
6hrs 10	A31 **E17 & E15 A6**
MACON	395 miles
7hr	A6 **E15**
LYON	471 miles
8hrs 50	A43 **E70 A48 E711**
GRENOBLE	537 miles
9hrs 26 | Head south to **Le Pont de-claix** and pick up
Tolls End the **N91** and **N94** via **Briancon**. Then head south along the **N94**, **D902**, **D86** and **D186** up to the resort. |

| RISOUL | |

KM	Distance	631miles *(1016km)*
⏱	Drive time	11 hours 35 mins
⛽	Fuel	£59
€	Tolls	£35

Top Lift
2750m.
Resort Height
1650m.
Vertical Drop
1100m.
Number of Runs
104
Longest Run
8km
Slopes
180km of piste
● ● Beginner
55% of the runs
● Intermediate
35% of the runs
● Advanced
10% of the runs

Cross-Country
40km of tracks
Snowboarding
Half-pipe & Park
Snow Season
Dec to May
Snowmaking
10% of pistes
Number of lifts
57
Up Lift Capicity
40,000 per hour
Mountain Cafes
5

On the Slopes - Risoul is located in the south of France, between Gap and Briancon, and combined with the neighbouring resort Vars, the whole area offers about 180 km of very good snowboarding, skiing and cross-country terrain. Although this is a low key resort, it is nevertheless a good one and a place that can boast good annual snow conditions, aided by the resorts high altitude. It's a mountain suited to everyone, and although the Risoul has a lot of good terrain on its own, the link with nearby Vars extends the possibilities even further. Long been a popular snowboard resort, skiers have been slow to catch on to the possibilities and are missing out – the mountain has plenty on offer from easy slopes for novice skiers to some cool back country areas for freeride snowboarders. Experts may look at the local piste map and come to the conclusion that there is not a lot for them to challenge, but they would be wrong, as there are lots of challenging steeps that would take a number of weeks rather, than days to conquer such as in Pic de Razies, Melezet and Platte De La Nonne, or Pic De La Mayt areas – not for the squeamish. Beginners have a good area to progress from, and if your are a first time boarder, then go to the Accueil to reach the snowboard kindergarten – a short and easy run that is perfect for your first bumps. Freestyle boarders should take De Cezier chair to reach Surfland, where the jibbing begins. This playground (which is akin to paradise), has a boardercross run, rails, quarter-pipes, and a pro-jump over a bus, and one of the best halfpipes in Europe.

Off the Slopes - Risoul is a small village where the inhabitants still treat you as a guest rather than a nuisance. There is a good selection of slopeside accommodation, with seven nights in an apartment costing from _390 per person. Eating out is cool at places like Snack Attack, but for night-life, head to the Yeti (little Holland), where you must drink more booze than the Dutch dude, then leave him on the floor and take off with his girlfriend.

Verdict - Excellent resort despite the slow lifts. Reasonable local services. 7/10

COST INDICATOR

Budget   Moderate   Very Expensive   Criminal

i - **Information** - 0033 (0) 492 460 260
www.risoul.com

✈ **Airports & Fly Drive Guide**

1st- Grenoble - 3 hrs 15
Le Pont de-Claix - **N91** and all routes via **Briancon** = **126 miles**

2nd- Lyon - 3 hrs 40
Grenoble, **N91** and all routes via **Briancon** = **158 miles**

3rd- Geneva (CH) - 4 hrs
A41 **E712**, Grenoble, **N91** all roads via **Briancon** = **182 miles**

France
Saint Lary

Mapping Page 49 E5

ROUTE PLANNER

CALAIS	0 miles

along the **A16** **E402**
Toll Road

AMIENS	94 miles
1hr 40	A16 **E402**
PARIS	167 miles
2hrs 50	Ring road south via Antony to the **A10** **E05**
ORLEANS	245 miles
4hrs 15	A71 **E09**
LIMOGES	413 miles
7hrs	A20 **E09**
MONTAAUBAN	499 miles
8hr 40	A62 **E09** **E72**
TOULOUSE	594 miles
10hrs 5	south around Toulouse, and pick up the **A64** **E80** via **Muret**.
Tolls End
LA BARTHE-de-NESTE	
D929	670 miles
ARREAU	665 miles
12hrs | D929, **D19** to the resort |

| ST LARY | |
9hr 22

KM	Distance	692 miles *(1114 km)*
⏱	Drive time	12 hours 10 mins
⛽	Fuel	£64
€	Tolls	£33

Top Lift
2450m.
Resort Height
1600m.
Vertical Drop
850m.
Number of Runs
40
Longest Run
4km
Slopes
90km of piste
● ● Beginner
74% of the runs
● Intermediate
14% of the runs
● Advanced
12% of the runs

Cross-Country
10km of tracks
Snowboarding
Half-pipe & Park
Snow Season
Dec to April
Snowmaking
15% of pistes
Number of lifts
32
Up Lift Capicity
25,200 per hour
Mountain Cafes
3

On the Slopes - This is a large and typical Pyrenean resort located in the South of the country and dates back to the 1950's. The main village of Saint Lary lies at 630 metres in the Aure Valley and above are two smaller villages, Saint Lary La Cabane at 1,600 metres, and Saint Lary Pla D'Adret at 1,700 metres. All three are connected by a series of lifts, with the upper villages reachable by road, or from Saint Lary by the cable car, which takes you to the slopes. If you think that most French ski resorts are massive purpose-built shams, St Lary should surely help change your perception – it's a very friendly place that gives you lots of fun both on the mountain and away from it. The slopes are wonderfully presented and the perfect place for beginners to get their legs, although it's a mountain that's best suited to those who have been on skis before. The easy blues spread out across the resort are perfect for learning on, with a mixture of chair lifts and drags to ferry you around. The simple runs reached from Saint Lary Pla D'Adret are the perfect starting point, before tackling the Vallon Du Portet trails. The Corniche is also a nice long easy blue run for intermediates and novices alike. However, this is a popular resort which results in a number of long lift queues, especially at weekends and during school holidays. The area only sets about 10km of cross-country tracks, but if you look out, you'll find more. Snowboarders who like to to get air will find the terrain park on the Espiaube very interesting with its boardercross circuit, lined with a kickers and hits. There is a good halfpipe lower down the mountain as well.

Off the Slopes - St Lary is laid out along a main street where you'll find chalets and hotels. Services are extremely good here, without the hustle and bustle of tourist traps. Although somewhat limited, most facilities are found in Saint Lary, rather than the other two villages. Eating and evening hangouts are quiet and tame and at the same time fairly inexpensive. The Latino and Les Chandelles are two of the most popular bars.

Verdict - A pleasant alternative to the big northern areas. Good facilities. 6/10

COST INDICATOR

Budget   Moderate   Very Expensive   Criminal

i - **Information** - 0033 (0) 562 395 081
www.saintlary.com

✈ **Airports & Fly Drive Guide**

1st- Toulouse (F) - 2 hrs 20
A64 **E80** via **ARREAU** D929, D19 = **95 miles**

2nd- Barcelona (S) - 6 hrs
Head north via **Lleida** along the **A2**, **N-240**, **C233**, **N230**, **D618**, **D125** and **D929** to the resort = **252 miles**

DRIVE TIME - nixon® www.nixonnow.com

Saint Martin

ROUTE PLANNER

CALAIS 0 miles
along the **A16 - A26**
E15 / E17
Toll Road

REIMS 168 miles 2hrs 55
A26 A4 E17 / 50

CHALONS en CHAMPAGNE 3hrs 15
A26 E17

TROYES 236 miles 4hrs
A5 E17 / 54

MARAC 295 miles 5hrs
A31 E17 / 21

DIJON 351 miles 6hrs 10
A39 E21

DOLE 363 miles 7hrs
A39 E21

BOURG-en-BRESSE 426 miles 7hrs 15
E21 A40

ALBERTVILE 537 miles 9hrs 30
Tolls End
N90 to Moutiers.
Then take the **D915 &**
D90 up to the resort.

ST MARTIN 7hr 58

Distance 566 miles *(911km)*
Drive time 10 hours 20 mins
Fuel £52
Tolls £35

Specifications

Top Lift 3200m.
Resort Height 1450m.
Vertical Drop 1500m.
Number of Runs 280
Longest Run 8km
Slopes 600km of piste
● Beginner 40% of the runs
◐ Intermediate 50% of the runs
● Advanced 10% of the runs

Cross-Country 120km of tracks
Snowboarding Half-pipe & Park
Snow Season Dec to May
Snowmaking 15% of pistes
Number of lifts 198
Up Lift Capicity 243,300 per hour
Mountain Cafes 43

On the Slopes - It's difficult to regard the tiny ski area of St Martin de Belleville as a resort in it's own right, as it is one of the base areas for the outer slopes of the massive Three Valleys ski region. With the terrain of Courchevel, Meribel, Val Thorens and the nearest neighbour, Les Menuires located practically on it's doorstep and accessible on the same lift ticket, you can access all the benefits of a mega resort, yet still enjoy the lower slopes of St Martin de Belleville as you ski on sunny, un-crowded slopes without having to join long queues. Getting to the slopes is a dawdle as there is a new gondola that takes you from the base area to the runs within five minutes. The type of users who will enjoy the slopes around the resort will be novice to intermediate skiers and snowboarders, but the more advanced can quickly and easily access the vast playgrounds around the Three Valleys – you won't go without for long. There are some okay off-piste areas close to home when conditions permit, but the more challenging terrain is to be found around the Three Valleys. St Martin de Belleville is not noted for vast amounts of natural snow, but the resort has done well to invest heavily in snowmaking to keep the lower altitude runs covered and useable through most of the season. One minor disappointment that beginners may notice is how little there is once they have mastered the main nursery slopes and Snowboarders may also find that this not a place for them if they like terrain parks and halfpipes. However, cross-country skiers should love this area. There are miles and miles of excellent tracks to explore, with routes through trees and along side open fields.

Off the Slopes - This is a lovely picture postcard resort full of character, charm with a warm French atmosphere. Local services are pleasant with rustic hotels and chalets dotted around the hilly village. Eating out and nightlife is rather limited, but that's not to say there aren't any options, there are some wonderful restaurants and some nice quite cosy bars.

Verdict - Wonderful resort with easy slopes, but it's all very basic. 5/10

COST INDICATOR

Budget   Moderate   Very Expensive   Criminal

i - **Information** - 0033 (0) 479 002 000
www.st-martin-belleville.com

Airports & Fly Drive Guide

1st- Grenoble - 2 hrs 20
A41, **E712** and all routes via Albertville = 105 miles

2nd- Geneva (CH) - 2 hrs 15
A41 E712 via **Annecy** & Albertville = 86 miles

3rd - Lyon - 2 hrs 25
A43 & E70 and all routes via Albertville = 112 miles

St Sorlin-d'Arves

ROUTE PLANNER

CALAIS 0 miles
along the **A16 - A26**
E15 / E17
Toll Road

REIMS 168 miles 2hrs 55
A26 A4 E17 / 50

CHALONS en CHAMPAGNE 3hrs 15
A26 E17

TROYES 236 miles 4hrs
A5 E17 / 54

MARAC 295 miles 5hrs
A31 E17 / 21

DIJON 351 miles 6hrs 10
A31 E17 & E15 A6

MACON 395 miles 7hrs
A6 E15

LYON 471 miles 8hrs 50
E70 A43, A430

CHAMBERY 533 miles 9hr 52
To La Chambery, then south down the **D926**
Tolls End to the resort.

ST SORLIN-d'ARVES

Distance 592 miles *(953 km)*
Drive time 10 hours 44 mins
Fuel £67
Tolls £35

Specifications

Top Lift 2250m.
Resort Height 1450m.
Vertical Drop 800m.
Number of Runs 110
Longest Run 7km
Slopes 300km of piste
● Beginner 45% of the runs
◐ Intermediate 45% of the runs
● Advanced 10% of the runs

Cross-Country 8km of tracks
Snowboarding Half-pipe & Park
Snow Season Dec to April
Snowmaking 16 cannons
Number of lifts 51
Up Lift Capicity 3,000 per hour
Mountain Cafes 4

On the Slopes - St Sorlin-d'Arves is relatively unknown outside of France. Located north east of Grenoble within the Maurinne Valley, it's a collection of resorts that includes Le Corbier and La Tonsure and form an up-and-coming circuit boasting over 300km of graded pistes which is constantly being expanded. Lifts connect much of the area and new lifts are being planned all the time. St Sorlin-d'Arves is not the biggest area here, but it is one of the more interesting both on the slopes and around the resort. Annual snow levels are good and lift lines are almost non-existent. The slopes are reached from the village centre and rise up over the La Blame and Les Persons Mountains. Most of the runs here are intermediate with very little for experts, however, Les Persons does hold some decent off-piste terrain. Skiers planning a week's holiday may find that another visit will be needed if you want to explore the whole region, but if you are only going to hang out at St Soling or up at St Jean, then a six day stay will be sufficient to get around every run. Beginners have a wonderful mountain that offers nursery slopes close to the village with plenty of slopes higher up on which to progress, in particular the slopes on Le Blame, or should you wish to go further afield then the green and blues that run down into Le Corbier. Snowboarding is as popular here as any place but the resort is not geared up for providing a terrain park, what's more 33 of the 51 lifts in the area are drag lifts, which won't please drag lift virgins.

Off the Slopes - St Sorlin is a pleasing village full of charm and character. It is neither expensive nor shoddy and will appeal to families who want a laid-back retreat offering good local amenities. There are a couple of hotels and a few self-catering apartments available, well located for the slopes and village area. The choice of restaurants is limited but nevertheless you can get a decent meal out at affordable prices. Nightlife is very quiet indeed, with only a couple of very laid-back bars to choose from.

Verdict - A friendly, enjoyable resort that is perfect for novices and families. 6/10

COST INDICATOR

Budget   Moderate   Very Expensive   Criminal

i - **Information** - 0033 (0) 479 597 330
www.saintsorlindarves.com

Airports & Fly Drive Guide

1st- Grenoble - 2 hrs
Le Pont de-Claix - **N526** & **D926** = 77 miles

2nd- Lyon - 2 hrs 25
A43 E70 Chambery & **D926** = 115 miles

3rd- Geneva (CH) - 2 hrs 30
A41 E71, A43 & D926 = 116 miles

DRIVE TIME - nixon • www.nixonnow.com

France
Serre Chevalier

Mapping Page 47 F7

Top Lift
3850m.
Resort Height
1200m.
Vertical Drop
1630m.
Number of Runs
111
Longest Run
8km
Slopes
250km of piste
● ● *Beginner*
20% of the runs
● *Intermediate*
68% of the runs
● **Advanced**
12% of the runs

Cross-Country
10km of tracks
Snowboarding
Half-pipe & Park
Snow Season
Dec to May
Snowmaking
15% of pistes
Number of lifts
76
Up Lift Capicity
70,700 per hour
Mountain Cafes
13

On the Slopes - There are a couple of points worth knowing about the Serre Chevalier region: one: it is an absolutely fantastic resort, quite simply one of the best in France, two: it can get extremely busy at certain periods. Stretched along the valley is a collection of small villages that give access to a mountain that is hard to beat. Not many resorts offer the amount of off-pistes, tree runs, moguls, gullies, powder fields and natural freestyle terrain as this gem of a place. They really do have it all here, despite the fact that many of the lifts are old and something of a trial in themselves, not to mention that there is occasionally the mother of all lifts queues. Serre Chevalier is a major resort and holds it's own in the big league. What also makes it stand out is that unlike the big purpose-built affairs, Serre Chevalier has developed over time and seldom resembles a theme park. There are old and new buildings, both on and off the slopes all of which blend in perfectly. This mountain is the ultimate adrenaline rush and no matter what standard of skier or snowboarder you are, you will love it and will want to return every season. Beginners have lots of nursery slopes throughout the area with some of the best around Le Monetiers, local ski schools are also particularly good with plenty of English speaking instructors. Snowboarders are particularly well catered for, with a boarder-cross circuit, a halfpipe with tunes, and lots of natural hits.

Off the Slopes - Serre Chevalier is a reasonably priced resort with lots of accommodation in a curious blend of a rustic yet modern setting. Briancon is the largest place to stay, but is not convenient for the main slopes. Chantemerle and Villeneuve (a few miles apart) offer the best facilities nearer the slopes and have plenty of restaurants to choose from, offering mainly traditional French dishes. Highly rated is the Noctambule and Le Glacier. Nightlife is a bit hit and miss, there are lively bars but also some expensive discos. Good hangouts are the Underground, the Yeti, X-treme's or the Frog.

ROUTE PLANNER

🛣️ **CALAIS**	0 miles	
	along the **A16 - A26**	
	E15 / E17	
	Toll Road	
➡️ **REIMS** 2hrs 55	168 miles	
	A26 A4 E17 / 50	
➡️ **CHALONS en CHAMPAGNE** 3hrs 15		
	A26 E17	
➡️ **TROYES** 4hrs	236 miles	
	A5 E17 / 54	
➡️ **MARAC** 5hrs	295 miles	
	A31 E17 / 21	
➡️ **DIJON** 6hrs 10	351 miles	
	A31 E17 & E15 A6	
➡️ **MACON** 7hrs	395 miles	
	A6 E15	
➡️ **LYON** 8hrs 50	471 miles	
	A43 E70 A48 E711	
➡️ **GRENOBLE** 9hrs 26	537 miles	
🚊 *Tolls End*	Head south to **Le Pont de-claix** and pick up the **N91** direction **Briancon.**	

➡️ **SERRE CHEVALIER**

📏 **Distance**	**600 miles** (997km)
🕐 **Drive time**	**10 hours 40 mins**
⛽ **Fuel**	**£55**
€ **Tolls**	**£35**

✈️ **Airports & Fly Drive Guide**

1st- Grenoble - **2 hrs 20**
➡️ Le Pont de-Claix - **N91** and all routes to **Briancon** = **95 miles**

2nd- Lyon - **2 hrs 30**
➡️ Grenoble, **N91** and all routes to **Briancon** = **122 miles**

3rd- Geneva (CH) - **3 hrs 10**
➡️ **A41 E712**, Grenoble, **N91** all roads to **Briancon** = **158 miles**

Verdict - A perfect mountain no matter what you're looking for, but expensive. **10/10**

COST INDICATOR
Budget   Moderate   Very Expensive   Criminal

i - **Information** - 0033 (0) 492 249 898
www.serre-chevalier.com

France
Tignes

Mapping Page 47 E8

Top Lift
3450m.
Resort Height
1550m.
Vertical Drop
1900m.
Number of Runs
65
Longest Run
10km
Slopes
300km of piste
● ● *Beginner*
8% of the runs
● *Intermediate*
69% of the runs
● **Advanced**
24% of the runs

Cross-Country
48km of tracks
Snowboarding
Half-pipe & Park
Snow Season
All year round
Snowmaking
40% of pistes
Number of lifts
97
Up Lift Capicity
110,000 per hour
Mountain Cafes
15

On the Slopes - Tignes is probably the most famous resort in Frances, surely the best all-round activity centre in the country. Tignes is in the super-league and this is an amazing mountain with an unbelievable amount of diverse terrain. You don't have to be a good skier to enjoy this place, but it says much for the mountain and diversity of terrain to find that experts also find plenty to keep them coming back. No other resort has this amount of easy accessible off-piste terrain and all of it is on a mountain with one of the best snow records in Europe. Visitors to Tignes first have to pass over an impressive dam (sufferers of vertigo should keep their eyes closed as you go over as it's a long way down) and is the close neighbour of Val d'Isere, which it is linked to via the slopes. By road the two areas are a considerable distance apart which help preserve the unique characteristics of each areas. Together they have some 300km of mountain terrain with pistes that are immaculately groomed and although not always necessary, snow cannons are used to top up any thin sections when they appear. Where Tignes can be let down is the minimal number of home runs for novices, but in general this is a good first-timer's resort. It's a top place for snowboarders to make good use of the natural terrain features and the ones who take advantage of the summer snow conditions. You can ski or snowboard at any time of the year thanks to the glacier, but during the summer, there are so many other sporting activities do to its impossible to list them all.

Off the Slopes - Tignes is a drab and ugly place, however most of its accommodation is located either on, or very close to the slopes. There are lots of apartment blocks, hotels and chalets to choose from, but nothing is cheap. Every type of food is available with a good selection of restaurants. Nightlife starts early and ends late – in fact, for some it never ends. This is a major party resort, but you will never have enough funds to keep going in the bars or clubs, as drinks prices are shocking.

ROUTE PLANNER

🛣️ **CALAIS**	0 miles	
	along the **A16 - A26**	
	E15 / E17	
	Toll Road	
➡️ **REIMS** 2hrs 55	168 miles	
	A26 A4 E17 / 50	
➡️ **CHALONS en CHAMPAGNE** 3hrs 15		
	A26 E17	
➡️ **TROYES** 4hrs	236 miles	
	A5 E17 / 54	
➡️ **MARAC** 5hrs	295 miles	
	A31 E17 / 21	
➡️ **DIJON** 6hrs 10	351 miles	
	A39 E21	
➡️ **DOLE** 7hrs	363 miles	
	A39 E21	
➡️ **BOURG-en-BRESSE** 7hrs 15	426 miles	
	E21, A40, N508, N90	
🚊 *Tolls End*		
➡️ **MOUTIERS** 10hrs	555 miles	
	D85, N90, D84 and **D902** to the resort.	

➡️ **TIGNES**

📏 **Distance**	**608 miles** (979km)
🕐 **Drive time**	**11 hours**
⛽ **Fuel**	**£56**
€ **Tolls**	**£30**

✈️ **Airports & Fly Drive Guide**

1st- Geneva (CH) - **2 hrs 40**
➡️ **A41 E712** south and all routes via **Moutiers** = **115 miles**

2nd- Grenoble - **3 hrs**
➡️ **A48, A41, E712** and all routes via **Moutiers** = **130 miles**

3rd- Lyon - **3 hrs 5**
➡️ **A43 & E70** and all routes via **Moutiers** = **137 miles**

Verdict - No1 French summer resort but spoiled by being too expensive. **10/10**

COST INDICATOR
Budget   Moderate   Very Expensive   Criminal

i - **Information** - 0033 (0) 479 400 440
www.tignes.com

DRIVE TIME - *nixon* www.nixonnow.com

Val d'Isere

Mapping Page 47 E8

Top Lift
3450m.
Resort Height
1550m.
Vertical Drop
1900m.
Number of Runs
129
Longest Run
4km
Slopes
150km of piste
● ● Beginner
8% of the runs
● Intermediate
68% of the runs
● Advanced
24% of the runs

Cross-Country
52km of tracks
Snowboarding
Half-pipe & Park
Snow Season
Nov to May
Snowmaking
22% of pistes
Number of lifts
97
Up Lift Capicity
110,000 per hour
Mountain Cafes
15

62

On the Slopes - There are two things that distinguish Val d'Isere from other resorts, on one hand you have a mountain with heaps of fantastic and adventurous terrain (some of the best in France in fact), and on the other hand, a resort that can be one of the most awful in Europe and through no fault of the French – the Brits have caught on here and made it their own. However the resort is linked by lift with Tignes and is one of the largest and best-known areas in France and with a massive 300km of linked piste and even more off-piste it's a little slice of heaven. Val's slopes are slightly more suited to beginners at the bottom as they have easier runs to get back to the resort at the end of the day. Beginners also have a couple of free lifts that service the base nursery slopes. On the main slopes, the two resorts share much the similar terrain and snowfall, although Val is slightly lower and so the late season snow melts quicker there. Snowboarders are generally more interested in Tignes as it's more geared up to providing half-pipes and terrain parks and in Val you are more likely to be traversing between slopes, which can be a strain on the old thigh muscles. Those who like to carve down long pistes have lots to get their teeth into especially around the Solaise area. Although this is not a great place for cross-country skiers, there are tracks to appeal, such as those Le Chatelard.

Off the Slopes - Val d'Isere is an ancient village that has resisted much of the sixties style architecture of neighbouring Tignes and has instead maintained a traditional French look. The big problem here is how damned expensive the place is as you simply can't get a cheap bed in any of the hotels or chalets, to do so you will need to base yourself outside Val in the likes of La Grangerie. On the plus side, with almost 100 restaurants, you can eat well here and there are cheap options. Nightlife, however, is expensive no matter where you end up and unfortunately many of the bars are simply dreadful, with way too many idiots overdoing après-ski and drinking beyond their means.

Verdict - Great slopes, but costly and somewhat pompous around town. **9/10**

COST INDICATOR

Budget   Moderate   Very Expensive   Criminal

i - **Information** - 0033 (0) 479 060 660
www.valdisere.com

ROUTE PLANNER

CALAIS 0 miles
along the **A16 - A26**
E15 / E17
Toll Road

→ **REIMS** 168 miles
2hrs 55   A26 A4 **E17 / 50**

→ **CHALONS en CHAMPAGNE**
3hrs 15   A26 **E17**

→ **TROYES** 236 miles
4hrs   A5 **E17 / 54**

→ **MARAC** 295 miles
5hrs   A31 **E17 / 21**

→ **DIJON** 351 miles
6hrs 10   A39 **E21**

→ **DOLE** 363 miles
7hrs   A39 **E21**

→ **BOURG-en-BRESSE** 426 miles
7hrs 15   **E21**, A40, N508, N90

Tolls End
10hrs   **MOUTIERS** 555 miles
D85, N90, **D84** and **D902** to the resort.

→ **VAL D'ISERE**

KM **Distance** 607 miles *(977km)*
⏱ **Drive time** 10 hours 55 mins
⛽ **Fuel** £55
€ **Tolls** £30

[map of Arcs, Coches, Tignes, Val d'Isere, Bonneva region]

✈ **Airports & Fly Drive Guide**

1st- Geneva (CH) - **2 hrs 35**
→ A41 **E712** south and all routes via **Moutiers** = **114 miles**

2nd- Grenoble - **3 hrs**
→ A48, A41, **E712** and all routes via **Moutiers** = **128 miles**

3rd- Lyon - **3 hrs 5**
→ A43 & **E70** and all routes via **Moutiers** = **136 miles**

Valmorel

Mapping Page 47 E7

Top Lift
2550m.
Resort Height
1250m.
Vertical Drop
1300m.
Number of Runs
50
Longest Run
9km
Slopes
150km of piste
● ● Beginner
44% of the runs
● Intermediate
40% of the runs
● Advanced
16% of the runs

Cross-Country
25km of tracks
Snowboarding
Half-pipe & Park
Snow Season
Dec to April
Snowmaking
70% of pistes
Number of lifts
56
Up Lift Capicity
51,500 per hour
Mountain Cafes
7

On the Slopes - Valmorel is a relatively new resort, which is both pleasant and well laid out. Despite having only been established around 20 years ago, it has grown into a friendly, family-orientated centre with slopes that will appeal to everyone and will make for a first class seven-day visit. As a fairly low-level resort, good snow cover is not always guaranteed, and there's not a huge amount of snowmaking in resort, so you can sometimes find yourself on threadbare slopes in the spring. Still, what's good is the convenience of the slopes to many of the hotels, providing good doorstep skiing and snowboarding for many visitors. What it doesn't offer, however, is a great deal of challenging terrain for advanced skiers and boarders and what there is is not particularly long and won't take too much time to conquer. Nevertheless, the slopes have been well planned and set out, making them ideal for leisurely intermediate piste skiing. Valmorel has 50 trails which are linked with St Francois Longchamp, the amount of terrain increases to over 160km, serviced by a series of easy-to-use, but rather slow lifts. Large queues are also a feature although they are manageable and you shouldn't spend more than fifteen minutes queuing in either area. To complement the resort's family reputation the local ski school is highly praised, as are the nursery slopes, which are all near the base lifts. Valmorel has yet to turn into snowboarder's paradise and even though the terrain does lend its self to some basic freeriding and good carving, there is not much to inspire boarders, nor come to that, is there a great deal of convenient cross-country skiing available near the resort.

Off the Slopes - Staying in Valmorel, you certainly get the feeling of being in a purpose-built French ski resort, but it's a nice feeling. Although small and with only an handful of hotels and apartments, what is on offers is of a high standard and it's a great place to bring a family with small children. Eating out is very limited, local attractions almost zero and nightlife very tame indeed, but it's all perfectly adequate.

Verdict - A pleasant family resort **5/10**

COST INDICATOR

Budget   Moderate   Very Expensive   Criminal

i - **Information** - 0033 (0) 479 098 555
www.valmorel.com

ROUTE PLANNER

CALAIS 0 miles
along the **A16 - A26**
E15 / E17
Toll Road

→ **REIMS** 168 miles
2hrs 55   A26 A4 **E17 / 50**

→ **CHALONS en CHAMPAGNE**
3hrs 15   A26 **E17**

→ **TROYES** 236 miles
4hrs   A5 **E17 / 54**

→ **MARAC** 295 miles
5hrs   A31 **E17 / 21**

→ **DIJON** 351 miles
6hrs 10   A39 **E21**

→ **DOLE** 363 miles
7hrs   A39 **E21**

→ **BOURG-en-BRESSE** 426 miles
7hrs 15   **E21** A40

Tolls End
10hrs   **ALBERTVILE** 537 miles
N90 towards **Moutiers**, taking the **D90** & **D990** and **D95** up to the resort.

→ **VALMOREL**

KM **Distance** 561 miles *(903km)*
⏱ **Drive time** 10 hours 15 mins
⛽ **Fuel** £52
€ **Tolls** £35

[map showing Montchavin le C, Champagny-en-Vanois, Valmorel, Méribel, St-Martin-de-Belleville region]

✈ **Airports & Fly Drive Guide**

1st- Geneva (CH) - **2 hrs 5**
→ A41 **E712** via **Annecy** & **Albertville** = **81 miles**

2nd- Grenoble - **2 hrs 15**
→ A41, **E712** and all routes via **Albertville** = **100 miles**

3rd - Lyon - **2 hrs 10**
→ A43 & **E70** and all routes via **Albertville** = **107 miles**

France

Valloire

Mapping **Page** 47 **F7**

Top Lift	3200m.
Resort Height	1800m.
Vertical Drop	1400m.
Number of Runs	67
Longest Run	5km
Slopes	120km of piste

●● *Beginner*
40% of the runs
● *Intermediate*
50% of the runs
● *Advanced*
10% of the runs

Cross-Country
5km of tracks
Snowboarding
Half-pipe & Park
Snow Season
Nov to Aug
Snowmaking
100 cannons
Number of lifts
47
Up Lift Capicity
51,900 per hour
Mountain Cafes
10

On the Slopes - Valloire is a great resort that appeals to most skiers and snowboarders, although not particularly snow-sure. Valloire and its linked cousin Valmeiner are located in the Maurienne valley, with both traditional villages dating back many years. However, it's Valloire that has developed into a modern ski resort while at the same time retaining its identity as an old French farming community. The slopes span out over three main sectors including the terrain in Valmenier, which actually lies over the mountain in a neighbouring valley. Valmenier is reached on the slopes via Crey du Quart, which is also the area that houses some of the best intermediate slopes, which make up the majority of the terrain here. There are challenges for experts; you only need to check out the blacks on Setaz area, to find out for yourself – it's just that there is little to test the serious skier or hardcore snowboarder. The resorts lifts get you around fairly quickly and lift lines are never a major problem except for holiday weekends, but what is often a let-down is the region's snow record as they have to rely on snow cannons particulary for the lower slopes. Still as the best beginners slopes are not at the base, at least novices don't have to learn on thin slivers of muddy stained snow. Cross-country skiers have a few nice areas to slide along when snow permits, while snowboarders can make good on some down some slopes that can be described as good freeriding slopes, but if this is your first snowboard holiday, then be aware that there's a lot of drag lifts here, some 17 in fact, which could prove a bit tricky for novices who have never used a drag before.

Off the Slopes - The resort has a relaxed and welcome feel to it, and fits the image of a rustic French mountain resort perfectly. The village is crammed with local facilities, and has some great accommodation to choose from, some good restaurants – the Gastilleur for instance – and some perfectly adequate bars for a quiet night's drinking without an overabundance of boozy idiots.

ROUTE PLANNER

🚗 **CALAIS** 0 miles
along the **A16 - A26**
E15 / E17
Toll Road

➡ **REIMS** 168 miles `2hrs 55`
A26 A4 E17 / 50

➡ **CHALONS en CHAMPAGNE** `3hrs 15`
A26 E17

➡ **TROYES** 236 miles `4hrs`
A5 E17 / 54

➡ **MARAC** 295 miles `5hrs`
A31 E17 / 21

➡ **DIJON** 351 miles `6hrs 10`
A31 E17 & E15 A6

➡ **MACON** 395 miles `7hrs`
A6 E15

➡ **LYON** 471 miles `8hrs 50`
E70 A43, A430

🅿 *Tolls End*

➡ **CHAMBERY** 533 miles `9hrs 50`
To La Chambery, then south down the **D902** to the resort.

⬇

➡ **VALLOIRE**

🚗 **Distance**	**592 miles**	*(953 km)*
⏱ **Drive time**	**10 hours 20 mins**	
⛽ **Fuel**	**£54**	
€ **Tolls**	**£35**	

✈ **Airports & Fly Drive Guide**

1st- Grenoble - 2 hrs 15
➡ Le Pont de-Claix - **N526** & **D902** = **110 miles**

2nd- Lyon - 2 hrs 20
➡ A43 **E70** Chambery & **D902** = **118 miles**

3rd- Geneva (CH) **- 2 hrs 25**
➡ A41 **E71**, A43 & **D902** = **120miles**

Verdict - In a word 'NICE' with good slopes, but not snow sure. **5/10**

COST INDICATOR

Budget   Moderate   Very Expensive   Criminal

𝒊 - **Information** - 0033 (0) 479 590 396
www.vallorie.net

France

Val Thorens

Mapping **Page** 47 **E7**

Resort Height	3200m.
Top Lift	2610m.
Vertical Drop	810m.
Number of Runs	46
Longest Run	4km
Slopes	150km of piste

●● *Beginner*
48% of the runs
● *Intermediate*
13% of the runs
● *Advanced*
13% of the runs

Cross-Country
10km of tracks
Snowboarding
Half-pipe & Park
Snow Season
Dec to April
Snowmaking
15% of pistes
Number of lifts
25
Up Lift Capicity
20,000 per hour
Mountain Cafes
4

On the Slopes - Val Thorens is one of the big guns in the Three Valleys and the highest built resort in Europe. The Three Valleys, offer 600km of piste and it will take dozens of trips before you get to know it all, that's why the 120km of high-altitude terrain on offer at Val Thorens should be more than enough for even a two week stay. Snowsure and with wonderful open pistes, this is a place for everyone, but despite it being a good mountain with excellent slopes, it can also be scarily busy, as this place is a favourite with tour operators. Val Thorens has been carefully designed so that you don't have to walk far from your accommodation to the slopes or to the shops and restaurants. However: the lifts fan out in all directions, giving instant access to the entire mountain, which is often open until June most years. Not surprisingly, the altitude means this resort enjoys long hours of sunshine and an excellent snow record. Val Thorens is not a place with much for cross-country skiers, but a top place for snowboarders with some great carving piste and a fun-park on the Caron area, which is wired up for sounds and comes loaded with toys.

Off the Slopes - Val Thorens resembles something of a holiday camp on a mountain. The obvious remit when planning this place was, 'get them in, pile them high, and don't worry about how the place looks or feels'. It's the perfect breeding ground for après-ski groups, who flock here by the bucket load. Around the resort, you'll find a number of shopping complexes and more than 45 places to eat, with enough accommodation to sleep 20,000 visitors, mostly in self-catering apartment blocks. Nightlife comes in the form of standard grade loud and boozy après-ski. However, it's not all gloom as there are a number okay hangouts free of tour reps misbehaving with their clients. Amongst the night-spots there is, the Red Fox for sing-a-long etc, the Frog and Roastbeef (what a lame name) a brit style pub, and the Underground, a late night haunt which sadly hasn't a clue what music is about.

ROUTE PLANNER

🚗 **CALAIS** 0 miles
along the **A16 - A26**
E15 / E17
Toll Road

➡ **REIMS** 168 miles `2hrs 55`
A26 A4 E17 / 50

➡ **CHALONS en CHAMPAGNE** `3hrs 15`
A26 E17

➡ **TROYES** 236 miles `4hrs`
A5 E17 / 54

➡ **MARAC** 295 miles `5hrs`
A31 E17 / 21

➡ **DIJON** 351 miles `6hrs 10`
A39 E21

➡ **DOLE** 363 miles `7hrs`
A39 E21

➡ **BOURG-en-BRESSE** 426 miles `7hrs 15`
E21 A40

🅿 *Tolls End*

➡ **ALBERTVILE** 537 miles `10hrs`
N90 to **Moutiers**. Then take the **D915** & **D117** up to the resort.

⬇

➡ **VAL THORENS** `7hr 58`

🚗 **Distance**	**576 miles**	*(927km)*
⏱ **Drive time**	**10 hours 40 mins**	
⛽ **Fuel**	**£54**	
€ **Tolls**	**£35**	

✈ **Airports & Fly Drive Guide**

1st- Geneva (CH) **- 2 hrs 36**
➡ A41 **E712** via Annecy & Albertville = **95 miles**

2nd- Grenoble - 2 hrs 40
➡ A41, **E712** and all routes via Albertville = **115 miles**

3rd- Lyon - 2 hrs 45
➡ A43 & **E70** and all routes via Albertville = **122 miles**

Verdict - Superb slopes, easy access, but pig ugly resort facilities. **8/10**

COST INDICATOR

Budget   Moderate   Very Expensive   Criminal

𝒊 - **Information** - 0033 (0) 479 000 808
www.valthorens.com

⏱ **DRIVE TIME -** *nixon* ® www.nixonnow.com

Germany

Resorts Featured
64 Feldberg
65 Garmisch
65 Schliersee
See page 29 for the index of all resorts.

64

DRIVE ON THE RIGHT

One way street

Autobahn *Motorway*

Customs post

Country identification

No Bicycles

Right turn permitted at red light

Motorway speed	**Open**
Rural speed	**100kph**
Urban speed	**50kph**
Alcohol limit	**50mgs**
Front seatbelts	✔
Rear seatbelts	✔
Kids in front seat	**12**
Legal age to drive	**18**
Warning triangle	Required
First aid kit	Required
Fire extinguisher	Advisable
Snowchains	Advisable

FACT FILE

Country - Bundesrepublik Deutschland
Location - Western Europe
Geography
Germany shares its borders with Austria, Belgium, Czech Republic, Denmark, France, Luxembourg Netherlands, Poland & Switzerland.
Highest Mountain - Zugspitze - 2963m
Coast line & Seas - Baltic Sea and North Sea
Land Area - 357,022 sq km (137,846 sq miles)
Capital - Berlin
Populartion - 82,163,475
Language - German
Religion - 34% Protestant, 34% Catholic, 36% others
Currecny - Euros
Time - GMT + 1 hour, (GMT + 2 hours between March & October)
Electricity Supply - 220volts
Communications - International Country code 0049
Fire 112
Police 110
Ambulance 110
National Tourism - 0049 (0) 231 1816 186
www.germany-tourism.de
Rail Information - www.bahn.de
Bus Information - www.germany-tourism.de
Air Information - www.germany-tourism.de
Weather Information - www.germany-tourism.de
Avalanche Information - 0049 (0) 89 92 14 1210
www.bayern.de/ifw/lwd/
www.wetteronline.de/bayern.htm

Passprts & Visa Requirments
	Passports	Visa
Australian	Yes	No
British	Yes	No
Canadian	Yes	No
USA	Yes	No
EU	ID	No

Duty Free - None EU travellers
200 cigarettes or 100 cigarillos or 50 cigars or 25g of tobacco. 1ltr of spirits over 22% or 21% of fortified wine or spirits up to 22% or 21% of sparkling wine or liqueur and 21 % of still wine. 50g of perfume and €175 worth of goods.
EU travellers - No tarrifs.

Motoring Organisations
ADAC
Am Westpark 8, 81373 Munchen
tel +49 (0) 89 76 76 0

Automobile von Deutschland
Lyoner Str. 16, 60528 Frankfurt
tel +49 (0) 69 66 06 0
http:// www.avd.de - e-mail: avd@avd.de

AIT   FIA

Top Lift	
1448m.	
Resort Height	
945m.	
Vertical Drop	
503m.	
Number of Runs	
23	
Longest Run	
3km	
Slopes	
50km of piste	
● *Beginner*	
60% of the runs	
● *Intermediate*	
30% of the runs	
● *Advanced*	
10% of the runs	

Cross-Country	
60km of tracks	
Snowboarding	
Half-pipe	
Snow Season	
Dec to April	
Snowmaking	
5% of pistes	
Number of lifts	
26	
Up Lift Capicity	
24,050 per hour	
Mountain Cafes	
5	

On the Slopes - Feldberg is situated in the Black Forest in the south of Germany and close to the French and Swiss borders. It's very popular with Germans, yet few skiers outside the country have ever heard of it, let alone visited. Feldberg doesn't rely purely on skiing or snowboarding for it's business, so having a mountain loaded, with lifts, restaurants and miles of terrain is not their ultimate aim – it's open year-round as a tourist and outdoor activities destination, which is obvious when you see how rather low-key everything is here. Feldberg is set at a relatively low altitude, which makes deep snow winters somewhat infrequent. Considering that they have not really invested in snowmaking, as back up when the real stuff is lacking, the season is often shorter than other Alpine environments. By no means is Feldberg a dull resort however, as there is a reasonable amount of terrain and plenty of small ski resort charm – if you are on your first ski holiday or don't fancy the busy French resorts, then Feldberg would be a good alternative. Most of the runs are of an easy nature with a handful of black runs for experts, but those who want to ski or snowboard as many kilometres as possible in a day would do better to go elsewhere. The 50 km of piste are spread out over two mountains and attracts a lot of families and groups at weekends, but the 26 lifts cope well and queues are simply not a problem. One group of users who should particularly enjoy it here are cross-country skiers. When there is good snow cover this region is famed for its acres of tracks through forests.

Off the Slopes - Feldburg is a cosy old town offering a good range of accommodation, from five star hotels to pensions. Around town you are warmly welcomed and presented with numerous and excellent local services, including ice-skating, swimming, an abundance of shops and nice restaurants. However, this is by no means a cheap place, which is evident when you dine out or hit one of the bars where the theme is German through-and-through.

Verdict Basic mountain where beginners can shine. Nice town, but pricey. **5/10**

COST INDICATOR
Budget   Moderate   Very Expensive   Criminal

i - **Information** - 0049 (0) 7655 8019
www.hochschwarzwald.de

ROUTE PLANNER

🏁 **CALAIS** 0 miles
along the **A16 - A26**
E15 / E17
Toll Road

REIMS xxx miles   2hrs 55
A4 E17 / 50

METZ 270 miles   3hrs 15
A4 E25 *Dir Strasbourg*
Tolls End

A35 north to the D4   6hrs 50
⚠ **Enter Germany** 401 miles
B500 to the E35 - 5

OFFENBURG 397 miles
E35 / 52, 5

FREIBURG IM BREISGAU   7hrs 25
433 miles

FELDBERG

KM Distance **463** miles *(745 km)*
Drive time **8** hours **10** mins
Fuel **£42**
Tolls **£27**

✈ **Airports & Fly Drive Guide**

1st- Basel (CH) - 40 minutes
E35, 5 and all routes north = **20 miles**

2nd- Strasbourg - 1 hr 50
10 / 5 E35 / 52 and all routes south = **75 miles**

3rd- Frankfurt - 3 hrs 30
E35, 5 and all routes south = **188 miles**

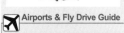

DRIVE TIME - **nixon** www.nixonnow.com

Germany
Garmisch

Mapping Page 88 B2

Top Lift
2830m.
Resort Height
720m.
Vertical Drop
1350m.
Number of Runs
60
Longest Run
3.2km
Slopes
72km of piste
● Beginner
49% of the runs
● Intermediate
49% of the runs
● Advanced
2% of the runs

Cross-Country
150km of tracks
Snowboarding
Half-pipe & Park
Snow Season
Nov to May
Snowmaking
13 cannons
Number of lifts
38
Up Lift Capacity
50,000 per hour
Mountain Cafes
12

On the Slopes - Garmisch, the biggest ski resort in Germany, is located in the south of the country an hour from Munich and a stone's throw from the Austrian border. Garmisch lives up to every impression of a traditional German town that you are likely to have formed in your mind – lederhosen, steins, bar women with large assets and a mountain to rival many French and Austrian ones. Garmisch is an extremely popular sporting town that, as well as providing dozens of sporting facilities, hosts numerous world ranking ski events including ski jumping and back in 1936, it hosted the Winter Olympics. Despite being less famous than nearby Austrian resorts and with consequently less international visitors, you can have a great time skiing or snowboarding on almost crowd-free slopes – apart from German holidays and weekends, when the ski area fills up with visitors from nearby Munich and Salzburg. The slopes sit below the summit of Germany's highest mountain, the Zugspitze and a cable car takes you to the very top – but the top of the mountain area is for sightseeing purposes and is not connected with the main ski slopes. There are actually five ski areas based around Garmisch, all of which can be visited by taking the local bus. On the main mountain, the slopes are divided into four sections and serviced by 38 lifts. The terrain here is mainly of an intermediate level, but adventurous skiers and freeride snowboarders will find plenty to keep them satisfied. Beginners have good nursery slopes around the lower sections to help their progression – as for cross-country skiers; there are loads of excellent tracks.

Off the Slopes - Garmisch caters well for it's visitors – there is a huge selection of places to stay, with services spread out over a wide area. Numerous events are held in the town all year round, which means that as well as being a little pricey; it can also be very busy. Restaurants are plentiful and cater for all tastes, if not all budgets. Nightlife is lively with a Bavarian theme, Euro pop and fine German beer.

Verdict - Not a particularly challenging place. Nice traditional hospitality. **6/10**

COST INDICATOR

Budget   Moderate   Very Expensive   Criminal

i - Information - 0049 (0) 8821 180 700
www.garmisch-partenkirchen.de

ROUTE PLANNER

🏠 **CALAIS** 0 miles
along the **A16 - A26**
E15 / E17
Toll Road

➡ **REIMS** 166 miles
2hrs 55   **A4 E17 / 50**

➡ **METZ** 270 miles
3hrs 15   **A4 E25** Dir Strasbourg
Tolls End

🛣 **A35** north to the **D4**
⚠ **Enter Germany** 401 miles
B500 to the **E35 - 5**

➡ **KARLSRUHE** 424 miles
7hrs 16   **A8 E52**
via Pforzheim

➡ **STUTTGART** 459 miles
7hrs 50   **A8 E52**

➡ **MUNICH** 589 miles
9hrs 58   Travel south of Munich heading for Garmisch along the **E533 A95, B2** and **B23** to the resort.

➡ **GARMISCH**

KM **Distance** 636 miles (1023 km)
⏱ **Drive time** 11 hours 30 mins
⛽ **Fuel** £59
€ **Tolls** £27

✈ **Airports & Fly Drive Guide**

1st- Innsbruck - 1 hr 15
➡ **A12 E60** north to **Germany** via the **177** and **B23** = **40 miles**

2nd- Munich - 1 hr 50
➡ **E533 A95, B2** and **B23** south = **80 miles**

3rd- Stuttgart - 3 hrs 15
➡ **A8, E52** and all routes via **Munich** = **164 miles**

Germany
Schliersee

Mapping Page 88 A3

Top Lift
1700m.
Resort Height
1175.
Vertical Drop
525m.
Number of Runs
31
Longest Run
3.2km
Slopes
35km of piste
● Beginner
24% of the runs
● Intermediate
62% of the runs
● Advanced
14% of the runs

Cross-Country
30km of tracks
Snowboarding
Half-pipe & Park
Snow Season
Dec to April
Snowmaking
0% of pistes
Number of lifts
13
Up Lift Capacity
13.700
Mountain Cafes
5

On the Slopes - Schliersee is popular with skiers and snowboarders from Munich and other nearby towns, which makes it busy yet particularly fun at weekends and during holiday periods – the rest of the time the resort is next to empty. For those who know their snowboard history, Schliersee is the hometown of the sports European carving legends Peter Bauer who, in the early days riding for Burton, made it look so easy as he carved up mountains with grace, style and at scary speeds. On the mountain there are two areas that make up the terrain – the Taubenstein slopes are the quieter ones and the runs are mainly intermediate, with a few easy runs and the odd testing section. The Taubenstein is also the spot where you will find the best powder after a dump, but as the snow record is patchy, expect powder days to be a bonus rather than the norm. Over on the Stumpfling-an-Sutten area, things are similar but as there is more choice it gets more crowded – the modern lift system copes well, however. Snowboarders have long graced these slopes and it has become a popular hangout, especially for freestylers who have a half pipe near the quad chair lift and a terrain park down by the Sonnenalm, which is loaded with all the normal facilities. Beginners have a good mountain even though the number of easy runs is limited in both choice and length.

Off the Slopes - Accommodation, shops, restaurants and other facilities can be found in either Schliersee itself or nearby Rottach. Schliersee is the bigger of the two towns with plenty of high quality services on offer, while smaller Rottach has less facilities and consequently fewer visitors – and lower prices. Both areas are notable for their good value for money and budget lodging and dining can be found if you look around. Evenings begin at the Braustuberl Bar, but watch out for the big waitresses who eat visitors for supper. Later, head for the Ski Alm Andreas where you can drink until late, listen to decent tunes and try your luck with a local.

Verdict - A bustling resort at weekends and appealing for beginners. **5/10**

COST INDICATOR

Budget   Moderate   Very Expensive   Criminal

i - Information - 0049 (0) 8026 60650
www.spitzingsee.de.

ROUTE PLANNER

🏠 **CALAIS** 0 miles
along the **A16 - A26**
E15 / E17
Toll Road

➡ **REIMS** 166 miles
2hrs 55   **A4 E17 / 50**

➡ **METZ** 270 miles
3hrs 15   **A4 E25** Dir Strasbourg
Tolls End

🛣 **A35** north to the **D4**
⚠ **Enter Germany** 401 miles
B500 to the **E35 - 5**

➡ **KARLSRUHE** 424 miles
7hrs 16   **A8 E52**
via Pforzheim

➡ **STUTTGART** 459 miles
7hrs 50   **A8 E52**

➡ **MUNICH** 589 miles
9hrs 58   Travel south of Munich heading for the **E45/52. A8.** Leave at junction 99 for the **B427** and **B307** via Miesbach to reach the resort.

➡ **SCHLIERSEE**

KM **Distance** 652 miles (1050 km)
⏱ **Drive time** 11 hours 20 mins
⛽ **Fuel** £59
€ **Tolls** £27

✈ **Airports & Fly Drive Guide**

1st- Innsbruck (A)- 1 hr 15
➡ **A12** north into **Germany** & **E45/60** & **B307** = **75 miles**

2nd- Munich - 1 hr 30
➡ **E533 and A8** and all routes south via Miesbach = **72 miles**

3rd- Salzburg (A)- 1 hr 35
➡ **E52/60** and the **B307** = **74 miles**

⏱ DRIVE TIME - 🏂 **nixon**® www.nixonnow.com

Resorts Featured
66   Cairngorm
67   Nevis Range
67   The Lecht
See page 29 for the index of all resorts.

DRIVE ON
THE LEFT

No Entry

No right turn

Height limit

Country identification

GB

Swing Bridge

Weight per axel limit

Motorway speed	70mph	
Rural speed	60mph	
Urban speed	30mph	
Alcohol limit	80mgs	
Front seatbelts	✔	
Rear seatbelts	✔	
Kids in front seat	12	
Legal age to drive	17	
Warming triangle	Advisable	
First aid kit	Advisable	
Fire extinguisher	Advisable	
Snowchains	Advisable	

FACT FILE

Country - United Kindgom of Great Britain & Nortern Ireland
Location - Western Europe
Geography
The UK has no land boarders with any international country.
Highest Mountain - Ben Nevis - 1344m
Coast line & Seas - Atlantic Ocean, North Sea
Land Area - 242,910 sq km (93,788 sq miles)
Capital - London
Populartion - 59,755,700
Language - English, Welsh, Gaelic
Religion - 54% Protestant,
10% Catholic, 36% others
Currecny - Pound Sterling
Time - GMT + 1 hour, (between March & October)
Electricity Supply - 240volts
Communications - International Country code 0044
Fire 999
Police 999
Ambulance 999
National Tourism - 0044 (020) 8563 3000
www.visitbritain.com
Rail Information - www.visitbritain.com
Bus Information - www.visitbritain.com
Air Information - www.visitbritain.com
Gateway International Airports
London - Edinburgh - Glasgow - Inverness
Weather Information - www.metro.govt.uk
Avalanche Information - www.sais.gov.uk

Passprts & Visa Requirments

	Passports	Visa
Australian	Yes	No
British	Yes	No
Canadian	Yes	No
USA	Yes	No
EU	ID	No

Duty Free - None EU travellers
200 cigarettes or 100 cigarillos or 50 cigars or 25g of tobacco. 1ltr of spirits over 22% or 21% of fortified wine or spirits up to 22% or 21% of sparkling wine or liqueur and 21 % of still wine. 50g of perfume and £145 worth of goods.
EU travellers - No tarrifs.

Motoring Organisations
RAC
89-91 Pall Mall, SW1Y 5HS London
tel +44 (0) 207 930 23 45 http:// www.rac.co.uk

AA
Norfolk House, Priestley Rd, Basingstoke
tel +44 (0) 990 44 88 66
e-mail: theaa.co.uk

 AIT FIA

Top Lift 1080m.
Resort Height 550m.
Vertical Drop 530m.
Number of Runs 28
Longest Run 3km
Slopes 37km of piste
● *Beginner* 34% of the runs
● *Intermediate* 62% of the runs
● **Advanced** 4% of the runs
Cross-Country 50km of tracks
Snowboarding Half-pipe
Snow Season Jan to April
Snowmaking 0% of pistes
Number of lifts 16
Up Lift Capicity -
Mountain Cafes 3

On the Slopes - The Cairngorms are a low-level mountain range, which many locals simply refer to as the 'Hills'. Recent years have seen numerous changes, in 2003 the area became a national park, yet prior to that, it was decided it would be a good idea to blow 20 million pounds on a funicular train to improve the access to the mountain. While it is true to say that the funicular has made access to the summit far easier in the summer months, during the winter it doesn't really matter as the mountain has such a poor snow record that the slopes seem to be closed far more than they are open. It's often said in these parts that if you can ski on the Cairngorms you will be able to ski anywhere, and there may be some truth in that, however, Scotland's snow record is getting worse every year and when there is enough for the lifts to open, the cost of buying a lift ticket and using the mountain facilities make it super expensive. On the plus side, when it does snow, the sun is out, and the kids are in school, you can have a great day on slopes that are best suited to intermediates with only the White Lady and West Wall for experts to try. Beginners will struggle to find a decent nursery slope, but with some good ski instruction facilities available by locals, help is at hand. Snowboarding took off here back in 1989 when Tony Brown opened the UK's first snowboard shop (The Snowboard Academy) – there is still a good local scene and a terrain park of sorts when snow permits.

Off the Slopes - Aviemore is only twenty minutes away with hotels, chalets, caravans, youth hostels and a bunk house. There are many other villages nearby that offer good lodging such as in Kincraig where you can stay at the likes of highly rated Ossian Hotel. Good facilities can also be found in Kingussie, Carrbridge or Grantown. The area has dozens of restaurants including good fast food outlets. Evenings are not aprés-ski style, they are Scottish: simple, welcoming and lively.

Verdict - Very poor snow record and pricey lifts, but good local facilities. **3**/10

COST INDICATOR

Budget   Moderate   Very Expensive   Criminal

i - **Information -** 0044 (0) 479 861 261
www.cairngormmountain.com

ROUTE PLANNER

LONDON 0 miles
along the **M1 - M6**
M6 - *(M6 Toll road cost from £2).*

→ **BIRMINGHAM** 98 miles
1hr 50   M6

→ **PRESTON** 215 miles
3hrs 50   M6

→ **CARLISE** 303 miles
5hrs 15   A74/M74

Enter Scotland

→ **GLASGOW** 394 miles
6hrs 50   M8- M73 - A80- M80

→ **STIRLING** 415 miles
7hrs 14   M9- A9

→ **PERTH** 447 miles
7hrs 55   A9

→ **AVIEMORE** 530 miles
9hrs 50   B9152

→ **CAIRNGORM**

KM **Distance** 539 miles (868 km)
Drive time 10 hours 15 mins
Fuel £48
Tolls

✈ **Airports & Fly Drive Guide**

1st- Inverness - 50 mins
→ B9039, A96, A9 and the B9152 = 36 miles

2nd- Aberdeen - 2 hrs 30
→ A944, and all routes east via Aviemore = 85 miles

3rd- Edinburgh - 2 hrs 50
→ M90 all routes north via Perth = 123 miles

DRIVE TIME - **nixon** www.nixonnow.com

Nevis Range

Top Lift	
1220m.	

Resort Height
100m.
Vertical Drop
580m.
Number of Runs
35
Longest Run
1.6km
Slopes
20km of piste
●● *Beginner*
65% of the runs
● *Intermediate*
25% of the runs
● *Advanced*
10% of the runs

Cross-Country
-
Snowboarding
Half-pipe & Park
Snow Season
Jan to April
Snowmaking
Zero
Number of lifts
12
Up Lift Capacity
9,600 per hour
Mountain Cafes
2

On the Slopes - Nevis Range has only been running as a ski resort since 1989 – back then it seemed like a good idea to invest in ski facilities as Scotland used to get regular snowfalls. The people who bankrolled the development may be regretting it now as far as the winter is concerned, but they have been pretty shrewd, here and rather than rely purely on snow and skiers in the winter, Nevis has become an year round resort with summer activities the money earner. A couple of years ago they opened a fantastic mountain bike trail set back into the contours of the land and there are plenty of other activities for summer visitors including a gondola that takes coach loads of pensioners up to the mountain café for a cup of tea. During the winter when the white stuff has fallen, the modern gondola and T-bars are a match for any lift system in the Alps. Where the Nevis Range differs considerably from the Alps is the totally unpredictable weather – largely a mixture of high winds and blizzards. The poor snow record may have something do to with the mountain's location close to the west coast; however, the resort's management shrug off weather related problems, and do their best to look after their visitors. If there is good snow cover, the slopes can get busy at weekends but are next to deserted during the week. The slopes, which have views across Ben Nevis, The UK's highest mountain, offer a choice of short runs for intermediates and some easy slopes for beginners, but there is nothing much here for advanced users. They don't build halfpipes here, however, there are some nice natural hits.

Off the Slopes - There is no accommodation near the slopes and the nearest town is Fort William a fifteen minute drive away, where you will find loads of places to book a bed with affordable rates ranging from £20 per person. The town has lots of decent shops and plenty of places to go for a meal; there are some nice restaurants and a couple of chip shops. Nightlife is very simple, rather loud in places, but nothing too heavy.

Verdict - Better in the summer for mountain biking. Good local amenities. **3**/10

COST INDICATOR

Budget   Moderate   Very Expensive   Criminal

i - **Information** - 0044 (0) 1397 705 825
www.nevisrange.co.uk

ROUTE PLANNER

✈ LONDON 0 miles
along the M1 - M6
M6 - *(M6 Toll road cost from £2).*

→ BIRMINGHAM 96 miles
1hr 50 M6

→ PRESTON 215 miles
3hrs 50 M6

→ CARLISE 303 miles
5hrs 15 A74/M74

Enter Scotland

→ GLASGOW 394 miles
6hrs 30 M8- M898, A82

→ CRIANIARICH 443 miles
8hrs A84, A85, A82

→ FORT WILLIAM 510 miles
9hrs 40 A82

→ NEVIS RANGE

KM **Distance** 516 miles *(830 km)*
⏱ **Drive time** 9 hours 50 mins
⛽ **Fuel** £48
€ **Tolls**

✈ Airports & Fly Drive Guide

1st- Inverness - 1 hr 45
→ A96 west and the A82 south = 72 miles

2nd- Glasgow - 2 hrs 20
→ A82 and all routes north via Crianiarich = 140 miles

3rd- Edinburgh - 3 hrs 15
→ M90 all routes north via Stirling = 138 miles

The Lecht

Top Lift
823m.
Resort Height
643.
Vertical Drop
183m.
Number of Runs
17
Longest Run
1km
Slopes
5km of piste
● *Beginner*
24% of the runs
● *Intermediate*
62% of the runs
● *Advanced*
14% of the runs

Cross-Country
-
Snowboarding
Half-pipe & Park
Snow Season
Dec to April
Snowmaking
10% of pistes
Number of lifts
12
Up Lift Capacity
8.700
Mountain Cafes
1

On the Slopes - Who says that size matters? Certainly not the people that run this tiny resort. Being Scotland's smallest has never bothered them much and in fact, none of the other Scottish resorts do as much or work as hard as they do at The Lecht to provide good activities all year round. Unlike the Cairngorms, they don't think they can compete with the Alps so things are kept in proportion and unlike the Glenshee and Glencoe, they don't want to sell up. The Lecht is the perfect all-Scottish family hangout, with or without snow. Like the rest of Scotland, real snow is not a foregone conclusion, so they have done something about it and installed snowmaking facilities, which really does help to keep the runs open when the other snow centres are closed. The Lecht also suffers slightly less from high winds – it does get windy and cold here, but being located lower and more sheltered than the slopes of Cairngorm and Glenshee has helped. The slopes are located on either side of the main through road to Aberdeen – an in the summer you could blink and miss it, the place is that small, yet it's big on heart and the slopes are the best by far in Scotland for beginners with nursery slopes right next to the car park and base lodge (the only lodge, actually). All the runs and lifts are named after birds of prey but perhaps cartoon characters would be more appropriate because none of the runs resemble the nature of an eagle owl. If you are an advanced skier or snowboarder and want long challenging runs go to France, but if you're a slow learning basic intermediate then an afternoon here won't hurt. Likewise easily pleased eight-year-old snowboarders will find the place a cool hangout.

Off the Slopes - You will find a small selection of local services back down the road in the village of Tomintoul, which is sleepy highland retreat with one shop a couple of hotels a through road. You can get a meal here and have a beer at night but don't expect a choice.

Verdict - Scotland's number 1 friendly resort and first class for beginners. **4**/10

COST INDICATOR

Budget   Moderate   Very Expensive   Criminal

i - **Information** - 0044 (0) 19756 51440
www.lecht.co.uk

ROUTE PLANNER

✈ LONDON 0 miles
along the M1 - M6
M6 - *(M6 Toll road cost from £2).*

→ BIRMINGHAM 96 miles
1hr 50 M6

→ PRESTON 215 miles
3hrs 50 M6

→ CARLISE 303 miles
5hrs 15 A74/M74

Enter Scotland

→ GLASGOW 394 miles
6hrs 30 M8- M73 - A80- M80

→ STIRLING 415 miles
7hrs 14 M9- A9

→ PERTH 447 miles
7hrs 55 A9

→ AVIEMORE 530 miles
9hrs 50 B9152, A95 to Grantown-on-Spey, A939 via Tomintoul.

→ THE LECHT

KM **Distance** 565 miles *(910 km)*
⏱ **Drive time** 9 hours 20 mins
⛽ **Fuel** £50
€ **Tolls**

✈ Airports & Fly Drive Guide

1st- Aberdeen - 1 hr 25
→ A944, and all routes east via Aviemore = 85 miles

2nd- Inverness - 1 hr 30
→ A96, A95, A939 Lecht Road = 54 miles

3rd- Edinburgh - 3 hrs 30
→ M90 all routes north via Perth = 160 miles

⏱ DRIVE TIME - nixon www.nixonnow.com

Italy

DRIVE ON
THE RIGHT

Parking
restrictions

68 Roundabout

Motorway
Autostrada

Town
Centre

Bypass
routing

Country
identification

On coming
traffic must
wait.

Bridge

Motorway speed	**130kph**
Rural speed	**80kph**
Urban speed	**50kph**
Alcohol limit	**80mgs**
Front seatbelts	✔
Rear seatbelts	✔
Kids in front seat	**12**
Legal age to drive	**18**
Warming triangle	Required
First aid kit	Advisable
Fire extinguisher	Advisable
Snowchains	Advisable

Photo - Tourist Office Prato Nevoso - Rider *Palo Bonelli*

Road Signs and Warnings

Centro Paese - *Town center*
Entrata - *Entrance*
Incrocio - *Crossroads*
Lavori in corso - *Roadworks ahead*
Parcheggio - *Parking ramp*
Passaggio a livello - *Train crossing*
Rallentare - *Slow*
Senso Vietato - *No entry*
Sosta Autorizzata - *Parking allowed during times shown*
Sosta Vietata - *No parking*
Stazione Di Polizia - *Police station*
Svolta - *Bend*
Tutte le Direzion - *All directions*
Uscita - *Exit*
Vietato Ingresso Veicoli - *No entry for vehicles*
Vietato Transito Autocarri - *Closed to heavy vehicles*

FACT FILE

Country - Repubblica Italiana
Location - Western Europe
Geography
Italy shares its land borders with
Austria, France, Slovenia and
Switzerland.
Highest Mountain
Mont Blanc - 4807m
Coast line & Seas
Tyrrhenian Sea, Adriatic Sea
the Mediterranean
Land Area
301,338 sq km (116,346 sq miles)
Capital - Rome
Populartion - 57,844,017
Language - Italian
Religion - 95% Roman Catholic
Currecny - Euros
Time
GMT + 1 hour, (GMT + 2 hours
between March & October)
Electricity Supply - 220volts
Communications
International Country code 00390
Fire 115
Police 112
Ambulance 118
National Tourism
0039 (0) 6 49711
www.enit.it
Rail Information - www.enit.it
Bus Information - www.enit.it
Air Information - www.enit.it
Gateway International Airports
Turin - Milan - Rome - Verona
Weather Information
www.enit.it
Avalanche Information
www.cai-svi.it
www.meteoitalia.it
Liguria 0039 010 53 20 49
Lombardia 0039 014 78 370 77
Piemonte 0039 0113 18 55 55
Sudtirol 0039 0417 27 11 77
Trentino 0039 0416 23 89 39
Valle d'Aosta 0039 0165 77 63 00
Veneto 0039 0436 792 21ss

Passsprts & Visa Requirments

	Passports	Visa
Australian	Yes	No
British	Yes	No
Canadian	Yes	No
USA	Yes	No
EU	ID	No

Duty Free - None EU travellers
200 cigarettes or 100 cigarillos or
50 cigars or 25g of tobacco. 1ltr of
spirits over 22% or 21% of fortified
wine or spirits up to 22% or 21% of
sparkling wine or liqueur and 21 %
of still wine. 50g of perfume and
€90 worth of goods.
EU travellers - No tarrifs

Motoring Organisations
Automobile Club d'Italia
Via Marsala
8-BP 2839, Roma
tel +39 (0) 6 49 981

Touring Club Italiano (TCI)
AITAIT   FIA
Corso Italia 10, 20122 Milano.
tel +39 (0) 2 53 599 540
http:// www.touringclub.it
e-mail: soci@touringclub.it

Italy
Andalo

Mapping Page 85 A8

Top Lift
2125m.
Resort Height
1050m.
Vertical Drop
986m.
Number of Runs
20
Longest Run
5km
Slopes
60km of piste
● ● Beginner
35% of the runs
● Intermediate
50% of the runs
● Advanced
15% of the runs

Cross-Country
15km of tracks
Snowboarding
Half-pipe & Park
Snow Season
Dec to April
Snowmaking
60% of pistes
Number of lifts
17
Up Lift Capicity
20,000 per hour
Mountain Cafes
11

On the Slopes - Andalo is located north of the city of Verona within the Brenta Dolomite mountains and unlike Italy's more popular resorts; it's a relatively quiet resort that mostly attracts skiers and snowboarders from the local area. There are very few UK based tour operators that have Andalo on their books, which helps keep the resort unspoiled, crowd-free and totally Italian in character. Andalo has been offering ski facilities for many years and while it's somewhat old-fashioned, it's constantly improving by adding new lifts and better mountain facilities. Snowmaking covers approximately 60% of the mountain to help things out when the natural snow is lacking, which is useful as Andalo doesn't have the most guaranteed of snow records. The snowmaking ensures that there is a decent amount of cover and the runs are kept in good condition until the spring. Andalo is a mountain that has a bit of everything to please all levels of both skiers and snowboaders. With the exception of a small amount of off-piste areas, experts don't have a great deal of challenging terrain, but beginners and intermediates are offered the best of the facilities with the slopes easily reached from the village, via the main gondola a chair lift. In terms of snowboarding Andalo is not the hottest mountain, although there are some good carving runs but no regular halfpipe or terrain park. Still the local ski school offers snowboard lessons and board hire is available in the village.

Off the Slopes - To get the best out of Andalo's village you have to put yourself out and search out the best spots, which is partly why it's such a pleasant and laid back village. Local services are of a high standard and the locals are very welcoming: what's more, Andalo is not expensive, with affordable accommodation available near the slopes and around the village you will find a selection of shops and a sports centre. There is a nightclub (of sorts) and a couple of bars but don't expect a lot of lively action – a meal in one of the restaurants is about the best it gets.

Verdict - Laid-back traditional resort that's good for intermediate skiers. 5/10

COST INDICATOR

Budget   Moderate   Very Expensive   Criminal

i - **Information -** 0039 (0) 461 585 836

ROUTE PLANNER

🚏 **CALAIS** 0 miles
along the **A16 - A26**
E15 / E17
Toll Road

➡ **REIMS** 168 miles
2hrs 53 **A4 E17 / 50**

➡ **METZ** 270 miles
4hrs 47 **A4 E25** *Dir Strasbourg*
Tolls End

🚏 **A35** north to the D4
⚠ **Enter Germany** 401 miles
B500 to the **E35 - 5**

➡ **KARLSRUHE** 424 miles
7hrs 16 **A8 E52** *via Pforzheim*

➡ **STUTTGART** 459 miles
7hrs 50 **A8 E52**

➡ **ULM** 523 miles
8hrs 55 **A7 E532**

➡ **KEMPTEN** 573 miles
9hrs 50 **A7 E532** south via
⚠ **Nesselwang** along the
B309 & B179.
Enter Austria 600 miles
Head south along the
B179 via the **Fernpaß**
to the **B189.**

➡ **INNSBRUCK** 658 miles
11hrs 50 **A13, Brenner Pass**
⚠ **Enter Italy** 681 miles
Toll Road **A22 E45** via Bolzano
Tolls End Pick up the **43 & S421**

➡ **ANDALO**

KM **Distance** 770 miles *(1240 km)*
🕐 **Drive time** 13 hours 55 mins
⛽ **Fuel** £71
€ **Tolls** £36

✈ **Airports & Fly Drive Guide**

1st- Verona - 1 hr 40
➡ A22 north via **Trento** = 83 miles

2nd- Innsbruck (A)- 2 hrs 10
➡ A22 **E45** via **Bolzano** and the 43 & **S421** = 114 miles

3rd- Milan - 3 hrs
➡ E64, A4 & A22 via **Trento** = 160 miles

Italy
Aprica

Mapping Page 85 A6

Top Lift
2309m.
Resort Height
1180m.
Vertical Drop
1129m.
Number of Runs
20
Longest Run
5km
Slopes
40km of piste
● ● Beginner
60% of the runs
● Intermediate
30% of the runs
● Advanced
10% of the runs

Cross-Country
10km of tracks
Snowboarding
Half-pipe
Snow Season
Dec to April
Snowmaking
10km of pistes
Number of lifts
24
Up Lift Capicity
15,000 per hour
Mountain Cafes
3

On the Slopes - A good resort for those wanting a relaxing ski holiday; particularly beginners. Aprica is a small place, not far from the Swiss border and Sondrio, and while its not anywhere near the most famous resort in Italy, it has it's fans, and a young family could do a lot worse. The resort is well-suited, if not perfect, for beginners or cruising intermediates who like wide-open and easily navigated pistes – if you're looking for lot's of well linked, steep trails and good off-piste powder you should look elsewhere. Aprica boasts an average of 350cm of natural snow a year, backed up with a snowmaking system where necessary. The slopes are split over two areas, with tight trees lining the slopes up to three-quarters the way up. The Magnetta area is the smaller of the two, with a handful of pisted trails, which includes a decent black home run, two short blues and a pointless red. It's on the second area, the Malga Palabione area is where the main action takes place. The slopes, which end on one side of the village, are a collection of short, easy runs that snake through trees, with steeper red runs above the tree line and where you will also find a steep black. It's beginners who will appreciate this mountain the most, with a good supply of nursery slopes that run the length of the village – most of these are serviced by draglifts, so if you haven't used one before then get ready for some embarrassment. Snowboarders are not blessed with a hardcore freeride mountain nor is there much for freestylers, but cross-country skiers have some nice tracks to glide along.

Off the Slopes - The village sits at an altitude of 1180m and is not one of the world's most attractive or interesting places. Local services tend to be a little simple, but the accommodation is reasonable and there is a sports centre, ice rink, swimming pool and an indoor climbing wall to help pass the time when you are not on the slopes. Evenings are very relaxed with only a handful of restaurants and bars to choose from and nothing loud or too lively.

Verdict - Good for families and affordable, but pig ugly place. 5/10

COST INDICATOR

Budget   Moderate   Very Expensive   Criminal

i - **Information -** 0039 (0) 349 746 113

ROUTE PLANNER

🚏 **CALAIS** 0 miles
along the **A16 - A26**
E15 / E17
Toll Road

➡ **REIMS** 168 miles
2hrs 53 **A4 E17 / 50**

➡ **METZ** 270 miles
4hrs 47 **A4 E25** *Dir Strasbourg*
Tolls End

🚏 **A35** north to the D4
⚠ **Enter Germany** 401 miles
B500 to the **E35 - 5**

➡ **KARLSRUHE** 424 miles
7hrs 16 **A8 E52** *via Pforzheim*

➡ **STUTTGART** 459 miles
7hrs 50 **A8 E52**

➡ **ULM** 523 miles
8hrs 55 **A7 E532**

➡ **KEMPTEN** 573 miles
9hrs 50 **A7 E532** south via
⚠ **Nesselwang** along the
B309 & B179.
Enter Austria 600 miles
Head south along the
B179 via the **Fernpaß**
to the **B189.**

➡ **INNSBRUCK** 658 miles
11hrs 50 **A13, Brenner Pass**
⚠ **Enter Italy** 681 miles
Toll Road **A22 E45** via Bolzano
Tolls End Pick up the **43 & 42**

➡ **APRICA**

KM **Distance** 828 miles *(1333 km)*
🕐 **Drive time** 16 hours
⛽ **Fuel** £77
€ **Tolls** £38

✈ **Airports & Fly Drive Guide**

1st- Verona - 2 hrs 32
➡ A22 north via **Trento** = 107 miles

2nd- Milan - 2 hrs 15
➡ E64, A4 & A22 via **Trento** = 97 miles

3rd- Innsbruck (A)- 3 hrs 30
➡ A22 **E45** via **Bolzano** and the 43 & **S421** = 146miles

🕐 DRIVE TIME - *nixon* www.nixonnow.com

Bardonecchia

ROUTE PLANNER

CALAIS 0 miles
along the **A16 - A26**
E15 / E17
Toll Road

REIMS 168 miles 2hrs 55
A4 **E17** / 50

CHALONS en CHAMPAGNE 3hrs 15
A26 **E17**

TROYES 236 miles 4hrs
A5 **E17** / 54

MARAC 295 miles 5hrs
A31 **E17** / 21

DIJON 351 miles 6hrs 10
A31 **E17** & **E15** A6

MACON 395 miles 7hrs
A6 **E15**

LYON 471 miles 8hrs
E70 A43, A430
N6 & 25
Tolls End *Access via Modane is possible via the pass.

Enter Italy 596 miles

MODANE 590 miles 10hrs 30
E70 & A32 along to the resort.

BARDONECCHIA

KM	Distance	**606 miles** (975km)
	Drive time	**11 hours 44 mins**
€	Fuel	**£63**
€	Tolls	**£35**

Top Lift
2750m.
Resort Height
1348m.
Vertical Drop
1402m.
Number of Runs
49
Longest Run
6km
Slopes
110km of piste
● ● Beginner
20% of the runs
● Intermediate
70% of the runs
● Advanced
10% of the runs

Cross-Country
5km of tracks
Snowboarding
Half-pipe
Snow Season
Dec to April
Snowmaking
20% of piste
Number of lifts
23
Up Lift Capicity
22,000 per hour
Mountain Cafes
11

70

On the Slopes - Bardonecchia is highly rated in Italy and is considered one of the country's best by international visitors – the resort's status with both Italy's royalty and elite has made it synonymous with high fashion and high prices. Located in the Susa valley close to the Frejus tunnel and the French border, Bardonecchia is an interesting resort, split over two mountain faces. It is best suited to intermediates, with a large choice of red runs that span the mountain from top to bottom of either area. The runs are well prepared and covered by over 90 snow cannons to help out when the snowfall is light. The area closest to the village is the smaller of the two, with mainly red pistes but also a long easy blue run from the top to the bottom. The other area, which is reached by shuttle bus, is much the same but on a bigger scale. Both areas are well suited to snowboarders and skiers who are looking for good freeride terrain. Some tight trees and nice backcountry spots make Bardonecchia a decent snowboarder's resort. Beginners will find the slopes are fine for them to learn the basics especially on the Campo Smith and Melezet areas, which have large nursery slopes – be warned, these popular areas can get busy. Cross-country skiers are left out in the cold a little in Bardonecchia – there are trails, but they're limited to a few short trails which are neither testing or very exciting.

Off the Slopes - Bardonecchia goes back to Roman times and is more of a mountain town than a resort as people work and live here rather than just play. Laid out along a wide open valley close to the Frejus tunnel, the town offers a host of facilities to cater for most tastes and interests. Hotels and restaurants are plentiful, however, and some are excellent. Nightlife is varied and caters mainly for those who like to sip, rather than gulp. This is not a place that goes in for hard core apres-ski (mercifully). The Medail is a popular hangout with the fashion set, but can get busy, especially over the weekend, when you can hardly move in the place.

Airports & Fly Drive Guide

1st- Turin - **1 hr 32**
A32 **E70** east via Susa = **60** miles

2nd- Grenoble (F) - **2 hrs 30**
A43, **E70** and all routes via Modane = **120** miles

3rd- Milan - **2 hrs 40**
A4 & **E64** and all routes via Torino = **142** miles

Verdict - Some excellent slopes, but resort lacks character. **6/10**

COST INDICATOR

Budget   Moderate   Very Expensive   Criminal

i - Information - 0039 (0) 122 99137

Bormio

ROUTE PLANNER

CALAIS 0 miles
along the **A16 - A26**
E15 / E17
Toll Road

REIMS 168 miles 2hrs 53
A4 **E17** / 50

METZ 270 miles 4hrs 47
A4 **E25** Dir Strasbourg
Tolls End

A35 north to the D4
Enter Germany 401 miles
B500 to the **E35** - 5

KARLSRUHE 424 miles 7hrs 16
A8 **E52** via Pforzheim

STUTTGART 459 miles 7hrs 50
A8 **E52**

ULM 523 miles 8hrs 55
A7 **E532**

KEMPTEN 573 miles 9hrs 50
A7 **E532** south via
Nesselwang along the B309 & B179.
Enter Austria 600 miles
Head south along the B179 via the Fernpaß to the B189.

INNSBRUCK 658 miles 11hrs 50
A13, Brenner Pass
Enter Italy 681 miles
Toll Road A22 **E45** via Bolzano
Tolls End Pick up the 38's

BORMIO

KM	Distance	**771 miles** (1241 km)
	Drive time	**14 hours 30 mins**
€	Fuel	**£71**
€	Tolls	**£36**

Top Lift
3010m.
Resort Height
1225m.
Vertical Drop
1787m.
Number of Runs
18
Longest Run
14km
Slopes
75km of piste
● ● Beginner
36% of the runs
● Intermediate
48% of the runs
● Advanced
16% of the runs

Cross-Country
15km of tracks
Snowboarding
Half-pipe & Park
Snow Season
Dec to May
Snowmaking
40% of pistes
Number of lifts
28
Up Lift Capicity
14,000 per hour
Mountain Cafes
13

On the Slopes - The Romans were the first to acknowledge the potential of the resort of Bormio, when they built a spa here fifteen hundred or so years ago and there have been regular visitors ever since. As a highly regarded resort with a good reputation for slope maintenance, the ski area of Bormio has grown from the first lifts being installed in the sixties into a major destination that hosts numerous top level ski events – in fact, the resort is going to stage the World Ski Championships in 2005. The result is that you have a mountain that has wonderful open pistes and great tree lined runs for all levels, but it's very popular with visitors from all over Europe flocking here in large numbers. The lift system is modern and efficient, however, and more than able to cope which means that queues are no bigger than any other international resort. Snow levels are favourable in Bormio and with half of the slopes covered by snowmaking, there is never a lack of snow. The runs cover two areas with an almost equal split of runs on each. Beginner and intermediates are the best served here, while advanced level skiers are left to choose from only a couple of short black runs. Advanced skiers and snowboarders may feel a little left out if big bowls are their thing, but there is some good off piste terrain and plenty of natural terrain features for the more adventurous to try. In the main Bormio is not particularly suited to freestylers but cross-country skiers, will find around 15km of trails to try but there are better places in Italy if that is your preference.

Off the Slopes - The town of Bormio is a rustic medieval place with a strong Italian identity and one that is very satisfying, with accommodation available on or near the pistes. Around town the is an air of glitz, but don't be fooled or put off as this is a nice affordable centre with some fine restaurants to choose from such as the Kuerc or the Talua. In the evenings, there is a relaxed air, while still being lively and good fun. Kings Club is the dancing spot.

Airports & Fly Drive Guide

1st- Innsbruck (A) - **2 hrs 40**
A22 **E45** via Bolzano and the 43 & 43 = **112** miles

2nd- Milan - **3 hrs**
E64, A4 & A22 via Trento = **130** miles

3rd- Verona - **3 hrs 40**
A22 north via Trento = **145** miles

Verdict - Fun resort, for all abilities. Attractive town with good services. **7/10**

COST INDICATOR

Budget   Moderate   Very Expensive   Criminal

i - Information - 0039 (0) 349 746 113

Italy
Canazei

Mapping Page **88 D3**

Top Lift
2638m.
Resort Height
1448m.
Vertical Drop
1190m.
Number of Runs
20
Longest Run
12km
Slopes
43km of piste
● ● *Beginner*
36% of the runs
● *Intermediate*
54% of the runs
● *Advanced*
10% of the runs

Cross-Country
20km of tracks
Snowboarding
Half-pipe & Park
Snow Season
Dec to April
Snowmaking
60% of piste
Number of lifts
16
Up Lift Capicity
20,000 per hour
Mountain Cafes
18

On the Slopes - Canazei is part the Dolomite Superski region, said to be the largest ski area in the world with over 1200 kilometres of terrain. Whatever the merits of this claim, Canazei does have a lot going for it. Located along the Fassa Valley, the resort is one of the many that make up the Sella Ronda circuit, a series of lift-linked mountain areas where thousands flock every weekend. There is something for everyone here – the area is vast and has every conceivable type of terrain on offer. Cross-country skiers can glide on around 90 km of measured tracks with a particularly nice long trail up on Vallungaa-Laangental area. Downhill skiers and snowboarders can do their thing on countless snow-sure slopes from one end of the circuit to the other – there is so much terrain that you would be hard pressed to cover it all , even if you were here for a whole season. Canazei itself sits at an altitude of 1440 metres and gives access to the Belvedere slopes, a tree covered area that will suit novices down to the ground. Those who want to get their teeth into more testing runs should visit one of the neighbouring centres such as the steeps on the Arraba area. The cross-country skiing is a bit limited, but there are some enjoyable trails with over 20km marked. Snowboarders of all religions should be able to enjoy this place as much as anyone else – there are lots of natural hits as well as a number of half-pipes and fun parks spread through out the area, including those at Canazei's Belvedere slopes.

Off the Slopes - Canazei is an old town with narrow streets and old buildings full of charm. The place is neither flash, nor expensive – accommodation, as with most local services, is simple and basic. There are a couple of hotels and some chalets to choose from, with an even greater selection in neighbouring villages. The restaurants are nearly all Italian styled and there are good options from pizza to pasta. Nightlife is nothing to write home about with a few simple bars and little else. Locals like to take it easy around here.

Verdict - A superb taste of Italy in a region with something for everyone. **8**/10

COST INDICATOR
Budget   Moderate   Very Expensive   Criminal

i - **Information** - 0039 (0) 462 601 113
www.fassa.com

ROUTE PLANNER

✈ **CALAIS** 0 miles
along the **A16 - A26**
E15 / E17
Toll Road

➡ **REIMS** 168 miles
2hrs 53 **A4 E17 / 50**

➡ **METZ** 270 miles
4hrs 47 **A4 E25** Dir Strasbourg
Tolls End

⚠ **A35** north to the D4
⚠ **Enter Germany** 401 miles
B500 to the **E35 - 5**

➡ **KARLSRUHE** 424 miles
7hrs 16 **A8 E52** via Pforzheim

➡ **STUTTGART** 459 miles
7hrs 50 **A8 E52**

➡ **ULM** 523 miles
8hrs 55 **A7 E532**

➡ **KEMPTEN** 573 miles
9hrs 50 **A7 E532** south via
⚠ **Nesselwang** along the
B309 & B179.
Enter Austria 600 miles
Head south along the
B179 via the **Fernpaß**
to the **B189.**

➡ **INNSBRUCK** 658 miles
11hrs 50 **A13, Brenner Pass**
⚠ **Enter Italy** 681 miles
Toll Road **A22 E45** via Bolzano
Tolls End Pick up the **12** and then the **48** via **Ora.**

➡ **CANAZEI**

ᴷᴹ **Distance** **746** miles (1200 km)
🕐 **Drive time** **13** hours **40** mins
⛽ **Fuel** **£68**
€ **Tolls** **£36**

✈ **Airports & Fly Drive Guide**
1st- Innsbruck (A)- **1 hr 50**
➡ **A22 E45** via **Bolzano** and the **43 & 43 = 88** miles

2nd- Verona - **2 hrs 30**
➡ **A22** north via **Trento** = **128** miles

3rd- Milan - **3 hrs 50**
➡ **E64, A4 & A22** via **Trento** = **200** miles

Italy
Cervinia

Mapping Page **84 A3**

Top Lift
3488m.
Resort Height
2050m.
Vertical Drop
1438m.
Number of Runs
129
Longest Run
8km
Slopes
200km of piste
● ● *Beginner*
16% of the runs
● *Intermediate*
65% of the runs
● *Advanced*
19% of the runs

Cross-Country
5km of tracks
Snowboarding
Half-pipe & Park
Snow Season
Dec to April
Snowmaking
25km of piste
Number of lifts
30
Up Lift Capicity
25,000 per hour
Mountain Cafes
18

On the Slopes - Located below the Matterhorn mountain that dominates the skyline, Cervinia will either excite you or bore you silly. Beginners and slow learning intermediates will find kilometre after kilometre of gentle and pleasant slopes, and while it has a large number of runs to choose from and a great snow record, there is something so bland about the resort that you could almost forget that you're in the shadow of one of the most recognisable mountains on the planet. Cervinia is linked to the famous Swiss resort of Zermatt, so if you do find it not to your liking, you can at least cross the border and try Zermatt's world-class slopes. Cervinia is a busy resort, but the lift system copes admirably, even though there are some trouble spots despite recent improvements to many of the older lifts. Cervinia can certainly boast about it's snow record, and while many low level resorts struggle and have to rely on snowmaking facilities, there is no such problem at Cervinia as the high altitude here means good regular dumps of fresh snow. Most of the mountain consists of red intermediate runs, but in truth many of them are over graded and a competent skier used to blue runs will manage them with ease, especially those on the lower slopes towards the village. Beginners should make for the Plan Maison area which is nice a gentle open expanse, with one of the only blue home runs, unless you have some balls and go for one of the reds. Cross-country skiers are going to find very little to keep them occupied, but freestyle skiers and snowboarders have plenty to keep them amused. Freeriders will find a few too many flats, but if carving is your gig, then this place is for you.

Off the Slopes - Cervinia has a number hotels and apartments that are located close to the slopes, but it's fair to say that it's not the most happening resort, nor is it one of the cheapest. Despite this, the resort is very popular with package tour operators who normally favour inexpensive resorts. Eating out is average, as is the nightlife which doesn't cut it at all.

Verdict - Great pistes for novices, snow sure slopes but an uninspiring resort. **6**/10

COST INDICATOR
Budget   Moderate   Very Expensive   Criminal

i - **Information** - 0039 (0) 166 949 136
www.cervinia.it

ROUTE PLANNER

✈ **CALAIS** 0 miles
along the **A16 - A26**
E15 / E17
Toll Road

➡ **REIMS** 168 miles
2hrs 53 **A4 E17 / 50**

➡ **CHALONS en CHAMPAGNE**
3hrs 15 **A26 E17**

➡ **TROYES** 236 miles
4hrs **A5 E17 / 54**

➡ **MARAC** 295 miles
5hrs **A31 E17 / 21**

➡ **DIJON** xxx miles
6hrs 10 **A31 E17 & E15 A6**

➡ **MACON** 396 miles
7hrs **A40 E62**

➡ **BOURG-en-BRESSE** 426 miles
7hrs 15 **A40 E62**

➡ **GENEVA** 491 miles
8hrs 20 **A40 E25 N506**,
direction **Chamonix.**
Mont Blanc.
Enter Italy

➡ **COURMAYEUR** 551 miles
9hr 40 **A5 E25** to the **406** via
Tolls End **Chatillon** to the resort.

➡ **CERVINIA**

ᴷᴹ **Distance** **606** miles (976 km)
🕐 **Drive time** **11** hours
⛽ **Fuel** **£55**
€ **Tolls** **£30**

✈ **Airports & Fly Drive Guide**
1st- Turin - **1 hr 55**
➡ **A5 EE612/E25** and **406** via **Chatillon = 75** miles

2nd- Milan - **2 hrs30**
➡ **E64 A4 E25** and **406** via **Chatillon = 118** miles

3rd- Geneva (CH) - **2 hrs 45**
➡ **Cluses - A40 E25 & D907** = **126** miles

71

DRIVE TIME - nixon www.nixonnow.com

Italy

Claviere

Mapping Page 47 F7

Top Lift
2300m.
Resort Height
1350m.
Vertical Drop
935m.
Number of Runs
20
Longest Run
6km
Slopes
50km of piste
● ● ● *Beginner*
26% of the runs
● ● ● *Intermediate*
60% of the runs
● *Advanced*
14% of the runs

Cross-Country
15km of tracks
Snowboarding
Half-pipe & Park
Snow Season
Dec to April
Snowmaking
10% of pistes
Number of lifts
11
Up Lift Capacity
11,000 per hour
Mountain Cafes
36

72

On the Slopes - A lovely village in a reasonable ski area with links to a much larger ski region. Perfect for those looking for the quiet life. Claviere is one of the resorts of the Milky Way ski region and is located right on the French/Italian border a mere stone's throw from the sprawling French resort of Montgenevre. On its own, Claviere is a small resort that has little to entice the international visitor, but with it's location and links to the Milky Way, bypassing this resort would be a mistake. Collectively, the area can boast over 400km of slopes with acres and acres of interesting terrain and a good snow record, 92 good lifts and hardly any queues – most of the time. The biggest let down is that navigating the Milky Way region is not as easy as you would expect, particularly on the Italian side. It is possible to link the resorts together by pistes and lifts, it takes some good piste map reading. The slopes that connect Claviere itself are very limited, with only a few red and blue runs and with the exception of two black runs on the Col de L'Alpet, it's certainly not a place where you will want to spend much time. The nursery slopes at the base are perfect for beginners and as most people are off exploring elsewhere in the Milky Way, the runs are generally crowd-free – its only on weekends, when the visitors from Turin are in attendance when things get a bit tight. Freestyle skiers and snowboarders are going to be a little disappointed on the slopes of Claviere itself, although the links to the Milky Way resorts means that a little exploration can pay dividends and provided you don't mind having to travel between areas, no one shold feel left out.

Off the Slopes - If all you want after a day on the slopes is a quiet, no-nonsense village free of crowds that won't hurt your bank balance, Claviere will do nicely. It's seriously laid back, with a couple of hotels, half a dozen restaurants and bars and a few shops for basic groceries and a postcard. You won't find tour reps making fools of themselves in the bars here.

Verdict - Basic slopes but a perfect village for those wanting a quiet time. **5/10**

COST INDICATOR
Budget   Moderate   Very Expensive   Criminal

i - **Information** - 0039 (0) 122 878 856

ROUTE PLANNER

🛂 **CALAIS** 0 miles
along the **A16 - A26**
E15 / E17
Toll Road

➡ **REIMS** 168 miles
2hrs 55 **A4 E17 / 50**

➡ **CHALONS en CHAMPAGNE**
3hrs 15 **A26 E17**

➡ **TROYES** 236 miles
4hrs **A5 E17 / 54**

➡ **MARAC** 295 miles
5hrs **A31 E17 / 21**

➡ **DIJON** 351 miles
6hrs 10 **A31 E17 & E15 A6**

➡ **MACON** 395 miles
7hrs **A6 E15**

➡ **LYON** 471 miles
8hrs **E70 A43, A430**
✈ **N6 & 25**
Tolls End *Access via Modane is possible via the pass.*

Enter Italy 596 miles

➡ **MODANE** 590 miles
10hr 30 **E70 & A32** along to the resort.

⬇

➡ **CLAVIERE**

🆖 **Distance** 622 miles *(1001 km)*
🕐 **Drive time** 11 hours 10 mins
⛽ **Fuel** £63
€ **Tolls** £35

✈ **Airports & Fly Drive Guide**

1st- Turin - 1 hr 35
➡ **A32 E70** east *via* Susa = 62 miles

2nd- Grenoble (F) - 2 hrs 38
➡ **A43, E70** and all routes via Modane = 110 miles

3rd - Milan - 2 hrs 45
➡ **A4 & E64** and all routes via Torino = 145 miles

Italy

Cortina

Mapping Page 88 D4

Top Lift
3243m.
Resort Height
1224m.
Vertical Drop
2020m.
Number of Runs
52
Longest Run
9km
Slopes
140km of piste
● ● ● *Beginner*
44% of the runs
● ● ● *Intermediate*
45% of the runs
● *Advanced*
11% of the runs

Cross-Country
80km of tracks
Snowboarding
Half-pipe & Park
Snow Season
Dec to Sept
Snowmaking
50% of pistes
Number of lifts
38
Up Lift Capacity
44,000 per hour
Mountain Cafes
25

On the Slopes - There are some resorts across Europe which set out to be different from the start, and Cortina is one of them. A playground of both the rich and famous, Cortina is a good mountain with lots of possibilities for all levels of skier and snowboarder, but the high class nature of the visitors means correspondingly high prices – a shame, as it means that not everyone can enjoy the benefits of the terrain that is on offer. The slopes are split into a series of expansive yet separate areas, which higher up are ideal for intermediates, while the lower areas are home to the main nursery slopes. Because of the layout of the area, some navigation is necessary which may even involve a bus ride between base stations to reach certain parts. The resort is best suited to beginner and intermediate users, with a good selection of well-marked trails for their enjoyment. Experts don't have a great deal to choose from with the steep run on the Cristallo about the best on offer. As for cross-country skiing, Cortina is one of the best around with some really good trails, which includes tracks through woods along an old railway line and around fields. Only in recent years has snowboarding been accepted on the slopes of Cortina, but at least the resort has started to provide some snowboard friendly services. The mountain is great for freeriding, but the attitude has meant that snowboarders have generally given the place the cold shoulder. Things are changing with the addition of a terrain park at Faloria, which has all the usual sculpted toys to get air off. However, cross-country skiers should be happy with the trails on offer around here, making this place one of the best around with over 80km of tracks.

Off the Slopes - Cortina is a big town with expensive hotels, expensive restaurants and expensive shops. It's possible to get a bed in a great place near to the slopes, but the price will put many off. Resort facilities are very good and more than adequate for any holiday. There are loads of good restaurants and a number of nightspots, but they tend to be pricey.

Verdict - Good resort with great facilities, but expensive. **8/10**

COST INDICATOR
Budget   Moderate   Very Expensive   Criminal

i - **Information** - 0039 (0) 4363 23123

ROUTE PLANNER

🛂 **CALAIS** 0 miles
along the **A16 - A26**
E15 / E17
Toll Road

➡ **REIMS** 168 miles
2hrs 53 **A4 E17 / 50**

➡ **METZ** 270 miles
4hrs 47 **A4 E25** *Dir Strasbourg*
Tolls End
✈ **A35** north to the D4
⛰ **Enter Germany** 401 miles
B500 to the **E35 - 5**

🛂 ➡ **KARLSRUHE** 424 miles
7hrs 16 **A8 E52** *via* Pforzheim

➡ **STUTTGART** 459 miles
7hrs 50 **A8 E52**

➡ **ULM** 523 miles
8hrs 55 **A7 E532**

➡ **KEMPTEN** 573 miles
9hrs 50 **A7 E532** south via
⛰ **Nesselwang** along the **B309 & B179.**
Enter Austria 600 miles
Head south along the **B179** via the **Fernpaß** to the **B189.**

➡ **INNSBRUCK** 658 miles
11hrs 50 **A13**, Brenner Pass
⛰ **Enter Italy** 661 miles
Toll Road **A22 E45** to **Varna**
Tolls End Pick up the **49** and then the **51** via **Carbonin.**

⬇

➡ **CORTINA**

🆖 **Distance** 766 miles *(1233 km)*
🕐 **Drive time** 13 hours 50 mins
⛽ **Fuel** £68
€ **Tolls** £36

✈ **Airports & Fly Drive Guide**

1st- Innsbruck (A)- 2 hrs 25
➡ **A22 E45** via **Bolzano** and the **43 & 43** = 110 miles

2nd- Verona - 3 hrs
➡ **A22** north via **Trento** = 155 miles

3rd- Milan - 4 hrs 30
➡ **E64, A4 & A22** via **Trento** = 242 miles

Italy
Courmayeur

Mapping Page 47 D8

Top Lift
2775m.
Resort Height
1225m.
Vertical Drop
1532m.
Number of Runs
28
Longest Run
10km
Slopes
100km of piste
● ● Beginner
25% of the runs
◐ Intermediate
60% of the runs
● Advanced
10% of the runs

Cross-Country
35km of tracks
Snowboarding
Half-pipe & Park
Snow Season
Dec to July
Snowmaking
365 cannons
Number of lifts
16
Up Lift Capicity
16,000 per hour
Mountain Cafes
24

On the Slopes - Courmayeur is an extremely popular resort located just over the border from the French resort of Chamonix and in the Shadow of Mt Blanc, Europe's second highest mountain. While not the highest resort in the world, the runs nevertheless hold their snow well and the slopes are covered by 365 snow cannons which help lay a base at the beginning of the season and add extra snow towards the end. Despite this, some of the lower runs are prone to thinning out and bare patches are visible in the late spring. If your apartment is not close to the main cable car, access to the slopes can be problematic. The predominantly intermediate runs start on the Cresta Youla at 2625 metres with descents back down in to the village via a sedate blue at the final stage. The main action takes place on the Lago Checrouit area, but despite the resort's reputation, Courmayeur is not the most challenging mountain – there is some great off-piste powder and you can sign up for heli-boarding should you fancy a real thrill, but the local slopes are not particularly challenging. Still, the Mont Blanc area is known as one of the most extreme regions in the world, so if you travel around you won't be disappointed. One group that may find the region a bit of a struggle are beginners, as the choice of blue runs are rather limited with the best novice's runs on the Pre de Pascal area of the Entreves cable car. Cross-country skies, on the other hand, are well catered for – lots of fantastic trails, both in the resort and the surrounding area.

Off the Slopes - The resort town is a mixture of old and new and a great holiday spot any time of year. Courmayeur is a fashionable place, so it's not cheap but there are plenty of good hotels and an abundance of boutiques for those who like to shop. The choice of restaurants is excellent, with something for all tastes but you'd be wise to check out the Red Lion or Pizzeria K2. In the evenings this place really comes alive and has a definite party feel to it. There are loads of bars; Roxy's, Cronox or Ziggy's are all popular.

Verdict - A wonderful resort for intermediates with excellent village services. **8**/10

COST INDICATOR

Budget   Moderate   Very Expensive   Criminal

i - **Information** - 0039 (0) 842 060
www.courmayeur.net

ROUTE PLANNER

🚗 **CALAIS** 0 miles
along the **A16 - A26**
E15 / E17
Toll Road

➡ **REIMS** 168 miles
2hrs 55 **A4 E17 / 50**

➡ **CHALONS en CHAMPAGNE**
3hrs 15 **A26 E17**

➡ **TROYES** 236 miles
4hrs **A5 E17 / 54**

➡ **MARAC** 295 miles
5hrs **A31 E17 / 21**

➡ **DIJON** xxx miles
6hrs 10 **A31 E17 & E15 A6**

➡ **MACON** 396 miles
7hrs **A40 E62**

➡ **BOURG-en-BRESSE** 426 miles
7hrs 15 **A40 E62**

➡ **GENEVA** 491 miles
8hrs 20 **A40 E25 N506,**
direction **Chamonix.**
Mont Blanc.

Enter Italy
Tolls End

⬇

➡ **COURMAYEUR**

KM **Distance** 553 miles *(890 km)*
🕐 **Drive time** 10 hours 10 mins
⛽ **Fuel** £52
€ **Tolls** £33

✈ **Airports & Fly Drive Guide**

1st- Geneva (CH) - **1** hr **30**
➡ Cluses - **A40 E25 & D907 =**
74 miles

2nd- Turin - 2 hrs
➡ **A5 EE612/E25** and **406** via
Chatillon = **94** miles

3rd- Milan - 2 hrs **30**
➡ **E64 A4 E25** and **406** via
Chatillon = **136** miles

Italy
Folgarida

Mapping Page 88 D2

Top Lift
2179m.
Resort Height
900m.
Vertical Drop
1279m.
Number of Runs
40
Longest Run
6km
Slopes
106km of piste
● ● Beginner
42% of the runs
◐ Intermediate
53% of the runs
● Advanced
5% of the runs

Cross-Country
30km of tracks
Snowboarding
-
Snow Season
Dec to April
Snowmaking
64% of piste
Number of lifts
26
Up Lift Capicity
26,700 per hour
Mountain Cafes
9

On the Slopes - Basic in all respects, but offers good access to other slopes in the region, however, Folgarida links with its bigger neighbours Madonna di Campiglio and Marilleva, all of which are located to the north of west of Trento. Together these northern resorts provide over 260km of slopes linked on the piste by a modern network of lifts that can transport over 26,700 individuals an hour – and what's more, although there is occasionally some congestion most lift queues are reasonable. Take Folgarida on its own and what you have is a very small resort that is both pleasing on the eye and easy on the pocket. This is also a place where you can ski on intermediate slopes above and below the tree line on crowd-free slopes. The resort sits at an altitude of 1400 metres with lifts up to 2500m via the Madonna. Folgarida is a well balanced alpine retreat nestled among trees and offering great scenery. Each year the area receives a healthy supply of snow and the pistes are well groomed on a daily basis, which is why this place tends to attract those who are not fussy but like to be pampered. Cross-country skiers will soon notice how good the trails, which snake the way through thick mountain forests, are. Snowboarders can ride from here, but in truth Madonna's slopes are better suited. While novices may not have a host of easy runs, what there is, is perfect for first timers with runs back down to the village that most novices should be able to manage.

Off the Slopes - Folgarida is a pleasant, low key alpine resort, which will suite families and those who want to stay away from the masses that accumulate over in Madonna. Although a small place, there are lots of places to get a bed at night, but little else as far as facilities are concerned – staying in Folgarida is more a case of bringing your own entertainment, groceries and a sense of fun. That said, there are half a dozen restaurants and you can have a night on the tiles without it costing the earth.

Verdict - Basic resort to appeal to novices. Nice pleasant village. **5**/10

COST INDICATOR

Budget   Moderate   Very Expensive   Criminal

i - **Information** - 0039 (0) 463 986 2723

ROUTE PLANNER

🚗 **CALAIS** 0 miles
along the **A16 - A26**
E15 / E17
Toll Road

➡ **REIMS** 168 miles
2hrs 53 **A4 E17 / 50**

➡ **METZ** 270 miles
4hrs 47 **A4 E25** *Dir Strasbourg*
Tolls End

🚗 **A35** north to the **D4**
🛈 **Enter Germany** 401 miles
B500 to the **E35 - 5**

🚗 **KARLSRUHE** 424 miles
7hrs 16 **A8 E52** *via Pforzheim*

➡ **STUTTGART** 459 miles
7hrs 50 **A8 E52**

➡ **ULM** 523 miles
8hrs 55 **A7 E532**

➡ **KEMPTEN** 573 miles
9hrs 50 **A7 E532** south via
🛈 **Nesselwang** along the
B309 & **B179**.
Enter Austria 600 miles
Head south along the
B179 via the **Fernpaß**
to the **B189**.

➡ **INNSBRUCK** 658 miles
11hrs 50 **A13, Brenner Pass**
🛈 **Enter Italy** 681 miles
Toll Road **A22 E45** via **Bolzano**
Tolls End Pick up the **43** & **42**

⬇

➡ **FOLGARIDA**

KM **Distance** 791 miles *(1274 km)*
🕐 **Drive time** 14 hours 10 mins
⛽ **Fuel** £68
€ **Tolls** £36

✈ **Airports & Fly Drive Guide**

1st- Verona - 2 hrs **10**
➡ **A22** north via **Trento**
= **105** miles

2nd- Milan - 3 hrs
➡ **E64, A4** & **A22** via **Trento**
= **129** miles

3rd- Innsbruck (A)- **2** hrs **40**
➡ **A22 E45** via **Bolzano** and
the **43** & **43** = **134** miles

🕐 DRIVE TIME - nixon. www.nixon.com

Foppolo

Mapping Page 85 A8

ROUTE PLANNER

Top Lift
2300m.
Resort Height
1600m.
Vertical Drop
550m.
Number of Runs
20
Longest Run
4km
Slopes
45km of piste
● ● *Beginner*
44% of the runs
● *Intermediate*
45% of the runs
● **Advanced**
11% of the runs

Cross-Country
5km of tracks
Snowboarding
–
Snow Season
Dec to April
Snowmaking
68 cannons
Number of lifts
12
Up Lift Capicity
7,500 per hour
Mountain Cafes
3

On the Slopes - Foppolo is located close to Bergamo and has a long history as a ski resort for those who like purpose-built resorts with easy access to the mountain and good local services. This place also appeals because as well as sustaining a good snow record, with slopes that don't get too busy, they also offer lifts that manage to move people without too many problems and queues that are kept to a minimum. The slopes are well looked after and the terrain is evenly split for novices and intermediates, but with very little to offer experts. There are only a few short blacks runs even though there are some areas where you can go off-piste in search of some powder and with a short bus ride link to San Simone, there is at least the option of finding a challenging run on neighbouring slopes, as long as you buy the joint lift pass. What is apparent wherever you go in this area is how laid back things are – the lifties are really cool and don't mind helping you out, the local ski school is very good and the instructors are friendly and many speak English. However, Foppolo is not the most interesting for cross-country skiers, as there are hardly any good areas and the trails that there are, are a bit dull and won't hold your attention for long. Likewise, this is not a place noted for snowboarding in terms of terrain parks or half-pipe. If you want to get air you will have to build your own kickers or search for the natural spots that there are. This is more of a freeriders resort with some interesting off-piste areas. Novices on skis or on a board, should take to this place as much of the terrain is rated beginner level with lots of easy to reach nursery slopes etc.

Off the Slopes - Foppolo is similar to other mountain villages in this area – traditional – but it's still a decent and affordable centre, perfect for a week's stay even though there are few local attractions off the mountain. There are no fancy sports centres and few shops, but at least accommodation is convenient, with doorstep skiing possible from a number of places. Eating out is very basic, as is nightlife.

CALAIS 0 miles
along the **A16 - A26**
E15 / E17
Toll Road

→ **REIMS** 168 miles
2hrs 53 **A4 E17 / 50**

→ **METZ** 270 miles
4hrs 47 **A4 E25** *Dir Strasbourg*
Tolls End
⚠ **A35** north to the **D4**
⚠ **Enter Germany** 401 miles
B500 to the **E35 - 5**

→ **KARLSRUHE** 424 miles
7hrs 16 **A8 E52** *via Pforzheim*

→ **STUTTGART** 459 miles
7hrs 50 **A8 E52**

→ **ULM** 523 miles
8hrs 55 **A7 E532**

→ **KEMPTEN** 573 miles
9hrs 55 **A7 E532** south via
⚠ **Nesselwang** along the
B309 & B179.
Enter Austria 600 miles
Head south along the
B179 via the **Fernpaß**
to the **B189.**

→ **INNSBRUCK** 658 miles
11hrs 50 **A13, Brenner Pass**
⚠ **Enter Italy** 681 miles
Toll Road **A22 E45** via **Bolzano**
Tolls End Pick up the **43 & 42**
BERGAMO
↓ **470**

→ **FOPPOLO**

KM **Distance** 913 miles (1469 km)
🕐 **Drive time** 15 hours 50 mins
⛽ **Fuel** £82
€ **Tolls** £38

✈ **Airports & Fly Drive Guide**
1st- Milan - 1 hr **40**
→ **E64, A4** & the **470** via
Bergamo **A4** = **60** miles

2nd- Verona - 2 hrs **30**
→ **A4** and **470** via Bergamo
= **110** miles

3rd- Turin - 3 hrs **20**
→ **A4 E64** via **Bergamo** and
the **470** = **150** miles

Verdict - Okay for a novice group but in the evenings, very dull and boring. **4/10**

COST INDICATOR

Budget   Moderate   Very Expensive   Criminal

i - **Information** - 0039 (0) 436 3231

La Thuile

Mapping Page 47 D8

ROUTE PLANNER

Top Lift
2642m.
Resort Height
1441m.
Vertical Drop
1200m.
Number of Runs
30
Longest Run
11km
Slopes
150km of piste
● ● *Beginner*
44% of the runs
● *Intermediate*
36% of the runs
● **Advanced**
20% of the runs

Cross-Country
25km of tracks
Snowboarding
Half-pipe & Park
Snow Season
Dec to April
Snowmaking
262 cannons
Number of lifts
36
Up Lift Capicity
26,000 per hour
Mountain Cafes
14

On the Slopes - La Thuile is a resort that is going from strength to strength and from popularity to popularity, perhaps something to do with being a close neighbour of Courmayeur. The resort has attracted many of those who want to enjoy the skiing on offer in the area, without having to endure its hustle and bustle. It may have something to do with the fact the terrain is very good, the snow record adequate and mountain facilities excellent. Located in the Aosta Valley, La Thuile links on the slopes with the French resort of La Rosiere, which is far smaller but together, they can match many others. All levels of mountain user will have something do here; there is a good helping of intermediate runs and some nice expert trails through tree lined areas. Not only that, beginner slopes are very good and although first timers won't be skiing or riding back into the village until they are more confident, there are lots of easy runs at altitude in La Thuile and La Rosiere which are covered with the same pass. Thanks to the efficient lift system, queues are close to zero and slopes crowd-free. Freeride skiers and snowboarders are in for a treat on these slopes with a mixture of trees and decent back-country to explore and you can sign up for heli-boarding if you're feeling brave. If cross-country skiing is your thing, then you to will pleasantly surprised with what is on offer.

Off the Slopes - The resort lies at the top of a winding road and what you find on arrival is not a fancy purpose built place overloaded with ugly apartment blocks, but a nice compact village with a sense of fun and simplicity about it. The resort is popular and tour operators ship in coach loads of visitors weekly, but they don't spoil the place and there is a good balance of local services with four star hotels and chalets. This resort has somewhat limited local attractions, with a swimming pool as its main amenity, but there is a fair selection of restaurants – for an all-round choice, La Lisse is hard to beat. Nightlife is tame, but fun; Bar Ruitor, the Bricole and Faanntasia are popular evening spots.

CALAIS 0 miles
along the **A16 - A26**
E15 / E17
Toll Road

→ **REIMS** 168 miles
2hrs 55 **A4 E17 / 50**

→ **CHALONS en CHAMPAGNE**
3hrs 15 **A26 E17**

→ **TROYES** 236 miles
4hrs **A5 E17 / 54**

→ **MARAC** 295 miles
5hrs **A31 E17 / 21**

→ **DIJON** xxx miles
6hrs 10 **A31 E17 & E15 A6**

→ **MACON** 396 miles
7hrs **A40 E62**

→ **BOURG-en-BRESSE** 426 miles
7hrs 15 **A40 E62**

→ **GENEVA** 491 miles
8hrs 10 **A40 E25 N506,**
direction **Chamonix.**
Mont Blanc.
Enter Italy

→ **COURMAYEUR** 553 miles
10hrs 10 **26**
Tolls End

→ **LA THULE**

KM **Distance** 563 miles (906km)
🕐 **Drive time** 10 hours 20 mins
⛽ **Fuel** £52
€ **Tolls** £33

✈ **Airports & Fly Drive Guide**
1st- Turin - 1 hr **45**
→ **A5 EE612/E25** and **406** via
Chatillon = **82** miles

2nd- Geneva (CH) - 1 hr **45**
→ Cluses - **A40 E25** & **D907** =
82 miles

3rd- Milan - 2 hrs **35**
→ **E64 A4 E25** and **406** via
Chatillon = **140** miles

Verdict - Good all-round mountain with nice slopes. Very basic resort. **8/10**

COST INDICATOR

Budget   Moderate   Very Expensive   Criminal

i - **Information** - 0039 (0) 165 884 179
www.lathuile.net

Italy
Limone

Mapping Page 53 B5

ROUTE PLANNER

CALAIS 0 miles		
	along the **A16 - A26**	
	E15 / E17	
	Toll Road	
REIMS 168 miles		
2hrs 53	**A26 A4 E17 / 50**	
CHALONS en CHAMPAGNE		
3hrs 15	**A26 E17**	
	Tolls End	
TROYES 236 miles		
	A5 E17 / 54	
MARAC 295 miles		
7hrs 16	**A31 E17 / 21**	
DIJON 351 miles		
7hrs 50	**A31 E17 & E15 A6**	
MACON 395 miles		
8hrs 55	**A6 E15**	
LYON 471 miles		
9hrs 50	**A43 E70 A48 E711**	
GRENOBLE 537 miles		
11hrs 50	**N90, A41, A32** and all routes via Turin to the the **A6.**	
Enter Italy 619 miles		
	A32, A6, E74 SP428, SR20, and all routes via **Cunoe SP422**	

LIMONE

KM Distance	**754 miles** *(1213km)*	
Drive time	**14 hours**	
Fuel	**£63**	
€ Tolls	**£39**	

Top Lift
2800m.
Resort Height
1032m.
Vertical Drop
1018m.
Number of Runs
46
Longest Run
-
Slopes
100km of piste
●● *Beginner*
20% of the runs
◐ *Intermediate*
70% of the runs
● *Advanced*
10% of the runs

Cross-Country
10km of tracks
Snowboarding
-
Snow Season
Dec to April
Snowmaking
15% of piste
Number of lifts
18
Up Lift Capicity
22,000 per hour
Mountain Cafes
7

On the Slopes - Limone is not the best known of resorts, but nevertheless it's popular with Italian and French visitors, partly due its location on the French/Italian border. It's a year-round holiday centre that attracts visitors for skiing in the winter and outdoor pursuits in the summer and therefore knows how to lay on good services. The views from the charming traditional village are spectacular, but in terms of offering skiers and snowboarders challenging terrain or a memorable trip, it's more difficult to see the appeal. Despite having a somewhat average snow record, Limone does have a number of decent slopes, but the large number of regular visitors must be keeping the best to themselves, because on the face of things, Limone does not particularly stand out from the crowd. Advanced skiers will soon have the place covered and if they have booked a two-week visit, they will soon be regretting it. Likewise, beginners will not be impressed with the poor choice of nursery slopes and the lack of gentle connecting pistes. However, piste hugging intermediate carvers on skis and snowboards, will have a super time with much of the mountain turned over to them and as lift lines are short and slopes uncrowded and easy to negotiate, Limone becomes a decent alternative to the rather better documented resorts. Not that snowboarders will be too bothered, as this is not a good snowboard resort simply because the terrain is rather dull and the resort is not interested in facilities long term. Cross-country skiers do get a decent amount of varied terrain to slide.

Off the Slopes - Limone is small rustic village and accommodation is a bit sparse with only a few hotels and B&B's to select from. Around the resort, local attractions include an art gallery, a cinema and sporting facilities. As well as a number of general shops there are over fifty restaurants to choose from and a number of bars, but don't expect to party hard – Limone is a quiet place and the locals like it that way.

Verdict - Low-key resort best suited to intermediates. **4/10**

COST INDICATOR
Budget   Moderate   Very Expensive   Criminal

i **- Information -** 0039 (0) 171 929 515
www.limone.net

Airports & Fly Drive Guide
1st- Nice - 1 hr 30
D2204 and routes north via Borgo San Dalmazzo = **68 miles**

2nd- Turin - 2 hrs 35
A6 and routes south via Cunoe = **92 miles**

3rd- Milan (A)- 3 hrs 35
A7, A21 south = **160 miles**

Italy
Livingo

Mapping Page 88 D1

ROUTE PLANNER

CALAIS 0 miles		
	along the **A16 - A26**	
	E15 / E17	
	Toll Road	
REIMS 168 miles		
2hrs 53	**A4 E17 / 50**	
METZ 270 miles		
4hrs 47	**A4 E25** *Dir Strasbourg*	
	Tolls End	
A35 north to the **D4**		
Enter Germany 401 miles		
	B500 to the **E35 - 5**	
KARLSRUHE 424 miles		
7hrs 16	**A8 E52** *via Pforzheim*	
STUTGART 459 miles		
7hrs 50	**A8 E52**	
ULM 523 miles		
8hrs 55	**A7 E532**	
KEMPTEN 573 miles		
9hrs 50	**A7 E532** south via	
Nesselwang along the **B309** & **B179.**		
	Enter Austria 600 miles	
	Head south along the **B179** via the **Fernpaß** to the **B189.**	
INNSBRUCK 658 miles		
11hrs 50	**A13, Brenner Pass**	
Enter Italy 681 miles		
Toll Road	**A22 E45** via Bolzano	
Tolls End	Pick up the **38** then the **301.**	

LIVINGO

KM Distance	**771 miles** (1240 km)	
Drive time	**13 hours 25 mins**	
Fuel	**£68**	
€ Tolls	**£36**	

Top Lift
2050m.
Resort Height
1032m.
Vertical Drop
940m.
Number of Runs
55
Longest Run
7km
Slopes
115km of piste
●● *Beginner*
44% of the runs
◐ *Intermediate*
45% of the runs
● *Advanced*
11% of the runs

Cross-Country
50km of tracks
Snowboarding
Half-pipe & Park
Snow Season
Dec to April
Snowmaking
15% of piste
Number of lifts
31
Up Lift Capicity
42,000 per hour
Mountain Cafes
6

On the Slopes - Perhaps the thing that Livigno is most famous for is it's its status as a tax-free haven, but there's far more to it than that. For example, there's a good rate of annual snowfall, it's set at a high altitude, which means that the snow stays better for longer, there's great skiing and snowboarding, particularly for beginners and intermediates and on top of that, there's good cross country options. On the downside, the resort itself is a little tacky and a little spread out, plus the slopes can get very busy. Still interested? Well, you should be – Livigno fulfils everything that a purpose built ski resort should. You can access the slopes with ease from numerous access points from both sides of the resort, with the main cluster of lower level nursery runs on the one side. In terms of terrain, intermediates and beginners are the best catered for with an abundance of blue and red runs for them to progress in the skiing and snowboarding. Experts are the ones who are let down, and despite a few marked out black trails, there is little of major interest and few demanding long steeps. You can find some off-piste terrain but you need to know where you're looking, which is best done with a local guide. Cross-country skiers have more than 50km of tracks that take in much of the mountain and although the trails are not the most spectacular, they are well laid out. Like much of Italy, Livigno took some time to recognise snowboarding, yet the resort has some great freeriding spots. In the past, there was not even sniff of a terrain park, but now Livigno has one of the largest parks in Europe.

Off the Slopes - If you're looking for any kind of consumer goods or for inexpensive drinking, Livigno has to be on your list of 'must visit' resorts, thanks to the tax-free policy. Accommodation is plentiful in the resort, with lots of basic hotels to cheap apartments and even a youth hostel. The resort is not fancy and even though it has an alpine appearance it is a bit tacky. Eating out is nothing to shout about while nightlife is a case of drink, drink even more then pass out.

Verdict - High altitude resort, but not for experts. Cheap by most standards. **7/10**

COST INDICATOR
Budget   Moderate   Very Expensive   Criminal

i **- Information -** 0039 (0) 342 996 379
www.aptlivingo.it

Airports & Fly Drive Guide
1st- Innsbruck (A)- 2 hrs 46
A22 E45 via Bolzano and the **43 & 43** = **112 miles**

2nd- Milan - 3 hrs 20
E64, A4 & A22 via Trento = **136 miles**

3rd- Verona - 3 hrs 40
A22 north via Trento = **146 miles**

DRIVE TIME - **nixon** www.nixon.com

Madesimo

Mapping Page 87 E6

ROUTE PLANNER

CALAIS	0 miles
	along the A16 - A26
	E15 / E17
	Toll Road
REIMS	xxx miles
2hrs 53	A4 E17 / 50
METZ	270 miles
4hrs 47	A4 E25 Dir Strasbourg
	Tolls End

A35 north to the D4
Enter Germany 401 miles
B500 to the E35 - 5

Enter Switzerland

BASEL	475 miles
8hr 10	E60, A3
ZURICH	523 miles
8hrs 55	A13, E43
CHUR	580 miles
10hrs	13 to the SS36 via Spiugen.

Enter Italy 631 miles
SS36

MADESIMO

KM Distance	643 miles (1035 km)
Drive time	11 hours 20 mins
Fuel	£58
€ Tolls	£32

Top Lift
2872m.
Resort Height
1550m.
Vertical Drop
1322m.
Number of Runs
25
Longest Run
3km
Slopes
80km of piste
● ● Beginner
20% of the runs
● Intermediate
70% of the runs
● Advanced
10% of the runs

Cross-Country
5km of tracks
Snowboarding
Half-pipe & Park
Snow Season
Dec to April
Snowmaking
22 cannons
Number of lifts
15
Up Lift Capicity
15,000 per hour
Mountain Cafes
4

On the Slopes - Until this point had you even heard of Maddesimo? No? Well, you are not alone – it's not even particularly well known in Italy, but those who are familiar with this rather special gem want to keep it to themselves and preserve what is on offer. Maddesimo may not be the biggest resort, nor has it got vast amounts of terrain, but what does offer is peace and quiet, high altitude slopes with good snow cover and excellent snowmaking for backup, along with terrain for all abilities. You won't find tour operators flooding the slopes with first timers in day-glo one piece suits, but you will find visitors who don't mind the two hour drive from Nice, because they know that when they get there, they'll be able to ski and snowboard on well maintained runs without needing a satellite navigation system in order to avoid crowds. Intermediates will generally get the best out of this mountain as most of the runs are basic with the odd scary bit to keep them on their toes. Experts, however, can have a good time, in particular on the Canalone run, which will be enough to fulfil even the most experienced speed freak. One of the joys of this mountain – apart for the short lift queues – is the diversity of the terrain and its features. One minute you can be knee deep in powder, the next chewing sticks as you weave through some thick wooded glades around the mid to lower sections. Beginners are better staying on the lower areas before venturing higher, as it is not the easiest mountain to master and there are not many novice runs higher up. Snowboarders, however, will be able to experience the big head rush you get when you jump off cliffs or pump down steep freeriding slopes such as the Val Di Lei area.

Off the Slopes - The village is a sprawling affair, with some good hotels and apartment rooms for hire. This is not an action town and local services are sparse but there is a sports centre, some shops and half a dozen or so restaurants and bars – don't expect to rock at night, quiet time is the order of the day here.

Verdict - A decent 'off the beaten track' resort, with nice intermediate slopes. 7/10

COST INDICATOR

Budget   Moderate   Very Expensive   Criminal

i - **Information** - 0039 (0) 3435 3015
www.

Airports & Fly Drive Guide

1st- Milan (CH) - 2 hrs 20
E35, A9, and all routes north via Arbedo = 82 miles

2nd- Turin - 4 hrs
A4 E64 and all routes north via Milan = 195 miles

3rd- Zurich - 2 hrs 40
E35, 2 and all routes south via Chur = 125 miles

Madonna di Campiglio

Mapping Page 85 A8

ROUTE PLANNER

CALAIS	0 miles
	along the A16 - A26
	E15 / E17
	Toll Road
REIMS	168 miles
2hrs 53	A4 E17 / 50
METZ	270 miles
4hrs 47	A4 E25 Dir Strasbourg
	Tolls End

A35 north to the D4
Enter Germany 401 miles
B500 to the E35 - 5

KARLSRUHE	424 miles
7hrs 16	A8 E52 via Pforzheim
STUTGART	459 miles
7hrs 50	A8 E52
ULM	523 miles
8hrs 55	A7 E532
KEMPTEN	573 miles
9hrs 50	A7 E532 south via

Nesselwang along the
B309 & B179.
Enter Austria 600 miles
Head south along the
B179 via the Fernpaß
to the B189.

INNSBRUCK	658 miles
11hrs 50	A13, Brenner Pass

Enter Italy 681 miles
Toll Road A22 E45 via Bolzano
Tolls End Pick up the 43 & 239

MA/DI CAMPIGLIO

KM Distance	803 miles (1293 km)
Drive time	14 hours 30 mins
Fuel	£68
€ Tolls	£36

Top Lift
2580m.
Resort Height
1520m.
Vertical Drop
985m.
Number of Runs
40
Longest Run
4km
Slopes
87km of piste
● ● Beginner
54% of the runs
● Intermediate
30% of the runs
● Advanced
16% of the runs

Cross-Country
30km of tracks
Snowboarding
Half-pipe & Park
Snow Season
Dec to April
Snowmaking
24 cannons
Number of lifts
25
Up Lift Capicity
30,700 per hour
Mountain Cafes
10

On the Slopes - Madonna Di Campiglio is one of the finest resorts in Italy and a favourite weekend destination for Milan's fashionable elite – and now increasingly popular with foreign visitors. Located north of Milan, close to Trento and 2 1/2 hours south of Innsbruck in Austria, this is a large modern resort that is spread out to offer access to the slopes from both sides of the town. You will find plenty of other resorts around the area that link up with Madonna, including the likes of Folgarida and Marilleva. In general the snow record for the whole area is pretty good and is backed up by lots of snowmaking facilities. The main slopes for Madonna are split in to three areas, Pradalago, Passo Groste or the Pancugolo, which are connected by a number of lifts and offer similar terrain on each area. The Pradalago slopes win the prize for being the largest area, however, but irrespective of which area you ride, beginner to intermediate will find that they are best served as the nursery slopes are ideal and well proportioned, with the best novice slopes at Campo Carlo Mango. Expert terrain may be a little short in supply, but what there is, is excellent with not just good off-piste slopes, but also challenging steep black pistes. It's not only Italy's skiers that like Madonna as it has gained a reputation amongst snowboaders, with top events being held here and attracting the biggest names in the sport – the local snowboard school is highly recommended. There are lots of good wooded trails for cross country fans, with something to suit entry level to advanced skiers.

Off the Slopes - The alpine-style village is somewhat expensive, with many of the hotels in the upper price brackets and little for budget-conscious visitors. The centre is car-free and loaded with shops, while restaurants are basic in style but good on service with pizzerias a favourite. Nightlife comes with a little too much glitz and The Cliffhanger and Stube are both popular hangouts.

Verdict - Snow-sure intermediate slopes. Resort can be expensive. 8/10

COST INDICATOR

Budget   Moderate   Very Expensive   Criminal

i - **Information** - 0039 (0) 4654 42000
www.

Airports & Fly Drive Guide

1st- Verona - 2 hrs
A22 north via Trento = 88 miles

2nd- Milan - 4 hrs
E64, A4 & A22 via Trento = 140 miles

3rd- Innsbruck (A)- 3 hrs
A22 E45 via Bolzano and the 43 & 43 = 146 miles

DRIVE TIME - *nixon* www.nixon.com

Passo Tonale

Italy

ROUTE PLANNER

✈	**CALAIS**	0 miles
	along the **A16 - A26**
	E15 / E17
	Toll Road
→	**REIMS** 168 miles	2hrs 53
	A4 E17 / 50
→	**METZ** 270 miles	4hrs 47
	A4 E25 Dir Strasbourg
	Tolls End
✈	**A35** north to the **D4**
⚠	**Enter Germany** 401 miles
	B500 to the **E35 - 5**
✈	**KARLSRUHE** 424 miles	7hrs 16
	A8 E52 via Pforzheim
→	**STUTTGART** 459 miles	7hrs 50
	A8 E52
→	**ULM** 523 miles	8hrs 55
	A7 E532
→	**KEMPTEN** 573 miles	9hrs 50
	A7 E532 south via
⚠	**Nesselwang** along the
	B309 & **B179**.
	Enter Austria 600 miles
	Head south along the
	B179 via the **Fernpaß**
	to the **B189**.
→	**INNSBRUCK** 658 miles	11hrs 50
	A13, Brenner Pass
⚠	**Enter Italy** 681 miles
Toll Road	**A22 E45** via **Bolzano**
Tolls End	Pick up the **43 & 42**

| → | **PASSO TONALE** |

KM	**Distance**	**800** miles *(1290 km)*
⏱	**Drive time**	**15** hours
⛽	**Fuel**	**£69**
€	**Tolls**	**£35**

Top Lift
3025m.
Resort Height
1883m.
Vertical Drop
1142m.
Number of Runs
28
Longest Run
7km
Slopes
80km of piste
● ● *Beginner*
20% of the runs
○ *Intermediate*
55% of the runs
● Advanced
24% of the runs

Cross-Country
24km of tracks
Snowboarding
Half-pipe & Park
Snow Season
Dec to April
Snowmaking
20km of piste
Number of lifts
28
Up Lift Capacity
32,000 per hour
Mountain Cafes
6

On the Slopes - The resort of Passo Tonale sits on top of the mountain pass of the same name and is not just a winter destination. Thanks to the resort's high altitude and the Presena Glacier, this is also a good summer ski and snowboard centre with good snow cover throughout the year. Strangely it's not common knowledge and despite having good sunny slopes and hardly any queues or busy slopes, Passo Tonale is still a relatively quiet place. UK tour operators do promote the resort in their brochures, but it is not to everyone's taste and perhaps the rather dull appearance and setting is to blame. Whatever, this is a place that is worth checking out and if you are a first timer to winter sports holidays, then it can fill most of your expectations. Passo Tonale is great for beginners, with some exceptionally good nursery slopes that are serviced by chair-lifts rather than dreaded drag lifts. The runs cover a large expanse and there are some great, wide-open pistes where carvers can fly down without too many obstacles getting in the way. Experts can feel at home here and will find that some of the challenging runs are just that. For instance if you don't treat the steep Cantiere run with respect or caution you could come unstuck. Snowboaders love this place, as there is something different to try out every run, and no matter what style of snowboarding takes your fancy, there is something for you have a go at. The off-piste is excellent, with the best terrain up on the Presena Glacier. Unfortunately there are no terrain parks, an oversight by the management for sure.

Off the Slopes - Given the rather bleak setting of the resort, the accommodation, restaurants, nightlife and local attractions won't be to everyone's liking, but nevertheless it caters well and has lots of amenities. There are all sorts of accommodation options, ranging from four star hotels to basic B&B's and even a campsite – not one for the winter, though. Prices are reasonable and overall it is an affordable place. Eating out options are limited, as are bars.

Verdict - An affordable resort that offers excellent slopes, year-round. **7/10**

COST INDICATOR

Budget   Moderate   Very Expensive   Criminal

i **- Information** - 0039 (0) 3649 1122
www.comune.ponte-di-legno.bs.it

| ✈ | **Airports & Fly Drive Guide** |
| **1st- Milan** - 2 hrs 25 |
| → | **E64, A4 & A22** via **Trento** |
| = **105** miles |
| **2nd- Verona** - 2 hrs 27 |
| → | **A22** north via **Trento** |
| = **114** miles |
| **3rd- Innsbruck** (A)- 2 hrs 50 |
| → | **A22 E45** via **Bolzano** and |
| the **43 & 43** = **145** miles |

Pila Aosta

Italy

ROUTE PLANNER

✈	**CALAIS**	0 miles
	along the **A16 - A26**
	E15 / E17
	Toll Road
→	**REIMS** 168 miles	2hrs 53
	A4 E17 / 50
→	**CHALONS en CHAMPAGNE**	3hrs 15
	A26 E17
→	**TROYES** 236 miles	4hrs
	A5 E17 / 54
→	**MARAC** 295 miles	5hrs
	A31 E17 / 21
→	**DIJON** xxx miles	6hrs 10
	A31 E17 & E15 A6
→	**MACON** 396 miles	7hrs
	A40 E62
→	**BOURG-en-BRESSE** 426 miles	7hrs 15
	A40 E62
→	**GENEVA** 491 miles	8hrs 20
	A40 E25 N506,
	direction Chamonix.
	Mont Blanc.
	Enter Italy 681 miles
	Past Courmayeur A5
	E25A4/5 head for Milan.
	Pick up the **A26** north
	and turn off at signs for
Tolls End	**Borgosesia** to reach the
	resort.

| → | **PILA AOSTA** |

KM	**Distance**	**687** miles *(1106 km)*
⏱	**Drive time**	**12** hours **20** mins
⛽	**Fuel**	**£58**
€	**Tolls**	**£36**

Top Lift
2750m.
Resort Height
1540m.
Vertical Drop
1210m.
Number of Runs
70
Longest Run
3.8km
Slopes
70km of piste
● ● *Beginner*
20% of the runs
○ *Intermediate*
72% of the runs
● Advanced
8% of the runs

Cross-Country
5km of tracks
Snowboarding
Half-pipe & Park
Snow Season
Dec to April
Snowmaking
12% of piste
Number of lifts
14
Up Lift Capacity
16,300 per hour
Mountain Cafes
8

On the Slopes - Pila is one of Italy's more interesting resorts and one that is still waiting to be discovered by the masses from other countries. Pila is a modern resort, which is linked by cable car to the Roman town of Aosta – but there's nothing ancient about the mountain, with its modern lifts and extensive snowmaking system. The slopes take in everything that you could wish for, from open powder fields to tight, wooded sections and well maintained pistes, all lending themselves nicely to beginners, intermediates and experts – it really wouldn't be an overstatement to say that Pila is a resort that has something to please all levels. Skiers who prefer big moguls fields and steep runs that take more than two turns to complete will find Pila much to there liking – the black run down from Piatta De Grevon is enough to give anyone something to think about and you really don't want to bail this one. Much of the mountain is made up of well-groomed red runs, which are ideal intermediate carving runs. Novices however, may find that much of the mountain is a bit tricky. Pila has long been a friend to snowboarders – back in the 80's, when the rest of Italy was only reading about snowboarding, Pila was way ahead and building pipes and running competitions. The mountain lends itsself particularly well to fast freeriding down gnarly steeps and through lots of tight trees. Cross-country skiers may want to give this place a miss. There is very little in terms of marked trails.

Off the Slopes - Pila is a welcoming resort, if a little sparse when it comes to facilities. The hotels that are available are good, as are the number of B&B's where reasonably-priced rooms are available. Apartments with rooms capable of sleeping groups of up to ten can also be rented around the resort. If Pila doesn't match your needs, then you may find Aosta a better option as it has more to offer in the way of accommodation, sports facilities, restaurants and bars. Wherever you stay, evenings are generally quiet, without any major events to report.

Verdict - A nice friendly mountain with great views and excellent red runs. **7/10**

COST INDICATOR

Budget   Moderate   Very Expensive   Criminal

i **- Information** - 0039 (0) 16552 1055
www.espace-de-pila.com

| ✈ | **Airports & Fly Drive Guide** |
| **1st- Milan** - 1 hr **44** |
| → | **E25** and all routes via |
| **Borgosesia** = **80** miles |
| **2nd- Turin** - 2 hrs |
| → | **E64 A4** and and all routes |
| via **Borgosesia** = **90** miles |
| **3rd- Verona** - 3 hr **20** |
| → | all routes via **Milan** and |
| **Borgosesia** = **168** miles |

DRIVE TIME - nixon ® www.nixon.com

Prato Nevoso

ROUTE PLANNER

CALAIS 0 miles
along the **A16 - A26**
E15 / E17
Toll Road

REIMS 168 miles
2hrs 53 **A4 E17 / 50**

CHALONS en CHAMPAGNE
3hrs 15 **A26 E17**

TROYES 236 miles
4hrs **A5 E17 / 54**

MARAC 295 miles
5hrs **A31 E17 / 21**

DIJON 351 miles
6hr 10 **A31 E17 & E15 A6**

MACON 395 miles
7hrs **A6 E15**

LYON 471 miles
8hrs 50 **E70 A43. N6**

Tolls End **Enter Italy** 596 miles
E70 A32

TURIN 650 miles
12hrs **A6, E717** to the **SP12**
and **SP5** via **Mondovi**
for the **SP5** and **SP37** to
the resort

PRATO NEVOSO

KM	Distance	**724 miles** *(1166 km)*
	Drive time	**13 hours 50 mins**
	Fuel	**£65**
	Tolls	**£43**

Top Lift
1950m.
Resort Height
1490m.
Vertical Drop
550m.
Number of Runs
15
Longest Run
-
Slopes
30km of piste
● *Beginner*
70% of the runs
○ *Intermediate*
35% of the runs
● **Advanced**
5% of the runs

Cross-Country
5km of tracks
Snowboarding
-
Snow Season
Dec to April
Snowmaking
15% of piste
Number of lifts
13
Up Lift Capacity
9,460 per hour
Mountain Cafes
2

On the Slopes - Prato Nevoso is neither big nor very well known despite the fact that it has been operating as a ski resorts since as far back as 1965. Located not far from the French border this is a resort that forms part of the Mondole ski circuit. Non-adventurous and ideal for slow learners who wet them selves at speeds above 2mph, this is really not one of the world's most interesting resorts. However, not everyone wants arse twitching steeps or bucket loads of deep powder. Some people prefer small mountains where the snow is irregular and lifts that go faster in reverse than forwards. But hey, this is still not a bad resort and if your have two young kids and plan a winter holiday with the whole family including the in-laws, uncles and aunts and the pets then look no further, this is a family retreat and although it is dull and not clever, it's adequate and good for a weeks simple fun. In fairness the resort is constantly upgrading its lift system and the 13 or so lifts can still up-lift over 9400 people an hour. Prato Nevoso has 30km of mainly beginner level runs and naff all for experts, however, when you add in the kilometres of pistes at Aresina, you have over 100km of terrain with areas of trees, some good off-piste powder spots and runs to take at speed. Cross-country skiers however, won't find much to shine on or talk about. They don't come much duller than this place for those who like to read a book as they ski. Snowboarders also won't be greatly enthused about what there is to offer here. The slopes are perfect if you have just brought your first board but don't know how to use them, like wise Euro-carvers wearing head bands, who like to pose along lift lines as they ride past at near walking pace, will love it here.

Off the Slopes - Prato Nevoso is purpose built but boring. Accommodation is extremely limited, although not expensive and local amenities are almost nonexistent, but you can get by with a couple of decent restaurants and a few nightspots. If you want to party hard, look elsewhere.

Verdict - Great for grannies first trip but dull to the extreme for the rest **5/10**

COST INDICATOR

Budget　　Moderate　　Very Expensive　　Criminal

i - Information - 0039 (0) 174 334 133

1st- Turin - 2 hrs 20
A6, E717 to the **SP37** via
Mondovi = 84 miles

2nd- Nice (F) - 3 hrs
**E74/80, A10, SS20, SP21,
SP5** and **SP237** = 110 miles

3rd- Lyon (F) - 4 hrs 45
E70 A43. N6 and all routes
via **Turin** and **Mondovi** = 245
miles

78

Sauze d'Oulx

ROUTE PLANNER

CALAIS 0 miles
along the **A16 - A26**
E15 / E17
Toll Road

REIMS 168 miles
2hrs 53 **A4 E17 / 50**

CHALONS en CHAMPAGNE
3hrs 15 **A26 E17**

TROYES 236 miles
4hrs **A5 E17 / 54**

MARAC 295 miles
5hrs **A31 E17 / 21**

DIJON 351 miles
6hr 10 **A31 E17 & E15 A6**

MACON 395 miles
7hrs **A6 E15**

LYON 471 miles
8hrs 50 **E70 A43, A430
N6 & 25**

Tolls End *Access via Modane is
possible via the pass.*

Enter Italy 596 miles
E70 A32

SAUZE d'OULX

KM	Distance	**616 miles** *(992 km)*
	Drive time	**11 hours 40 mins**
	Fuel	**£61**
	Tolls	**£37**

Top Lift
2823m.
Resort Height
1382m.
Vertical Drop
1441m.
Number of Runs
-
Longest Run
7km
Slopes
400km of piste
● *Beginner*
15% of the runs
○ *Intermediate*
62% of the runs
● **Advanced**
25% of the runs

Cross-Country
24km of tracks
Snowboarding
Half-pipe & Park
Snow Season
Dec to April
Snowmaking
75km of pistes
Number of lifts
15
Up Lift Capacity
94,000 per hour
Mountain Cafes
15

On the Slopes - The Milky Way is a huge ski circuit that is home to a number of resorts, among them Sauze d'Oulx, one of the most popular in the region. Over the years, Sauze has gained a bit of a down market reputation that has a British feel to it as it's not a quaint comfortable retreat. This is a place where groups of package holiday-makers fill up the slopes during the day and party hard in the evenings. The slopes are idea for intermediate and slow learners as there are a good number of well connected and wide open pistes, which are mainly above the tree line and although the snow record here is hit and miss, the runs are well maintained. The uplift is not one of the resort's strong points and with a number of rather old chair lifts, getting around all the slopes can take some time – but at least queues are not a major problem. If you have never tried skiing or snowboarding before, then you might find Sauze's slopes a bit daunting, especially if you are a really slow learner. On the other hand, if you have a few snow trips under your belt, then you will find this place hard to beat. The intermediate runs are excellent and will make a carver out of most who try it. Experts are not going to be so engrossed, although there are runs to send a shiver down the spine including some great off-piste areas. In terms of snowboarding, this place is best for those who like flat pistes.

Off the Slopes - While Sauze d'Oulx is package tour heaven, cheap and a bit run down it's very lively and a lot fun if you come with an open mind. There are plenty of centrally located hotels with very reasonable rates along with apartment rooms for groups and B&B's for those on their own. Dining out doesn't have to cost the earth, as there is a good selection of restaurants with prices and menus to suit all tastes. But apart from eating out and drinking, the resort doesn't have much else to offer – the bars and discos are all very busy and stay open late, however, Nothing is too flash and prices for booze reasonable, however, watch out for over zealous tour reps on ego trips.

Verdict - Ideal for intermediates, but not the quietest place – cheap, though. **7/10**

COST INDICATOR

Budget　　Moderate　　Very Expensive　　Criminal

i - Information - 0039 (0) 122 858 009

1st- Turin - 1 hr 30
A32 E70 east via **Rivoli** =
56 miles

2nd - Milan - 2 hrs 45
A4 & E64 and all routes via
Turin = 137 miles

3rd - Lyon (F) - 2 hrs 50
E70 A43, A430, N6 via
Oulx = 140 miles

Italy
Sestriere

Mapping Page 47 F8

ROUTE PLANNER

CALAIS 0 miles	
along the **A16 - A26** **E15 / E17** *Toll Road*	
REIMS 168 miles	2hrs 53
A4 E17 / 50	
CHALONS en CHAMPAGNE	3hrs 15
A26 E17	
TROYES 236 miles	4hrs
A5 E17 / 54	
MARAC 295 miles	5hrs
A31 E17 / 21	
DIJON 351 miles	6hr 10
A31 E17 & E15 A6	
MACON 395 miles	7hrs
A6 E15	
LYON 471 miles	8hrs 10
E70 A43, A430 **N6 & 25**	
Tolls End *Access via Modane is possible via the pass.*	
Enter Italy 596 miles	
E70 A32	

Top Lift
2823m.
Resort Height
1350m.
Vertical Drop
1330m.
Number of Runs
118
Longest Run
7km
Slopes
400km of piste
● ● *Beginner*
15% of the runs
◑ *Intermediate*
60% of the runs
● *Advanced*
25% of the runs

Cross-Country
24km of tracks
Snowboarding
Half-pipe
Snow Season
Dec to April
Snowmaking
950 cannons
Number of lifts
20
Up Lift Capicity
94,000 per hour
Mountain Cafes
17

On the Slopes - Large, modern and a 2006 host resort for the winter Olympics, Sestriere is an all-round resort that should appeal to every level of skier and snowboarder – it's also one of the more popular resorts of the Milky Way network of resorts. The 118 plus runs are well pisted and even though reliable snow is not assured, the resort has so many snow cannons that snow cover of some sort is always possible – the lifts are extremely efficient and no-one stands in a queue for more than a few minutes except for the busiest of weekends and over holidays. Experts can go home content after a week on a mountain with good steep sections and some fabulous off-piste areas. Intermediates are in for a major treat with almost 60% of the marked runs to suit them and if you go home the same standard as you arrived you need to get your self treated by a shrink. Beginners also have places suited to them, with good local nursery slopes set out in a convenient manner and if Sestriere's slopes are not enough, there are plenty more to choose from within the region – not all are lift linked, however. Should you have a late night on the tiles and can't make the slopes during the day don't fret, because the slopes are lit twice a week for night skiing and snowboarding. Snowboarders who do get out of bed have a mountain with endless freeriding spots and some awesome natural hits to get big airs from. Resonable cross-crountry resorts with a few interesting tracks dotted around the mountain.

Off the Slopes - The resort is going through many changes and getting a major face-lift for the Olympics, a good thing as Sestriere is a rather ugly modern affair. However, it offers excellent facilities with apartment accommodation the main form of lodging, where prices are reasonable and deals are available. The resort has a number of attractions and drinking is not the only thing that takes place here. However, if you do fancy pints then why not try Pinky's or the Irish Igloo bar, both are popular haunts with locals and visitors alike.

SESTRIERE	
KM **Distance** 625 miles *(1006 km)*	
⏱ **Drive time** 12 hours 10 mins	
⛽ **Fuel** £62	
€ **Tolls** £37	

Verdict - This is an all-round mountain with a nice resort to back it up. **8/10**

COST INDICATOR

Budget | Moderate | Very Expensive | Criminal

i **- Information -** 0039 (0) 122 755 444

✈ **Airports & Fly Drive Guide**

1st- Turin - **1 hr 40**
➡ **A32 E70** east via **Rivoli** = 65 miles

2nd - Milan - **2 hrs 55**
➡ **A4 & E64** and all routes via Turin = 146 miles

3rd - Lyon (F) - **3 hrs**
➡ **E70 A43, A430, N6** via Oulx = 148 miles

Italy
Val Gardena

Mapping Page 88 D3

ROUTE PLANNER

CALAIS 0 miles	
along the **A16 - A26** **E15 / E17** *Toll Road*	
REIMS 168 miles	2hrs 53
A4 E17 / 50	
METZ 270 miles	4hrs 47
A4 E25 Dir Strasbourg	
Tolls End	
A35 north to the **D4**	
⚠ **Enter Germany** 401 miles **B500** to the **E35 - 5**	
KARLSRUHE 424 miles	av1hr 35
A8 E52 via Pforzheim	
STUTTGART 459 miles	7hrs 50
A8 E52	
ULM 523 miles	8hrs 55
A7 E532	
KEMPTEN 573 miles	9hrs 50
A7 E532 south via	
⚠ **Nesselwang** along the **B309 & B179.**	
Enter Austria 500 miles Head south along the **B179** via the **Fernpaß** to the **B189.**	
INNSBRUCK 658 miles	11hrs 50
A13, Brenner Pass	
⚠ **Enter Italy**	
Toll Road **A22 E45** via **Chiusa**	
Tolls End Then pick up the **242** and the **243** to the resort.	
VAL GARDENA	

Top Lift
2454m.
Resort Height
1563m.
Vertical Drop
890m.
Number of Runs
70
Longest Run
9km
Slopes
1200km of piste
● ● *Beginner*
30% of the runs
◑ *Intermediate*
60% of the runs
● *Advanced*
10% of the runs

Cross-Country
98km of tracks
Snowboarding
Half-pipe & Park
Snow Season
Dec to April
Snowmaking
400 cannons
Number of lifts
80
Up Lift Capicity
86,400 per hour
Mountain Cafes
18

On the Slopes - Val Gardena, or Selva Val Gardena as it's more properly known, is located in one most amazing parts of the Dolomites and, in partnership with numerous other resorts, is a major player when it comes to linked ski networks. Set amongst some spectacular scenery, this area should always be on your short list when flicking through the winter holiday brochures. Massive rock cliffs form the backdrop to a mountain with huge possibilities and endless enjoyment – which can be tested a little when you're battling the crowds and waiting in endless lift queues. This area doesn't have the best annual snow record and the resort is rather dated and not the most convenient for the slopes — don't let that point put you off as there is plenty here to counter any negatives. The runs are perfect for most levels, although advanced skiers and hardcore freeriding snowboarders may find it lacking in testing terrain. It's those in the middle ranks who will get the best out of this place, as most of the runs are marked red on the piste map, but it would be fair to say that some slopes are a bit overrated and provided you have your wits about you, can be tackled by those who normally stick to blue runs. Snowboarders who can't find anything to content themselves within a region of around 1200km of piste should really try a different sport. Like wise, and if cross-country skiing is your pleasure, if you can't make do with the 100km of trails that you will find here, you need to give up and try bowls.

Off the Slopes - Val Gardena is not to everyone's taste and isn't the sort of place you would want a postcard of. You will find comfortable hotels and various apartment blocks, but not all are the most convenient – still, there dozens of shops and numerous restaurants to choose from as well as a cinema, skating, swimming pools and a sports centre. Nightlife is tame and although there are loads of bars, mainly with a traditional theme, late night sessions don't seem to be very popular around here.

KM **Distance** 738 miles *(1188 km)*	
⏱ **Drive time** 13 hours 20 mins	
⛽ **Fuel** £60	
€ **Tolls** £34	

Verdict - Something for everyone and a reasonably priced resort. **8/10**

COST INDICATOR

Budget | Moderate | Very Expensive | Criminal

i **- Information -** 0039 (0) 471 795 122
www.valgardena.it

✈ **Airports & Fly Drive Guide**

1st- Innsbruck (A) - **1 hr 40**
➡ **A13**, Brenner Pass south via **Chiusa** = 80 miles

2nd- Verona - **2 hrs 30**
➡ **A22** north via **Trento** = 127 miles

3rd- Milan - **3 hrs 50**
➡ **E64, A4 & A22** via **Trento** = 200 miles

⏱ **DRIVE TIME -**  *nixon* www.nixon.com

Norway

Photo - Norwegian Tourism

Resorts Featured
80 **Geilo**
81 **Hemsedal**
81 **Voss**

80 *See page 29 for the index of all resorts.*

DRIVE ON THE RIGHT

Information

Passing place

Joining traffic has priority

Country identification

2 hours parking

Weight per axel limit

Motorway speed	**90kph**	
Rural speed	**80kph**	
Urban speed	**50kph**	
Alcohol limit	**50mgs**	
Front seatbelts	✔	
Rear seatbelts	✔	
Kids in front seat	**-**	
Legal age to drive	**18**	
Warming triangle	Advisable	
First aid kit	Advisable	
Fire extinguisher	Advisable	
Snowchains	Advisable	

FACT FILE

Country - Kongeriket Norge
Location - Western Europe (North)
Geography
Norway shares its land borders with Finland, Russia and Sweden.
Highest Mountain - Glittertind - 2470m
Coast line & Seas - The Atlantic Ocean, Norweigan Ocean, North Sea and the Artic Sea
Land Area - 323,759 sq km (125,004 sq miles)
Capital - Oslo
Popualrtion - 4.5 million
Language - Norwegian
Religion - 86% Evangelical Lutherans
Currecny - Krone
Time - GMT + 1 hour, (GMT + 2 hours between March & October)
Electricity Supply - 220volts
Communications - International Country code 0047
Fire 110
Police 112
Ambulance 113
National Tourism - 0047 (0) 24 14 46 00
www.visitnorway.com
Rail Information - www.nsb.no
Bus Information - www.visitnorway.com
Air Information - www.visitnorway.com
Weather Information - www.dnmi.no
Avalanche Information - www.dnmi.no
www.powderguide.no

Passprts & Visa Requirments

	Passports	Visa
Australian	Yes	No
British	Yes	No
Canadian	Yes	No
USA	Yes	No
EU	ID	No

Duty Free - **None EU travellers**
200 cigarettes or 100 cigarillos or 50 cigars or 25g of tobacco. 1ltr of spirits over 22% or 21% of fortified wine or spirits up to 22% or 21% of sparkling wine or liqueur and 21 % of still wine. 50g of perfume and NOK3500 worth of goods.
EU travellers - No tarrifs.

Motoring Organisations
Kongelig Norsk Automobilklub
Cort Adelersgate 16, 0254 Oslo
tel +47 21 60 49 00

Norges Automobil-Forbund
tel +47 22 34 14 00
fax +47 22 33 13 72
http:// www.naf.no
e-mail: naf@naf.no

Photo - Tourist Office Geilo

Top Lift
1173m.
Resort Height
800m.
Vertical Drop
275m.
Number of Runs
32
Longest Run
4km
Slopes
33km of piste
● *Beginner*
34% of the runs
● *Intermediate*
46% of the runs
● **Advanced**
20% of the runs
Cross-Country
220km of tracks
Snowboarding
Half-pipe & Park
Snow Season
Nov to May
Snowmaking
20 cannons
Number of lifts
18
Up Lift Capicity
21,000 per hour
Mountain Cafes
7

On the Slopes - Geilo is Norway's answer St Moritz; a resort that is neither big nor adventurous, but highly fashionable with Norway's jet set who want to pose rather than take part – which is fine as it leaves the slopes to the real skiers and snowboarders. Located in the Hallingdal valley, Geilo is easy to reach despite being a four-hour drive from Oslo (which is where many of the visitors travel from – weekends and holiday can be unpleasantly busy). The slopes are spread out over two separate mountain areas, which receive a good covering of snow annually and the bulk of the runs are found on the Geilo side, with a small offering on the area known as Vestil. Neither area is particularly steep, nor do they offer much in terms of adventure and the only way to visit both is by road. Most of the runs at Geilo are rated intermediate and apart from a few black slopes and consequently the resort is best suited to beginner and intermediate skiers – many of the red runs are over cautiously rated and can soon be tackled by the more adventurous. What Geilo lacks in challenging terrain it more than makes up for keen freestyle skiers and snowboarders, with three superb terrain parks that have a variety of features rated for beginners to advanced riders. The parks all boast pipes and a series of well-sculpted hits with fun boxes and rails to session. Another plus for Geilo is the amount of amazing cross-country trails in the area.

Off the Slopes - Geilo is not going to win an awful lot of prizes in the facilities awards, yet what there is, is decent enough – a smattering of shops and a generous offering of hotels and cabins abound, but every thing is spread out and there is little for the budget traveller. Pepe's Pizza restaurant is good, but expensive by other European country's standards. The locals are welcoming, however and despite spendy prices for drinks, you can have a good night out. Lille Blaa, which is a snowboarder's hangout, is good for a beer as is the Bukkespranget pub.

Verdict - Reasonable terrain for most users, and fantastic terrain parks. **4/10**

COST INDICATOR

Budget   Moderate   Very Expensive   Criminal

i - **Information** - 0047 (0) 3209 5900
www.geilo.com

Mapping Page 110 A5

ROUTE PLANNER

OSLO	0 miles
	along the E18
DRAMMEN	11 miles
12mins	E134
KONGSBERG	52 miles
1hr 5	E134, 40
RODBERG	62 miles
1hr 50	40
GEILO	

KM	**Distance** 152 miles (245km)
⏱	**Drive time** 3 hours 20 mins
⛽	**Fuel** £15
£	**Tolls**

✈ **Airports & Fly Drive Guide**
1st- Oslo - 3 hrs 20
E18 south, E134 west & 40 north = 152 miles

⏱ DRIVE TIME - nixon® www.nixon.com

Norway

Hemsedal

Mapping Page 117 E5

ROUTE PLANNER

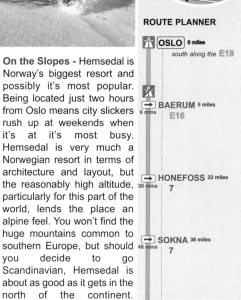

OSLO	0 miles	south along the E18
BAERUM	5 miles	6 mins · E16
HONEFOSS	22 miles	30 mins · 7
SOKNA	38 miles	48 mins · 7
GOL	120 miles	2hrs 40 · 52
HEMSEDAL		

Top Lift
1498m.
Resort Height
650m.
Vertical Drop
800m.
Number of Runs
38
Longest Run
6km
Slopes
38km of piste
● *Beginner*
50% of the runs
● *Intermediate*
26% of the runs
● **Advanced**
24% of the runs

Cross-Country
90km of tracks
Snowboarding
Half-pipe & Park
Snow Season
Nov to May
Snowmaking
30% of pistes
Number of lifts
17
Up Lift Capicity
23,000 per hour
Mountain Cafes
5

On the Slopes - Hemsedal is Norway's biggest resort and possibly it's most popular. Being located just two hours from Oslo means city slickers rush up at weekends when it's at it's most busy. Hemsedal is very much a Norwegian resort in terms of architecture and layout, but the reasonably high altitude, particularly for this part of the world, lends the place an alpine feel. You won't find the huge mountains common to southern Europe, but should you decide to go Scandinavian, Hemsedal is about as good as it gets in the north of the continent. Frequent storms and occasionally harsh winds deposit plenty of natural snow in the resort and there is an extensive snowmaking system to help out should things get patchy. Getting around is made easy by the quick and modern lift system which totals sixteen lifts, the majority of which are draglifts – which won't please novices. The easy runs can be reached from one of the five chair lifts, however, so the less experienced don't need to worry too much. The 38 runs are largely rated easy or intermediate, but there is still terrain for more advanced skiers and snowboarders in the form of some interesting trails with moguls and steep off-piste areas. Freestylers are well catered for with what is widely acknowledged as one of the best terrain parks in Europe and lots of good back-country terrain. Cross-country skiers have over 90km of tracks and while this is not the hottest cross-county resort it offers way more terrain than most European resorts.

Off the Slopes - Hemsedal is a basic and low-key place and accommodation is mixed with a good choice of quality hotels and almost affordable self-catering chalets. The resort also has some good local facilities, which includes a gym, a bowling alley and for those who like to practice their swing, winter golfing. In the evenings Hemsedal really comes to life for the party animals, but if you like your evenings quiet and relaxed you will be best off relaxing in your accommodation. Hot spots are the Hemsedal Café and Skogstads.

Distance 140 miles *(225 km)*
Drive time 3 hours 10 mins
Fuel £14
Tolls

Airports & Fly Drive Guide

Verdict - One of Scandinavia's best resorts especially for beginners. **6/10**

1st- Oslo - 3 hrs 10
E18 south, E16 north & 7, 52 north = **140 miles**

COST INDICATOR

Budget   Moderate   Very Expensive   Criminal

i - **Information** - 0047 (0) 3205 5030
www.hemsedal.com

Norway

Voss

Mapping Page 116 FS

ROUTE PLANNER

OSLO	0 miles	along the E18
DRAMMEN	11 miles	10 mins · E134
KONGSBERG	52 miles	1hr 5 · E134, 40
GEILO		7
VOSS		

Top Lift
945m.
Resort Height
57m.
Vertical Drop
645m.
Number of Runs
12
Longest Run
4km
Slopes
42km of piste
● *Beginner*
40% of the runs
● *Intermediate*
60% of the runs
● **Advanced**
0% of the runs

Cross-Country
60km of tracks
Snowboarding
Half-pipe & Park
Snow Season
Dec to April
Snowmaking
N/A
Number of lifts
10
Up Lift Capicity
8,500 per hour
Mountain Cafes
2

On the Slopes - A small resort with a big name, with good novice and intermediate slopes but little to offer experts. Voss has long been a leading ski resort in Norway and much favoured by nationals and visitors alike, despite being somewhat small. What's more important than how well known a place is, is that it has something to offer its visitors and Voss certainly fills that criteria. Located in the shadow of Mount Hangur and a stone's throw from some spectacular fjords, Voss is one of the those lake side towns that offers practically every type of winter and summer sport going. However, being a popular all year round tourist destination can have its drawbacks, mainly the crowds lining up at the lift stations at weekends and during holiday periods and the expensive prices for most services. The slopes, which link directly to the town by a cable car, are not what experts favour and with no real black runs, there is little to test the advanced. With the exception of the area above the Superbodega, 60% of the terrain is rated as red, which will please intermediates until they realise there is only a total of 12 trails in all and suddenly 60% doesn't sound so impressive. The easy runs are well defined and easy to reach and while not extensive, are perfectly adequate for beginners. Snowboarders are much in evidence and those who know the score will find some good freeriding can be achieved in the Bodega and Superbodega areas. There is a terrain park of sorts, but it is not well maintained, nor is it extensive. Cross-country facilities do exist, although users might find the diversity of trails not up to the standards of other resorts.

Off the Slopes - Voss is a pleasant town, with good facilities and lots of good accommodation. Fleischer's is the best hotel and also offers apartment rooms for hire. Alternatively you could book into the Voss Youth Hostel with cheap bunks (well cheap by most standards). Evenings can be very lively and are best spent in the Hotel Jar or in the Pentagon basement bar, but at around a fiver a pint, its not cheap.

Distance 240 miles *(386 km)*
Drive time 5 hours 30 mins
Fuel £24
Tolls

Airports & Fly Drive Guide

Verdict - Small resort with Olympic history but little to offer experts. **5/10**

1st- Oslo - 5 hrs 30
E18 south, E134 west & 7 north = **240 miles**

COST INDICATOR

Budget   Moderate   Very Expensive   Criminal

i - **Information** - 0047 (0) 5651 1212

DRIVE TIME - nixon. www.nixon.com

Spam

Spain

Resorts Featured
82 **Baqueria Beret**
83 **La Molina**
83 **Sierra Nevada**
See page 29 for the
index of all resorts.

82

See page 29 for the
index of all resorts.

FACT FILE

Country - Estado Espanol
Location - Western Europe (South)
Geography
Spain shares its land borders with Andorra, France
and Portugal.
Highest Mountain - Mulhacen - 3482m
Coast line & Seas - The Atlantic Ocean
and the Mediterranean
Land Area - 504,782 sq km (194,897 sq miles)
Capital - Madrid
Populartion - 41 million
Language - Spanish, Catalan, Galician and Basque
Religion - majority are Roman Catholic
Currecny - Euros
Time - GMT + 1 hour, (GMT + 2 hours between
March & October)
Electricity Supply - 220volts
Communications - International Country code 0034
Fire 080
Police 092
Ambulance 092
National Tourism - www.tourspain.es
Rail Information - www.renfes.es
Bus Information - www.tourspain.es
Air Information - www.tourspain.es
Weather Information - www.inm.es
Avalanche Information - www.ubes/allus/allaus.htm
www.ics.es/allus/maincas.html
www.inmes.es

Passprts & Visa Requirments

	Passports	Visa
Australian	Yes	No
British	Yes	No
Canadian	Yes	No
USA	Yes	No
EU	ID	No

Duty Free - None EU travellers
200 cigarettes or 100 cigarillos or 50 cigars or 25g of
tobacco. 1ltr of spirits over 22% or 21% of fortified wine
or spirits up to 22% or 21% of sparkling wine or liqueur
and 21 % of still wine. 50g of perfume and €37 worth of
goods.
EU travellers - No tarrifs.

Motoring Organisations
RACE
Jose Abascal, 10 28003 Madrid
tel +34 91 594 74 75

RACC - tel +34 93 495 50 35

Federation Espanola de Automvilismo
(FEA) - tel +34 91 729 94 30

DRIVE ON
THE RIGHT

Heavy
Traffic

Dangerous
Descent

Give Way

Country
identification

E

Dead end

Road leads
to canal
or river

Motorway speed	120kph
Rural speed	90kph
Urban speed	50kph
Alcohol limit	50mgs
Front seatbelts	✔
Rear seatbelts	✔
Kids in front seat	-
Legal age to drive	18
Warming triangle	Required
First aid kit	Advisable
Fire extinguisher	Advisable
Snowchains	Advisable

Baqueria Beret

Top Lift
2515m.
Resort Height
1500m.
Vertical Drop
1015m.
Number of Runs
46
Longest Run
5km
Slopes
71km of piste
● Beginner
44% of the runs
● Intermediate
46% of the runs
● Advanced
10% of the runs

Cross-Country
25km of tracks
Snowboarding
Half-pipe & Park
Snow Season
Dec to April
Snowmaking
20 cannons
Number of lifts
26
Up Lift Capicity
28,700 per hour
Mountain Cafes
6

On the Slopes - Skiing and
snowboarding is generally
not the first thing that springs
to mind when you think of
Spain, so its no wonder that
Baqueria Beret is not a com-
monly known-name outside
the country. While Sierra
Nevada is the most famous of
the Spanish resorts, Baqueria
Beret is by far the biggest of
them and has been since
being established back in
1965. Today, this is a popular
and snow sure resort with a
modern and efficient lift system capable of carrying over
30,000 visitors an hour up the
slopes. Located in the
Pyrenees close to the French
border, good snowfalls are
common and with decent
snow making, the runs are
usually well covered with
snow. In the latter part of the
season, things tend to warm
up quick quickly so expect a
fair amount of slush on the
lower slopes by mid March. Still, with few queuing problems, you're unlikely to have to spend
too much time in a lift line and its not long
before you are heading up the mountain to
where the better snow is. Most of the slopes will
particularly appeal to beginners and intermediates, but there are a few notable spots for
advanced skiers and snowboaders to check out
– most of which is off-piste. Freestylers who
enjoy terrain parks are in for a shock, as there
is only a poor effort and although a half-pipe is
occasionally constructed, it is poorly maintained. If you want to get air, then seek out a
local rider who will show you the best hits, or
simply build your own. In the same way, cross-
country skiers are not going to be over
impressed with the quality of tracks to explore.

Off the Slopes - The village is a dull and ugly
affair, with tall apartment blocks that blight out
the skyline. That said, there are some good
hotels and self-catering options and with prices
generally lower than in France, it is an affordable resort. Baqueria Beret has a good selection of restaurants and no one should go hun-
gry – La Sidreia is highly recommended for
Spanish and local dishes. The village has loads
of bars and evenings are very entertaining, lively and a bit rowdy but a lot of fun.

Verdict - Lively resort with good,
snow sure slopes, ugly village though. **7/10**

COST INDICATOR

Budget   Moderate   Very Expensive   Criminal

i - **Information** - 0034 (0) 9736 39010
www.baquerias.es

ROUTE PLANNER

🏨 **CALAIS** 0 miles
along the A16 E402

Toll Road

→ **ARRAS** 69 miles
1hr 13 **A11 E15**

→ **PARIS** 162 miles
2hrs 44 Ring road south via
Antony to the A10 E05

→ **ORLEANS** 245 miles
4hrs 14 **A71 E09**

→ **VIERZON** 297 miles
5hrs 6 **A20 E09**

→ **MONTAUBAN** 572 miles
9hrs 40 **A62 E09 E72**

→ **TOULOUSE** 585 miles
10hrs south around Toulouse,
✈ pick up the **A64 E80**
Tolls End to Junction 17 - **D33.**

→ **MONTREJEAU** 659 miles
11hrs 14 **D33 - N125**

→ **FOS** 680 miles
11hrs 45 ⛰ **Enter Spain**
N125 via Fos

VIELHA 698 miles
28

↓

→ **BAQUERIA BERET**
9hr 22
KM **Distance** 697 miles (1122 km)
🕐 **Drive time** 12 hours 10 mins
⛽ **Fuel** £62
€ **Tolls** £32

✈ **Airports & Fly Drive Guide**

1st- Toulouse (F) - **2 hrs**
→ **A64 E80**, D3, N125 via
Montrejeau = **105 miles**

2nd- Barcelona (S) - **4 hrs 30**
→ C16, 16, 260, 145, 1 = **205**
miles

Spain
La Molina

Mapping Page 49 F7

ROUTE PLANNER

CALAIS	0 miles	along the A16 E402

Toll Road

ARRAS 69 miles	1hr 13	A11 E15
PARIS 162 miles	2hrs 44	Ring road south via Antony to the A10 E05
ORLEANS 245 miles	4hrs 14	A71 E09
VIERZON 297miles	5hr 6	A20 E09
MONTAUBAN 572 miles	9hrs 40	A62 E09 E72
TOULOUSE 585 miles	10hrs	south around Toulouse, pick up the A61 E80 then the A66 E09

Tolls End

PAMIERS 630 miles	10hrs 45	N20 E09

Enter Spain 700 miles
152 south via Alp

Top Lift
2540m.
Resort Height
1600m.
Vertical Drop
875m.
Number of Runs
25
Longest Run
4km
Slopes
40km of piste
● *Beginner*
52% of the runs
● *Intermediate*
37% of the runs
● *Advanced*
11% of the runs

Cross-Country
5km of tracks
Snowboarding
Half-pipe
Snow Season
Dec to April
Snowmaking
25% of pistes
Number of lifts
15
Up Lift Capacity
16,300 per hour
Mountain Cafes
4

On the Slopes - La Molina is a Pyrenean resort that is slowly gaining national and international recognition. Tour operators have yet to make La Molina a place where they can make money by buying up the best hotel beds and shipping out loads of package holiday groups – but it's only a matter of time before they cotton on to the wonders of this high altitude, tree-covered mountain nestled at the far end of the Moxero mountains. If you want a trip to a mountain that has yet to learn the term 'lift line rage' then pencil La Molina in. There are two areas Tosa de Alp and its neighbour Masella, that offer both the action seeker and the 'more reserved, plenty to do – unfortunately they're not linked by lift and access to both will involve a short bus trip. Masella is the bigger of the two areas and the place where you will find some of the best powder fields and more interesting off-piste including some tight tree lines mid way. If there is a criticism then it's the lack of expert terrain – there are some steep sections but nothing very demanding. Beginners are in for a good time and a weeks stay will not be a waste of time. The nursery slopes are ideal and with a good local ski school on hand, first timers should progress. With regards to snowboarding, the resort has been quick to cotton on, with a nice sized pipe and a cool terrain park area located on Marsella. Despite this mountain having a gentle pitch and being covered in trees, when it comes to cross-country skiing, La Molina is a bit of a let down. There are a few tracks to check out, but the choice is extremely limited and not all are easy to get to.

Off the Slopes - With some good slope side accommodation at reasonable rates, La Molina is a good family resort. You can wine, dine and sleep in La Molina but should that not be enough, then a good alternative would be to base down in Puigcerda, which is only ten minutes away. Local attractions include a small sports centre, a couple of shops and a number of bars, with Sommy's Bar a local hot spot.

KM **Distance**	**716 miles** (1153 km)
⏱ **Drive time**	**12 hours 50 mins**
⛽ **Fuel**	**£65**
€ **Tolls**	**£36**

Verdict - Simple resort with a good family appeal and a nice village. **6/10**

COST INDICATOR

Budget   Moderate   Very Expensive   Criminal

i - Information - 0034 (0) 7289 2031

✈ Airports & Fly Drive Guide

1st- Barcelona (S) - 3 hrs
→ C17, via Vic and Oris to the N-152 & GI-400 = 110 miles

2nd- Toulouse (F) - 3 hr 5
→ A61 E80 and all routes south via Foix = 125 miles

3rd- Madrid (S) - 9 hrs 40
→ A7 E15 north and all routes via Barcelona = 399 miles

Spain
Sierra Nevada

Mapping Page 71 E5

ROUTE PLANNER

MADRID	0 miles	down the E5 via Gelaf

	1hr 35	
BAILEN 190 miles	4hrs 25	323 E902

GRANADA xxx miles
395

SIERRA NEVADA	9hr 22	

Top Lift
3102m.
Resort Height
2100.
Vertical Drop
1002m.
Number of Runs
54
Longest Run
6km
Slopes
66km of piste
● *Beginner*
35% of the runs
● *Intermediate*
45% of the runs
● *Advanced*
20% of the runs

Cross-Country
8km of tracks
Snowboarding
Half-pipe & Park
Snow Season
Dec to April
Snowmaking
260 cannons
Number of lifts
20
Up Lift Capacity
31,965
Mountain Cafes
5

On the Slopes - There are not many places in the world where you can ski in the morning on snow-covered mountains, then spend an afternoon skinny-dipping in the Mediterranean – but you can at Sierra Nevada, located in the deep south of Spain and a short drive from the coastline near Grenada. On a clear day it's possible to see the Atlas Mountains in Morocco from the peak of Veleta on Sierra Nevada. Much favoured by Spain's royals and the Gucci set, the best time to catch the snow is generally in mid February, and even though the resort has snowmaking facilities, the temperatures often prevent their use. The slopes are serviced by 20 lifts which fan out from the base, but despite being able to uplift over 31,000 skiers an hour, lift lines can be a real hassle with bottle necks on many of the lifts – weekends can be a particular problem as this place is very popular. Still, negatives aside one can have a great time skiing or snowboarding here as the slopes are nicely laid out with most of them coloured red, making it an ideal spot for intermediates who like to take things easy. There are not too many shocks here; the advanced terrain is limited to a few short trails, although there is a sizeable off-piste section close to the main pistes. This is an excellent resort for beginners, with good nursery slopes at Borreguiles which are easy and convenient to get to. The local ski school is also good and caters for all levels and all ages. However, snowboard instruction is still a bit primitive, and only basic tution is available for novices to intermediate level.

Off the Slopes - The resort is fairly modern in as much that it is quite crowded, but everything is within walking distance and despite being an expensive place, it's both welcoming and lively. Apartments offer the cheapest lodging and are well situated for the village centre. Local attractions are bit limited but dining out is of a high standard with some good restaurants to choose from. If you like to party, then you will love Sierra as the nightlife is both good and varied.

KM **Distance**	**292 miles** (470km)
⏱ **Drive time**	**8 hours 10 mins**
⛽ **Fuel**	**£33**
€ **Tolls**	**£48**

Verdict - Interesting place with decent slopes. Great nightlife. **5/10**

COST INDICATOR

Budget   Moderate   Very Expensive   Criminal

i - Information - 0034 (0) 9582 49100
www.sierranevadaski.com

✈ Airports & Fly Drive Guide

1st- Madrid - xx hr
→ E05 and all routes south via Granada = xx miles (xxkm)

2nd- Malaga - xx hr
→ 331, 359, A92 via Granada = xx miles (xxkm)

⏱ DRIVE TIME - nixon www.nixon.com

Sweden

Resorts Featured

84 Baqueria Beret
85 La Molina
85 Sierra Nevada
See page 29 for the index of all resorts.

84

DRIVE ON THE RIGHT

Stop

Flervags-stopp

Lane indicator

No right turn

Country identification

Footpath

Tunnel

Motorway speed	**110kph**
Rural speed	**90kph**
Urban speed	**50kph**
Alcohol limit	**20mgs**
Front seatbelts	✔
Rear seatbelts	✔
Kids in front seat	-
Legal age to drive	**18**
Warming triangle	Required
First aid kit	Advisable
Fire extinguisher	Advisable
Snowchains	Advisable

FACT FILE

Country - Konungariket Sverige
Location - Western Europe (North)
Geography
Sweden shares its land borders with Finland and Norway.
Highest Mountain - Kebnekaise - 2111m
Coast line & Seas - Baltic Sea
Land Area - 449,964 sq km (173,732 sq miles)
Capital - Stockholm
Populartion - 8.9 million
Language - Swedish
Religion - 86% Evangelical Lutherans
Currecny - Krona
Time - GMT + 1 hour, (GMT + 2 hours between March & October)
Electricity Supply - 230volts
Communications - International Country code 0046
Fire 112
Police 112
Ambulance112
National Tourism - www.visit-sweden.com
Rail Information - www.samtrafiken.se
Bus Information - www.visit-sweden.com
Air Information - www.visit-sweden.com
Weather Information - www.visit-sweden.com
Avalanche Information - www.smhi.se

Passprts & Visa Requirments

	Passports	Visa
Australian	Yes	No
British	Yes	No
Canadian	Yes	No
USA	Yes	No
EU	ID	No

Duty Free - None EU travellers
200 cigarettes or 100 cigarillos or 50 cigars or 25g of tobacco. 1ltr of spirits over 22% or 21% of fortified wine or spirits up to 22% or 21% of sparkling wine or liqueur and 21 % of still wine. 50g of perfume and SKR17000 worth of goods.
EU travellers - No tarrifs.

Motoring Organisations
Kung Automobil Klubben
tel ++46 (0) 8 678 00 55
Svenska Bilsportforbundet
tel ++46 (0) 8 626 33 00
Motormannens Riksforbund
10435 Stockholm
tel ++46 (0) 8 690 38 00
www.motormannen.se

Top Lift	1275m.
Resort Height	380m.
Vertical Drop	895m.
Number of Runs	100
Longest Run	6.5km
Slopes	82km of piste
● *Beginner*	60% of the runs
● *Intermediate*	40% of the runs
● *Advanced*	10% of the runs
Cross-Country	290km of tracks
Snowboarding	Half-pipe & Park
Snow Season	Nov to May
Snowmaking	20 cannons
Number of lifts	18
Up Lift Capicity	48,00 per hour
Mountain Cafes	18

On the Slopes - . Think of Sweden and the usual things that spring to mind are blondes, Abba and bullet-proof cars. Sweden has a healthy ski and snowboard scene, however, and the best of the country's resorts can boast some serious offerings – Åre is one them. Although located some distance from Stockholm, it's a resort worth visiting if you are planning a Swedish snow holiday as the largest area of linked slopes in Sweden, it's an excellent example of a family-orientated resort. Are has a good snow record with well maintained slopes, but it's a mountain that is prone to high winds and frequent changing weather patterns. It can also be very busy and long lift queues do exist – what's more, as a resort that attracts Sweden's more affluent crowd, Are is scarily expensive both on and off the slopes. The cross-country skiing here is awesome with over 290km of wooded and open tracks to explore and thanks to floodlights in some areas, you can even go for a slide in the evenings. The main downhill slopes are stretched along the shore of lake Aresjon and cover a number of well-defined areas, with the main slopes laid out above. Overall this is a mountain that favours learners and those who can handle red runs – experts will be largely disappointed, even though there are some good off-piste areas and a few white-knuckle descents. Most areas will appeal to beginners, but if you want to stay away from the crowds, then the runs at Duved may be more appealing. In general this is a decent freestyle skier and snowboarder's resort, but the halfpipe and park are not up to much.

Off the Slopes - Åre offers plenty of accommodation, both in the town or one of the surrounding villages. No matter where you stay, it's going to be expensive and a good proportion of the accommodation is not convenient for the slopes. Still, there are lots of attractions off the slopes and some good restaurants to choose from. Nightlife is also enjoyable and lively, if expensive.

Verdict - A good mountain, with good intermediate runs. Hellish expensive. **6/10**

COST INDICATOR

Budget   Moderate   Very Expensive   Criminal

i **- Information -** 0046 (0) 647 17720
www.areresort.se

ROUTE PLANNER

STOCKHOLM	0 miles	*north along the* E4
UPPSALA	39 miles	40 mins · E4
MEHEDEBY		E4
HAGASTROM		E4
SODERHAMM		E4
SUNDSVALL	230 miles	4hrs · E14
OSTERSUND	345 miles	6hrs 25 · E14
KROKOM		E14
JARPEN		E14
ARE		

Distance 410 miles *(660 km)*
Drive time 7 hours 50 mins
Fuel £38
Tolls

✈ **Airports & Fly Drive Guide**

1st - Ostersund 1 hr
E14 north = **55 miles**

2nd - Stockholm - 7 hrs 50
E4 & E14 north = **410 miles**

DRIVE TIME - *nixon* www.nixon.com

Sweden

Riksgransen

Mapping Page 127 D7

ROUTE PLANNER

Top Lift
910m.
Resort Height
500m.
Vertical Drop
410m.
Number of Runs
20
Longest Run
2km
Slopes
22km of piste
● *Beginner*
40% of the runs
● *Intermediate*
55% of the runs
● *Advanced*
5% of the runs

Cross-Country
8km of tracks
Snowboarding
Park
Snow Season
Feb to June
Snowmaking
-
Number of lifts
6
Up Lift Capicity
75,00 per hour
Mountain Cafes
2

On the Slopes - Riksgransen is located just 125 miles south of the Arctic Circle and unlike its more southern cousins, it only opens in February yet stays open until early summer. Due to the northerly latitude, the days are long and the nights short and you can quite easily ski or snowboard in warm weather conditions after most pubs in the UK would have called 'last orders'. You can even go heliskiing/boarding at midnight. Riksgransen is a tiny resort and ever since snowboarding took off, it has become a major freestyle skiers and snowboarder's hangout – but it's the snowboarder's who have made it famous and you can rarely open a snowboard magazine without seeing a big air shot taken from some where around here. The slopes are ideal for freeriding and natural freestyle as there are so many wind lips, kickers and gullies. There is a pipe on occasions, but most choose to go natural. 40% of the runs are graded as beginner runs, but the resort is not particularly suited to their needs and first timers are better off in Bjorkliden, which about 20 minutes away near Kiruna. Advanced skiers do have a number of fast spots, but like snowboarders, this place is better for skiers on short skis who like do hit jumps. Cross-country skiers would also be wasting their time here, the terrain is far too uneven and there are no real tracks of any note and those that do exist won't take too much time to conquer. However, if you don't mind going it alone and making your own paths, then there will be areas to explore outside the main circuit.

Off the Slopes - Riksgransen is over 20 hours from Stockholm, so it's no wonder that it hasn't developed into a resort, as we know it. With the exception of the ski lifts, there is simply nothing here other than the Riksgransen Hotel, which is where you sleep, eat, drink and party. The hotel has a good restaurant, which serves traditional Swedish food. With no resort facilities apart from a spa, the obvious thing to do is party with the other outback enthusiast that makes it here.

🛣 **OSLO (N)**
north along the E4

🛣 **UPPSALA** 40 miles
40 mins E4

→ **GAVLE**
E4

→ **HARNOSAND**
E4

→ **OMSKOLDSVVIK**
E4

→ **VASTERBOTTENS LAN**
E4

→ **TORE** 570 miles
9hrs 30 E10

↓

→ **RIKSGRANSEN**

KM **Distance 848 miles** *(1365 km)*
🕐 **Drive time 15 hours 40 mins**
⛽ **Fuel £77**
€ **Tolls**

Verdict - Nice resort, which will appeal to skiers and snowboarders alike. **5/10**

✈ **Airports & Fly Drive Guide**
1st- Stockholm - 15 hrs 40
→ E4 north = 848 miles

COST INDICATOR

Budget Moderate Very Expensive Criminal

🄸 - Information - 0046 (0) 9804 0080
www.riksgransen.nu

Sweden

Salen

Mapping Page 118 E3

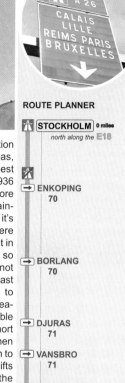

ROUTE PLANNER

Top Lift
930m.
Resort Height
400.
Vertical Drop
330m.
Number of Runs
110
Longest Run
10km
Slopes
155km of piste
● *Beginner*
55% of the runs
● *Intermediate*
25% of the runs
● *Advanced*
20% of the runs

Cross-Country
350
Snowboarding
Half-pipe & Park
Snow Season
Nov to April
Snowmaking
60 cannons
Number of lifts
79
Up Lift Capicity
101,700
Mountain Cafes
38

On the Slopes - A collection of four independent areas, Salen is Sweden's biggest resort and dates back to 1936 as a ski area. Salen has more than 155km of well maintained slopes and while it's not 100% snowsure, there has been heavy investment in snowmaking technology so when the real stuff is not forthcoming, they can blast out enough man-made to keep the slopes going all season long. What is noticeable about the slopes is how short they are – if you ski fast then you may find that you seem to be standing in line for lifts longer than carving the pistes. Queues are pretty short, however, and the lifts are so well laid out and close to the runs that getting around the pistes is easy. Beginners who have never used draglifts will have to learn quickly as 71 of the lifts are drags of one sort or another. The short runs may suit first timers and intermediates that are working on their technique, but they can become a bit tedious if you are at an advanced level. Experts have some decent steep black runs to enjoy, so its not all bad news – the Adam and Pernilla are two runs that will test most. If off-piste powder is your thing then you may want to look elsewhere, but you can bob in and out of wooded sections. Salen is hard to beat for cross-country skiers, with more than 350km of mapped out tracks, many of which snake along wooded paths that are a joy in themselves. Sometimes, there are more cross-country skiers here than their down hill cousins. This is also a hot spot for freestyle skiers and snowboarders, with Tandalen the designated freestyle area where you will find fantastic snowparks.

Off the Slopes - There are over 50,000 beds set aside for tourists in and around Salen, so you should be able to find something to suit. Prices vary depending on how close you stay to the slopes, but in general nothing is cheap in a resort that is well suited to families. There are dozens of good restaurants, excellent sporting attractions and plenty of bars where nightlife is intense.

🛣 **STOCKHOLM** 0 miles
north along the E18

🛣

→ **ENKOPING**
70

→ **BORLANG**
70

→ **DJURAS**
71

→ **VANSBRO**
71

→ **MALUNG**
71

→

→ **LIMA**
71

→ **TRANSTRAND**
71

↓

→ **SALEN**

KM **Distance 253 miles** *(407 km)*
🕐 **Drive time 6 hours 30 mins**
⛽ **Fuel £27**
€ **Tolls**

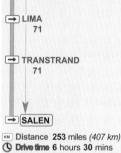

Verdict - A good, fun mountain for families and intermediates. **6/10**

✈ **Airports & Fly Drive Guide**
1st - Stockholm - 6 hr 23
→ E18 , 70 and 71 north = 253 miles

COST INDICATOR

Budget Moderate Very Expensive Criminal

🄸 - Information - 0046 (0) 280 18700
www.salen.com

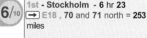

85

🕐 DRIVE TIME - nixon® www.nixon.com

Switzerland

DRIVE ON THE RIGHT

86

Motorway

Level Crossing

Postal vehicle has priority

Slow Lane

Slippery when wet

Country identification

Tunnel, lights compulsory

Bend in main road

Motorway speed	120kph
Rural speed	80kph
Urban speed	50kph
Alcohol limit	80mgs
Front seatbelts	✔
Rear seatbelts	✔
Kids in front seat	7
Legal age to drive	18
Warming triangle	Required
First aid kit	Advisable
Fire extinguisher	Advisable
Snowchains	Advisable

Photo - K2 Snowboards

Road Signs and Warnings

Abstand halten - *Maintain distance*
Altstadt - *Oldtown*
Anfang -*Start, beginning*
Anschluß - *Junction*
Ausfahrt - *Exit*
Autobahnkreuz -*Autobahn junction*
Bauarbeiten - *Roadworks*
Bei Nässe - *During wet conditions*
Belegt - *Full*
Durchfahrt verboten *No through traffic*
Einbahnstraße - *One-way street*
Einfahrt - *Entrance*
Fahrbahnwechsel - *Change lanes*
Fahrtrichtung - *Direction of travel*
Freiefahrt - *Road is clear*
Frostchäden - *Frost damage*
Gefahr/gefährlich - *Danger, risk*
Glatteisgefah - *Icy road*

Grenze - *Border*
Grenze Kontrolle - *Customs inspection*
Kfz - *Motor vehicle*
Langsam fahren - *Drive slowly*
Licht einschalten - *Turn on lights*
Links einbiegen -*Turn left*
Nur - *Only*
Parkplatz - *Parking lot*
Polizei - *Police*
Radweg kreutz - *Bicycle-path crossing*
Raststätte - *Service area*
Rechts einbiegen - *Turn right*
Rechts fahren - *Keep right*
Rollsplitt - *Loose Material*
Sackgasse - *Dead end, cul-de-sac*
Schülerlotse - *School crossing guard*
Sperrgebiet - *Restricted area*
Sperrung - *Closure*

Spur - *Traffic lane*
Stadtzcentrum - *Town center*
Straße -*Street*
Straßenschäden - *Road damage*
Streugut - *Road salt/sand*
Tankstelle - *Fuel station*
Überholen verboten - *No passing*
Umleitung - *Detour*
Unfall - *Accident; drive with care*
Verboten - *Prohibited*
Verengte Fahrbahn - *Road narrows*
Verkehr - *Traffic*
Vorfahrt - *Priority (right of way)*
Vorfahrtstraße - *Priority road*
Vorsicht - *Be careful*
Weg - *Way, lane*
Zufahrt frei - *Access permitted*

FACT FILE

Country - Schweizerische Eidgenossenschaft, Confederation Sussie, Confederazione Svizzera
Location - Western Europe
Geography
Switzerland shares its borders with Austria, France, Germany, Italy and Liechtenstein.
Highest Mountain
Duffourspitze - 4634m
Coast line & Seas
Land locked
Land Area
41,284 sq km (15,940 sq miles)
Capital - Bern
Popularion - 7,164,444
Language - 70% German, 30% French, Italian and Romansch.
Religion - 43% Catholic and 47% Protestant
Currecny - Swiss Franc
Time
GMT + 1 hour, (GMT + 2 hours between March & October)
Electricity Supply - 220volts
Communications
International Country code 0041
Fire 118
Police 117
Ambulance 144
National Tourism
0041 (0) 288 11 11
www.myswitzerland.com
Rail Information - www.sbb.ch
Bus Information
www.myswitzerland.com
Air Information
www.myswitzerland.com
Gateway International Airports
Bern, Geneva, Zurich
Weather Information
www.myswitzerland.com
Avalanche Information
www.slf.ch
www.meteoschweiz.ch
0041 (0) 848 800 187

Passsprts & Visa Requirments

	Passports	Visa
Australian	Yes	No
British	Yes	No
Canadian	Yes	No
USA	Yes	No
EU	ID	No

Duty Free - None EU travellers
200 cigarettes or 100 cigarillos or 50 cigars or 25g of tobacco. 1ltr of spirits over 22% or 21% of fortified wine or spirits up to 22% or 21% of sparkling wine or liqueur and 21 % of still wine. 50g of perfume and SFr100 worth of goods.
EU travellers - No tarrifs

Motoring Organisations
Touring Club Suisse (TCS)
Chemin de Blandonnetcase postale 820
tel ++41 (0) 22 417 27 27

Automobile Club de Suisse
tel ++41 (0) 31 328 31 11
fax ++41 (0) 31 311 03 10
http:// www.acs.ch
e-mail: acszv@acs.ch

Switzerland
Adelboden

Mapping Page 86 D3

ROUTE PLANNER

Top Lift 2355m.	**On the Slopes** - Adelboden and its linked neighbour of Lenk, are a couple of unassuming, low-key resorts, which deserve more attention than they presently receive. It's an area where you can happily spend a week on a pleasing mountain where skiers and snowboarders of all abilities can improve their technique. Not far from here are some of Switzerland's big, glitzy resorts such as Wengen, but you don't need razzmatazz to have fun and while Wengen attracts the jet-set, Adelboden gets the more discerning visitor. The slopes are on a medium sized mountain, and consequently the snow record is not always what one would like it to be, and with only a small snow-making set-up, it's wise to plan your visit to coincide with the best snow. There are some 56 lifts that cover the	
Resort Height 1355m.		
Vertical Drop 1000m.		
Number of Runs 65		
Longest Run 7km		
Slopes 170km of piste		
● Beginner 40% of the runs		
● Intermediate 50% of the runs		
● Advanced 10% of the runs		

CALAIS 0 miles
along the A16 - A26
E15 / E17
Toll Road

REIMS 168 miles 2hrs 55
A4 E17 / 50

METZ 270 miles 4hrs 47
A4 E25

Tolls End

STRASBOURG 384 miles 6hrs 30

Enter Germany 470 miles
N4

OFFENBURG 397 miles 6hrs 48
E35 - A5

Enter Switzerland
E35 - A5

BASEL 474 miles 8hrs
E25 - A2, A1, A6

BERN 540 miles 9hrs
E27 - A12

SPIEZ 554 miles 9hr 25
Then take all routes via **Wimmis** to **Frutigen**, and pass through following all local signs to the resort.

Cross-Country 25km of tracks	
Snowboarding Half-pipe & Park	
Snow Season Dec to April	
Snowmaking 20km of pistes	
Number of lifts 56	
Up Lift Capicity 30,000 per hour	
Mountain Cafes 18	

two resorts, which makes getting around the mountain easy – there are times long queues occur however, and note that although Lenk is reachable via the pistes it's not straightforward and some prior planning will help. The slopes are split in five sections and offer a similar style of terrain in each area – the mountain is particularly suits beginner to intermediate carvers who like gentle, crowd-free slopes but beginners also have a mountain that will please, with good nursery slopes in the village and ample higher slopes to progress on. Snowboarders, who want to learn the basics, will find that the local snowboard school gives good advice on how and where to go and cross-country skiers are also reasonably well catered for with a nice selection of interesting tracks to explore.

Off the Slopes - Adelboden is Swiss through-and-through – a charming and welcoming old style village complete with cows with big bells. Accommodation options are very good; the Hotel Bellevue is highly rated, as is the Pension Bodehutti, which is close to the slopes. The village offers a good level of facilities as well as having a varied selection of restaurants. Evenings here are based around a few quiet drinks in one of the many traditional bars.

ADELBODEN

Distance 572 miles *(920 km)*
Drive time 10 hours 15 mins
Fuel £52
Tolls £15

Verdict - Good all-round, all-level resort that is just about affordable. **7/10**

COST INDICATOR

Budget   Moderate   Very Expensive   Criminal

i - **Information** - 0041 (0) 673 8080
www.adelboden.ch

Switzerland
Andermatt

Mapping Page 87 D5

ROUTE PLANNER

Top Lift 2965m.	**On the Slopes** - For the skier or snowboarder looking for a wonderfully traditional resort that still has great snow and terrain, they would be hard pressed to find one better than Andermatt. While it may not be large, or particularly modern it does offer excellent snow – and plenty of it every year – some superb off-piste powder fields and a mountain evenly matched for all levels of visitor. Despite being a small resort, Andermatt can cut it with the big boys and there are not many similar places that can offer as much deep powder, or testing terrain as this. The resort's reputation has not gone unnoticed, however — both with locals and foreign visitors and the drawback is that it has become a very popular resort with both locals and visitors from the rest of Europe. While the slopes can get busy at	
Resort Height 1445m.		
Vertical Drop 1520m.		
Number of Runs 56		
Longest Run 5km		
Slopes 56km of piste		
● Beginner 30% of the runs		
● Intermediate 40% of the runs		
● Advanced 30% of the runs		

CALAIS 0 miles
along the A16 - A26
E15 / E17
Toll Road

REIMS 168 miles 2hrs 55
A4 E17 / 50

METZ 270 miles 4hrs 47
A4 E25

Tolls End

STRASBOURG 384 miles 6hrs 30

Enter Germany 470 miles
N4

OFFENBURG 397 miles 6hrs 48
E35 - A5

Enter Switzerland
E35 - A5

BASEL 474 miles 8hrs
E25 - A2, A1, A6

LUZEN 513 miles 9hrs 10
E35 - 2

WASSEN
E35

Cross-Country 20km of tracks	
Snowboarding Half-pipe & Park	
Snow Season Dec to April	
Snowmaking None	
Number of lifts 13	
Up Lift Capicity 4,200 per hour	
Mountain Cafes 4	

times, the lift system generally copes well and apart from early morning bottlenecks and the weekend rushes for the main cable car, queues are minimal most of the time. The terrain is split into three areas with the slopes on the mighty Gemsstock the highest of the bunch. The bulk of skiers and snowboarders tend to start out on the Natschen slopes, which lie just above the resort and offer a number of easy runs back down into the village. Natschen is also the place where beginners will find the best selection of easy slopes to practice on and when they have got the basics down, they can ski home down a sedate blue trail that runs through open trees. Intermediates and advanced skiers are better off taking the cable car to the summit of the Gemsstock, where they will find a choice of either a steep black or intermediate red that will have them catching their breath by the end.

Off the Slopes - Andermatt is a wonderful village, oozing with tradition. There are numerous hotels and some wonderful B&B's with very reasonable rates. There are a good number of restaurants that serve traditional style food although there's not a huge variety of choice between the menus of different eateries. Local services and evening distractions are good.

ANDERMATT

Distance 559 miles *(900 km)*
Drive time 10 hours 5 mins
Fuel £50
Tolls £15

Verdict - Excellent snow record with some testing steeps. Basic village. **8/10**

COST INDICATOR

Budget   Moderate   Very Expensive   Criminal

i - **Information** - 0041 (0) 887 1454
www.andermatt

Airports & Fly Drive Guide

1st- Bern - 1 hr 20
E25, A6 and all routes via
Spiez = **38** miles

2nd- Zurich - 2 hrs 50
A8 and all routes south via
Spiez = **118** miles

3rd- Geneva - 3 hrs
All routes via **Lausanne** &
Aigle - 11 = **140** miles

Airports & Fly Drive Guide

1st- Zurich- 1 hr 50
E41 & E35 and all routes
via Wassen = **78** miles

2nd- Bern - 2 hrs
8 and all routes east via
Wassen = **88** miles

3rd- Geneva - 3 hrs 40
E35 - A1, A9, and all routes
via Bern & Wassen = **190** miles

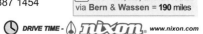

DRIVE TIME - nixon www.nixon.com

Anzere

ROUTE PLANNER

CALAIS 0 miles	along the A16 - A26 E15 / E17 Toll Road
REIMS 168 miles 2hrs 55	A4 E17 / 50
METZ 270 miles 4hrs 47	A4 E25
Tolls End	
STRASBOURG 384 miles 6hrs 30	
Enter Germany 470 miles	N4
OFFENBURG 397 miles 6hrs 48	E35 - A5
Enter Switzerland	E35 - A5
BASEL 474 miles 8hrs	E25, A2, A12, A9
BERN 540 miles 9hrs	E27 - A12
MONTREUX 592 miles 9hrs 25	E27, A9
SION	A9
ANZERE	

KM **Distance**	618 miles (995 km)
Drive time	11 hours 40 mins
Fuel	£57
€ **Tolls**	£15

Top Lift
2362m.
Resort Height
1423m.
Vertical Drop
930m.
Number of Runs
24
Longest Run
4.8km
Slopes
40km of piste
● Beginner
40% of the runs
● Intermediate
50% of the runs
● Advanced
10% of the runs

Cross-Country
14km of tracks
Snowboarding
Half-pipe & Park
Snow Season
Dec to April
Snowmaking
5% of piste
Number of lifts
12
Up Lift Capacity
9,250 per hour
Mountain Cafes
3

On the Slopes - Anzere is wonderful family destination, close to Crans-Montana and located above the small town of Sion around three hours from Geneva. Anzere tends to be largely ignored in favour of the bigger places by the tour operators although isn't to say that it is without a loyal following – you only need to be around early on a weekend to find out for yourself, as the early morning lifts queues can be quite lengthy. The mainly south-facing slopes offer a number of slopes that are mainly suited to beginner and intermediate skiers and snowboarders and set at a high altitude, the slopes get a lot of sun, but they also receive annual snowfalls in excess of 800 cm a season, which is pretty impressive by most European standards. The terrain is a little lacking for advanced users and competent skiers and snowboarders are unlikely to find a whole lot of adventurous terrain to hold their attention beyond a day or two. If you're simply looking for out of a winter snow holiday, in a quite unassuming resort where you can have a relaxing week on snow while catching a few mid day rays at lunchtime and just chill in the evenings, then Anzere will fit the bill nicely. The nursery slopes are very good and with a couple of excellent local ski and snowboard schools, pave the way well for novices to progress to bigger and better things. The cross-country skiing is a little disappointing, with very little to offer in terms of marked out tracks. Likewise this is not a hot snowboarder's mountain for the advanced, although beginners and intermediates should get on well.

Off the Slopes - The resort is mainly purpose-built and designed in a traditional Swiss style making it not only a pleasing village, but also a very convenient one for both the slopes and for local facilities. There are some excellent and well-appointed hotels near the village centre and lots of self-catering chalets to rent. While there may not be an overabundance of restaurants, bars or shops, those local facilities that are available – including a good sports centre – are of a high standard.

Verdict - Fine for beginners, but not for experts. Nice village centre. **5/10**

COST INDICATOR

Budget   Moderate   Very Expensive   Criminal

 Information - 0041 (0) 2739 92805

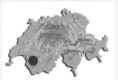

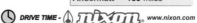

✈ Airports & Fly Drive Guide

1st- Geneva - 2 hrs 15
➡ E25,A9 and all routes via Montreux = 110 miles

2nd- Bern - 2 hrs 30
➡ All routes south via Montreux = 112 miles

3rd - Zurich - 3 hrs 40
➡ All routes south via E35 Andermatt = 185 miles

Arosa

ROUTE PLANNER

CALAIS 0 miles	along the A16 - A26 E15 / E17 Toll Road
REIMS 168 miles 2hrs 55	A4 E17 / 50
METZ 270 miles 4hrs 47	A4 E25
Tolls End	
STRASBOURG 384 miles 6hrs 30	
Enter Germany 470 miles	N4
OFFENBURG 397 miles 6hrs 48	E35 - A5
Enter Switzerland	E35 - A5
BASEL 474 miles 8hrs	E35 A2, A3, E60
ZURICH 524 miles 9hrs	E43, A3
LANDQUART 573miles	E43, A13
CHUR 598 miles 10hrs 15	
AROSA	

KM **Distance**	616 miles (992 km)
Drive time	11 hours 30 mins
Fuel	£58
€ **Tolls**	£15

Top Lift
2655m.
Resort Height
1800m.
Vertical Drop
855m.
Number of Runs
55
Longest Run
5km
Slopes
70km of piste
● Beginner
38% of the runs
● Intermediate
56% of the runs
● Advanced
6% of the runs

Cross-Country
30km of tracks
Snowboarding
Half-pipe & Park
Snow Season
Dec to April
Snowmaking
10km of pistes
Number of lifts
14
Up Lift Capacity
22,000 per hour
Mountain Cafes
7

On the Slopes - Most people have a pre-formed impression of what a Swiss resort is like – most would expect to see snow-covered peaks, and a quaint village with wooden chalets, and Arosa lives up to the image perfectly; picture postcard stuff right down to the village clock. One visit is enough to make you want to keep coming back for more, time after time. Even though Arosa is not promoted by all UK tour operators, its still a busy resort but despite this you seldom spend more than a few minutes in any lift line. Not only does this high-altitude resort have a reliable snow record, it also has pistes to suit everyone, with wide-open runs laid out above the tree lines and long runs back down into the village. Keen skiers or hardcore snowboarders may find the lack of challenging runs a bit of a let down as there are only a couple of black runs, which are deemed by some as overrated. Even so, the off-piste opportunities are very good. There is a decent amount of freeride terrain that means snowboarders have made Arosa a popular hangout, despite the fact that the terrain park is a bit dull, freestylers still seem to like it here. Some cross-country skiers rate a resort by the amount of kilometres of tracks available, but this not always a good measure, because there's only 30km of tracks here, yet this place has some of the best trails in the country and is highly rated.

Off the Slopes - The resort is a bit disjointed and not everything is easily accessed, but there are plenty of slope side beds, albeit at a high price. Arosa is well known for being expensive and if you plan to do some holiday shopping here make sure your credit card is fully loaded. Being a laid back resort, dining out is both mellow and traditional – there are dozens of restaurants with something for everyone. The Kacheelofa-Stubil is a highly rated restaurant as is the Pizzeria da Gianni. In the evenings the village is fairly quiet with a number of cosy bars where locals like to take it easy. The popular hangouts are the Sitting Bull, Grischuna, and the Mexicalito. There all are basic but okay.

Verdict - Traditional resort with great scenery and excellent slopes **7/10**

COST INDICATOR

Budget   Moderate   Very Expensive   Criminal

Information - 0041 (0) 378 7020
www.arosa.ch

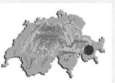

✈ Airports & Fly Drive Guide

1st- Zurich - 3 hrs
➡ All routes south via E35, A13, A3 to Chur = 105 miles

2nd - Innsbruck (A) - 4 hrs
➡ All routes via the Arlberg to the A14 = 148 miles

3rd - Geneva - 5 hrs 30
➡ All routes east via Zurich and Chur = 260 miles

Switzerland
Champery

Mapping Page 86 E2

ROUTE PLANNER

Top Lift
2275m.
Resort Height
1050m.
Vertical Drop
1225m.
Number of Runs
60
Longest Run
4km
Slopes
100km of piste
● Beginner
50% of the runs
● Intermediate
40% of the runs
● Advanced
10% of the runs

Cross-Country
10km of tracks
Snowboarding
Half-pipe & Park
Snow Season
Dec to April
Snowmaking
10% of pistes
Number of lifts
36 -(220 in area)
Up Lift Capicity
20,300 per hour
Mountain Cafes
10

On the Slopes - Champery is a great resort with good links to the massive Portes du Soleil area that extends the available skiing from 100km of pistes in the immediate area to over 650km in the Portes du Soleil, and linked by more than 220 lifts with a combined up-lift rate of 225,000 people. Awesome. The main thing is whether or not all this terrain is any good and whether it suits its visitors. It has to be said that not only is this a super area that offers endless opportunities for all levels. Champery's slopes are not particularly well suited for beginners, as the number of easy runs are limited to a few, fairly steep novice slopes that can be a bit tricky for total first timers, especially children. On the other hand those individuals who like to feel the wind on their face as they reach Mach six, can do so on various steep blacks. The best of the challenging terrain is not actually around Champery, but in other parts of the Portes du Soleil, however. Good off-piste can often be found on the slopes of the neighbouring resort of Les Crosets. Champery itself is a quiet mountain where lift queues are kept to a minimum and where the snow cover is reasonable, even though the snowmaking facilities are not on par with what is on offer elsewhere if the real stuff is lacking. The cross-country terrain is okay, if limited, but the resort has rigged up floodlights, so if you fancy burning of the fondue after supper, you can go out and do a few laps. Snowboards are confined to daylight riding and there are better places to ride in the region, for instance in nearby Les Crosets.

Off the Slopes - Champery is Switzerland through and through, complete with rustic wooden chalets and excellent local facilities. There is a nice choice of hotels, mainly two and three star, as well as variety of self-catering chalets. The resort has a family feel to it and facilities are excellent. There are loads of restaurants with pizza available for the kids and should you fancy doing something different, why not visit the bell foundry. But if booze is your thing, don't expect to party hard here.

CALAIS 0 miles
along the A16 - A26
E15 / E17
Toll Road

REIMS 168 miles
2hrs 55 A4 E17 / 50

METZ 270 miles
4hrs 47 A4 E25

Tolls End

STRASBOURG 384 miles
6hrs 30

⚠ **Enter Germany** 470 miles
N4

OFFENBURG 397 miles
6hrs 48 E35 - A5

⚠ **Enter Switzerland**
E35 - A5

BASEL 474 miles
8hrs E25 - A2, A1, A6

BERN 540 miles
9hrs E27 - A12

MONTREUX 592 miles
9hrs 25 E27, A12

BEX
Leave the E27 A12 and follow all local signs to the resort.

CHAMPERY

KM **Distance** 520 miles *(837 km)*
🕐 **Drive time** 10 hours 5 mins
⛽ **Fuel** £50
€ **Tolls** £15

✈ **Airports & Fly Drive Guide**
1st- Geneva - 2 hrs 15
A1, A9 and all routes via Montreux = 80 miles

2nd- Bern - 2 hrs 30
All routes south via Montreux = 82 miles

3rd - Zurich - 3 hrs 45
All routes south via E35
Andermatt = 156 miles

Verdict - Good resort within the Portes du Soleil area. Nice local services. **7**/10

COST INDICATOR

Budget   Moderate   Very Expensive   Criminal

i - **Information** - 0041 (0) 479 2020
www.champery.ch

Switzerland
Crans Montana

Mapping Page 86 E3

ROUTE PLANNER

Top Lift
3000m.
Resort Height
1500m.
Vertical Drop
1500m.
Number of Runs
60
Longest Run
12km
Slopes
160km of piste
● Beginner
38% of the runs
● Intermediate
50% of the runs
● Advanced
12% of the runs

Cross-Country
40km of tracks
Snowboarding
Half-pipe & Park
Snow Season
Dec to April
Snowmaking
18km of pistes
Number of lifts
35
Up Lift Capicity
41,000 per hour
Mountain Cafes
14

On the Slopes - Crans-Montana is not only a big mountain, but also a large resort town that packs in just about everything you could possibly want in a winter holiday destination. The town's size can have drawbacks, for instance most visitors will find that they have to take a bus from their accommodation to the slopes and the town does lack a 'cosy' feel somewhat. Still, you go to Crans Montana to ski, and it's on-hill that the resort excels in a superb way. The mountain is serviced by an extremely efficient modern lift system, which is able to eliminate lift queues most of the time. The runs cover a vast area, which allows skiers and snowboarders to spread out and prevent piste jams. Most runs are red intermediate ones and if you don't fancy off-piste skiing, some experts might find the ski area a little easy, with not enough variation. If you do like to get away from the pistes, however, then you might want to sign up with a guide and check out the slopes around the Chetseronor or take the Plaine Morte tour. Snowboarding has been popular here since day one; one of Europe's first snowboard schools was founded here back in the eighties. The slopes will leave the average user more than content even though they get a lot of sun on a regular basis, which tends to soften them up when you don't want them to. Cross-country will find plenty of interesting tracks to try out, such as those around the golf course, or up around the Plans Mayens area.

Off the Slopes - Crans-Montana can accommodate over 40,000 visitors, with hotels and apartments the main attraction – be prepared to have to catch the bus or take a taxi to get around as everything is fairly spread out. Shopping is almost as big a draw here as the skiing, with loads of quality shops to browse around. Countless restaurants produce every type of menu known, but it all comes with a price tag. Likewise, nightlife is both full-on and lively, but not cheap. Check out Amadeus Bar and Constellation, both have a party crowd and decent sounds.

CALAIS 0 miles
along the A16 - A26
E15 / E17
Toll Road

REIMS 168 miles
2hrs 55 A4 E17 / 50

METZ 270 miles
4hrs 47 A4 E25

Tolls End

STRASBOURG 384 miles
6hrs 30

⚠ **Enter Germany** 470 miles
N4

OFFENBURG 397 miles
6hrs 48 E35 - A5

⚠ **Enter Switzerland**
E35 - A5

BASEL 474 miles
8hrs E25 - A2, A1, A6

BERN 540 miles
9hrs E27 - A12

MONTREUX 592 miles
9hrs 10 E27, A1, A9

SION

CRANS MONTANA

KM **Distance** 557 miles *(897 km)*
🕐 **Drive time** 10 hours 15 mins
⛽ **Fuel** £50
€ **Tolls** £15

✈ **Airports & Fly Drive Guide**
1st- Bern - 2 hrs 30
All routes south via Montreux = 76 miles

2nd- Geneva - 2 hrs 35
E25, A1, A9 and all routes via Montreux = 116 miles

3rd - Zurich - 3 hrs 50
All routes south via E35
Andermatt = 190 miles

Verdict - Great slopes, but the town is big and somewhat unwelcoming. **9**/10

COST INDICATOR

Budget   Moderate   Very Expensive   Criminal

i - **Information** - 0041 (0) 485 0404
www.crans-montana.ch

🕐 **DRIVE TIME** - nixon www.nixon.com

Davos

Mapping Page 87 D7

Top Lift
2845m.
Resort Height
1550m.
Vertical Drop
2000m.
Number of Runs
75
Longest Run
9.5km
Slopes
320km of piste
● ● *Beginner*
30% of the runs
● *Intermediate*
50% of the runs
● **Advanced**
20% of the runs

Cross-Country
75km of tracks
Snowboarding
Half-pipe & Park
Snow Season
Nov to April
Snowmaking
20km of piste
Number of lifts
54
Up Lift Capicity
36,500 per hour
Mountain Cafes
17

On the Slopes - Davos seems to be more famous as an international talking shop rather than one of Switzerland's premier ski and snowboard resorts these days, which is a real shame. To say that this resort is truly amazing is an understatement and while the town is rather impersonal, the mountains that surround it are as good as it gets – if you fail to have a good time or don't go home impressed, take up racing snails in a cardboard box. Davos altitude usually ensures a good level of snow, covering pistes that are spread over five mountain areas stretching from Davos Dorf to Klosters. The large amount of terrain means that the crowds are well dispersed throughout the region, which helps to keep lift queues to a minimum. What's more, the recent addition of a new gondola means the queues that used to exist at Davos Dorf, are now all but a thing of the past. From the moment you first hit the slopes in the morning, to your last run at night, your day will be filled with an endless choice of well-groomed pistes. It's well worth taking time in the morning to plan your day and study the piste map carefully as not all the runs connect up, however. The best place for beginners to start is on the nursery slopes at Bolgen, after which you should head up to the wide easy pistes on Parsenn. When it comes to snowboarding, look no further, Davos it is; there's even a snowboard hotel in the town. The whole area has 'ride me' written all over it and is total, full on fun, especially on the Jakobshorn where you'll find two pipes and a snowpark.

Off the Slopes - There is simply not enough room here to detail what Davos has to offer – suffice to say that it is a big mountain town, packed with every size and shape of hotel, guesthouse and pension possible and although prices tend to be high wherever you stay, some deal are possible. Around the town, there are dozens of shops, sporting attractions; zillions of restaurants and loads of nightspots from life music bars with young crowds to cabaret and casino's.

Verdict - Truly awesome, particularly for snowboarders. Big town. 10/10

COST INDICATOR

Budget   Moderate   Very Expensive   Criminal

i - **Information** - 0041 (0) 415 2121
www.davos.ch

ROUTE PLANNER

CALAIS 0 miles
along the A16 - A26
E15 / E17
Toll Road

→ **REIMS** 168 miles
2hrs 55   A4 E17 / 50

→ **METZ** 270 miles
4hrs 47   A4 E25

Tolls End

→ **STRASBOURG** 384 miles
6hrs 30

⚠ **Enter Germany** 470 miles
N4

→ **OFFENBURG** 397 miles
6hrs 48   E35 - A5

⚠ **Enter Switzerland**
E35 - A5

→ **BASEL** 474 miles
8hrs   E25 - A2, A1, A6

→ **ZURICH** 524 miles
9hrs   E43, A3

→ **LANDQUART** 573 miles
10hrs   28

28 via **Klosters**

→ **DAVOS**

KM **Distance** 616 miles *(992 km)*
🕐 **Drive time** 10 hours 50 mins
⛽ **Fuel** £55
€ **Tolls** £15

✈ **Airports & Fly Drive Guide**
1st- Zurich- 2 hrs 20
→ All routes south via A3 to Landquart = 98 miles

2nd - Innsbruck (A) - 2 hrs 30
→ All routes via the Arlberg to the A14 = 110 miles

3rd- Geneva - 4 hrs 50
→ All routes via the A1and Zurich to the 28 = 261 miles

Engelberg

Mapping Page 87 D5

Top Lift
3020m.
Resort Height
1050m.
Vertical Drop
1970m.
Number of Runs
44
Longest Run
4km
Slopes
80km of piste
● ● *Beginner*
30% of the runs
● *Intermediate*
60% of the runs
● **Advanced**
10% of the runs

Cross-Country
40km of tracks
Snowboarding
Half-pipe & Park
Snow Season
Dec to April
Snowmaking
20% of pistes
Number of lifts
24
Up Lift Capicity
23,000 per hour
Mountain Cafes
9

On the Slopes - Engelberg is located in the centre of the country, two hours south of Zurich. This rather stunning part of Switzerland that boasts spectacular mountain scenery is worth visiting just for the views alone. While Engelberg may not be a famous resort nor does it have vast numbers of runs it is noteworthy for good reliable snowfalls, but year round skiing and snowboarding on the Titlis glacier. During the winter, skiing and snowboarding tales place on the Standi-Titlis area, which is reached from the village via the six-person gondola that takes you up to Trubsee. At this level the runs are perhaps more suited to beginners and intermediates that any others, but continue to the summit and experts will be bursting with excitement as they find some great off-piste slopes. In truth, experts are most likely to benefit from the terrain on offer as with the exception of the nursery slopes on the Standi, there just aren't enough easy runs. For more confident skiers it's a different story, however, with most of the mountain rated at intermediate level although there are some advanced runs to try out. Snowboarders have long been aware of what Engelberg has to offer, with superb back-country terrain to head for, and as well as having a snowpark and basic half-pipe, the Titlis glacier is a popular location for summer snowboard camps open to any one who can ride – or who wants to learn. For cross-country skiers this is also a mountain that rates highly.

Off the Slopes - This is a delightful traditional Swiss village full of character and charm laid out in such at manner that's it easy to get around. Accommodation is offered in hotels and apartments with some good deals available, either by booking direct or through a tour operator. The resort provides good local amenities and excellent sporting facilities. Most of the restaurants are based in hotels but there are also some fast food outlets for those on a budget or on the go. In the evenings, things don't really rock, but this is still a lively resort with some nice bars to check out.

Verdict - Fine intermediate's mountain and a very welcoming village. 7/10

COST INDICATOR

Budget   Moderate   Very Expensive   Criminal

i - **Information** - 0041 (0) 639 7777
www.engelberg.ch

ROUTE PLANNER

CALAIS 0 miles
along the A16 - A26
E15 / E17
Toll Road

→ **REIMS** 168 miles
2hrs 55   A4 E17 / 50

→ **METZ** 270 miles
4hrs 47   A4 E25

Tolls End

→ **STRASBOURG** 384 miles
6hrs 30

⚠ **Enter Germany** 470 miles
N4

→ **OFFENBURG** 397 miles
6hrs 48   E35 - A5

⚠ **Enter Switzerland**
E35 - A5

→ **BASEL** 474 miles
8hrs   E35 A2, A3, E60

→ **OLTEN**
9hrs   E35 - A2

LUZEN
E35 - A2

→ **STANS** 522 miles
9hrs 20   Follow directions up to the resort.

→ **ENGELBERG**

KM **Distance** 535 miles *(861 km)*
🕐 **Drive time** 10 hours
⛽ **Fuel** £50
€ **Tolls** £15

✈ **Airports & Fly Drive Guide**
1st- Zurich - 1 hr 50
→ E41, A2 and all routes via Stans = 64 miles

2nd - Bern - 2 hrs
→ A8 and all routes east via Stans = 85 miles

3rd- Geneval - 3 hrs 40
→ A1, A2 Olten and all routes south via Stans = 185 miles

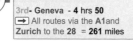
🕐 DRIVE TIME - **nixon** ● www.nixon.com

Switzerland
Films / Laax

Mapping Page 87 D6

Top Lift	3020m.
Resort Height	1100m.
Vertical Drop	1763m.
Number of Runs	92
Longest Run	15km
Slopes	241km of piste

● ● Beginner — 30% of the runs
● Intermediate — 45% of the runs
● Advanced — 26% of the runs

Cross-Country — 55km of tracks
Snowboarding — Half-pipe & Park
Snow Season — Dec to Sept
Snowmaking — 30% of pistes
Number of lifts — 29
Up Lift Capacity — 41,200 per hour
Mountain Cafes — 17

On the Slopes - Flims/Laax are two resorts that are joined together on the mountain via a number of interconnecting lifts. Situated south of Zurich, the region is one of Switzerland's best kept secrets outside of the country – some of the best off-piste sections are a secret to all but the locals, so you will have to know where to find them. Laax is the first of the two, which is the access point for the Vorab glacier where you can ski and snowboard year round. If you have never skied here before then definitely put these two on your short list because you won't be disappointed. An excellent lift system, reasonable snow falls, and wide open pistes all help make this spot a gem, yet the region has yet to be exploited by the UK market – it seems that only the Swiss and some of their cousins from Germany have cottoned on. Where some resorts are either one thing or the other, Flims and Laax are a mixture of everything and whether you are a beginner, expert, cross-country skier or a freestyle loving snowboarder, you will find something to appeal to you. It's also good to find a resort that truly doesn't have long lift lines with the exception of the busiest weekend periods. Cross-country tracks stretch to over 60km of tracks and some are extremely enjoyable making this a great place to glide around in a leisurely manner. The snowboard scene is big here, and as well as being a resort that hosts loads of events all year round, the mountain offers both freestyles and carvers some fantastic terrain, for all levels.

Off the Slopes - Both villages offer an excellent choice of accommodation with plenty of hotels and apartments close to the slopes. Laax is the bigger of the two, but both have about the same amount of off hill facilities and prices are similar in both, which are in the mid to high bracket. Flims is home to a good pizza joint called Pomodor, but on the whole eating out is a bit too costly for what is on offer. Nightlife on the other hand is cool, and revellers can be heard partying hard most nights, especially those in the Angel bar in Flims.

Verdict - Superb all-round mountain with great pistes. Nice villages also. **9/10**

ROUTE PLANNER
CALAIS 0 miles — along the A16 - A26 E15 / E17 Toll Road
REIMS 168 miles 2hrs 55 — A4 E17 / 50
METZ 270 miles 4hrs 47 — A4 E25
Tolls End
STRASBOURG 384 miles 6hrs 30
Enter Germany 470 miles — N4
OFFENBURG 397 miles 6hrs 48 — E35 - A5
Enter Switzerland — E35 - A5
BASEL 474 miles 8hrs — E25 - A2, A1, A6
ZURICH 524 miles 9hrs — E43, A3
LANDQUART 573 miles 10hrs — E43, A13
TAMINS
FLIMS / LAAX

Distance 614 miles (988 km)
Drive time 10 hours 40 mins
Fuel £55
Tolls £15

COST INDICATOR
Budget — Moderate — Very Expensive — Criminal

i - Information - 0041 (0) 920 9200
www.alpenarena.ch

Airports & Fly Drive Guide
1st- Zurich - 2 hrs — All routes south via the A3 to Tamins = 96 miles
2nd- Innsbruck (A) - 3 hrs — All routes via the Arlberg to the A14 = 145 miles
3rd- Geneva - 4 hrs 40 — All routes along the A2, A3 to Tamins = 260 miles

---

Switzerland
Grindelwald

Mapping Page 86 D4

Top Lift	2970m.
Resort Height	1035m.
Vertical Drop	1467m.
Number of Runs	195
Longest Run	15m
Slopes	200km of piste

● ● Beginner — 30% of the runs
● Intermediate — 50% of the runs
● Advanced — 20% of the runs

Cross-Country — 25km of tracks
Snowboarding — Half-pipe & Park
Snow Season — Dec to April
Snowmaking — 35% of psites
Number of lifts — 44
Up Lift Capacity — 40,000 per hour
Mountain Cafes — 21

On the Slopes - Grindelwald is set below the north face of the mighty Eiger and quite simply, the scenery and mountain setting is stunning and truly hard to beat. This is an awesome place in terms of the skiing and snowboarding opportunities, which are aided by the fact that Grindelwald shares the mountain with its extremely highbrow neighbour, Wengen. The slopes are lovingly groomed and if you stay on the main base runs or the slopes just above the village on the Oberjoch area, then you will find plenty of easy runs mixed with some interesting intermediate slopes. In an area this size and altitude, you would expect an excellent snow record, which is close to the truth, but some of the lower runs often get poor cover or wear through quite easily. Still it's only a minor hitch, as generally the snow is good here, especially on the Wengen side. However, what is a real pain are the lift queues throughout the season – the worst being the queues for the Grund train, which can be worst than waiting for a train at Charing Cross in London. The other slight let down here is the lack of expert terrain – in general, unless you are prepared to go way off-piste there's not a lot to challenge the most demanding skier or snowboarder. On the other hand there's lots for snowboarders to enjoy, which includes a good snowpark and decent halfpipe. In a country known for it's excellent cross-country facilities the area around Grindelwald is very good, however, with most of the tracks set out around the lower areas around the resort, good snow cover is not always assured.

Off the Slopes - Grindelwald is a good all-round holiday village made up largely of chalets and expensive hotels. The resort sits both sides of the main road and is a fun place where a family with children are well catered for. The facilities are excellent and cater for all, but although this is cheaper than nearby Wengen, it's still an expensive place. Nightlife is very typical for this region, lively, and styled at après fans with bar games and other nonsense.

Verdict - Breathtaking scenery and good for beginners and intermediates. **8/10**

ROUTE PLANNER
CALAIS 0 miles — along the A16 - A26 E15 / E17 Toll Road
REIMS 168 miles 2hrs 55 — A4 E17 / 50
METZ 270 miles 4hrs 47 — A4 E25
Tolls End
STRASBOURG 384 miles 6hrs 30
Enter Germany 470 miles — N4
OFFENBURG 397 miles 6hrs 48 — E35 - A5
Enter Switzerland — E35 - A5
BASEL 474 miles 8hrs — E25 - A2, A1, A6
BERN 540 miles 9hrs — E25 - A6, A8
INTERLAKEN 565 miles 9hrs 40
GRINDELWALD

Distance 576 miles (927 km)
Drive time 10 hours 20 mins
Fuel £53
Tolls £15

COST INDICATOR
Budget — Moderate — Very Expensive — Criminal

i - Information - 0041 (0) 854 1212
www.grindelwald.ch

Airports & Fly Drive Guide
1st- Bern - 1 hr 20 — E25, A6, A8 and all routes via Interlaken = 43 miles
2nd - Geneva - 3 hrs — A1, A6, A8 and all routes via Interlaken = 144 miles
3rd- Zurich - 2 hrs 30 — 8 and all routes south via Interlaken = 95 miles

DRIVE TIME - nixon www.nixon.com

Gstaad

Mapping Page 86 E3

ROUTE PLANNER

CALAIS 0 miles	
along the A16 - A26	
E15 / E17	
Toll Road	
REIMS 168 miles 2hrs 55	A4 **E17 / 50**
METZ 270 miles 4hrs 47	A4 **E25**
Tolls End	
STRASBOURG 384 miles 6hrs 30	
Enter Germany 470 miles	N4
OFFENBURG 397 miles 6hrs 48	**E35 - A5**
Enter Switzerland	**E35 - A5**
BASEL 474 miles 8hrs	**E25 - A2, A1, A6**
BERN 540 miles 9hrs	**E27 - A12**
MONTREUX 592 miles 9hrs 25	**E27, A9**
AIGLE	11 following all local signs to the resort.
GSTAAD	

KM Distance	**536** miles (863 km)
Drive time	**9** hours **50** mins
Fuel	**£50**
€ Tolls	**£15**

Top Lift
3000m.
Resort Height
1050m.
Vertical Drop
995m.
Number of Runs
60
Longest Run
4km
Slopes
240km of piste
● ● Beginner
60% of the runs
● Intermediate
30% of the runs
● Advanced
10% of the runs

Cross-Country
60km of tracks
Snowboarding
Half-pipe & Park
Snow Season
Nov to October
Snowmaking
12km of piste
Number of lifts
66
Up Lift Capicity
-
Mountain Cafes
6

92

On the Slopes - Gstaad is a destination that not only attracts large numbers of visitors every season, it is also popular with the rich and well-informed set, giving the place an upmarket feel. Gstaad could hardly be described as an expert's mountain, with only a limited amount of steep terrain to choose from, yet despite that, the off-piste challenges are pretty good. The trees around the Wispile are good fun and offer some interesting skiing and snowboarding, furthermore with the option to go heli-skiing or boarding (not cheap, it has to be said) the backcountry areas make up for the tame and unchallenging main runs. On the pistes, the lifts are set out in such a way that getting around poses no real problems and hardly any time is lost in lift queues. With many runs favouring intermediate users, this is a mountain that is ideally suited to anyone who wants to progress, but the slopes often throw up a few surprises, so you will need to have your wits about you. Although the season here is much the same as any other Swiss resort (in general November to April), the glacier Les Diablerets is close at hand, so if you fancy a summer trip then head there and you can ski all year round. For snowboarders there is a boarder-cross and a snowpark, but this place doesn't really cut it as a top snowboard destination – the opposite can be said for cross-country facilities, as this is a great destination for sliding along scenic tracks. The tracks up at the Sparenmoors are first class and unlike the lower areas, will usually have good snow cover.

Off the Slopes - Gstaad is definitely not one of the most convenient resorts, although it's a pleasant and friendly town, it is something of a hassle when its comes to access to the slopes and much of the accommodation – most people are going to have to catch a ski bus to reach the base lifts. There are, however, plenty of quality apartments and chalets if you want to go self-catering but it's worth noting that Gstaad is an expensive resort all round. For a reasonably priced meal check out hotel Olden.

Verdict - Good intermediate slopes, let down by a disjointed, expensive town. **7**/10

COST INDICATOR

Budget　Moderate　Very Expensive　Criminal

i **- Information -** 0041 (0) 748 8181
www.gstaad

Airports & Fly Drive Guide

1st- Bern - 1 hr 26
E25, A6 and all routes via Saanen = **50** miles

2nd - Geneva - 2 hrs
All routes via Lausanne & Aigle - 11 = **96** miles

3rd - Zurich - 3 hrs
A6 - all routes south via Saanen = **130** miles

Klosters

Mapping Page 87 D7

ROUTE PLANNER

CALAIS 0 miles	
along the A16 - A26	
E15 / E17	
Toll Road	
REIMS 168 miles 2hrs 55	A4 **E17 / 50**
METZ 270 miles 4hrs 47	A4 **E25**
Tolls End	
STRASBOURG 384 miles 6hrs 30	
Enter Germany 470 miles	N4
OFFENBURG 397 miles 6hrs 48	**E35 - A5**
Enter Switzerland	**E35 - A5**
BASEL 474 miles 8hrs	**E35 A2, A3, E60**
ZURICH 524 miles 9hrs	**E43, A3**
LANDQUART 573 miles 10hrs	28
KLOSTERS	

KM Distance	**610** miles (982 km)
Drive time	**10** hours **40** mins
Fuel	**£55**
€ Tolls	**£15**

Top Lift
2844m.
Resort Height
1191m.
Vertical Drop
2031m.
Number of Runs
76
Longest Run
10km
Slopes
170km of piste
● ● Beginner
35% of the runs
● Intermediate
50% of the runs
● Advanced
15% of the runs

Cross-Country
30km of tracks
Snowboarding
Half-pipe & Park
Snow Season
Dec to April
Snowmaking
-
Number of lifts
31
Up Lift Capicity
31,000 per hour
Mountain Cafes
12

On the Slopes - Forget the pictures you see in the tabloids and the impression that you may have that Klosters is about Prince Charles and his sons dodging the paparazzi, Klosters is not solely about various royals or famous wannabes; it's a major mountain that offers excellent skiing and snowboarding. You may have the impression that the town would be made up of a vast number of mansions around a mega-developed town, but you would be very wrong. Klosters is a place that any skier or snowboarder, no matter what their ability, can have great week in. With the exception of some of the lower areas, the snow is pretty reliable and the season extends until mid-April mostly. The runs seldom get too crowded, but the Gotschna cable car can be a nightmare on a Saturday morning when the crowds try to access the mountain after breakfast. While some might say that Klosters is a little overrated, most would agree that the off-piste terrain is excellent and can be very testing – please note that these mountains can be hostile, so only go off-piste with the assistance of a knowledgeable local guide. For beginners, the slopes on Madrisa are rather appealing while intermediates — whether on two skis or a snowboard – will find the series of red trails down from Gotschnagrat are wonderful places to test your ability to the limit. The area known as Schifer is great for intermediates also. There is a terrain park here for freestyle skiers and snowboarders, in the main the facilities at Davos are better. Like wise, Klosters has around 30km of cross-country tracks with more trails available at Davos.

Off the Slopes - Klosters is an old village that is full of real character and not a purpose-built eyesore. This is a quiet resort with expensive hotels and chalets and not much in between. Eating out is also an expensive affair, but at least you can get a decent pizza at Alberto's. Evenings are fairly quiet; they don't go in for hardcore late night partying here although there is a selection of simple traditional bars.

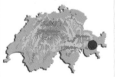

Verdict - Klosters is a good place to ski and snowboard, but not cheap. **7**/10

COST INDICATOR

Budget　Moderate　Very Expensive　Criminal

i **- Information -** 0041 (0) 410 2020
www.klosters.ch

Airports & Fly Drive Guide

1st- Zurich - 2 hrs 5
All routes south via A3 to Landquart = **92** miles

2nd - Innsbruck (A) - 2 hrs 40
All routes via the Arlberg to the A14 = **114** miles

3rd - Geneva - 4 hrs 30
All routes via the A1and Zurich to the 28 = **255** miles

Switzerland
Leysin

Mapping Page 86 E2

Top Lift
2200m.
Resort Height
1300m.
Vertical Drop
900m.
Number of Runs
30
Longest Run
6km
Slopes
120km of piste
● Beginner
30% of the runs
● Intermediate
50% of the runs
● Advanced
20% of the runs

Cross-Country
40km of tracks
Snowboarding
Half-pipe & Park
Snow Season
Dec to April
Snowmaking
20% of pistes
Number of lifts
19
Up Lift Capacity
18,000 per hour
Mountain Cafes
6

On the Slopes - Leysin is not a place widely known by UK skiers, although many snowboarders have become acquainted with the resort as many world ranking snowboard events are staged on the mountain and indeed Channel 4 TV hosted its 'Board Stupid' programme from here (sad pop stars on snowboards plugging crap albums mainly). For the rest of us, Leysin is an unusual place and in some ways doesn't resemble a resort in the traditional sense at all. Stretched out up the face of a steep hill, access to Leysin takes the form of a drive up a long and winding road. To get to the slopes you only need to drive a short distance to reach the base access point where you get on the gondola and from the top you are presented with slopes that are mainly intermediate level with some areas that will also please experts. In general, the snow record is fairly good, but the lower areas – where most of the nursery slopes are located – can often thin out in the spring. If you like to ski trees, then Leysin is a place for you, despite the immediate off-piste slopes being a bit limited. One reason why the resort has become popular with snowboarders, is the fact that the resort management have been very active in providing good freestyle facilities on the mountain and in staging big events that attract some of the biggest names in snowboarding — all the greats have ridden here, including Terje Haakonsen and Daniel Franck.

Off the Slopes - Leysin is a traditional village that is home to an American college, some big hotels and modern apartment blocks. There is also a very good bunk house, should you be on a tight budget. The Vagabond has good rates and as well as a cafe, there is also a lively bar. Chalet Ermina, at the other end of the village, is a fine place to stay and serves a mean breakfast. Around the village are some fine restaurants that serve mainly traditional Swiss dishes. Nightlife is also good and as well as some cool bars, there are a couple of lively discos, a cinema and a sports centre but most things in the resort are expensive.

ROUTE PLANNER

🏠 **CALAIS** 0 miles
along the **A16 - A26**
E15 / E17
Toll Road

➡ **REIMS** 168 miles
2hrs 55 **A4 E17 / 50**

➡ **METZ** 270 miles
4hrs 47 **A4 E25**

Tolls End

➡ **STRASBOURG** 384 miles
6hrs 30

⚠ **Enter Germany** 470 miles
N4

➡ **OFFENBURG** 397 miles
6hrs 48 **E35 - A5**

⚠ **Enter Switzerland**
E35 - A5

➡ **BASEL** 474 miles
8hrs **E25 - A2, A1, A6**

➡ **BERN** 540 miles
9hrs **E27 - A12**

➡ **MONTREUX** 592 miles
9hrs 25 **E27, A9**

🏠 **AIGLE**
11 following all local signs up to the resort.

➡ **LEYSIN**

KM **Distance** 517 miles (832 km)
🕐 **Drive time** 9 hours 40 mins
⛽ **Fuel** £48
€ **Tolls** £15

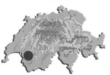

Verdict - Super cool hangout loved by snowboarders. Basic resort. **8/10**

COST INDICATOR

Budget   Moderate   Very Expensive   Criminal

i - **Information** - 0041 (0) 2449 42244
www.leysin.ch

✈ **Airports & Fly Drive Guide**

1st- Geneva - 1 hr 45
➡ All routes via **Lausanne &**
Aigle - 11 = 76 miles

2nd- Bern - 2 hrs
➡ **A12** and all routes south
via **Vevey = 78 miles**

3rd- Zurich - 3 hrs 15
➡ **A1, A12** - and routes south
via **Vevey = 152 miles**

Switzerland
Murren

Mapping Page 86 D4

Top Lift
2970m.
Resort Height
1650m.
Vertical Drop
2175m.
Number of Runs
26
Longest Run
16km
Slopes
215km of piste
● Beginner
30% of the runs
● Intermediate
50% of the runs
● Advanced
20% of the runs

Cross-Country
5km of tracks
Snowboarding
Half-pipe & Park
Snow Season
Dec to April
Snowmaking
34% of pistes
Number of lifts
44
Up Lift Capacity
9,200 per hour
Mountain Cafes
7

On the Slopes - Murren is loosely linked with the ski areas of Wengen and Grindelwald, but unlike its close neighbours, it is an altogether different resort. Of course there are some similarities – being located so close to each other, the three have the same pattern of snowfall and terrain and all three share a joint lift pass which covers the Jungfrau region. Murren stands out from the other two resorts in that it is seen as the little brother and as a result, is often far less crowded than the others. While there are not so many runs as can be found at the other resorts, the terrain is just as adventurous and offers some wonderful runs from the summit of the Schilthorn back down into the village – the top section is not for the faint of heart. From the summit you'll have to conquer a short, but fairly steep black piste before it mellows out via a couple of blue runs before turning red and then into a steep black again. While it could fairly be said that Murren is not over supplied with black runs, the challenging terrain that is available is exactly that. What's more, off-piste terrain over in the Blumental area is wonderful. Whatever grade you are, there are a lot of cliffs around here, some are even close to runs and netted off, so be careful wherever you go. There are some nice nursery slopes for beginners just above the village and off the Schiltgrat chair lift, but in general Murren doesn't have a lot of nursery slopes and some that are coloured blue can be a bit testing for younger first timers. There is a good terrain park located on the Schiltgrat slopes loaded with toys to get air off and there is also a decent size halfpipe. In terms of cross-country skiing, this is not the most interesting place.

Off the Slopes - Murren is a delightful resort, at high altitude and reachable by cable car or the funicular train. The whole place is straight from a picture postcard with small streets and quaint chalets. There are not many hotels to select from but the choices are good with rates to suite most pockets. Dining out and nightlife is both good and lively, but not over the top.

ROUTE PLANNER

🏠 **CALAIS** 0 miles
along the **A16 - A26**
E15 / E17
Toll Road

➡ **REIMS** 168 miles
2hrs 55 **A4 E17 / 50**

➡ **METZ** 270 miles
4hrs 47 **A4 E25**

Tolls End

➡ **STRASBOURG** 384 miles
6hrs 30

⚠ **Enter Germany** 470 miles
N4

➡ **OFFENBURG** 397 miles
6hrs 48 **E35 - A5**

⚠ **Enter Switzerland**
E35 - A5

➡ **BASEL** 474 miles
8hrs **E25 - A2, A1, A6**

➡ **BERN** 540 miles
E25 - A6, A8

➡ **INTERLAKEN** 565 miles
9hrs 40 To Lauterbrunnen
then access by train

➡ **MURREN**

KM **Distance** 577 miles (929 km)
🕐 **Drive time** 12 hours 23 mins
⛽ **Fuel** £60
€ **Tolls** £15

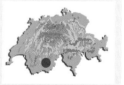

Verdict - Good resort located in a fantastic setting, with lots of charm. **7/10**

COST INDICATOR

Budget   Moderate   Very Expensive   Criminal

i - **Information** - 0041 (0) 856 8686
www.wengenmurren.ch

✈ **Airports & Fly Drive Guide**

1st- Bern - 3 hrs 20
➡ **E25, A6, A8** and all routes
via **Interlaken = 43 miles**

2nd- Zurich - 4 hrs 30
➡ **8** and all routes south via
Interlaken = 94 miles

3rd- Geneva - 5 hrs
➡ **A1, A6, A8** and all routes
via **Lauterbrunnen = 144 miles**

🕐 DRIVE TIME - **nixon**® www.nixon.com

Nendaz

ROUTE PLANNER

CALAIS 0 miles
along the A16 - A26
E15 / E17
Toll Road

REIMS 168 miles
2hrs 55 A4 E17 / 50

METZ 270 miles
4hrs 47 A4 E25

Tolls End

STRASBOURG 384 miles
6hrs 30

Enter Germany 470 miles
N4

OFFENBURG 397 miles
6hrs 48 E35 - A5

Enter Switzerland
E35 - A5

BASEL 474 miles
8hrs E25 - A2, A1, A6

BERN 540 miles
9hrs E27 - A12

MONTREUX 592 miles
9hrs 25 E27, A9

SION
follow all local
signs to the resort.

NENDAZ

KM **Distance**	546 miles	(880 km)
Drive time	10 hours 20 mins	
Fuel	£52	
€ **Tolls**	£15	

Top Lift
3300m.
Resort Height
1365m.
Vertical Drop
1935m.
Number of Runs
196
Longest Run
15km
Slopes
177km of piste
● ● *Beginner*
37% of the runs
○ *Intermediate*
57% of the runs
● *Advanced*
6% of the runs

Cross-Country
24km of tracks
Snowboarding
Half-pipe & Park
Snow Season
Dec to April
Snowmaking
5% of piste
Number of lifts
41
Up Lift Capicity
25,000 per hour
Mountain Cafes
8

On the Slopes - Nendaz is slap-bang in the middle of Switzerland's famous Four Valleys region and unlike its close cousin Verbier, this is a quiet place that not many are aware of. It's a shame, really because like Verbier and other mountain resorts in the area, there is a lot going on and Nendaz is left relatively crowd-free, although some lift queues do exist. The terrain is not vast but with lots of alternatives in the area, there's always something else to check out. Snow cover here is good and the fact that the slopes are high up usually means a long season with good cover over most of the runs all the time, which is important when you see how little snowmaking facilities exist. In general, beginners and intermediates are the ones who will get the most out of these slopes with some great intermediate slopes on the pistes at Siviez, which connects with both Verbier and Nendaz. Experts are better off visiting Verbier itself, which is where you will find some high altitude extreme terrain that needs to be treated with respect and while you can get to Verbier via an array of lifts it's not something that can be done quickly – it's probably better to take one of the ski buses. While advanced skiers might not like Nendaz's offerings, beginners should love it with some excellent wide-open nursery slopes up at Tracouet. There is a terrain park here, but freestyle skiers and snowboarders tend to prefer the goings on up in Verbier, where things are more orginaised. Cross-country skiers have 20km of tracks to explore around a pleasant landscape where the trails are simple and not over testing *(perfect for granny on her first OAP snow holiday)*.

Off the Slopes - Nendaz is a large modern resort built with a discerning eye. New chalets blend in well, the whole place has a welcoming feel and it is very much geared to looking after its visitors. The sheer number of available beds makes booking a room here easy. Restaurants are also plentiful and despite Nendaz being expensive both dining out and nightlife are very good and offer value for money.

Verdict - Not bad as an alternative to Verbier, but not hot for experts. **7**/10

COST INDICATOR

Budget   Moderate   Very Expensive   Criminal

i - **Information** - 0041 (0) 289 5589
www.nendaz.ch

Saas Fee

ROUTE PLANNER

CALAIS 0 miles
along the A16 - A26
E15 / E17
Toll Road

REIMS 168 miles
2hrs 55 A4 E17 / 50

METZ 270 miles
4hrs 47 A4 E25

Tolls End

STRASBOURG 384 miles
6hrs 30

Enter Germany 470 miles
N4

OFFENBURG 397 miles
6hrs 48 E35 - A5

Enter Switzerland
E35 - A5

BASEL 474 miles
8hrs E35 A2, A3, E60

BERN 540 miles
9hrs E27 - A12

THUN 540 miles
9hrs 10 A6, 223

VISP 594 miles
10hrs 50

SAAS FEE

KM **Distance**	610 miles	(982 km)
Drive time	12 hours 40 mins	
Fuel	£59	
€ **Tolls**	£15	

Top Lift
3500m.
Resort Height
1800m.
Vertical Drop
1700m.
Number of Runs
40
Longest Run
9km
Slopes
100km of piste
● ● *Beginner*
25% of the runs
○ *Intermediate*
50% of the runs
● *Advanced*
25% of the runs

Cross-Country
10km of tracks
Snowboarding
Half-pipe & Park
Snow Season
All year round
Snowmaking
5km of pistes
Number of lifts
32
Up Lift Capicity
26,000 per hour
Mountain Cafes
8

On the Slopes - Saas Fee is a well-known and very popular location, and it's not just in the winter that the resort welcomes snow sports enthusiasts – it's Switzerland's number one summer ski and snowboard mountain as well. Despite the reputation that this mountain has gained over the years, there are plenty of things to annoy you like the fact that it is actually quite small and although good snow may have fallen, the weather often causes the lifts to close down. What's more, it is not a very challenging mountain and most experienced skiers and snowboarders would be able to complete all the runs within a few days. That said, there is some testing terrain with trees up on the Plattjen area and the runs off the Hinterallalin are not to be scoffed at. What is noticeable here during the winter is how cold it can get and how shaded the slopes are, which has the effect of keeping the snow surface hard and often icy. Despite this, it is possible to ski and ride powder – but don't blink or you will miss it. It's also fair to say that it is very popular with freestyle skiers and snowboarders in the off season as the resort is one of the few in the world that maintains their pipe and terrain park almost all year round. Steeper sections quickly get mogul led-out, which is not particularly attractive for novice skiers and most snowboarders. Beginners have little to complain about, with plenty of nursery slopes both close to the village, mid way and up at the top. Cross-country skiing is not the most interesting here although there are some nice tracks.

Off the Slopes - This is a traditional resort with a modern outlook. The car-free status of the village means that the only vehicles allowed are electric powered ('milk floats' that are owned by hotels). There are plenty of tour operators that offer package deals and with over 50 hotels and loads of self-catering options, there is lots to choose from. Not noted for is cuisine, Saas Fee still has some fine restaurants, while nightlife is fantastic and thanks to the obvious snowboard culture, its bang up to date.

Verdict - Picturesque mountain town, especially suitable for intermediates. **7**/10

COST INDICATOR

Budget   Moderate   Very Expensive   Criminal

i - **Information** - 0041 (0) 958 1858
www.saas-fee.ch

Switzerland
Savoginin

Mapping Page 87 D6

ROUTE PLANNER

🛫	**CALAIS**	0 miles
	along the A16 - A26 E15 / E17	
	Toll Road	
➡	**REIMS** 168 miles	
2hrs 55	A4 E17 / 50	
➡	**METZ** 270 miles	
4hrs 47	A4 E25	
	Tolls End	
➡	**STRASBOURG** 384 miles	
6hrs 30		
⛰	**Enter Germany** 470 miles	
	N4	
➡	**OFFENBURG** 397 miles	
6hrs 48	E35 - A5	
⛰	**Enter Switzerland**	
	E35 - A5	
➡	**BASEL** 474 miles	
8hrs	E35 A2, A3, E60	
➡	**ZURICH** 524 miles	
9hrs	E43, A3	
	LANDQUART	
⛷	**CHUR**	
➡	**TAMINS** 583 miles	
10hrs		
➡	**SAVOGNIN**	

KM	**Distance**	627 miles *(1009 km)*
🕐	**Drive time**	11 hours
⛽	**Fuel**	£57
€	**Tolls**	£15

Top Lift 2713m.
Resort Height 1210m.
Vertical Drop 1513m.
Number of Runs 27
Longest Run 7km
Slopes 80km of piste
● *Beginner* 35% of the runs
◐ *Intermediate* 63% of the runs
● **Advanced** 2% of the runs

Cross-Country 40km of tracks
Snowboarding Half-pipe & Park
Snow Season Nov to April
Snowmaking 10% of pistes
Number of lifts 17
Up Lift Capicity 16,140 per hour
Mountain Cafes 7

On the Slopes - Savognin is not a well known resort with most skiers and you're unlikely to find it featured in many tour operator's brochures – their loss, because not only is it a good family-orientated resort, but also one that is not plagued by crowds plus the locals are extremely friendly and make visitors feel welcome. Two hours from Zurich, Savognin is a spot where you can ski on nice sunny pistes that are serviced by just seventeen lifts, laid out in a way to maximise your time on the snow rather than in queues. Intermediate level skiers and novice snowboarders are the ones most attracted to this mountain, as some sixty percent of pistes are marked red with only a small percentage of black runs. There are a few steep sections such as the Pro Spinatsch under the Tiggignas chair lift, but really experts are better off going to nearby St Moritz (if you can afford it) or in the other direction, to Davos. Each season the mountain gets an average 450cm of snow, so there is not a great deal of need for the snowmaking system that has been installed although it is fired up here and there to lend a hand when necessary. While much of the mountain is of an intermediate standard, Savognin is an excellent beginner's mountain with well-groomed nursery slopes near the village, but most of the runs are serviced by drag lifts so those not familiar with T-bars might find they take a little getting used to. Snowboarding is popular here, particularly with locals and while the pipe is not always maintained, you only need to ask and the management will sort it for you. It's more fun to hook up with some local groms who like to build their own kickers and do their own thing. Cross-country skiing is also quite good here but the trails can be a little too similar to one another.

Off the Slopes - Savognin is a pleasant no fuss village full of everything that is Switzerland. What's more this is a resort with a surprisingly good number of local facilities. Accommodation comes in the standard format of hotel, chalets and pensions with reasonable room rates available. Nightlife is definitely very low key.

Verdict - Basic intermediate mountain with good slopes. Excellent village. **6/10**

COST INDICATOR
Budget   Moderate   Very Expensive   Criminal

i - **Information** - 0041 (0) 8168 42222
www.graubuenden.ch/savognin

✈ **Airports & Fly Drive Guide**
1st - Zurich - **2 hrs 22**
➡ All routes south along the A3, A13 via **Tamins** = **110 miles**
2nd - Innsbruck (A) - **3 hrs 20**
➡ All routes via the **Arlberg** to the A14 = **133 miles**
3rd - Geneva - **5 hrs**
➡ All routes via **Zurich** and **Tamins** = **272 miles**

Switzerland
St Moritz

Mapping Page 87 D7

ROUTE PLANNER

🛫	**CALAIS**	0 miles
	along the A16 - A26 E15 / E17	
	Toll Road	
➡	**REIMS** 168 miles	
2hrs 55	A4 E17 / 50	
➡	**METZ** 270 miles	
4hrs 47	A4 E25	
	Tolls End	
➡	**STRASBOURG** 384 miles	
6hrs 30		
⛰	**Enter Germany** 470 miles	
	N4	
➡	**OFFENBURG** 397 miles	
6hrs 48	E35 - A5	
⛰	**Enter Switzerland**	
	E35 - A5	
➡	**BASEL** 474 miles	
8hrs	E25 - A2, A1, A6	
	ZURICH 524 miles	
	E43, A3	
	LANDQUART	
⛷	**CHUR**	
➡	**ST MORITZ**	

KM	**Distance**	651 miles *(1048 km)*
🕐	**Drive time**	11 hours 30 mins
⛽	**Fuel**	£59
€	**Tolls**	£15

Top Lift 3305m.
Resort Height 1770m.
Vertical Drop 1169m.
Number of Runs 47
Longest Run 5km
Slopes 354km of piste
● *Beginner* 16% of the runs
◐ *Intermediate* 70% of the runs
● **Advanced** 14% of the runs

Cross-Country 150km of tracks
Snowboarding Half-pipe & Park
Snow Season Dec to Sept
Snowmaking 70km of pistes
Number of lifts 56
Up Lift Capicity 33,000 per hour
Mountain Cafes 12

On the Slopes - St Moritz possibly at the top of the league when it comes to high class, and somewhat snobby ski resorts. It is a playground for the seriously well heeled, to the point where mere mortals will struggle to afford a trip there. Many of St Moritz' visitors don't even bother with the mountain, and spend most of their time sitting on balconies, seeing and being seen, or enjoying the quality – but expensive – shops. This is possibly a good thing, because while the pose patrol are doing their thing away from the action, those who take their skiing and snowboarding seriously can roam around the slopes with ease – with the exception of some of the lower level mountain restaurants where a few fur-clad idiots do manage to get to. Irrespective of the distractions, St Moritz does manage to achieve a well-maintained mountain with a good lift system and plenty of snowmaking – although they don't often need it. The main pisted slopes are essentially superb for intermediates, while simply adequate for beginners. Experts should really try the off-piste terrain, because that is where St Moritz shines and comes in to its own – there is a huge amount of fantastic backcountry powder bowls and endless tree lines and as so few people take the time or effort to check it out, you can be sure to find lots of untracked slopes. Snowboarders will enjoy this superb freeride resort, but they may receive the cold shoulder from some of the more traditional ski crowd.

Off the Slopes - It seems strange that a resort that attracts so much money and attitude, can be so damn ugly and resemble Peckham in south London rather than an alpine hideaway – it only goes to show that money can't buy taste. No matter where you stay or where you shop prices are high, but if you can afford it there are plenty of quality hotels. The resort has lots of restaurants, but you won't dine out on the cheap. If you have a gold credit card, then try the Bumann's, seriously expensive but serious good. However, in terms of night life, its expensive and generally very poor in all aspects.

Verdict - Excellent off-piste terrain that is spoiled by an overrated resort. **6/10**

COST INDICATOR
Budget   Moderate   Very Expensive   Criminal

i - **Information** - 0041 (0) 837 3333
www.stmoritz.ch

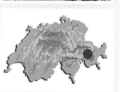

✈ **Airports & Fly Drive Guide**
1st - Zurich - **3 hrs**
➡ All routes south along the A3, A13 via **Chur** = **134 miles**
2nd - Innsbruck (A) - **2 hrs 45**
➡ All routes via the **Arlberg** to the A14 = **115 miles**
3rd - Geneva - **5 hrs 30**
➡ All routes via **Zurich** and **Chur** = **296 miles**

🕐 **DRIVE TIME** - *nixon* ® www.nixon.com

Verbier

Top Lift
3330m.
Resort Height
1500m.
Vertical Drop
1830m.
Number of Runs
77
Longest Run
15
Slopes
241km of piste
● ◑ *Beginner*
40% of the runs
◑ *Intermediate*
40% of the runs
● **Advanced**
20% of the runs

Cross-Country
40km of tracks
Snowboarding
Half-pipe & Park
Snow Season
All year round
Snowmaking
50km of piste
Number of lifts
95
Up Lift Capicity
41,400 per hour
Mountain Cafes
37

On the Slopes - Verbier is Switzerland's number one resort and highly rated by skiers and snowboarders alike. There is one major downside for what is otherwise a superb all-round mountain – money, fame and snobbery, Verbier has them all, making it one of Europe's most expensive resorts. Unlike many other highbrow resorts, Verbier has got something to shout about with a mountain to match anything in the world. Quite apart from the terrain on offer, the scenery is truly breath taking – the sun seems to shine almost constantly on this mountain, which in general receives a good covering of snow every year, especially on the higher slopes. And thanks to the Mont Fort Glacier, there is enough snow to allow for skiing or snowboarding all year meaning you can visit in August should you wish. Lift queues are a bit of a problem here, but with the introduction of new lifts things are rapidly improving – the new gondola that takes you to Les Attelas has done much to ease things. Known for its extreme terrain, Verbier is a magnet for experts, but be warned, some of the slopes are extremely steep – the couloirs of Mont Gele and Les Attelas are serious stuff, so take care. There are tamer areas in the region, however, with most of the mountain suited to intermediates. Beginners are also presented with good nursery slopes close to the village, and should you require instruction, the local ski school has a very good reputation and takes all ages at any level.

Off the Slopes - Verbier is a large place, but even so it's also a pleasant one with excellent local services and accommodation options from hotels to apartments and even a bunkhouse. There are some great shops and excellent restaurants around the resort, such as the Rosalp, which is a wonderful experience. Evenings are full on in Verbier, with some really good bars and clubs, but you need some serious cash to totally enjoy yourself. Check out the Farinet, the Vaux, Pub Mont Fort or Nelsons, all offer something different and are pretty cool.

Verdict - A fantastic mountain that will please all users. Expensive resort. **10/10**

COST INDICATOR

Budget　　Moderate　　Very Expensive　　Criminal

i - **Information** - 0041 (0) 775 3888
www.verbier.ch

96

ROUTE PLANNER

CALAIS 0 miles
along the A16 - A26
E15 / E17
Toll Road

→ **REIMS** 168 miles
2hrs 55　**A4 E17 / 50**

→ **METZ** 270 miles
4hrs 47　**A4 E25**

Tolls End

→ **STRASBOURG** 384 miles
6hrs 30

⚠ **Enter Germany** 470 miles
N4

→ **OFFENBURG** 397 miles
6hrs 48　**E35 - A5**

⚠ **Enter Switzerland**
E35 - A5

→ **BASEL** 474 miles
8hrs　**E25 - A2, A1, A6**

→ **BERN** 540 miles
9hrs　**E27 - A12**

→ **MONTREUX** 592 miles
9hrs 25　**E27, A9**

→ **MARTIGNY**
10hrs　21 follow all local signs to the resort.

→ **VERBIER**

KM Distance 630 miles *(1014 km)*
Drive time 3 hours 5 mins
Fuel £69
Tolls £15

✈ Airports & Fly Drive Guide

1st- Geneva - 2 hrs 10
→ All routes via **Lausanne & Martigny = 100 miles**

2nd - Bern - 2 hrs 20
→ **E27, A12, A9** and all routes via **Martigny = 102 miles**

3rd- Zurich - 3 hrs 40
→ **A1, A12, A9** and all routes via **Martigny = 176 miles**

Villars

Top Lift
2120m.
Resort Height
1300m.
Vertical Drop
913m.
Number of Runs
52
Longest Run
5km
Slopes
99km of piste
● ◑ *Beginner*
40% of the runs
◑ *Intermediate*
50% of the runs
● **Advanced**
10% of the runs

Cross-Country
45km of tracks
Snowboarding
Half-pipe & Park
Snow Season
All year round
Snowmaking
5km of pistes
Number of lifts
35
Up Lift Capicity
16,000 per hour
Mountain Cafes
9

On the Slopes - Villars is a small resort that links up with the Les Diablerets glacier (Glacier 3000 as it likes to be called now) and while it is neither a fashionable resort nor a high one, Villars is a simple place with a family feel. The runs are evenly split and should best please beginners and intermediates, with very few expert slopes. Snow conditions lower down are not always fantastic, but having a glacier in your back yard means that there is always snow to play on higher up. Unless you're staying close to the main gondola, you may find you have to catch a shuttle bus from the end of the village, which can make getting on the mountain a bit of a pain. Once up, things are no worse than any other resort of this size, and even-though some queues do form at certain points, the runs are not bad on the whole. Given that the terrain is not the most challenging, experts might find the slopes a little tedious, but there are some nice off-piste areas to explore, so it would be unfair to dismiss Villars out of hand for the more experienced, but overall it's intermediates who will gain the most out of visit. The red runs on the Grand Chamossaire or those up at Floriettaz are ideal carving areas. Iseneau also has a couple of nice blue runs where novices can have a good time, but the bulk of the nursery slopes are located around the village and as well as them often being rather crowded, they can also lack snow later in the season. Snowboarders save this place for the end of season snowboard bash, but other than that this is not a hot spot – the runs up on the glacier offer far more interest. Villars is a good spot for cross-country skiers with nice tracks.

Off the Slopes - Villars is an old village and looks the part – traditional style chalets are the main choice of accommodation and are dotted around a fairly wide area. The village has lots going on and if you decided to have a day off from skiing there is a tennis court, swimming pool, and ice-rink. There's also a fair selection of hotel-based restaurants and a handful of bars, but no major action. The Mini Bar is okay.

Verdict - Good destination for a family looking for a traditional resort. **6/10**

COST INDICATOR

Budget　　Moderate　　Very Expensive　　Criminal

i - **Information** - 0041 (0) 495 3232
www.villars.ch

ROUTE PLANNER

CALAIS 0 miles
along the A16 - A26
E15 / E17
Toll Road

→ **REIMS** 168 miles
2hrs 55　**A4 E17 / 50**

→ **METZ** 270 miles
4hrs 47　**A4 E25**

Tolls End

→ **STRASBOURG** 384 miles
6hrs 30

⚠ **Enter Germany** 470 miles
N4

→ **OFFENBURG** 397 miles
6hrs 48　**E35 - A5**

⚠ **Enter Switzerland**
E35 - A5

→ **BASEL** 474 miles
8hrs　**E25 - A2, A1, A6**

→ **BERN** 540 miles
9hrs　**E27 - A12**

MONTREUX 592 miles
E27, A9

→ **AIGLE**
10hrs 15　11 following all local signs to the resort.

→ **VILLARS**

KM Distance 604 miles *(972 km)*
Drive time 10 hours 30 mins
Fuel £58
Tolls £15

✈ Airports & Fly Drive Guide

1st- Geneva - 1 hrs 40
→ **A1** and all routes east via **Aigle = 75 miles**

2nd - Bassel - 2 hrs 40
→ **E25 - A6, A12** and all routes via **Aigle = 133 miles**

3rd- Zurich - 3 hrs 10
→ All routes via **Bern** and **Aigle = 151 miles**

Switzerland
Wengen

Mapping Page 86 D4

ROUTE PLANNER

✈ CALAIS	0 miles	
	along the A16 - A26	
	E15 / E17	
	Toll Road	
➡ REIMS	168 miles	2hrs 55
	A4 E17 / 50	
➡ METZ	270 miles	4hrs 47
	A4 E25	
	Tolls End	
➡ STRASBOURG	384 miles	6hrs 30
⚠ Enter Germany	470 miles	
	N4	
➡ OFFENBURG	397 miles	6hrs 48
	E35 - A5	
⚠ Enter Switzerland		
	E35 - A5	
➡ BASEL	474 miles	8hrs
	E25 - A2, A1, A6	
➡ BERN	540 miles	9hrs
	E25 - A6, A8	
➡ INTERLAKEN	565 miles	9hrs 25
LAUTERBRUNNEN		

Top Lift
2971m.
Resort Height
1275m.
Vertical Drop
1050m.
Number of Runs
53
Longest Run
7km
Slopes
200km of piste
● ● Beginner
50% of the runs
● Intermediate
25% of the runs
● Advanced
25% of the runs

Cross-Country
20km of tracks
Snowboarding
Half-pipe & Park
Snow Season
Nov to April
Snowmaking
35km of pistes
Number of lifts
44
Up Lift Capicity
20,200 per hour
Mountain Cafes
20

On the Slopes - While not at the very top of the league for snobby resorts, Wengen runs a close second and is a spot where the chic crowd come to show off and socialise. This is a place where people come to show of their new all- in-one designer ski suits with fur collars and gold embroidered motifs, *(truly hideous style of clothing that belong to the 70's and 80's, look shocking and should be banned from all mountains)*. Still, in a place where stray dogs wear over boots, the mountain is pretty damn good and famed for some excellent steep pistes. The terrain will appeal to all serious skiers and snowboarders. Set below the Eiger and the mighty Jungfrau mountains, which rise to over 4000 metres, the slopes offer similar opportunities to those located in nearby Grindelwald, which is linked by gondola and a series of other lifts. But unlike Grindelwald, Wengen has more intermediate slopes and is substantially larger in area – to be fair; the two resorts are so closely linked on the piste, that it's hard to separate them. Access to the mountain is either via a cable car ride that leaves the village centre or by taking the old mountain train and once up users are presented with lots of wide-open, intermediate runs but few advanced slopes. Some of the best steeps are those around Eigergletscher where you will be tested to the full, you can also try the Lauberhorn but don't go anywhere near it unless you are sure of your ability – it's a fearsome downhill run used for World Cup races There are good nursery slopes near the village but the ones down to Grindelwald are nicer.

Off the Slopes - Despite the resort's obvious upper class appeal and prices to match, Wengen is still a wonderful village with excellent facilities. Hotels, rather than self-catering or chalets, are the preferred form of accommodation and a room in one of the more basic hotels cost more than €45 a night. Eating out is popular with lots of hotel restaurants serving Swiss cuisine; the Bernerhof does good food. Those of you who like party towns won't like Wengen; quiet evenings are the norm around here.

KM **Distance**	573 miles (922 km)	
⏱ **Drive time**	12 hours 30 mins	
⛽ **Fuel**	£60	
€ **Tolls**	£15	

Verdict - Wengen offers great slopes with amazing views. Expensive town. **8/10**

COST INDICATOR

Budget   Moderate   Very Expensive   Criminal

✈ **Airports & Fly Drive Guide**
1st- Bern - 3 hrs 30
➡ E25, A6, A8 and all routes via Interlaken = **40** miles

2nd - Zurich - 4 hrs 30
➡ 8 and all routes south via Interlaken = **90** miles

3rd- Geneva - 5 hrs
➡ A1, A6, A8 and all routes via Interlaken = **140** miles

ℹ - **Information** - 0041 (0) 855 1414
www.wengen-muerren.ch

Switzerland
Zermatt

Mapping Page 86 F4

ROUTE PLANNER

✈ CALAIS	0 miles	
	along the A16 - A26	
	E15 / E17	
	Toll Road	
➡ REIMS	168 miles	2hrs 55
	A4 E17 / 50	
➡ METZ	270 miles	4hrs 47
	A4 E25	
	Tolls End	
➡ STRASBOURG	384 miles	6hrs 30
⚠ Enter Germany	470 miles	
	N4	
➡ OFFENBURG	397 miles	6hrs 48
	E35 - A5	
⚠ Enter Switzerland		
	E35 - A5	
➡ BASEL	474 miles	8hrs
	E35 A2, A3, E60	
BERN	540 miles	
	E27 - A12	
➡ THUN	540 miles	9hrs 10
	A6, 223	
➡ VISP	594 miles	

Top Lift
3820m.
Resort Height
1620m.
Vertical Drop
2200m.
Number of Runs
77
Longest Run
15km
Slopes
250km of piste
● ● Beginner
22% of the runs
● Intermediate
50% of the runs
● Advanced
28% of the runs

Cross-Country
10km of tracks
Snowboarding
Half-pipe & Park
Snow Season
All year round
Snowmaking
45km of pistes
Number of lifts
71
Up Lift Capicity
75,200 per hour
Mountain Cafes
38

On the Slopes - Zermatt offers great skiing and snowboarding, high altitude slopes, lots of sun, classic wide open runs, first class piste grooming, lots of powder, heli-skiing, a cool terrain park and a delightful village. Everything is there for visitors to enjoy a major holiday, but the extremely high prices and snobby attitude can be off-putting. Zermatt really is a top resort that will make a week's stay a very memorable one, both on and off the slopes. Located below the Matterhorn, the views from the town are just stunning and worth the trek to take a few photographs, if nothing else. The area is split into four areas – including the Italian resort of Cervina – all of which can be accessed from the same lift ticket. There are some 71 lifts in the region, but expect to have to wait in queues in the morning especially if you want to catch the Matterhorn cable car, which has so many people packed tightly, you travel in near darkness. The snow record throughout the region is good and with the assistance of plenty of snowmaking, means that snow cover is usually guaranteed. What's more, with the snow that collects over the winter on the Klein Matterhorn glacier, it means that you can play on these slopes throughout the month of July. Zermatt will appeal to all levels of skiers and snowboarders, but is best suited to intermediates and expert visitors. In truth, it's not really a resort for beginners, as there a too few nursery slopes to choose from and the best areas can often be crowded with ski schools. Zermatt entices snowboarders from all over the world and offers great backcountry trails, a fantastic world-class terrain park and a big halfpipe.

Off the Slopes - You will find traditional buildings amid an air of snobbery and money in Zermatt, Still, all visitors are welcome and should you choose to stay in one of the many hotels or chalets, you will find a high standard all over. Zermatt is renowned for its fine restaurants, with great dining in many places. Nightlife is highly rated here, even if it is a bit heavy on the tour rep lead après style partying.

➡ ZERMATT		
KM **Distance**	616 miles (992km)	
⏱ **Drive time**	13 hours 20 mins	
⛽ **Fuel**	£60	
€ **Tolls**	£15	

Verdict - An excellent all-round mountain. Expensive, though. **9/10**

COST INDICATOR

Budget   Moderate   Very Expensive   Criminal

✈ **Airports & Fly Drive Guide**
1st- Bern - 4 hrs 50
➡ A6 and all routes east via Visp = **82** miles

2nd - Geneva - 5 hrs 10
➡ A1, A9 and all routes south via Visp = **148** miles

3rd- Zurich - 6 hrs 10
➡ A,4 A2 and all routes south via Visp = **155** miles

ℹ - **Information** - 0041 (0) 966 8100
www.zermatt.ch

Switzerland, my kind of place

day 1

Switzerland is a quick getaway with only 1 1/2 hours flight time. For the best deals check out www.swiss.com/uk

The Swiss Travel System is the most comprehensive, fully integrated public transport network in the world. Find tickets & youth passes at www.rail.ch

We settled right into our cozy chalet in Engelberg. There's no place like home, except for a Swiss mountain hut.

day 3

Transfering to the Jungfrau is oh so easy. Just sit back and have a beer on the train as you soak up the scenery.

For spectacular views, take a trip on the highest railway in Europe, the Jungfraujoch. Go to www.jungfrau.ch

After a great day in the powder, enjoy a night cap in one of the charming restaurants or bars in Grindelwald.

day 5

WIN!!!!

A 3 night break for two to the Jungfrau Destination! For your chance to win, enter at www.MySwitzerland.com

We decided to try our luck in a half pipe contest on our last day in the Jungfrau Region. Look at Rick go!

The Jungfrau Region isn't just about hitting the pipe - there's Tina enjoy-ing the the powder on a bluebird day.

We had to have one last air on th quarter pipe we built before gettin back on the road.

day 2

The centrepiece of Engelberg is the giant Titlis at 3020m. Make your way up the revolving Titlis Rotair cable car to find some great snowboarding.

Off the slopes, head to The Yucatan for a taste of its legendary apres ski atmosphere and Mexican food.

We rounded off our first day in Engelberg with the traditional thrill of a bit of downhill boarding.

day 4

Snowboarders make the pilgrimmage to Wengen for the natural pipes of the Snowboard Valley on Kleine Scheidegg.

Relax in the revolving restaurant at the top of the Schilthorn in Muerren and take in the Bernese Alps.

Here are the boys having it in the backcountry. This was some of the lightest powder we've ever had.

Why not go out for one last drink and dance with friends before leaving this promised land...

While the rest of the group decided to have one last meal with the great friends we made in Switzerland.

Packages to Engelberg and the Jungfrau Region start from as little as £230. Phone 00800 100 200 30 or visit www.MySwitzerland.com

Land Rover Dealers

Armstrong Massey Land Rover
York
01937 531 531

Barretts Land Rover
Ashford
01233 506 070

Barretts Land Rover
Canterbury
01227 475 475

Beadles Land Rover
Sidcup
0208 309 1100

Broadfields Land Rover
Bishops Stortford
01279 465 657

Bushbury Land Rover
Wolverhampton
01902 393 200

Caffyns Land Rover
Lewes
01273 473 186

Cambrian Land Rover
Aberystwyth
01970 624 841

Charles Douglas Land Rover
Aylesbury
01296 610 061

Charles Douglas Land Rover
Hull
01482 645 413

Charles Douglas Land Rover
Luton
01582 568 600

Charles Douglas Land Rover
Driffield
01377 217 191

Charles Douglas Land Rover
Pickering
01751 477 177

Charles Hurst Land Rover
Belfast
02890 383 544

Chipperfield Land Rovers
Kings Langley
01923 263 030

Colliers Land Rover
Birmingham
0121 382 5566

Conwy Land Rover
Llandudno Junctior
01492 580 000

Copley Land Rover
Halifax
01422 363 340

County Land Rover
Barnstable
01271 349 232

Croall Bryson Land Rover
Kelso
01573 224 345

Donnelly Land Rover
Dungannon
02887 722 887

Droitwich Land Rover
Droitwich
01905 797 777

Duckworth Land Rover
Market Rasen
08704 842 101

Evans Halshaw Land Rover
Solihull
0121 745 5566

Evans Halshaw Land Rover
Stoke
01782 219 500

Farnell Land Rover
Bradford
01274 482 998

Farnell Land Rover
Leeds
01943 871 100

Frank Ogg Land Rover
Elgin
01343 559 820

Gateway Land Rover
Newport
01633 271 888

Gatwick Land Rover
Crawley
01293 531 222

Gordon Lamb Land Rover
Chesterfield
01246 269 000

Green Lane Land Rover
Gloucester
01452 715 700

Greens Land Rover
Haverfordwest
01437 771 555

Guy Salmon Land Rover
Coventry
02476 839 500

Guy Salmon Land Rover
Knutsford
01565 632 525

Guy Salmon Land Rover
Leeds
01132 425 500

Guy Salmon Land Rover
Sheffield
01142 765 655

Guy Salmon Land Rover
Stockport
0161 474 7799

Guy Salmon Land Rover
Stratford Upon Avon
01789 414 696

Guy Salmon Land Rover
Thames Ditton
0208 339 0200

Guy Salmon Land Rover
Wakefield
01924 242 422

H R Owen Land Rover
Bury St Edmunds
01284 706 705

H R Owen Land Rover
Colchester
01206 216 900

H R Owen Land Rover
Kensington
0207 590 5900

H R Owen Land Rover
Park Royal
0208 992 2299

Hadley Green Land Rover
Barnet
0208 440 8252

Hammond Land Rover
Halesworth
01986 834 700

Hartwell Land Rover
Northampton
0870 904 9050

Hartwell Land Rover
Oxford
0870 904 9150

Hartwell Land Rover
St Helens
0870 904 9880

Harwoods Land Rover
Croydon
01737 552 202

Harwoods Land Rover
Pulborough
01798 872 407

Heathwood Land Rover
Ashford
01784 244 033

Hereford Land Rover
Hereford
01531 640 746

Hillendale Land Rover
Nelson
01282 723 723

Hunt Grange Land Rover
Tonbridge
01732 353 637

Hunters Land Rover
Bristol
0870 607 0842

Hunters Land Rover
Derby
01332 545 000

Hunters Land Rover
Guildford
01483 568 262

Hunters Land Rover
Kings Lynn
01553 760 507

Hunters Land Rover
Norwich
01603 788 887

Hunters Land Rover
Southampton
02380 215 800

J V Like Land Rover
Brecon
01497 842 100

Jacksons Land Rover
Guernsey
01481 230 999

Jacksons Land Rover
Jersey
01534 635 555

James Edwards Land Rover
Preston
01995 640 888

James Edwards Land Rover
Chester
01244 373 333

Kentdale Land Rover
Kendal
01539 814 444

Kings Land Rover
Newport
01983 520 555

Lakeland Land Rover
Coniston
01539 441 317

Lancaster Land Rover
Reading
01189 658 400

Lindacre Land Rover
Ipswich
01473 744 222

Lloyd Land Rover
Carlisle
01228 599 000

Lookers Land Rover
Chelmsford
01245 611 111

Lookers Land Rover
Hadleigh
01702 559 933

M J Fews Land Rover
Wotton Under Edge
01453 844 131

Macrae and Dick Land Rover
Inverness
01463 668 980

Marshall Land Rover
Bedford
01234 355 655

Marshall Land Rover
Cambridge
01223 377 700

Marshall Land Rover
Lincoln
01522 877 200

Marshall Land Rover
Melton Mowbray
01664 480 033

Marshall Land Rover
Peterborough
01733 566 767

Matford Land Rover
Exeter
01392 825 825

Medway Land Rover
Maidstone
01622 699 750

Merlin Land Rover
Cardiff
02920 713 100

Merlin Land Rover
Doncaster
01302 323 344

Merlin Land Rover
Nottingham
01159 578 000

Morrisons Land Rover
Stirling
01786 814 888

Mylchreest Land Rover
Douglas
01624 623 481

Ottons Land Rover
Salisbury
01722 414 400

Paramount Land Rover
Swansea
01792 311 500

Parks Land Rover
Ayr
01292 653 000

Parkside Land Rover
Boston
01205 722 110

Pentland Land Rover
Edinburgh
0131 273 2000

Pilling Land Rover
Welwyn Garden City
01707 299 334

Ribblesdale Land Rover
Settle
01729 822 323

Riders Land Rover
Truro
01872 263 377

Ripon Land Rover
Ripon
01765 646 464

Rocar Moores Land Rover
Huddersfield
01484 516 016

Rockside Land Rover
Bury
0161 761 1121

Roger Young Land Rover
Saltash
01752 849 999

Rossleigh Land Rover
Cupar
01334 659 910

Rossleigh Land Rover
Durham
0191 383 1555

Rossleigh Land Rover
Edinburgh
0131 669 9133

Rossleigh Land Rover
Milton Keynes
01908 518 100

Rossleigh Land Rover
Newcastle
0191 229 3000

Rossleigh Land Rover
Perth
01738 474 200

Rossleigh Land Rover
Stockton On Tees
01642 644 444

Royal Ascot Land Rover
Ascot
01344 870 383

Shields Land Rover
Inverclyde
01479 784 4631

Shields Land Rover
Glasgow
0141 876 1001

Shukers Land Rover
Ludlow
01584 877 231

Shukers Land Rover
Shrewsbury
01743 450 045

Stafford Land Rover
Stafford
01785 214 140

Stratstone Land Rover
Mayfair
0207 514 0400

Sturgess Land Rover
Leicester
01162 470 074

T H White Land Rover
Swindon
01793 852 381

T P Topping Land Rover
Enniskillen
02866 323 475

Taggarts Land Rover
Motherwell
01698 276 076

Taunton Land Rover
Taunton
01823 412 559

Testers Land Rover
Edenbridge
01732 863 303

Three Counties Land Rover
Stourbridge
01384 424 288

Town & County Land Rover
Aberdeen
01224 871 219

Trinity Land Rover
Hinckley
01455 622 300

Webbers Land Rover
Basingstoke
01256 300 615

Wessex Land Rover
Portsmouth
02392 325 555

Westover Land Rover
Christchurch
01202 462 222

Williams Land Rover
Manchester
0161 232 5000

Wooburn Green Land Rover
High Wycombe
01628 525 252

Yeovil Land Rover
Yeovil
01935 426 600

LAND ROVER MAGS

Land Rover Monthly
01359 240 066
www.LRM.co.uk

Land Rover Enthusiast
01491 202 522
www.landroverenthusiast.com

Land Rover Owner International
01733 468 231
www.LRO.com

Land Rover World
020 8774 0600
www.landroverworld.co.uk

4 X 4 DRIVING

4x4 Events
phone - 01792 862 669
www.4x4events.co.uk

4 Play OFF Road Driving
phone - 01275 332 174
www.4playoffroaddriving.co.uk

Johnsons Off Road School
phone - 01386 761 515
www.offroadschool.co.uk

Lee James 4x4 Ltd
phone - 08453 30 98 30
www.leejames4x4.co.uk

The Elite Trading Company
phone - 01832 601 112

100

Ultra Adventure Driving
phone - 0800 328 7407

Whitecliff 4x4
phone - 01594 834 666

www.4x4funday.com
details on 4x4 events
phone - 01686 413 151

AIRLINES

Air France
phone - 0845 082 0162
www.airfrance.com/uk

Air Scotland
phone - 0141 848 4990
www.air-scotland.com

Alitalia
phone - 0870 544 8259
www.alitalia.co.uk

Austrian Airlines
phone - 020 7766 0300
www.austrianairlines.co.uk

Bmibaby
phone - 0870 264 2229
www.flybmi.com

British Airways
phone - 0845 77 333 77
www.britishairways.com

British Midlands
phone - 0870 607 0555
www.flybmi.com

Continental Airlines
phone - 0800 776464
www.continental.com

Czech Airlines
phone - 0870 444 3747
www.czechairlines.com

EasyJet
phone - 0870 6 000 000
www.easyjet.com

Finnair
phone - 020 7408 1222
www.finnair.com

Iceland Express
phone - 0870 850 0737
www.icelandexpress.com

Lufthansa
phone - 0845 773 7747
www.lufthansa.com

Ryanair
phone - 0871 246 0000
www.ryanair.com

SAS Scandinavian Airline
phone - 0870 607 2772
www.scandinavian.net

Swiss International Air lines
phone - 0845 601 0956
www.swiss.com

Virgin Atlantic Airways
phone - 0293 450 150
www.virgin.atlantic.com

AIRPORTS

Aberdeen
phone - 01224 722 331
www.baa.co.uk

Belfast International
phone - 028 442 2888
www.belfastairport.com

Birmingham International
phone - 0870 733 5511
www.bhx.co.uk

Bristol International
phone - 0870 121 2747
www.bristolairport.co.uk

Edinburgh
phone - 0131 333 1000
www.baa.co.uk

Glasgow International
phone - 0141 887 1111
www.baa.co.uk

Liverpool - John Lennon
phone - 0870 750 8484

London Gatwick
phone - 0870 000 2468
www.baa.com

London Heathrow
phone - 0870 000 0123
www.baa.co.uk

Luton
phone - 01582 405 100
www.london-luton.com

Manchester
phone - 02161 489 3000
www.manchesterairport.co.uk

AIR TRAVEL

Airport Transfer Service
phone - 0033 450 536 397

Alpine Cab Company (The)
phone - 0033 450 731938
www.alpinecabco.com

www.a2bairports.co.uk
online booking for flights

www.ebookers.com
budget priced global flights

www.expedia.co.uk
Flights, car, hire hotels etc.

www.lastminute.com
All sorts of travel services

www.opodo.co.uk
worldwide travel deals

www.skyscanner.net
budget priced airline fares

www.travelocity.co.uk
budget priced global flights

www.whichbudget.com
information on cheap airlines

BREAKDOWN

AA
phone - 0800 0852 840
www.theAA.com

Greenflag Motoring
phone - 0800 400 638
www.greenflag.com

RAC
phone - 0800 550 055
www.rac.co.uk

CAR HIRE

Alamo Rent A Car
phone - 0870 400 4580
www.goalamo.com

Avis Rent A Car
phone - 0870 606 0100
www.avis.co.uk

Budget Car & Van Rental
phone - 0800 181 181
www.budget.co.uk

easyCar
phone - 0906 333 3333
www.europcar.co.uk

Europcar
phone - 0845 722 2525
www.europcar.co.uk

Eurostyle
phone - 020 7624 1313
sales@eurostyle.uk.com

Hertz UK
phone - 0870 48 48 48
www.hertz.co.uk

Holiday Autos
phone - 0870 400 0099
www.europcar.co.uk

CROSSING THE CHANNEL

Brittany Ferries
www.brittanyferries.co.uk

Norfolkline
phone - 0870 870 1020
www.norfolkline.com

P&O North Sea Ferries
phone - 0870 129 6002
www.ponsf.com

P&O Portsmouth
phone - 0870 242 4999
www.poportsmouth.com

P&O Stena Line
phone - 0870 600 0600
www.posl.com

P&O Sea France
phone - 08705 711 711
www.seafrance.com

Superfast Ferries
phone - 0870 055 1234
www.superfast.com

DRY SKI SLOPES

Alford Ski Centre
phone - 01975 563024

Alpine Snowsports Aldershot
phone - 01252 325889
www.alpinesnowsports.co.uk

Alston Adventure Centre
phone - 01434 381886
www.alstontraining.co.uk

Ancrum Outdoor Centre
phone - 01382 435911

Bearsden Ski & Board
phone - 0141 943 1500
www.skibearsden.co.uk

Bishop Reindorp Ski Cnt
phone - 01483 504988
www.brski.co.uk

Bowles Outdoor Cnt
phone - 01892 665 665

Brentwood Park Centre
phone - 01277 211994

Bromley Ski Cnt
phone - 01689 876812

Calshot Activities Centre
phone - 023 8089 2077

Cardiff Ski & Board Cnt
phone - 029 2056 1793
www.skicardiff.com

Christchurch Ski Centre
phone - 01202 499155

Craigavon Golf & Ski Cnt
www.craigavon.gov.uk
Dan-yr-ogof Ski Slopes
phone - 01639 730284

Exeter & District Ski Club
phone - 01392 211422
exeterclub@ntlworld.com

Firpark Ski Centre
phone - 01259 751772

Folkestone Sports Centre
phone - 01303 850 333
www.folkestoneski.co.uk

Glasgow Ski/Board Centre
phone - 0141 427 4991
www.ski.glasgow.org

Glenmore Lodge
phone - 01479 861256
www.glenmorelodge.org.uk

Gloucester Ski/Board Centre
phone - 08702 400375
www.gloucesterski.com

Gosling Ski Centre
phone - 01707 384384
www.goslingsports.co.uk

Halifax Ski/Board Centre
phone - 01422 340760
darren@lineone.net

Hemel Ski Centre
phone - 01442 241321
www.hemel.ski.co.uk

SNOW AND DRIVER SERVICES

High Actions' Avon Ski Cnt
phone - 01934 852335
www.highaction.co.uk

John Nike - Bracknell
phone - 01344 789000
John Nike - Chatham
phone - 01634 827979
www.jnll.co.uk

John Nike - Llandudno
phone - 01492 874707
www.jnll.co.uk

John Nike - Plymouth
phone - 01752 600220
www.jnll.co.uk

Kendal Ski Club
phone - 01539 732948
sec.kendal@cwcom.net

Kidsgrove Ski Centre
phone - 01782 784908
www.ski.kidsgrove.co.uk

John Nike - Swadlincote
phone - 01283 217200
www.jnll.co.uk

Loch Rannoch Centre
phone - 01882 632201
www.lochrannoch.hotel.co.uk

Midlothian Ski Centre
phone - 0131 445 4433
www.midlothian.gov.uk

Mount Ober Ski Centre
phone - 028 9079 5666
mt.ober@ukonline.co.uk

Newmilns Ski Slope
phone - 01560 322320

Norfolk Ski Club
phone - 01003 662781
www.norfolkskiclub.co.uk

Pendle Ski Club
phone - 01200 425222

Plas y Brenin
phone -01690 720214

Polmonthill Ski Centre
phone - 01324 503835

Pontypool Ski Centre
phone - 01495 756955

Rhiwgoch Ski Centre
phone - 01766 540578
www.logcabins.skiwales.co.uk

Runcorn Ski/Board Centre
phone - 01928 701965
www.runcornskicentre.co.uk

Sandown Ski Centre
phone - 01372 467132
www.sandownsports.co.uk

Sheffield Ski Village
phone - 0114 276 9459
www.sheffieldskivillage.co.uk

Ski Pembrey
phone - 01554 834443

Ski Rossendale
phone - 01706 226457
www.ski.rossendale.co.uk

Southampton Ski Centre
phone - 023 8079 0970

Stoke Ski Centre
phone - 01782 204159
www.stokeskicentre.co.uk

Suffolk Ski Centre
phone - 01473 602347
www.suffolkskicentre.co.uk

Tallington Ski/Board Cnt
phone - 01778 344990
www.waspdirect.com

Telford Ski Centre
phone - 01952 586862
www.telfordleisure.co.uk

The Ackers
phone - 0121 772 5111
www.ackers.adventure.co.uk

Torquay Alpine Ski Club
phone - 01803 313350
www.skitorquay.co.uk

Warrnwell Snow Zone
phone - 01305 853245

Wellington Sports Centre
phone - 01823 663010

Whickham Thorns Centre
phone - 0191 433 5767
www.gateshead.gov.uk

Wycombe Summit
phone - 01494 474711
www.wycombesummit.co.uk

Yeovil Ski Centre
phone - 01935 421702

IN-CAR ENTERTAINMENT

Auto Audio Installations
phone - 020 8838 8839
blair@autoaudio.uk.com

Alpine Electronics
phone - 02476 719 500
www.alpine.com

Braybrook's In-Car Audio
phone - 01992 500 292
www.braybrooks.com

INSURANCE SERVICES

AA Five Star Europe
phone - 0800 0852 840
www.theAA.com

ABC Holiday Extras
phone - 0870 8444020
www.abctravelinsurance.co.uk

Atlas Insurance
phone - 020 7609 5000
www.atlasdirect.net

Autohome
phone - 0800 371 280
www.autohome.co.uk

BIBA
phone - 020 7623 9043
www.biba.org.uk

Blackwater Travel Indemnity
phone - 01621 855553

British Activity Holiday
phone - 020 7251 6821
www.ansell.co.uk

Columbus Direct
phone - 020 7375 0011
www.columbusdirect.com

Direct Line Travel Insurance
phone - 0845 246 8704
www.directline.com/travel

Direct Travel Insurance
phone - 01903 812345
www.direct.travel.co.uk

Douglas Cox Tyrie
phone - 01708 385969

Eagle Star
phone - 0800 33 800
www.eaglestar.co.uk

Endsleigh Insurance
phone - 020 7436 4451
www.endsleigh.co.u

Europ Assistance
phone - 01444 442442
www.europ-assistance.co.uk

First Assist Group
www.firstassist.co.uk

Fogg Travel Insurance
phone - 01623 631 331
www.fogginsurance.co.uk

Greenflag Motoring
phone - 0800 400 638
www.greenflag.com

James Hampden
phone - 01530 416 369
www.jameshampden.com

Leisurecare Insurance
phone - 01793 750 150

Liverpool Voctoria
phone - 0800 373 905
www.liverpool-victoria.co.uk

Matthew Gerard Insurance
phone - 01483 730 900

Medicover
phone - 0870 735 3600
www.medi-cover.co.uk

Mondial Assistance
www.mondial-assistance.co.uk

Primary Insurance Group
phone - 0870 444 3434
www.primaryinsurance.co.uk

Privilege Insurance
phone - 0845 246 0311

Quoteline Direct
phone - 0870 444 0870

RAC
phone - 0800 550 055
www.rac.co.uk

Select Travel Insurance
phone - 08707 370870
sxp@inter.group.co.uk

Ski Club of Great Britain
phone - 020 8410 2000
www.skiclub.co.uk

ski-insurance.co.uk
phone - 0870 755 6101
www.ski-insurance.co.uk

Skisure.com
www.skisure.insurance.co.uk

Snowcard Insurance Services
phone - 01327 262805
www.snowcard.co.uk

Sportscover Direct Ltd
phone - 0117 922 6222
www.sportscover.co.uk

Supreme Travel
phone - 01355 260547
www.travelinsurance-uk.com

Travel Insurance Club Ltd
phone - 01702 423398
www.ticdirect.co.uk

Travel Protection Group plc
phone - 028 9032 6585

World Ski & Snowboard Club
phone - 0870 757 2288
www.worldski.co.uk

World Cover Direct
phone - 0800 365 121
www.worldcover.com

Worldwide Travel Insurance
phone - 01892 833338
www.worldwideinsure.com

MOTOR SPORTS

Onethousandevents Ltd
phone - 01625 573 659

Chequered Flag Awnings
phone - 01694 781 544

Rally-Europe Ltd
phone - 01234 353 003

Everyman Motor Racing
phone - 01455 841 670

Rally Drive
phone - 01430 827162

Chris Birkbeck International Rally School
phone - 01287 677 512

Thruxton Motorsport Centre
phone - 01264 882222 -
info@thruxtonracing.co.uk

NATIONAL INFORMATION

Andorran Embassy
phone -020 8874 4806

Austrian National Tourism
phone - 020 7629 0461
www.austria.tourism.at

Croatia
phone - 02 8563 7979
www.coatia.hr

Czech Tourist Authority
phone - 020 7631 0427
www.czechtourism.com

Finnish Tourist Board
phone - 020 7365 2512
www.finland-tourism.com

French Tourist Office
phone - 09068 244123
www.franceguide.com

German Tourist Office
phone - 09001 600100
www.germany-tourism.de

Italian State Tourist Office
phone - 020 7399 3562
www.enit.it

Norwegian Tourist Board
phone - 0906 302 2003
www.visitnorway.com

Portugal Information
phone - 0906 364 0610
www.portugalinsite.com

Romanian Tourist Office
phone - 020 7224 3692
www.romaniatourism.com

Scottish Tourist Board
phone - 0845 22 55 121
ski.visitscotland.com

Slovenian Tourist Office
phone - 0870 225 5305
www.slovenia.tourism.si

Spanish Tourist Office
phone -020 7486 8077
www.tourspain.co.uk

Swedish Tourism
phone - 00800 3080 3080
info@swetourism.org.uk
www.visit.sweden.com

Switzerland Tourism
phone - 00800 100 200 30
info.uk@switzerland.com
www.MySwitzerland.com

RADAR ALERT SYSTEMS

Radar Direct
phone -0800 374 782
www.radardirect.co.uk

M4 Marketing
phone -01744 602 756
www.speedtrapfinder.com

ROAD CAMERA ALERT

Blackspot Interactive Ltd
phone -01327 855 586
www.blackspot.com

Kane Gear
phone -0870 881 188
www.kanegear.com

Networx Automotive
phone -0870 350 1345
www.networxautomotive.com

Snooper UK
phone -0870 787 0700
www.snooperuk.com

SpeedCamerasUK
phone -0800 328 0934
www.speedcamerasuk.com

ROOF RACKS & BOXES

DAP Ltd
www.skidrive.co.uk

GT Towing
phone -0870 787 0700
www.gttowing.co.uk

Lakeland Roof Box Company
phone -8700 766 326
www.roofbox.co.uk

Motor Traveller
phone -01753 833 442
www.carbox.co.uk

Thule Ltd
www.thule.co.uk

SNOW AND DRIVER SERVICES

SNOW CLUBS & ORGANISATIONS

British Association of Snowsport Instructors (BASI)
phone - 01479 861717
www.basi.org.uk

British Ski & Snowboard Fed
phone - 0131 445 7676
www.bssf.co.uk

British Ski Club for the Disabled BSCD
www.bscd.org.uk

British Snowboard Ass (BSA)
phone - 0131 445 2428
www.thebsa.org

English Ski Council
phone - 0121 501 2314
www.englishski.org

Ski Club of Great Britain
phone - 0845 458 0780
www.skiclub.co.uk

Snowsport Scotland
phone - 01314454151
www.snsc.demon.co.uk

Snowsport Wales
phone - 029 2056 1904
www.snowsportwales.net

The Uphill Ski Club
phone - 01479 861272
www.uphillskiclub.co.uk

World Ski & Snowboard Ass
phone - 0870 7572288
www.worldski.co.uk

SNOW COURSES

British Ski & Snowboard Sch
phone - 01237 451 099

British Ski Academy
phone - 020 8399 1181

The Development Centre
www.tdcski.com

EurekaSki
phone - 01326 375 710

Lauralee Bowie Ski Adventures
phone - 00 1604 689 7444

The International Academy
phone - 02920 672 500

Mountain Tracks
phone - 020 8877 5773
www.mountaintracks.co.uk

Nonstopski
phone - 020 8772 7852

TOptimum Ski Courses
phone - 01279 641 951
www.optimumski.com

Peak Leaders
phone - 01337 860 079
www.peakleaders.co.uk

Piste To Powder Adventures
phone - 01661 824 318

Rookie Academy
www.rookieacademy.co.nz

Ski Club of Great Britain
phone - 0845 458 0780
www.skiclub.co.uk

Ski Company (The)
phone - 0870 241 2085
www.theskicompany.co.uk

Ski Instructors Training
phone - 0800 328 0345

Ski Le Gap
www.teamexcel.net

The Telemark Ski Company
phone - 01535 644 069
www.telemarkskico.com

Top Ski
phone - 0033 4 79 06 14 80

SNOW HELI-SKI/BOARD

Air Valle
www.airvalle.it

SNOW RECRUITMENT

Jobs in the Alps
phone - 01536 771 150
www.jobs-in-the-alps.com

Natives
phone - 08700 463 377
www.natives.co.uk

SNOWBOARD HIRE

Ellis Brighams
phone -
www.ellis-brighams.com

The Snowboard Academy
phone - 01479 810 362

SNOW PUBLICATIONS

Daily Mail Ski & Snowboard
phone - 020 8515 2000

Document Snowboard
phone - 01733 293 250

Fallline
phone - 01733 293 250

Good Ski Guide
phone - 020 7332 2000

Ski & Board
phone - 0845 458 0780

Snow Magazine
phone - 01442 879 555

Snowboard UK
phone - 01202 735 090

Snowmole
phone - 0207 801 9410
www.snowmole.com

The Good Skiing & Snowboarding Guide
email: books@which.net

The Snowboard Guide
phone - 0034 952 141 276

Where to Ski & Snowboard
phone - 01373 835 208

White Lines Snowboard
phone - 01235 536 229

World Snowboard Guide
phone - 020 734 0674
www.worldsnowboardguide.com

SNOW SPORTS SHOPS

Countryside
phone - 0800 279 4799
www.countryside.co.uk

Ellis Brighams
www.ellis-brighams.com
Head Office - 0161 833 0746
Aviemore - 01479 810 175
Bristol - 01179 741 157
Chester - 01244 318 311
Fort William - 01397 706 220
Leeds - 011977 522 040
Liverpool - 01151 709 6912
London Covent Garden
         - 0207 395 1010
London Kensington
         - 0207 937 6889
Manchester Castlefield
         - 0161 833 0746
Manchester Deansgate
         - 0161 834 7278
Milton Keynes Xscape
         - 01908 609 122
Tamworth Snowdome
         - 01827 590 47

Ski Bartlett
phone - 020 8848 0040
www.skibartlett.com

Snow & Rock
phone -
www.snowandrock.com

SNOW TRAVEL AGENTS

Alpine Answers
phone - 020 8871 4656
www.alpineanswers.co.uk

Avant-ski
phone - 0191 285 8141
www.avant-ski.com

Iglu.com
phone - 020 8542 6658
www.iglu.com

Independent Ski Links
phone - 01964 533905
www.ski-links.com

JP Global Travel
phone - 0131 538 8455
www.jpglobaltravel.co.uk

Kwik Ski
phone - 01268 457746
www.kwik-ski.co.uk

Ski Expectations
phone - 01799 531888
ski.expectations@virgin.net

Ski Line
phone - 020 8650 5900
www.skiline.co.uk

Ski McNeill
phone - 028 9066 6699
www.skimcneill.com

Ski Solutions
phone - 020 7471 7700
www.skisolutions.com

Ski & Surf
phone - 020 8958 2418
www.skisurf.com

Ski Travel Centre
phone - 0141 649 9696
www.ski-travel-centre.co.uk

Skiers Travel
phone - 0870 010 0032
www.skiers-travel.co.uk

Snow Finders
phone - 01858 466 888
www.snowfinders.com

Snow Line
phone - 0870 333 0064
www.snow-line.co.uk

SNOW TOUR OPERATORS

Absolute Ski
(for Meribel in France)
phone - 01788 822100
www.absoluteski.com

Airtours
phone - 0800 916 0623
www.airtours.co.uk

Albus Travel
(for St Anton in Austria)
phone - 01449 711952
www.albustravel.com

Alpine Action Chalets
(for the 3 Valleys in France)
phone - 01903 761986
www.alpine-action.co.uk

Alpine Answers Select
phone - 020 8871 4656
www.alpineanswers.co.uk

Alpine Escapes
(for Morzine in France)
phone - 00 33 450 74739
www.alpine.escapes.com

Alpine Events
phone - 020 7622 2265
www.alpineevents.co.uk

Alpine Tours
(For Austria and Italy)
phone - 01227 738388
sales@alpinetours.co.uk

Snow Sense
phone - 0131 662 4487
www.snowsense.co.uk

Alpine Weekends
phone - 020 8944 9762
www.alpineweekends.com

Alps2Go
(for Morzine in France)
phone - 01908 585548
www.alps2go.com

Altitude Holidays
(for Courchevel in France)
phone - 0870 870 7669
www.altitudeholidays.com

American Ski Hotels
(for France & North America)
phone - 01892 511894
www.awwt.co.uk

American Ski Classics
(for North America)
phone - 020 8392 6660
www.americanskiclassics.com

APT Holidays Ltd
(for France)
phone - 01268 783878
www.apt.holidays.co.uk

Aravis Alpine Retreat
(for St Jean.de.Sixt & La Clusaz in France)
phone - 020 8878 8760
www.aravis.retreat.com

Avant-skl
(for France)
phone - 0191 285 8141
www.avant.ski.com

Balkan Holidays
(for Bulgaria, Slovenia & Romania)
phone - 0845 130 1114
www.balkanholidays.co.uk

Barreelli Ski Cholets in
(for Champogny & Les Houches in France)
phone - 0870 220 1500
www.barrelliski.co.uk

Belvedere Chalets
(for Meribel in France)
phone - 01264 738 257
www.belvedereproperties.net

Bigfoot Travel
(for Chamonix in France)
phone - 0870 300 5874
www.bigfoot.travel.co.uk

Bladon Lines
phone - 020 8780 8800
bladonlines@inghams.co.uk
www.inghams.co.uk

Board and Lodge
(for Chamonix in France)
phone - 020 7916 2275
www.boardnlodge.com

Bonne Nelge Ski Holidays
(for Meribel in France)
phone - 01270 256966
www.bonne-neige-ski.com

Borderline
(for Bareges in France)
phone - 00 33 562 926895
info@bordertinehols.com
www.borderlinehols.com

Canadian Powder Tours
(for Fernie in Caanada)
phone - 001 250 423 3019
www.canadianpowdertours.com

Canterbury Travel
(for Lapland)
phone - 01923 822388
www.laplandmagic.com

The Chalet Company
(for Morzine & Ardent - France)
phone - 0871 717 4208
00 33 450 79 68 40
www.thechaletco.com

The Chalet Group
(for France)
phone -00 33 479 013500
www.chaletgroup.com

Chalet Kiana
(for Les Contamines in France)
phone - 00 33 450 915518
www.chaletkiana.com

Chalet Number One
(for Ste-Foy in France)
phone - 01572 717259
www.chaletnumberone.com

Les Chalets de St Martin
(for St Martin in France)
phone - 01202 473255
www.leschalets.co.uk

Chatet Snowboard
(for snowboarding in France)
phone - 0870 800 4020
www.csbmountainholidays.com

Chalets 'Unlimited'
phone - 0191 285 8141
www.avant.ski.com

Chalet World
phone - 01743 231 199
www.chaletwortd.co.uk

Challenge Activ
(for Morzine in France)
phone - 0871 717 4113
www.challenge.activ.com

Chamonix Lodge
(for Chamonix in France)
phone - 00 33 674 601167
www.chamonixlodge.com

Chez Jay Ski Chalets
(Les Arcs & La Plagne- France)
phone - 01843 298030
www.chezjayski.com

Classic Ski Limited
phone - 01590 623400
www.classicski.co.uk

Club Europe Schools Skiing
phone - 0800 496 4996
www.club-europe.co.uk

Club Med
phone - 08453 676767
www.clubmed.co.uk

Club Pavilion
phone - 0870 241 0427
www.conceptholidays.com

Collineige Chamonix
(for Chamonix in France)
phone - 01276 24262
www.collineige.com

Connick Ski
phone - 00 33 450 732212
www.connickski.com

Contiki Coach
phone - 020 8290 6422
www.contiki.com

Cooltlp Mountain Holidays
(for Meribel in France)
phone - 01964 563563
www.cooltip.com

Corporate Ski Company (The)
phone - 020 7627 5500

Crystal
phone - 0870 160 6040
www.crystalski.co.uk

Descent International
(for France & Switzerland)
phone - 020 7384 3854
www.descentco.uk

Les Deux Chalets
(for Meribel in France)
phone - 01303 246966
www.chaletdelauney.co.uk

Directski.com
(Andorra, Austria, France & Italy)
phone - 0800 587 0945
www.directski.com

Elegant Resorts
phone - 01244 897333
www.elegantresorts.co.uk

Equity School Ski
phone - 01273 299299

www.equityschooltravel.co.uk

Equity Ski
phone - 01273 298298
www.equityski.co.uk

Ema Low Hotel
phone - 0870 750 6820
www.emalow.co.uk

Esprit Ski
(for Europe & North America)
phone - 01252 618300
www.esprit.holidays.co.uk

Eurotunnel Motoring Holidays
(for France)
phone - 0870 333 2001
www.eurotunnel.com

The Family Ski Company
(for France)
phone - 01684 540333
www.familyski.co.uk

Fantiski-Skizk
(for Val-d'Isere in France)
phone - 01622 861533
www.fantiski.co.uk

Finlays
(for France)
phone - 01573 226611
www.finlayski.com

First Choice
phone - 0870 754 3477
www.firstchoice.co.uk/ski

FlexiSki
phone - 0870 909 0754
www.flexiski.com

Fraser Ralston
(for Chamonix in France)
phone - 028 9042 4662
www.chamonix.uk.com

Freedom Holidays
(for Chatel in France)
phone - 01798 861888
www.freedomholidays.co.uk

French Freedom Holidays
(for France)
phone - 01724 290660
www.french.freedom.co.uk

Frontier Ski
(for Canada)
phone - 020 8776 8709
www.frontier.ski.co.uk

Frosty's Ski & Snowboard
(for St.jean.de.Sixt in France)
phone - 00 33 450 023728
www.frostys.co.uk

Frozenplanet.co.uk
(for the Alps)
phone - 07947 331606
www.frozenplanetco.uk

Glacier Dayz
(for Champagny in France)
phone - 01925 485389
www.glacierdayz.com

Haig Ski
(for Chatel in France)
phone - 00 33 450 811947
www.haigski.com

Handmade Holidays
phone - 01285 642 555
www.handmadeholidays.co.uk

Hannibals Holidays
(for Serre-Chevalier in France)
phone - 01233 813105
www.hannibals.co.uk

Headwater Holidays
(for cross-country skiing trips)
phone - 01606 720199
www.headwaterholidays.co.uk

High Mountain Holidays
(for Les Praz in France)
phone - 01993 775540
www.highmountain.co.uk

Huski
(for Chamonix in France)
phone - 020 7938 4844
www.huski.com

Independent Ski Links
phone - 01964 533905
www.ski-links.com

Inghams
phone - 020 8780 4433
www.inghams.co.uk

Inntravel
(for cross-country skiing trips)
phone - 01653 617 920
www.inntravel.co.uk

Interhome
(for the European Alps)
phone - 020 8891 1294
www.interhome.co.uk

International Academy
(for school trips)
phone - 029 2067 2500
www.internationalacademy.com

Interski Group
(for Italy)
phone - 01623 456333
www.interski.co.uk

Kuoni Holidays
(for Switzerland)
phone - 01306 747000
www.kuoni.co.uk

Lagrange Holidays
(for France & Andorro)
phone - 020 7371 6111
www.lagrangeholidays.co.uk

The Last Resort
(for St Jean-de-Sixt in France)
phone - 0800 652 3977
www.lastresort.info

Le Ski
(for Courchevel, Vald'Isere & La Tania in France)
phone - 0870 754 4444
www.leskicom

Lotus Supertravel
(for Europe & US)
phone - 020 7962 9933
www.supertravel.co.uk

Made to Measure Holidays
phone - 01243 533333
www.mtmhols.co.uk

Mark Warner
phone - 0870 770 4226
www.markwarner.co.uk

MasterSki
(Christian ski holidays)
phone - 020 8942 9442
www.mastersun.co.uk

McNab Mountain Sports
(for snowboarding in Argentiere in France)
phone - 01546 830243
www.mcnab.co.uk

Meriski Chalet
(for Meribel in France)
phone - 01285 648518
www.meriskico.uk

MGS Ski
(for Val.Cenis in France)
phone - 01799 525984
www.mgsskL.com

Momentum Ski
phone - 020 7371 9111
www.momentumski.com

Moswin Tours
(for German resorts)
phone - 0116 271 9922
www.moswin.com

Mountain Highs
(for Morzine in France)
phone - 0121 550 9321
www.mhighs.dircon.co.uk

Mountain Tracks
(for Chamonix in France)
phone - 020 8877 5773
www.mountaintracks.co.uk

Neilson
phone - 0870 333 3347
www.neilson.com

Neilson School Groups
(for school trips to North America & Eurape)
phone - 01833 3620
www.skierswortd.com

Optimum Ski
(for Les Arcs in France)
phone - 08702 406198
www.optimumski.com

Oxford Ski Company
(for the Alps)
phone - 01451 810300
www.oxfordski.com

Panorama Holidays
phone - 08707 505060
www.panoramaholidays.co.uk

Peak Leisure
(for Ste-Foy in France)
phone - 01256 397010
www.peak-leisure.co.uk

Peak Retreats
phone - 0870 770 0408
www.peakretreats.co.uk

Peak Ski
(for Verbier Switzerland)
phone - 01442 832629
www.peak-ski.co.uk

PGL Ski Europe
(for school trips)
phone - 01989 768168
www.pgl.co.uk

PGL Teenski
(teenagers ski trips)
phone - 01989 767767
www.pgl.co.uk

Piste Artiste Ltd
(for Champery in France)
www.pisteartiste.com

Plus Travel
(for Switzerland)
phone - 020 7734 0383
www.plustravel.co.uk

Powder Byrne
(for Europe)
phone - 020 8246 5300
www.powderbyrne.com

Powder Skiing in North America Limited
(for heli-skiing in Canada)
phone - 020 7736 8191

Premiere Neige
(for Ste-Foy in France)
phone - 0709 2000 300
www.premiere-neige.com

Ramblers Holidays
(for cross country skiing)
phone - 01707 331133
www.ramblersholidays.co.uk

Re-lax Holidays
(for Switzerland)
phone - 020 8360 1185
www.re-laxholidays.co.uk

Rocketski
phone - 01273 262626
info@rocketski.com
www.rocketski.com

Scott Dunn Latin America
(for South American trips)
phone - 020 8682 5030
www.scottdunn.com

Scott Dunn Ski
phone - 020 8682 5050
www.scottdunn.com

Silver Ski
(for France)
phone - 01622 735544
www.silverski.co.uk

Simon Butler Skiing
(for Megeve in France)
phone - 0870 873 0001
www.simonbutlerskiing.co.uk

Simply Ski
(for chalet holidays)
phone - 020 8541 2209
www.simplyski.co.uk

Ski 'n' Action
(Le Praz - in France)
phone - 01707 251696
www.ski-n-action.com

Ski 2
phone - 01962 713330
www.ski-2.com

Ski Activity Holidays
phone - 01738 840888
www.skiactivity.com

Ski Addiction
(for Chatel in France & St Anton in Austria)
phone - 01580 819354
www.skiaddiction.co.uk

Ski All America
(for Canada and USA)
phone - 08701 676 676
www.skiallamerica.com

Skialot
(for Chatel in France)
phone - 020 8363 8326
www.skialot.com

Ski Amis
(for La Plagne in France)
phone - 020 7692 0850
www.skiamis.com

Ski Arrangements
(for North America & Europe)
phone - 08700 110565
www.skiarrangements.com

SkiAway Holidays
(for the Pyrenees & France)
phone - 01903 824823
www.tourplanholidays.com

Ski Balkantours
(for Eastern Europe)
phone - 028 9024 6795
www.balkan.co.uk

Ski Barrett-Boyce
(for Megeve in France)
phone - 01737 831184
www.skibb.com

Ski Basics
(for Meribel in France)
phone - 01225 444143
www.skibasics.co.uk

Ski Beat
(for La Plagne, Les Arcs, Val d'Isere & La Tania in France)
phone - 01243 780405
www.skibeat.co.uk

Ski Blanc
(for Meribel in France)
phone - 020 8502 9082
www.skiblanc.co.uk

Ski Bon
(for Meribel in France)
phone - 020 8668 8223
www.skibon.com

SkiBound
(for school trips)
phone - 0870 900 3200
www.skibound.co.uk

Ski Chamois
(for Morzine in France)
phone - 01302 369006
www.skichamois.co.uk

Ski Club of Great Britain *(trips for club members)*
phone - 0845 458 0780
www.skiclub.co.uk

Ski Company (The)
phone - 0870 241 2085
www.theskicompany.co.uk

Ski Cuisine
(for Meribel in France)
phone - 01702 589543
www.skicuisine.co.uk

Ski Deep
(La Tania & Le Praz in France)
phone - 00 33 479 081905
info@skideep.com
www.skideep.com

105

Ski Etoile
(for Montgenevre & Argentiere in France)
phone - 01588 640442
www.skietoile.co.uk

Ski Expectations
(for Europe)
phone - 0799 531888
www.skiexpectations.com

Ski Famille
(for Les Gets in France)
phone - 0845 644 3764
www.skifamille.co.uk

Ski France
phone - 0870 787 3402
www.skifrance.co.uk

SkiGower
(school trips in Switzerland)
phone - 01527 851411
www.skigower.co.uk

Ski Hame
(for the 3 Valleys in France)
phone - 01875 320157
www.skihame.co.uk

Ski Hillwood
(for Austria, Canada & France)
phone - 01923 290700
www.hillwood.holidays.co.uk

Ski Hiver
(for Peisey / Les Arcs in France)
phone - 023 9242 8586
www.skihiver.co.uk

Ski Independence
(for Canada, Europe & USA)
phone - 0870 555 0555

Ski La Cote
(for La Chapelle d'Abondance in France)
phone - 01482 668357

Ski Leisure Direction
(for France)
phone - 020 8324 4042
www.leisuredirection.co.uk

Ski Life
(for self-drive in France)
phone - 0870 429 2180
www.skiinglife.co.uk

Ski Line
(for Europe & North America)
phone - 020 8650 5900
www.skiline.co.uk

Ski Link
(for France)
phone - 01983 812883
www.ski.link.co.uk

Ski McNeill
(for Europe & USA)
phone - 028 9066 6699
www.skimcneill.com

Ski Miquel
phone - 01457 821200
www.miquelhols.co.uk

Ski Morgins
phone - 01568 770681
www.skimorgins.com

Ski Morzine
(for Morzine in France)
phone - 01372 470104
www.skimorzine.com

Ski Olympic
(for France)
phone - 01302 328820
www.skiolympic.com

Ski Peak
(for Vaujany in France)
phone - 01428 608070
www.skipeak.com

SkiPlan Travel Service
phone - 01273 774778
sales@topstravel.co.uk

Ski Rosie
(Chatel & Morgins in France)
Phone - 00 33 450813100
rosie@skirosie.com
www.skirosie.com

Ski Safari
(for Canada, Chile & USA)
phone - 01273 223680
www.skisafari.com

Skisafe Travel
(for Scotland)
phone - 0141 812 0925
www.osatravel.co.uk

Ski Scott James
(for Argentiere in France)
phone - 01845 501139
www.skiscottjames.co.uk

Ski Solutions
phone - 020 7471 7777
www.skisolutions.com

Ski Success
(For Italy & USA)
phone - 01225 764205
www.success-tours.co.uk

Ski Supreme
(for coach & self-drive trips)
phone - 01355 260547
www.skisupreme.co.uk

Ski Total
(for Europe & Canada)
phone - 08701 633633
www.skitotal.com

Ski-Val
(for France & Austria)
phone - 0870 746 3030
www.skival.co.uk

Ski Verbier
(for Verbier in Switzerland)
phone - 020 7385 8050
www.skiverbier.com

Ski Weekend
(for weekend trips)
phone - 0870 060 0615
www.skiweekend.com

Ski Weekends & Snowboard Breaks
(for the 3 Valleys in France)
phone - 01375 396688
www.skiweekends.com

Ski Wild
(for Austria)
phone - 0870 746 9668
www.skiwild.co.uk

Ski with Julia
(for Switzerland)
phone - 01386 584478
www.skijulia.co.uk

Skiworld
(for Europe & North America)
phone - 0870 241 6723
www.skiworld.ltd.uk

Ski Yogi
(for Italy)
phone - 01799 531886
www.skiexpectations.com

Sloping Off
(for coach trips)
phone - 01725 552833
www.equity.co.uk

Slovenija Pursuits
(for Slovenija & Austria)
phone - 0870 220 0201
www.slovenijapursuits.co.uk

Snowbizz Vacances
(for Puy-St-Vincent in France)
phone - 01778 341455
www.snowbizz.co.uk

Snowcoach
(for Andorra, Austria & France)
phone - 01727 866177
www.snowcoach.co.uk

Snowfocus
(for Chatel in France)
phone - 01392 479555
www.snowfocus.com

Snowlife
(for La Clusaz in France)
phone - 01534 863630
www.snowlife.co.uk

Snowline
(for France)
phone - 020 8870 4807
www.snowline.co.uk

Snowscape
(for Austria)
phone - 01905 357760
www.snowscape.co.uk

Solo's
(for singles trips)
phone - 08700 720700
www.solosholidays.co.uk

Source (La)
(for Villard-Reculas in France)
phone - 01707 655988
www.lasource.org.uk

Stanford Skiing
(for Megeve in France)
phone - 01223 477644
www.stanfordskiing.co.uk

St Anton Ski Company
(for St Anton in Austria)
phone - 00 43 676 495 3438
com www.atlas.co.uk/ski

Susie Ward Alpine Holidays
(for Chatel in France)
phone - 01872 553055
www.susieward.com

Swiss Travel Service
(for Switzerland)
phone - 0870 191 7175
www.swisstravel.co.uk

Thomson Ski & Snowboarding
phone - 0870 606 1470
www.thomson.ski.co.uk

Top Deck
phone - 020 7244 8000
www.topdecktravel.co.uk

Tops Ski Chalets & Club Hotels
(for France)
phone - 01273 774666
www.topstravel.co.uk

Trail Alpine
(for Morzine in France)
phone - 0870 750 6560
www.trailalpine.co.uk

Trailfinders
(for North America)
phone - 0845 050 5900
www.trailfinders.com

United Vacations Ski Freedom USA & Canada
(for North America)
phone - 0870 606 2222
www.unitedvacations.co.uk

Uptoyou.com
phone - 0845 070 0203
www.uptoyou.com

Val d'Isere A La Carte
phone - 01481 236800
www.skivaldisere.co.uk

Vanilla Ski
(for Seez - La Rosiere in France)
phone - 01932 860696

Vertical Reality at Verbler Ltd
(for Verbier in Switzerland)
phone - 01268 452337

VIP
(for Val d'Isere in France)
phone - 00 8875 1957
www.valdisere.co.uk

Virgin Ski
(for USA)
phone - 0870 220 2788
www.virginholidays.co.uk/snow

Waymark Holidays
(for cross-country skiing trips)
phone - 01753 516477
www.waymarkholidays.com

Weekends in Val d'Isere
phone - 020 8944 9762
www.val-disere.ski.com

White Roc
phone - 020 7792 1188
www.whiteroc.co.uk

World Skiers
phone - 0870 757 2288
www.worldskiers.com

YSE
(for Val-d'Isere in France)
phone - 020 8871 5117
www.yseski.co.uk

SNOW CHAINS

Land Rover
www.landrover.com
for the Snowtraction System or snowchain STC7905.

Brindley Chains Ltd
phone - 01925 825555
www.brindley-chains.co.uk

Car Parts Direct
phone - 01332 290 833
www.carparts-direct.co.uk

DAP Ltd
phone - 01223 323 488
www.skidrive.co.uk

GT Towing
phone - 0870 787 0700
www.gttowing.co.uk

Motor Traveller
phone - 01753 833 442
www.carbox.co.uk

RUD Chains Ltd
phone - 01227 276 611
www.carbox.co.uk

Snowchains Europroducts
phone - 01732 884 408
www.snowchains.co.uk

Snowchains Ltd
phone - 01732 884 408
www.snowchains.co.uk

Spikes Spiders
phone - 01706 819 365
www.spikesspiders.com

TYRES & WHEELS

Bronco 4x4 Ltd
phone - 01538 398 555
sales@bronco4x4.com

Spikes Spiders
phone - 01706 819 365
www.spikesspiders.com

MST Ltd
phone - 01684 577 208

Red Rock 4X4
phone - 01834 812 812
redrock4x4sales@aol.com

Vredestein UK Ltd
phone - 01933 677770

West Coast Off Road
phone - 0870 787 9014

WEATHER INFO

www.snow-forecast.com

www.thefirstresort.com

www.skiclub.co.uk

www.snow-forecast.com

WEB SNOW SERVICES

Beater Outdoor Adventure
www.beater.com

Beater Outdoor Adventure
www.Ellis-brighams.com

Beater Outdoor Adventure
www.finches-ski.com

Mountain Equipment Co-op
www.mec.ca

mySimon
www.mysimon.com

Rel
www.rei.com

Snow + Rock
www.snowandrock.com

www.goski.com

www.ifyouski.com

www.iglu.com

www.packyourskis.com

www.ski.co.uk.com

www.skifrance.co.uk.com

www.travel-spot.co.uk

Mapping Legend and Contents

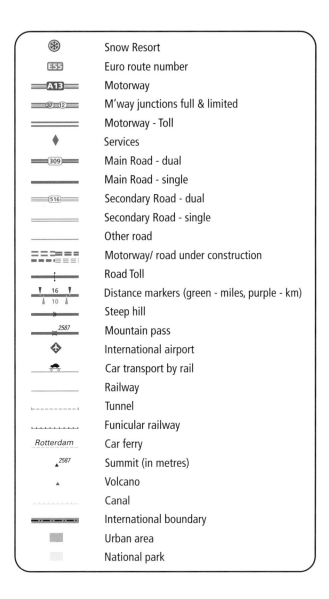

✳	Snow Resort
E55	Euro route number
A13	Motorway
37 12	M'way junctions full & limited
	Motorway - Toll
♦	Services
309	Main Road - dual
	Main Road - single
516	Secondary Road - dual
	Secondary Road - single
	Other road
	Motorway/ road under construction
	Road Toll
16 10	Distance markers (green - miles, purple - km)
≫	Steep hill
2587	Mountain pass
✈	International airport
	Car transport by rail
	Railway
	Tunnel
	Funicular railway
Rotterdam	Car ferry
▲2587	Summit (in metres)
▲	Volcano
	Canal
	International boundary
	Urban area
	National park

Contents

© Collins Bartholomew Ltd 2004   RY11665 / 770
Produced for Ice Publishing by Collins Bartholomew

Collins Bartholomew, an Imprint of HarperCollinsPublishers
77-85 Fulham Palace Road, Hammersmith, London W6 8JB
www.collinsbartholomew.com

1:1 000 000

1 centimetre to 10 kilometres

0	10	20	30	40	50	60	70	80 km

0		10		20		30		40		50 miles

1 inch to 16 miles

pics 1 & 2 Tourist office Val d'Isere

Resort Index A to Z Index (see from page 27 for resort guides)

Index to place names
Please note that this is a *selective* index of place names

A

B

Georgsmarienhütte 33 D7
Gera 95 D7
Geraardsbergen 35 C6
Gérardmer 43 D5
Geretsried 88 A3
Gerlingen 43 C8
Germencik 193 D8
Germering 91 F6
Germersheim 37 F7
Gernika-Lumo 57 B5
Gernsbach 43 C7
Gerpinnes 35 D7
Gerstetten 90 E4
Gersthofen 91 E6
Gerwisch 95 B7
Gerzat 46 D2
Gescher 33 E5
Getafe 62 D4
Gevelsberg 33 F6
Gevgelija 185 B6
Gex 47 C6
Ghedi 82 A1
Gheorghe Doja 177 D7
Gheorgheni 169 D5
Gherăești 169 D6
Gherla 168 D2
Ghidigeni 169 F8
Ghimbav 177 B5
Ghimeș-Făget 169 E5
Ghimpați 177 E5
Ghindari 168 E4
Giannitsa 185 C6
Giardini-Naxos 75 C6
Giarmata 167 F5
Giarre 75 D6
Giaveno 47 F8
Gibellina Nuova 74 C2
Gibraltar 69 E5
Gien 41 E5
Giengen an der Brenz 91 E5
Gießen 37 C8
Gifhorn 95 A5
Gijón-Xixón 55 A7
Gilău 167 D8
Gilching 91 F6
Gillingham *GB* 31 D7
Gilze 32 F2
Gingelom 35 C7
Ginosa 77 B5
Gioia del Colle 77 B6
Gioia Tauro 75 B7
Gioiosa Ionica 75 B8
Gioiosa Marea 75 C5
Giovinazzo 77 A5
Girifalco 75 A8
Girișu de Criș 167 D6
Giromagny 43 E5
Girona 59 C7
Girov 169 D6
Gislaved 104 A3
Gisors 34 F3
Gistel 34 B4
Giubiasco 85 A5
Giugliano in Campania 76 B1
Giulianova 78 A4
Giurgiu 177 F5
Givet 35 D7
Givors 46 E4
Givry *B* 35 D6
Giżycko 152 F2
Gjirokastër 184 E2
Gjøvik 117 E7
Gladbeck 33 F5
Gladenbach 37 C7
Gladsakse 103 D7
Glanerbrug 33 D5
Glarus 87 C6
Glasgow 21 D5
Glauchau 95 E8
Gleisdorf 164 C4
Glenrothes 21 C6
Glina *RO* 177 E6
Glinde 99 C5
Gliwice 158 F4
Glodeni *MD* 169 B8
Gloggnitz 164 A4
Głogów 97 C7
Głogówek 158 F3
Glossop 27 D5
Gloucester 29 B7
Głowno 159 B6
Głubczyce 158 F3
Głuchołazy 158 F2
Glückstadt 33 A8
Głuszyca 97 E7
Glyfada 191 D7
Gmünd *A* 93 D5
Gmunden 89 A6
Gniew 154 C4
Gniewkowo 154 E4
Gniezno 101 F8
Gnjilane 180 E3
Goch 32 F4
Göd 166 B2
Godalming 31 E5
Godech 181 C5
Godega di Sant'Urbano 88 E4
Gödöllő 166 B2
Goes 32 F1
Gogolin 158 E3
Gogoșu *RO* 175 E7
Goicea 176 F2
Goirle 32 F3
Goito 82 A1
Goldach 87 B6
Gołdap 152 E3
Goleniów 101 D5
Golub-Dobrzyń 154 E4
Gondomar *E* 54 E2
Gondomar *P* 60 B3
Gönen 189 E6
Gonfreville-l'Orcher 34 F1
Gonnesa 80 E1
Gonnosfanadiga 80 E2
Gonzaga 82 B2
Goole 27 D7
Goor 33 D5
Göppingen 90 E4
Góra *PL* 97 C7
Góra Kalwaria 157 G2
Goražde 173 E8
Gorgonzola 85 B5
Gorgota 177 D6
Gorinchem 32 E3
Gorizia 89 E6
Gorlice 160 D2
Görlitz 97 D5
Gorna Oryakhovitsa 182 C3
Gornești 168 D3
Gornja Radgona 164 C4
Gornji Milanovac 174 F4
Gorseinon 28 C4
Gorssel 32 D4
Görükle 189 D8
Gorzów Wielkopolski 101 E5
Gosforth *GB* 21 F8
Goslar 95 B5
Gospić 172 C3
Gosport 29 D8
Gossau 43 F8
Gostivar 179 F8
Gostyń *PL* 97 B8
Gostynin 155 F5
Göteborg 107 D6
Götene 107 B8
Gotha 95 D6
Gotse Delchev 185 A8
Göttingen 94 C4
Götzis 87 C6
Gouda 32 E2
Gournay-en-Bray 34 F3
Goussainville 41 B5
Gozzano 84 B4
Grabs 87 C6
Gračanica *BIH* 173 C7
Grâce-Hollogne 35 C8
Gradačac 173 B7
Grădiștea *RO* 177 E7
Grado *E* 55 B6
Grado *I* 89 F6
Gräfelfing 91 F7
Gräfenhainichen 95 C8
Grafing bei München 91 F7
Gragnano 76 B2
Grajewo 156 C4
Grammichele 75 E5
Granada 69 B8
Granarolo dell'Emilia 82 C3
Grand-Couronne 34 F2
Grande-Synthe 34 C3
Grândola 66 C2
Grangemouth 21 C5
Granollers 59 D6
Gransee 100 E3
Grantham 27 F7
Granville 39 C6
Grassano 76 B4
Grasse 52 D4
Graulhet 49 C8
Grave 32 E4
Gravelines 34 C3
Gravellona Toce 84 A4
Gravesend 31 D6
Gravina di Catania 75 D5
Gravina in Puglia 77 B5
Gray 42 F3
Grays 31 D6
Graz 164 C3
Grazzanise 76 A1
Great Harwood 27 D5
Great Malvern 29 B7
Great Yarmouth 31 B8
Grebănu 177 B7
Greenock 20 D4
Greifswald 100 B3
Greiz 95 E8
Grenå 103 B5
Grenade 49 C7
Grenchen 43 F5
Grenoble 47 E6
Greve in Chianti 82 E2
Greven *D* 33 E6
Grevena 184 E4
Grevenbroich 37 B5
Grevenmacher 36 E4
Grevesmühlen 99 C6
Grez-Doiceau 35 C7
Griesheim 37 E7
Grieskirchen 92 F4
Grigiškės 153 E7
Grigoriopol 170 C3
Grimbergen 35 C6
Grimma 95 D8
Grimmen 100 B2
Grimsby 27 D8
Grimstad 106 B2
Grindsted *DK* 102 D2
Grivița *RO* 177 D7
Grobbendonk 35 B7
Gröbenzell 91 F6
Grocka 174 D4
Grodków 158 E2
Grodzisk Mazowiecki 157 F2
Grodzisk Wielkopolski 97 A7
Groenlo 33 E5
Grójec 157 G2
Gronau (Westfalen) 33 D5
Groningen 33 B5
Großenhain 96 D3
Großenkneten 33 C7
Groß-Enzersdorf 93 F8
Grosseto 81 E3
Groß-Gerau 37 E7
Großostheim 37 E8
Großräschen 96 C4
Grosuplje 89 E8
Grottaferrata 78 C2
Grottaglie 77 C6
Grottaminarda 76 A2
Grottammare 78 A4
Grotte 74 D3
Grou 32 B4
Grudziądz 154 D4
Grugliasco 84 C3
Gruiu 177 D6
Grumăzești 169 C6
Grumo Appula 77 A5
Grums 113 C5
Grünberg 37 C8
Grünstadt 37 F7
Grybów 161 E2
Gryfice 101 C5
Gryfino 100 D4
Gryfów Śląski 97 D6
Guadalajara 63 C5
Guadix 71 E5
Gualdo Cattaneo 78 A2
Gualdo Tadino 83 F5
Gualtieri 82 B1
Guarda 61 C5
Guardavalle 75 B8
Guardiagrele 79 C5
Guardia Sanframondi 76 A2
Guastalla 82 B1
Gubbio 82 E4
Guben 97 B5
Gubin 97 B5
Guebwiller 43 E5
Guer 39 E5
Guérande 38 F4
Guéret 45 C7
Gueugnon 46 B3
Gugești 177 B7
Guglionesi 79 C6
Guichen 39 E5
Guidonia-Montecelio 78 C2
Guildford 31 E5
Guilherand 46 F4
Guimarães 54 F2
Guînes 31 E8
Guingamp 38 C3
Guipavas 38 C2
Guisborough 27 B6
Guise 35 E5
Gujan-Mestras 48 A3
Gulbene 151 B8
Gŭlŭbovo *BG* 182 E4
Gummersbach 37 B6
Gundelfingen 43 D6
Günzburg 91 E5
Gunzenhausen 91 D6
Gura Humorului 169 B5
Gura Ocniței 177 D5
Gura Șuții 177 D5
Gura Văii 169 E7
Gura Vitioarei 177 C5
Gurghiu 168 D4
Gur'yevsk 152 D1
Gusev 152 E3
Guspini 80 E2
Gussago 85 B7
Gustavsberg 115 C6
Güstrow 99 C8
Gütersloh 33 E7
Gvardeysk 152 E2
Gyál 166 C2
Gyomaendrőd 166 D4
Gyömrő 166 C2
Gyöngyös 166 B3
Győr 165 A6
Gyula 167 D5

H

Haacht 35 C7
Haag 93 F5
Haaksbergen 33 D5
Haaltert 35 C6
Haapsalu 146 C4
Haar 91 F7
Haarlem 32 D2
Habay-la-Neuve 35 E8
Habo 107 C8
Hadamar 37 D7
Haddington 21 C7
Haderslev 102 E3
Hadımköy 189 B8
Hadleigh 31 C7
Hadsten 102 C4
Hagen 33 F6
Hagenow 99 D6
Hagfors 113 B6
Haguenau 43 C6
Haiger 37 C7
Hailsham 31 F6
Hainburg an der Donau 93 F8
Hainichen 96 D3
Hajdúböszörmény 167 B5
Hajdúdorog 167 B5
Hajdúhadház 167 B6
Hajdúnánás 161 H2
Hajdúsámson 167 B6
Hajdúszoboszló 167 C5
Hajnówka 157 E6
Halásztelek 166 C2
Hălăucești 169 C7
Halberstadt 95 B6
Hălchiu 169 F5
Halden 107 A5
Haldensleben 95 A6
Hale 27 E5
Halesowen 29 A7
Halifax 27 D5
Halle *B* 35 C6
Halle (Saale) 95 C7
Halle (Westfalen) 33 E7
Hällefors 113 B7
Hallein 89 A5
Halle-Neustadt 95 C7
Hall in Tirol 88 B3
Hallsberg 108 A3
Hallstahammar 114 C3
Halluin 35 C5
Halmeu 161 H5
Halmstad 103 B7
Halstead 31 C7
Halstenbek 99 C5
Halsteren 32 F2
Haltern 33 E6
Halver 37 B6
Ham *F* 35 E5
Hamar 117 E8
Hamburg 99 C5
Hämeenlinna 143 D6
Hameln 33 E8
Hamilton 21 D5
Hamina 144 E4
Hamm 33 E6
Hamme 35 B6
Hammel 102 C3
Hammelburg 90 A4
Hammerfest 129 B5
Hamminkeln 33 E5
Hamois 35 D7
Hamont 32 F3
Ham-sur-Heure 35 D6
Handlová 163 D5
Hangö 143 F5
Hanko 143 F5
Hannover 94 A4
Hannoversch Münden 94 C4
Hannut 35 C7
Haparanda 135 C6
Haradok 149 F4
Hard 87 B6
Hardenberg 33 D5
Harderwijk 32 D3
Harelbeke 35 C5
Haren 33 B5
Haren (Ems) 33 C6
Harjavalta 142 C4
Hârlău 169 C7
Harlingen 32 B3
Harlow 31 D6
Harnes 34 D4
Härnösand 119 A8
Harpenden 31 C5
Harrislee 98 A4
Harrogate 27 C6
Hârșova 171 D1
Harstad 127 C5
Harsum 94 B4
Hartberg 164 B4
Hartlepool 27 B6
Harwich 31 C7
Haselünne 33 C6
Haslemere 31 E5
Haslev 103 E6
Hasparren 48 D2
Hasselt *B* 35 C8
Hasselt *NL* 32 D4
Haßfurt 91 B5
Hässleholm 103 C8
Haßloch 37 F7
Hastings 31 F7
Hațeg 175 B8
Hatfield 27 D6
Hattem 32 D4
Hattersheim am Main 37 E7
Hattingen 33 F6
Hatvan 166 B3
Haubourdin 34 C4
Haugesund 110 C1
Hautmont 35 D6
Hauzenberg 92 E3
Havant 30 F4
Havârna 169 A6
Havelberg 99 E8
Haverfordwest 28 B3
Haverhill 31 C6
Havířov 162 B4
Havixbeck 33 E6
Havlíčkův Brod 93 C6
Havran 189 F5
Havsa 189 A5
Hawick 21 E7
Haxby 27 C6
Hayange 36 F4
Hayrabolu 189 B5
Hayvoron 170 A4
Haywards Heath 31 E6
Hazebrouck 34 C4
Heanor 27 E6
Hechingen 43 D8
Hechtel 35 B8
Heddesheim 37 F7
Hedemora 113 A8
Hedge End 29 D8
Heemskerk 32 D2
Heemstede 32 D2
Heerde 32 D4
Heerenveen 32 C4
Heerhugowaard 32 C2
Heerlen 36 C4
Heers 35 C8
Heesch 32 E3
Heeze 32 F3
Heide 98 B4
Heidelberg 37 F8
Heidenau 96 D4
Heidenheim an der Brenz 91 E5
Heilbronn 43 B8
Heiligenhaus 33 F5
Heiligenstadt Heilbad 95 C5
Heiloo 32 C2
Heinola 143 C8
Heinsberg 36 B4
Heist-op-den-Berg 35 B7
Hekelgem 35 C6
Helegiu 169 E6
Helensburgh 20 C4
Hellevoetsluis 32 E1
Hellín 71 B8
Helmbrechts 91 A7
Helmond 32 F3
Helmstedt 95 A6
Helsingborg 103 C7
Helsinge 103 C6
Helsingfors 143 F7
Helsingør 103 C7
Helsinki 143 F7
Helston 28 F3
Hemel Hempstead 31 D5
Hemmingen *D* 94 A4
Hemsbach 37 F8
Hendaye 48 D2
Hengelo *NL* 32 E4
Hengelo *NL* 33 D5
Hénin-Beaumont 34 D4
Henley-on-Thames 31 D5
Hennebont 38 E3
Hennef (Sieg) 37 C6
Hennigsdorf Berlin 96 A3
Heppenheim (Bergstraße) 37 E8
Herborn 37 C7
Herbrechtingen 91 E5
Herceg-Novi 178 E4
Herdecke 33 F6
Hereford 29 B6
Herent 35 C7
Herentals 35 B7
Herford 33 E8
Héricourt 43 E5
Herisau 43 F8
Herk-de-Stad 35 C7
Herlev 103 D7
Hermagor 89 C6
Hermsdorf 95 D7
Hernani 48 D1
Herne *B* 35 C6
Herne *D* 33 F6
Herne Bay 31 D7
Herning 102 C2
Hérouville-St-Clair 39 B7
Herrenberg 43 C8
Hersbruck 91 C7
Herselt 35 B7
Herstal 35 C8
Herten 33 F5
Hertford 31 C6
Herve 35 C8
Herzberg *D* 96 C3
Herzberg am Harz 95 C5
Herzebrock-Clarholz 33 E7
Herzele 35 C6
Herzogenaurach 91 C6
Herzogenbuchsee 43 F6
Herzogenburg 93 E6
Hesdin 34 D3
Hespérange 36 F4
Hessisch Lichtenau 94 D4
Hessisch Oldendorf 33 D8
Heswall 26 E4
Hettstedt 95 C7
Heusenstamm 37 E8
Heves 166 B4
Hexham 21 F7
Heysham 26 C4
Heythuysen 35 B8
Heywood 27 D5
Hiddenhausen 33 D7
High Wycombe 31 D5
Hilchenbach 37 B7
Hildburghausen 91 A6
Hilden 37 B5
Hildesheim 94 B4
Hille *D* 33 D8
Hillegom 32 D2
Hillerød 103 D6
Hilpoltstein 91 D6
Hilversum 32 D3
Himberg 93 F7
Hîncești 170 D2
Hinckley 27 F6
Hindley 26 D4
Hinnerup 102 C4
Hinwil 43 F8
Hirson 35 E6
Hirtshals 106 D4
Hitchin 31 C5
Hjo 108 C2
Hjørring 106 E4
Hlinsko 93 B7
Hlohovec 162 E3
Hlučín 162 B4
Hlyboka 169 A5
Hlybokaye 149 F2
Hobro 102 B3
Hochdorf *CH* 43 F7
Höchstadt an der Aisch 91 B6
Hoddesdon 31 D6
Hódmezővásárhely 166 E4
Hodonín 93 D8
Hoek van Holland 32 E1
Hoensbroek 35 C8
Hoeselt 35 C8
Hoevelaken 32 D3
Hoeven 32 F2
Hof *D* 91 A7
Hofgeismar 37 A8
Hofheim am Taunus 37 D7
Hofors 114 A3
Höganäs 103 C7
Hoghiz 168 F4
Hohenems 87 C6
Hohenmölsen 95 D7
Hohenstein-Ernstthal 95 E8
Hokksund 111 B7
Holbæk *DK* 103 D6
Holboca 169 C8
Holešov 162 C3
Holíč 93 D8
Hollabrunn 93 E7
Hollola 143 D7
Holmestrand 111 C7
Holmfirth 27 D5
Holstebro 102 C2
Holten 33 D5
Holyhead 26 E2
Holzkirchen 88 A3
Holzminden 37 A8
Holzwickede 33 F6
Homberg (Efze) 37 B8
Homburg 37 F6
Homécourt 36 F4
Homocea 169 E7
Hondarribia 48 D2
Hønefoss 111 A7
Honfleur 39 A8
Honiton 29 D6
Honley 27 D5
Hoofddorp 32 D2
Hoogerheide 32 F2
Hoogeveen 33 C5
Hoogezand-Sappemeer 33 B5
Hoogkarspel 32 C3
Hoogkerk 33 B5
Hoogstraten 32 F2
Hoogvliet 32 E2
Höör 103 C8
Hoorn 32 C3
Hopfgarten im Brixental 88 B4
Horb am Neckar 43 C7
Hörby 103 D8
Horezu 176 C2
Horgen 43 F7
Horia *RO* 169 D7
Horley 31 E6
Horn *A* 93 E6
Horn-Bad Meinberg 33 E8
Hørning 102 C4
Horodok 160 D6
Horsens 102 D3
Horsham 31 E5
Hørsholm 103 D7
Horst 32 F4
Hörstel 33 D6
Horten 111 C7
Horw 86 C4
Horwich 26 D4
Hösbach 37 E8
Hosszúpályi 167 C6
Hotarele 177 E6
Houdain 34 D4
Houghton le Spring 21 F8
Houten 32 E3
Houthalen 35 B8
Houthulst 34 C4
Hove 31 F6
Hövelhof 33 E8
Höxter 33 E8
Hoyerswerda 96 C4
Hoylake 26 E4
Hradec Králové 93 A6
Hranice *CZ* 162 C3
Hrasnica 173 E7
Hrastnik 89 D8
Hrodna 156 C6
Hrubieszów 160 B6
Hückelhoven 36 B4
Hückeswagen 37 B6
Hucknall 27 E6
Huddersfield 27 D5
Hude (Oldenburg) 33 B7
Hudești 169 A6
Hudiksvall 119 C7
Huedin 167 D8
Huelva 67 E5
Huércal-Overa 71 E7
Huesca 57 D8
Huéscar 71 D6
Huissen 32 E4
Huittinen 142 C4
Huizen 32 D3
Hüllhorst 33 D8
Hulst 32 F1
Hultsfred 108 D4
Humenné 161 F3
Humpolec 93 C6
Hundested 103 C6
Hunedoara 167 F8
Hünfeld 94 E4
Hungen 37 D8
Huntingdon 31 B6
Hürth 37 C5
Huși 169 D8
Husum *D* 98 A4
Huy 35 D8
Hwlffordd 28 B3
Hyères 52 E3
Hythe *GB* 29 D8
Hythe *GB* 31 E7
Hyvinkää 143 E7

I

Ialoveni 170 D2
Ianca *RO* 176 F3
Ianca *RO* 177 C8
Iara 168 E2
Iași 169 C8
Ibbenbüren 33 D6
Ibi 72 B3
Ibrány 161 H3
Ichtegem 34 B4
Idar-Oberstein 37 E6
Idrija 89 E7
Idstein 37 D7
Ieper 34 C4
Iernut 168 E3
Ighiu 168 F2
Igis 87 C6
Iglesias 80 E2
Ignalina 151 F7
Igoumenitsa 184 F2
Igualada 59 D5
Iisalmi 140 C4
IJmuiden 32 D2
IJsselmuiden 32 D4
IJsselstein 32 E3
Ikast 102 C3
Ikhtiman 181 E6
Ilava 162 D4
Iława 155 D5
Ilford 31 D6
Ilfracombe 28 D4
Ílhavo 60 C2
Ilirska Bistrica 89 F7
Ilkeston 27 E6
Ilkley 27 C5
Illertissen 87 A7
Illingen 37 F5
Illkirch-Graffenstaden 43 C6
Íllora 69 B8
Illzach 43 E5
Ilmenau 95 E6
Ilsede 95 A5
Iłża 157 H2
Imatra 145 C5
Immenstadt im Allgäu 87 B7
Immingham 27 D7
Imola 82 C3
Imperia 53 C6
Imphy 46 B2
Impruneta 82 E2
İmroz 187 D7
Imst 87 C8
Inca 73 D6
İncirliova 193 D8
Incisa in Val d'Arno 82 E3
Inđija 174 C4
Ineu *RO* 167 E6
Infiesto 55 B7
Ingelheim am Rhein 37 E7
Ingelmunster 35 C5
Ingolstadt 91 D7
Inis 24 C3
Inis Córthaidh 25 D6
Innsbruck 88 B3
Inowrocław 154 E3
Însurăței 177 C8
Întorsura Buzăului 177 B5
Inverness 19 F5
Ioannina 184 F3
Ion Creangă 169 D7
Ion Luca Caragiale 177 D5
Iordăcheanu 177 C6
Ipotești 169 B6
Ipsala 187 C8
Ipswich 31 C7
Irakleio 194 E4
Irshava 161 G5
Irsina 76 B4
Irún 48 D2
Irunea 48 E2
Irvine 20 D4
Isaccea 171 C2
Isaszeg 166 B2
Isbergues 34 C4
Ischia 76 B1
Iseo 85 B6
Iserlohn 33 F6
Isernhagen 94 A4
Isernia 79 D5
Isla Cristina 67 F5
Islaz 176 F3
Ismaning 91 F7
Isny im Allgäu 87 B7
Isola del Gran Sasso d'Italia 78 B4
Isola della Scala 82 A2
Isola del Liri 78 D4
Isola di Capo Rizzuto 77 F6
Isperikh 177 F7
Ispica 75 F5

The full 60'000 places index, with map reference and page number, can be found at - www.snow-atlas.com

Orimattila 143 D8
Oristano 80 D2
Orivesi 143 B6
Orlea 176 F3
Orléans 40 E4
Orlová 162 B4
Ormož 164 D4
Ormskirk 26 D4
Orneta 155 C6
Orosei 80 C4
Orosháza 166 E4
Oroszlány 165 B7
Orsay 40 C4
Orşova 175 D7
Ortaca 197 B8
Ortaklar 193 D8
Orta Nova 76 A4
Orte 78 B2
Orthez 48 D3
Ortigueira 54 A3
Ortona 79 B5
Orvault 39 F6
Orvieto 78 A1
Oryakhovo 176 F2
Orzesze 158 F4
Orzinuovi 85 C6
Orzysz 152 F3
Osby 104 C4
Oschatz 96 D3
Oschersleben (Bode) 95 B6
O Seixo 54 E2
Osica de Sus 176 E3
Osijek 165 F8
Osimo 83 E6
Osio Sotto 85 B6
Oskarshamn 105 A7
Oslo 111 B8
Osmangazi 189 D8
Osnabrück 33 D7
Osny 40 B4
Oşorhei 167 D6
Osøyri 110 A2
Ospitaletto 85 B6
Oss 32 E3
Ostellato 82 B3
Ostend 34 B4
Osterhofen 92 E2
Osterholz-Scharmbeck 33 B8
Ostermundigen 47 A8
Osterode am Harz 95 C5
Ostiglia 82 B2
Ostra *I* 83 E5
Ostrava 162 B4
Östringen 37 F8
Ostróda 155 C6
Ostrov *CZ* 92 A2
Ostrov *RO* 177 E8
Ostrov *RUS* 149 B2
Ostroveni 176 F2
Ostrowiec Świętokrzyski 159 D8
Ostrów Mazowiecka 155 E8
Ostrów Wielkopolski 158 C3
Ostrzeszów 158 C3
Ostuni 77 B7
Osuna 69 B5
Oswestry 26 F4
Oświęcim 159 F5
Oţelu Roşu 175 B7
Otley *GB* 27 C5
Otmuchów 93 A8
Otopeni 177 D6
Otradnoye 145 F8
Otranto 77 C8
Otrokovice 162 C3
Ottaviano 76 B1
Ottersberg 33 B8
Ottignies 35 C7
Ottobrunn 91 F7
Ottweiler 37 F5
Otwock 157 F3
Oud-Beijerland 32 E2
Oudenaarde 35 C5
Oudenbosch 32 F2
Oudenburg 34 B4
Oud-Gastel 32 F2
Oud-Turnhout 32 F3
Ouistreham 39 B8
Oulainen 135 F6
Oullins 46 D4
Oulu 135 D7
Oulunsalo 135 E7
Oupeye 35 C8
Ourense 54 D3
Outokumpu 141 E6
Outreau 31 F8
Ovada 53 A7
Ovar 60 B2
Overath 37 C6
Overijse 35 C7
Overpelt 35 B8
Ovidiu 171 E2
Oviedo 55 B6
Oxelösund 109 B6
Oxford 29 B8
Oxted 31 E6
Oyonnax 47 C6
Oyten 33 B8
Ożarów 159 D8
Ożarów Mazowiecki 157 F2
Ózd 161 H1
Ozersk 152 E3
Ozieri 80 B2
Ozimek 158 E4
Ozoir-la-Ferrière 41 C5
Ozorków 159 B5
Ozzano dell'Emilia 82 C3

P

Pabianice 159 C5
Paceco 74 C1
Pachino 75 F6
Pacy-sur-Eure 40 B3
Paczków 93 A8
Paderborn 33 E8
Padeş 175 C8
Padiham 27 D5
Padina *RO* 177 D7
Padinska Skela 174 C4
Padova 82 A3
Padrón 54 C2
Padula 76 C3
Paese 88 F4
Pagani 76 B2
Paide 147 C6
Paignton 29 E5
Paimio 142 E4
Paimpol 38 C4
Paisley 21 D5
Pajęczno 159 D5
Pakość 154 E3
Pakruojis 150 E4
Paks 165 D8
Palafrugell 59 C8
Palagianello 77 B6
Palagiano 77 B6
Palagonia 75 E5
Palaiseau 41 C5
Palamós 59 C8
Palanga 150 E1
Palazzolo Acreide 75 E5
Palazzolo sull'Oglio 85 B6
Palazzo San Gervasio 76 B4
Palencia 56 E2
Palermo *I* 74 C2
Palestrina 78 C2
Paliano 78 C3
Palma Campania 76 B2
Palma del Río 67 D8
Palma de Mallorca 65 E8
Palma di Montechiaro 74 E3
Palmanova 89 E6
Palmela 66 C2
Palmi 75 B7
Palo del Colle 77 A5
Palomares del Río 67 E7
Palombara Sabina 78 C2
Păltinoasa 169 B5
Pamiers 49 E7
Pamplona 48 E2
Panagyurishte 181 E7
Pančevo 174 D4
Panciu 169 F7
Pâncota 167 E6
Pandino 85 C6
Pănet 168 E3
Panevėžys 151 E5
Pângărați 169 D6
Panicale 78 A1
Panningen 32 F4
Pantelimon *RO* 177 E6
Paola 76 E4
Pápa 165 B6
Papenburg 33 B6
Papendrecht 32 E2
Parabita 77 D8
Paraćin 175 F6
Parainen 142 E4
Paray-le-Monial 46 C3
Parchim 99 D7
Parczew 157 G5
Pardubice 93 B6
Parets del Vallès 59 D6
Pargas 142 E4
Paris 41 C5
Pârjol 169 D6
Parkano 139 F5
Parla 62 D4
Parma 82 B1
Pärnu 147 E5
Pârscov 177 C6
Partanna 74 D2
Parthenay 44 B4
Partinico 74 C2
Partizánske 162 E4
Pasai Donibane 48 D1
Paşcani 169 C6
Pasewalk 100 D4
Pasiàn di Prato 89 E5
Pasiano di Pordenone 89 E5
Pasłęk 155 C5
Passau 92 E3
Passy 47 D7
Pastavy 151 F8
Pasvalys 151 D5
Pásztó 163 F6
Pătârlagele 177 C6
Patchway 29 C6
Paterna 64 F3
Paternò 75 D5
Patos 184 C1
Patra 190 C3
Pattensen 94 A4
Patti 75 C5
Pau 48 D4
Pauillac 44 E3
Păunești 169 F7
Pavia *I* 85 C5
Pavia di Udine 89 E6
Pavilly 34 F2
Pavlikeni 182 C3
Pavullo nel Frignano 82 C2
Payerne 47 B8
Pazardzhik 181 E7
Pazin 83 A6
Peacehaven 31 F6
Peć 179 D7
Peccioli 82 E1
Pécel 166 C2
Pechea 171 B1
Pechory 148 F1
Pecica 167 F5
Pecq 35 C5
Pécs 165 E7
Pederobba 88 E4
Pedroso *P* 60 B2
Peer 35 B8
Pegnitz 91 B7
Peine 95 A5
Peiraias 191 D7
Peißenberg 88 A2
Peiting 87 B8
Pelago 82 E3
Pelhřimov 93 C6
Pélissanne 51 D7
Pelplin 154 C4
Penafiel 60 B3
Peñarroya-Pueblonuevo 67 C8
Penarth 29 C6
Pendlebury 27 D5
Peniche 60 F1
Penicuik 21 D6
Penmarch 38 E2
Penne *I* 78 B4
Penrith 21 F7
Penzance 28 F2
Penzberg 88 A3
Pepinster 35 C8
Perama *GR* 191 D6
Perchtoldsdorf 93 F7
Perechyn 161 G4
Perehins'ke 161 F6
Peretu 176 F4
Perg 93 F5
Pergine Valsugana 85 A8
Pergola 83 E5
Periam 167 F5
Périgueux 45 E5
Periș 177 D5
Perișoru 177 E8
Peristerio 191 D7
Perleberg 99 D7
Pernes-les-Fontaines 51 C7
Pernik 181 D5
Pero 85 B5
Péronnas 47 C5
Péronne 34 E4
Perpignan 50 F3
Perros-Guirec 38 C3
Pershore 29 A7
Perstorp 103 C8
Perth 21 C6
Pertuis 51 C8
Perugia 82 F4
Perushtitsa 181 E8
Péruwelz 35 D5
Perwez 35 C7
Pesaro 83 D5
Pescantina 82 A2
Pescara 79 B5
Peschiera del Garda 82 A1
Pescia 82 D1
Peshkopi 179 F8
Peshtera 181 F7
Pesnica 164 D4
Peso da Régua 60 B4
Pessac 44 F3
Pétange 36 F4
Peterborough 27 F7
Peterhead 19 F8
Peterlee 21 F8
Petersberg 90 A4
Petersfield 31 E5
Petershagen *D* 33 D8
Petilia Policastro 75 A8
Petrer 72 B3
Petrești *RO* 176 D4
Petricani 169 C6
Petrich 185 B7
Petrila 176 B1
Petrinja 164 F4
Petrodvorets 145 F7
Petroşani 176 B1
Petrovac *CS* 175 E6
Petrovaradin 174 C3
Peyrehorade 48 D3
Pézenas 50 D4
Pezinok 162 E3
Pfaffenhofen an der Ilm 91 E7
Pfarrkirchen 92 E2
Pforzheim 43 B7
Pfullendorf 43 E8
Pfullingen 43 C8
Pfungstadt 37 E7
Philippeville 35 D7
Piacenza 85 C6
Piana degli Albanesi 74 C2
Pianella 78 B4
Pianoro 82 C2
Piaseczno *PL* 157 F2
Piastów 157 F2
Piatra Neamț 169 D6
Piatra Olt 176 E3
Piatra Şoimului 169 D6
Piazza Armerina 74 D4
Piazzola sul Brenta 82 A3
Picassent 64 F3
Picerno 76 B3
Piechowice 97 E6
Piedimonte Matese 76 A1
Piedras Blancas 55 A6
Piekary Śląskie 159 F5
Pieksämäki 140 F4
Pieńsk 97 D5
Pierrelatte 51 B6
Piešťany 162 E4
Pieszyce 97 E7
Pietra Ligure 53 B6
Pietraperzia 74 D4
Pietrasanta 82 D1
Pieve di Cento 82 B2
Pieve di Soligo 88 E4
Pignataro Maggiore 76 A1
Pijnacker 32 E2
Piła 101 D7
Pilas 67 E6
Piława Górna 97 E8
Pilis 166 C3
Piliscsaba 165 A8
Pilisszentiván 165 A8
Pilisvörösvár 165 A8
Pinarhisar 189 A6
Pińczów 159 E7
Pineda de Mar 59 D7
Pinerolo 47 F8
Pineto 78 B4
Pinhal Novo 66 B2
Pinneberg 98 C4
Pinos-Puente 69 B8
Pinto 62 D4
Pioltello 85 B5
Piombino 81 D2
Piombino Dese 88 F4
Pionerskiy 155 A6
Pionki 157 H3
Piossasco 47 F8
Piotrków Trybunalski 159 C6
Piove di Sacco 82 A4
Piovene Rocchette 85 B8
Pipirig 169 C5
Piran 83 A6
Pirkkala 143 C5
Pirmasens 37 F6
Pirna 96 D4
Pirot 180 C4
Pisa *I* 82 E1
Piscu 171 B1
Piscu Vechi 175 F8
Písek *CZ* 92 C4
Pishchanka 170 A2
Pisogne 85 B6
Pisticci 77 C5
Pistoia 82 D2
Pisz 155 D8
Piteå 134 D3
Pitești 176 D4
Pithiviers 41 D5
Pitkyaranta 145 B8
Pittem 35 C5
Piwniczna-Zdrój 161 E1
Pizzighettone 85 C6
Pizzo 75 A7
Plabennec 38 C2
Plaisance-du-Touch 49 D7
Plaisir 40 C4
Planegg 91 F7
Plasencia 61 D7
Plattling 92 D2
Plauen 91 A7
Plenița 175 E8
Plérin 38 C4
Pleszew 158 B3
Plettenberg 37 B6
Pleven 181 B8
Pljevlja 179 C6
Płock 155 F5
Ploemeur 38 E3
Ploërmel 39 E5
Ploiești 177 C5
Plön 99 B5
Płońsk 155 F6
Plopeni 177 C5
Plopii-Slăvitești 176 F3
Plopșoru 176 D1
Plosca 176 F4
Ploufragan 38 C4
Plougastel-Daoulas 38 D2
Plouzané 38 D1
Plovdiv 181 E8
Plungė 150 E2
Pluvigner 38 E4
Plymouth 28 E4
Plzeň 92 B3
Pniewy *PL* 97 A7
Pobiedziska 97 A8
Pocking 92 E3
Podari 176 E2
Poddębice 159 B5
Poděbrady 93 A6
Podenzano 53 A8
Podgorica *CS* 179 E6
Podoleni 169 D6
Podu Iloaiei 169 C7
Podujevo 180 D2
Poduri 169 E6
Podu Turcului 169 E7
Poggiardo 77 D8
Poggibonsi 82 E2
Poggio Renatico 82 B3
Poggio Rusco 82 B2
Pogoanele 177 D7
Pogradec 184 C3
Poiana Câmpina 177 C5
Poiana Lacului 176 D3
Poiana Mare 175 F8
Poiana Mărului 176 B4
Poiana Teiului 169 C5
Poienarii Burchii 177 D5
Poieni 167 D8
Poienile de Sub Munte 168 B3
Poirino 53 A6
Poissy 40 B4
Poitiers 45 B5
Pola de Laviana 55 B7
Pola de Lena 55 B6
Pola de Siero 55 B7
Polanica-Zdrój 93 A7
Połaniec 159 E8
Polatsk 149 F3
Połczyn Zdrój 101 C6
Polessk 152 D2
Polgár 161 H2
Polgárdi 165 C8
Police 100 D4
Polichni 185 C7
Policoro 77 C5
Polignano a Mare 77 B6
Polistena 75 B7
Polkowice 97 C7
Polla 76 C3
Pollença 73 C6
Pollenza 83 F6
Polski Trŭmbesh 182 C3
Poltár 163 E6
Põlva 147 E8
Polygyros 185 D8
Pomarance 82 F2
Pomáz 166 B2
Pomezia 78 D2
Pomorie 183 D7
Pompei 76 B1
Pompey 42 C4
Ponferrada 55 D5
Poniatowa 157 H4
Ponsacco 82 E1
Pont-à-Celles 35 D6
Pont-à-Mousson 42 B4
Pontarlier 47 B7
Pontassieve 82 D3
Pont-Audemer 34 F1
Pontault-Combault 41 C5
Pontchâteau 39 F5
Pont-de-Roide 43 F5
Pont-du-Château 46 D2
Ponteareas 54 D2
Pontecagnano Faiano 76 B2
Pontecorvo 78 D4
Pontedera 82 E1
Ponte di Piave 88 E4
Pontefract 27 D6
Ponte nelle Alpi 88 D4
Pontenure 85 C6
Ponte San Nicolò 82 A3
Ponte San Pietro 85 B6
Pontevedra 54 D2
Pontevico 82 A1
Pontinha 66 B1
Pontinia 78 D3
Pontivy 38 D4
Pont-l'Abbé 38 E2
Pontoise 40 B4
Pontonnyy 145 F7
Pontremoli 85 E6
Pont-Ste-Maxence 34 F4
Pont-St-Esprit 51 B6
Pontypool 29 B6
Pontypridd 29 C5
Poole 29 E7
Poperinge 34 C4
Popești *RO* 167 C7
Popești-Leordeni 177 E6
Popoli 78 C4
Popovo 182 C4
Poppi 82 E3
Poprad 161 F1
Popricani 169 C8
Porcari 82 D1
Porcia 89 E5
Pordenone 89 E5
Poręba 159 E5
Pori 142 C3
Porkhov 148 F4
Pornic 39 F5
Porrentruy 43 F5
Porsgrunn 106 A3
Portadown 23 C6
Portalegre 60 F4
Portchester 29 D8
Port-de-Bouc 51 D7
Portes-lès-Valence 46 F4
Port Glasgow 20 D4
Porthcawl 29 C5
Portici 76 B1
Portimão 66 F2
Portishead 29 C6
Port Láirge 25 D6
Portlaoise 23 F5
Porto *P* 60 B2
Porto do Son 54 C1
Porto Empedocle 74 E3
Portoferraio 81 E2
Portogruaro 89 E5
Portomaggiore 82 B3
Porto Recanati 83 E6
Porto San Giorgio 83 F6
Porto Sant'Elpidio 83 F6
Portoscuso 80 F1
Porto Tolle 82 B4
Porto Torres 80 B1
Porto-Vecchio 53 F8
Portsmouth 29 D8
Port-St-Louis-du-Rhône 51 D7
Port Talbot 29 C5
Portugalete 56 B4
Port-Vendres 50 F4
Porvoo 143 E8
Posada *E* 55 B6
Pößneck 95 E7
Poșta Câlnău 177 C7
Postojna 89 E7
Potcoava 176 E3
Potenza 76 B4
Potenza Picena 83 E6
Potlogi 177 D5
Potsdam 96 A3
Potters Bar 31 D6
Poulton-le-Fylde 26 C4
Pouzauges 44 B3
Považská Bystrica 162 D4
Poviglio 82 B1
Póvoa de Varzim 54 F2
Povoletto 89 E6
Poysdorf 93 E8
Požarevac 175 D5
Požega *CS* 174 F3
Požega *HR* 165 F7
Poznań 97 A8
Pozoblanco 70 B2
Pozuelo de Alarcón 62 C4
Pozzallo 75 F5
Pozzuoli 76 B1
Pozzuolo del Friuli 89 E5
Prabuty 155 C5
Prachatice 92 D4
Prades *F* 49 F8
Praha 93 B5
Praia a Mare 76 D4
Praid 168 E4
Praszka 158 D4
Prata di Pordenone 89 E5
Prato 82 D2
Pratola Peligna 78 C4
Pratteln 43 F6
Pravia 55 B6
Predappio 82 D3
Predeal 177 B5
Preetz 99 B5
Preganziòl 88 F4
Preiļi 151 D8
Prejmer 169 F5
Premià de Mar 59 D6
Premnitz 95 A8
Prenzlau 100 D3
Přerov 162 C3
Preševo 180 E3
Presicce 77 D8
Prešov 161 F2
Pressbaum 93 F7
Prestatyn 26 E3
Preston *GB* 26 D4
Prestwick 20 E4
Preutești 169 C6
Preveza 190 B1
Priboj *CS* 179 B6
Příbram 92 B4
Priego de Córdoba 69 B7
Prienai *LT* 153 E5
Prievidza 163 D5
Prijedor 173 B5
Prijepolje 179 C6
Prilep 185 B5
Prinsenbeek 32 F2
Priolo Gargallo 75 E6
Priozersk 145 D7
Priština 180 D2
Pritzwalk 99 D8
Privas 46 F4
Priverno 78 D3
Prizren 179 E8
Prizzi 74 D3
Probištip 180 F4
Procida 76 B1
Profondeville 35 D7
Prokuplje 180 C3
Prostějov 93 C8
Proszowice 159 F6
Provadiya 183 C6
Provins 41 C6
Prudhoe 21 F8
Prudnik 158 F3
Prundeni 176 D3
Prundu 177 E6
Prundu Bârgăului 168 C3
Pruszcz Gdański 154 B4
Pruszków 157 F2
Przasnysz 155 E7
Przemków 97 C6
Przemyśl 160 D4
Przeworsk 160 D4
Przysucha 157 H2
Pskov 148 F2
Pszczyna 163 B5
Ptolemaida 185 D5
Ptuj 164 D4
Puchenii Mari 177 D6
Puchheim 91 F6
Púchov 162 D4
Pucioasa 177 C5
Puck 154 A4
Puçol 64 E3
Pudsey 27 D6
Puente-Genil 69 B6
Puertollano 70 B4
Puerto Real 68 D3
Pui 175 B8
Pula *HR* 83 B6
Pula *I* 80 F2
Puławy 157 H3
Pulheim 37 B5
Pulsano 77 C6
Pułtusk 155 F7
Purkersdorf 93 F7
Purmerend 32 D3
Pŭrvomay *BG* 182 E3
Pushkinskiye Gory 149 B3
Püspökladány 167 C5
Pustoshka 149 D4
Puszczykowo 97 A8
Pusztaszabolcs 165 B8
Putignano 77 B6
Putnok 161 G1
Putte *B* 33 B7
Putten 32 D3
Püttlingen 37 F5
Puurs 35 B6
Pyle 29 C5
Pyrgos *GR* 190 E3
Pyrzyce 101 E5
Pyskowice 158 F4
Pytalovo 149 B2

Q

Quakenbrück 33 C7
Qualiano 76 B1
Quarrata 82 D2
Quartu Sant'Elena 80 E3
Quattro Castella 82 C1
Quedlinburg 95 B6
Queluz 66 B1
Querfurt 95 C7
Quesnoy-sur-Deûle 34 C4
Questembert 38 E4
Quiberon 38 F3
Quickborn 99 C5
Quierschied 37 F5
Quiévrain 35 D5
Quiliano 53 B6
Quimper 38 D2
Quimperlé 38 E3
Quinzano d'Oglio 85 C6

R

Raahe 135 E6
Raalte 32 D4
Raamsdonksveer 32 E2
Rabastens 49 C7
Rabka 163 C7
Răcăciuni 169 E7
Racale 77 D8
Racalmuto 74 D3
Răcari 177 D5
Racconigi 53 A5
Răchitoasa 169 E7
Racibórz 158 F4
Ráckeve 165 B8
Rădăuți 169 B5
Radeberg 96 D4
Radebeul 96 D3
Radevormwald 37 B6
Radlje ob Dravi 89 C8
Radnevo 182 E4
Radolfzell am Bodensee 43 E8
Radom 157 H2
Radomir 181 D5
Radomsko 159 D5
Radovanu 177 E6
Radoviš 185 A6
Radovljica 89 D7
Răducăneni 169 D8
Radviliškis 150 E4
Radymno 160 D4
Radziejów 154 F4
Radzymin 155 F8
Radzyń Podlaski 157 G4
Raeren 36 C4
Raffadali 74 D3
Râfov 177 D6
Ragusa 75 F5
Rahden 33 D7
Raisio 142 E4
Raismes 35 D5
Rakamaz 161 H2
Rakhiv 168 A3
Rakitovo 181 F7
Rákóczifalva 166 D4
Rakovník 92 A4
Rakovski 181 E8
Rakvere 147 B7
Ramacca 75 D5
Rambervillers 42 D4
Rambouillet 40 C4
Râmnicu Sărat 177 B7
Râmnicu Vâlcea 176 C3
Ramonville-St-Agne 49 D7
Ramsbottom 27 D5
Ramsgate 31 D8
Rånåsfoss 111 B8
Randazzo 75 C5
Randers 102 B4
Rankweil 87 C6
Raon-l'Étape 43 D5
Rapallo 53 B8
Rapla 147 C6
Rapperswil 43 F8
Raseiniai 150 F4
Răşinari 176 B2
Raška 179 C8
Râşnov 177 B5
Rasony 149 E3
Rastatt 43 C7
Rastede 33 B7
Ratekau 99 C6
Rathenow 95 A8
Ratingen 33 F5
Ratzeburg 99 C6

The full 60'000 places index, with map reference and page number, can be found at - **www.snow-atlas.com**

Tarnów *PL* 159 F7
Tarnowskie Góry 158 E4
Tarquinia 78 B1
Tarragona 58 E4
Tàrrega 58 D4
Tarrio 54 B2
Tărtășești 177 D5
Tartu 147 E8
Tarutyne 170 F3
Tarvisio 89 D6
Tășnad 167 C7
Tassin-la-Demi-Lune 46 D4
Tát 165 A8
Tata 165 A8
Tatabánya 165 A8
Tătărani 176 C4
Tatarbunary 170 F4
Tauberbischofsheim 90 C4
Taucha 95 C8
Taufkirchen *D* 91 F7
Taunton 29 D6
Tauragė 150 F2
Taurianova 75 B7
Taurisano 77 D8
Tăuții-Măgherăuș 167 B8
Tavagnacco 89 E5
Tavarnelle Val di Pesa 82 E2
Tavernes de la Valldigna 72 A3
Taverny 41 B5
Taviano 77 D8
Tavira 66 F4
Tavistock 28 E4
Tczew 154 C4
Teaca 168 D3
Teano 76 A1
Techirghiol 171 E2
Tecuci 169 F8
Tegelen 32 F4
Teggiano 76 C3
Téglás 167 B6
Teglio 85 A6
Teignmouth 29 E5
Teiuș 168 E2
Tekirdağ 189 C6
Telciu 168 C3
Telega 177 C5
Telford 26 F4
Telfs 88 B2
Telgte 33 E6
Telšiai 150 E2
Teltow 96 A3
Temerin 174 B3
Tempio Pausania 80 B3
Templin 100 E3
Temse 35 B6
Teningen 43 D6
Tepecik *TR* 189 B8
Teplice 96 E4
Teramo 78 B4
Terborg-Silvolde 32 E4
Terespol 157 F6
Tergnier 35 F5
Terlizzi 77 A5
Termini Imerese 74 C3
Termoli 79 C6
Terneuzen 32 F1
Terni 78 B2
Ternitz 164 A4
Terracina 78 E3
Terralba 80 D2
Terranova da Sibari 77 E5
Terranuova Bracciolini 82 E3
Terrasini 74 C2
Terrassa 59 D6
Terrasson-Lavilledieu 45 F6
Teruel 63 D8
Tervel 177 F8
Tervuren 35 C7
Tessenderlo 35 B7
Teterow 99 C8
Teteven 181 D7
Tétouan 69 F5
Tetovo *MK* 179 F8
Tettnang 87 B6
Teufen 43 F8
Tewkesbury 29 B7
Thale (Harz) 95 B6
Thalwil 43 F7
Thame 30 D4
Thann 43 E5
Thatcham 29 C8
Thessaloniki 185 C7
Thetford 31 B7
Theux 35 D8
Thiene 88 E3
Thiers 46 D2
Thionville 36 F4
Thisted 102 A2
Thiva 191 C6
Thizy 46 D4
Tholey 37 F5
Thônes 47 D7
Thonon-les-Bains 47 C7
Thornbury 29 C6
Thornton 26 C4
Thouars 44 A4
Thuin 35 D6
Thuir 50 F3
Thun 86 D3
Thurles 25 C5
Țibana 169 D7
Țibănești 169 D7
Tibro 108 B2
Țicleni 176 D1
Tidaholm 107 C8
Tiel 32 E3
Tielt 35 C5
Tienen 35 C7
Tiengen 43 E7
Tierp 115 A5
Țifești 169 F7
Țigănești 176 F4
Tighina 170 D3
Tiha Bârgăului 168 C3
Tilburg 32 F3
Tilbury 31 D6
Tileagd 167 D7
Tilehurst 29 C8
Timișoara 167 F5
Timrå 119 B7
Tinca 167 D6
Tineo 55 B5
Tinqueux 35 F6
Tipperary 24 D4
Tiranë 184 B2
Tirano 85 A7
Tiraspol 170 D3
Tire 193 D8
Tirschenreuth 91 B8
Tisău 177 C6
Tismana 175 C8
Tiszaalpár 166 D3
Tiszacsege 167 B5
Tiszaföldvár 166 D4
Tiszafüred 166 B4
Tiszakécske 166 D3
Tiszalök 161 H2
Tiszalúc 161 H2
Tiszaújváros 161 H2
Tiszavasvári 161 H2
Titel 174 C4
Tito 76 B3
Titu 177 D5
Tivat 179 E5
Tiverton 29 D5
Tivoli 78 C2
Tłuszcz 155 F8
Todi 78 A2
Todirești *RO* 169 B5
Todirești *RO* 169 C6
Todirești *RO* 169 D7
Todmorden 27 D5
Toijala 143 C6
Tokaj 161 H2
Tokod 165 A8
Tököl 165 B8
Toledo 62 E3
Tolentino 83 F6
Tolmezzo 89 D5
Tolmin 89 D6
Tolna 165 D8
Tolosa *E* 48 E1
Tomar 60 E3
Tomaszów Lubelski 160 C5
Tomaszów Mazowiecki 157 H1
Tomelilla 104 D4
Tomelloso 63 F5
Tomești *RO* 169 C8
Tonbridge 31 E6
Tønder 102 F2
Tongeren 35 C8
Tonnay-Charente 44 D3
Tonneins 49 B5
Tonnerre 41 E7
Tønsberg 111 C7
Toplița *RO* 168 D4
Topoľčany 162 E4
Topoloveni 176 D4
Topolovgrad 182 F4
Topraisar 171 E2
Torano Castello 76 E4
Torbalı 193 C8
Torchiarolo 77 C7
Torelló 59 C6
Torgau 96 C3
Torgelow 100 C4
Torhout 35 B5
Torigni-sur-Vire 39 B7
Torino 84 C3
Toritto 77 B5
Tornesch 98 C4
Tornio 135 B6
Törökbálint 165 B8
Törökszentmiklós 166 C4
Torquay 29 E5
Torre Annunziata 76 B1
Torre del Campo 69 A8
Torre del Greco 76 B1
Torredonjimeno 69 A7
Torrejón de Ardoz 62 C4
Torrelavega 56 B2
Torremaggiore 79 D6
Torremolinos 69 D6
Torrent 64 F3
Torre-Pacheco 72 D2
Torre Santa Susanna 77 C7
Torres Novas 60 F2
Torres Vedras 60 F1
Torrevieja 72 C3
Torrita di Siena 82 F3
Torrox 69 C7
Tórshavn 18 B2
Tortolì 80 D3
Tortona 53 A7
Tortora 76 D4
Tortoreto 78 A4
Tortorici 75 C5
Tortosa 58 F3
Toruń 154 E4
Toscolano-Maderno 85 B7
Tostedt 98 D4
Toszek 158 E4
Totana 71 D8
Tótkomlós 166 E4
Totnes 29 E5
Totton 29 D8
Toul 42 C3
Toulon 51 E8
Toulouges 50 F3
Toulouse 49 D7
Tourcoing 35 C5
Tourlaville 39 A6
Tournai 35 C5
Tournan-en-Brie 41 C5
Tournefeuille 49 D7
Tournon-sur-Rhône 46 F4
Tournus 46 B4
Tours 40 F2
Towcester 30 C4
Trabotivište 181 F5
Tradate 85 B5
Traian *RO* 169 D7
Traiskirchen 93 F7
Trakai 153 E6
Tralee 24 D2
Trá Li 24 D2
Tranås 108 C3
Tranbjerg 102 C4
Trani 77 A5
Trapani 74 C1
Trappes 40 C4
Trasacco 78 C4
Traun 92 F4
Traunreut 89 A5
Traunstein *D* 89 A5
Travagliato 82 A1
Travemünde 99 B6
Traversetolo 82 C1
Travnik 173 D6
Trbovlje 89 D8
Trebaseleghe 88 F4
Třebíč 93 C7
Trebinje 178 D4
Trebisacce 77 D5
Trebišov 161 G3
Trebnje 89 E8
Trebur 37 E7
Trecastagni 75 D6
Trecate 84 C4
Tredegar 29 B5
Tréguier 38 C3
Treia *I* 83 F6
Trélazé 39 F7
Trelleborg 103 E8
Tremelo 35 C7
Trenčín 162 D4
Trento 85 A8
Treorchy 29 C5
Trepuzzi 77 C7
Trescore Balneario 85 B6
Trets 51 D8
Treuchtlingen 91 D6
Trevi 78 A2
Treviglio 85 B6
Treviso 88 E4
Trévoux 46 D4
Trezzo sull'Adda 85 B6
Tricarico 76 B4
Tricase 77 D8
Tricesimo 89 D5
Trier 37 E5
Trieste 89 F6
Trifești *RO* 169 D7
Triggiano 77 A6
Trikala 185 F5
Třinec 163 B5
Tring 31 C5
Trinitapoli 76 A4
Trino 84 C4
Tripoli 190 E4
Tritenii de Jos 168 E2
Trivento 79 C5
Trivero 84 B3
Trnava *SK* 162 E3
Trofa 54 F2
Trogir 172 E4
Troia 76 A3
Troina 75 D5
Troisdorf 37 C5
Trollhättan 107 C6
Tromsø 127 A7
Trondheim 120 E4
Troon 20 D4
Tropea 75 B7
Trossingen 43 D7
Trostberg 91 F8
Trouville-sur-Mer 39 A8
Trowbridge 29 C7
Troyan 181 D8
Troyes 41 D7
Trstenik *CS* 179 B8
Truro 28 F3
Trușești 169 B7
Truskavets' 161 E5
Trŭstenik *BG* 181 B7
Trutnov 97 E7
Tryavna 182 D3
Trzcianka *PL* 101 E7
Trzebiatów 101 B5
Trzebinia 159 F5
Trzebnica 97 C8
Trzemeszno 154 F3
Tržič 89 D7
Tübingen 43 C8
Tubize 35 C6
Tuchola 154 D3
Tuchów 160 D2
Tudela 57 E6
Tudora 169 B6
Tudor Vladimirescu 171 B1
Tufești 171 C1
Tui 54 E2
Tukums 150 B4
Tulach Mhór 23 F5
Tulcea 171 C2
Tullamore 23 F5
Tulle 45 E7
Tullins 47 E5
Tulln 93 E7
Tulnici 169 F6
Tulucești 171 B1
Tumba 109 A7
Tunbridge Wells, Royal 31 E6
Tura 166 B3
Turceni 176 D1
Turčianske Teplice 163 D5
Turda 168 E2
Turek 158 B4
Tŭrgovishte 183 C5
Turgutlu 193 C8
Turi 77 B6
Turka 161 F5
Túrkeve 166 C4
Turku 142 E4
Turnhout 32 F2
Turnov 97 E5
Turnu Măgurele 176 F4
Tursi 77 C5
Turț 161 H5
Tuscania 78 B1
Tuszyn 159 C5
Tutrakan 177 E6
Tuttlingen 43 E8
Tuusula 143 E7
Tuzla *BIH* 173 C8
Tuzla *RO* 171 E2
Tvøroyri 18 C2
Tvrdošín 163 C6
Tvŭrditsa 182 D4
Twardogóra 158 C3
Twello 32 D4
Twistringen 33 C7
Tyachiv 161 H6
Tychy 159 F5
Tynemouth 21 F8
Tyrnavos 185 E6

U

Úbeda 69 A8
Überherrn 37 F5
Überlingen 43 E8
Ubrique 69 D5
Ubstadt-Weiher 37 F8
Uccle 35 C6
Uckfield 31 E6
Uddevalla 107 C6
Uden 32 F3
Udenhout 32 F3
Udești 169 B6
Udine 89 E5
Ueckermünde 100 C4
Uelzen 99 E6
Uetendorf 47 B8
Uetersen 98 C4
Uetze 95 A5
Ugento 77 D8
Ugine 47 D7
Uherské Hradiště 162 D3
Uherský Brod 162 D3
Uhingen 90 E4
Uitgeest 32 D2
Uithoorn 32 D2
Uithuizen 33 B5
Újfehértó 167 B6
Újkígyós 167 E5
Újszász 166 C3
Ukmergė 151 F6
Ula *TR* 197 B7
Ulcinj 179 F6
Ulft 32 E4
Üllő 166 C2
Ulm 90 E4
Ulmeni *RO* 167 C8
Ulmeni *RO* 177 E7
Ulmu *RO* 177 C7
Ulricehamn 107 D8
Ulvenhout 32 F2
Ulverston 26 C4
Ul'yanovka 170 A4
Umbertide 82 F4
Umbrărești 169 F8
Umeå 138 B2
Ümraniye 189 B8
Ungheni *MD* 169 C8
Ungheni *RO* 168 E3
Ungureni *RO* 169 B6
Uničov 93 B8
Unirea *RO* 168 E2
Unna 33 F6
Unterägeri 43 F7
Unterhaching 91 F7
Unterschleißheim 91 F7
Upplands-Väsby 115 C5
Uppsala 115 B5
Urbania 82 E4
Urbino 82 E4
Urdorf 43 F7
Urechești *RO* 177 B7
Uricani 175 C8
Urk 32 C3
Urla 193 C7
Urlați 177 C6
Uroševac 180 E2
Urtenen 47 A8
Urziceni *RO* 177 D6
Ushachy 149 F3
Usingen 37 D7
Üsküdar 189 B8
Uslar 94 C4
Ussel *F* 45 E8
Uster 43 F7
Ústí nad Labem 96 E4
Ústí nad Orlicí 93 B7
Ustka 101 A7
Ustroń 163 B5
Ustrzyki Dolne 161 E4
Utena 151 F7
Utiel 63 E8
Utrecht 32 E3
Utrera 67 F7
Uttoxeter 27 F5
Uusikaupunki 142 D3
Uxbridge 31 D5
Uzès 51 C6
Uzhhorod 161 G4
Užice 174 F3
Uzunköprü 188 B4

V

Vaals 36 C4
Vaasa 138 D3
Vaassen 32 D4
Vác 166 B2
Văcărești 177 D5
Vado Ligure 53 B7
Vadsø 130 C3
Vadstena 108 B3
Vadu Moldovei 169 C6
Vadu Pașii 177 C7
Vaduz 87 C6
Vagney 42 D4
Vágur 18 C2
Vaiano 82 D2
Vairano Patenora 76 A1
Vaison-la-Romaine 51 B7
Valandovo 185 B6
Valašské Meziříčí 162 C4
Valbom 60 B2
Valbonne 52 D4
Valdagno 85 B8
Valdemoro 62 D4
Valdepeñas 71 B5
Val-de-Reuil 34 F2
Valderice 74 C1
Valdobbiadene 88 E4
Valea Călugărească 177 C6
Valea Doftanei 177 C5
Valea lui Mihai 167 C6
Valea Lungă *RO* 177 C5
Valea Moldovei 169 C5
Valea Râmnicului 177 C7
Valea Seacă *RO* 169 C6
Valea Stanciului 176 F2
Valeggio sul Mincio 82 A2
Valence *F* 46 F4
Valence *F* 49 B6
Valencia 64 F3
Valenciennes 35 D5
Văleni *RO* 169 D8
Vălenii de Munte 177 C5
Valentigney 43 F5
Valenza 53 A7
Valenzano 77 A5
Valga 147 F7
Valguarnera Caropepe 74 D4
Valjevo 174 E3
Valka 147 F7
Valkeakoski *FIN* 143 C6
Valkenswaard 32 F3
Valladolid 55 F8
Vallauris 52 D4
Vall de Uxó 64 E3
Vallentuna 115 C5
Vallet 39 F6
Vallo della Lucania 76 C3
Valls 58 E4
Valmadrera 85 B5
Valmiera 147 F6
Valmontone 78 C3
Valognes 39 A6
Valongo *P* 60 B3
Valréas 51 B7
Valu lui Traian 171 E2
Valverde del Camino 67 E6
Vama *RO* 169 B5
Vammala 143 C5
Vámospércs 167 C6
Vânatori 169 F7
Vânătorii Mici 177 E5
Vânători-Neamț 169 C6
Vanda 143 E7
Vänersborg 107 B6
Vânju Mare 175 E8
Vannes 38 E4
Vantaa 143 E7
Varallo 84 B4
Vărăști 177 E6
Varaždin 165 D5
Varazze 53 B7
Varberg 103 A6
Vărbilău 177 C5
Varde 102 D2
Varel 33 B7
Varėna 153 F6
Varennes-Vauzelles 46 A2
Varese 85 B5
Variaș 167 F5
Varkaus 141 F5
Varna *BG* 183 C7
Värnamo 104 A4
Varnsdorf 97 D5
Várpalota 165 B7
Varsseveld 33 E5
Vasa 138 D3
Vásárosnamény 161 H4
Vasilați 177 E6
Vaslui 169 D8
Västerås 114 C4
Västerhaninge 109 A7
Västervik 109 D5
Vasto 79 C5
Vasvár 165 C5
Vaterstetten 91 F7
Vatra Dornei 168 C4
Vaulx-en-Velin 46 D4
Vauvert 51 C6
Vaux-le-Pénil 41 C5
Växjö 105 B5
Vecchiano 82 D1
Vechelde 95 A5
Vechta 33 C7
Vecsés 166 C2
Vedea *RO* 177 F5
Vedelago 88 F4
Veendam 33 B5
Veenendaal 32 E3
Veghel 32 F3
Veglie 77 C7
Vejen 102 D3
Vejer de la Frontera 68 E4
Vejle *DK* 102 D3
Velbert 33 F5
Veldhoven 32 F3
Velen 33 E5
Velenje 89 D8
Veles 180 F3
Vélez-Málaga 69 C7
Velika Gorica 164 F4
Velika Plana *CS* 175 E5
Veliki Preslav 183 C5
Veliko Tŭrnovo 182 C3
Velingrad 181 F7
Velké Meziříčí 93 C7
Veľký Krtíš 163 F6
Velletri 78 D2
Vellinge 103 E7
Vellmar 94 C4
Velten 100 F3
Velyka Mykhaylivka 170 D4
Velykyy Bereznyy 161 F4
Venafro 78 D4
Venaria 84 C3
Vence 52 C4
Vendas Novas 66 B3
Vendôme 40 E3
Venezia 82 A4
Vénissieux 46 D4
Venlo 32 F4
Vennesla 106 C1
Venosa 76 B4
Venray 32 F4
Ventimiglia 53 C5
Ventspils 150 A2
Verbania 84 A4
Vercelli 84 C4
Verdalsøra 121 D5
Verden (Aller) 33 C8
Verdun 42 B3
Veresegyház 166 B2
Verești 169 B6
Vergato 82 C2
Verín 54 E4
Verkhovyna 168 A3
Verl 33 E7
Vernești 177 C7
Verneuil-sur-Avre 40 C3
Vernier 47 C6
Vernio 82 D2
Vernole 77 C8
Vernon 40 B3
Vernouillet 40 C3
Veroia 185 D6
Verolanuova 85 C6
Veroli 78 D3
Verona 82 A2
Versailles 40 C4
Versmold 33 E7
Versoix 47 C6
Vertou 39 F6
Verucchio 82 D4
Verviers 35 C8
Verwood 29 D7
Verzuolo 53 A5
Veselí nad Moravou 162 D3
Vesoul 42 E4
Veszprém 165 C7
Vésztő 167 D5
Veternik 174 C3
Vetlanda 108 E3
Vetovo *BG* 177 F6
Vetralla 78 B1
Veurne 34 B4
Vevey 47 C7
Veyre-Monton 46 D2
Viadana 82 B1
Viana do Castelo 54 E1
Vianen 32 E3
Viareggio 82 D1
Viarmes 41 B5
Viborg 102 B3
Vibo Valentia 75 B7
Vic 59 C6
Vícar 71 F6
Vicchio 82 D3
Vicenza 82 A3
Vichy 46 C2
Vico del Gargano 79 C8
Vico Equense 76 B1
Vicovu de Jos 169 B5
Vicovu de Sus 169 B5
Victoria *RO* 176 B3
Videle 177 E5
Vidin 175 F8
Vidra *RO* 169 F7
Vidra *RO* 177 E6
Vielsalm 36 D4
Vienenburg 95 B5
Vienne 46 E4
Viernheim 37 F7
Viersen 32 F4
Vierzon 40 F4
Vieste 79 C8
Vietri sul Mare 76 B2
Vif 47 F6
Vigarano Mainarda 82 B3
Vigasio 82 A2
Vigevano 85 C5
Vigliano Biellese 84 B3
Vignola 82 C2
Vigo 54 D2
Vigodarzere 82 A3
Vigone 47 F8
Vigonza 82 A3
Viișoara *RO* 168 E2
Viladecans 59 E6
Vila do Conde 54 F2
Vilafranca del Penedès 59 E5
Vila Franca de Xira 66 B2
Vilagarcía de Arousa 54 C2
Vilalba 54 B3
Vilanova de Arousa 54 D2
Vila Nova de Famalicão 54 F2
Vila Nova de Gaia 60 B2
Vila Nova de Ourém 60 E2
Vilanova i la Geltrú 59 E5
Vilar de Andorinho 60 B2
Vila Real 54 F3
Vila-real de los Infantes 64 E3
Vila Real de Santo António 66 F4
Vilaseca de Solcina 58 E4
Vilassar de Mar 59 D6
Vila Viçosa 66 B4
Viljandi 147 E6
Vilkaviškis 152 E4
Villa Bartolomea 82 A2
Villabate 74 C3
Villablino 55 C6
Villa Carcina 85 B7
Villacarrillo 71 C5
Villa Castelli 77 B7
Villach 89 C6
Villacidro 80 E2
Villa d'Almè 85 B6
Villadose 82 B3
Villadossola 84 A4
Villafranca de los Barros 67 C6
Villafranca di Verona 82 A2
Villafranca Tirrena 75 C6
Villajoyosa-La Vila Joíosa 72 B4
Villa Literno 76 A1
Villamartín 67 F8
Villanueva de Córdoba 70 C3
Villanueva de la Serena 67 B7
Villaputzu 80 E3
Villarosa 74 D4
Villarrobledo 63 F6
Villa San Giovanni 75 C7
Villasor 80 E2
Villaviciosa 55 B7
Villefontaine 47 E5
Villefranche-de-Rouergue 49 B8
Villefranche-sur-Mer 53 C5
Villefranche-sur-Saône 46 D4
Villena 72 B2
Villeneuve-d'Ascq 35 C5
Villeneuve-lès-Avignon 51 C7
Villeneuve-Loubet 52 D4
Villeneuve-sur-Lot 49 B6
Villeneuve-sur-Yonne 41 D6
Villers-Cotterêts 35 F5
Villers-lès-Nancy 42 C4
Villers-sur-Glâne 47 B8
Villeurbanne 46 D4
Villingen 43 D7
Villorba 88 E4
Vilnius 153 E7
Vilsbiburg 91 E8
Vilshofen 92 E3
Vilvoorde 35 C6
Vimercate 85 B5
Vimmerby 108 D4
Vinaròs 58 F3
Vinci 82 D2
Vineuil *F* 40 E3
Vinga 167 F5
Vingåker 108 A4
Vinica *MK* 180 F4
Vinkovci 165 F8
Vințu de Jos 168 F2
Vipiteno 88 C3
Vire 39 C7
Viriat 47 C5
Virkkala 143 F6
Viron 191 D7
Virovitica 165 E6
Virton 35 F8
Vis 79 A8
Visaginas 151 E8
Visby *S* 109 D7
Visé 35 C8
Viseu 60 C4
Vișeu de Jos 168 B3
Vișeu de Sus 168 B3

Vişina *RO* 176 D4
Visoko 173 D7
Visp 84 A3
Visselhövede 98 E4
Viterbo 78 B1
Vitoria-Gasteiz 57 C5
Vitré 39 D6
Vitrolles 51 D7
Vitry-le-François 41 C8
Vittel 42 D3
Vittoria 75 E5
Vittorio Veneto 88 E4
Vitulazio 76 A1
Viveiro 54 A4
Vize 189 A6
Vizille 47 F6
Viziru 171 C1
Vizzini 75 E5
Vlaardingen 32 E2
Vladičin Han 180 D4
Vladimirescu 167 F5
Vlăhiţa 169 E5
Vlašim 93 B5
Vlasotince 180 D4
Vleuten 32 E3
Vlijmen 32 E3
Vlissingen 32 F1
Vlorë 184 D1
Vlotho 33 D8
Vöcklabruck 92 F3
Voerde (Niederrhein) 33 F5
Voghera 53 A7
Vöhringen *D* 91 F5
Voineşti *RO* 169 C7
Voineşti *RO* 176 C4
Voiron 47 E5
Voitsberg 89 B8
Vojens 102 E3
Volda 116 B2
Volendam 32 D3
Völkermarkt 89 C8
Volketswil 43 F7
Völklingen 37 F5
Volos 185 F7
Volosovo 148 B3
Volovăţ 169 B5
Volovets' 161 G5
Volpago del Mòntello 88 E4
Volpiano 84 C3
Volta Mantovana 82 A1
Volterra 82 E2
Voluntari 177 E6
Voorburg 32 E2
Voorschoten 32 E2
Voranava 153 F7
Vorden 32 E4
Vordingborg 103 F6
Vorona 169 B6
Vorst 35 B7
Võru 147 F8
Voss 116 F3
Vosselaar 32 F2
Voula 191 D7
Vranje 180 D3
Vranov nad Topľou 161 F3
Vratsa 181 C6
Vrbas 174 B3
Vrchlabí 97 E6
Vreden 33 E5
Vrhnika 89 E7
Vriezenveen 33 D5
Vrnjačka Banja 179 B8
Vršac 175 C5
Vsetín 162 C4
Vsevolozhsk 145 F7
Vučitrn 179 D8
Vught 32 F3
Vukovar 173 A8
Vulcan *RO* 175 C8
Vulcan *RO* 176 B4
Vulcăneşti 171 B2
Vûlchedrûm 176 F1
Vulturu *RO* 177 B8
Vûrshets 181 C6
Vyalikaya Byerastavitsa 156 D6
Vyborg 145 D5
Vyerkhnyadzvinsk 149 E2
Vylkove 171 B4
Vynnyky 160 D6
Vynohradiv 161 H5
Vyritsa 148 B4
Vyškov 93 C8
Vysoké Mýto 93 B7
Vyzhnytsya 168 A4

W

Waalre 32 F3
Waalwijk 32 F3
Waarschoot 35 B5
Wąbrzeźno 154 D4
Wachtebeke 35 B6
Wächtersbach 37 D8
Waddinxveen 32 E2
Wadebridge 28 E3
Wädenswil 43 F7
Wadern 37 F5
Wadersloh 33 E7
Wadgassen 37 F5
Wadowice 163 B6
Wageningen 32 E3
Waghäusel 37 F7
Wągrowiec 101 D8
Waiblingen 43 C8
Waidhofen an der Thaya 93 D6
Waidhofen an der Ybbs 93 F5

Waimes 36 D4
Wakefield 27 D6
Wałbrzych 97 E7
Walcourt 35 D6
Walcheren 35 D7
Wałcz 101 D7
Wald *CH* 43 F8
Waldbröl 37 C6
Waldkirch 43 D6
Waldkraiburg 91 F8
Waldshut 43 E7
Walferdange 36 E4
Wallasey 26 D4
Walldorf *D* 37 E7
Walldorf *D* 37 F8
Walldürn 43 A8
Wallisellen 43 F7
Walsall 27 F5
Walsrode 98 E4
Waltershausen 95 D5
Walton-on-Thames 31 D5
Wangen im Allgäu 87 B7
Wanze 35 D8
Warburg 33 F8
Wardenburg 33 B7
Ware 31 C6
Waregem 35 C5
Wareham 29 E7
Waremme 35 C8
Waren 99 C8
Warendorf 33 E7
Warka 157 G2
Warlingham 31 E6
Warminster 29 D7
Warnsveld 32 D4
Warrington 26 E4
Warstein 33 F7
Warszawa 157 F2
Warwick 29 A8
Washington 21 F8
Wasilków 156 D5
Wasselonne 43 C6
Wassenaar 32 D2
Wassenberg 36 B4
Waterford 25 D6
Waterloo 35 C6
Waterlooville 30 E4
Watford 31 D5
Wattwil 43 F8
Wavre 35 C7
Wedel (Holstein) 98 C4
Weener 33 B6
Weert 32 F4
Weesp 32 D3
Wegberg 36 B4
Węgorzewo 152 F2
Węgrów 155 F8
Wehl 32 E4
Wehr 43 E6
Weiden in der Oberpfalz 91 B8
Weil am Rhein 43 E6
Weilburg 37 D7
Weil der Stadt 43 C8
Weilerswist 37 C5
Weilheim in Oberbayern 88 A2
Weimar 95 D6
Weinfelden 43 E8
Weingarten 87 B6
Weinheim 37 F8
Weinsberg 37 F8
Weinstadt 43 C8
Weißenburg in Bayern 91 D6
Weißenfels 95 D7
Weißenhorn 91 F5
Weißwasser 97 C5
Weiz 164 B3
Wejherowo 154 A3
Welkenraedt 36 C4
Wellingborough 31 B5
Wellington *GB* 29 D6
Wells 29 D6
Wels 92 F4
Welver 33 F7
Welwyn Garden City 31 C6
Wendelstein 91 C6
Wenden 37 C6
Wendlingen am Neckar 43 C8
Wennigsen (Deister) 94 A4
Werdau 95 E8
Werder *D* 95 A8
Werdohl 33 F6
Werl 33 F7
Wernau 43 C8
Werne 33 F6
Wernigerode 95 B6
Wertheim 90 B4
Werther (Westfalen) 33 E7
Wervik 35 C5
Wesel 33 F5
Wesoła 157 F2
Wesseling 37 C5
West Bridgford 27 F6
West Bromwich 27 F5
Westbury 29 C7
Westerlo 35 B7
Westerstede 33 B7
Westervoort 32 E4
West Kirby 26 E4
Westmalle 32 F2
Weston-super-Mare 29 C6
Wetteren 35 C6
Wettingen 43 F7
Wetzikon 43 F8
Wetzlar 37 C7
Wevelgem 35 C5
Wexford 25 D7
Weybridge 31 D5
Weyhe 33 C8

Weymouth 29 E7
Whitburn 21 D5
Whitby 27 B7
Whitehaven 26 B3
Whitley Bay 21 E8
Whitstable 31 D7
Whittlesey 27 F8
Wichelen 35 C6
Wickford 31 D7
Wicklow 23 F7
Widnau 87 B6
Widnes 26 E4
Więcbork 101 D8
Wiefelstede 33 B7
Wiehl 37 C6
Wieleń 101 E7
Wieliczka 159 F6
Wieluń 158 D4
Wien 93 F7
Wiener Neustadt 93 F7
Wierden 33 D5
Wieringerwerf 32 C3
Wiesbaden 37 D7
Wiesloch 37 F8
Wiesmoor 33 B6
Wigan 26 D4
Wigston 27 F6
Wijchen 32 E4
Wijk bij Duurstede 32 E3
Wil 43 F8
Wildeshausen 33 C7
Wilhelmshaven 33 A7
Wilkau-Haßlau 95 E8
Willebroek 35 B6
Willich 33 F5
Wilmslow 27 E5
Wilnsdorf 37 C7
Wimborne Minster 29 D7
Wimereux 31 F8
Winchester 29 D8
Windsor 31 D5
Wingene 35 B5
Winnenden 43 B8
Winschoten 33 B5
Winsen (Aller) 99 E5
Winsen (Luhe) 99 D5
Winsford 26 E4
Winterberg 37 B7
Winterswijk 33 E5
Winterthur 43 F7
Wintzenheim 43 D5
Wipperfürth 37 B6
Wisbech 27 F8
Wishaw 21 D5
Wisła 163 B5
Wismar 99 C7
Wissembourg 43 B6
Witham 31 C7
Witkowo *PL* 154 F3
Witney 29 B8
Witnica *PL* 101 F5
Witten 33 F6
Wittenbach 43 F8
Wittenberge 99 E7
Wittenheim 43 E5
Wittingen 99 E6
Wittlich 37 E5
Wittmund 33 A6
Wittstock 99 D8
Witzenhausen 94 C4
Władysławowo 154 A4
Włocławek 154 F4
Włodawa 157 G6
Włoszczowa 159 E6
Wodzisław Śląski 158 F4
Woerden 32 E2
Wohlen *CH* 43 F7
Wohlen *CH* 47 A8
Woippy 42 B4
Wojkowice 159 F5
Woking 31 E5
Wokingham 31 D5
Wolbrom 159 F6
Wołczyn 158 D3
Wolfen 95 C8
Wolfenbüttel 95 B5
Wolfhagen 33 F8
Wolfratshausen 88 A3
Wolfsberg 89 C8
Wolfsburg 95 A6
Wolgast 100 B3
Wolin 100 C4
Wolkersdorf 93 E8
Wolmirstedt 95 A7
Wołomin 155 F7
Wołów 97 C8
Wolsztyn 97 B7
Wolvega 32 C4
Wolverhampton 27 F5
Wombwell 27 D6
Wommelgem 35 B7
Woodbridge 31 C8
Wootton Bassett 29 C7
Worb 47 B8
Worcester 29 A7
Wörgl 88 B4
Workington 21 F6
Worksop 27 E6
Wormerveer 32 D2
Worms 37 E7
Wörth am Rhein 43 B7
Worthing 31 F5
Wrecsam 26 E4
Wrexham 26 E4
Wrocław 97 D8
Wronki *PL* 101 E7
Września 101 F8

Wschowa 97 B7
Wünnenberg 33 F8
Wunsiedel 91 B7
Wunstorf 94 A4
Wuppertal 33 F6
Würselen 36 C4
Würzburg 90 B4
Wurzen 95 C8
Wuustwezel 32 F2
Wymondham 31 B7
Wyrzysk 101 D8
Wysokie Mazowieckie 157 E4
Wyszków 155 F8

X

Xanten 33 F5
Xanthi 187 B6
Xàtiva 72 A3
Xinzo de Limia 54 E3
Xirivella 64 F3

Y

Yakoruda 181 F6
Yambol 183 E5
Yampil' 170 A1
Yatağan 197 A7
Yavoriv *UA* 160 D5
Ybbs an der Donau 93 F5
Y Drenewydd 26 F3
Yeadon 27 C5
Yecla 72 B2
Yenihisar 193 E8
Yeovil 29 D6
Y Fenni 29 B6
Ylivieska 139 B6
Ylöjärvi 143 B5
York 27 C6
Youghal 25 E5
Yssingeaux 46 F3
Ystad 103 E8
Yutz 36 F4
Yverdon 47 B7
Yvetot 34 F1
Yvoir 35 D7
Yzeure 46 B2

Z

Zaandam 32 D2
Žabalj 174 C4
Ząbki 157 F2
Ząbkowice Śląskie 97 E8
Zábřeh 93 B8
Zabrze 158 F4
Zadar 172 D2
Zafferana Etnea 75 D6
Zafra 67 C6
Żagań 97 C6
Zagon 169 F6
Zagorje ob Savi 89 D8
Zagreb 164 E4
Zaječar 175 F7
Zakopane 163 C7
Zakynthos 190 D2
Zalău 167 C8
Zalaegerszeg 165 C5
Zalaszentgrót 165 C6
Zaltbommel 32 E3
Zambrów 156 D4
Zamora 55 F7
Zamość *PL* 160 B5
Zandhoven 35 B7
Zandvoort 32 D2
Zăneşti 169 D6
Zapolyarnyy 130 E4
Zaprešić 164 E4
Zaragoza 57 F8
Zarasai 151 E4
Zarautz 48 D1
Zărneşti *RO* 176 B4
Zărneşti *RO* 177 C7
Žarnovica 163 E5
Żarów 97 D7
Żary 97 C5
Žatec 92 A3
Zaventem 35 C7
Zavidovići 173 C7
Zawadzkie 158 E4
Zawiercie 159 E5
Zbąszyn 97 A6
Zbąszynek 97 A6
Žďar nad Sázavou 93 C7
Zduńska Wola 159 C5
Zdzieszowice 158 F3
Zedelgem 35 B5
Zehdenick 100 E3
Zeist 32 E3
Zeitz 95 D8
Zele 35 B6
Zelenogorsk 145 E6
Zelenogradsk 152 D1
Zelhem 32 E4
Zella-Mehlis 95 E5
Zell am See 89 B5
Zelów 159 C5
Zelzate 35 B6
Zemeş 169 E6
Zemst 35 C6
Zemun 174 D4
Zenica 173 D7

Zerbst 95 B7
Zero Branco 88 F4
Zetea 168 E4
Zetel 33 B7
Zeulenroda 95 E7
Zeven 33 B8
Zevenaar 32 E4
Zevenbergen 32 F2
Zevio 82 A2
Zgierz 159 B5
Zgorzelec 97 D5
Zhabinka 157 F6
Zhovkva 160 D6
Zhydachiv 161 E6
Žiar nad Hronom 163 E5
Ziębice 97 E8
Zielona Góra *PL* 97 B6
Zielonka 155 F7
Zierikzee 32 F1
Žilina 163 C5
Zimnicea 176 F4
Zirc 165 B7
Zirndorf 91 C6
Zistersdorf 93 E8
Zittau 97 D5
Zlaté Moravce 162 E4
Zlatna 167 F8
Zlatograd 187 B6
Zlín 162 C3
Złocieniec 101 D6
Złotoryja 97 D7
Złotów 101 D8
Żmigród 97 C8
Žnin 154 E3
Znojmo 93 D7
Zoersel 32 F2
Zoetermeer 32 E2
Zofingen 43 F6
Zogno 85 B6
Zografos 191 D7
Zola Predosa 82 C2
Zolder 35 B8
Zollikofen 47 A8
Zollikon 43 F7
Zomergem 35 B5
Zonhoven 35 C8
Zonnebeke 34 C4
Zorleni 169 E8
Zornotza 56 B4
Żory 158 F4
Zossen 96 A3
Zottegem 35 C6
Zrenjanin 174 C4
Zschopau 96 E3
Zubieta *E* 48 D1
Zuchwil 43 F6
Zug 43 F7
Zuidhorn 32 B4
Zuidlaren 33 B5
Zuidwolde 33 C5
Zülpich 37 C5
Zulte 35 C5
Zumarraga 48 E1
Zundert 32 F2
Županja 173 B8
Zürich 43 F7
Żuromin 155 E6
Zutendaal 35 C8
Zutphen 32 D4
Zvolen 163 E5
Zvorište 169 B6
Zvornik 173 C8
Zweibrücken 37 F6
Zwettl 93 E6
Zwevegem 35 C5
Zwickau 95 E8
Zwiesel 92 D3
Zwijndrecht *B* 35 B6
Zwijndrecht *NL* 32 E2
Zwoleń *PL* 157 H3
Zwolle 32 D4
Zwönitz 95 E8
Żychlin 159 A5
Żyrardów 157 F1
Żywiec 163 B6

Key to Map Pages

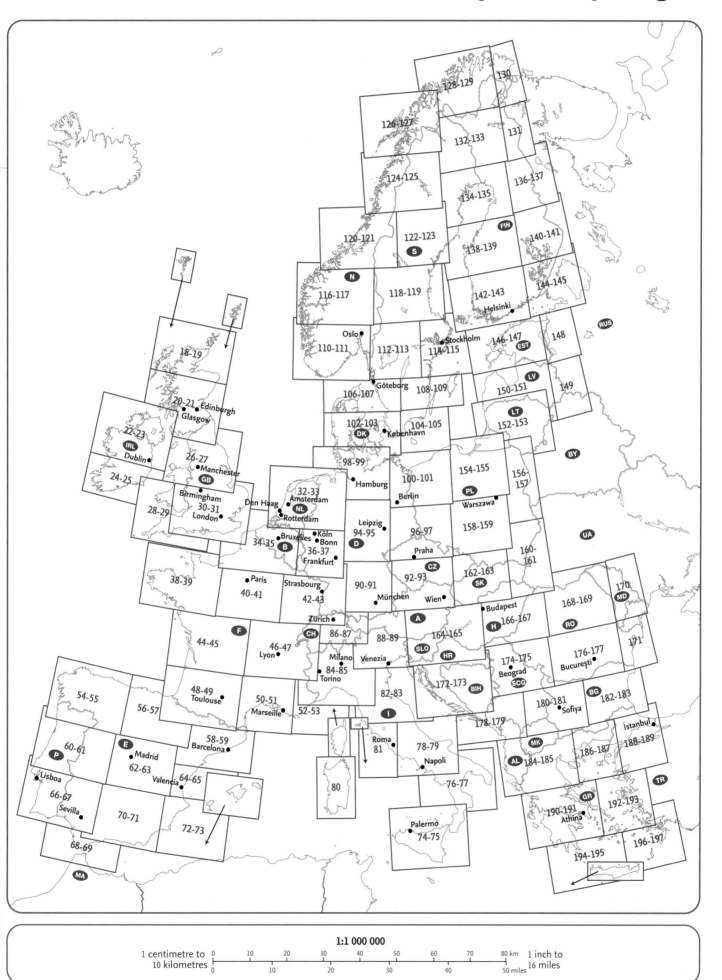

1:1 000 000

1 centimetre to
10 kilometres

0 10 20 30 40 50 60 70 80 km

0 10 20 30 40 50 miles

1 inch to
16 miles

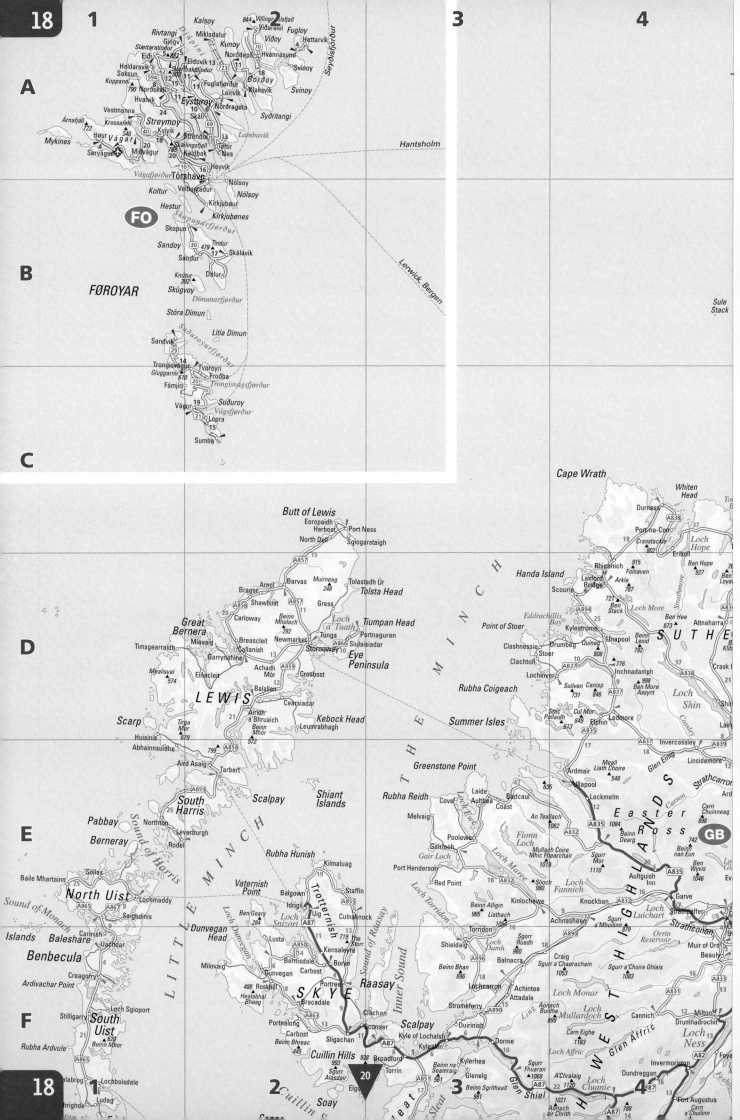

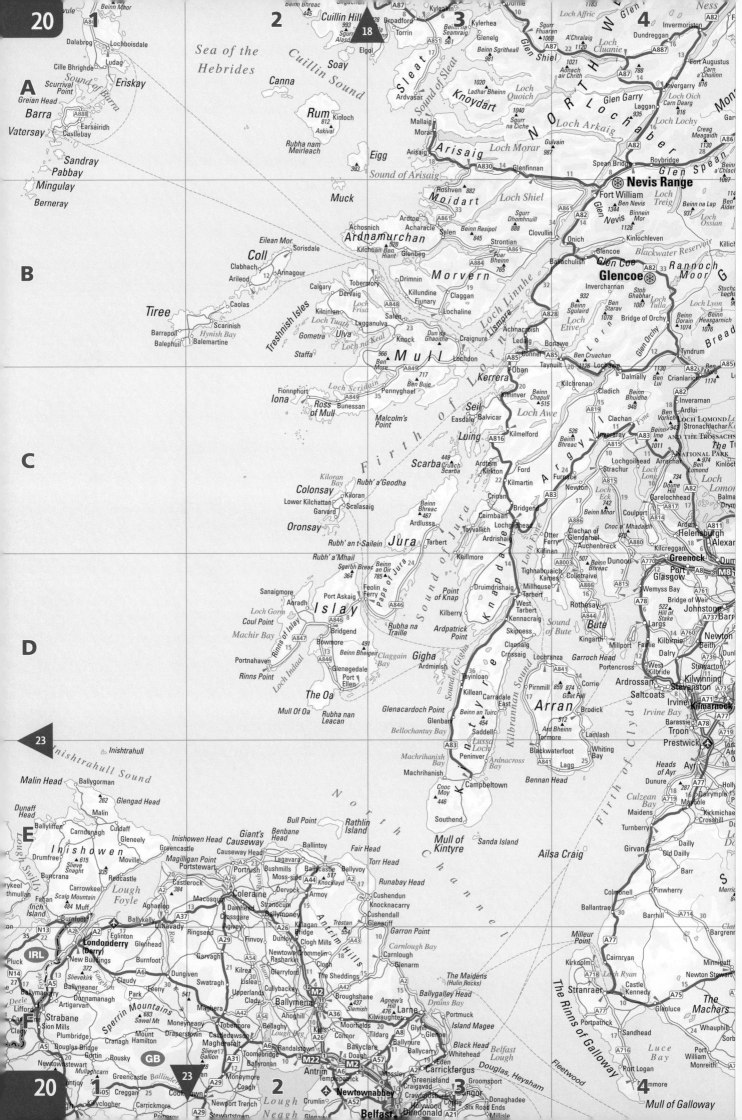

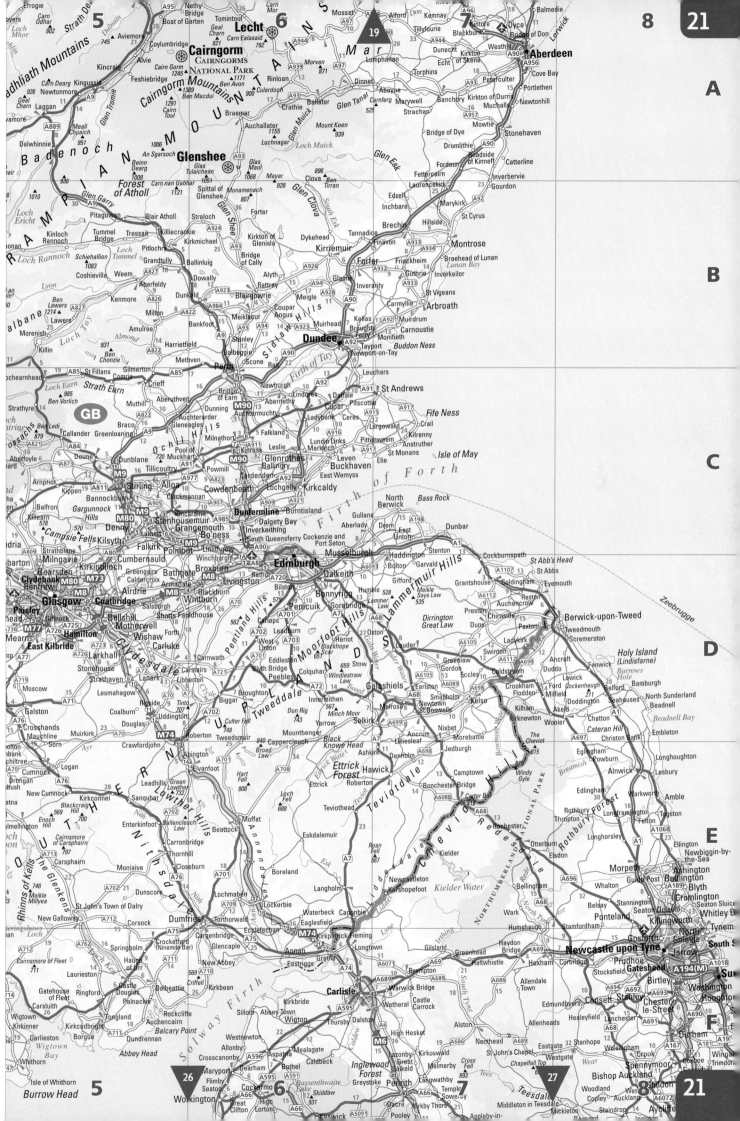

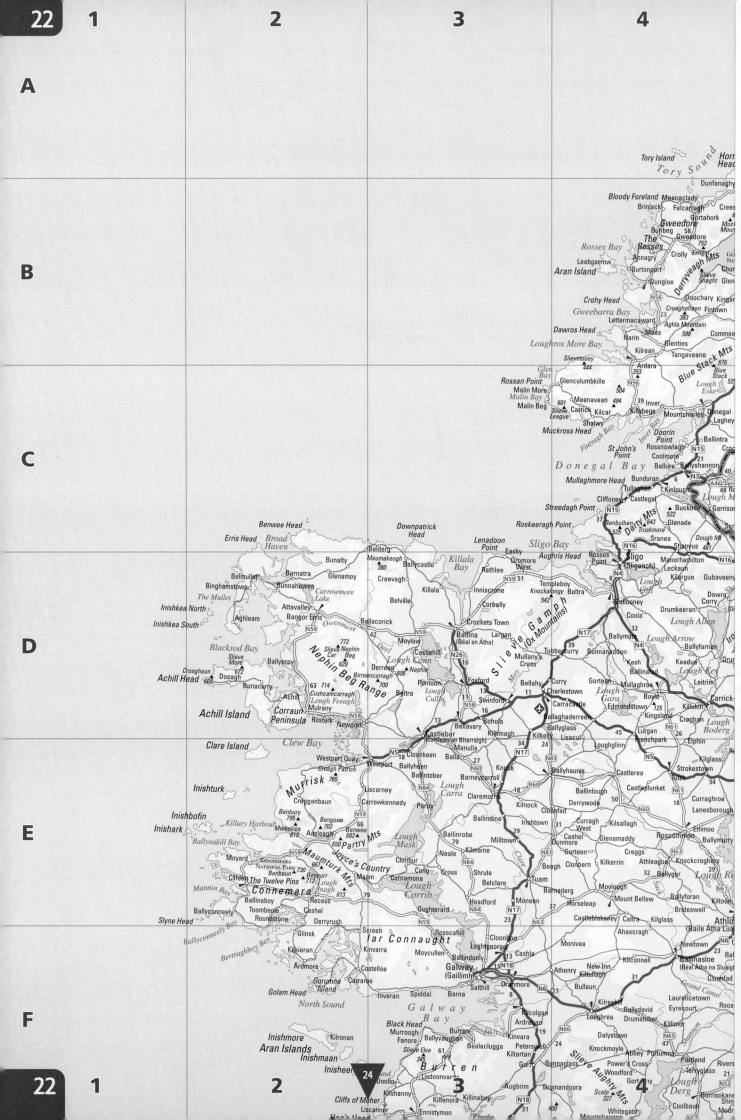

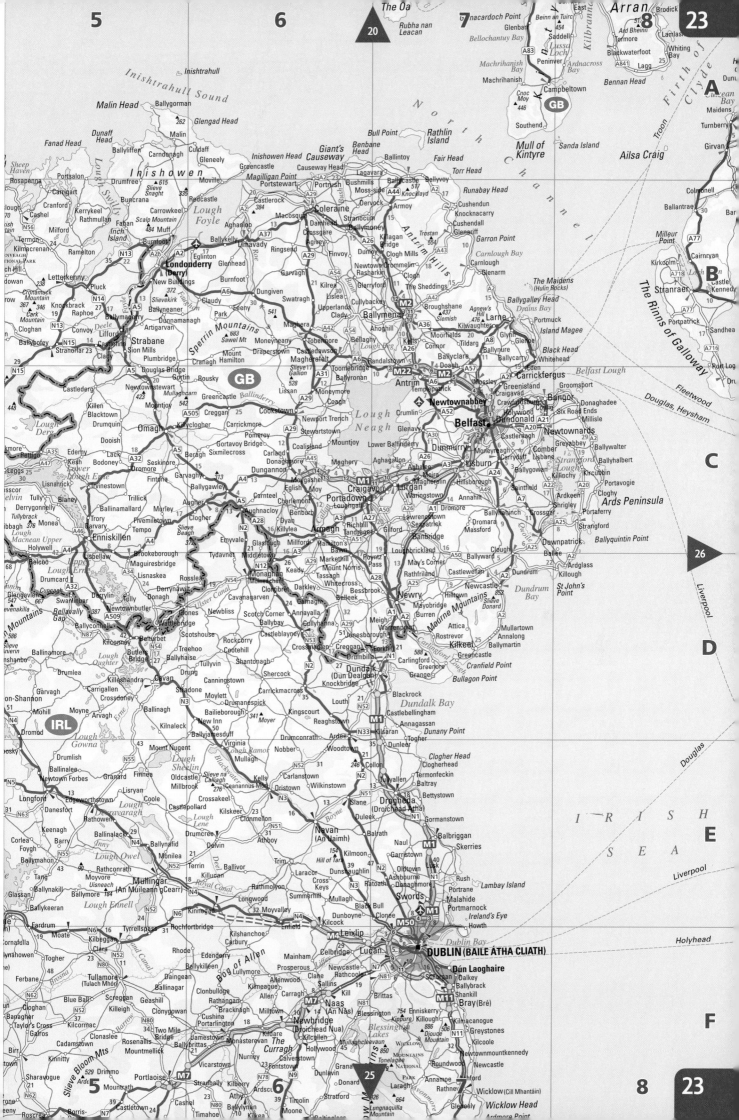

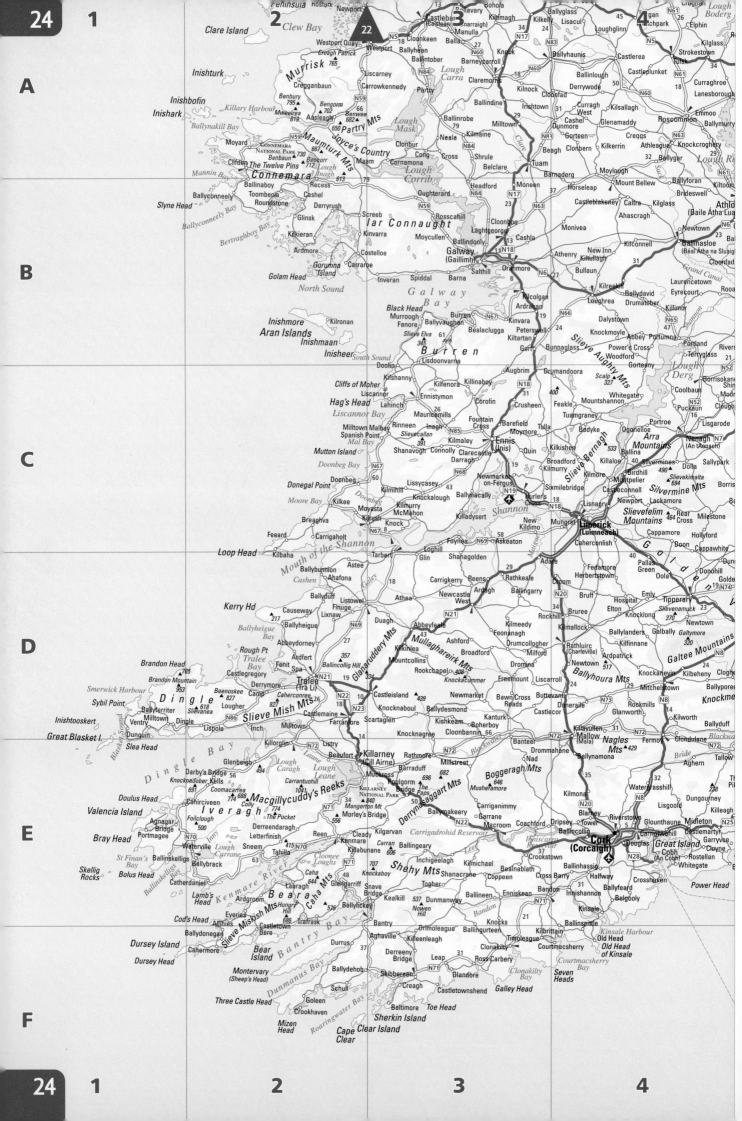

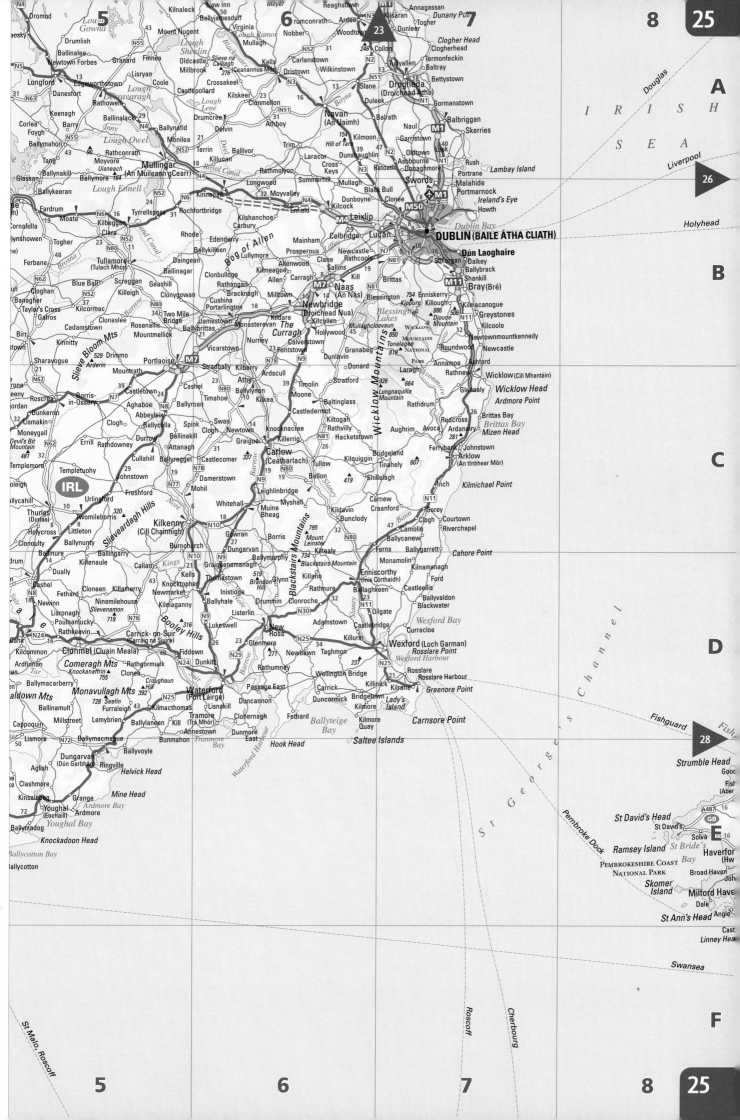

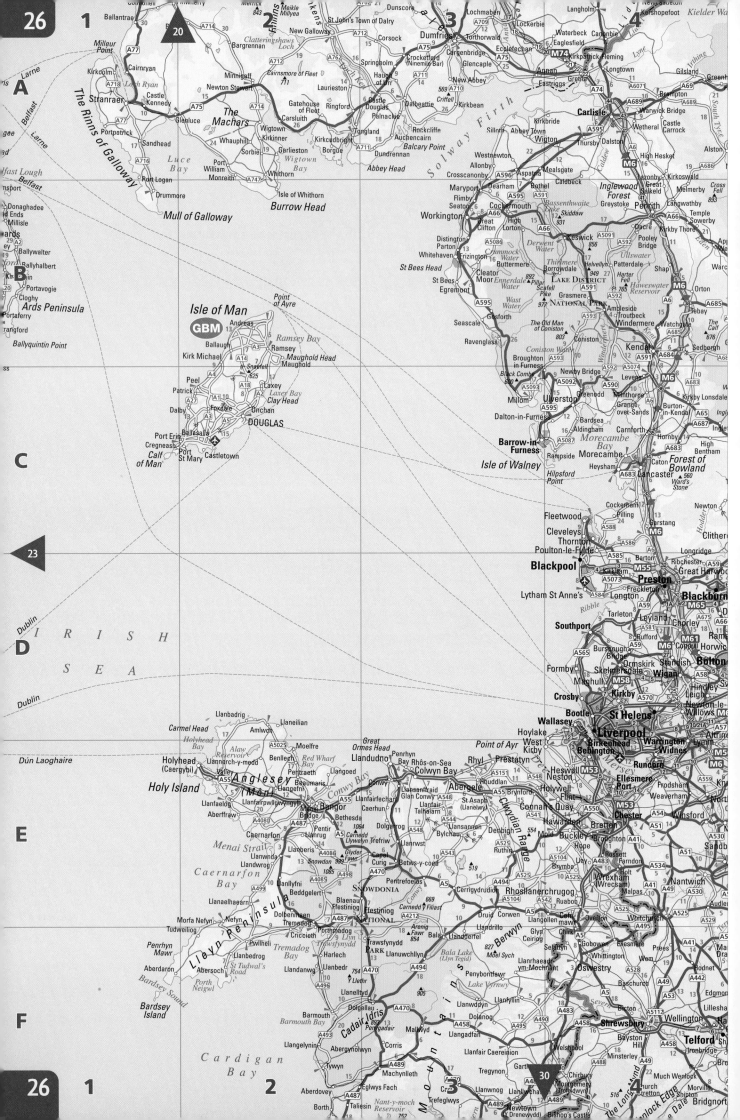

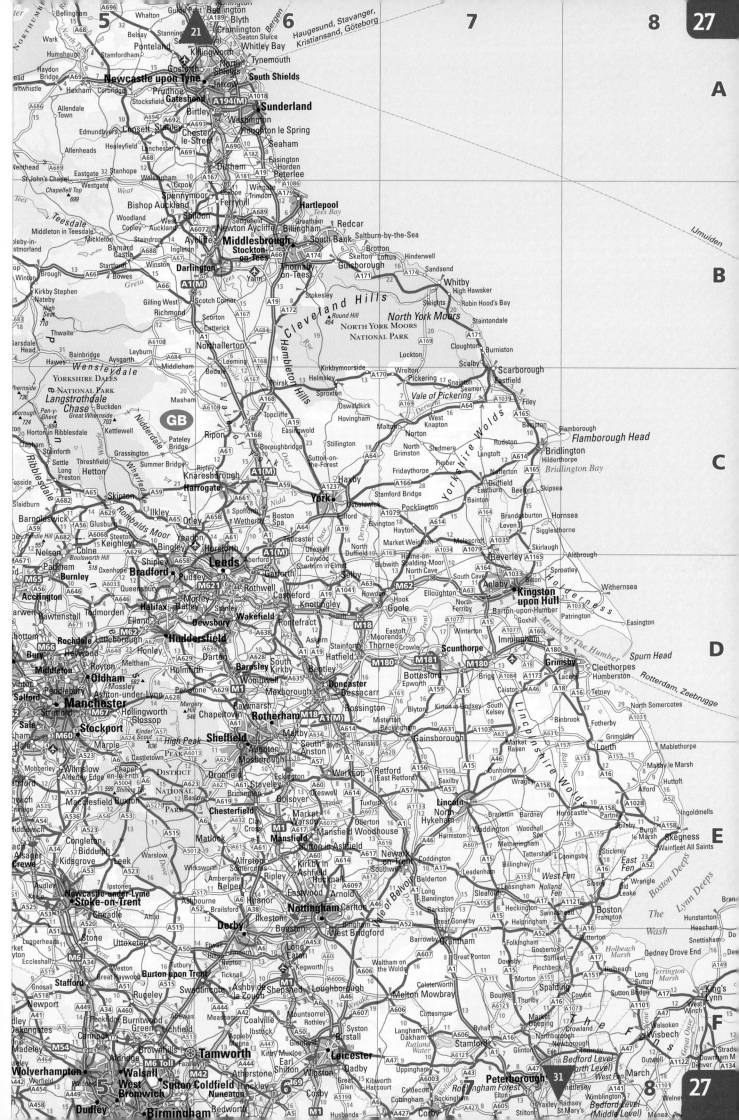

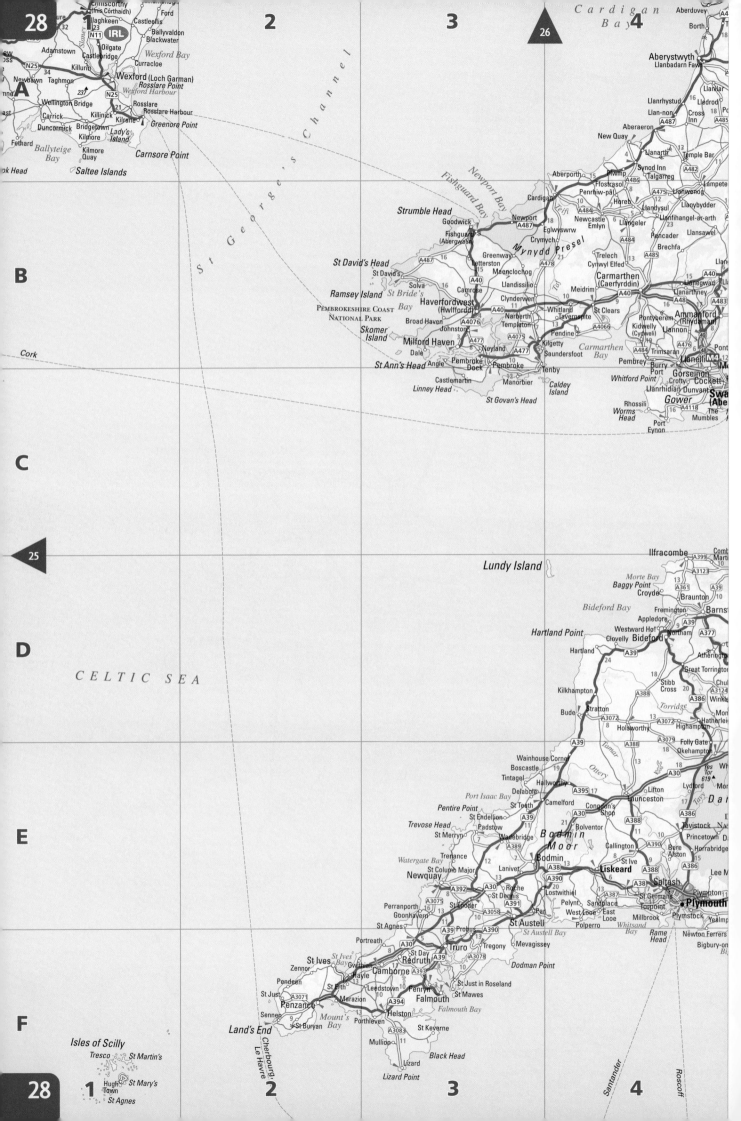

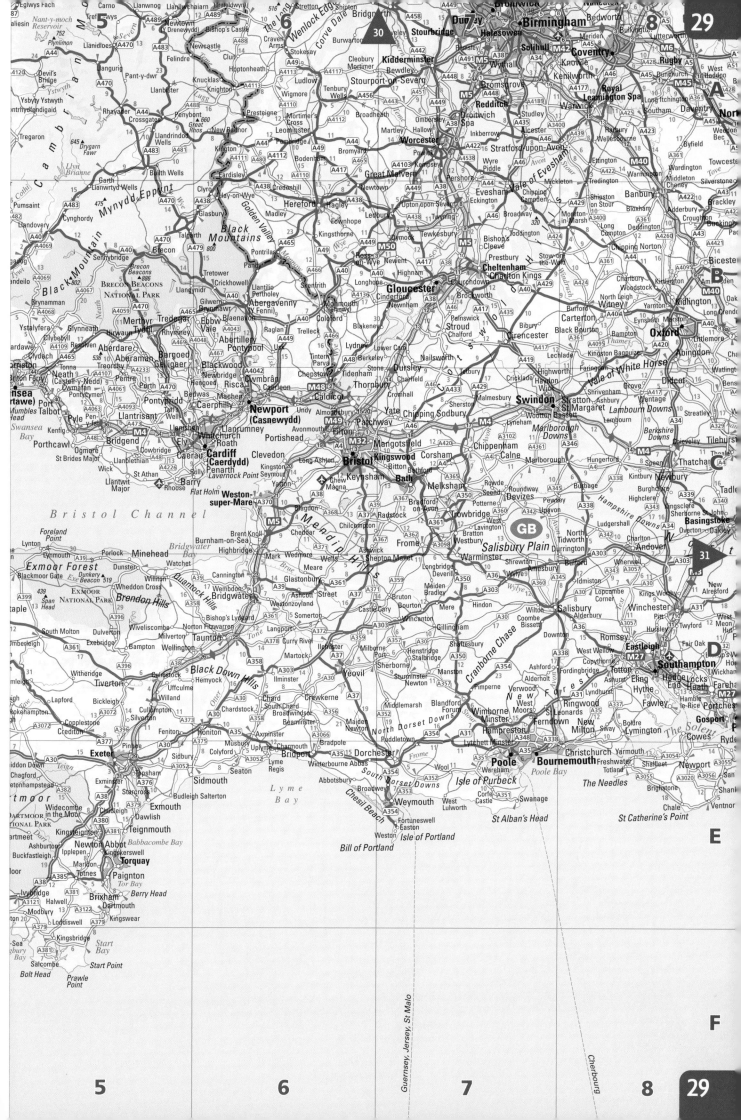

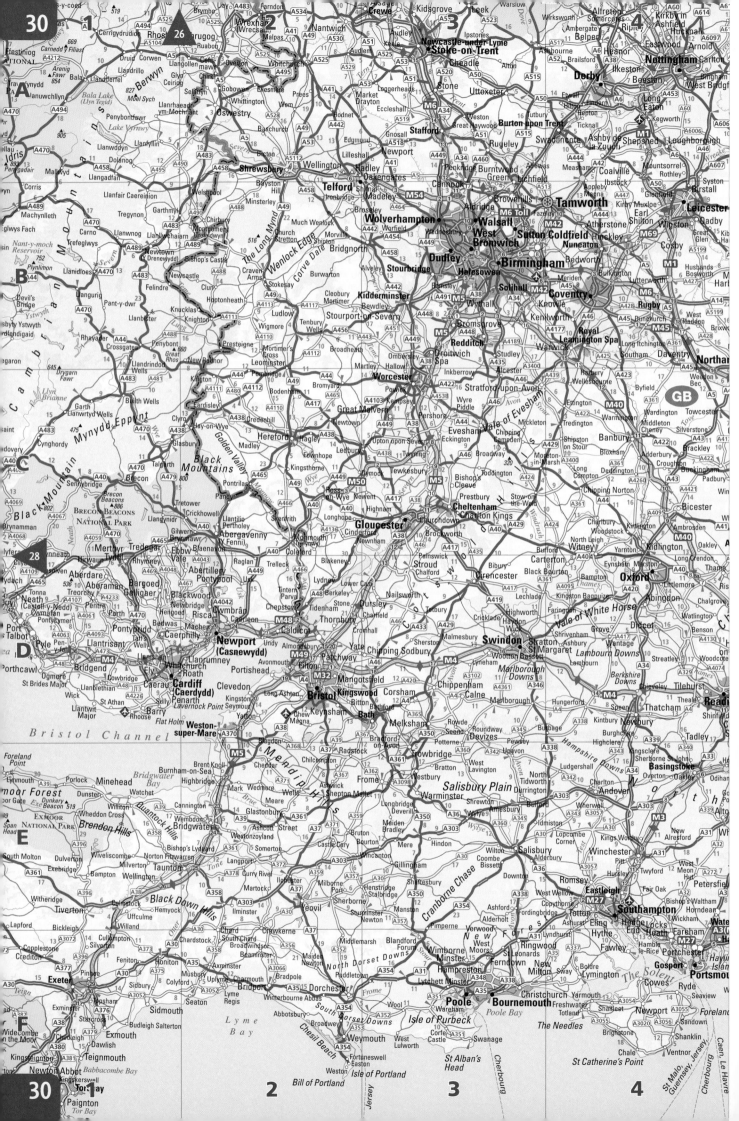

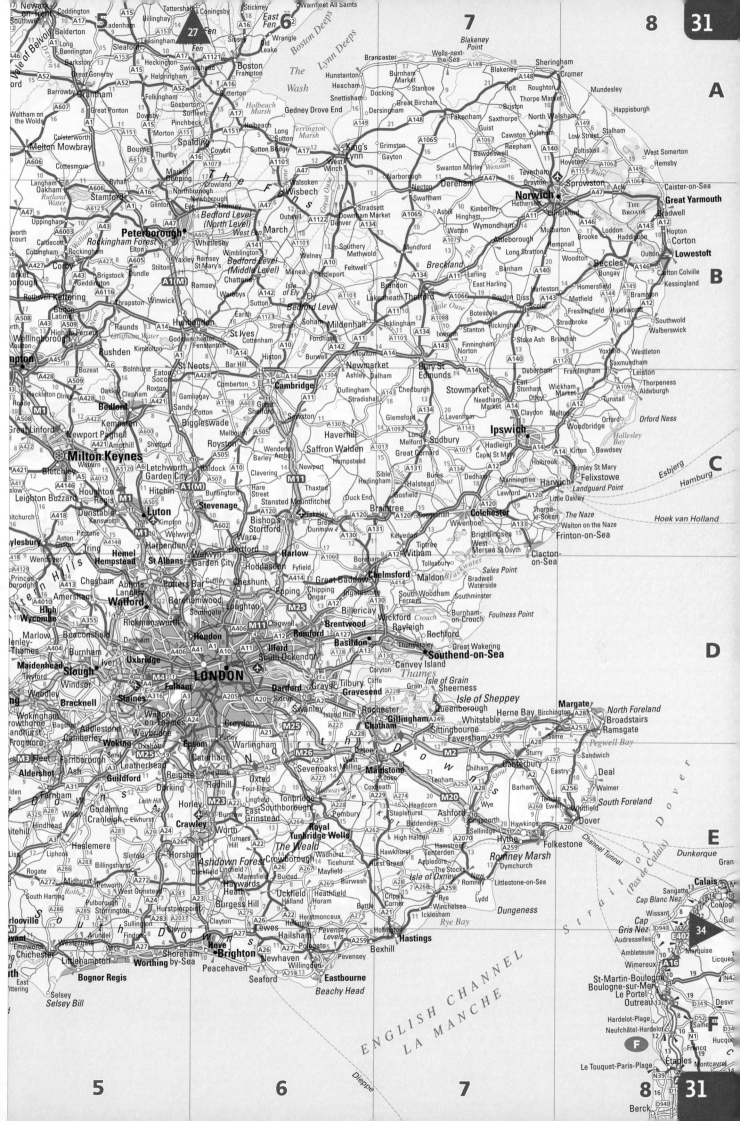

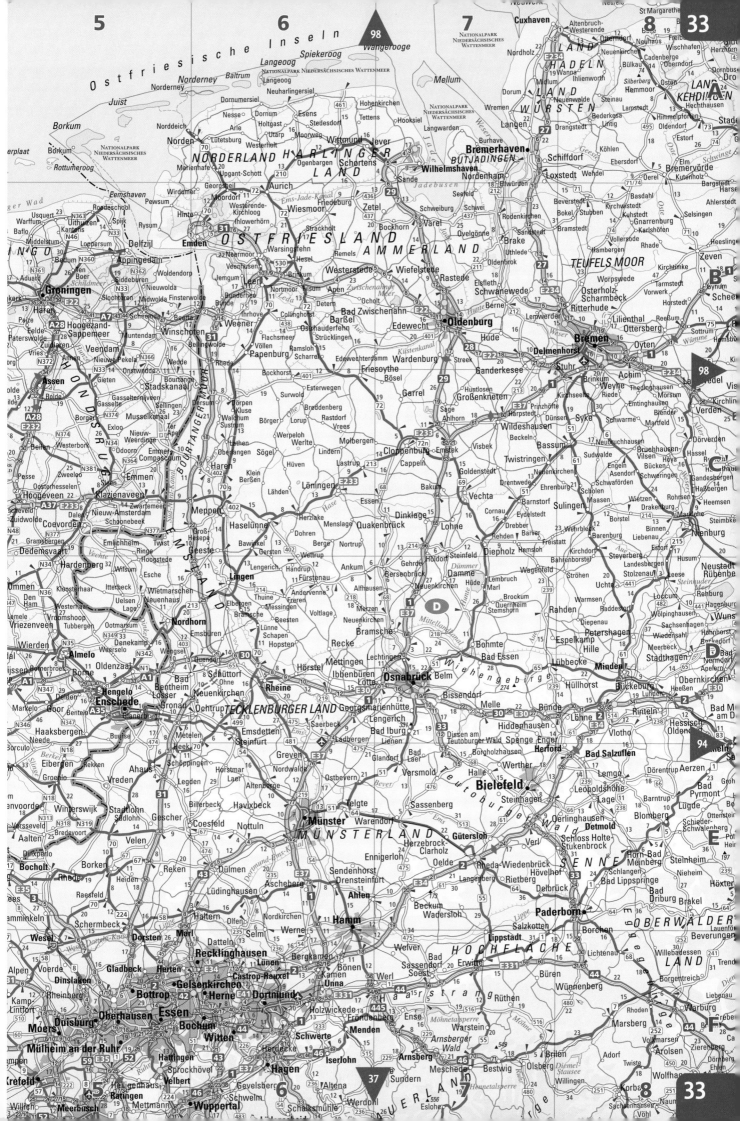

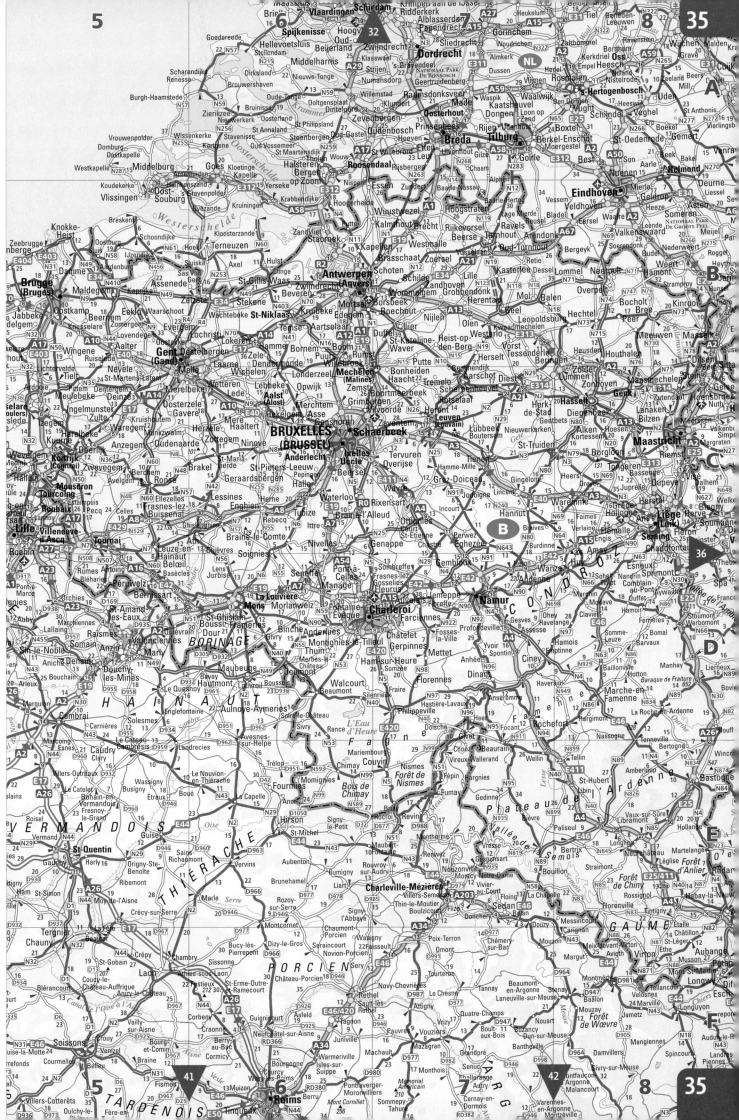

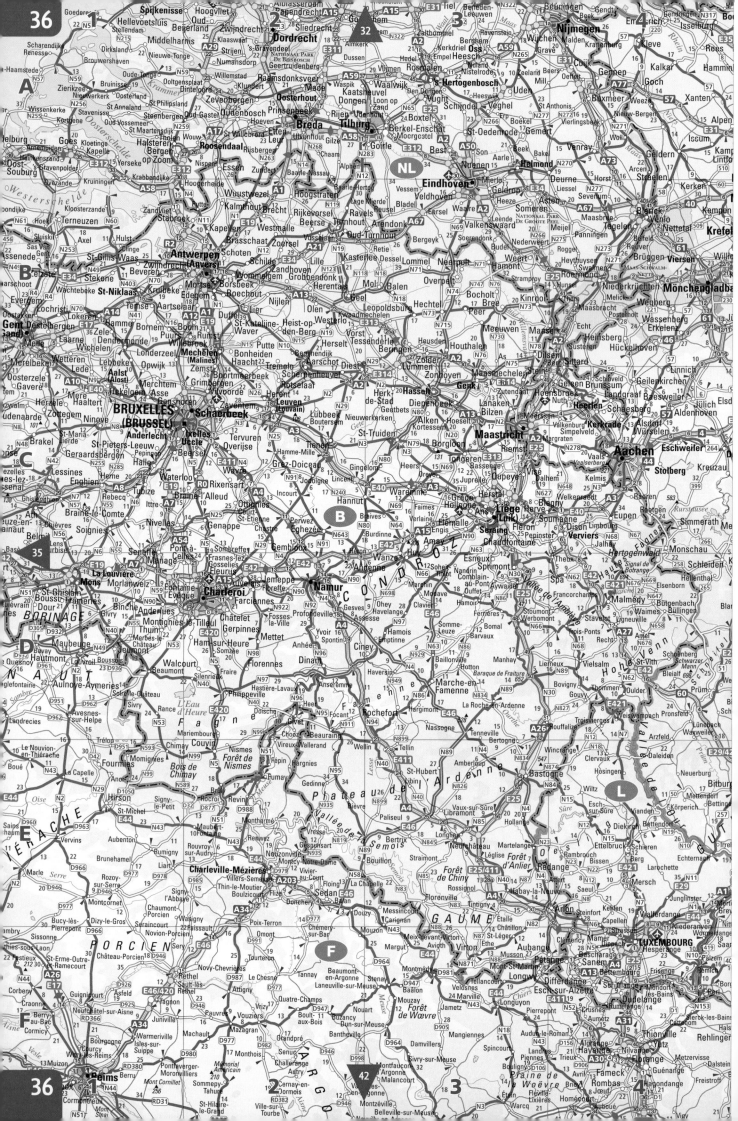

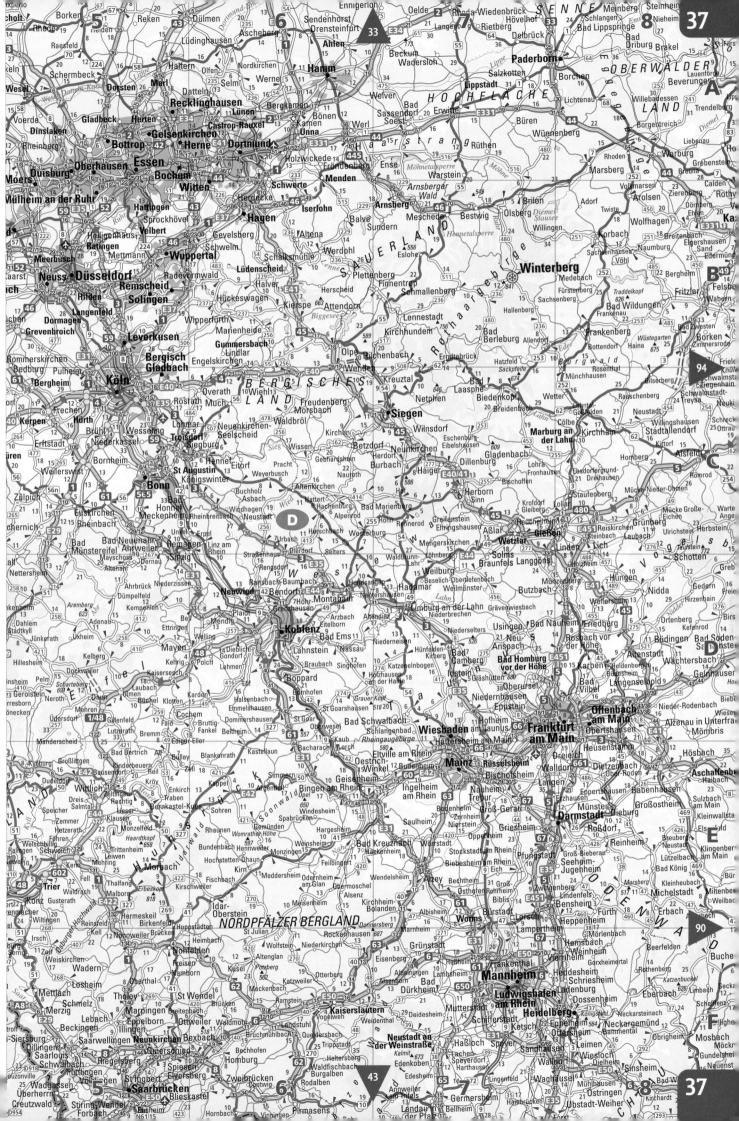

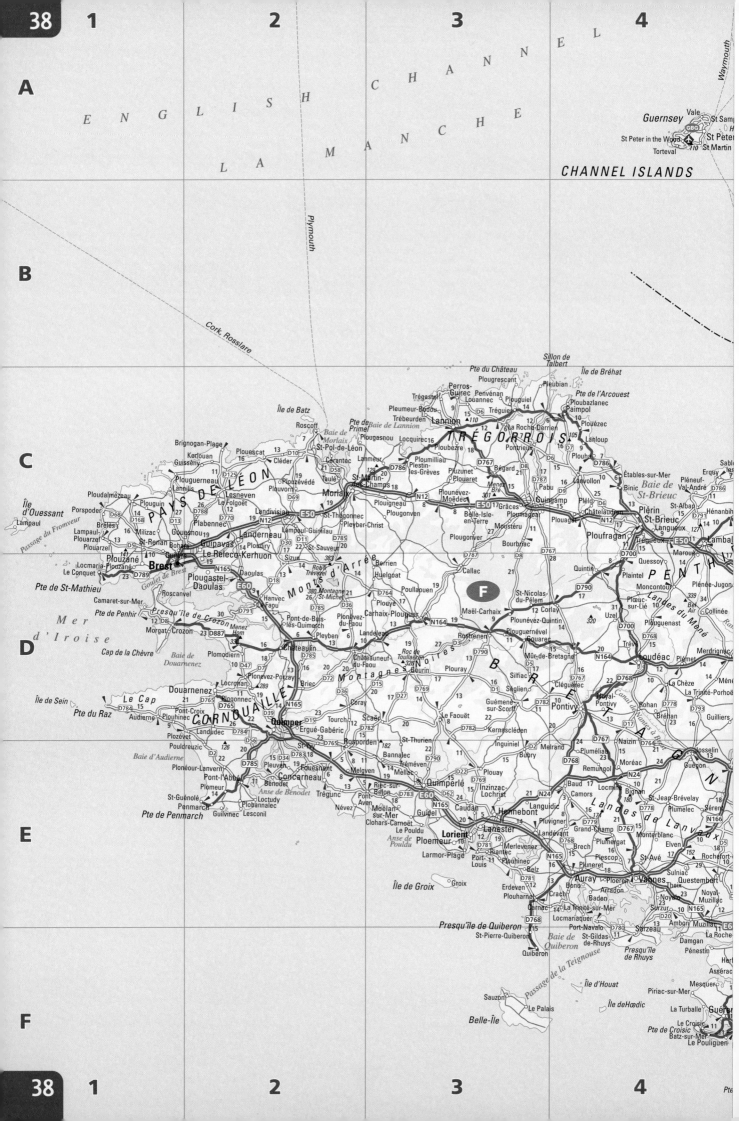

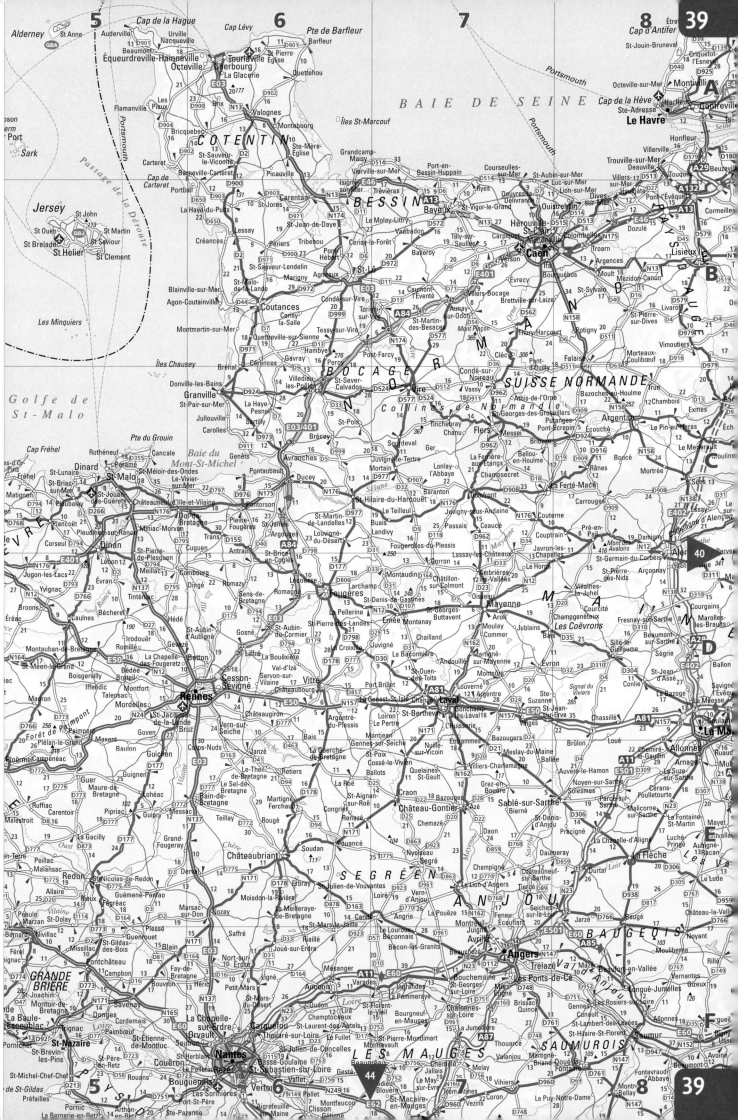

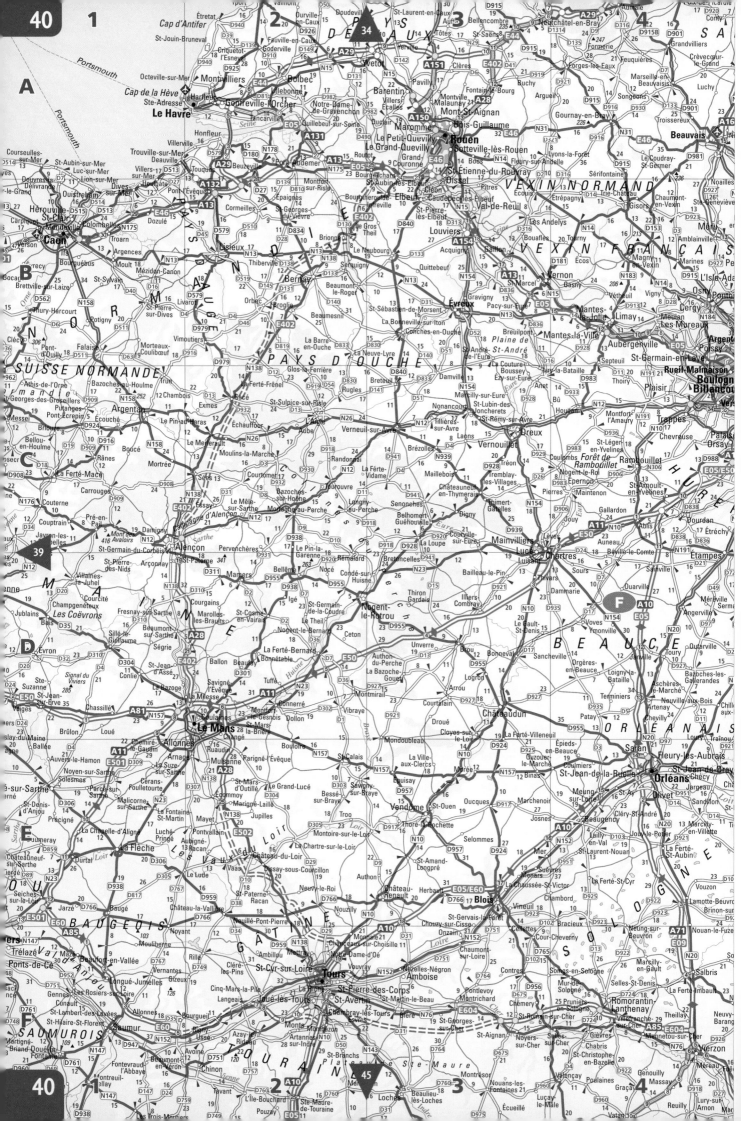

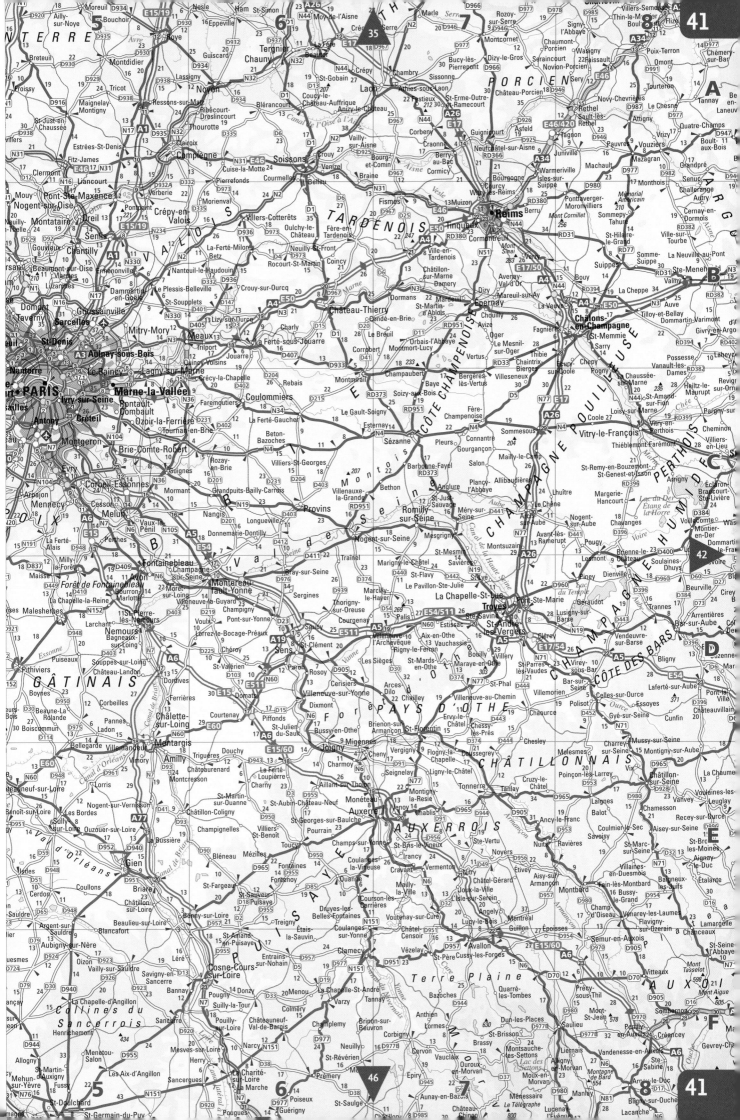

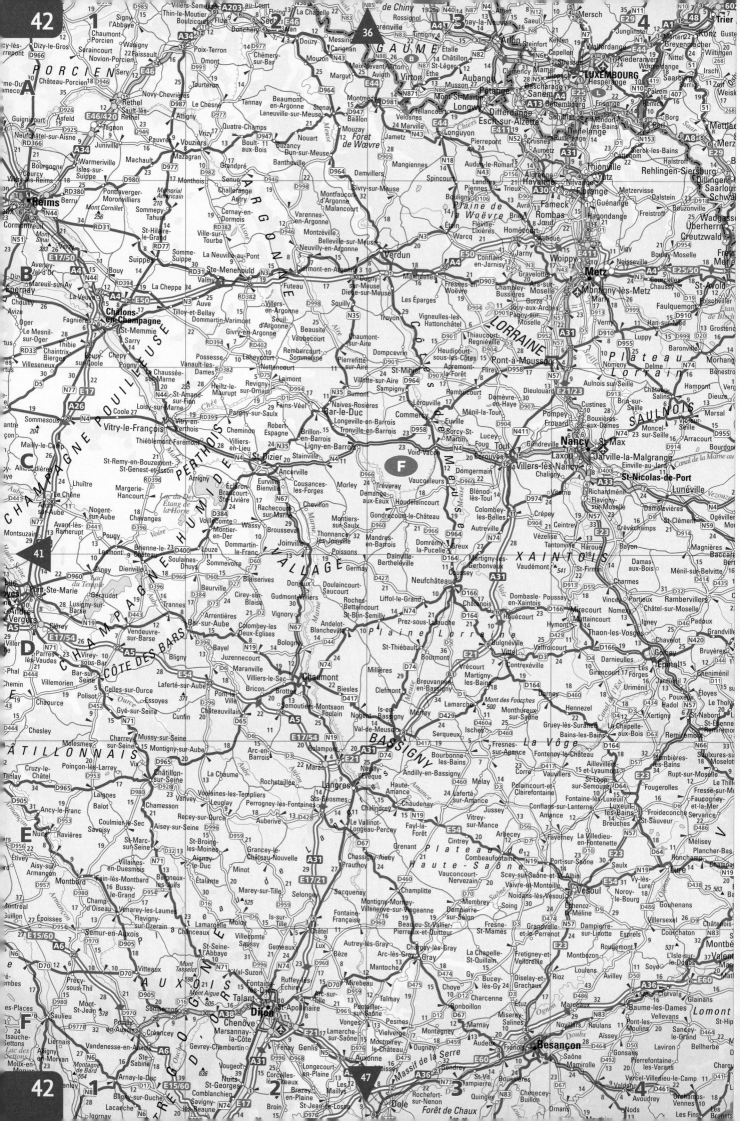

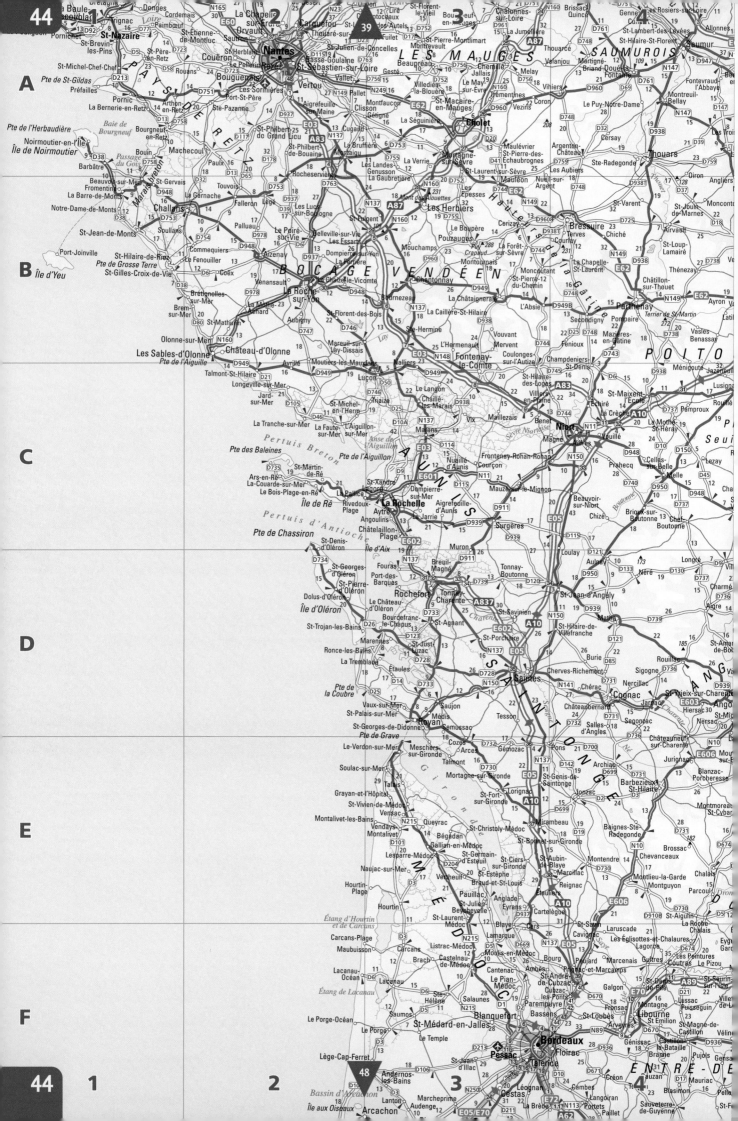

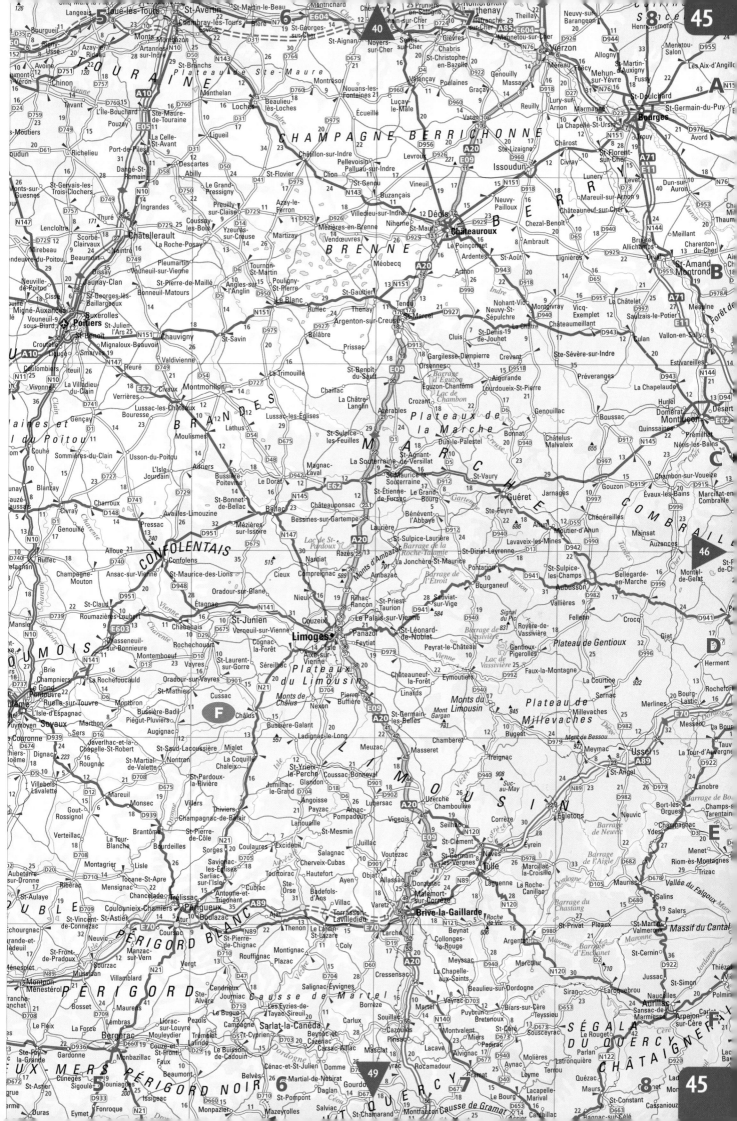

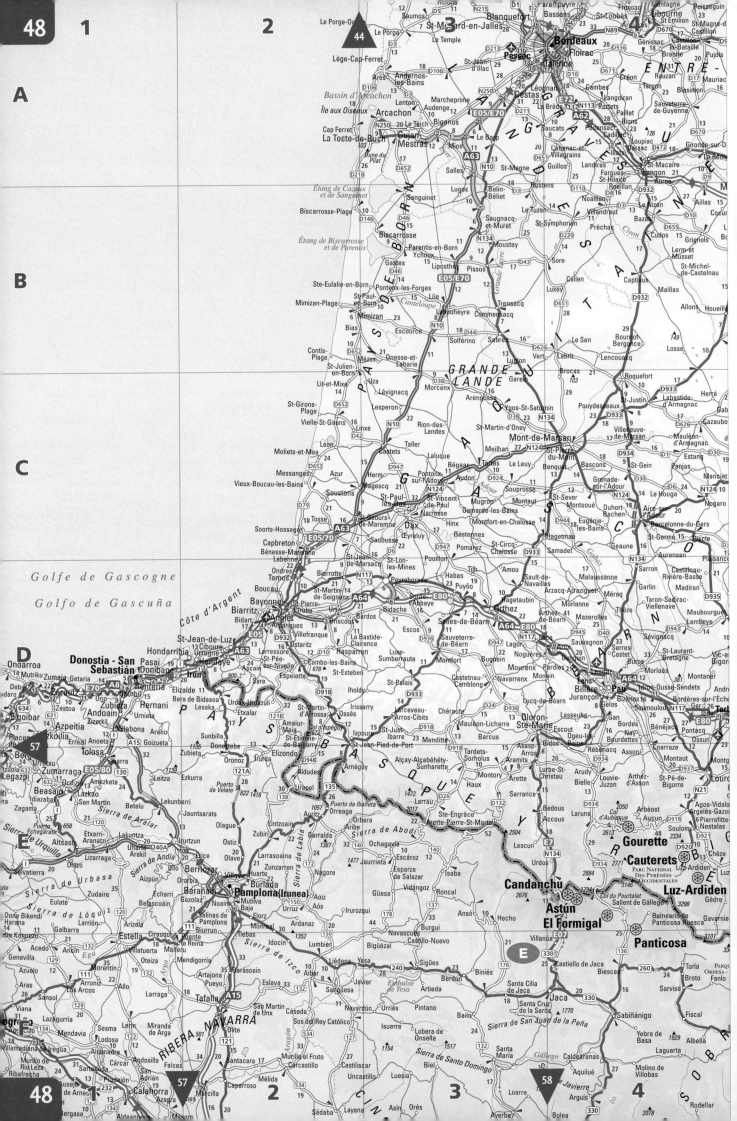

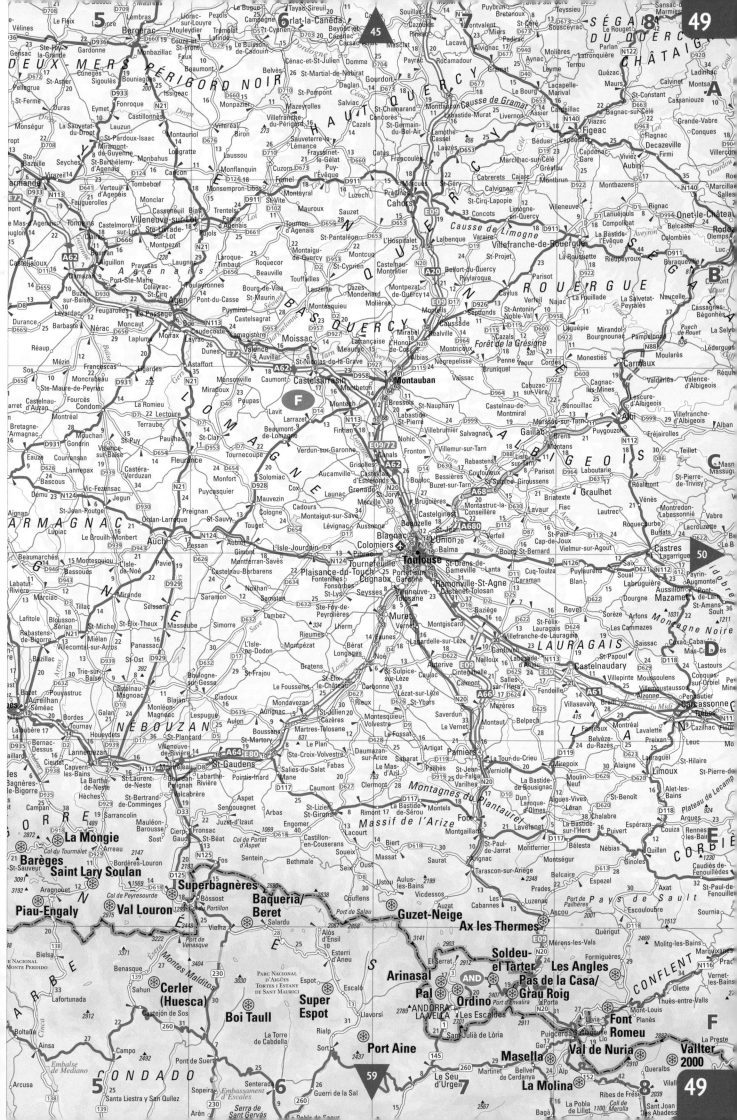

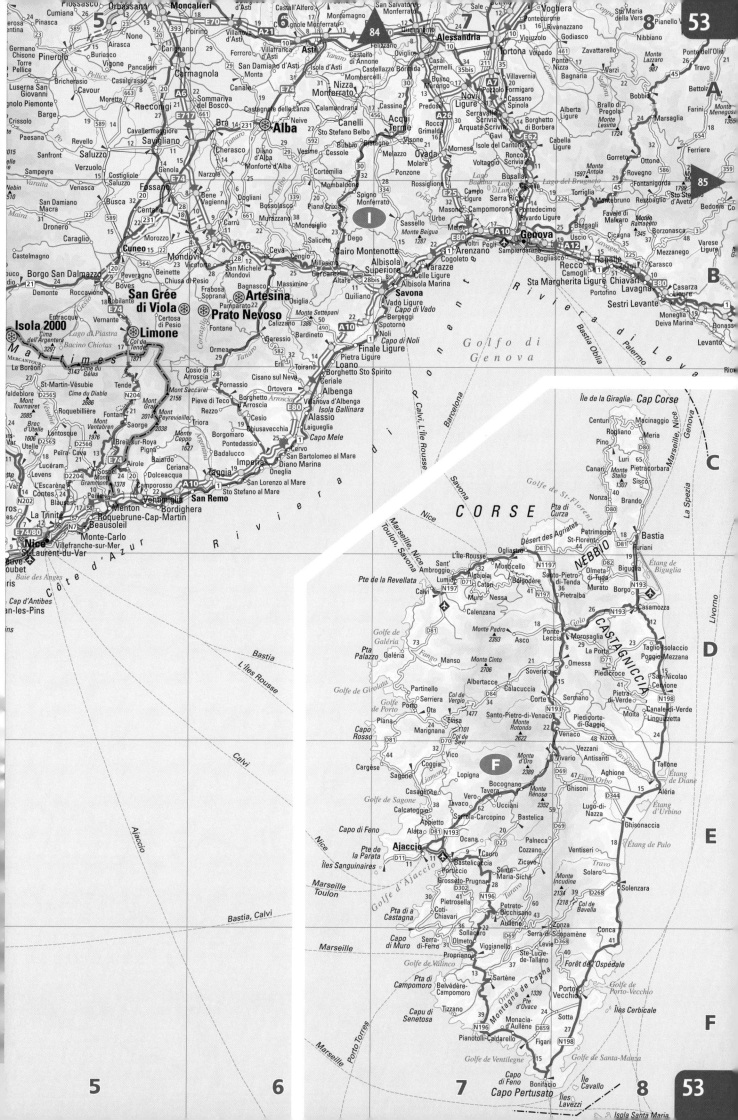

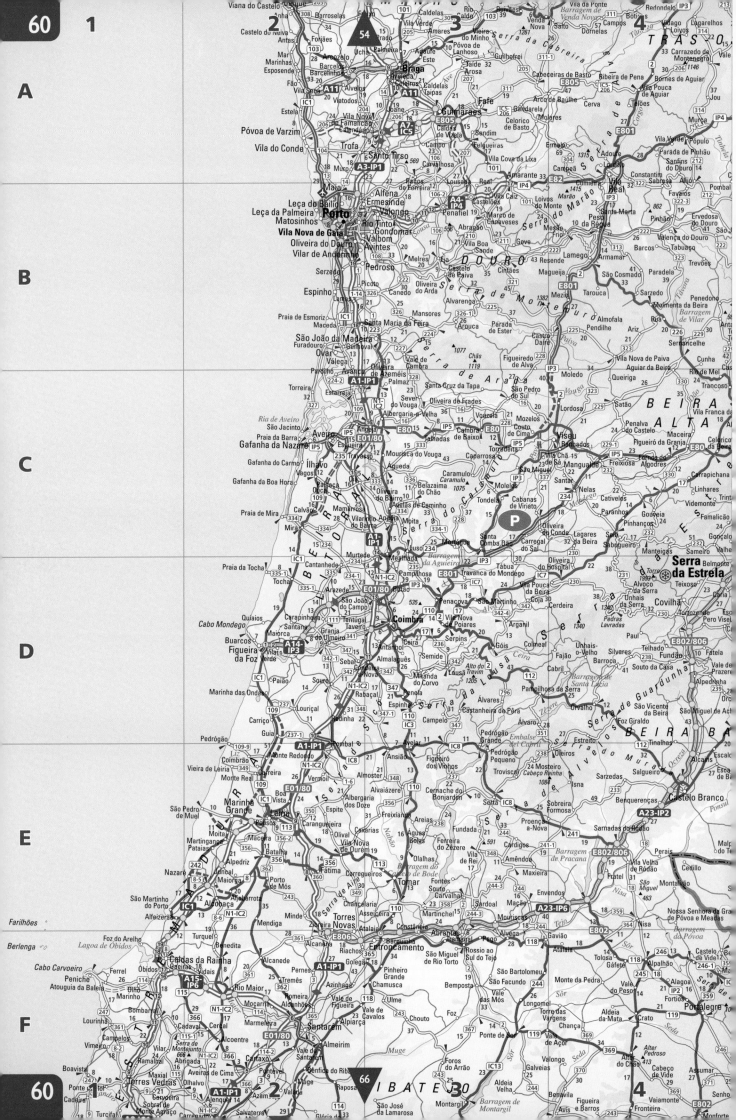

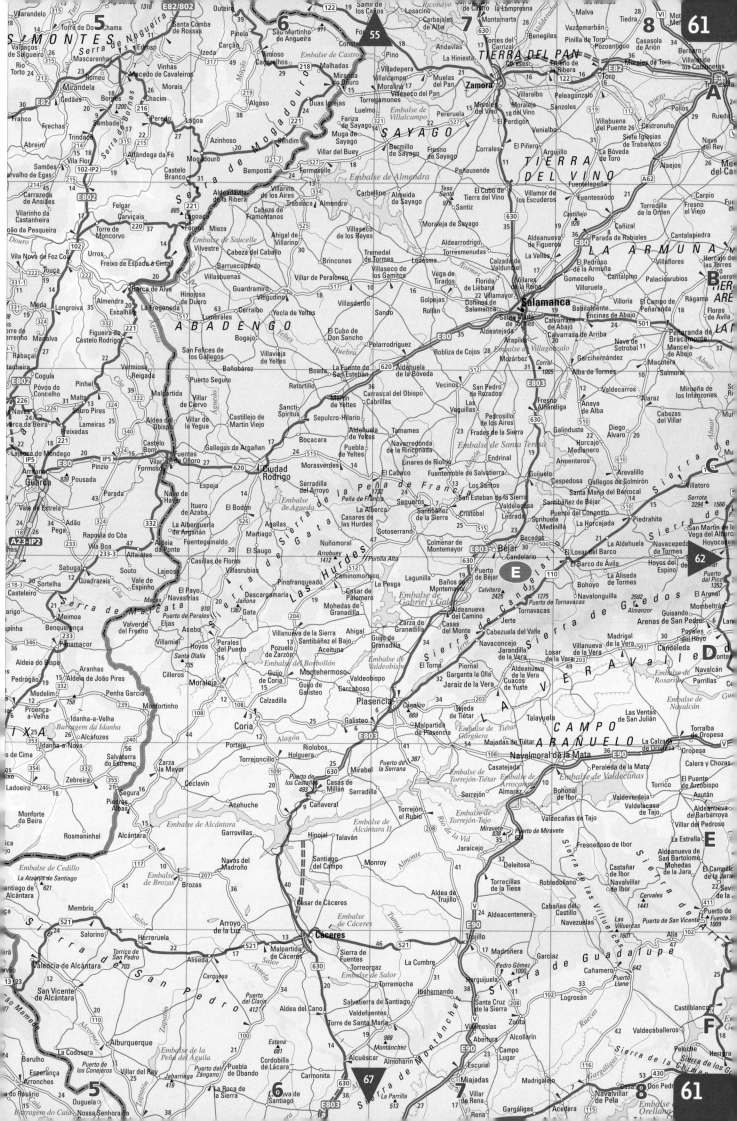

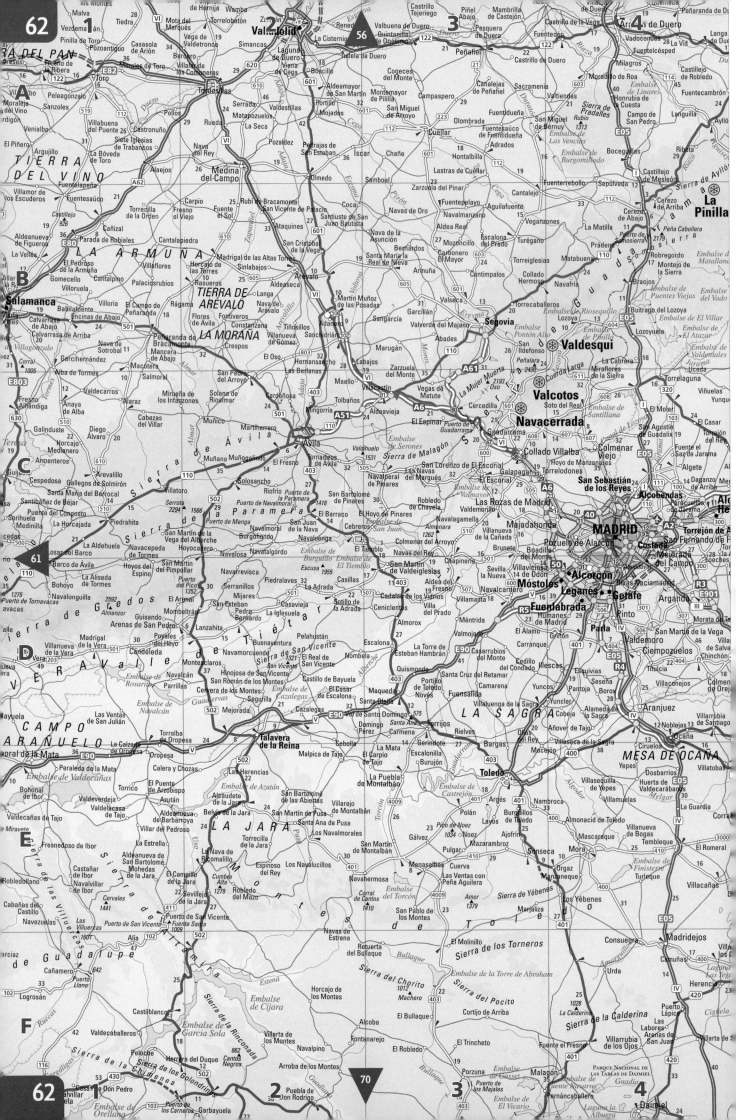

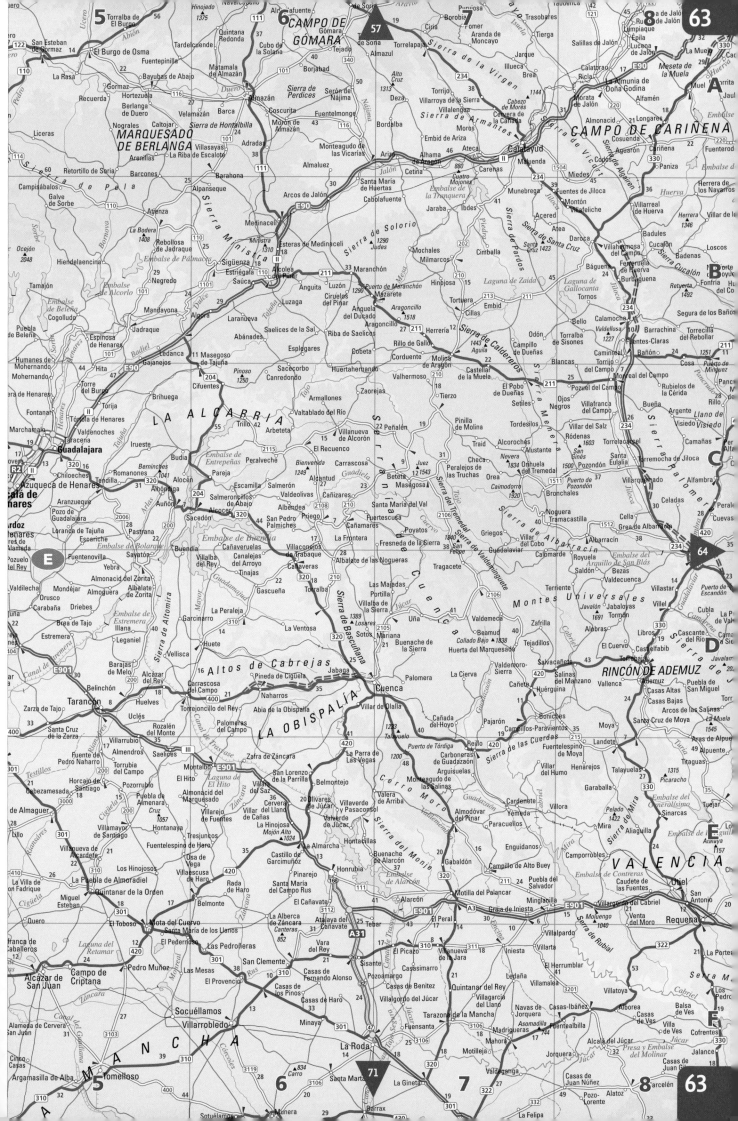

Zaragoza

CAMPO DE CARIÑENA

LLANOS DE CARDIEL

M O N E G R O S

DESIERTO DE CALANDA

Alcañiz

Calatayud

Daroca

E

Teruel

RINCÓN DE ADEMUZ

Montes Universales

Sierra de Javalambre

EL MAESTRAZGO

BAIX EBRE

Tortosa

Vinaròs

Benicarló

Peñíscola

Alcalá de Xivert

Oropesa

Benicasim

Castelló de la Plana

Almassora

Vila-real de los Infantes

Burriana

Nules

Moncófar

Sagunto

El Port

Puçol

Puig

Massamagrell

Meliana

Alboraya

Valencia

Torrent

Catarroja

Silla

Sueca

Cullera

VALENCIA

Requena

Utiel

Golfo de Valencia

Eivissa, Palma de Mallorca

Costa del

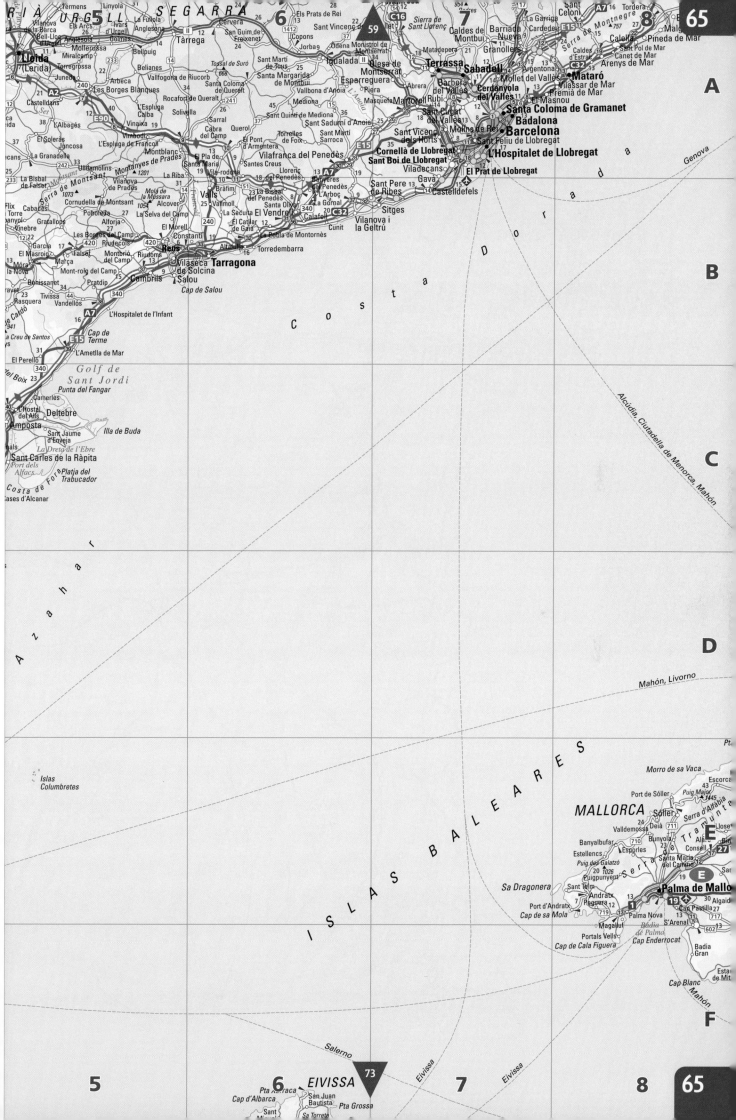

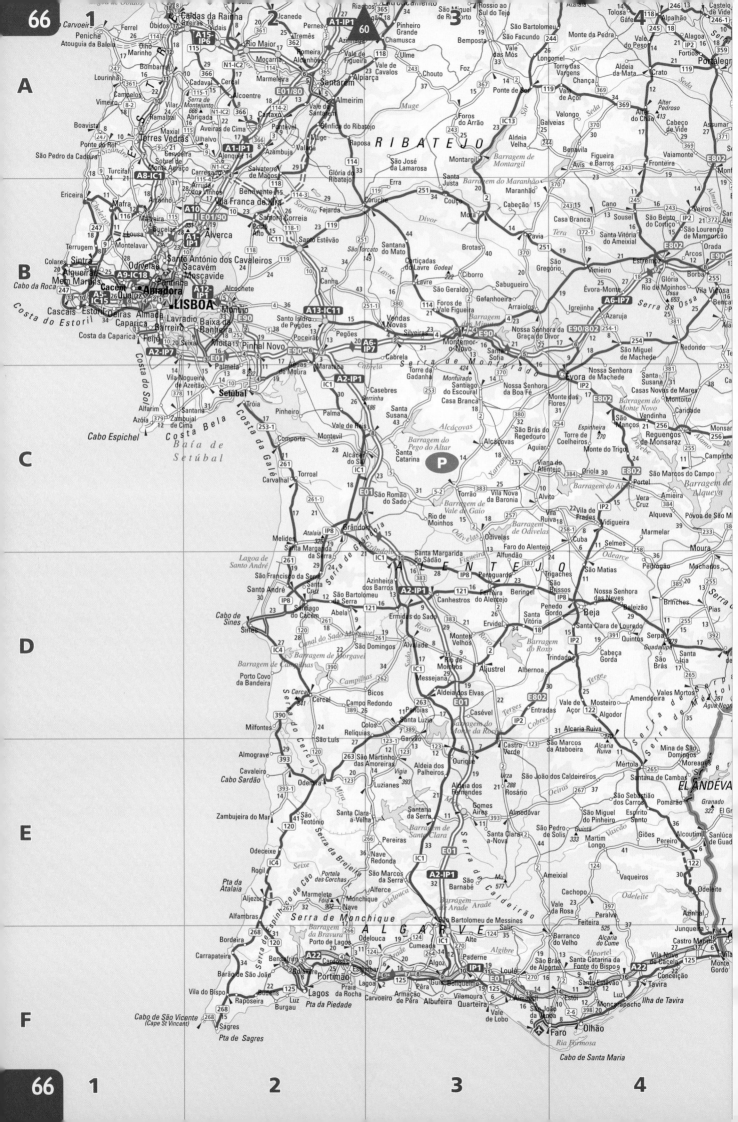

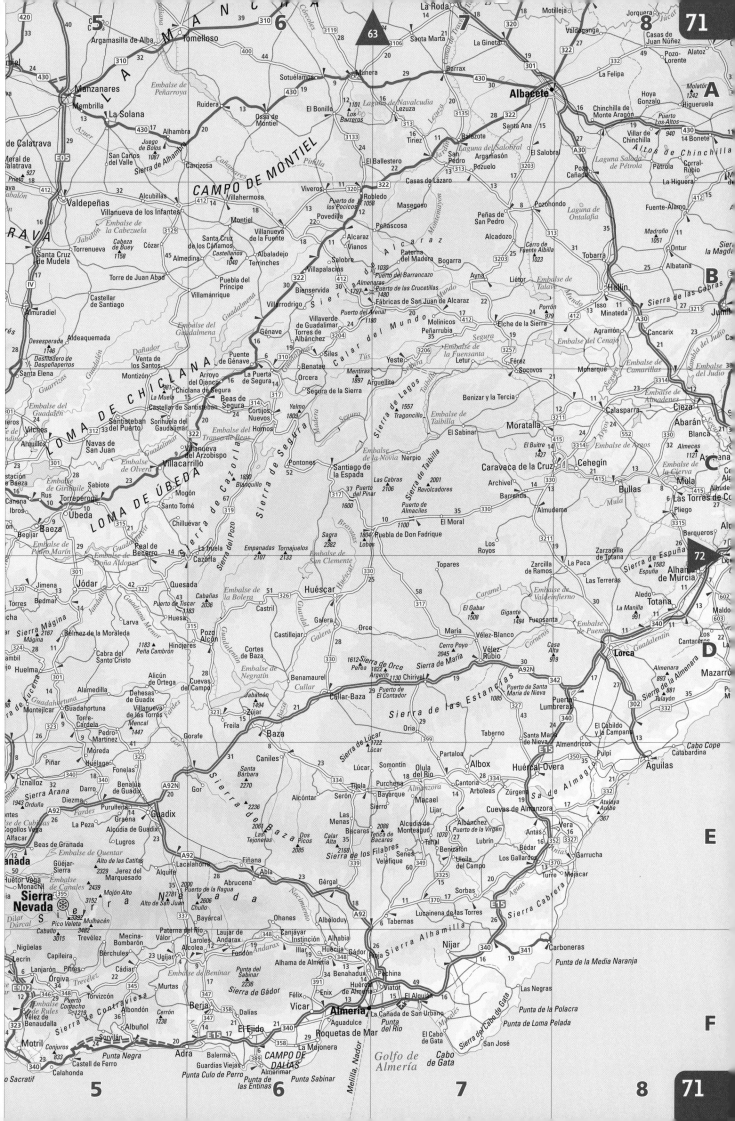

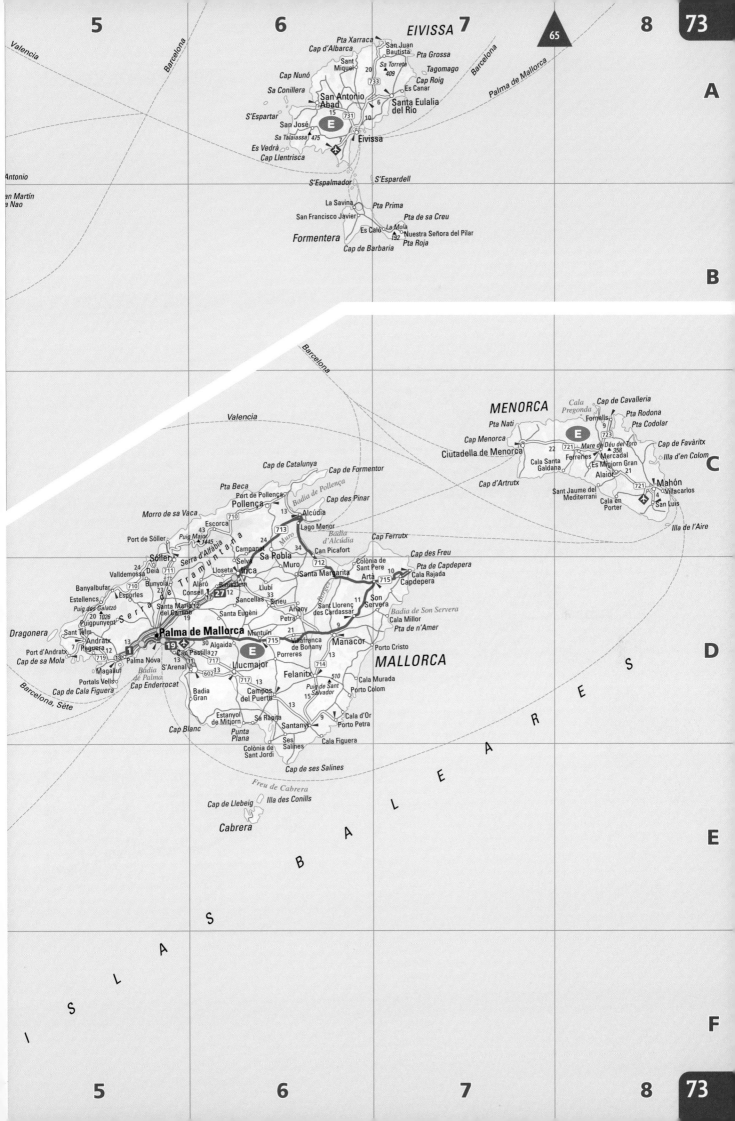

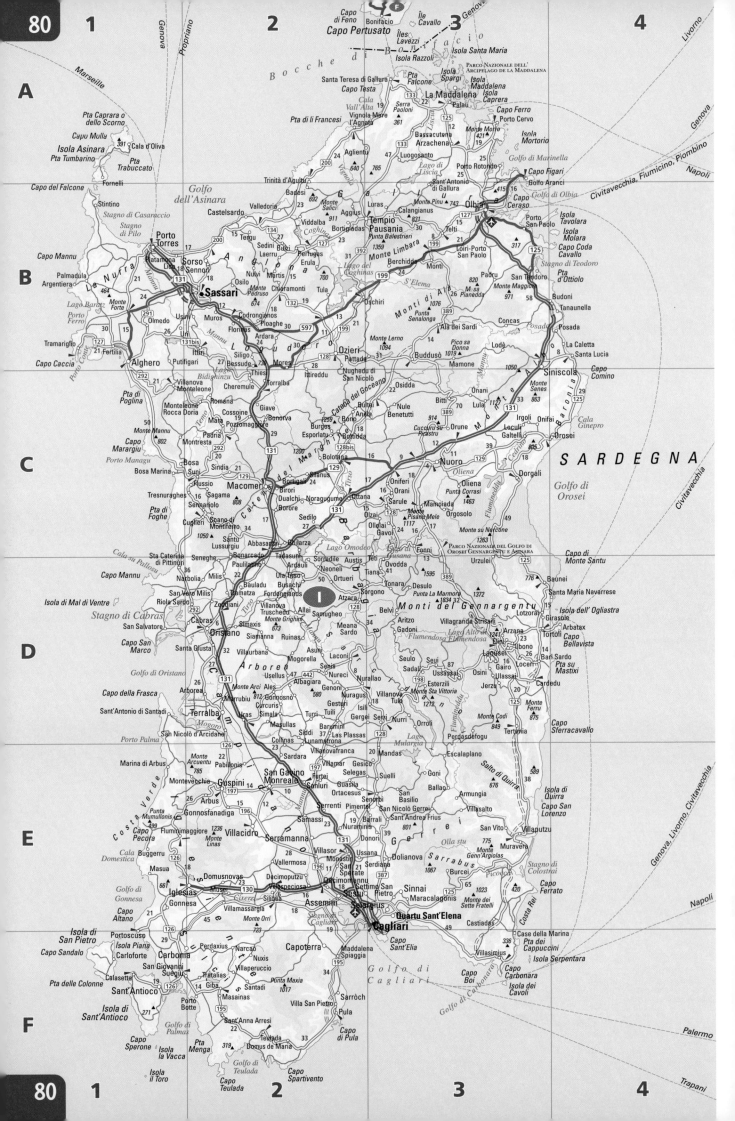

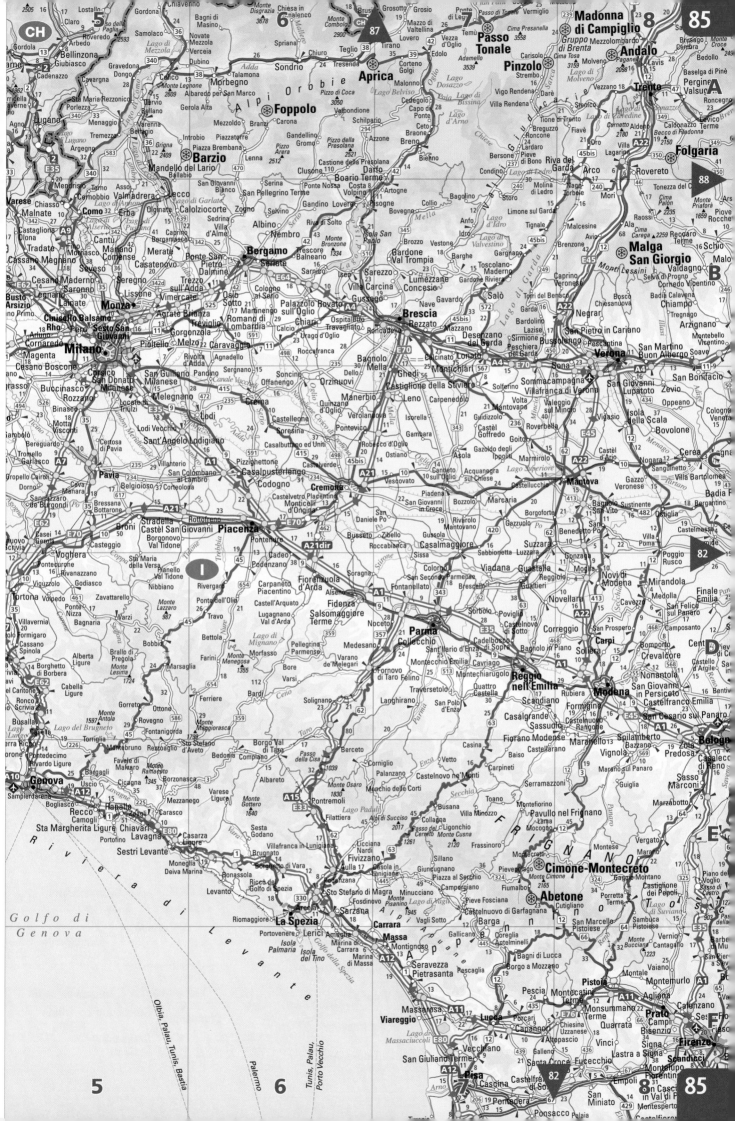

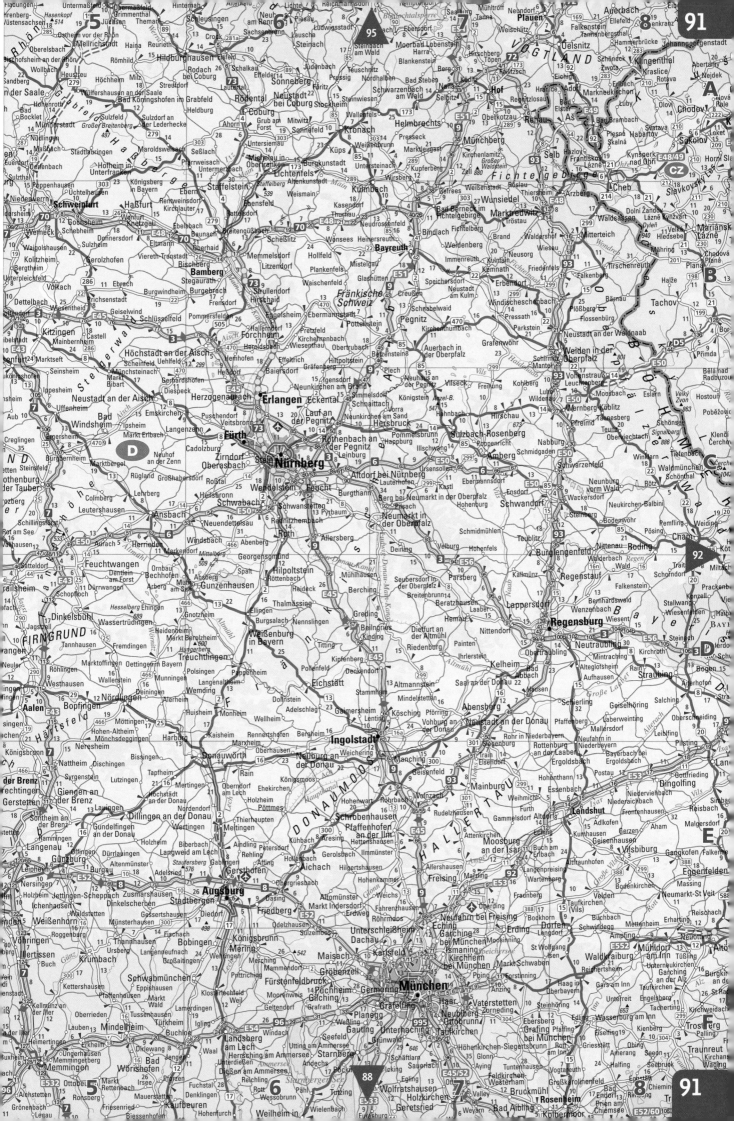

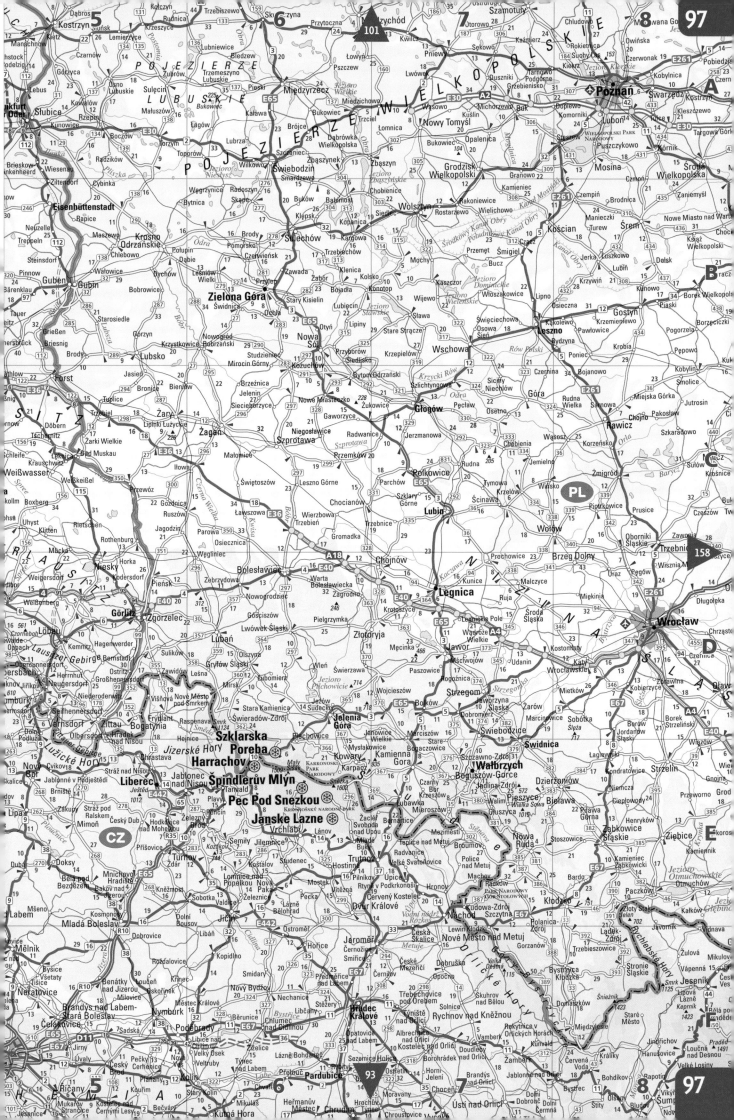

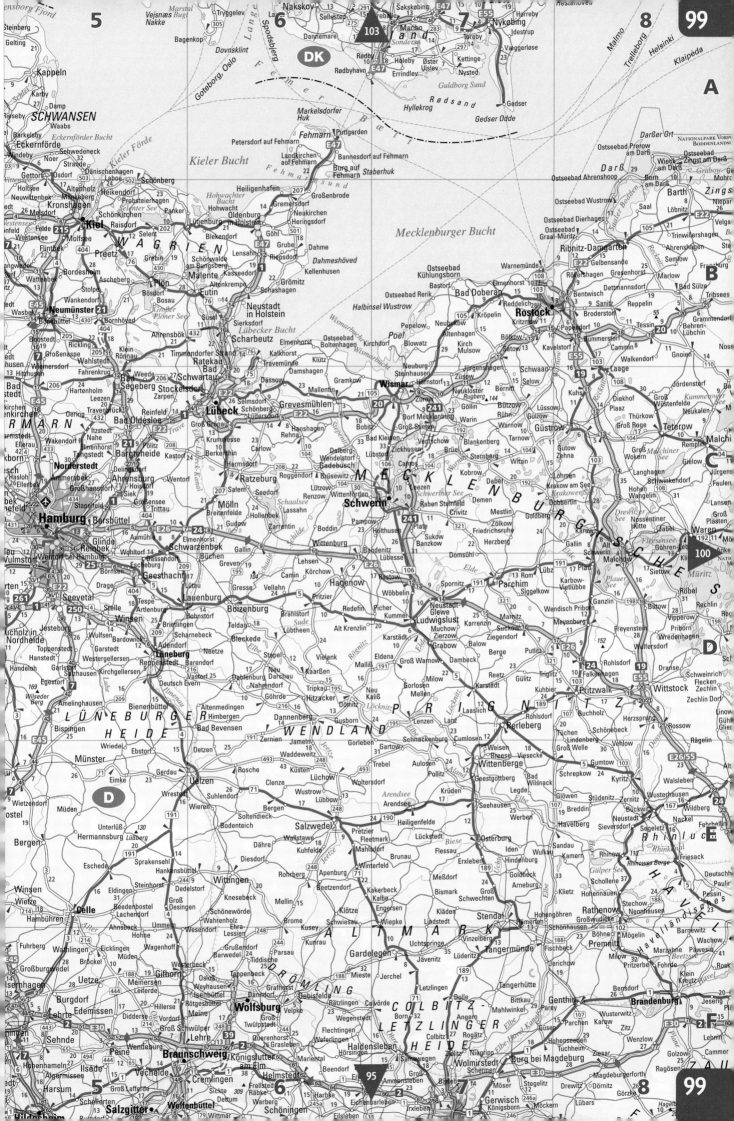

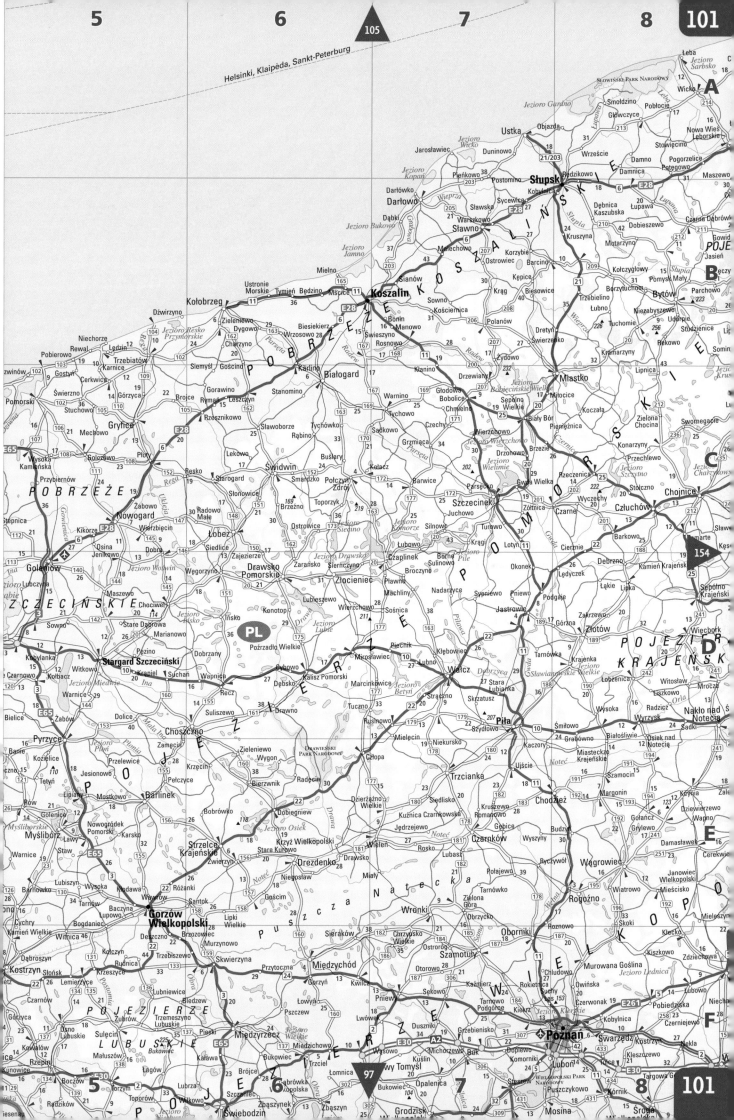

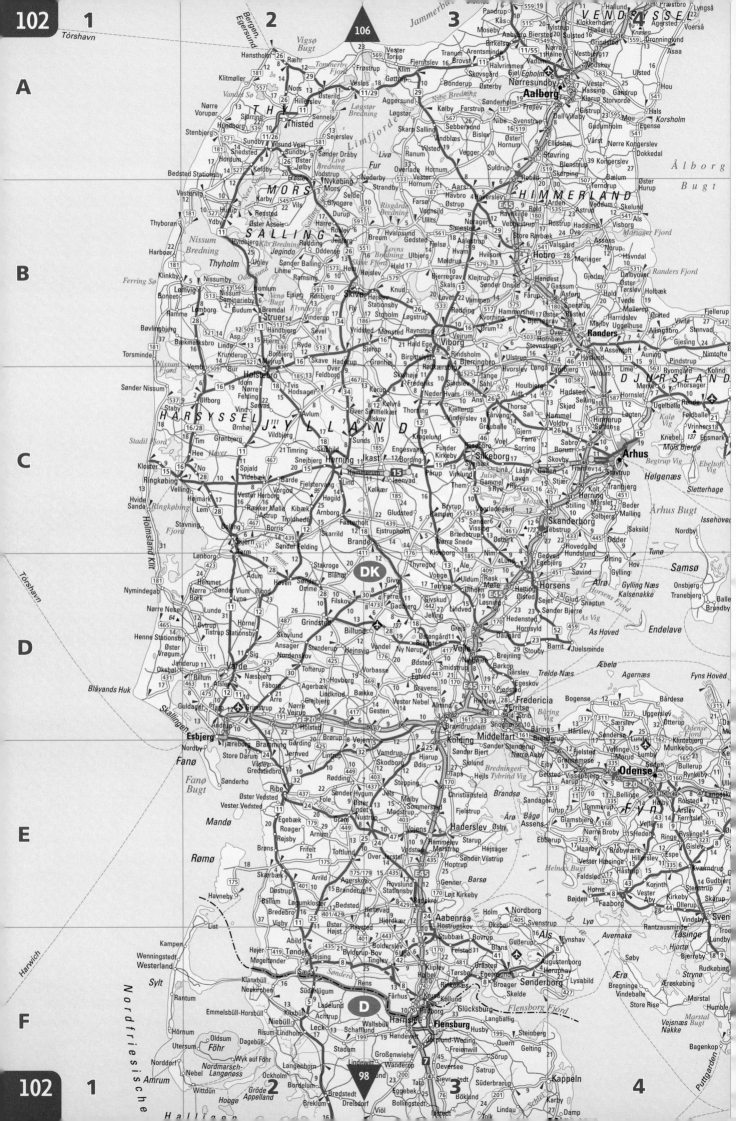

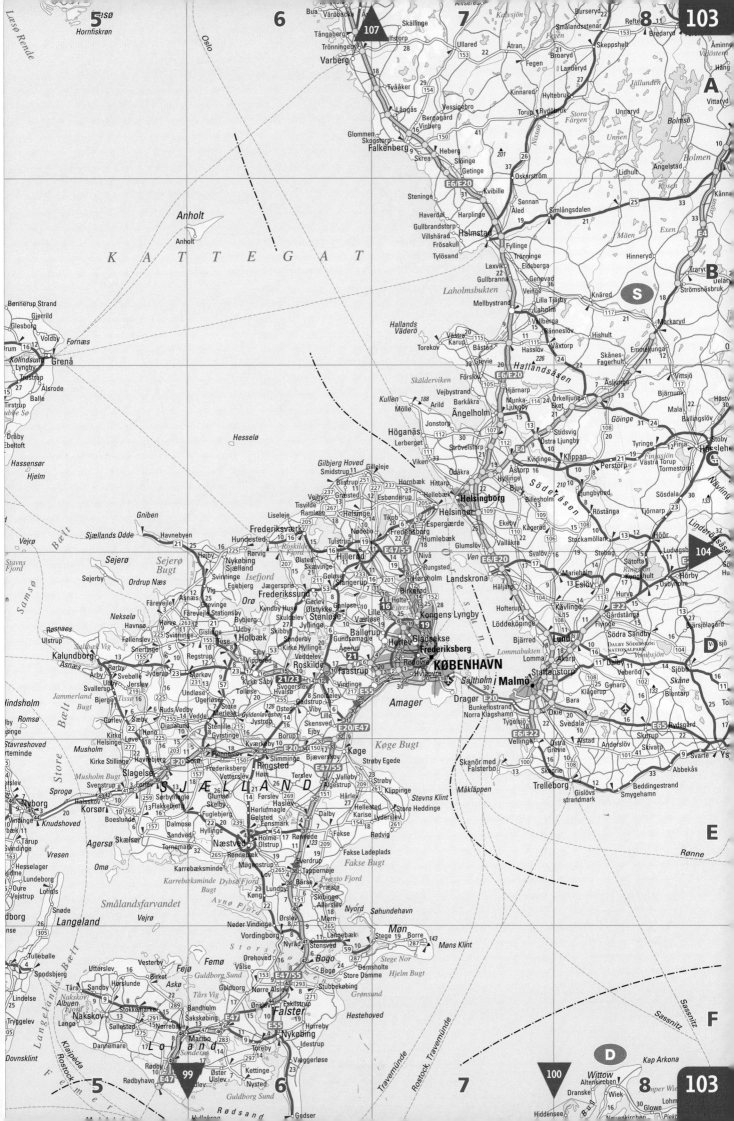

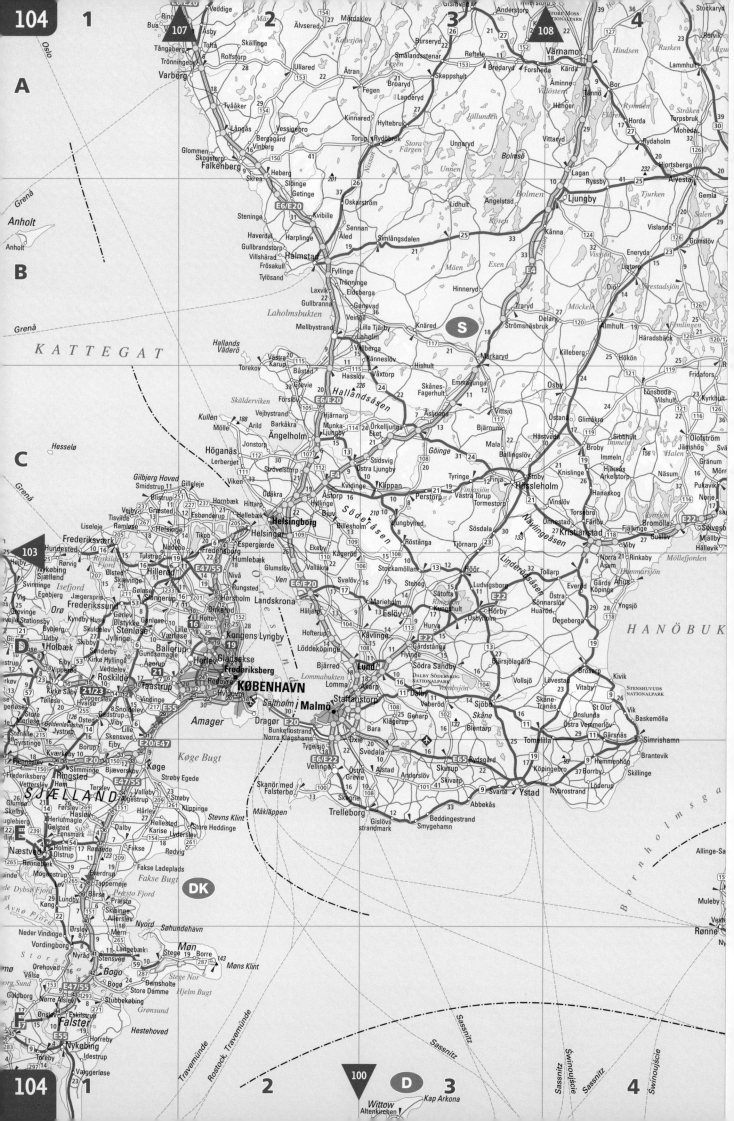

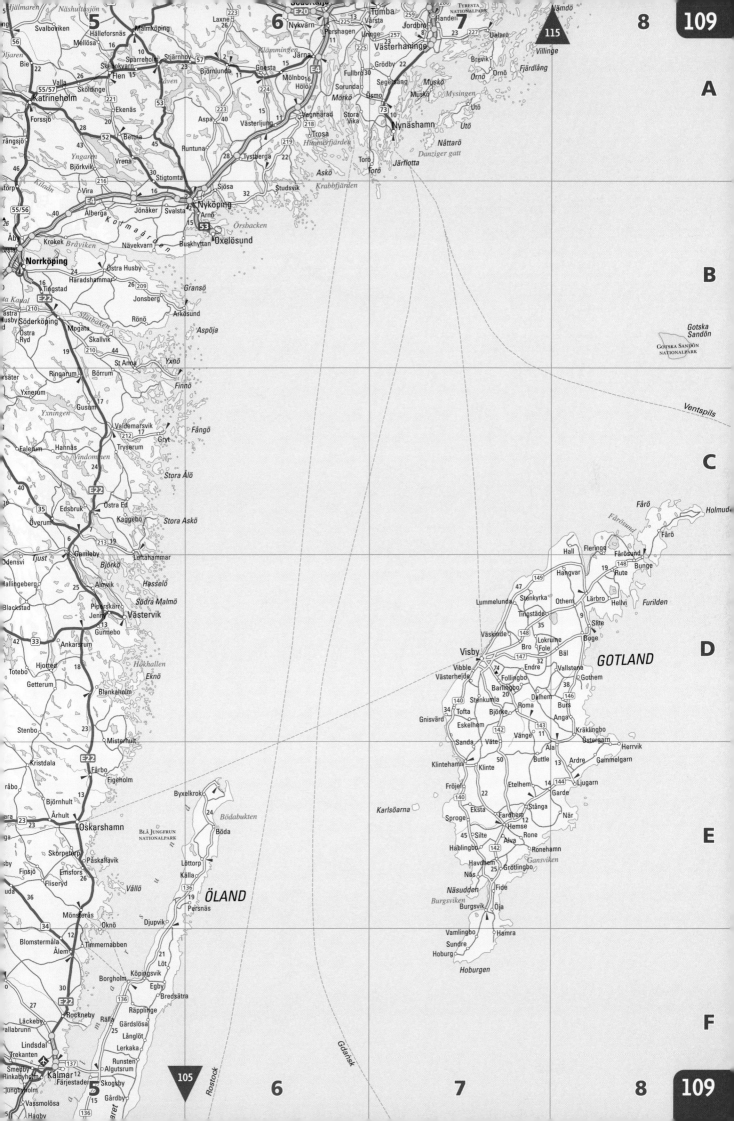

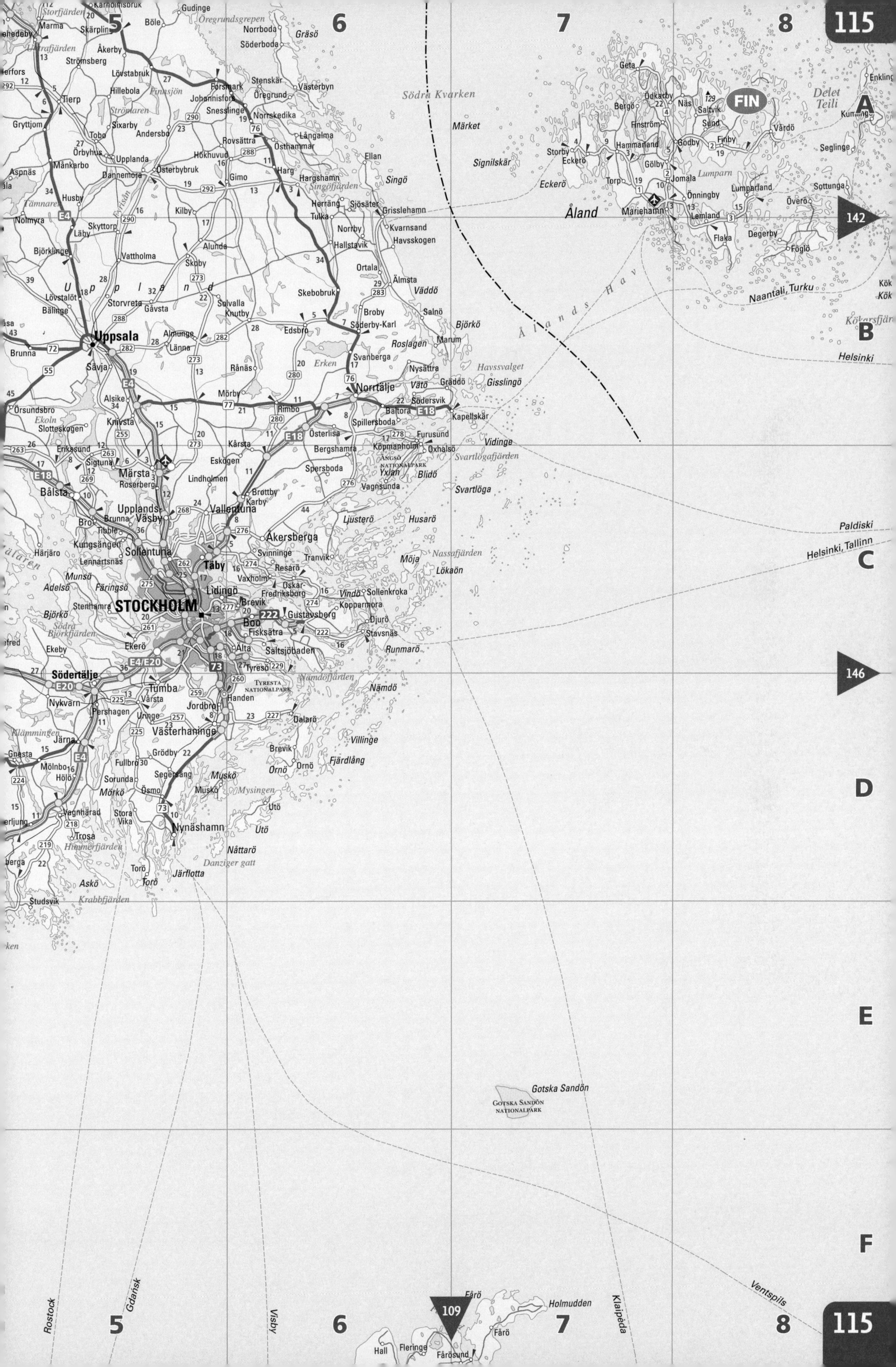
5
6
7
8
A
B
C
D
E
F
142
146
109
FIN
Åland
Mariehamn
Geta
Bergö
Ödkarby
Näs
Saltvik
Sund
Finström
Hammarland
Godby
Finby
Vårdö
Storby
Eckerö
Gölby
Jomala
Torp
Önningby
Lumparland
Lumparn
Lemland
Flaka
Degerby
Föglö
Sottunga
Överö
Seglinge
Kumlinge
Enklinge
Delet
Teili
Kökar
Kökarsfjärden
Naantali, Turku
Helsinki
Paldiski
Helsinki, Tallinn
Ventspils
Klaipėda
Visby
Gdańsk
Rostock
Ålands Hav
Södra Kvarken
Märket
Signilskär
Eckerö
Gräsö
Norrboda
Söderboda
Öregrundsgrepen
Gudinge
Karlholmsbruk
Storfjärden
Marma
Skärplinge
Böle
Åkerby
Strömsberg
Untrafjärden
Lövstabruk
Hillebola
Finnsjön
Tierp
Strömaren
Gryttjom
Sixarby
Toba
Andersbo
Forsmark
Johannisfors
Snesslinge
Stenskär
Öregrund
Västerbyn
Norrskedika
Långalma
Östhammar
Rovsättra
Hökhuvud
Gimo
Österbybruk
Dannemora
Upplanda
Örbyhus
Månkarbo
Aspnäs
Husby
Tämnaren
Nolmyra
Skyttorp
Läby
Björklinge
Vattholma
Alunda
Skoby
Kilby
Uppland
Lövstalöt
Bälinge
Storvreta
Gåvsta
Solvalla
Knutby
Uppsala
Almunge
Länna
Brunna
Sävja
Rånäs
Edsbro
Ellan
Singö
Hargshamn
Singöfjärden
Harg
Herräng
Sjösäter
Grisslehamn
Tulka
Kvarnsand
Norrby
Havsskogen
Hallstavik
Ortala
Älmsta
Väddö
Skebobruk
Salnö
Broby
Söderby-Karl
Björkö
Roslagen
Marum
Svanberga
Erken
Nysättra
Havssvalget
Gisslingö
Norrtälje
Vätö
Gräddö
Södersvik
Baltora
Kapellskär
Spillersboda
Rimbo
Mörby
Alsike
Knivsta
Örsundsbro
Ekoln
Slotteskogen
Österlisa
Bergshamra
Furusund
Köpmanholm
Oxhalsö
Vidinge
Svartlögafjärden
Ängsö nationalpark
Yxlan
Blidö
Svartlöga
Kårsta
Eskogen
Lindholmen
Spersboda
Vagnsunda
Eriksund
Sigtuna
Märsta
Rosersberg
Bålsta
Upplands-Väsby
Bro
Brunna
Tibble
Brottby
Karby
Vallentuna
Ljusterö
Husarö
Kungsängen
Lennartsnäs
Härjäro
Sollentuna
Åkersberga
Svinninge
Tranvik
Möja
Nassafjärden
Täby
Resarö
Vaxholm
Oskar-Fredriksborg
Lökaön
Munsö
Adelsö
Färingsö
Lidingö
Vindö
Sollenkroka
Stenhamra
STOCKHOLM
Brevik
Kopparmora
Björkö
Södra Björkfjärden
Boo
Gustavsberg
Djurö
Fisksätra
Stavsnäs
Ekeby
Ekerö
Älta
Saltsjöbaden
Runmarö
Södertälje
Tyresö
Nämdöfjärden
Tumba
Tyresta nationalpark
Nämdö
Nykvarn
Vårsta
Handen
Pershagen
Jordbro
Dalarö
Uringe
Västerhaninge
Klämmingen
Järna
Villinge
Gnesta
Gröddby
Brevik
Ornö
Fjärdlång
Mölnbo
Hölö
Fullbro
Sorunda
Segersäng
Muskö
Mörkö
Ösmo
Mysingen
Utö
Vagnhärad
Stora Vika
Nynäshamn
Trosa
Himmerfjärden
Nåttarö
Danziger gatt
Torö
Järflotta
Askö
Krabbfjärden
Studsvik
Gotska Sandön
Gotska Sandön nationalpark
Fårö
Holmudden
Hall
Fleringe
Fårösund

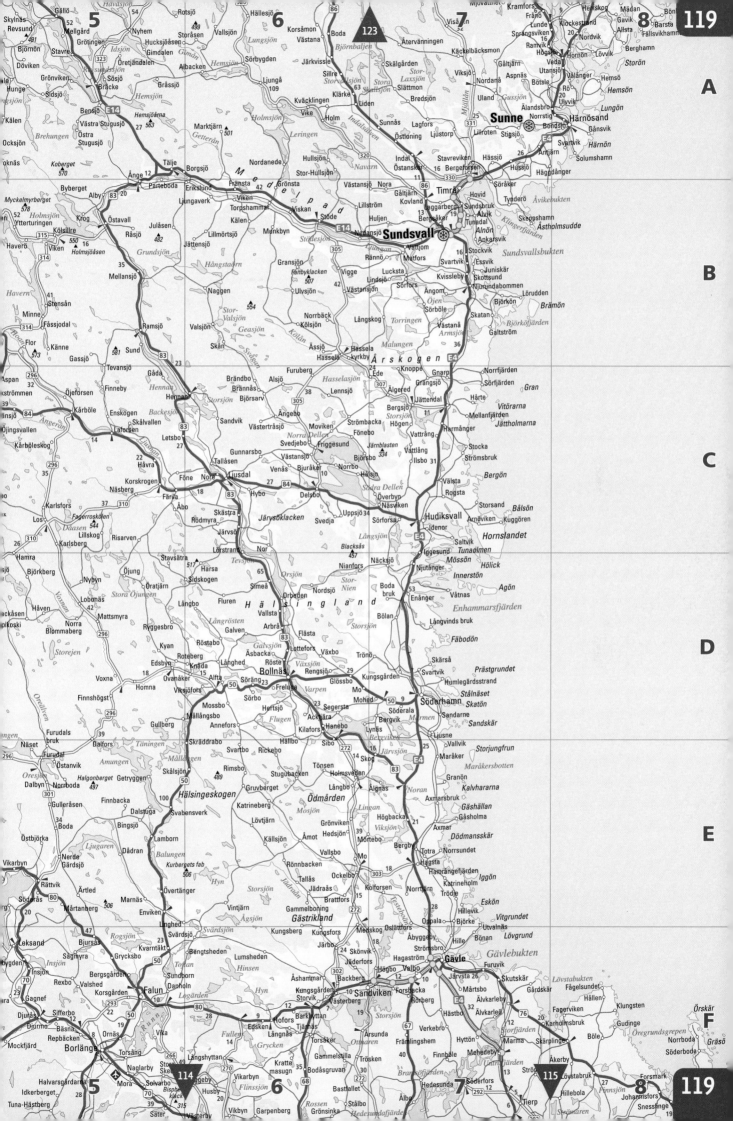

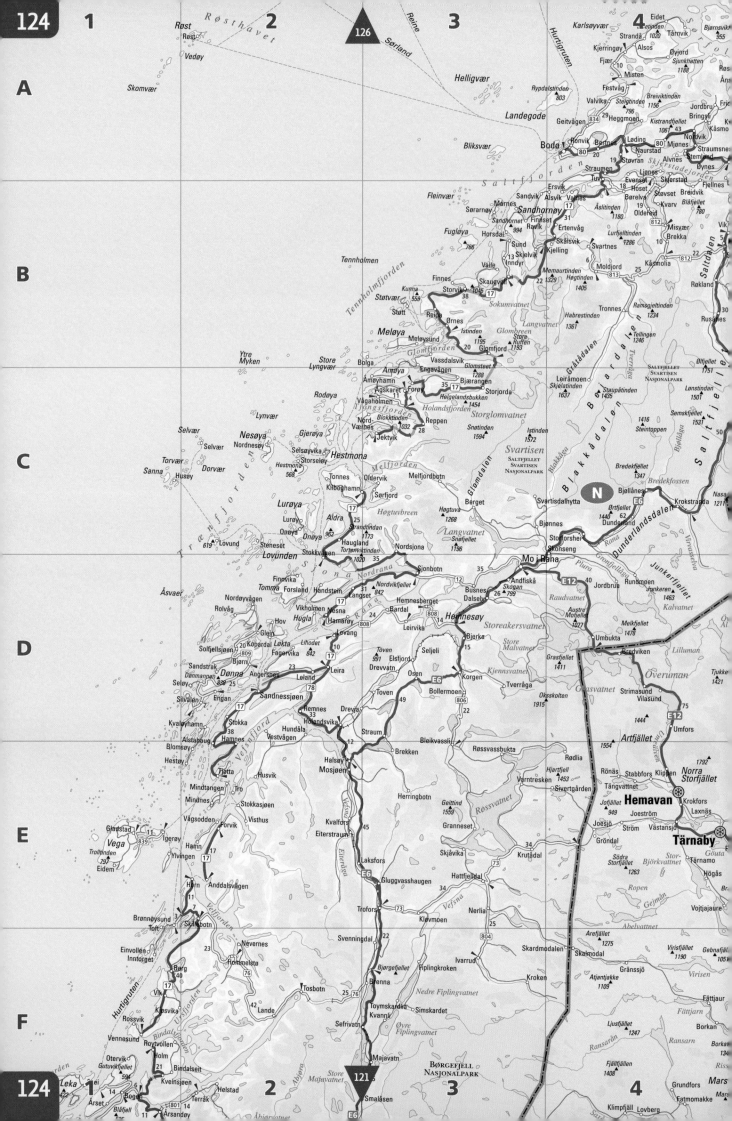

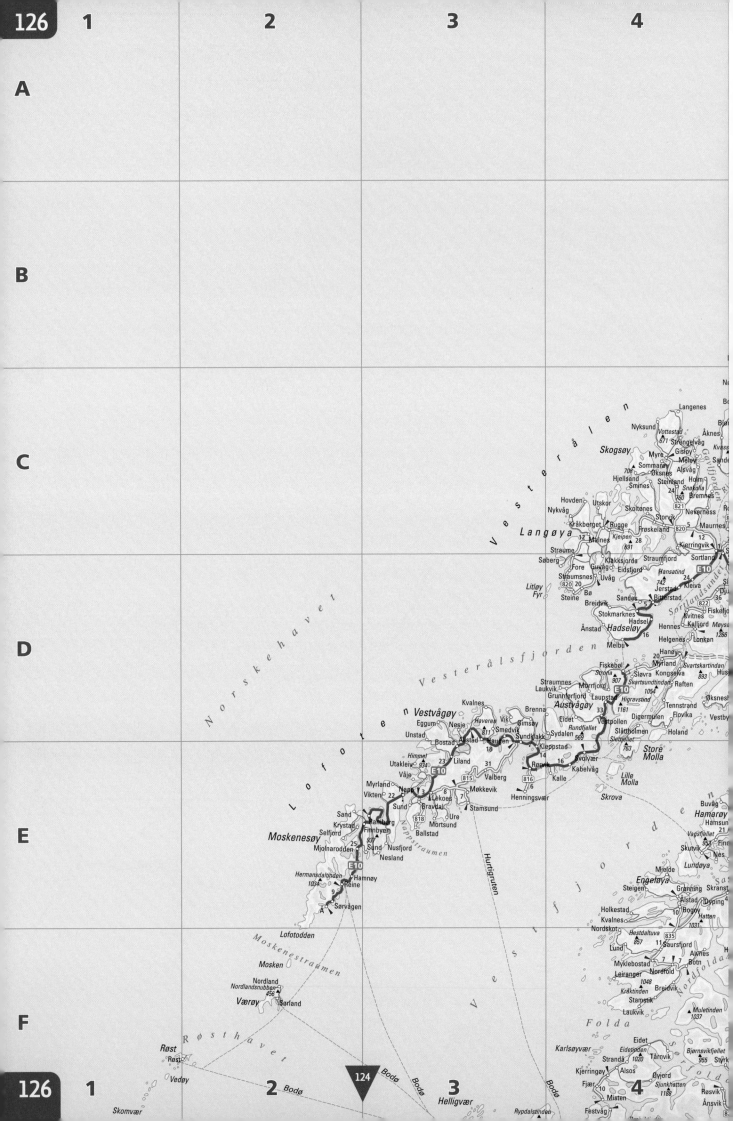

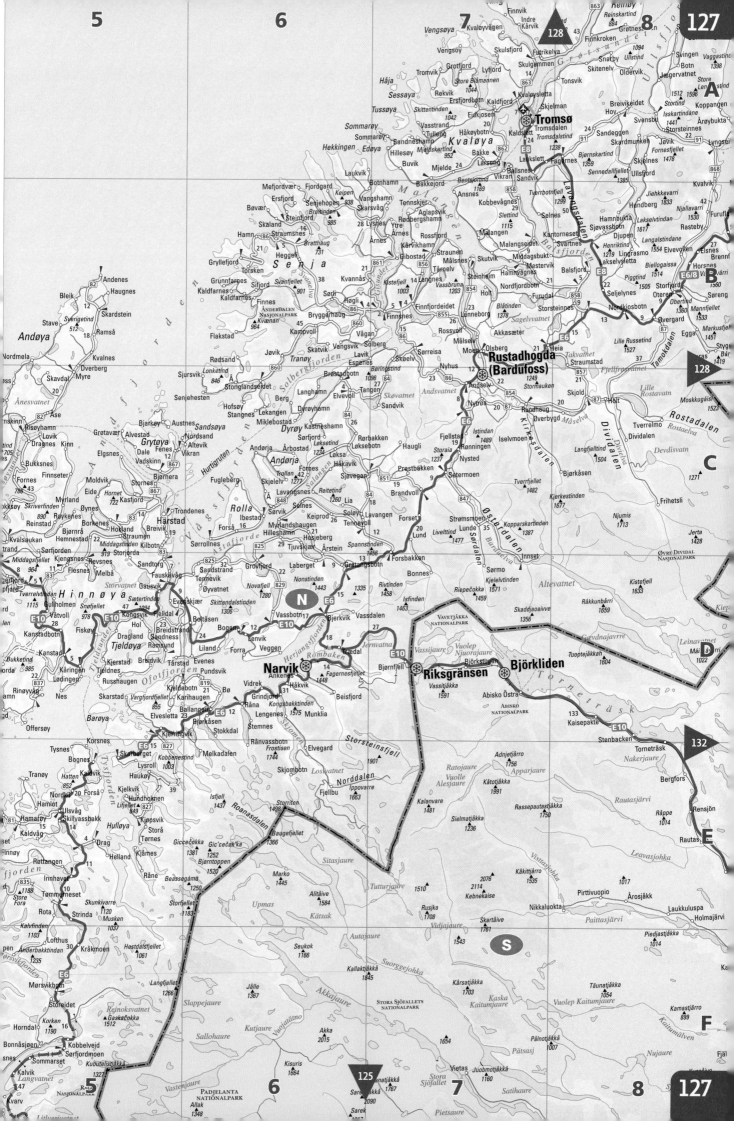

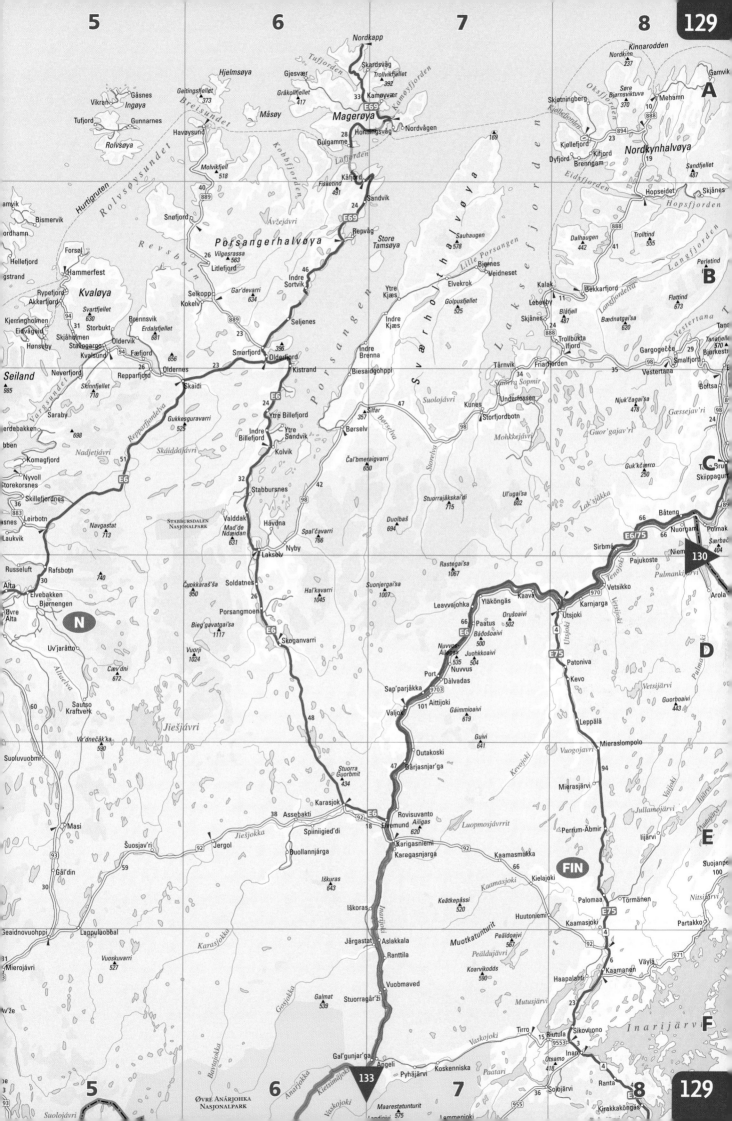

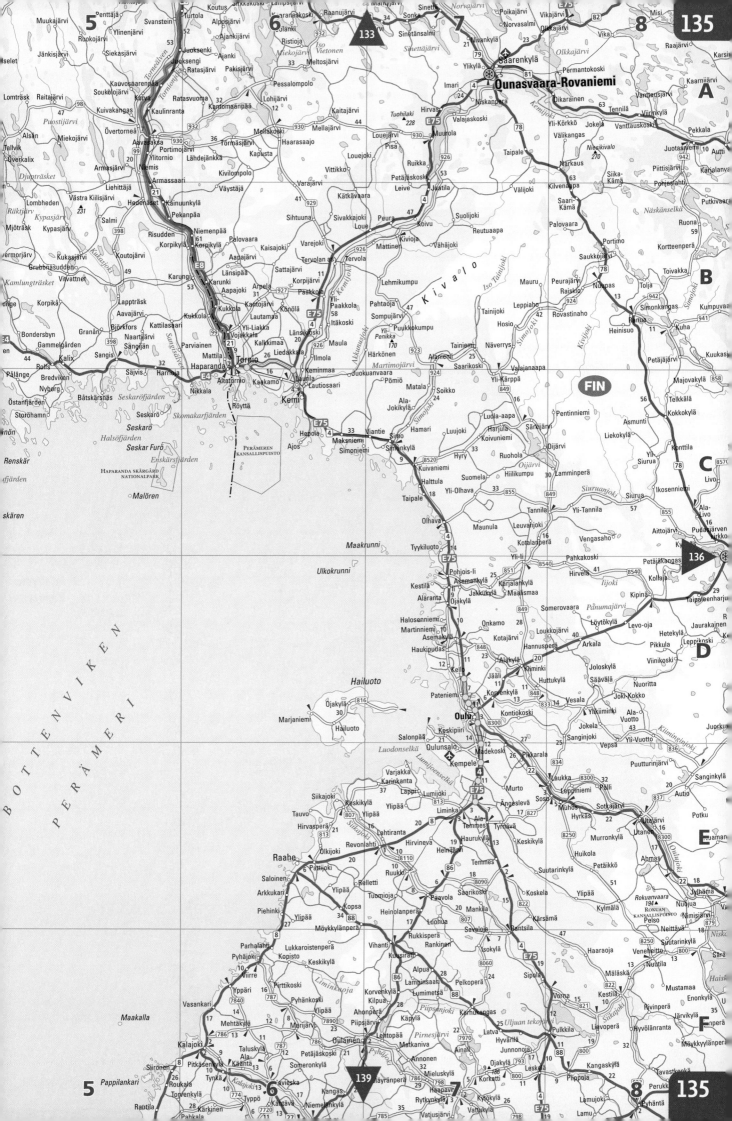

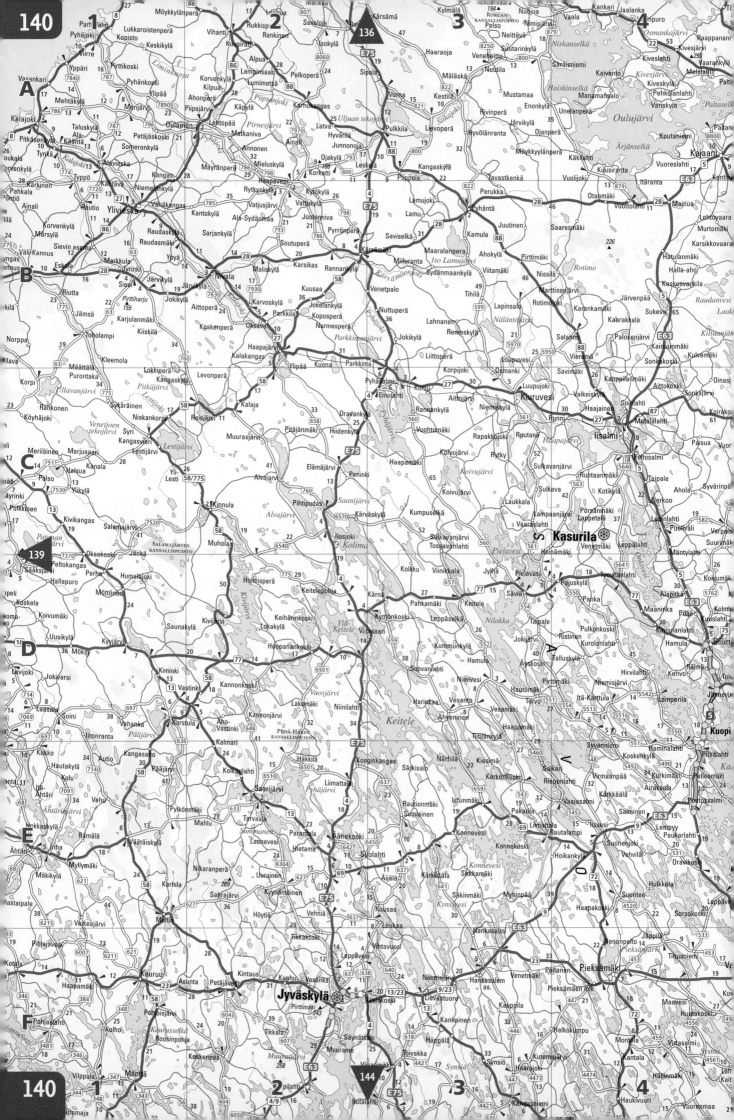

1
2
3
4
A
B
C
D
E
F
138
115
146
Kaskinen (Kaskö)
Pjelax
Myrkky
Luovankylä
Kauhajoki
Pantäne
Ikkelänjärvi
Ilvesjoki
Kristinestad (Kristiinankaupunki)
Tjöck
Karijoki
Lappfjärd
Dagsmark
Hyyppä
Panttikylä
Nummijärvi
Nummikoski
Sara
Uuro
Kauhajärvi
Heikkilä
Träskvik
Härkmeri
Vanhakylä
Villamo
Kärjenkoski
Lauhanvuoren kansallispuisto
Lauhavuori
Kauhanevan-Pohjankankaan kansallispuisto
Perä-Hyyppä
Karvia
Sarvela
Alkkia
Karvianjärvi
Skaftung
Isojoki
Sarviluoma
Suomijärvi
Ömossa
Vesijärvi
Suojoki
Kodesjärvi
Jyllinkoski
Kantti
Sideby
Kalltäsk
Honkajoki
Kuvaskangas
Lauttijärvi
Pyntäinen
Ala-Honkajoki
Korvaluoma
Kuusijoki
Merikarvia
Tuorila
Siikainen
Pohjankangas
Ouran saaristo
Alakylä
Venesjärvi
Niinisalo
Jämijärvi
Kööritilä
Leväsjoki
Kankaanpää
Hämeenkangas
Isojärvi
Honkakoski
Vihteljärvi
Pomarkku
Ahlainen
Reposaari
Mäntyluoto
Noormarkku
Lassila
Lavia
Pihlava
Kyläsaari
Söörmarkku
Harjakangas
Karhijärvi
Säppi
Pori
Preiviiki
Harjunpää
Viasvedenlahti
Viasvesi
Kaasmarkku
Ulvila
Kullaa
Sääksjärvi
Putaja
Kiikoinen
Frittala
Niemenkylä
Lattomeri
Nakkila
Luvia
Harjavalta
Kauvatsa
Äetsä
Kiikka
Kuivalahti
Kokemäki
Riste
Keikyä
Olkiluoto
Panelia
Irjanne
Peipohja
Puurijärven ja Isonsuon kansallispuisto
Lapijoki
Eurajoki
Kiukainen
Huittinen
Rauma
Eura
Köyliönjärvi
Lappi
Köyliö
Kankaanpää
Vuorenmaa
Rihtniemi
Unaja
Iso-Vimma
Kodiksami
Säkylä
Vermuntila
Kodisjoki
Hinnerjoki
Pyhäjärvi
Pyhäjoki
Vampula
Ihode
Otajärvi
Honkilahti
Koskenkylä
Pyhäranta
Pyhämaa
Alastaro
Kammela
Untamala
Heinijoki
Virttaa
Laitila
Yläne
Oripää
Vekara
Lyökki
Laajoki
Karjalankylä
Varsinais-Suomi
Uusikaupunki
Kalanti
Uusikartano
Karjalan kirkonkylä
Mynäjoki
Aurajoki
Lahti
Isokari
Pöytyä
Lokalahti
Vehmaa
Mynämäki
Tortinmäki
Karinainen
Kaurissalo
Rautila
Pyhe
Mietoinen
Nousiainen
Valpperi
Vahto
Aura
Askainen
Nummi
Paattinen
Kustavi
Taivassalo
Lemu
Masku
Tarvasjoki
Jurmo
Etelä-Vartsala
Hakkenpää
Merimasku
Rusko
Maaria
Lieto
Iniön aukko
Naantali
Raisio
Fiskö
Äva
Brändö
Turku (Åbo)
Littoinen
Paimio
Piikkiö
Kaarina
Geta
Rymättylä
Enklinge
Torsholma
Kakskerta
Sauvo
Bergö
Näs
Björkö
Lappo
Ödkarby
Saltvik
Delet Teili
Finström
Sund
Kumlinge
Mossala
Pargas (Parainen)
Godby
Hammarland
Vårdö
Houtsala
Eckerö
Emby
Seglinge
Karuna
Gölby
Torp
Jomala
Lumparn
Houtskär
Nagu
Attu
Mjösund
Tjuda
Kimito
Önningby
Lumparland
Sottunga
Korpo
Eckerö
Åland
Mariehamn
Jungfruskär
Storlandet
Kihti Skiftet
Lemland
Överö
Korpoström
Kirjais
Östermark
Björkboda
Flaka
Degerby
Föglö
Dragsfjärd
Västanfjärd
Dalsbruk (Taalintehdas)
Stockholm
Ålands Hav
Alskär
Aspö
Nötö
Högsåra
Hankoniemi
Kökar
Karlby
Hellsö
Kökarsfjärde
Jurmofjärden
Björkö
Gullkronafjärd
Hitis
Rostock
Helsinki
Jurmo
Skärgårdshavets nationalpark
Vänö
Örö
Rosala
Hangö västra fjärd

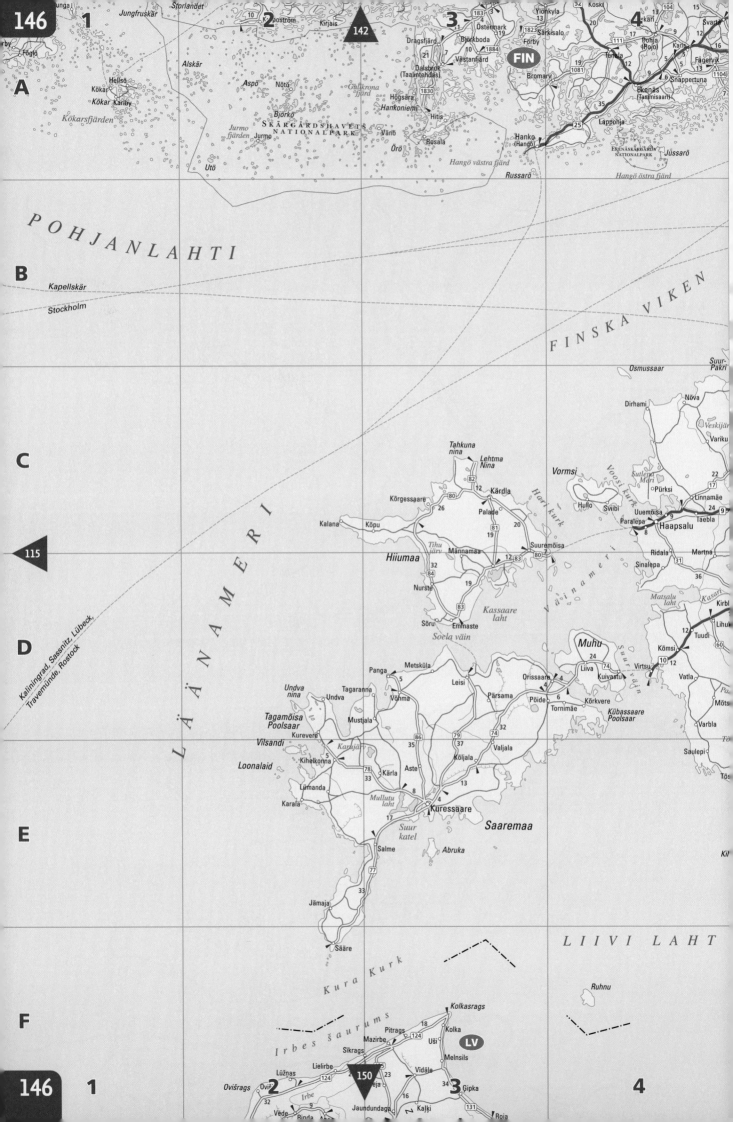

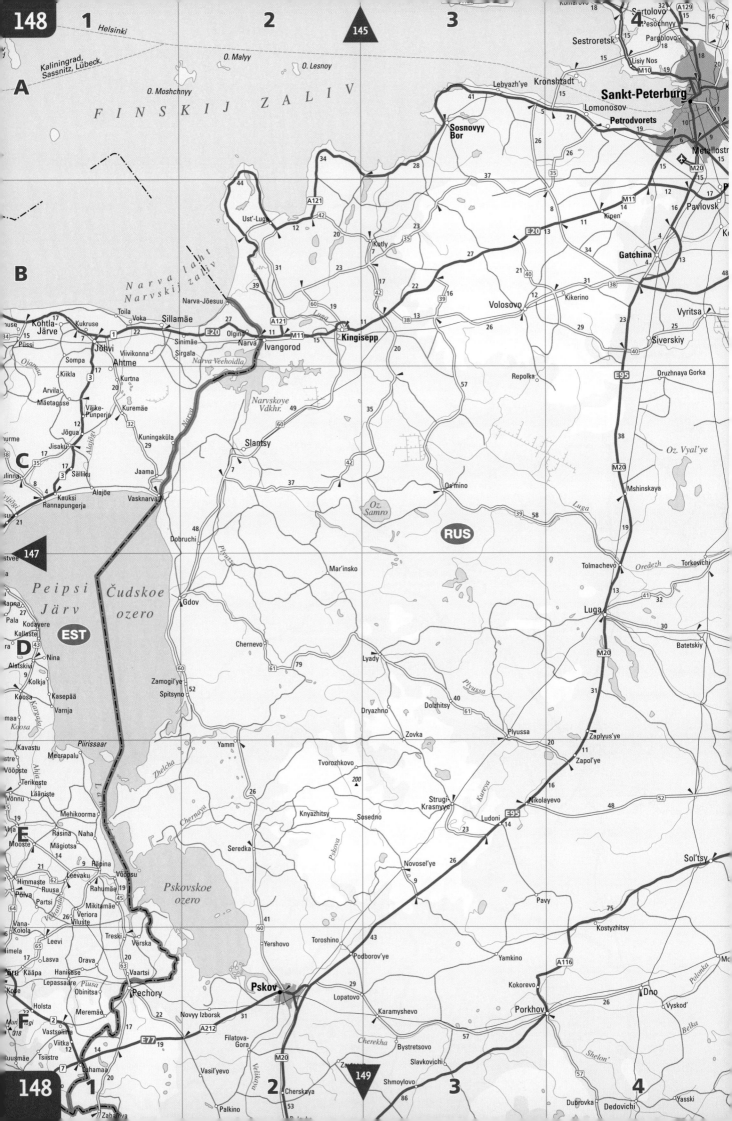

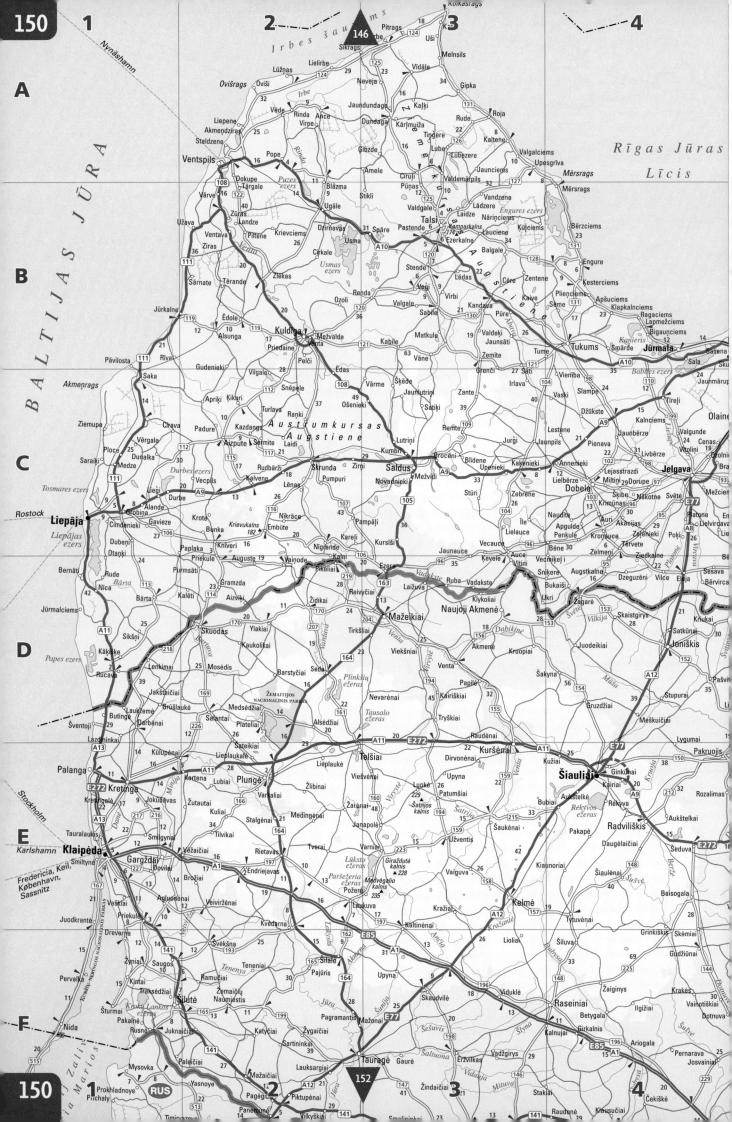

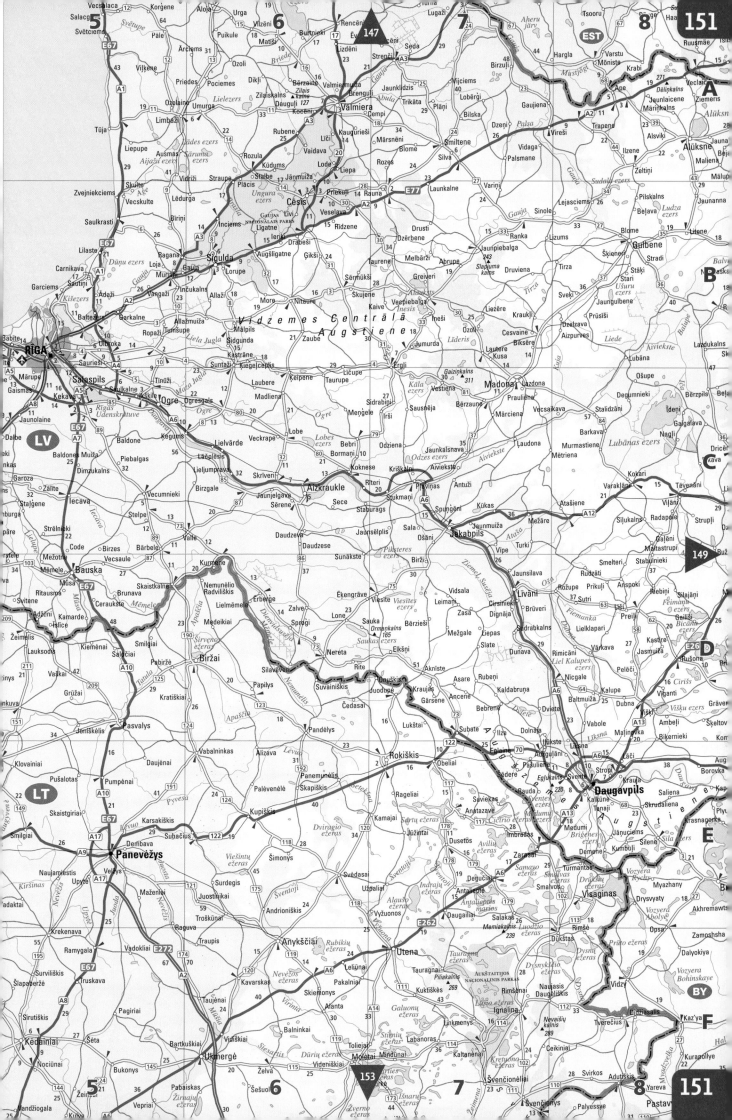

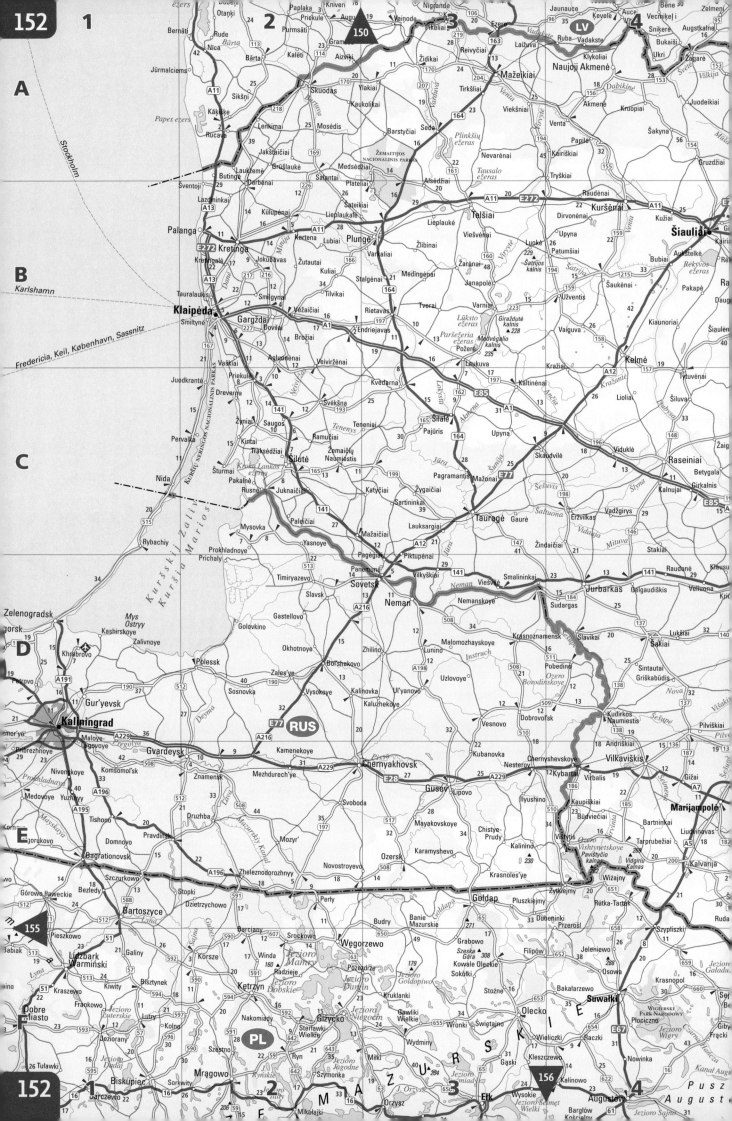

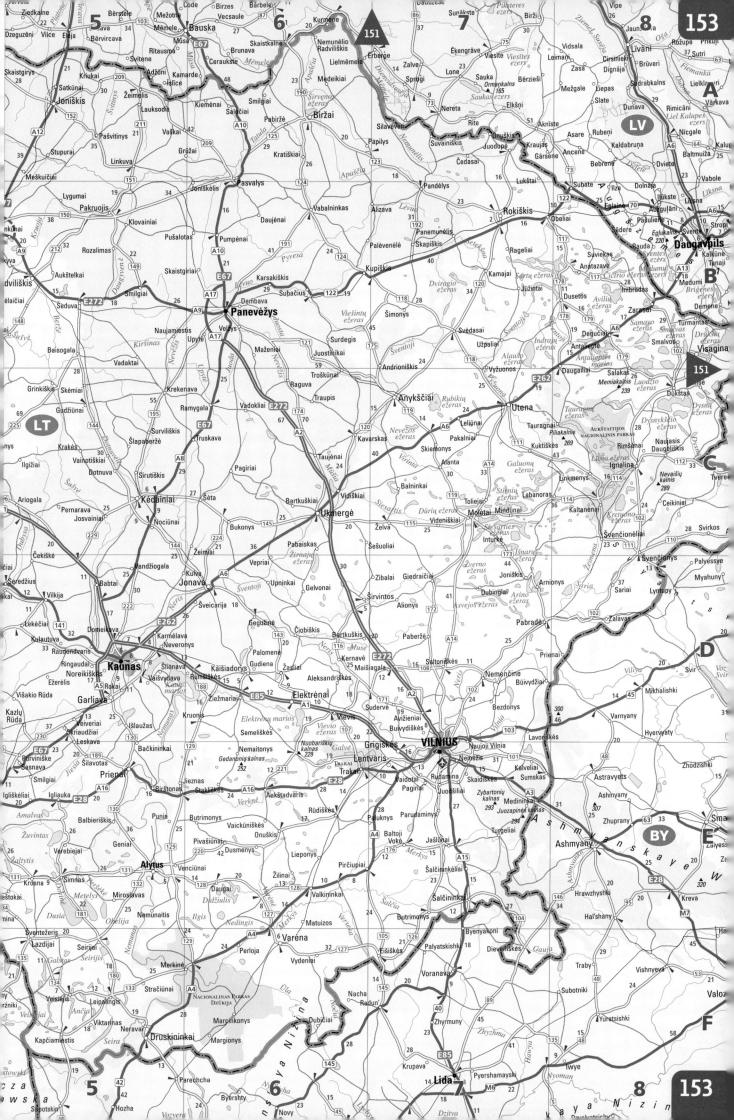

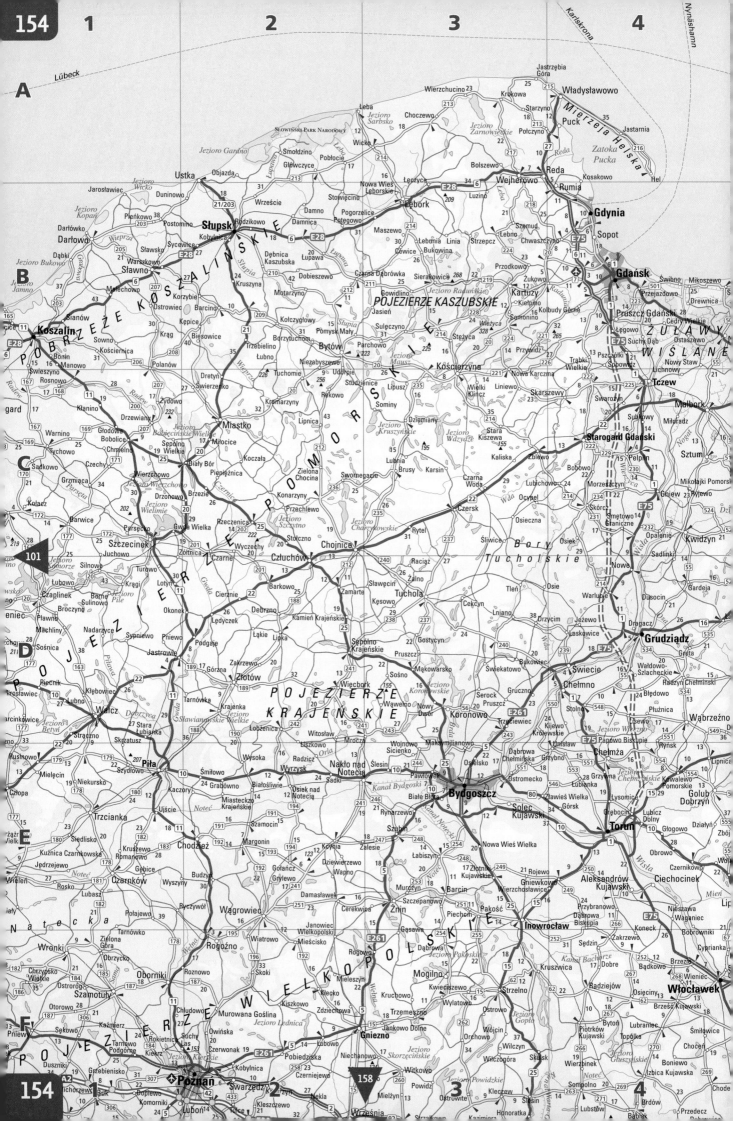

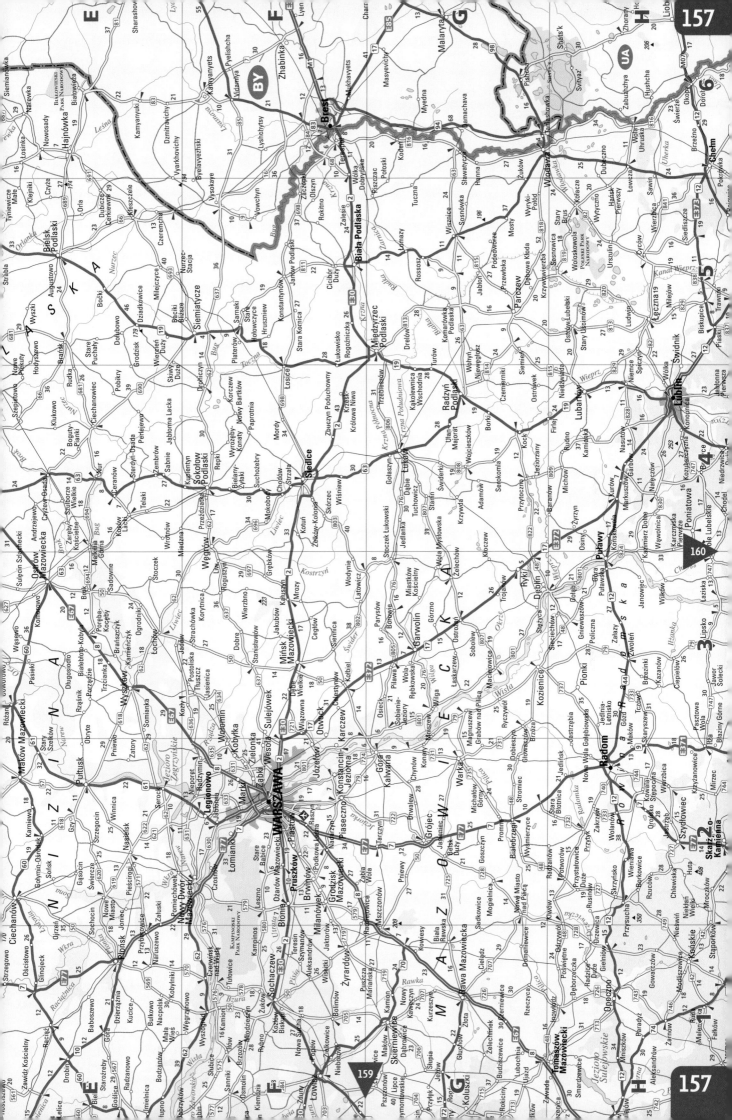

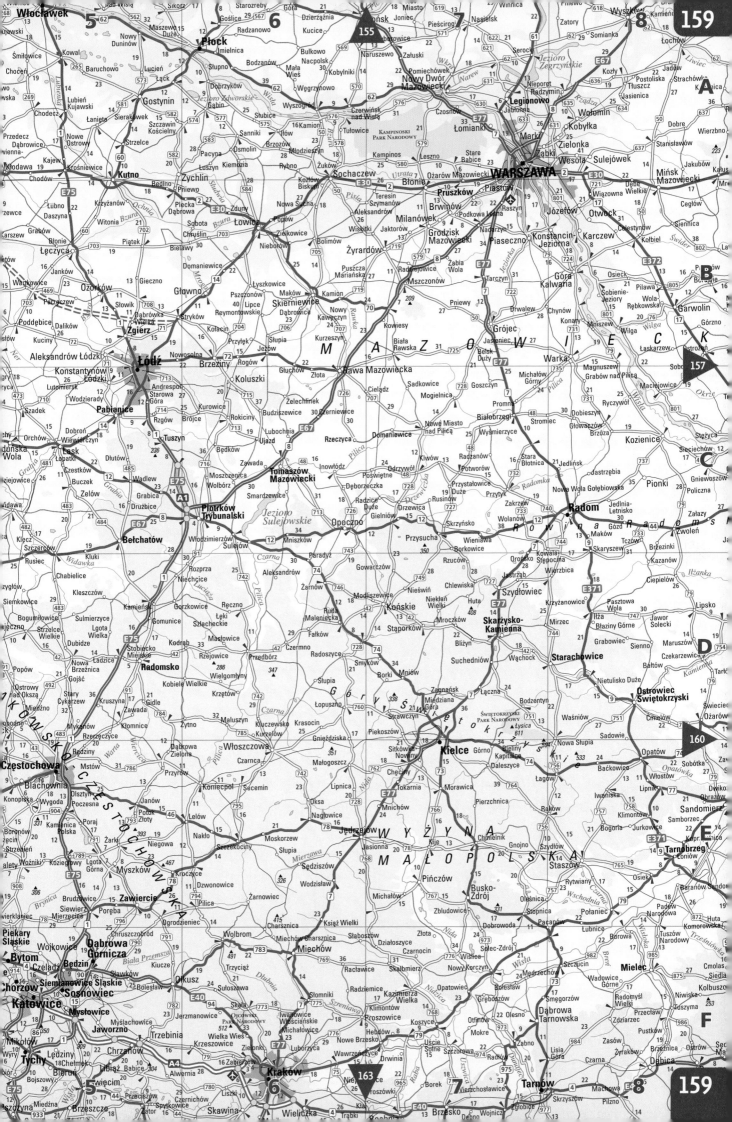

158
CZ
A
93
165
PŁASKOWYŻ GŁUBCZYCKI
Orlické Hory
Rychlebské Hory
Hrubý Jeseník
Žďárské Vrchy
Oderské vrchy
Moravskoslezské Beskydy
Javorník
Chřiby
Ždánický Les
Malé Karpaty
Biele Karpaty
Považský Inovec
TRIBEČ
Pohronská pahorkatina
Marchfeld
Hradec Králové
Pardubice
Chrudim
Náchod
Kłodzko
Nysa
Prudnik
Głuchołazy
Kędzierzyn-Koźle
Racibórz
Opava
Ostrava
Havířov
Frýdek-Místek
Šumperk
Jeseník
Krnov
Bruntál
Svitavy
Litomyšl
Olomouc
Prostějov
Přerov
Kroměříž
Zlín
Vsetín
Valašské Meziříčí
Nový Jičín
Brno
Blansko
Vyškov
Hodonín
Břeclav
Znojmo
Třebíč
Jihlava
Uherské Hradiště
Trenčín
Považská Bystrica
Púchov
Piešťany
Trnava
Nitra
Nové Zámky
Topoľčany
Senica
Skalica
Malacky
Pezinok
Senec
Galanta
Šaľa
Dunajská Streda
Šamorín
BRATISLAVA
WIEN
Tulln
Stockerau
Korneuburg
Klosterneuburg
Hollabrunn
Mistelbach
Schwechat
Mödling
Baden
Bad Vöslau
Traiskirchen
Wiener Neustadt
Eisenstadt
Neusiedler See
Mosonmagyaróvár

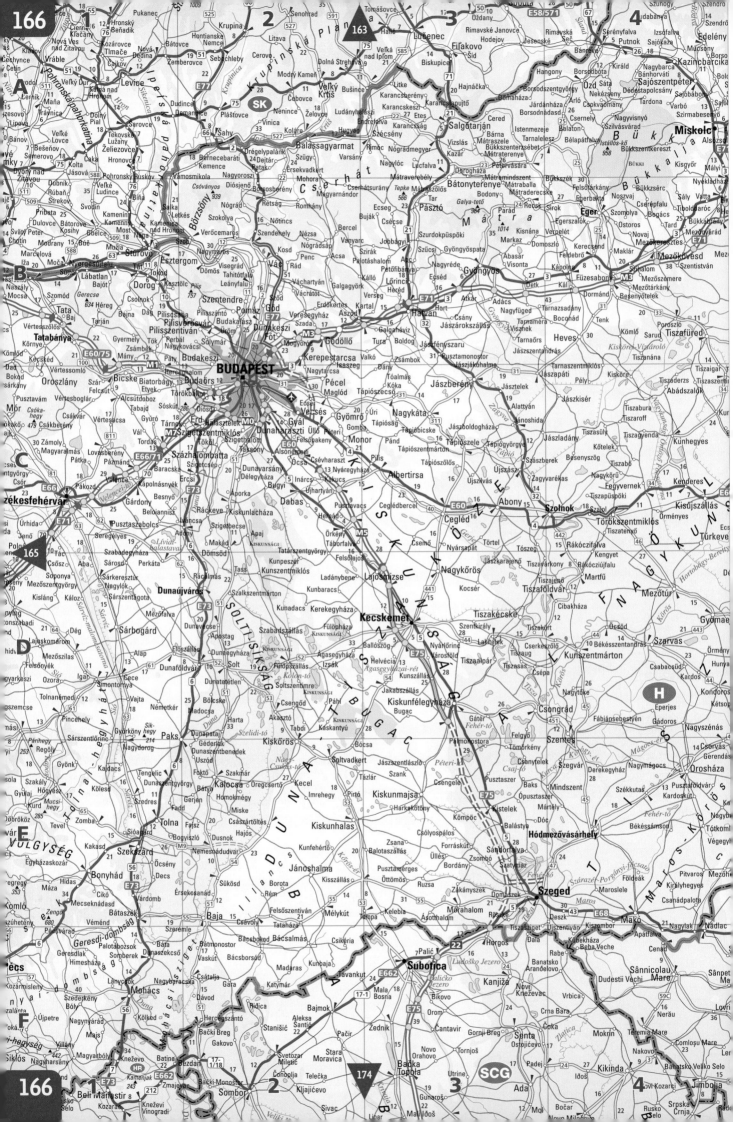

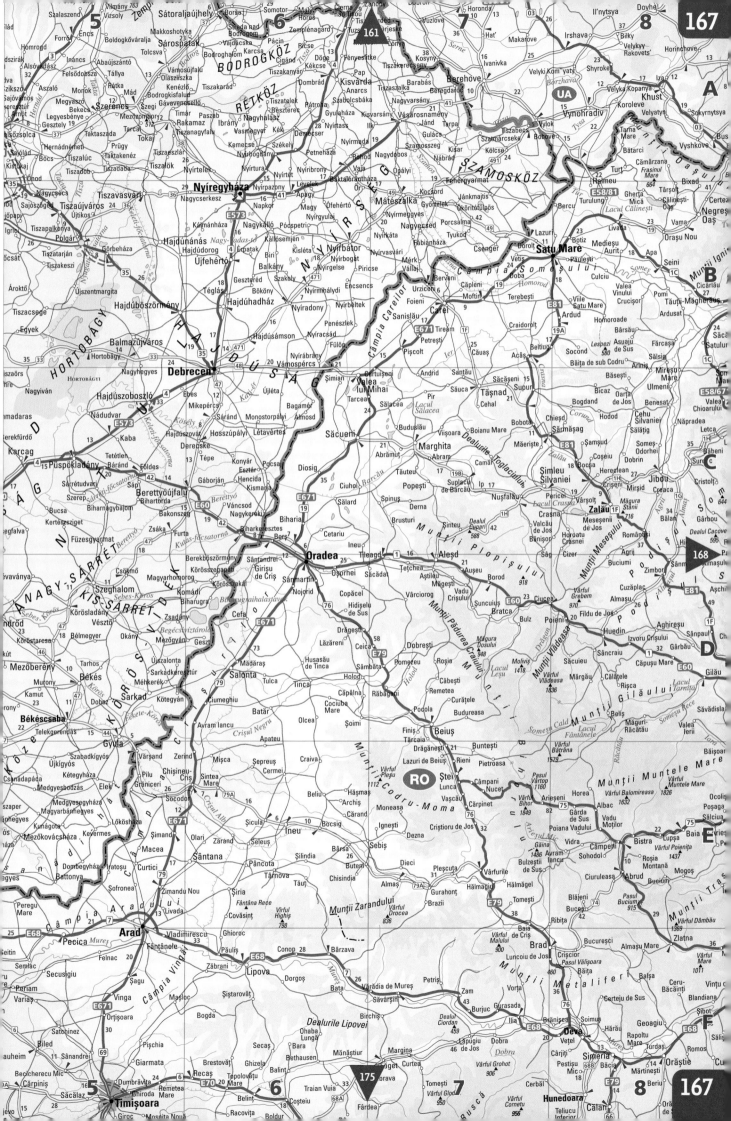

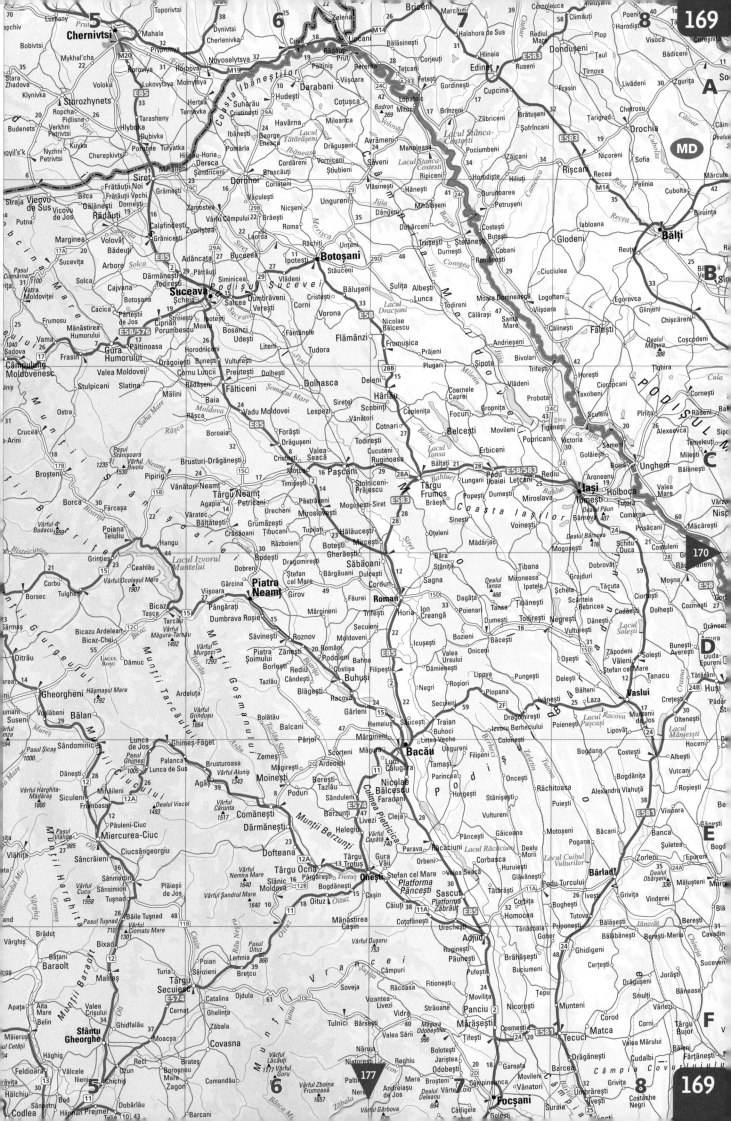

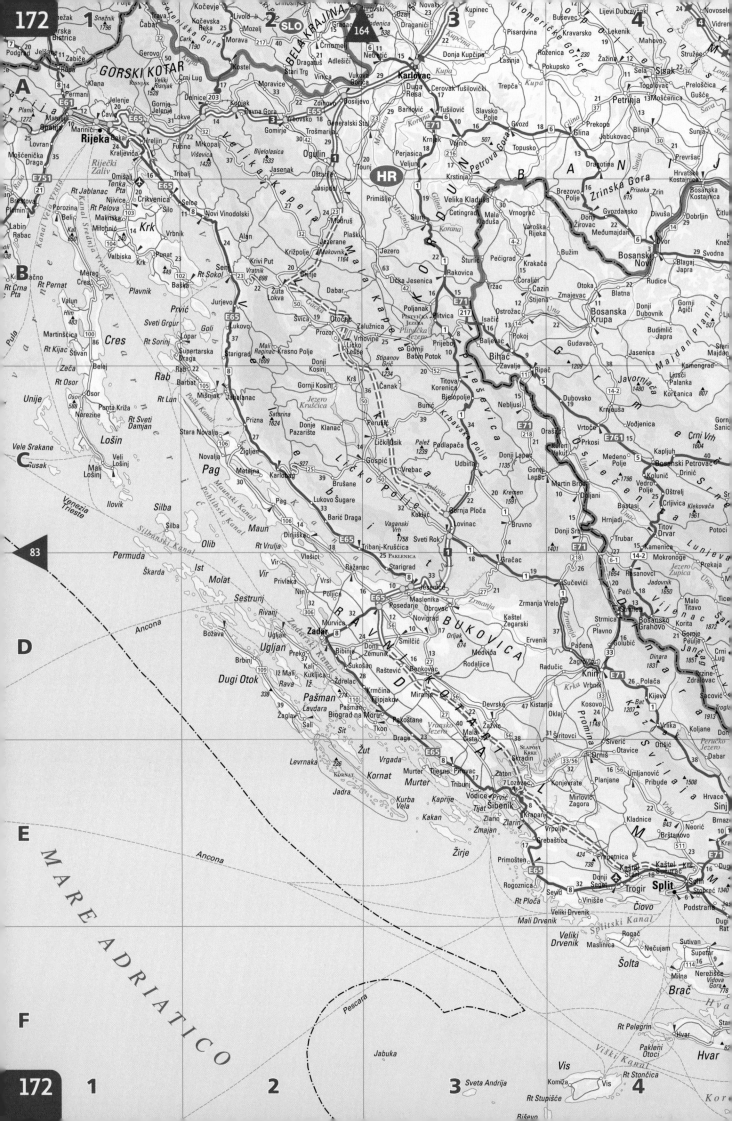

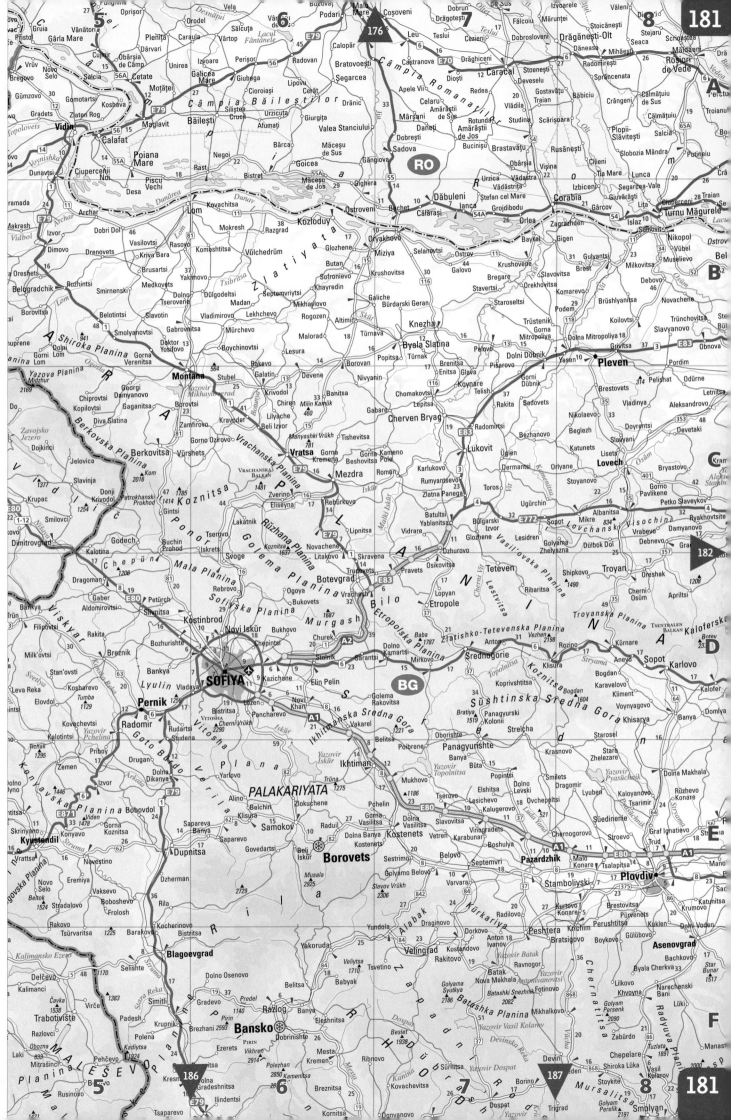

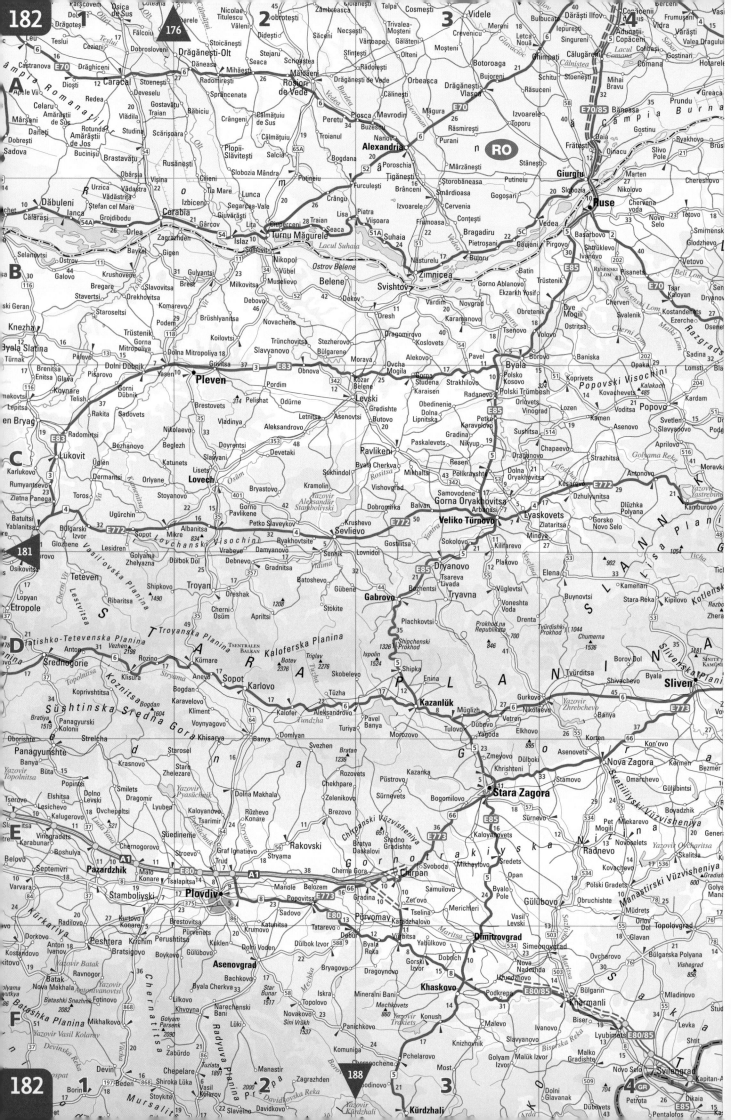

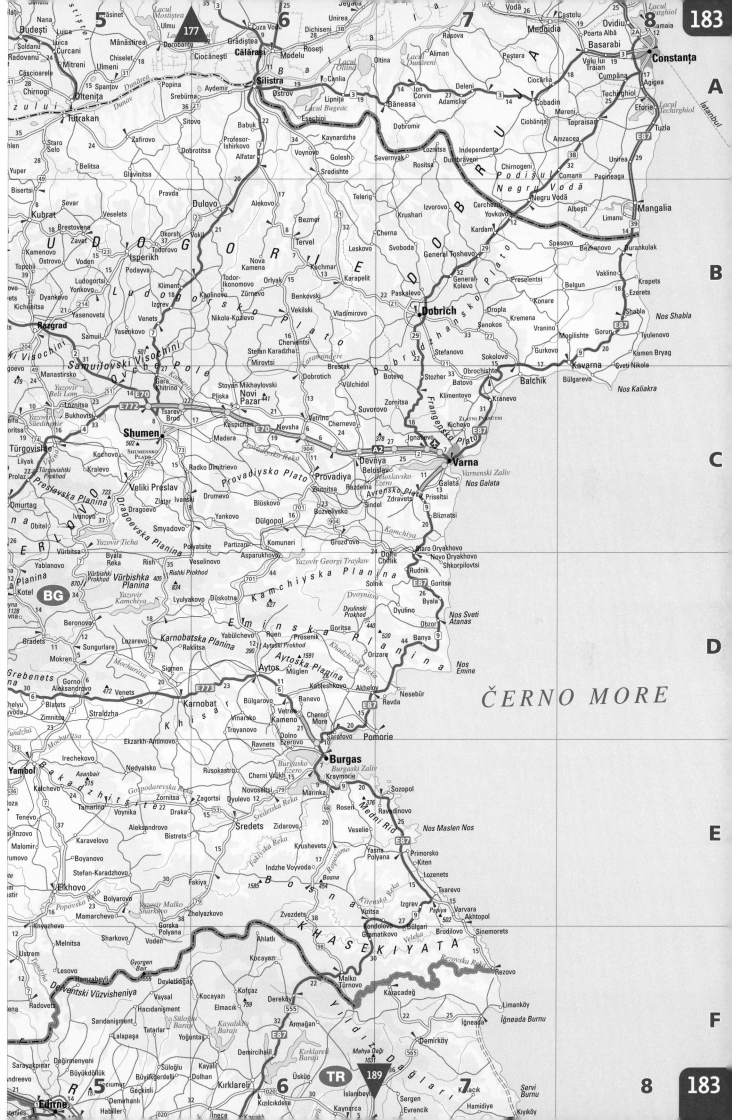

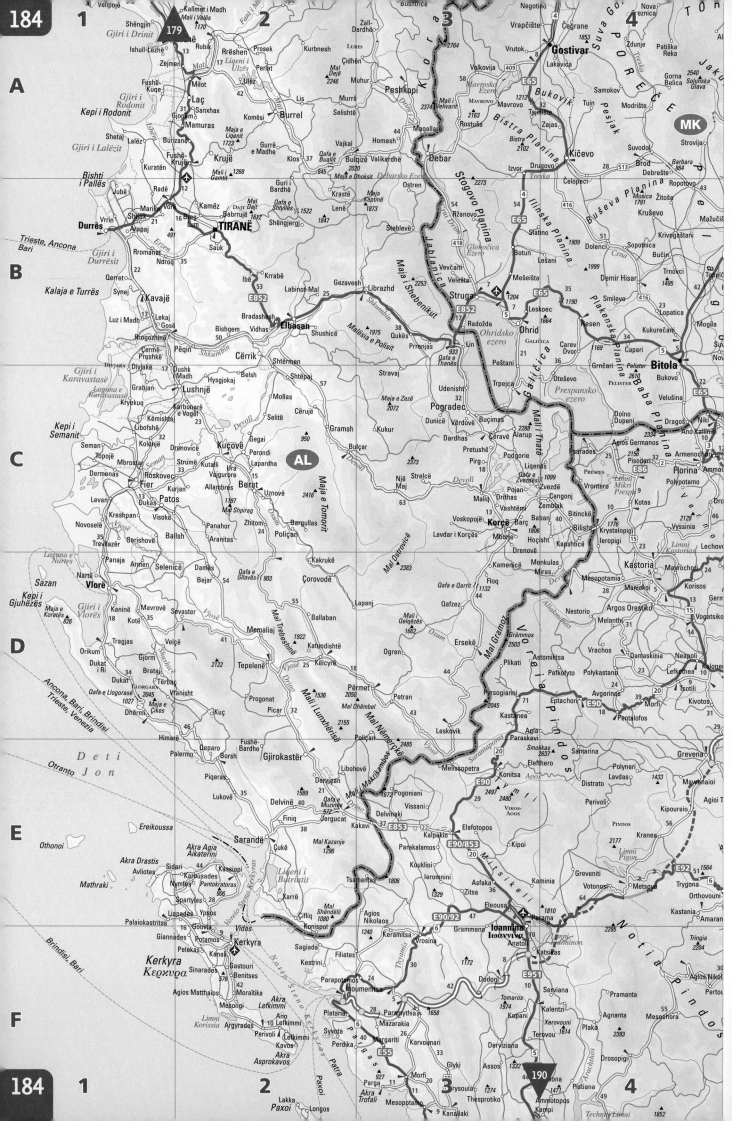

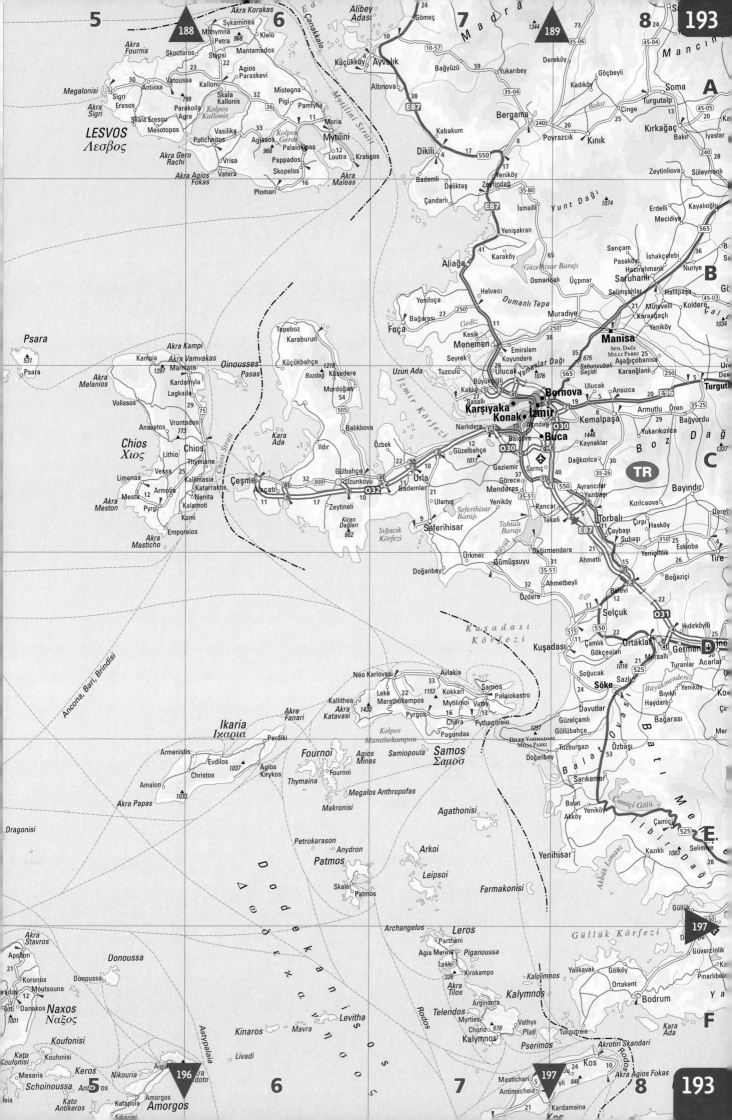

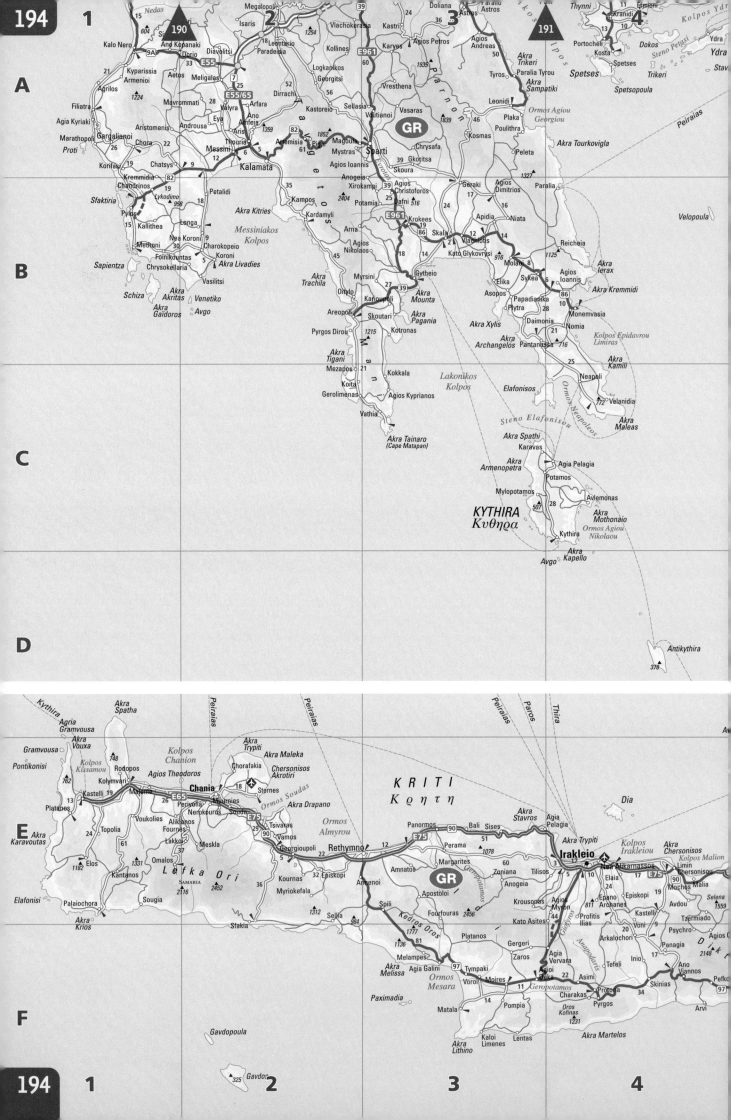

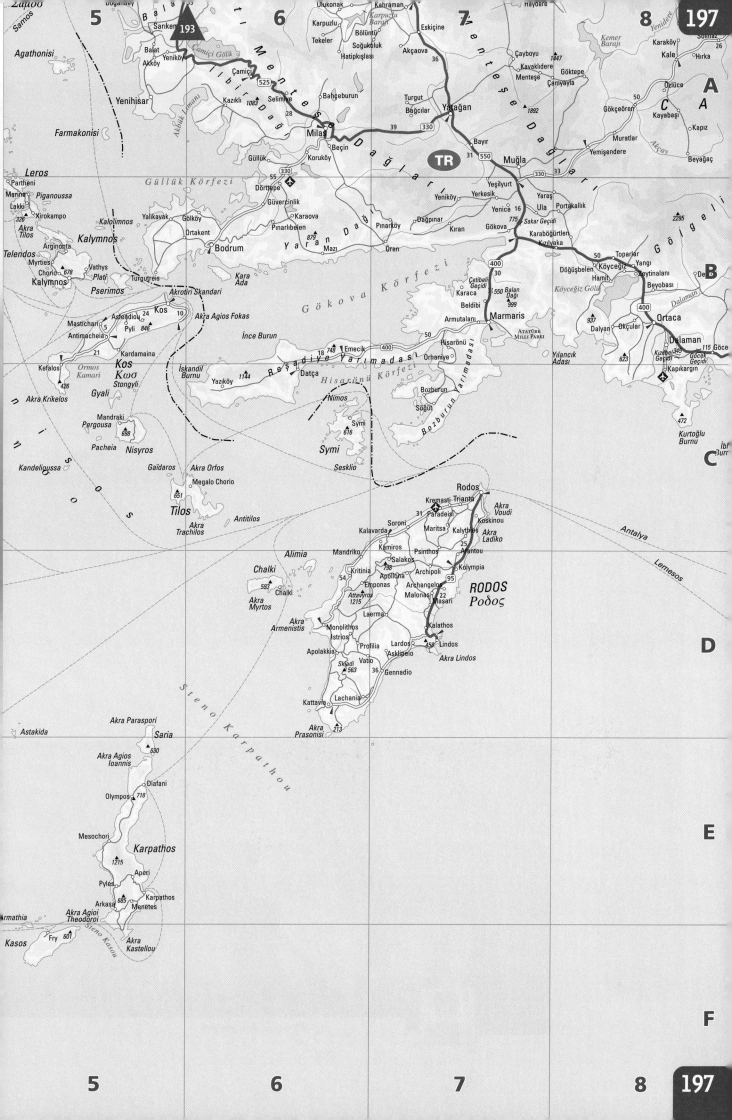